T5-AEZ-615

CULTURAL DIVERSITY
and
CANADIAN EDUCATION

THE CARLETON LIBRARY SERIES

A series of original works, reprints, and new collections of source material relating to Canada, issued under the supervision of the Editorial Board, Carleton Library Series, Carleton University Press Inc., Ottawa, Canada.

CULTURAL DIVERSITY and CANADIAN EDUCATION

ISSUES AND INNOVATIONS

EDITED BY

John R. Mallea
&
Jonathan C. Young

CARLETON UNIVERSITY PRESS
OTTAWA - CANADA

ISBN 0-88629-007-4 (paperback)

Printed and bound in Canada

Carleton University Press gratefully acknowledges the support extended to its publishing programme by the Canada Council and the Ontario Arts Council.

Publication of the present work has been made possible by a subvention from the Multiculturalism Program, Government of Canada. However, The Minister of State for Multiculturalism and the Multiculturalism Directorate disclaim any responsibility in whole or in part for the views and opinions expressed and for the completeness or accuracy of information included in this publication.

Canadian Cataloguing in Publication Data

Main entry under title:
Cultural diversity and Canadian education

(Carleton library series ; 130)
ISBN 0-88629-007-4

1. Education—Canada—Addresses, essays, lectures. 2. Pluralism (Social sciences)— Addresses, essays, lectures. 3. Multiculturalism—Canada—Addresses, essays, lectures. I. Mallea, John R. II. Young, J. C. (Jonathan C.) III. Series: The Carleton library ; no. 130.

LA412.C84 1983 370.19'34'0971 C84-090007-4

Distributed by:
Oxford University Press
70 Wynford Drive
DON MILLS, Ontario, CANADA, M3C 1J9.
(416)441-2941

FOR OUR PARENTS

Contents

Preface

Patriation of the Canadian constitution in 1982, with an amending formula and a Charter of Rights and Freedoms, was a major event born of intense political struggle and conflict. The government of Quebec refused to join with the rest of the provinces and the federal government in bringing home the constitution. It did so, moreover, in large part because the minority language education rights embedded in the new constitution ran directly counter to the provisions of its provincial language legislation — Bill 101. This fact alone ensures that issues of language, culture and education will continue to figure prominently in debates over Canada's future.

The complex web of relationships surrounding language, culture and education has been the subject of considerable comment and analysis during the past two decades. A veritable flood of reports, studies, books and articles dealing with one aspect or another of these relationship has threatened to engulf even the most persistent and discerning of readers in the area. At least this is how it appears to the editors of the present text as they and their students have attempted to untangle this web in seminars focusing on the provision of education in a culturally diverse society. This text is a result of these efforts and it is intended to be of assistance to others who are seeking to understand the appropriate role of schooling in contemporary Canada. Responsibility for the selections and the organizational format we have chosen, of course, is ours and ours alone.

The text is divided into six separate but related sections. Competing visions of Canadian pluralism are identified and the debate over the formal role of the school discussed. Education policy and practice regarding language and culture are highlighted, as is the crucially important question of cultural transmission. The school curriculum, viewed as a selective version of society's core values, knowledges and skills, is analysed in terms of how well it reflects the cultural experience and contributions of minority Canadians. A section describing programs, existing and proposed, is provided and the text closes with a look at issues and innovations in policy and practice.

Many of the materials presented here have appeared in print before, but are not equally accessible to the general reader. Taken together, a sense of the changing temporal and substantive nature of the relationship between cultural diversity and education. Perceptions of the role and significance of publicly funded education in the maintenance and development of minority languages and cultures, for example, underwent considerable modification in the 1960s and 1970s. Policies and legislation were enacted in a variety of jurisdictions. School curricula and textbooks slowly began to reflect the realities of racial, linguistic and cultural pluralism. Conventional theory and institutions came under attack and struggles were waged to make them more representative of minority needs and aspirations. Here and there innovations appeared, attracted support and were replicated. Elsewhere fierce opposition to change was encountered and struggles continue. Conflict not consensus characterizes the current debate. Schools are expected to contribute both to the promotion of cultural diversity and the maintenance of social cohesion. Dilemmas, ambiguities and contradictions abound. But at least one thing is clear. The search for responsive educational patterns to the realities of a multiracial, multi-ethnic Canada is far from complete.

J.R.M.
J.C.Y.

Introduction: Cultural Diversity and Canadian Education

J. R. MALLEA

Canada has long expressed support for the political principle that cultural diversity is a valuable and enriching quality of national life.[1] The nation's cultural diversity was in fact a major determinant of the particular form of federalism adopted at Confederation. The importance of education in this regard, moreover, was fully recognized. Its potentially divisive nature led the framers of the British North America Act to move education "out of the national political system and into the sub-systems of the provinces where the differences could flourish."[2]

The declared intent of these arrangements was to ensure "that all Canadians could retain their historic cultural identities while at the same time sharing economically, militarily and in international affairs in the benefits of a larger nation." Promise, however, has not always been matched by achievement. Conflict not consensus, controversy not harmony, has more often than not characterized the efforts of minority ethnic groups to translate educational aspirations into practice. The provisions of the British North America Act have not proved adequate to deal with the language of education issue. As a result, Acadians, Franco-Ontarians, Franco-Manitobans, and other French-speaking minorities at various times and in various contexts, have discovered that provincial autonomy in educational matters has worked to their disadvantage.[3]

Far from adopting a positive stance towards differences in language and culture, public schools have until fairly recently gone out of its way to eradicate them. Assimilation, not appreciation of differences, has been the policy, conformity not diversity, the goal.[4] As Hodgetts pointed out, "Although we laugh at ourselves for doing so, and perhaps have convinced each other that today things are different, in actual fact we are continuing to teach a white, Anglo-Saxon, Protestant, political and constitutional history of Canada."[5] The portrayal of Canada's ethnic groups other than English or French in Alberta's senior high schools has also been described as woefully inadequate. School textbooks generally do not represent a pluralist model of Canadian culture, but continue to portray a consensus, non-controversial view of society. In the universities, too, there has been a well-documented and widespread neglect of Canadian issues and problems, including those relating to cultural diversity.[6]

It is a truism that educational systems and institutions are shaped and guided by the societies that establish them. Educational goals reflect societal goals. Disagreement over major societal issues therefore is often reflected in formal institutions of learning, particularly when the disagreement centres on what form society and its institutions are to take.

In a culturally and linguistically diverse society this inevitably involves contentious issues of culture, language and ethnic relations. These issues have long been the source of considerable uncertainty and debate in education, for Canadians have traditionally viewed formal schooling as the major institution for the transmission of society's core values and beliefs. Not surprisingly, therefore, when disagreements over these values and beliefs arise, they are reflected in the schools. Their impact over the last two decades, moreover, has increased.

The reasons for this are many and complex and cannot be dealt with adequately in an introductory essay. It is worth noting, however, several important changes that have exercised a major influence. The Canadian economy developed rapidly after the Second World War bringing in its train widespread social and cultural change. The Quiet Revolution in Quebec brought about fundamental shifts in individual and collective expectations. Nationalism flourished and demands for greater sovereignty increased. Outside Quebec, francophone minorities sought to assert themselves. Massive immigration occurred and the ethnic composition of the population changed dramatically, resulting in the aggregate size of the "other" ethno-cultural groups approaching that of francophones. Minority ethnic groups — especially in Western Canada — forcefully brought their contributions and concerns to national attention. In addition, growing alienation among the native peoples led to a more militant expression of their needs and efforts to obtain greater control over the forces of development that threatened to engulf them.

Changing Ethnic Composition

Four major periods of settlement that have exercised a profound impact on the ethnic composition of Canada's population can be identified. The first, the pre-European period, extended over ten thousand years and led to scattered occupation of the territory by the native peoples. The second coincided with that of French colonization up to 1760. The third, following the ceding of Canada to Britain at the Treaty of Paris in 1763 and the American Declaration of Independence (1776) was characterized by the arrival of large numbers of British immigrants and Loyalists, resulting in the French being outnumbered by the middle of the nineteenth century. The fourth period coincided to a large extent with the settlement of the prairies, resulting in the addition of immigrants from other ethno-cultural backgrounds to the already established aboriginal, French and British groups.

Census statistics from 1871 to 1971 (see Table 1) reveal that those of British ethnic origin, while falling in overall numerical strength, have continued to form the majority throughout the period. French Canadians have not suffered the same overall decline in strength as the British group. Since 1951, however, their overall percentage of the population has been falling. The largest percentage increase in the population has occurred in the category termed the "other" ethnic groups. As early as 1921, it is worth emphasizing, these groups formed between 30 and 40 per cent of the prairie population. Fifty years later, in 1971, they formed 25.3 per cent of the total population. The culturally and linguistically diverse native peoples made up 1.4 per cent of the population.

Ambiguities surrounding the definition of ethnicity have led to considerable debate over the interpretation of census figures based on ethnic origin.[7] It is worth noting, for example, that ethnic origin is not a necessarily valid indicator or approximation of the Canadian population's real ethnic affiliations. Mother tongue or the language of the home are probably better indicators. Even these may well be inadequate when one considers that other elements such as kinship patterns, religious affiliations, national background and phenotypical features also play an important role in defining one's ethnicity. What the statistics for 1971 do reinforce is that numerically anglophones form a majority in Canadian society and that the population is made up of two major linguistic groups: anglophones and francophones. Territorial duality, moreover, approximates linguistic duality. Francophones form the majority in Quebec, while anglophones form a massive majority in the rest of Canada. In the course of the last twenty-five years, this division has become more distinct. On the one hand, over 90 per cent of the population claiming English as their mother tongue are to be found outside Quebec; on the other, over 80 per cent of those claiming French as their mother tongue reside within its borders.[8]

Furthermore, the English language exerts considerable assimilative power among all groups. The extent to which younger French Canadians outside of Quebec are being assimilated to English has been vividly documented.[9] The Federation of Francophones outside

TABLE 1: Number and Composition of Canadian Population According to Ethnic Origin, 1871 to 1971

Year	*All Origins*		*British*		*French*		*Native*[a]		*Other*[b]	
	Number (×1,000)	%	*Number (×1,000)*	%	*Number (×1,000)*	%	*Number (×1,000)*	%	*Number (×1,000)*	%
1871[c]	3,486	100.0	2,111	60.5	1,083	31.1	23	0.7	269	7.7
1901[c]	4,623	100.0	2,619	56.7	1,606	34.7	38	0.8	360	7.8
1901[d]	5,371	100.0	3,063	57.0	1,649	30.7	128	2.4	531	9.9
1911[d]	7,207	100.0	3,999	55.5	2,062	28.6	106	1.5	1,040	14.4
1921[d]	8,788	100.0	4,869	55.4	2,453	27.9	113	1.3	1,353	15.4
1931[d]	10,377	100.0	5,381	51.9	2,928	28.2	129	1.2	1,939	18.7
1941[d]	11,507	100.0	5,716	49.7	3,483	30.3	126	1.1	2,182	18.9
1951[d]	13,648	100.0	6,372	46.7	4,309	31.6	165	1.2	2,802	20.5
1951[e]	14,009	100.0	6,710	47.9	4,319	30.8	165	1.2	2,815	20.1
1961[e]	18,238	100.0	7,997	43.8	5,540	30.4	220	1.2	4,481	24.6
1971[e]	21,568	100.0	9,624	44.6	6,180	28.7	313	1.4	5,451	25.3

Source: Royal Commission on Bilingualism and Biculturalism (1970), p. 257; Dominion Bureau of Statistics (1953), table 34; and Statistics Canada (1973*b*), cat. no. 92–723, table 2.

Notes: a Erratic movements of population of Indian and Inuit origin are explained largely by changes in census practices, in particular with respect to assignation of Métis. As for rest of Canadian population, origin of natives is determined through paternal line since 1951, while in previous censuses, special criteria were used to enumerate them: from 1911 to 1931, they were defined by maternal line; in 1941, all Métis were counted separately; prior to 1911, they seem to have been included, as a rule, in the native population.

b. This residual category also includes those who did not declare their origin in cases where these were not distributed. However, numbers seem to be negligible and probably have no effect on the *general* picture of evolution of numbers and relative size of this category.

c. Comprises only Nova Scotia, New Brunswick, Quebec, and Ontario.

d. Does not include Newfoundland.

e. Includes Newfoundland.

TABLE 2: Population According to Ethnic Origin, Mother Tongue and Home Language, Canada, 1971

	Number (×1,000)				
Origin or Language	*Ethnic Origin (1)*	*Mother Tongue (2)*	*Home Language (3)*	*Index of Ethnolinguistic Continuity (2)÷(1) (4)*	*Index of Linguistic Continuity (3)÷(2) (5)*
British or English	9,624	12,974	14,446	1.35	1.11
French	6,180	5,794	5,546	0.94	0.96
Native	313	180	137	0.58	0.76
Other,	5,451	2,620	1,439	0.48	0.55
of which:					
German	1,317	561	213	0.43	0.38
Italian	731	538	425	0.74	0.79
Ukrainian	581	310	145	0.53	0.47
Dutch	426	145	36	0.34	0.25
Scandinavian[a]	385	84	10	0.22	0.12
Polish	316	135	71	0.43	0.53
Hungarian	132	87	51	0.66	0.59
Greek	124	104	87	0.84	0.84
Chinese	119	95	78	0.80	0.82
Yugoslav[b]	105	74	29	0.70	0.39
Total	21,568	21,568	21,568	—	—

Source: Statistics Canada (1973*b*), cat. no. 92–723; *idem* (1973*c*), cat. no. 92–725; and *idem* (1973*d*), cat. no. 92–726.

Notes: a. Includes Danes, Icelanders, Norwegians, and Swedes.

b. Includes Croatians, Serbs, and Slovaks.

Quebec has also demonstrated the marginality of Francophone communities. Linguistic transfers among members of the other ethnic groups have largely been in the direction of English. "Outside Quebec, the situation is very clear. English remains intact, or very nearly, and attracts all. French, as well as the 'other' languages, has a low preservation rate and attracts nothing. The same situation exists with the 'other' languages in Quebec."[10]

TABLE 3: Linguistic Continuity, Persistence, and Transfers, 1971

Region and Mother Tongue	*Continuity Index (%)*	*Rate of Persistence (%)*	*% of Linguistic Transfers*	
			Toward English	*Toward French*
QUEBEC				
English	112.6	92.5	—	83.5
French	100.1	98.4	92.0	—
Native	89.1	85.1	89.4	10.6
Other,	71.4	67.0	70.5	29.5
of which:				
German	45.4	40.9	80.8	19.2
Italian	79.9	76.8	46.1	53.9
Ukrainian	70.2	63.6	87.4	12.6
CANADA WITHOUT QUEBEC				
English	111.3	99.2	—	21.1
French	73.0	70.2	99.1	—
Native	75.3	69.8	99.6	0.4
Other,	52.1	49.1	99.5	0.5
of which:				
German	37.7	35.8	99.7	0.3
Italian	78.6	73.8	98.1	1.9
Ukrainian	45.8	41.9	99.9	0.1

Source: Statistics Canada (1975), cat. no. 92–776, tables 1 and 2.

Since the Second World War, francophones have become concentrated more and more in Quebec, and other groups have increasingly been losing their ancestral languages. Native languages have also been increasingly threatened.

Statistics drawn from the 1971 census for children aged five years and over, attending school full-time, confirm the pervasive drawing power of English. As Table 4 indicates, percentages showing the language most spoken at home are in each case smaller than those for both mother tongue and ethnic origin. It also shows that the use of French as the mother tongue in the home is declining somewhat. Among those of native origin, almost half do not have a native language as their mother tongue, and of those that do even fewer use it most frequently in the home. The drawing power of English among the other ethnic groups is even more dramatic. Out of a total of 23.9 per cent who indicate that their background is neither native nor British or French, only 6.6 per cent gave their mother tongue as other than English or French and only 4.2 per cent reported that it was their home language. Differences nevertheless exist among these groups. Assimilation to English does not form a homogeneous or monolithic pattern. It is more marked among children of north European ancestry than it is, say, among those of Italian ancestry.

TABLE 4: Population Five Years and Over, Attending School Full-time, by Ethnic Origin, Mother Tongue, and Language of Home, 1971

	Ethnic Origin		*Mother Tongue*		*Language of Home*	
	No.	*%*	*No.*	*%*	*No.*	*%*
Total:	5,938,315	100	5,938,315	100	5,938,315	100
BRITISH/ ENGLISH	2,663,360	44.8	3,859,740	65.0	4,086,315	68.8
FRENCH	1,763,935	29.7	1,609,560	27.1	1,572,685	26.4
INDIAN/ ESKIMO	100,110	1.7	53,375	0.9	41,145	0.7
OTHERS:	1,410,910	23.8	415,640	7.0	237,795	4.0
–German	344,120	5.8	79,665	1.3	32,235	0.5
–Italian	187,305	3.1	111,455	1.9	82,745	1.4
–Jewish	77,305	1.2	—	—	—	—
–Netherlands	134,245	2.3	17,535	0.3	4,240	0.1
–Polish	80,725	1.4	18,075	0.3	10,025	0.2
–Scandinavian	96,505	1.6	—	—	—	—
–Ukrainian	143,335	2.4	41,250	0.7	18,700	0.3
–Asian	74,845	1.2	—	—	—	—
–Others and Unknown	272,535	4.6	147,665	2.4	89,855	1.5

Source: Statistics Canada, 1971 Census of Canada. Population; The School Population. Cat. 92–742 Vol. 1, Part 5 (Bulletin 1.5–2).

Ethnic Revitalization

If we were to examine census statistics alone, especially at a single point in time, one might conclude that, as language is an important indicator of ethnicity, the latter is becoming a progressively less important factor in Canadian affairs. To do so, however, would prove misleading. There is a surprising amount of evidence, not only in Canada, to indicate a worldwide resurgence of ethnicity as a social and political force. Irrespective, it seems, of political boundaries, ideologies and economic systems, ethnicity is attracting attention in modernized and modernizing societies alike.

Why this is so remains unclear. Part of the answer, though, may lie in a fuller and more complete understanding of the role of ethnicity in the process of modernization itself. Does there, as some believe, exist a basic incompatibility between the universalizing forces of modernity and the distinctive cultural patterns associated with ethnicity? Is development synonymous with modernization and does the process so pervade our lives that the differences defining ethnic groups will of necessity vanish over time? Or is it possible that development can be fostered in ways that do not infringe on cherished ethnic norms and values? Have countries such as Canada, the United States and the Soviet Union (which take on the overall appearance of highly developed industrial societies) overestimated the extent to which modernization has occurred? Have they overlooked the persistence of traditional norms and values as a result? Might ethnicity, in an increasingly impersonal, mass society unsure of its goals and values, provide the basis for positive self-identity and continued growth? Can identification with one's linguistic and ethno-cultural background provide communal man with social relationship more enduring and less instrumental than those arising out of legal rights, occupation and social status?

Answers to these complex questions are difficult to find. Yet it is these and similar questions (as the contents of this text underline) which have absorbed so much of the energy and attention of Canadians of late. At the federal level, milestones in this quest include the Royal Commission on Bilingualism and Biculturalism (1963), the Official Languages Act (1969), the policy of "Multiculturalism Within a Bilingual Framework" (1971), The Task Force on Canadian Unity (1979), and the Canada Act (1982). Quebec's Quiet Revolution in the late fifties and early sixties, the Commissions of Inquiry into Education (1962), The Position of the French Language and Language Rights (1968) and subsequent language Bills 85 (1968), 63 (1969), 22 (1974), and Bill 101 (1977) reflect similar sometimes competing efforts to resolve these questions.

In other provinces, too, contemporary issues of language and culture have been addressed. In 1968 Ontario passed a law guaranteeing education in French for its Franco-Ontarian minority. In 1969 New Brunswick passed an Official Languages Act establishing equality of status for English and French and equal rights in education for the two linguistic groups. A year later the Manitoba government passed Bill 133, which gave francophones the legal right to schooling in French and removed the earlier restriction that French could only be used as a language of instruction for up to half a day. In Saskatchewan the Education Act (1978) guaranteed access to education in French. Prince Edward Island in 1980 amended its School Act to provide for instruction in both the official languages. Across the country, in British Columbia, a comprehensive policy statement on education in the two official languages was published in 1981. In the last decade, too, following the lead of the federal government, five provinces (Alberta, British Columbia, Manitoba, Ontario and Saskatchewan) have adopted provincial multiculturalism policies and have tried in varying degrees to translate their normative principles into educational practice.

Multiculturalism Within a Bilingual Framework

Given the complexity of the issues under consideration, it is useful in this context to examine the federal government's policy of Multiculturalism within a Bilingual Framework in some detail. Introduced into the House of Commons in 1971, where it won overwhelming support from the three major political parties, the policy explicitly rejected assimilation as an undesirable and unacceptable goal. According to the Prime Minister, his government considered the "melting pot" approach to be an inappropriate response to the realities of Canadian cultural diversity. Rather, the time was now "overdue for the people of Canada to become more aware of the rich tradition of the many cultures we have in Canada." What was being called into being was a new vision of Canadian society, one which refused to sacrifice diversity in the name of unity and which placed the cultures of many groups on an equal footing.

The policy embraces a variety of goals. It seeks to preserve basic human rights, increase citizen participation, develop Canadian identity, reinforce Canadian unity, encourage cultural diversity and eliminate discrimination. It reaffirms the principle of individual freedom of choice, and takes pains to point out that membership in an ethnic group should not place constraints on it. Such membership is, nevertheless, considered of major importance in helping combat the alienating effects of mass society "in which mass-produced culture and entertainment and large impersonal institutions threaten to denature and depersonalize man." The policy also reflects a belief that confidence in one's individual identity, strengthened by a sense of belonging, provides an acceptable and necessary base for national unity.

> The more secure we feel in one particular social context, the more we are free to explore our identity beyond it. Ethnic groups often provide people with a sense of belonging which can make them better able to cope with the rest of society than they would as isolated individuals. Ethnic loyalties need not, and usually do not, detract from wider loyalties to community and country.[11]

Accepting this interpretation of the benefits of ethnic group membership, the federal government's position "that there cannot be one cultural policy for Canadians of British and French origin, another for the original peoples, and yet a third for all others" is both logical and persuasive. Its corollary, moreover, is equally clear. That is, if the many cultures in Canada are seen as a heritage to treasure, then the attempt to ensure their continuance and development should help in the breakdown of discriminatory attitudes and cultural jealousies.

Despite these ringing assertions, indeed perhaps because of them, the policy has been heavily criticized. Many consider it to be a political ploy aimed at gaining the support of the minority ethnic groups. Others view it as representing a political compromise that attempts to straddle two competing models of Canadian society: pluralism and dualism. Still others believe that as a statement of public policy it suffers from a distinct absence of conceptual support and stands in serious need of further development.

Negative reaction to the policy has coalesced around six basic criticisms. The first, made mainly, although by no means exclusively, by francophones in Quebec, claims that the policy distorts historical and sociological realities because Canada possesses two main cultures as well as two official languages. Culture and language, these critics protest, are indivisible. It is therefore contradictory to have a policy of multiculturalism alongside a policy of official bilingualism. It is also politically dangerous in that it serves to erode the already shaky confidence that French Canadians have in the federal government's ability to protect their language and culture. The second is that made by the native peoples who, while roundly rejecting the "founding nations" interpretation of Canadian society, also found scant comfort in a policy that scarcely seemed to recognize their existence and made no mention of aboriginal rights.

A third criticism suggests that the policy erroneously reinforces the belief that Canada's non-official language groups represent a homogeneous element in the population. Critics point out that while these groups share some important characteristics in common, they also vary widely along a number of important variables. For example, they possess differing views of themselves and their place in Canadian society. Thus while some seem to have lost interest in their heritage languages and cultures, others work vigorously to maintain and enhance them in a Canadian context. The fourth of the six criticisms centres around the argument that the policy represents a conflicting and often contradictory response to poorly defined issues. The fifth is related. It is based on the view that ethnic and social stratification are closely related in Canada and that the policy stresses group maintenance (as opposed to individual development) and therefore helps preserve values which are inimicable to the socio-economic mobility of minority group members. The sixth and final criticism is the most general and perhaps the most telling. The present policy, it is argued, emphasizes style over substance and thus enables the government to praise the values of individualism and pluralism simultaneously.

Governments can only do so, however, where ethnic communities are intent upon assimilation or as long as they are too politically underdeveloped to make their existence forcefully known to the obvious majority.

> The conceptual trick is to acknowledge diversity of cultures within the society but assume that culture deals mainly with styles and cooking recipes and has relatively little impact on ambitions, moral judgements and public goals. If ethnicity is this shallow, then things that really matter to individuals will hardly be affected, and it will not impinge on important national decisions.[12]

Once assimilation is rejected and ethnic communities assert themselves, however, the discrepancies between democratic ideology and ethnic reality are harder to justify and maintain.

Both of these developments have occurred in Canada. Assimilation has come under strong challenge and linguistic and cultural minority groups are engaging increasingly in their own political development. Passage of the Canada Act (1982) is a case in point. The Charter of Rights and Freedoms states that it shall be interpreted in a manner consistent with the preservation and enhancement of the multicultural heritage of Canadians. It also includes clauses dealing with aboriginal rights and minority language educational rights. But it is precisely these last two areas of rights that have proved to be the most contentious and have led to renewed protest and legal challenges. The search for agreement on these issues is obviously far from over.

A similar lack of agreement can be observed in the world of scholarship and education. Little consensus, for example, exists among social scientists as to which theories of social change are most helpful in responding to the dynamics of an evolving Canadian society. Two recent critics, following a review of leading theories (including those of Parsons and Marx and their disciples) found all of them wanting in that none allowed for alternatives to the inevitability of the futures they portrayed. They proposed instead a model of an evolving Canadian society in which linguistic, ethnic and regional diversity — institutionalized in all sectors of society — would find expression.[13] What forms these institutions might take in publicly funded systems of schooling is, as we shall see, a crucial but largely unresolved issue in both educational theory and practice. One reason for this is that the term "multicultural education" is itself a source of confusion. Its use is characterized more by currency than consensus. So great, indeed, is the ambiguity associated with it, that one commentator suggests it might best be consigned to the "conceptual graveyard."[14] Another considers it a labyrinth of largely unexamined assumptions.[15]

The Pluralist Dilemma in Education

Not surprisingly, schools are experiencing difficulty in translating radically different expectations into policy and practice. These expectations, involving issues of individual and collective rights, majority-minority relations, social cohesion and control, highlight the complexities of education in a multi-ethnic state. Ambiguities, contradictions and paradoxes abound. In Canada, they pose, in particularly acute forms, what has been termed the pluralist dilemma in education.[16]

This dilemma arises out of the need to strike an appropriate balance between the educational goals of ethnic minority groups on the one hand, and those of the larger society on the other. Or to put it another way, schools are expected, at one and the same time, to respond to cultural diversity and to promote social cohesion and national integration. The task has never been an easy one. Schools reflect society and while they "can help to develop and transmit certain political orientations that must be shared, within a certain range of variations, by most members of any ongoing system,"[17] difficulties obviously arise when there is little agreement as to what these orientations are or should be.

In multi-ethnic societies, moreover, this already complex task is made more so by the acute tension that often exists between competing centripetal and centrifugal forces or tendencies.

> Centripetal tendencies refer both to cultural trends such as acceptance of common values, styles of life, etc., as well as structural features like increased participation in a common set of groups, associations, and institutions. . . . Conversely, centrifugal tendencies among subordinate groups are those that foster separation from the dominant group or

> from societal bonds in one respect or another. Culturally this most frequently means retention and presentation of the group's distinctive traditions in spheres like language, religion, recreation, etc., together with the particularistic values associated with them. . . .[18]

All societies require elements of centripetality if they are to function effectively, but multi-ethnic societies have to learn to live with greater measures of centrifugality than their more homogeneous counterparts. Thus the extent to which majority and minority groups share a tendency, whether centripetal or centrifugal, determines whether or not an agreed-upon form of accommodation can be achieved. Where they differ markedly, as, say, over the language of instruction in schools, controversies arise and conflicts often result.

The extent to which schools serve the interests of dominant groups in multi-ethnic societies is a second major element of the pluralist dilemma. Again, traditionally, the school has been viewed as the major formal agency by which selected values, knowledges, skills and attitudes, deemed necessary for the continuation of a society, have been transmitted from one generation to the next. But in stratified societies, responsibility for their selection has rested largely in the hands of the dominant group defined as "that collectivity within a society which has as pre-eminent authority to function both as guardians and sustainers of the controlling value systems, and prime allocators of rewards in the society."[19] In Canada, this has led John Porter and Denis and Murphy, among others, to emphasize the relationship between ethnic and social stratification and to question the school's role in the conservation of the vertical mosaic. Elsewhere, Bullivant considers the issue of whether schools promote the life chances of children from the dominant group over those of other ethnic groups. Bernstein views the school and its curriculum as vehicles of social reproduction, and Carnoy has described the school as an agent of cultural imperialism.[20]

In Canada, the pluralist dilemma is further exacerbated by the lack of any clearly formulated concept of educational policy set in the framework of broader national policies. The absence of clearly defined and agreed upon goals is the result; a fact noted by the Organisation for Economic Co-operation and Development examiners in the mid 1970s when they observed that "the sooner a workable path toward stating definite goals is found, the sooner the acceptable criteria for making reform decision will be discovered, and the better the prospects will be for the further development of the Canadian educational system."[21] Progress in this direction is at best mixed. The Council of Ministers of Education of Canada have noted the absence of any clearly articulated sense of Canadian society, its values and needs. In a similar vein, Hodgetts and Gallagher concluded that "any analysis of progress, however, does not inspire confidence that a generation of truly well-informed young Canadians, sensitive to the interests and concerns of their fellow Canadians or of Canadian society as a whole, is near at hand." In higher education, the contribution of colleges and universities to the study and resolution of pan-Canadian issues remains a pressing federal concern.[22]

Not surprisingly, despite sincere efforts in some jurisdictions to respond responsibly and imaginatively to the educational needs and aspirations of minority groups, the pluralist dilemma in education also looms particularly large at the school board level. Thus while assimulation has been repeatedly questioned as a worthwhile social goal, little agreement has been reached over the last two decades as to what specific school goals, policies and practices should replace it. Schools are experiencing serious role conflicts as a result.

Such lack of agreement poses important pedagogical questions for educational decision-makers and practioners. Are minority children's previous cultural and linguistic experiences to be viewed in additive or subtractive terms? That is, are they to be viewed as a valuable foundation upon which to build, or as experiences that hinder school-based learning? If the latter, how does such a position differ from the now socially unacceptable assimilationist position? If the former, how is this position to be reflected in educational policy and practice? Are heritage languages, for example, to be included in the regular school day as part of the formal curriculum, or are they to be seen as "extra-curricular" activities or the responsibility of specific ethnic community groups?

Resolution of the Dilemma?

As the Preface indicates, the contents of the text that follows constitutes a modest effort to clarify and illuminate the substance and boundaries of the pluralist dilemma in Canadian education. This introductory essay, therefore, will not close with a specific set of neat conclusions. The subject is too complex and problematic for that. Rather it will end with a concise summary of the major challenges to be faced. At the national level, for example, resolution of the dilemma will depend upon the development of a form of revised federalism that reconciles the historic principle of dualism with the contemporary realities of a multi-racial, multi-ethnic state.[23] At the provincial level, resolution of the pluralist dilemma will differ according to region, but will involve the challenge of creating legislation and policies enabling the legitimate educational aspirations of official and non-official language groups to be reflected in institutional and structural as well as normative terms.[24] At the municipal level, school boards will face increasing demands for special interest groups seeking changes in the organization of schooling so as to provide greater responsiveness to minority group requests for bilingual and bicultural programs and the appointment of well-qualified teachers and staff from the minority communities. How well we respond to these challenges is of course a matter for the future. No one today, however, can argue that the main outlines of the dilemma have not become increasingly clear.

Notes

Tables 1, 2 and 3 are reprinted, by permission of The Institute for Research on Public Policy, from R. Breton, J.G. Reitz, and V.F. Valentine. *Cultural Boundaries and the Cohesion of Canada* (Montreal: The Institute for Research on Public Policy, 1980).

1. R.L. Watts, *Multicultural Societies and Federation* (Ottawa: Information Canada, 1970).
2. J.R. Mallory, "The Evolution of Federalism in Canada," paper presented as part of a seminar on Federal-Provincial Relations (Ottawa: mimeo, 1976), p. 2.
3. R. Cook, "Presentation to First Session of Destiny Canada Conference, Final Report" (Toronto: mimeo, York University, 1977), p. 15.
4. C.J. Jaenen, "Cultural Diversity and Education," in N. Byrne and J. Quarter, *Must Schools Fail?* (Toronto: McClelland and Stewart, 1972), pp. 199–217.
5. A.B. Hodgetts, *What Culture? What Heritage?* (Toronto: The Ontario Institute for Studies in Education, 1968), p. 20.
6. See, for example, M. Lupul, "The Portrayal of Canada's 'Other' Peoples in Senior High School History and Social Studies Textbooks in Alberta, 1905 to the Present," paper presented to the 54th Annual Meeting of the Canadian Historical Association, University of Alberta, Edmonton, June 6, 1975; D. Pratt, "The Social Role of School Textbooks," in E. Zureik and R. Pike, (eds.), *Socialization and Values in Canadian Society* (Toronto: McClelland and Stewart, 1975), pp. 100–26; and T. Symons, *To Know Ourselves,* Vols. I and II (Ottawa: Association of Universities and Colleges of Canada, 1975).
7. See, for example, N. Ryder, "The interpretation of origin Statistics," *Canadian Journal of Economics and Political Science*, 21, no. 3 (1955), pp. 466–79, and J. Porter, "Ethnic Pluralism in Canadian Perspective," in N. Glazer, and D.P. Moynihan, (eds.), *Ethnicity; Theory and Experience* (Cambridge, Mass.: Harvard University Press, 1975), pp. 267–304.
8. Breton, p. 26.
9. R.J. Joy, *Language in Conflict* (Toronto: McClelland and Stewart, 1972).
10. Breton, *Cultural Boundaries,* p. 33.
11. P.E. Trudeau, Federal Government's Response to Book IV of the Royal

Commission on Bilingualism and Biculturalism. Document tabled in the House of Commons by the Prime Minister, October 8, 1971, p. 3.
12. C. Enloe, *Ethnic Conflict and Political Development* (Boston: Little, Brown and Company, 1973), pp. 60–61.
13. L. Marsden, and E. Harvey, *Fragile Confederation: Social Change in Canada* (Toronto: McGraw-Hill, Ryerson), 1979.
14. M.D. Stent, W.P. Hazard, and H.S. Rivlin, *Cultural Pluralism in Education: A Mandate for Change* (New York: Appleton-Century Crofts, 1973).
15. P. Carlson, "Towards a definition of local level multicultural education," *Anthropology and Education Quarterly*, 7, no. 4 (1976), pp. 26–30.
16. Similar issues are coming under increasing scrutiny elsewhere. In the United States the popular notion that the common school served as the crucible of the American melting pot has been challenged by Colin Greer in his book *The Great School Legend: A Revisionist Interpretation of American Public Education* (New York: Basic Books, 1972), and alternatives advocating greater responsiveness to diversity are being advanced. In Britain, too, the role of the school in this regard is being re-evaluated; see H. Townsend and E. Brittan, "Multicultural Education: Needs and Innovation," Preliminary Report of the Schools Council Education for a Multiracial Society Project: Schools Working Paper 50 (London: Evans/Methuen Educational, 1973). In Australia, Brian Bullivant in his book *Race, Ethnicity, and Curriculum* (South Melbourne: The Macmillan Co. of Australia, 1981), documents similar developments.
17. D. Easton, "The Function of Formal Education in a Political System," *The School Review*, 65, no. 3 (1957), p. 311.
18. R.A. Schermerhorn, *Comparative Ethnic Relations: A Framework for Theory and Research* (New York: Random House, 1970), p. 81.
19. Ibid., pp. 12–13.
20. See J. Porter, "Dilemmas and Contradictions of a Multi-Ethnic Society," *Transactions of the Royal Society of Canada*. Series 4, 10 (1972), pp. 193–205; A. Denis and R. Murphy, "Schools and the Conservation of the Vertical Mosaic," Paper presented at the National Conference of the Canadian Ethnic Studies Association, Laval University, Quebec, 1977, 25pp; B. Bernstein, "On the classification and framing of educational knowledge," in M.F.D. Young, (ed.), *Knowledge and Control, New Directions for the Sociology of Education* (London: Collier-Macmillan, 1971), pp. 47–69; M. Carnoy, *Education as Cultural Imperialism* (New York: David McKay Company, 1974).
21. Organization for Economic Co-operation and Development, *Reviews of National Policies for Education: Canada* (Paris: OECD, 1976).
22. See Council of Ministries of Education, *Provincial Social Studies/Social Sciences Programs in Canada as of 1978–79* (Toronto: The Council, 1978); A.B. Hodgetts, and P. Gallagher, *Teaching Canada for the '80s* (Toronto: OISE, 1978); and F. Fox, "An address to the Association of Universities and Colleges of Canada" (Ottawa: Secretary of State, 1981).
23. J.R. Mallea, "Minority-Language Education in Québec and Anglophone Canada" in R. Bouthis, Ed., *Language Conflict and Planning in Québec* (Clevedon, Avon: Multilingual Matters, Ltd., 1984.
24. J.R. Mallea, "Cultural Diversity and Canadian Education: A Review of Contemporary Developments" in R. Samuda et al., *Multiculturalism: Social and Educational Issues* (Toronto: Alleyn and Bacon Ltd., 1984.

Part One

IMAGES OF CANADIAN SOCIETY

Educational issues invariably form part of larger questions of purpose and value within the wider society. It is arguable, moreover, that if the contribution of a society's educational systems is to be most effectively organized, some consensus should exist around the core values, skills and knowledges that they are expected to promote. Where such consensus is absent, their task is rendered all the more difficult. This is the situation in Canada today with respect to society's view of linguistic and cultural diversity and its value.

This section presents major and differing interpretations of the Canadian response to cultural diversity, both past and present. Other perspectives, of course, exist, and reference to some of these can be found in later sections of the text. But these five papers, we believe, speak to central concerns surrounding the issue of Canadian linguistic and cultural diversity and the societal framework that might best respond to its presence.

Howard Palmer, in his article "Reluctant Hosts: Anglo-Canadian Views of Multiculturalism in the Twentieth Century," traces the growth of contemporary interest in cultural pluralism. He reminds us that questions of language and culture in Canada have always been surrounded by public controversy. Summarily rejecting the view that Anglo-Canadians have always sought to promote cultural diversity, he contends that Anglo-conformity was the prevailing ideology prior to World War Two. As a result, new arrivals traditionally had to conform to the values and institutions of the major society. In the postwar years, however, shifts have taken place in the predominant ideology. Assimilation took on overtones of the "melting pot," immigrants were increasingly seen as having more to offer than their labour, and ethnic differences came to be increasingly accepted. These changes contributed to the exploration of differing models of cultural pluralism in the 1960s and 1970s. Throughout these two decades, he argues, and especially since the announcement of the federal policy "Multiculturalism Within A Bilingual Framework" (1971), Canadians have witnessed a debate between proponents of assimilation versus multiculturalism, between proponents of biculturalism and multiculturalism, and between different proponents of multiculturalism.

Not surprisingly, the policy "Multiculturalism Within A Bilingual Framework" (See Appendix) has received little support among French Canadians. Many of its critics consider the policy to be a contradiction in terms. Chief among these is Guy Rocher. A Québécois sociologist of the front rank, Rocher has four major reservations about the federal government's policy. He believes, first, that it will jeopardize the future of bilingualism in the official languages. Secondly, it is a regrettable example of distinguishing between language and culture — one that will prove detrimental to French Canadians. Thirdly, he does not consider it to be an adequate basis for nationhood. Rather, he is of the opinion that Canada could probably have gained a great deal culturally if it had retained the idea of two central cultural communities serving as a focal point around which the other communities could group and find support. Fourthly, he sees the policy as a retrograde step in that it down-grades the idea of French Canadians as partners with the English-speaking community in the country's sociological structure. This new way of viewing the Canadian state, in his view, favours the English-speaking community and adversely affects francophones within and without Quebec.

A second Western Canadian scholar, the late Robert Painchaud, takes a different tack. He takes the view that the federal policy essentially relegates francophones, especially those outside Quebec, to the status of "just another ethnic group," thereby denying what he believes to be the fundamentally bicultural nature of Canadian confederation. He is also skeptical of how Canada can "give concrete support to twenty-five or fifty different cultures when one of its two cultures — or, rather, one of its two forces — has so much difficulty winning acceptance after having discovered and founded this country." Drawing a clear distinction between federal and provincial responsibilities, he quotes approvingly the position of the Association Culturelle Franco-Canadienne de la Saskatchewan which recommends the federal government concern itself with "the basic duality" of the country, leaving the provinces to attend to the needs of the other ethnic groups.

The final contribution to this opening section is the late John Porter's article "Dilemmas and Contradictions of a Multi-Ethnic Society." Here Porter adopts what may be termed a liberal assimilationist position, arguing that a policy of multiculturalism serves to reinforce and perpetuate ethnic stratification. Energies expended on ethnic group maintenance, he contends, only reduces the social and economic mobility of individuals, thereby helping preserve the Canadian "vertical mosaic" in which class lines coincide with ethnic lines. For Porter, the choice facing Canadians is "between ethnic stratification that results from ethnic diversity and the greater possibilities for equality that result from a reduction of ethnicity as a salient feature of a modern society." He comes down firmly in favour of reducing the contemporary emphasis on ethnicity, and advocates a limited role for ethnic groups in which they would serve as temporary, "psychic" shelters to help immigrants make the adjustment to mainstream Canadian society.

Reluctant Hosts: Anglo-Canadian Views of Multiculturalism in the Twentieth Century

HOWARD H. PALMER

Introduction

The way in which Anglo-Canadians have reacted to immigration during the twentieth century has not simply been a function of the numbers of immigrants or the state of the nation's economy. The immigration of significant numbers of non-British and non-French people raised fundamental questions about the type of society which would emerge in English-speaking Canada; hence, considerable public debate has always surrounded the issue of immigration in Canada. The questions which have repeatedly been raised include the following: Were the values and institutions of Anglo-Canadian society modelled exclusively on a British mould and should immigrants be compelled to conform to that mould? Or, would a distinctive identity emerge from the biological and cultural mingling of Anglo-Canadians with new immigrant groups? Would cultural pluralism itself give English-speaking Canada a distinctive identity? These three questions reflect the three theories of assimilation which have dominated the twentieth century debate over immigrant adjustment.

The assimilation theory which achieved early public acceptance was Anglo-conformity. This view demanded that immigrants renounce their ancestral culture and traditions in favour of the behaviour and values of Anglo-Canadians. Although predominant prior to the Second World War, Anglo-conformity fell into disrepute and was replaced in the popular mind by the "melting pot" theory of assimilation. This view envisaged a biological merging of settled communities with new immigrant groups and a blending of their cultures into a new Canadian type. Currently, a third theory of assimilation — "cultural pluralism" or "multiculturalism" — is vying

---

SOURCE: Revised by the author from an address to the Second Canadian Conference on Multiculturalism. First published in the conference report, *Multiculturalism as State Policy,* by the Canadian Consultative Council on Multiculturalism, (and subsequently published in R. Douglas Francis and Donald B. Smith, eds., *Readings in Canadian History: Post-Confederation*). Reproduced by permission of the Minister of Supply and Services, Canada.

for public acceptance. This view postulates the preservation of some aspects of immigrant culture and communal life within the context of Canadian citizenship and political and economic integration into Canadian society.[1]

There has been a recent burgeoning of historical and sociological research on Anglo-Canadian attitudes toward ethnic minorities. Much of this research contradicts the view which has been advanced by some Anglo-Canadian historians[2] and politicians that Anglo-Canadians have always adopted the "mosaic" as opposed to the American "melting pot" approach. Much of this rhetoric has simply been wishful thinking. Perhaps immigrant groups did not "melt" as much in Canada as in the United States, but this is not because Anglo-Canadians were more anxious to encourage the cultural survival of ethnic minorities. There has been a long history of racism and discrimination against ethnic minorities in English-speaking Canada, along with strong pressures for conformity to Anglo-Canadian ways.

The "Settlement" Period and the Predominance of Anglo-conformity: 1867–1920

Among the several objectives of the architects of the Canadian confederation in 1867, none was more important than the effort to accommodate the needs of the two main cultural communities. There was virtually no recognition of ethnic diversity aside from the British-French duality. This is, of course, somewhat understandable since at the time of confederation, only eight percent of the population of three and one half million were of non-British[3] or Non-French ethnic origin. There were, however, significant numbers of people of German and Dutch origin, well-established black and Jewish communities as well as a few adventurers and entrepreneurs from most European ethnic groups now in Canada.

The proportion of people of other than British, French, or native origin in Canada remained small until nearly the turn of the century; the United States proved more attractive for most European emigrants. In fact it was attractive for many Canadians as well, and the Dominion barely maintained its population. But with the closing of the American frontier which coincided with improving economic conditions in Canada and an active immigration promotion campaign by Wilfrid Laurier's Liberal government, many immigrants began to come to the newly opened land of western Canada in the late 1890s.[4] Immigration policy gave preference to farmers, and most non-British immigrants came to farm in western Canada. However, some immigrants ended up working in mines, laying railway track, or drifting into the urban working class.[5] During this first main wave of immigration between 1896 and 1914, three million immigrants, including large numbers of British labourers, American farmers and eastern European peasants came to Canada. Within the period of 1901 and 1911, Canada's population rocketed by 43 per cent and the percentage of immigrants in the country as a whole topped 22 per cent. In 1911, people of non-British and non-French origin formed 34 per cent of the population of Manitoba, 40 per cent of the population of Saskatchewan, and 33 per cent of the population of Alberta.

Throughout the period of this first large influx of non-British, non-French immigrants, (indeed up until the Second World War), Anglo-conformity was the predominant ideology of assimilation in English-speaking Canada.[6] For better or for worse, there were few proponents of either the melting pot or of cultural pluralism. Proponents of Anglo-conformity argued that it was the obligation of new arrivals to conform to the values and institutions of Canadian society — which were already fixed. During this period when scarcely anyone questioned the verities of God, King and country, there was virtually no thought given to the possibility that "WASP" values might not be the apex of civilization which all men should strive for.

Since at this time the British Empire was at its height, and the belief in "progress" and Anglo-Saxon and white superiority was taken for granted throughout the English-speaking world, a group's desirability as potential immigrants varied almost directly with its members physical and cultural distance from London (England) and the degree to which their skin pigmentation conformed to Anglo-Saxon white. Anglo-Canadians regarded British and American immigrants as the most desirable.[7] Next came northern and western Europeans who were regarded as culturally similar and hence assimilable. They were followed by central and eastern Europeans, who in the eyes of Clifford Sifton and immigration agents, had a slight edge on Jews and southern Europeans, because they were more inclined to go to and remain on the land. These groups were followed in the ethnic pecking order by the "strange" religious sects, the Hutterites, Mennonites and Doukhobors, who were invariably lumped together by public officials and the general public despite significant religious and cultural differences between them. Last, but not least (certainly not least in the eyes of those British Columbians and their sympathizers elsewhere in the country who worried about the "Asiatic" hordes) were the Asian immigrants — the Chinese, Japanese and East Indians (the latter of whom were dubbed "Hindoos," despite the fact that most were Sikhs). Running somewhere close to last were black immigrants, who did not really arise as an issue because of the lack of aspiring candidates, except in 1911, when American blacks were turned back at the border by immigration officials because they allegedly could not adapt to the cold winters in Canada; a curious about-face for a department which was reassuring other American immigrants that Canadian winters were relatively mild.[8]

As might be expected, prevailing assumptions about the relative assimilability of these different groups were quickly transformed into public debate over whether immigrants whose assimilability was problematic should be allowed into the country. During this first wave of immigration, considerable opposition developed to the entry of central, southern and eastern European immigrants, Orientals, and to the three pacifist sects. Opposition to these groups came from a variety of sources, for a variety of reasons. But one of the most pervasive fears of opinion leaders was that central, southern and eastern Europeans, and Orientals would wash away Anglo-Saxon traditions of self-government in a sea of illiteracy and inexperience with "free institutions."[9] Many English-Canadian intellectuals, like many American writers at the time, thought that North America's greatness was ensured so long as its Anglo-Saxon character was preserved. Writers emphasized an Anglo-Saxon tradition of political freedom and self-government and the "white man's" mission to spread Anglo-Saxon blessings.[10] Many intellectuals and some politicians viewed Orientals and central southern and eastern European immigrants as a threat to this tradition and concluded that since they could not be assimilated they would have to be excluded. The introduction in Canada of a head tax on Chinese immigrants, a "gentlemen's agreement" with Japan which restricted the number of Japenese immigrants, the passing of orders-in-council which restricted immigration from India, the gradual introduction of restrictive immigration laws in 1906, 1910 and 1919 relative to European immigration and the tightening of naturalization laws was based in considerable part on the assumptions of Anglo-conformity — immigrants who were culturally or racially inferior and incapable of being assimilated, either culturally or biologically, would have to be excluded.[11] Those who rose to the immigrants' defence argued almost entirely from economic grounds: immigration from non-British sources was needed to aid in economic development, not because it might add anything to Canada's social or cultural life.

Although the trend toward restrictionism during the early 1900s seemed to indicate a government trend toward Anglo-conformity in response to public pressure, for the most part between 1867 and 1945 there was no explicit federal government policy with regard to the role of non-British and non-French ethnic groups in Canadian society. It was generally assumed, however, that immigrants would eventually be assimilated into either English-Canadian or French-Canadian society. A recent careful study of Clifford Sifton's attitudes toward immigrant groups in Canadian society concludes Sifton assumed that central and eastern Europeans "... would be 'nationalized' in the long run through their experience on the land. ..."[12] The federal government's concern was tied to the economic consequences of immigration, while schools, the primary agents of assimilation, were under provincial jurisdiction. The federal government had encouraged Mennonites and Icelanders to settle in blocks in Manitoba during the 1870s and had given them special concessions (including local autonomy for both and military exemptions for the Mennonites) to entice them to stay in Canada rather than move to the United States.[13] But this was not because of any conscious desire to make Canada a cultural mosaic, nor was it out of any belief in the value of cultural diversity. Block settlements, by providing social and economic stability, were simply a way of getting immigrants to settle in the west and remain there.[14] The government policy was pragmatic and concerned primarily with economic growth and "nation building"; there was little rhetoric in immigration propaganda picturing Canada as a home for oppressed minorities who would be able to pursue their identities in Canada.

Provincial governments were faced with the problems of assimilation more directly than the federal government since the provinces maintained jurisdiction over the educational systems. The whole question of the varying attitudes of provincial authorities toward assimilation is much too complex to outline in this article; suffice it to say that with some notable exceptions (like the bilingual school system in Manitoba between 1896 and 1916, and the school system which was established for Hutterites in Alberta), Anglo-conformity was the predominant aim of the public school system and was an underlying theme in the textbooks.

Anglo-conformity was most pronounced during the First World War as nationalism precipitated insistent hostility to "hyphenated Canadianism" and demanded an unswerving loyalty. For many Anglo-Canadians during the war, loyalty and cultural and linguistic uniformity were synonymous. During the war, western provincial governments acted to abolish the bilingual schools which had previously been allowed.[15] The formation of the Union government of Conservatives and Liberals during the war was an attempt to create an Anglo-Saxon party, dedicated to "unhyphenated Canadianism" and the winning of the war; even if this meant trampling on the rights of immigrants through press censorship and the imposition of the War Time Elections Act which disfranchised "enemy aliens" who had become Canadian citizens after March 21, 1902.[16] Various voluntary associations like the YMCA, IODE, National Council of Women, Canadian Girls in Training, Girl Guides, Big Brothers and Big Sisters Organizations and Frontier College, as well as the major Protestant denominations, also intensified their efforts to "Canadianize" the immigrants, particularly at the close of the war when immigrant support for radical organizations brought on anti-radical nativist fears of the "menace of the alien."[17] The pressures for conformity were certainly real, even if English-Canadians could not always agree completely on the exact nature of the norm to which immigrants were to be assimilated.

All the major books on immigration prior to 1920, including J.S. Woodsworth's *Strangers Within Our Gates*, J.T.M. Anderson's *The Education of the new Canadian,* Ralph Connor's *The Foreigner*, Alfred Fitzpatrick's *Handbook for New Canadians,* C.A. Magrath's *Canada's Growth and Some Problems Affecting It,* C.B. Sissons's *Bilingual Schools in Canada*, and W.G. Smith's *A Study in Canadian Immigration*, were based on the assumptions of Anglo-conformity. To lump all these books together is of course to oversimplify, since they approached the question of immigration with varying degrees of nativism (or anti-foreign sentiment) and humanitarianism. Nor were all of the voluntary organizations' attempted "Canadianization" work among immigrants motivated solely by the fear that immigrants would undermine the cultural homogeneity of English-speaking Canada. Many of these writers and organizations saw their work with the immigrants as a means of fighting social problems and helping immigrants achieve a basic level of political, social and economic integration into Canadian society. But it cannot be denied that their basic assumption was that of Anglo-conformity. Cultural diversity was either positively dangerous, or was something that would and should disappear with time, and with the help of Anglo-Canadians.

Perhaps it should be emphasized that the individuals advocating Anglo-conformity were not just the reactionaries of their day. Protestant Social Gospellers (including J.S. Woodsworth, later one of the founders of the CCF) who played such a prominent role in virtually all the reform movements of the pre-World War One period (including women's rights, temperance, and labour, farm and penal reform) believed that immigrants needed to be assimilated to Anglo-Canadian Protestant values as part of the effort to establish a truly Christian society in English-speaking Canada.[18] Women's groups pushing for the franchise argued that certainly they deserved the vote if "ignorant foreigners" had it, and joined in the campaign to Canadianize the immigrants who "must be educated to high standards or our whole national life will be lowered by their presence among us."[19]

But there was a central contradiction in Anglo-Canadian attitudes toward ethnic minorities. Non-Anglo-Saxon immigrants were needed to open the west and to do the heavy jobs of industry. This meant not only the introduction of culturally distinctive groups, but groups which would occupy the lower rungs of the socio-economic system. The pre-1920 period was the period of the formation of, and the most acute expression of what was later called the "vertical mosaic." Anglo-Canadians were not used to the idea of cultural diversity, nor the degree of class stratification which developed during this period of rapid settlement and industrialization. The answer to all the problems of social diversity which the immigrants posed was assimilation. The difficulty however with achieving this goal of assimilation was not only the large numbers of immigrants, or the fact that not all (or even a majority) of them wanted to be assimilated. One of the major factors preventing assimilation was discrimination by the Anglo-Canadian majority.

The basic contradiction, then, of Anglo-Canadian attitudes as expressed through the "Canadianization" drives was the tension between the twin motives of humanitarianism and nativism — between the desire to include non-British immigrants within a community and eliminate cultural differences and the desire to stay as far away from them as possible because of their presumed undesirability. This contradiction was graphically revealed at the national conference of the IODE in 1919. The women passed one resolution advocating a "Canadianization campaign" to "propagate British ideals and institutions," to "banish old world points of view, old world prejudices, old world rivalries and suspicion" and to make new Canadians 100 per cent British in language, thought, feeling and impulse." Yet they also passed another resolution protesting "foreigners" taking British names.[20]

It does not appear that this was simply a case of the Anglo-Canadian majority being divided between those who wanted to pursue a strategy of assimilation, and those who wanted to pursue a strategy of subordination and segregation. Certainly there was some division along these lines, but as suggested by the IODE resolutions, discrimination and anglo-conformity were often simply two different sides of the same coin — the coin being the assumption of the inferiority of non-Anglo-Saxons.

What developed throughout English-speaking Canada during this period was a vicious circle of discrimination. Non-Anglo-Saxons were discriminated against because they were not assimilated, either culturally or socially, but one of the reasons they were not assimilated was because of discrimination against them. As one researcher noted in a 1917 report on "Social Conditions in Rural Communities in the

Prairie Provinces," the group "clannishness" of immigrants which was so widely deplored by the public was caused as much by the prejudice of the English as it was by the groups' desire to remain different.[21]

There is no need to catalogue here the extensive patterns of social, economic and political discrimination which developed against non-Anglo-Saxons.[22] Patterns of discrimination parallelled preferences of immigrant sources with northern and western Europeans encountering relatively little discrimination, central and southern Europeans and Jews encountering more discrimination and non-whites encountering an all pervasive pattern of discrimination which extended to almost all aspects of their lives. Discrimination was one of the main factors which led to the transference (with only a few exceptions) of the same ethnic "pecking order" which existed in immigration policy to the place each group occupied in the vertical mosaic, with the British (especially the Scots) on top, and so on down to the Chinese and blacks who occupied the most menial jobs.[23] Non-British and non-French groups not only had very little economic power; they also would not even significantly occupy the middle echelons of politics, education or the civil service until after the Second World War.

The ethnic stereotypes which developed for eastern European and Oriental groups emphasized their peasant origins. These stereotypes played a role in determining the job opportunities for new immigrants and functioned to disparage those who would climb out of their place. Opprobrious names such as "Wops," "Bohunks" and especially "foreigner" indicated class as well as ethnic origin and these terms were used as weapons in the struggle for status. The very word "ethnic" carried, for many people, such an aura of opprobrium that even recently there have been attempts to expurgate the use of the word. Ethnic food and folklore were regarded by most Anglo-Canadians as not only "foreign," but "backward" and lower class. Folklorist Carole Henderson has aptly described the views of Anglo-Canadians toward folklore (views which continue to the present day): "Except for members of some delimited regional and usually ethnic, subcultures such as Newfoundlanders or Nova Scotian Scots, most Anglo-Canadians simply fail to identify folklore with themselves, and tend to consider such materials to be the . . . unimportant possessions of the strange, foreign or 'backward people in their midst'."[24]

The 1920s and the Emergence of Melting Pot Ideas

The 1920s brought the second main wave of non-British and non-French immigrants to Canada and saw the emergence of the second ideology of assimilation, the "melting pot." During the early 1920s both Canada and the United States had acted to further restrict immigration from southern, central and eastern Europe and from the Orient. Chinese were virtually excluded from Canada, and central, southern and eastern Europeans were classified among the "non-preferred" and restricted category of immigrants. But by the mid-1920s several powerful sectors of Canadian society, including transportation companies, boards of trade, newspapers and politicians of various political persuasions, as well as ethnic groups, applied pressure on the King government to open the immigration doors.[25] These groups believed that only a limited immigration could be expected from the "preferred" countries and that probably only central and eastern Europeans would do the rugged work of clearing marginal land. The railways continued to seek immigrants to guarantee revenue for their steamship lines, traffic for their railways and settlers for their land. With improving economic conditions in the mid-twenties, the federal government responded to this pressure and changed its policy with respect to immigrants from central and eastern Europe.

While continuing to emphasize its efforts to secure British immigrants, in September 1925, the Liberal government of Mackenzie King entered into the "Railways Agreement" with the CPR and CNR which brought an increased number of central and eastern Europeans. The Government authorized the railways to encourage potential immigrants of the "non-preferred" countries to emigrate to Canada and to settle as "agriculturalists, agricultural workers and domestic servants."[26]

Through this agreement, the railways brought to Canada 165,000 central and eastern Europeans and 20,000 Mennonites. They represented a variety of ethnic groups and a diversity of reasons for emigrating. Most of the Ukrainian immigrants were political refugees. Poles, Slovaks and Hungarians were escaping poor economic conditions. German-Russians and Mennonites were fleeing civil war, economic disaster and the spectre of cultural annihilation in Russia.[27] Often they chose Canada since they could no longer get into the United States because of its quota system and the Canadian route was the only way they could get to North America. With this new wave of immigration, the proportion of the Canadian population that was not of British, French, or native origin, rose to more than 18 per cent by 1931.

In responding to this new wave of immigration, many opinion leaders held to an earlier belief that Canada should be patterned exclusively on the British model, and continued to advocate Anglo-conformity. In national periodicals and newspapers during the

1920s, the emphasis which was placed on the need to attract British immigrants was related to this assumption that Anglo-conformity was essential to the successful development of Canadian society. "Foreign" immigrants was related to this assumption that Anglo-conformity was Britishers to maintain Anglo-Saxon traditions.[28] R.B. Bennett, later to become the Conservative prime minister during the early 1930s, attacked melting pot ideas in the House of Commons and argued "These people [continental Europeans] have made excellent settlers: . . . but it cannot be that we must draw upon them to shape our civilization. We must still maintain that measure of British civilization which will enable us to assimilate these people to British institutions, rather than assimilate our civilization to theirs . . ."[29]

The influx of new immigrants from central and eastern Europe during the mid and late twenties also aroused protests from a number of nativist organizations such as the Ku Klux Klan, The Native Sons of Canada, and the Orange Order who were convinced that Canada should "remain Anglo-Saxon."[30] Nativist sentiment in western Canada was most pronounced in Saskatchewan where one of its leading spokesmen was George Exton Lloyd, an Anglican bishop and one of the founders of the Barr colony at Lloydminster.

In a torrent of newspaper articles and speeches, Lloyd repeated the warning that Canada was in danger of becoming a "mongrel" nation: "The essential question before Canadians today is this: Shall Canada develop as a British nation within the empire, or will she drift apart by the introduction of so much alien blood that her British instincts will be paralyzed?"[31] According to Lloyd, Canada had but two alternatives: it could either be a homogeneous nation or a heterogeneous one. The heterogeneous or melting pot idea had not worked in the United States (as evidenced by large numbers of unassimilated immigrants at the outbreak of the First World War), and could not, he argued, work in Canada. With Lloyd, as with other individuals and organizations promoting Anglo-conformity at this time, one gets the distinctive feeling that they were on the defensive. Like other English-speaking Canadians who had a strong attachment to Britain and the Empire, Lloyd saw a threat to Canada's "British" identity, not only in the increasing numbers of "continental" immigrants, but also in the declining status of things British as Canadians moved towards a North American based nationalism which did not include loyalty to the British Empire as its primary article of faith.[32]

During the late 1920s, a new view of assimilation, the melting pot, developed greater prominence. This view of assimilation, which arose partly as a means of defending immigrants against nativist attacks from people like Lloyd, envisioned a biological merging of Anglo-Canadians with immigrants and a blending of their cultures into a new Canadian type. Whereas Lloyd and other nativists argued that since immigrants could not conform to Anglo-Canadian ideals they should be excluded, a new generation of writers argued that assimilation was indeed occurring, but to a new Canadian type.[33] Since assimilation was occurring, nativist fears were unwarranted. Indeed, immigrants would make some valuable cultural contributions to Canada during the process of assimilation. Although these writers did not all use the melting pot symbol when discussing their view of assimilation, one can lump their ideas together under the rubric of the melting pot because they did envisage the emergence of a new society which would contain contributions from the various immigrant groups.

Most of these writers who defended continental European immigration did not seriously question the desirability of assimilation. Robert England, a writer and educator who worked for the CN, had read widely enough in anthropological sources to be influenced by the cultural relativism of Franz Boas and other anthropologists and did in his writing question the desirability of assimilation.[34] But most of these writers were concerned primarily with attempting to promote tolerance toward ethnic minorities by encouraging their assimilation, and many became involved in programs to facilitate this assimilation.

Advocates of Anglo-conformity and the melting pot both believed that uniformity was ultimately necessary for unity, but they differed on what should provide the basis of that uniformity. Advocates of the melting pot, unlike the promoters of Anglo-conformity, saw assimilation as a relatively slow process, and saw some cultural advantages in the mixing that would occur.

There was not, however, always a clear distinction between Anglo-conformity and the melting pot. Rhetoric indicating that immigrants might have something more to offer Canada than their physical labour was sometimes only a thinly veiled version of Anglo-conformity; the melting pot often turned out to be an Anglo-Saxon melting pot. For example, John Blue, a prominent Edmonton promoter and historian, wrote in his history of Alberta in 1924 that the fears about foreign immigration destroying Canadian laws and institutions had proved groundless. "There is enough Anglo-Saxon blood in Alberta to dilute the foreign blood and complete the process of assimilation to the mutual advantage of both elements."[35]

There were a variety of reasons for the development of melting pot ideas during the 1920s.[36] The growth of an autonomous Canadian nationalism helped the spread of such ideas. Some English-Canadian opinion leaders began to discuss the need for conformity to an exclusively Canadian norm rather than a "British" norm. One of the arguments that John W. Dafoe, the influential editor of the *Winnipeg Free Press* and J.S. Ewart, a constitutional lawyer, used in support of their view of Canadian nationalism was that non-British immigrants could not be expected to feel loyalty to the British Empire.[37]

Melting pot advocates tended to the people who had some personal experience with immigrants, and recognized both the intense pride that immigrants had in their cultural backgrounds as well as the rich cultural sources of those traditions. But they also lived in a time when recognition of ethnicity meant mostly Anglo-Canadian use of ethnicity as a basis of discrimination or exploitation. It was also a time when some ethnic groups were still close enough to their rural peasant roots that ethnic solidarity was often not conducive to upward mobility. The view of most melting pot advocates that the disappearance of ethnicity as a basis of social organization would increase the mobility opportunities of the second generation was based on a sound grasp of the realities of the day. The life-long campaign of John Diefenbaker for "unhyphenated Canadianism" and "one Canada" grew out of this experience with ethnicity as something that could be used to hinder opportunities, and was consistent with his emphasis on human rights, rather than group rights.[38]

The 1930s

Although immigration was severely cut back during the depression of the 1930s, the role of ethnic minorities in English-speaking Canada continued to be a major public concern. Paradoxically, although the depression witnessed the high point of discrimination against non-Anglo-Saxons, it was also during the 1930s that the first major advocates of cultural pluralism in English-speaking Canada began to be heard.

The depression affected non-Anglo-Saxon immigrants more than most other groups in the society. These immigrants, because of their language problems and lack of specialized skills, were concentrated in the most insecure and therefore most vulnerable segments of the economy. Since immigrants were the last hired and the first fired, a large proportion were forced onto relief. Government officials were gravely concerned about the way immigrants seemed to complicate the relief problem. Calls by some officials for deportation as the solution to the relief problem were heeded by the federal government; sections 40 and 41 of the Immigration Act (still essentially the same act as the one which existed in 1919) provided for deportation of non-Canadian citizens on relief and government officials took advantage of the law to reduce their relief rolls.

While there was some continuing concern over the assimilation of non-British and non-French immigrants during the 1930s, most Anglo-Canadians were more concerned about protecting their jobs.[39]

Prior to the depression, most Anglo-Saxons were content to have the foreigners do all the heavy work of construction, and the dirty work of the janitors and street sweepers. But as the economy slowed down, these jobs became attractive. Whereas the pre-depression attitude was "let the foreigners do the dirty work," the depression attitude became "how come these foreigners have all of our jobs?" The 1930s also saw the high point of anti-semitism as the patterns of discrimination which had hindered the desires of second generation Jews for entry into the professions were extended into a vicious and virulent anti-semitism by fascist groups.[40]

Barry Broadfoot's book *Ten Lost Years* also makes it clear that discrimination and prejudice flourished during the depression. In the transcripts of his interviews with the "survivors" of the depression, one is struck by the all-pervasiveness of derogatory ethnic epithets in interviewees' recollections of their contact with immigrants. One does not read of Italians, Chinese or Poles. One reads of "Dagos," "Wops," "Chinks," "Polacks," "Hunyaks."[41] One survivor of the depression, waxing philosophical, gives explicit expression to the prevailing attitudes of the time. He compares how the depression affected people from R.B. Bennett down to "the lowest of the low," "some bohunk smelling of garlic and not knowing a word of English. . . ."[42] Another survivor recalls that her boy had great difficulty finding work during the depression, and went berserk because of the blow to his self-esteem when the only job he could find was "working with a bunch of Chinks. . . ."[43]

The vicious circle of discrimination became perhaps even more vicious during the 1930s as non-Anglo-Saxons' political response to the depression further poisoned attitudes toward them. The discrimination and unemployment which non-Anglo-Saxons faced was an important factor in promoting the support of many for radical political solutions to the depression, in either communist or fascist movements. Indeed, the vast majority of the support for the communists throughout Canada, and for the fascists in western Canada, came from non-Anglo-Saxons.[44] Ethnic support for these two movements, and the conflict between left and right within most central and eastern European groups and the Finns, was seen as further evidence of the undesirability of non-Anglo-Saxons. The existence of fascist and communist movements in Canada was not of course due simply to the presence of immigrants bringing "old world" ideas. The leaders in both movements were predominantly of British origin,[45] and their "ethnic" support came more from immigrants reacting to depression conditions than from immigrants bringing to

Canada old world ideas. But the depression gave further support to the notion of non-Anglo-Saxons being unstable politically; one more proof along with immigrant drinking, garlic eating and the legendary violence at Slavic weddings, that non-Anglo-Saxons were in dire need of baptism by assimilation. Deporting immigrant radicals was seen as one alternative to assimilation and the federal government did not hesitate to use this weapon.[46]

The relationship in the public mind between ethnicity, lower social class origins, and political unsoundness explains why during the late 1920s so many second-generation non-Anglo-Saxons who were anxious to improve their lot economically made deliberate attempts to hide their ethnic background, such as by changing their names. Ethnic ties were clearly disadvantageous for those non-Anglo-Saxons seeking economic security or social acceptance. The experience of the second generation in English-speaking Canada was similar to the second-generation experience as described by a historian writing about ethnic groups in the United States. "Culturally estranged from their parents by their American education, and wanting nothing so much as to become and to be accepted as Americans, many second generation immigrants made deliberate efforts to rid themselves of their heritage. The adoption of American clothes, speech, and interests, often accompanied by the shedding of an exotic surname, were all part of a process whereby antecedents were repudiated as a means of improving status."[47]

Despite the continuing dominance of the old stereotypes concerning non-Anglo-Saxons and the continuing dominance of assimilationist assumptions, the 1930s also saw the emergence of the first full-blown pluralist ideas in somewhat ambiguous form in John Murray Gibbon's book *The Canadian Mosaic* and in the writings of Watson Kirkconnell, then an English professor at the University of Manitoba. These writers were much more familiar than earlier writers with the historical backgrounds of the ethnic groups coming to Canada, and they were influenced by a liberalism which rejected the assumptions of Anglo-Saxon superiority. Gibbon, a publicity agent for the Canadian Pacific Railway, wrote his book as an expansion of a series of CBC radio talks on the different ethnic groups of Canada. He traced the history of each group and related their contributions to Canadian society. Although he was concerned with the preservation of folk arts and music, he also went out of his way to alleviate fears of unassimilability by discussing individuals' assimilation as well as the "cement" of common institutions which bound the Canadian mosaic together. Although Gibbon was not the first writer to use the mosaic symbol, he was the first to attempt to explore its meaning in any significant way.

Kirkconnell was an essayist, poet and prolific translator of European verse from a number of European languages. His writing on ethnic groups was based on a different approach than Gibbon's. He tried to promote tolerance toward "European Canadians" by sympathetically portraying the cultural background of the countries where the immigrants originated and by demonstrating the cultural creativity of European immigrants in Canada through translating and publishing their creative writing.[48] In his writing he attacked the assumptions of Anglo-conformity, and advocated a multicultural society which would allow immigrants to maintain pride in their past.

> . . . it would be tragic if there should be a clumsy stripping-away of all those spiritual associations with the past that help to give depth and beauty to life . . . If . . . we accept with Wilhelm von Humboldt 'the absolute and essential importance of human development in its richest diversity,' then we shall welcome every opportunity to save for our country every previous element of individuality that is available.[49]

Kirkconnell was not advocating complete separation of ethnic groups so that they might be preserved. He believed that assimilation needed to occur in the realm of political and economic values and institutions but he hoped that some of the conservative values and folk culture of immigrants could be preserved.

Kirkconnell did not ignore the political differences within ethnic groups. Indeed, with the outbreak of the Second World War he wrote a book in which he attempted to expose and combat both fascist and communist elements in different ethnic groups.[50] But he was also active in attempts to bring various other factions of eastern European groups together in order to alleviate public criticism of divisions within ethnic groups.[51]

These advocates of pluralism believed that ethnic diversity was not incompatible with national unity. Unity need not mean uniformity. They believed that recognition of the cultural contributions of non-Anglo-Saxon groups would heighten the groups' feeling that they belonged to Canada and thus strengthen Canadian unity. But Gibbon and Kirkconnell were voices crying in the wilderness — a wilderness of discrimination and racism.

After 1945: The Emergence of Multiculturalism

The war period and early postwar period was a transitional time with respect to attitudes toward immigration and ethnicity. Although the war brought renewed hostility toward enemy aliens, a number of developments during the war eventually worked to undermine ethnic prejudice. During the arrival of the third wave of immigration in the late 1940s and 1950s, many prewar prejudices lingered, and ethnic minorities encountered considerable pressures for conformity. But for a variety of intellectual, social and demographic reasons, the ideology of cultural pluralism has been increasingly accepted in the post-World War Two period. The decline of racism and the growing influence of theories about cultural relativism opened the way for the emergence of pluralist ideas. The arrival of many intellectuals among the postwar political refugees from eastern Europe and the growth in the number of upwardly mobile second- and third-generation non-Anglo-Canadians, some of whom felt that they were not being fully accepted into Canadian society, increased the political pressures at both federal and provincial levels for greater recognition of Canada's ethnic diversity. Some suggested that this could be achieved through the appointment of senators of a particular ethnic origin, or through the introduction into the school curriculum of ethnic content and of ethnic languages as courses (and sometimes as languages of instruction).[52]

These demands for greater government recognition of "other ethnic groups" increased during the 1960s in response to the French-Canadian assertion of equal rights and the Pearson government's measures to assess and ensure the status of the French language and culture. In 1963 the Royal Commission on Bilingualism and Biculturalism was appointed to "inquire into and report upon the existing state of bilingualism and biculturalism in Canada and to recommend what steps should be taken to develop the Canadian Confederation on the basis of an equal partnership between the two founding races, taking into account the contribution made by the other ethnic groups to the cultural enrichment of Canada." Many non-British, non-French groups, particularly the Ukrainians, opposed the view that Canada was bicultural. By 1961, 26 per cent of the Canadian population was of other than British or French ethnic origin; over two hundred newspapers were being published in languages other than French and English; there were fairly well-defined Italian, Jewish, Slavic and Chinese neighbourhoods in large Canadian cities, and there were visible rural concentrations of Ukrainians, Doukhobors, Hutterites and Mennonites scattered across the western provinces: thus, how was it possible for a royal commission to speak of Canada as a *bi*cultural country?

This feeling that biculturalism relegated all ethnic groups who were other than British or French to the status of second-class citizens helps explain the resistance some of these groups expressed to the policies and programs that were introduced to secure the status of the French language in Canada. The place of the so-called other ethnic groups in a bicultural society became a vexing question for federal politicians, who had originally hoped that steps to ensure French-Canadian rights would go a long way towards improving inter-ethnic relations in Canada. The partial resolution of this dilemma was the assertion in October 1971 by Prime Minister Trudeau that, in fact, Canada is a *multi*cultural country and that steps would be taken by the federal government to give public recognition to ethnic diversity through the introduction of a policy of multiculturalism. Several provinces with large numbers of non-Anglo Canadians have also initiated their own policies of multiculturalism.

Although most political leaders in English-speaking Canada have accepted and proclaimed the desirability of Canada's ethnic diversity, the Canadian public has not given unanimous support to pluralism. The debate over the place of ethnic groups in Canadian life continues, focusing on such questions as: Does the encouragement of pluralism only serve to perpetuate the vertical mosaic, in which class lines coincide with ethnic lines, or does it help break down class barriers by promoting acceptance of the legitimacy of cultural differences? Are the goals of current government policy — cultural pluralism and equality of opportunity — mutually compatible? Does the encouragement of ethnic group solidarity threaten the freedom of individuals in these groups, or can ethnic groups provide a liberating, rather than a restricting, context for identity? Does the encouragement of cultural diversity serve to perpetuate old-world rivalries, or will the recognition of the contributions of Canada's ethnic groups heighten their feeling that they belong in Canada and thus strengthen Canadian unity? Is government talk of multiculturalism just a way to attract the ethnic vote, or is positive action necessary to preserve cultural pluralism when cultural diversity throughout the world is being eroded by the impact of industrial technology, mass communication and urbanization? Does the encouragement of multiculturalism simply heighten the visibility of the growing numbers of non-whites in the country and hinder their chances of full acceptance as individuals into Canadian life, or is a public policy of multiculturalism essential to an effective campaign against racism? The nature of these arguments suggest that the prevailing assumptions about immigration and ethnicity have changed over time in English-speaking Canada. They also suggest that the discussion about the role of immigration and ethnic groups in Canadian life is still an important, and unfinished, debate.

Notes

1. For a discussion of these three ideologies of assimilation in the United States, see Milton Gordon, *Assimilation in American Life* (New York, 1964).
2. L.G. Thomas, "The Umbrella and the Mosaic: The French-English Presence and the Settlement of the Canadian Prairie West," in J.A. Carroll, ed., *Reflections of Western Historians* (Tucson, Arizona, 1969), pp. 135–52; Allan Smith, "Metaphor and Nationality in North America," *Canadian Historical Review* 51 no. 3 (September, 1970).
3. The Canadian census has consistently classed the Irish as part of the British group.
4. Howard Palmer, *Land of the Second Chance: A History of Ethnic Groups in Southern Alberta* (Lethbridge, 1972); Norman Macdonald, *Canada Immigration and Colonization, 1841–1903* (Toronto, 1967); Harold Troper, *Only Farmers Need Apply* (Toronto, 1972).
5. Donald, Avery, "Canadian Immigration Policy and the Foreign Navvy," *Canadian Historical Association Reports*, 1972; Edmund Bradwin, *Bunkhouse Man* (New York, 1928); H. Troper and R. Harney, *Immigrants* (Toronto, 1975).
6. Donald Avery, "Canadian Immigration Policy, 1896–1919: The Anglo-Canadian Perspective," (Ph.D. thesis, University of Western Ontario, 1973); Cornelius Jaenan, "Federal Policy Vis-à-Vis Ethnic Groups," unpublished paper, Ottawa, 1971; Howard Palmer "Nativism and Ethnic Tolerance in Alberta, 1880–1920" (thesis, University of Alberta, 1971); and "Nativism and Ethnic Tolerance in Alberta, 1920–1972," (Ph.D. thesis, York University, 1973).
7. H. Palmer, "Nativism and Ethnic Tolerance in Alberta, 1880–1920," Chapters 1 and 2; Troper, *Only Farmers Need Apply;* D.J. Hall, "Clifford Sifton: Immigration and Settlement Policy, 1896–1905" in H. Palmer, ed., *The Settlement of the West* (Calgary, 1977), pp. 60-85.
8. H. Troper, "The Creek Negroes of Oklahoma and Canadian Immigration, 1909–11," *Canadian Historical Review* (September, 1972), p. 272–88.
9. Rev. George Bryce, "Past and Future of Our Race," *Proceedings,* Canadian Club of Toronto, 1911, p. 6–7; C.A. Magrath, *Canada's Growth and Problems Affecting It* (Ottawa, 1910); Goldwin Smith in *Weekly Sun,* Feb. 1, 1899, Sept. 17, 1902, Sept. 23, 1903, May 18, 1904, Aug. 16, 1905; W.A. Griesbach, *I Remember* (Toronto, 1946), pp. 214–17, 220–21.
10. Carl Berger, *A Sense of Power* (Toronto, 1970), p. 117–88.
11. James Morton, *In The Sea of Sterile Mountains* (Vancouver, 1973); W.P. Ward, "The Oriental Immigrant and Canada's Protestant Clergy, 1858–1925," *B.C. Studies,* 22 (Summer, 1974), p. 40–55; Ted Ferguson, *A White Man's Company* (Toronto, 1975).
12. Hall, "Clifford Sifton: Immigration and Settlement Policy, pp. 79–80.
13. W.L. Morton, *Manitoba, A History* (Toronto, 1957), p. 161, 162.
14. J.B. Hedges, *Building the Canadian West* (New York, 1939); Frank Epp, *Mennonites in Canada, 1786–1920* (Toronto, 1974).
15. Cornelius J. Jaenen, "Ruthenian Schools in Western Canada 1897–1919," *Paedagogica Historica,* International Journal of the History of Education, 10, no. 3 (1970), pp. 517–41, Avery, "Canadian Immigration Policy," pp. 374–420.
16. Ibid., p. 408.
17. Kate Foster, *Our Canadian Mosaic* (Toronto, 1926); J.T.M. Anderson, *The Education of the New Canadian* (Toronto, 1918); C.B. Sissons, *Bi-Lingual*

Schools in Canada (Toronto, 1917); W.G. Smith, *Building the Nation* (Toronto, 1922). For a discussion of some of the concrete activities involved in these "Canadianization" programs, see Harney and Troper, *Immigrants,* Chapter 4.

18. J.S. Woodsworth, *Strangers Within our Gates* (Winnipeg, 1909); Marilyn Barber, "Nationalism, Nativism and the Social Gospel: The Protestant Church Response to Foreign Immigrants in Western Canada, 1897–1914" in Richard Allen, ed., *The Social Gospel in Canada* (Ottawa, 1975), pp. 186–226.
19. Quoted in Barbara Nicholson, "Feminism in the Prairie Provinces to 1916" (M.A. thesis, University of Calgary, 1974), p. 71. For the views of womens' groups on immigration and the role of immigrants in Canada society, see ibid., pp. 83–85, 86, 114, 121, 133, 165–69, 186–87.
20. Reported in *Lethbridge Herald,* May 29, 1919.
21. J.S. Woodsworth, "Social Conditions in Rural Communities in the Prairie Provinces" (Winnipeg, 1917), p. 38.
22. For a fairly extensive chronicling of patterns of discrimination against a number of minority groups, see Morris Davis and J.F. Krauter, *The Other Canadians* (Toronto, 1971).
23. For an analysis of the various causes of ethnic stratification (settlement patterns, time of arrival, immigrant and ethnic occupations, ethnic values, language barriers and discrimination and exploitation) see Book IV, *Report of the Royal Commission on Bilingualism and Biculturalism* (Ottawa, 1969), Chapter 2.
24. Carole Henderson, "The Ethnicity Factor in Anglo-Canadian Folkloristics," *Canadian Ethnic Studies,* 7, no. 2, forthcoming.
25. *Canadian Annual Review*: 1923, p. 264–65; 1924–25, p. 190–92.
26. *Canada Year Book,* 1941, p. 733.
27. Olha Woycenko, *The Ukrainians in Canada* (Winnipeg, 1967); Victor Turek, *Poles in Manitoba* (Toronto, 1967), p. 43; J.M. Kirschbaum, *Slovaks in Canada* (Toronto, 1967), p. 101; Edmund Heier, "A Study of German Lutheran and Catholic Immigrants in Canada formerly residing in Czarist and Soviet Russia" (M.A. thesis, University of British Columbia, 1955), Chapter 3.
28. R.B. Bennett, House of Commons *Debates,* June 7, 1929, p. 3925–7.
29. Ibid.
30. H. Palmer, "Nativism in Alberta, 1925–1930," *Canadian Historical Association Reports* (1974), pp. 191–99.
31. G.E. Lloyd, "National Building," *Banff Crag and Canyon,* Aug. 17, 1928.
32. A.R.M. Lower, *Canadians in the Making* (Don Mills Ontario, 1958), Chapters 22, 27.
33. J.S. Woodsworth, "Nation Building," *University Magazine,* 1917, pp. 85–99, F.W. Baumgartner, "Central European Immigration," *Queen's Quarterly* (Winter, 1930), pp. 183–92; Walter Murray, "Continental Europeans in Western Canada," *Queen's Quarterly* (1931); P.M. Bryce, *The Value of the Continental Immigrant to Canada* (Ottawa, 1928), E.L. Chicanot, "Homesteading the Citizen: Canadian Festivals Promote Cultural Exchange," *Commonwealth* (May, 1929), pp. 94–95; Chicanot, "Moulding a Nation," *Dalhousie Review* (July, 1929), pp. 232–37. J.H. Haslam, "Canadianization of the Immigrant Settler," *Annals* (May, 1923), pp. 45–49; E.H. Oliver, "The Settlement of Saskatchewan to 1914," *Transactions of the Royal Society* (1926), pp. 63–87; Agnes Laut, "Compar-

ing the Canadian and American Melting Pots," *Current Opinion,* 70 (April, 1921), pp. 458–62; Kate Foster, *Our Canadian Mosaic* (Toronto, 1926). Robert England, "Continental Europeans in Western Canada," *Queen's Quarterly* (1931).

34. Robert England, *The Central European Immigrant in Canada* (Toronto, 1929).
35. John Blue, *Alberta Past and Present* (Chicago, 1924), p. 210.
36. There were some advocates of the melting pot prior to 1920, but it did not gain widespread acceptance until the 1920s. See H. Palmer, "Nativism in Alberta, 1880–1920," Chapter 1; Marilyn Barber, "Nationalism, Nativism, and the Social Gospel."
37. Douglas Cole, "John S. Ewart and Canadian Nationalism," *Canadian Historical Association Report,* (1969), p. 66.
38. John Diefenbaker, *One Canada* (Toronto, 1975), p. 140, 141, 218–19, 274.
39. H. Palmer, "Nativism in Alberta, 1920–1972," Chapter 3.
40. James Gray, *The Roar of the Twenties* (Toronto, 1975) Chapter 11; Lita-Rose Betcherman, *The Swastika and the Maple Leaf* (Don Mills, Ontario, 1975).
41. Barry Broadfoot, *Ten Lost Years,* p. 25, 70, 76, 132, 156–64, 186, 279.
42. Ibid., p. 132.
43. Ibid., p. 186.
44. Ivan Avakumovic, *The Communist Party in Canada: A History* (Toronto, 1975), p. 66–67; Betcherman, *The Swastika and the Maple Leaf*, Chapter 5.
45. Ibid.
46. H. Palmer, "Nativism in Alberta, 1920–1972," Chapter 3.
47. M.A. Jones, *American Immigration* (Chicago, 1960), p. 298. For fictional treatments of the second generation's repudiation of the ethnic past in an attempt to become accepted, see John Marlyn, *Under the Ribs of Death* (Toronto, 1951) and Magdalena Eggleston; *Mountain Shadows* (New York, 1955), p. 122. See also, *Change of Name* (Toronto: Canadian Institute of Cultural Research, 1965).
48. Watson Kirkconnell, *The European Heritage, A Synopsis of European Cultural Achievement* (London, 1930); *Canadian Overtones* (Winnipeg, 1935). For a complete listing of Kirkconnell's work, see the list in his memoirs, *A Slice of Canada* (Toronto, 1967), p. 374–75. For an assessment of his work, see J.R.C. Perkin, ed., *The Undoing of Babel* (Toronto, 1975).
49. W. Kirkconnell, trans., *Canadian Overtones,* preface.
50. Watson Kirkconnell, *Canada Europe and Hitler* (Toronto, 1939).
51. W. Kirkconnell, *A Slice of Canada*.
52. For documentary evidence of changing ethnic attitudes in the postwar era and the emergence of multiculturalism as an idea and as a governmental policy, see H. Palmer, *Immigration and the Rise of Multiculturalism* (Toronto, 1975), Chapter 3.

The Ambiguities of a Bilingual and Multicultural Canada

GUY ROCHER

The Trudeau government's redefinition of the Canadian nation and the consequences this redefinition is likely to have for Canada's cultural and political future have not yet been sufficiently recognized. In the document presented in the House of Commons by the Prime Minister on October 8, 1971, the Trudeau government revealed its response to the recommendations of Volume IV of the Royal Commission on Bilingualism and Biculturalism, and put forward concrete measures which it intended to adopt in order to implement its chosen policy. This very important document has not received the attention it deserved. In it is to be found the image of Canadian society and its future held by the government which presides over it.

This document is of special interest to sociologists. It contains a statement of policy, and it is evident that this statement rests upon a particular sociological analysis of Canadian society. Therefore, the sociologist may both judge the quality of this sociology on which the Canadian government bases its position, and take a stand on the substance of the debate itself.

I should like first to identify the document's innovative element relative to existing conceptions of Canada, then to proceed to explain briefly the basis upon which this innovation rests, and finally to express my personal judgment of the new definition of Canada adopted by the Trudeau government.

A review of some recent history will provide a better understanding of the change brought about by the present government of Canada.

THE POSITION OF THE LAURENDEAU-DUNTON COMMISSION

The mandate given by the Pearson government, on July 19, 1963, to

---

SOURCE: Paper presented at a session on Multiculturalism in Canada at the annual meeting of the Canadian Association of Sociology and Anthropology, May 30, 1972, under the title "Les ambiguïtés d'un Canada bilingue et multiculturel." Reprinted by permission of the author.

the Royal Commission of Inquiry into Bilingualism and Biculturalism contained a clear expression of an image of Canadian society. The new commission, created under the terms of an order-in-council, was in fact charged with: "recommending the measures to be taken in order that Canadian Confederation may develop according to the principle of equality between its two founding peoples, taking into account the contribution of other ethnic groups to the cultural enrichment of Canada."

Later, the same order-in-council speaks of the "basically bicultural nature of our country and the subsequent input of other cultures." Thus, in setting out the mandate creating the Laurendeau-Dunton Commission, the Pearson government was stating clearly its image of Canadian reality as bilingual and bicultural, composed of two founding peoples, and enriched by the contribution of a large number of other ethnic groups.

This same definition was adopted by the commission. Throughout its report, the commission speaks of Canada as a country composed of two societies, one francophone, the other anglophone, or of "two dominant cultures, the English and the French," or of "two communities" forming the central core of the Canadian nation. Ever-greater numbers of cultural and ethnic groups, whose contribution is important, were added to these two original societies. Canada, with its policy of open immigration, has never given the impression of a country which wished to be a melting pot; rather, it has adopted a liberal attitude toward the ethnic groups which came to enrich it.

Following the example of the Pearson government, the Laurendeau-Dunton Commission also expressed the desire that this policy continue. It recognized that, in practice, new Canadians integrate with one or the other of the two principal communities, the anglophone or the francophone. The question was how this integration was to continue to occur. There was no question of the ethnic groups ceasing to serve as a sociological environment for the new Canadians and to enrich the Canadian cultural heritage with their contribution.

THE TRUDEAU GOVERNMENT'S POSITION

In its declaration of October 8, 1971, the Trudeau government stated: "Not only is the Government responding in a positive manner to the Commission's recommendations, but also, in order to respect the spirit of Volume IV, it wishes to go beyond these recommendations in order to ensure Canada's cultural diversity." By expressing itself in this way, the government was at the very least twisting the truth somewhat, for in reality the government's stance is clearly at variance with the mandate which had been given to the commission and with the conclusions reached by this latter body. In fact, although the Trudeau government retains the image of a bilingual Canada, it completely rejects that of a bicultural Canada. It rejects the idea of two founding peoples, two societies, two dominant cultures, and opts for another image of Canada: that of a multicultural nation. The October 8, 1971 document states: "We are of the belief that cultural pluralism is the very essence of the Canadian identity. . . . To say that we have two official languages is not to say that we have two official cultures; no culture is in and of itself more "official" than any other. . . . The term "biculturalism" does not properly depict our society; the word "multiculturalism" is more apt in this regard." In concrete terms, the government sets itself the objective of "encouraging cultural diversification within a bilingual framework."

This official stand of the Canadian government constitutes an important innovation: it breaks with the image of a unitary country as well as with that of a bicultural one. Moreover, it is an innovation which has substantial practical consequences, realized in the form of the investment of millions of dollars in various programs designed to support Canadian cultural diversity.

THE BASES FOR THIS NEW POSITION

Let us attempt to pursue in somewhat greater depth the analysis of this evolution of the Canadian government's view. Apart from the political, or even electoral, aims which were imputed to the Trudeau government, how does the government justify its innovation?

It seems to me that, in contrast to the Pearson government and the Commission on Bilingualism and Biculturalism, the image of Canada put forward by the Trudeau government has a new foundation or a new base. The Laurendeau-Dunton Commission and the Pearson government position was based on a point of view which was both historical and sociological. The concept of two nations was supported by two facts, one historical and the other sociological. First, it was seen that, historically, the country originated in two communities — anglophone and francophone — which provided the principal social and political structures still in evidence. Secondly, it was recognized that new Canadians integrate with one or the other of these two communities, both from the linguistic and from the cultural standpoint, even though they may maintain links with the culture of the country from which they or their forefathers emigrated.

In contrast, the Trudeau government's position relies on what I would call psycho-sociological foundations. The document of October 8, 1971 expresses it as follows:

> One of man's fundamental needs is a feeling of belonging, and much of our contemporary social malaise — among all age groups — exists because this need has not been met. Ethnic groups are by no means the only means of satisfying this need to belong, but they have played a very important role in Canadian society. Ethnic pluralism can help us to overcome or to avoid the homogenization or depersonalization of a mass society. Vital ethnic groups can give second-, third- and later-generation Canadians the feeling that they are linked to the traditions and peoples of various parts of the world and various periods of time.

The ethnic community thus appears to the Trudeau government as one of the primary groups able to fulfill contemporary man's need for identity and security, and to counter the anonymity and anomie of the mass society.

It is also through an appeal to social psychology that the document explains how multiculturalism can simultaneously serve Canadian unity; "The greater our feeling of security in a given social context, the more we are free to explore our identity outside this context. Ethnic groups give people a feeling of belonging which enables them to face society better than they could as isolated individuals. Fidelity to one's own culture does not necessarily, and does not usually, diminish the even greater fidelity towards the collectivity and towards the country."

This distinction between the historico-sociological foundations and the psycho-sociological foundations of an image of Canada may seem theoretical. However, it does indeed appear to be at the source of two very different concepts of Canada. The first emphasizes the central role of two original communities, to which is grafted the cultural impact of all the other ethnic groups. The second emphasizes instead the multiplicity of the ethnic groups, their absolute cultural as well as political equality, within the framework of Canada's official bilingualism.

THE DANGERS INHERENT IN THIS POSITION

I now wish to develop the reasons why I feel this concept of Canadian society to be ambiguous, faulty and dangerous in its longer-term implications. I have three principal objections:

Bilingualism

First, the distinction between language and culture constitutes one of the most debatable basic implications of the Trudeau government's position. Official bilingualism for Canada is thus detached from the cultural support upon which it relied up to now. In particular, official bilingualism, which as is known only too well, has practically no sociological roots since the majority of Canadians, whether anglophone or francophone, are not bilingual, takes on a very artificial character. Within the new context of multiculturalism, the fragile Canadian bilingualism likely risks being only a vestige of a past which can easily be abandoned or possibly denied. Bilingualism could have had some meaning inasmuch as it symbolized the marriage of two linguistic and cultural communities within Canadian Confederation. But when this idea of two cultural communities is abandoned in favour of Canada's multicultural nature, bilingualism becomes an abstraction, the symbol of a past which no longer corresponds to the present. Under these conditions, it can be foreseen that maintaining a bilingualism with such shallow roots will be found to be more and more difficult. In setting aside the historical basis for biculturalism, one will soon find no reason to maintain an artificial bilingualism. It may then be that Canada can be defined just as well as a unilingual country, or as a country where four, five or six languages are official.

It is not necessary to go far afield to find the ambiguities of bilingualism in a multicultural context; they appear in the Trudeau government statement of October 8, 1971. While proclaiming the distinction between language and culture, the Trudeau government announced that it would "take measures with a view to supplying educational materials for a non-official language. . . . Acquiring the language of one's forefathers is an important part of the development of a cultural identity." Here we see the Trudeau government recognize the link between language and culture, after denying this same link when it was a question of biculturalism and bilingualism. Furthermore, the federal government announced that it would do something for non-official languages which it has never done in establishing French in education outside Quebec. The logical outcome of the policy set out by the Trudeau government is the imminent establishment of multilingualism to replace bilingualism.

In Montreal, there already exists the kind of bilingualism which the policy of multiculturalism will lead to. Among new Canadians, the bilingualism currently practised is English-Greek, English-Italian, English-German bilingualism; English-French bilingualism is almost non-existent.

National Identity

The second important reservation which I have with respect to multiculturalism is that I do not believe it constitutes the basis for a nation. The Canadian nation, as defined by the Trudeau government, no longer has a central cultural core which is clearly identifiable. Canada would be a sort of microcosm or meeting-place for all the nations of the world, represented here by groups of greater or lesser numerical size, all having an equal right to recognition and financial support of the Canadian government. Canada probably could have been greatly enriched if it had been able to maintain the idea of two cultural communities serving as poles for groupings of the other ethnic groups. Instead of this, there is proposed to us a nebulous sort of image constituted by an undefined number of different cultures, which the Trudeau government would wish to see interact but to which it proposes no common denominator.

I perceive a sense of failure in this stance taken by the Trudeau government: it is recognized that there is no Canadian culture, either anglophone or francophone. Whereas the idea of biculturalism put forward the image of a Canada with a certain internal structure, the concept of multiculturalism offers us the absence of a national culture as its program. I wonder what kind of nation can really exist on a basis which is so fluid and so noncommittal.

The Francophone Community

Finally, I wish to emphasize very briefly that, for the French-Canadian community, this new multicultural policy is a large step backwards which has as yet, I think, gone unrecognized by French Canadians. For several generations, French Canadians have struggled to gain a recognition of a bilingualism which would not only be a recognition of French as an official language, but at the same time a recognition of the French-Canadian community as the counterpart of the English-Canadian community in the Canadian sociological structure. By detaching bilingualism from biculturalism, the Trudeau government betrays all the hopes which French Canadians could have placed in bilingualism as they perceived it; that is, closely linked to the biculturalism of which it was both a symbol and an essential condition.

Of the two main linguistic and cultural communities, anglophone and francophone, it is obviously the francophone community which will suffer the most from this new multicultural policy, and which can feel threatened by it. In reality, since the anglophone community is predominant everywhere but in Quebec, and even there is also very powerful, it will necessarily remain the centre of attraction for all the other ethnic cultures. On the other hand, in this new context the francophone community will see its position and its status decline rapidly. With economic forces already acting to its disadvantage, it will become more and more secondary in the midst of all the other cultures which will compose the new Canadian mosaic.

It is my personal belief that, as French Canadians become aware of this new situation, the Quebec separatist option will appear to be a desirable solution to an increasing number of French Canadians. I fear that the cultural fragmentation proposed to us by the October

1971 declaration of the Canadian government will in fact prove a plan for destroying Canadian Confederation. A multicultural Canada offers too few chances for the future survival and flourishing of the French-Canadian culture. The creation of an independent francophone Quebec will then appear to be the one final chance for a North American francophone nation whose future is inevitably uncertain.

The Franco-Canadians of Western Canada and Multiculturalism

ROBERT PAINCHAUD

The policy of multiculturalism put forward by the federal government in 1971 has not as yet generated much enthusiasm in French Canada. Nor, it should be added, has it received much support from what may loosely be termed English Canada. My purpose here is to examine the attitudes of the French-speaking population vis-à-vis the program which resulted from the recommendations contained in Book IV of the Royal Commission on Bilingualism and Biculturalism. More specifically, this brief survey deals only with the French-speaking community of western Canada. Others far more knowledgeable of the relations between linguistic and cultural groups in Ontario, Quebec and the Maritimes will, hopefully, examine the reaction of their French-speaking compatriots to multiculturalism.

In any event, it seems appropriate to isolate the Canadian West in a study of the relationships between the French-speaking and "ethnic" communities. Interestingly, bilingualism remains under attack in the West, while multiculturalism finds there some of its strongest advocates. My contention is that the sensitivity of the francophone communities across the prairies and in British Columbia to continuing criticisms of a bilingual Canada explains their reluctance to support and promote multiculturalism. It should be said immediately that this does not suggest that other ethnocultural communities are blamed for the difficulties experienced by the promoters of bilingualism. It reveals instead the insecurity which permeates the French-speaking minorities in that region of Canada as well as their fear that somehow multiculturalism will undermine their position as one of the cornerstones of Canadian society.

SOURCE: *Multiculturalism as State Policy*, Second Canadian Conference on Multiculturalism, Ottawa, 13–15 February 1976, pp. 29–46. Reproduced by permission of the Minister of Supply and Services, Canada.

The French Fact in Western Canada

Basic to an understanding of the French-speaking position on the contribution of other linguistic and cultural groups to the development of a Canadian identity is the troubled history of the francophone population in the Canadian West. The Manitoba Act of 1870 gave the first province to join Confederation after 1867 a set of institutions which reflected the prevailing duality at Red River between the French-speaking (Catholic) and English-speaking (Protestant) populations. It appeared that both Quebec and Ontario would share equally in the development of the northwest. Yet, within a decade, the number of French-Canadian immigrants from Quebec or the New England states failed to keep pace with the large influx of Ontarians and other immigrant groups, with the result that Manitoba soon witnessed what Professor W.L. Morton characterizes as "the triumph of Ontario democracy."[1] Nonetheless, the French-speaking leadership in western Canada maintained that this new region of Canada must continue to provide for the recognition of at least the two societies transplanted from central Canada. The protracted battles over schools in Manitoba and in what became Saskatchewan and Alberta reinforced that determination. Nor were they alone in advocating a pan-Canadian view of Canadian-*Canadien* society. Much of the French-Canadian elite from Quebec, among them Henri Bourassa, lent support to their cause. Thus, underlying the actions and posture of the French-speaking spokesmen of the West on linguistic and cultural questions was and is a strong belief in the basic duality of Canada itself.

There prevailed until quite recently a second opposing viewpoint which perceived the past and future of the country in different terms. To summarize the view briefly: Canada was essentially an English country, and as far as the West was concerned there was no place for the perpetuation of any form of duality in a region composed of many peoples of various backgrounds. What was required was the integration, if not the total assimilation, of incoming groups into what could only be an English-speaking community. One historian has concluded that Ontarians won the "struggle for cultural dominance" in the West and that the Canadianization "process" of other immigrant groups in the quarter century prior to the outbreak of World War One amounted to "an implicit slap at French Canada."[2] The objective was to favour the English language above all others, to promote British institutions over "foreign" inventions, to replace group loyalties by individual attachment to a Canadian way of life, and to achieve these goals within one generation.

Interestingly enough, the French-speaking minorities of western

Canada, in their struggle to retain or recover what they believed to be entrenched rights for their language and institutions, found allies in the European groups of Catholic faith. Acting on the belief that language and faith were inextricably mixed, French-speaking leaders, especially the clergy, sought to create a community of interests between the francophone elements — Métis, French-Canadian, French, Belgian and Swiss — and the arriving Slavic and Germanic peoples. The marked opposition of the 1880s to "foreign" immigration gave way in the 1890s and early 1900s to full encouragement of this type of immigration. While continuing, therefore, to press the federal government for measures and programs that would either facilitate the repatriation of thousands of French-Canadians living in the United States or assist in the movement of significant numbers of European French-speaking to western Canada, lay and clerical leaders welcomed the growing number of German, Flemish, Polish and Ruthenian settlers. Archbishop Adélard Langevin of St. Boniface, a dominant figure in the French and Catholic communities of western Canada, told one of his more active colonization agents in 1898 that only by reinforcing their position could they expect to resolve the critical schools questions which were deemed fundamental for their development: "Immigration must be encouraged more than ever, especially French immigration, but I exclude no one, be he Galician, Russian or German. All Catholics are welcome but the French doubly so."[3]

Within a decade, partly as a result of the judicious exploitation of the bilingual clause contained in the 1897 Laurier-Greenway Agreement, the Franco-Manitoban *collectivité* became so identified with the ethnic groups in the province that they were seen as "just another ethnic group."[4] Consequently, when a new provincial administration moved during World War One to "Canadianize" the numerous nationalities within its borders by abolishing the controversial clause and by proclaiming English as the sole language of instruction in all public schools, no exception was made for the French-speaking population. The *Manitoba Free Press*, which at times recognized the special position occupied by the francophone group but also attacked the program of "balkanization" nurtured largely by a predominantly French-speaking clergy, concluded on March 26, 1916, that the solution was to

> either stick to one language, or to go on not to bilingualism but to multi-lingualism. This country must be either English-speaking or polyglot. It is politically impossible to give special privileges by law to the French and deny them to other and more numerous non-English speaking races.

And so, in 1916, following decisive legislation pushed through the legislature by the Norris government, the Franco-Manitoban community suffered a serious blow both to its status as a charter group in the province and to its attempts to recover the rightful place of its language and culture at the official level. Needless to say, the francophone groups in the other western provinces found themselves in the same position.

It is worthwhile to pause here and consider the importance of these developments. The predicament that led the embattled French-speaking collectivities west of the Great Lakes to join with other minority groups in the pursuit of collective survival raises difficult questions. One is the cause of the failure on the part of the French-speaking leadership across western Canada to attract settlers from Quebec and elsewhere in order to increase the number of settlements of French origin across the prairies. The second question relates to the image that other ethnocultural groups have of the French-speaking community and to the debate over what distinguishes "culture" from "folklore."

Why did French Canada fail to assert itself more forcefully in western Canada? Explanations range from its lack of a frontier mentality to considerations of larger economic issues.[5] There is also a *nationaliste* interpretation which attributes the small numbers of French-speaking migrants and immigrants to the West to systematic opposition by an Anglo-Saxon majority determined to prevent the extension of the French fact west of Quebec.[6] This simplistic interpretation by contemporary Québécois historians, however, does not hold true. First, those who subscribe to it forget that francophone leaders in western Canada accused not the Anglo-Saxons, but rather the political, journalistic and clerical elites of Quebec for their own lack of interest in supporting the movement of French Canadians towards the Canadian prairies. The absence, therefore, of strong French-speaking communities which could only extend the influence of Quebec says a great deal about their view of Canada and of French Canada in the half century following Confederation. Second, one suspects that these *nationalistes* are intent on dismissing the French-speaking minorities as "dead ducks" and on blaming others for it. Clearly, the object is to exclude the minorities from the Quebec-Canada confrontation over matters of sovereignty and independence.

The image of French-speaking ethnocultural groups developed by the other ethnocultural groups was, according to Professor J.E. Rea, the result of the forced assimilation of these latter groups into an Ontario model of Canada. In his view, the persistence of French-Canadian culture in western Canada is a "continuing reminder of the price these 'new Canadians' had to pay for acceptance" into the

English-speaking whole. To which he adds that the B and B Commission "discovered the greatest resentment toward French Canada among those immigrant groups of the West whose own cultural heritage had been emasculated." He ends by asking what prospects there can be for a multicultural society in western Canada if French Canada is ghettoized or if it loses its identity.[7] Thus, the strategy of inter-ethnic cooperation developed in the 1896–1916 period sought to reverse the trend towards the "melting-pot" ideal. Have leaders in the ethnocultural communities sufficiently recognized that the French-speaking clergy especially offered its encouragement and extended generous assistance to Polish, German, Ukrainian and Flemish groups desirous of retaining their language and culture?

Relations between the francophone and ethnic communities in western Canada changed significantly in the years after 1920. A growing separation replaced the rapprochement of earlier years. In part this resulted from the organization of national churches and societies to give expression to the needs of the non-French groups. On the other hand, the French-speaking minorities disassociated themselves from ethnic issues, preferring instead to pursue their goals of linguistic and cultural survival independently. It is worthwhile recalling, however, that the private French radio stations organized in the prairie provinces after World War Two made available their facilities to interested ethnocultural groups in the 1950s and 1960s. The outcry that followed the abandonment of this policy in recent years attests to the importance of that collaboration.

Briefly then, for better or for worse, the history of western Canada reveals that the survival of the French Fact — at least in the period before 1920 — was inextricably linked to that of other ethnocultural groups. With that in mind, we may now turn to an examination of the years since the start of the Quiet Revolution. There is no doubt that events in Quebec had an impact on the consciousness of English Canada and that they very much influenced the nature and the course of cultural developments on the rest of Canada.

The French Fact and Multiculturalism in the West

How did Franco-Canadians in western Canada receive the announcement of the multiculturalism policy tabled by the Government of Canada in Parliament in October 1971?

Even before the Prime Minister's statement to the House of Commons, there were mixed feelings about the implications of the recommendations contained in Book IV of the B and B Report.

Publication of the latter, following so closely upon the enactment of the Official Languages Act, prevented francophone leaders from devoting much time to reconciling the one with the other. They were almost completely immersed in working out the impact that the Official Languages Act could have on the French-speaking *collectivités*. It is not surprising, therefore, that they concentrated their energies on revitalizing and restructuring, and in some cases on abolishing, outmoded practices and institutions. There is no doubt that the long-awaited legislation, and especially its promise of direct federal support, injected a renewed sense of confidence in the future.

Nonetheless, some groups considered the links between francophone and ethnocultural problems. Thus, in November 1970, the ACFC (Association Culturelle Franco-Canadienne de la Saskatchewan), in a brief to the joint Parliamentary Committee on the Constitution, rejected the melting-pot concept because it feared that cultural uniformity could lead to repression, prejudice and the quenching of creativity. It favoured instead the freedom of cultural expression for all — native peoples, Ukrainians, Italians, French and English. Furthermore, it argued that each province should decide which language, or languages, would be made official. "Any language other than English or French should be allowed to be made official in any province of Canada, or in any city or political region under provincial jurisdiction."[8] Finally, while proposing that French and English remain the only two official languages at the federal level, and that federal bilingual districts be established in each of the provincial capitals, the association's presentation adopted the following stance on the recognition of other cultures:

> Up to now, there has been a tendency in Canada to speak in terms of two cultural communities, anglophone and francophone, almost to the exclusion of other cultural communities, such as groups speaking Indian and Métis, Eskimo, Italian, Ukrainian and so forth. If these realities of Canadian culture are not given positive encouragement in our constitution, we fear that their subjection to unconscious harmful suppression will continue, on the pretext that they do not come within the law. Any new constitution should not only recognize these cultural communities but also recommend the establishment of official "cultural regions." These regions would be entitled to various supplementary federal services by way of emphasizing the importance of their contribution to the Canadian mosaic. Just as in the case of bilingual districts, these cultural regions would also be given official recognition by the provinces, and could have one or several "official" languages designated by them.
>
> In short, we support the creation of bilingual districts for regions in which the English and French cultures predominate, and of cultural

regions for areas in which cultures other than the English and French cultures deserve special recognition.[9]

Thus, the Franco-Canadians of Saskatchewan drew a clear distinction between federal and provincial responsibilities in linguistic and cultural matters. Let the former, they suggested, concern itself with the basic duality of the country, and the latter attend to the needs and aspirations of other groups.

No such distinction emerged from the Manitoba Mosaic Congress held in Winnipeg in October 1970. Most of the French-speaking delegates stormed out of a plenary session dealing with the problem of defining and delimiting the extent of linguistic and cultural rights. They were protesting both against the failure of the congress to support resolutions recognizing French and English as the official languages of Manitoba, and the attempt to give other languages recognition as Canadian languages with protection under the Official Languages Act.[10] The editor of *La Liberté et le Patriote,* the French weekly serving both the Manitoba and Saskatchewan communities, had anticipated difficulties before the opening of the congress. He welcomed the beginning of a serious dialogue among the various ethnic groups, as well as between them and "les autres" (presumably the French and Anglo-Saxon groups), on "the possibilities of working together to create a bilingual Canada in which each cultural identity will be able not only to survive, but also to flourish and enhance the general character of the country by making its own special contribution." One concern was that

> . . . in their efforts to maintain their ethnic or cultural identity, more often than not the majority of these groups attacked their problems alone, sometimes at the expense of others, in particular the French Canadians, who are considered to be in a more privileged position than the other groups.

Nonetheless, he invited the Franco-Manitobans to attend the congress, while perhaps not involving themselves too much in the discussions, limiting themselves to a defence of the French fact in Canada and in Manitoba and to lending moral support to other groups desirous of obtaining some protection for their identity. He concluded the editorial by restating for the occasion the theme of the special mission that French-speaking minorities, and especially that of Manitoba, could play on the Canadian scene:

> Obviously, transplanted Quebecers who have not adapted here are not going to hope that such a congress will be a success. They have not even succeeded in convincing new-Canadian groups of the validity of their own goals, and seem to have lost any interest in doing so. It is up to francophones in the rest of the country to develop the potential for a

> bilingual, multicultural Canada. The next ten years will tell whether this was a pipe dream . . . Manitoba today, with its ethnocultural complexity, is being invited to move still further ahead into the future. This cannot be accomplished without the participation of Franco-Manitobans. . . .[11]

Little public discussion ensued, as even the weeklies turned their attention to the October Crisis and the accompanying debate. Unfortunately, no one thought later of returning to the unresolved cultural issues.

If the reaction to Book IV was varied, there was at least a response. Such was not the case late in 1971 when the Prime Minister made public his government's multiculturalism policy. The event went largely unnoticed in official circles and in the francophone press of western Canada. None of the weeklies commented upon the principles or the programs contained in the Prime Minister's statement to the House of Commons. Yet they could have asked themselves what was meant by a policy of "multiculturalism within a bilingual framework." Was biculturalism laid to rest? What did the view that Canada could recognize no official culture or cultures signify for the French-speaking minorities? How might Franco-Canadians and their numerous associations contribute to a rapprochement between peoples of different languages or cultures? Their silence almost suggests disapproval.

One plausible explanation is that the French-speaking communities across the prairies and in British Columbia were so involved in taking advantage of the new climate of opinion generated in most parts of the country in favour of the concept of a bilingual Canada that they failed to interest themselves in the concerns of other ethnocultural groups. Never before, at least not since the late nineteenth century, had the French fact enjoyed so many advantages. The years after 1968 were golden years. Assisted by grants from the federal government, each of the provincial associations (the Franco-Manitoban Society, the French-Canadian Association of Alberta, and the Federation of Franco-Columbians) undertook programs of social animation aimed at revitalizing dispirited populations. There followed a reawakening that led to wider and greater participation in educational, social, cultural and economic issues affecting the *collectivités*. Initiatives made possible by federal and/or provincial assistance included financing for cultural centres, teachers' colleges, tours by local and Québécois or Acadian chansonniers, cooperative ventures, festivals, and much more. The purchase by Radio-Canada of the three private radio stations operated for over twenty years by francophone groups in each of the prairie provinces added to federal participation in the field of public communications. French-language television programming reached more communities, although there remains room for improvements in this area. It appeared that a feeling of *épanouissement* (flowering) would replace the defensiveness of *la survivance* (survival).

In the midst of these developments, Franco-Canadians did not involve themselves much in inter-cultural activities. In Manitoba, they organized a pavilion on one occasion for the very successful Folklarama held during the summer months, but have not participated in recent years. To the suggestion that the Franco-Manitobans reconsider their position, the French editor of the bilingual *St. Boniface Courier* objected that

> . . . we are not ethnics. Incidentally, this editor firmly believes that we would find ourselves in a most pitiful situation if it weren't for the federal policy of bilingualism and biculturalism. After all, this is just about the only thing keeping us alive!
>
> We are not an ethnic group, but does that necessarily mean that France, the country of origin for all of us, should not make some effort to participate in Folklarama, the "festival of nations"?[12]

This rather strange commentary thus concludes that native-born francophones are somehow non-ethnic, while the French from Europe constitute an ethnic group. Let only the latter join "folkloric" festivals, while the former engage in "cultural" projects! French-speaking members of arts or folk councils often discovered that this type of attitude led francophone groups to decline invitations to join inter-cultural events.

Franco-Canadian spokesmen have ready explanations for what many western Canadians view as a ghetto mentality. Apart from the oft-repeated argument that French-speaking people are not "just another ethnic group," they insist that English Canadians (read Anglo-Saxons), whom they perceive as the other "founding race" of Canada, are never spoken of as "ethnics" either. They fail to see, therefore, why the French-speaking population should be included, at least in terms of western Canada, in events or festivals celebrating "ethnic" traditions. Furthermore, they point to the multiplicity of cultural happenings offered by francophone groups and organizations, insisting that they are open to the public. In their view, they are bound to uphold the French fact in the West. Admittedly, the language barrier prevents many of their co-citizens from appreciating their programs, but they maintain that the latter emanate from the only community capable of giving life to Canada's other official language. How many multicultural activities, they ask, are presented in a bilingual (French-English) framework? Their answer to this question is that ethnic groups in western Canada are part and parcel of anglophone culture. In effect, this amounts to the view that there are two majority cultures in Canada.

Over the years, these same francophone leaders maintained that once the French-speaking communities had recovered much lost ground, they would be open to greater interaction with other ethnocultural groups. In the last twelve months, however, they have expressed concern over the permanence of federal and provincial support for the furtherance of the French fact in the West. The uneasiness over the future of programs until now administered by a separate section within the Secretary of State's department led to the appointment of a special task force, funded by that same department, to inquire into the needs and problems of the francophone minorities six years after the implementation of the Official Languages Act. The briefs submitted to this *Groupe de travail sur les minorités de langue française* embody revealing attitudes and positions on the relationships between bilingualism, biculturalism and multiculturalism.

The briefs touching upon the wants of the Fransaskois and of the Franco-Albertains detail the achievements of recent years and plead for the maintenance of at least the support made available to them since 1968–69. The ACFC summarizes its position thus:

> We believe that our work between 1968 and 1975 was extremely important both for its application to francophones and on the level of Canadian unity. Indeed, ever since our Association first received support from the Secretary of State Department, while there were many false starts, still there were stunning successes that could not otherwise have been accomplished. Armed with these early experiences, we are confident that in the future we will be able to step up our development program in order to permanently counteract the anglicization of our members.[13]

Neither this Saskatchewan mémoire nor that of Alberta's ACFA addresses itself to the multiculturalism policy; both associations admit to the heavy burdens placed on them in the pursuit of bilingual and bicultural goals.

The brief from La Fédération des Franco-Colombiens on the other hand emphatically states that the French fact and bilingualism are the only ways by which Canada can give itself a cultural identity distinct from that of the United States. Its authors then attack the deplorable status of the francophone minorities whose incapacity to develop themselves "... is certainly not the result of persecution and hypocrisy on the part of certain provincial governments with anglophone majorities and on the part of many individual anglophones." It is in this context that the following paragraph on the place of multiculturalism should be read:

> ... bilingualism and multiculturalism must not be confused. Multiculturalism in Canada will only be achieved when bilingualism finally

flourishes. We must have no illusions since certain provinces, British Columbia in particular, still refuse to accept the French fact. This lack of tolerance toward biiingualism has all too often been disguised by the excuse of multiculturalism. Such an attitude thwarts any attempts to achieve the desired national unity. Let us abandon multiculturalism and strive to achieve bilingualism on a national scale. When this objection has been reached, new Canadians will have the support of strong and culturally flourishing francophones in their efforts to obtain respect for their languages and cultures.[14]

While admitting that the monies spent under terms of the bilingualism program are substantial, the federation argues that the French-speaking minorities actually receive *less* assistance than groups coming under the multiculturalism grants ($3,025,000 as compared to $10 million). They make the point that the bilingualism policy makes no sense unless there are bilingual people!

A somewhat more moderate, but nonetheless pointed, brief was submitted by La Société Franco-Manitobaine. It too stresses the importance of bilingualism as a *sine qua non* for the achievement of national unity. The SFM believes that progressively the provincial governments should assume responsibility for the épanouissement of the francophone minorities, but since they cannot presently count on receiving solid and satisfactory support from them, it therefore remains essential that the federal government continue to cater to their needs. But after rendering an approving judgment on federal measures introduced over the last ten years in favour of the francophone minorities, its authors speak out against two developments which threaten these same minorities. They claim, in the first instance, that federal authorities are losing interest in the French fact beyond the borders of Ontario in the west and of New Brunswick in the east. They attribute this to the pessimistic interpretations which Québécois presumably advance in Ottawa with respect to the value of the minorities in the assertion of the French fact in Canada generally. Studies based on the 1971 census data apparently draw negative conclusions on the future of the French-speaking minorities.

The second development detrimental to the Franco-Manitobans and their compatriots in other provinces comes from western Canada. The SFM's brief explains it this way:

Another reaction from Western Canada, where the Liberal Party has a great deal of difficulty getting solid support from the electorate, tends to view the francophone minority in the West as just another ethnic group. This has resulted in pressure to make the federal bilingualism policy evolve into a policy of multiculturalism whereby francophone minorities would have no right to special treatment as such. Hence there is pressure to make the internal organization of the Secretary of

> State Department evolve in this direction. The SFM feels that both these trends, which have opposite aims but similar effects, have not yet succeeded in seriously undermining the federal government's bilingualism policy. In our view, this would be a simplistic approach that would have disastrous middle- and long-term effects on the nature of the Canadian Confederation. It would present to French Canadians in the East and West the image of English Canada as a dominant majority, along the lines of the American "melting pot," denying French any status outside Quebec, northern Ontario and New Brunswick. Certainly there can be no question of seriously offering the "ethnic" minorities in the West any more than limited support for cultural and folkloric survival. No French-speaking minority can be satisfied with such a situation.[15]

The message is clear: five or even ten years of federal and/or provincial concern do not atone for sixty years of neglect; bilingualism must take priority over multiculturalism; the federal government must continue to act as the guardian of the francophone community, because of its national status and because of the provincial government's ". . . considerable hesitation, delays and many refusals when Franco-Manitoban organizations request special grants to carry out educational, socio-economic and cultural activities in French."

The reluctance of the provincial government in asserting the "statut spécial" of the Franco-Manitoban community would be the result of "strong pressure to make it move in the direction of the multicultural approach described above."[16] Clearly, the days of l'épanouissement have not arrived.

The final report of the task force submitted to the Secretary of State in November 1975 reflects the deep-felt anxieties of the French-speaking minorities across the country, beyond Quebec that is. "C'est le temps ou JAMAIS," it proclaims from its title page. There follows a lengthy analysis of the development of the federal government's bilingualism policy and its assistance program for minority language communities, beginning with the 1963 appointment of a Royal Commission on Bilingualism and Biculturalism. It proceeds happily along through the enactment of the Official Languages Act which "*. . . was meaningful only because there were francophone minorities outside Quebec and because these minorities had and should have a real future.*"[17] The multiplier effect created by the legislation on improving relations between Canadians rested in part on the very existence of French-speaking minorities outside of Quebec which had maintained the French fact over many decades of often heroic struggles. Task force members conclude that the years between 1969 and 1972 testify to the realization of, or at least the promise of, a bilingual and bicultural Canada.

According to the authors of the report, the pattern was altered by the two federal elections held in 1972 and 1974, as well as by an anglophone "backlash" which forced a downgrading of the bilingual-bicultural program. Instead, they continue, "*multiculturalism* is now proposed as the solution to all problems, but for the French-speaking minorities it is the *death sentence of bilingualism.*"[18]

The first Canadian conference on multiculturalism, held in 1973, and the appointment of a Minister of State for multiculturalism, were followed by the imposition of a ceiling on grants intended for the official language minority groups. In their view, the francophone minorities had fulfilled their role in the Quebec-Canada confrontation by demonstrating that there could be a viable French fact in almost all regions of Canada. Having thus saved Confederation, the minorities were relegated to a position where their maintenance depended upon the tolerance or intolerance of the majority.[19]

This most important and revealing document goes on to say much more about the unique problems of the French-speaking minorities, all of which warrants close study by those concerned with such things. But its analysis of events and trends of recent years contains flaws. In the first place, it assumes that bilingualism and multiculturalism are competing and mutually exclusive policies. Furthermore, the chain of events does not bear the interpretation that the multiculturalism policy resulted from a backlash in English Canada (whatever that is) following the 1972 federal election or that it signified the end of a biculturalism policy adopted after 1969. Does this mean that the cabinet favoured a biculturalism policy, while at the same time preparing a multiculturalism policy announced in October 1971, *one full year before* the general election? The members of the Groupe de travail would have done better to consider the view that the multiculturalism policy was designed to bolster the Liberal party's support among ethnocultural communities. Would not yet another interpretation suggest that the federal government sought to reconcile the interests of both the francophone and other ethnocultural communities by proclaiming an Official Languages Act in 1969, followed by a cultural policy two years later which embodied the recognition of all cultures in the all-encompassing phrase of "multiculturalism within a bilingual framework"? An ambiguous statement that, which still leaves many unanswered questions while appealing to all. (The latter comment of course does not apply to those die-hards in Canada who oppose both bilingualism and multiculturalism.)

Relations today between Ottawa and the French-speaking minorities have not reached a breaking point; that is unlikely to happen. But this latest manifesto of what is often referred to as the diaspora reveals the degree of dependency on the federal government. One wonders how federal politicians will receive a report prepared by associations largely funded by federal departments and severely critical of Ottawa's policies in a related field. Will attacks on the multiculturalism program harm the cause of the francophone minorities? Will federal authorities appreciate the complex and deep-rooted anxieties which gave rise to their ethnocentrism? How will other ethnocultural groups react to the apparent refusal of the francophone community to accept multiculturalism? The end result may be to supply the numerous critics of bilingualism and multiculturalism with evidence of the divisiveness of both policies.

No good will result from a condemnation of the francophone outlook on linguistic and cultural issues arising out of the recognition by the federal government of Canada's multicultural fabric. An understanding of the self-image of French-speaking minorities offers the best guarantee for a dialogue urgently needed. Before considering the prospects for a rapprochement, however, may we now turn to a brief examination of three major concerns to leaders of the Franco-Canadian communities in western Canada on the eve of a period of decisions.

The Future of the French Fact in Western Canada

Paradoxically, the French-speaking communities in western Canada experience life and death at the same time. On the one hand, unprecedented social and cultural developments in the 1960s and 1970s hold the promise of a bright future. To illustrate, *Le Cercle Molière*, which is now attracting growing audiences across the West, has developed into a semi-professional theatre group. . . . Its programs have included dramas and children's plays written by local playwrights.

On the other hand, however, leaders in the francophone community as well as observers from without point to signs of disintegration which are slowly, but inevitably, strangling the western *collectivités*. The former archbishop of Saint-Boniface, Mgr. Maurice Baudoux, who devoted his life to the Church and to the survival of francophone culture in each of the three prairie provinces, told a Royal Society of Canada colloquium in June 1975 of the "dépersonnalisation culturelle" which increasingly alienates the younger generation from the legacy handed down by their fathers and forefathers. His observations, added to those of others, focus on three subjects of major concern to Franco-Canadians: the census of 1971, immigration and relations with Quebec.

Richard Arès, in a detailed study of the 1971 census, makes disturbing comments on the future of the French-speaking minorities, both in western Canada and elsewhere. A sample of his remarks attests to the seriousness of the situation. On Saskatchewan: "In Saskatchewan, French survival is turning into a tragedy." On Alberta: "This is another province where French survival is turning into a tragedy." On the West generally: "In the western provinces the situation of French is not rosy, in fact it is pitiful. It has continued to deteriorate from one decade to the next. . . . The struggle for survival is becoming increasingly a matter of heroism, a superhuman undertaking."[20]

For Arès, one composite table summarizes the present state of these minorities:

Overall Situation of the French Group in Western Canada in 1971

Province	*Ethnic origin*		*Mother tongue*		*Language usually spoken*	
Manitoba	86,515	8.8%	60,545	6.1%	39,600	3.9%
Saskatchewan	56,200	6.1	31,605	3.4	15,930	1.7
Alberta	94,665	5.8	46,500	2.8	22,700	1.4
British Columbia	96,550	4.4	38,035	1.8	11,505	0.5
Total	33,930	5.8%	176,685	3.1%	89,735	1.6%

From it, he draws the following conclusions:

> This table says it all, showing the huge losses suffered by the group of French origin in its everyday struggle for survival. From ethnic origin to mother tongue the loss is 157,245, and from mother tongue to language usually spoken the loss is 86,950. Added together these two figures give a total loss of 244,200 in Western Canada. This is cultural and linguistic genocide!
>
> French doubtless continues to survive in these areas, but only at the cost of a constant, exhausting struggle that is so costly as to be Pyrrhic in nature. More Canadians of French origin fall in the fight than survive.[21]

The University of Montreal demographer, Jacques Henripin, sounds a more ominous note in a research paper prepared as background for the Green Paper on Immigration. Assessing the future role of French-speaking minorities outside Quebec in the equilibrium between francophone and anglophone populations in Canada, he comes to the following conclusion:

> In fact, it could be said that French Canadians living outside Quebec contribute more to the English language than to French. No matter how much this group grows. Its contribution will go to the English language.

> Thus francophone communities outside Quebec are gradually disappearing. . . . The adoption of English by people of French origin is following a roughly geometric progression and in 1971 it was realized that almost half had lost their language of origin.
>
> That is one of the conclusions of my research. It seems to me that there is not much room for hope, in the light of what has happened, for the survival of francophone communities outside Quebec and for the areas bordering Quebec.[22]

Not surprisingly, francophone leaders in Western Canada do not share this almost fatalistic prediction. Nonetheless, they admit that the data pose serious questions about the future viability of their communities, but they insist that it would be premature to dismiss the resiliency of proud and resourceful minorities.

The concern over the latest census figures became apparent during public discussion on the Green Paper dealing with Canada's immigration policies. In its brief, La Société Franco-Manitobaine argued that "the disproportion between the number of anglophone and francophone immigrants is a fundamental departure from the government's bilingualism policy, since it threatens to wipe out those of us who are trying to survive as a viable francophone community in Western Canada." It asks how Canada could "give concrete support to twenty-five to fifty different cultures when one of its two cultures — or rather, one of its two forces — has had so much difficulty winning acceptance after having discovered and founded this country."[23]

Its authors further insisted that there are opportunities in western Canada for French-speaking immigrants intent on working and living in a francophone milieu, and called upon Ottawa to so inform prospective immigrants. Finally, the society indicated that it had reservations about renewed Quebec interest in immigration questions:

> We welcome, for example, the Quebec government's current interest in immigration, especially francophone immigration, an area which it has long neglected. On the other hand, we francophone minorities view with disfavour the Quebec government's tendency to proclaim itself *the* protector of French culture in Canada. We believe this role is equally the responsibility of the federal government and we would like to see it assume its responsibilities in this regard.[24]

This growing dependency on Ottawa causes concern because of the accompanying estrangement of the minorities *vis-à-vis* Quebec. Traditionally, the ties between the mother province of French Canada and the diaspora have been close. Franco-Canadian leaders from the West have argued since the entry of the northwest into Confederation that their *collectivités* were the vanguard of the French fact beyond the Great Lakes. But even in the late nineteenth century, there were indications that all was not well between them. Lay and clerical leaders from the prairies felt that their counterparts in Quebec were not sufficiently concerned about extending the French fact in western Canada. They said as much in private and in public exchanges. Typical was the biting comment of *L'Echo de Manitoba* in 1902 accusing the Québécois of direct responsibility for the unhappy schools questions:

> Over the past thirty years it would have been easy for you to send us a contingent of 2,000 immigrants each year, from among the masses rushing to the United States. . . .
>
> Then we would never have had a school problem. It should be pointed out in passing that it is you and you alone in the province of Quebec who are responsible for what has happened to the Manitoban minority.[25]

Of course, the western minorities could not subsist without assistance from Quebec. Indeed, during the fifty years that followed the loss of education rights in 1915, private and governmental assistance from Quebec greatly succoured these distant communities. It was therefore natural for Premier Jean Lesage to pose as the champion of all of French Canada in the 1960s.

That part of the *politique de grandeur* was shortlived as Quebec turned to more pressing priorities. Many francophones outside that province understood the need for the Quiet Revolution and remained confident that the new Quebec would one day resume the leadership of French Canada. But the debate between the proponents of a French Quebec and those of a French Canada soon alienated most francophones from outside Quebec. As the gulf developed, the latter turned more and more to Ottawa for the affirmation of the French fact across the country. The federal government readily assumed this function, thereby rediscovering a role it had played in Confederation until the 1890s.

This development, of itself, did not cause concern within the ranks of the francophone minorities. What did, and still does, cause anxiety is the widespread feeling that Ottawa's interest in the minorities will wane as the independentist clamour in Quebec dies down.[26] At that point, and should the involvement of various Quebec ministries in extending various forms of aid to these same minorities also decrease, the isolation of highly vulnerable francophone communities would lead to a final and complete disintegration of their social fabric. In that they would resemble other ethnocultural groups similarly threatened.

What is the connection between these three areas of concern to the French-speaking minorities and the policy of multiculturalism?

Concern about the apparent trends found in the 1971 census, concern about the possibility of adding more non-francophones to Canada's population, and concern about the implications of estrangement from Quebec and growing dependency on the federal government, help explain, in my view, the reluctance on the part of the francophone minorities to bless multiculturalism. They insist that high priority must be accorded to entrenching in law and especially in practice the policy of bilingualism. Also prompting their defence of bilingualism are the negative comments all too frequently heard from many quarters in western Canada: bilingualism is described as an "attempt to force French down our throats," as "wasteful," "divisive," "disturbingly pushy," "useless," "shameful," or "retrograde." Regrettably, rather than find allies and supporters for bilingualism among the other ethnocultural groups who understand and appreciate the value and merits of linguistic and cultural diversity, too many francophone leaders tend to associate attacks on bilingualism with multiculturalism. Others believe that because of the key role of the French-speaking minorities in Confederation, and given their presently precarious existence in western Canada, the federal government should pursue a vigorous policy of bilingualism *and* biculturalism. Their argument is that western Canadians generally should learn far more than they do at present about French Canada before receiving assistance to pursue other linguistic and cultural activities. Thus, biculturalism as a complement of bilingualism must precede any policy of multiculturalism.

To summarize, it is quite clear that the uncertain fate and future of the French fact in western Canada explains the hesitation on the part of most francophones, and the outright opposition of others, to support the policy of multiculturalism.

Perspectives for the Future

What lies ahead? What are the prospects for a rapprochement between French-speaking and other ethnocultural communities on multiculturalism?

First, they must recognize that far more unites them than divides them. They share common concerns about assimilation forces operating against them. Education questions remain vital in their struggle to preserve and develop their languages and cultures. The so-called ethnic press and the French-speaking weeklies are similarly plagued by financial and distribution problems. Above all, perhaps, history reveals that they sought to impress upon western Canada and Canada the marks of a distinctive society based on the wealth of their cultures. There is no doubt that this country benefited from the diversity they added to it. What separates them is fear, suspicion and the lack of a dialogue.

Secondly, the Franco-Canadians of western Canada must understand that bilingualism and multiculturalism are not adversary but complementary policies. Multiculturalism can only strengthen the existence of the French fact and can greatly assist the cause of bilingualism. There are spokesmen within the francophone communities who understand this, but it would be useful and important for each of the official associations (SFM, ACFC, ACFA, and the FCC) to adopt resolutions in favour of the policy of multiculturalism. If the francophone collectivities fail to support programs designed to assist other ethnocultural communities urgently in need of linguistic and cultural "recovery," they will one day find themselves is isolated within western Canada. What is worse, they would then face a hostile and unyielding bloc of assimilated groups determined not to extend to the French-speaking element any special privileges. The francophone groups, which more than other groups appreciate the value of diversity as opposed to uniformity, must recognize that they have no monopoly either on culture or on the right to cultural survival. And, while they do enjoy advantages in the area of linguistic rights, they must come to understand that other groups may wish to retain their language for cultural purposes. Ways must be found, therefore, to overcome the fear that multiculturalism will harm bilingualism.

Thirdly, non-French-speaking ethnocultural groups must be patient with the francophone communities. Let them distinguish clearly between bilingualism and multiculturalism. Are they prepared to assist their French-speaking co-citizens in seeking recognition of the existence of a French Canada *a mari usque ad mare?* Will they join with French-speaking parents who seek to obtain French language schools in their area? Are they willing to accept that their children will have to acquire perhaps two official languages before undertaking the study of their cultural language? The burden on their shoulders is indeed a heavy one, and one that has not as yet received the recognition it deserves.

Fourthly, the federal and provincial governments must be more sensitive to both the francophone and other ethnocultural communities. Why is it that some provincial governments in western Canada refuse to recognize the French fact in their province? How prepared are governments generally to entrench the rights of French Canadians in the West and in Canada on the one hand, and to legislate the rights of other linguistic and cultural groups on the other hand? Has the federal government abandoned the concept of biculturalism, or does it seek to promote multiculturalism as the expression of a cultural heritage within what could be termed loosely "French Canada" and "English Canada"? Is multiculturalism to be encouraged primarily in terms of "folklore"? Will Radio-Canada and the CBC continue — assuming of course that they have actually begun — to provide an outlet for multiculturalism only in the two official languages? These and many other questions are left unanswered. No dialogue between Canada's peoples and their governments can begin until these problems have been explored.

In the final analysis, however, the future of the French fact in Canada as well as the future of multiculturalism will depend on the willingness of Canadians to respect and cherish their diversity. Only then can there be unity.

Notes

1. W.L. Morton, *Manitoba, A History,* 2nd ed. (Toronto: University of Toronto Press, 1961), pp. 199–233.
2. J.E. Rea, "The Roots of Prairie Society" in D. Gagan, ed., *Prairie Perspectives* (Toronto: Holt, Rinehart and Winston, 1970), pp. 50–51.
3. Archives de l'Archevêché de Saint-Boniface, *Fonds Langevin,* St.-Boniface, April 5, 1898, Lengevin to Father Jean Gaire.
4. For a discussion of the objectives, strategy and implications of this issue, see Gilbert Comeault, "Les rapports de Mgr L.-P.-A. Langevin avec les groupes ethniques minoritaires et leurs répercussions sur le statut de la langue française au Manitoba, 1895-1916," *Sessions d'étude de la Société Canadienne d'Historie de l'Eglise Catholique* (1975), pp. 65–85.
5. See Arthur Silver, "French Canada and the Prairie Frontier, 1870–1890," *Canadian Historical Review*, Vol. I (1969), pp. 11–36; also Albert Faucher, "L'émigration des Canadiens-français au XIXe siècle: position du problème et perspective", in *Recherches Sociographiques,* Vol. 3 (Sept-Dec. 1964), pp. 277–318; and Gilles Paquet, "L'émigration des Canadiens-français vers la Nouvelle-Angleterre, 1870–1890: prises de vues quantitatives," in ibid., pp. 319–70.
6. For example, see Michel Brunet, *Québec-Canada Anglais* (Montreal: éditions HMH, 1969), pp. 215–16, 227.
7. See Rea, "Roots of Prairie Society," pp. 53–54.
8. "L'Association Culturelle Franco-Canadienne de la Saskatchewan et la Constitution," *La Liberté et le Patriote*, January 27, 1971.
9. Ibid.
10. See Report of Manitoba Mosaic (Winnipeg, 1971).
11. "La mosaïque culturelle du Manitoba," *La Liberté et le Patriote,* October 7, 1970.
12. "L'éternelle question," *St. Boniface Courier,* August 20, 1975. See my own response in the *St. Boniface Courier,* August 27 and September 3, 1975, also reprinted in *La Liberté,* September 3, 1975.
13. See "Mémoire de l'A.C.F.C. présenté au Groupe de travail sur les minorités de langue française," October 19, 1975. See also "Mémoire de

l'Association Canadienne-Française de l'Alberta au Groupe de Travail sur les minorités de langue française" (1975).

14. "Mémoire de la Fédération des Franco-Colombiens présenté au Groupe de travail sur les minorités de langue française," Vancouver, September 26, 1975.
15. "Mémoire de la Société Franco-Manitobaine présenté au Groupe de travail sur les minorités de langue française," September 30, 1975.
16. Ibid., p. 7.
17. "Une hypothèque à long terme avec responsabilités conjointes," report submitted to the Secretary of State by the Task Force on French-Language Minorities, November 7, 1975, p. 12 (underlining in original).
18. Ibid., p. 19 (underlining in original).
19. Ibid., p. 20.
20. Richard Arès, *Les positions — ethniques, linguistiques et religieuses — des Canadiens français à la suite du recensement de 1971 (Montréal: Les Editions Bellarmin, 1975), pp. 93, 04, 203.*
21. *Ibid., p. 96.*
22. *La Liberté*, 14 mai 1975. See also Jacques Henripin, "L'immigration et le déséquilibre linguistique."
23. "Mémoire de La Société Franco-Manitobaine à la Commission parlementaire sur l'immigration," June 1975, pp. 4, 5.
24. Ibid., p. 9.
25. Quotes in *La Patrie* (Montreal), January 24, 1902.
26. See Richard Arès, *Qui fera l'avenir des minorités francophones au Canada* (Saint-Boniface, La Société Historique de Saint-Boniface, 1972, pp. 11–15.

Dilemmas and Contradictions of a Multi-ethnic Society

JOHN PORTER

The decade of the 1950s was notable for a naïve belief in the affluent society; that of the 1960s for its concern with poverty. It would appear that the 1970s is to be the decade of organized minorities. Although all minorities take on the appearance of reality once they are organized, some are more real than others. Indians and other non-whites are something more than a statistical group because they live mainly in distinct cohesive communities and have distinctive physical charactersitics. On the other hand the pseudo-minorities who make their appeals with the rhetoric of liberation from oppression — youth, women, and homosexuals to take some examples — are at least at their present stage of organization statistical categories that lack sociological coherence. Though they may act like real minorities with a degree of readiness for confrontation, these pseudo and statistical minorities are more like interest or pressure groups invoking the right of association ultimately to influence those in power.

Policy responses of governments and other powers groups to organized minorities have produced a new terminology: positive discrimination, preferential hiring, or benign quotas. These policy responses are quite different from human rights legislation, fair employment practices legislation, and the like, which provide individuals, not groups or collectivities, with rights, enforceable in the courts, against discrimination. Perhaps it is a measure of the failure of these instruments fashioned as they were for the individual that people have had to organize as minorities to redress grievances when it becomes apparent that deprivation is concentrated within particular statistical groups in the social structure. But the new instruments focused as they are on groups, and providing what might be called group rights — say to proportional representation within all institutional hierarchies — constitute a radical departure from a

SOURCE: *Transactions of the Royal Society of Canada,* 10, no. 2 (1972), pp. 193–205. Reprinted by permission of the author and the Royal Society of Canada.

society organized on the principle of individual achievement and universalistic judgments, towards one organized on group claims to representation on the basis of particular rather than universal qualities.

The new ideas are pervasive, and can even be found in the *Eighth Annual Review* of the Economic Council of Canada, where there is a discussion of social indicators.[1] Among these indicators there would be one to deal with the distributive aspects of economic outputs, but with groups as well as individuals considered as recipients (age, sex, and ethnic groups, for example).

No liberal social scientist would argue against social reform, or the elimination of poverty, or the provision of opportunity. He might be concerned, however, with what is an important shift of emphasis in the decade of the organized minority where claims are made by people not as individuals but as members of minority groups. When discrimination and deprivation are measured in terms of group membership, as ultimately they are, then the reduction of these conditions seems most easily achieved through positive discrimination in which institutions, corporations, and universities, for example, are required to maintain quotas throughout their hierarchical structures to make them representative with respect to minorities. Here is the first dilemma, for such policies will raise problems for the individual since in order to make his claims he will have to determine the minorities to which he belongs, and one can visualize a somewhat complex passbook arrangement indicating the answers. One's memberships could cross-cut in several ways making it necessary to calculate the maximum advantage. Thus in a preferential employment and career program one's prospects for advancement would be greatly enhanced by being, say, non-white, of non-English mother tongue, female, under 30 (or perhaps over 50), and lesbian.[2]

The possibilities are endless since societies can be viewed as intersecting sets of minorities and majorities defined by an infinite number of criteria, all of different relevance at different times.

If the epoch of the individual comes to an end, the rise of the meritocracy which Michael Young so feared[3] will be prevented by positive discrimination which does not use merit as the principal criterion of selection. It might be difficult to make judgments about which of the two would lead, if not to the good, at least to the better society. With the individualized achievement of the meritocracy — as all who have studied the problem know — the educational and opportunity structures have been class-biased and even the criteria of merit have been class-tinged. (In the age of organized minorities the criteria of selection are seen to be tinged by race, sex, age, and heterosexuality.)

It is important to be aware of the kinds of problems that are likely to emerge when we deal with inequality on the basis of group rather than individual claims. I want now to deal with some problems in the context in which we are more accustomed to talking about minorities; that is, ethnic minorities.

In discussions of the relations between ethnic minorities and majorities, the dominant theme seems to be that of equality; equality of legal, political, and social rights, equality of opportunity, and equality of economic well-being. The unequal distribution of things that are valued in the society is also the dominant theme in the analysis of social class. It would seem that ethnic differentiation and social class differentiation, or social stratification, are often the same thing in societies that are made up of various ethnic groups. The political quest of modern democracies has been to overcome inequalities, although there is a good deal of dispute about definitions and means.

To understand the interplay between ethnic inequalities and class inequalities it is important to look at how ethnic differentiation within a society develops. In most historical instances it has been through conquest or migration. In the case of conquest the victors enslave their victims in varying degrees or relegate them to inferior statuses and forms of work. This can be seen in the successive conquests over centuries, which hardened into the classical caste system in India. It can also be seen in the quasi-caste systems of Central and South America, and in North America where the descendants of the indigenous groups in both the United States and Canada represent one of the most visible underclasses to be found anywhere. In the developing nations of the third world, ethnic pluralism has resulted from the transporting of indentured labour groups from their original habitats to another for specific kinds of economic activities, or it has resulted from European powers bringing into administrative units, convenient for their own purposes, tribal groups of very differing cultures.

For new nations developed in formerly unpopulated regions, such as the United States and Canada, ethnic differentiation has arisen through immigration, which was determined by the host or charter group who got there first, or who conquered and determined the conditions under which other groups might enter. These conditions ranged from unfree slave immigration to free selective immigration under which the host society made invidious judgments about the appropriateness of various groups for particular jobs. Migration is an economic process by which one factor of production, labour, moves with the other factor, capital. The entire process is selective; people get sorted out according to their believed-in qualities or aptitudes for different economic activities. We can see in our time the building up of stratification systems through ethnic migrations. In the United States it is the Puerto Rican and the Black moving into urban areas. In England it is the migration of the coloured Commonwealth. Throughout western Europe, it is the migration of Italian, Spanish, and Portuguese labour, 80 per cent of it unskilled, and sometimes with a minimum of social and legal rights.

Economic forces have created the inequalities of ethnic stratification. There are jobs that the host or conquering groups do not want to do or consider demeaning, servicing jobs for example. Or stratification is necessary for the building up of a labour force of a particular type of economy — the plantation economy where labour force needs have been met most frequently through slavery or indentured labour. Or, as with the Canadian west, a region can be developed with a more or less freely moving migration. Over time this marked differentiation at the period of entry can either harden into a permanent class system, or change in the direction of absorption, assimilation, integration, and acculturation as a result of which the relationship between ethnicity and class disappears. The stratification order that exists, hardened or modified, has a subjective counterpart in the evaluations that are made about the standing or place of various ethnic groups in the population and the degrees of social distance (that is, the degree of intimacy which they are prepared to engage in with members of other groups) that prevail between people of different groups. These subjective counterparts can be determined with considerable precision. It would seem then that the promotion of flourishing ethnic communities is directly opposed to absorption, assimilation, integration, and acculturation and could lead to a permanent ethnic stratification and thus is likely to interfere with the political goal of individual equality. Such a contradiction is in the hypothesis of a colleague, Frank Vallee, in his study of French-Canadian communities outside Quebec, communities that are like immigrant ethnic groups anywhere else in Canada in that they are spatially dispersed and without territory. His hypothesis is as follows:

> the more a minority group turns in upon itself and concentrates on making its position strong, the more it costs its members in terms of their chances to make their way as individuals in the larger system . . .
>
> Among ethnic minority groups which strive to maintain language and other distinctions, motivations to aspire to high-ranking social and economic positions in the larger system will be weak, unless, of course, it is characteristic of the ethnic groups to put a special stress on educational and vocational achievement . . .[4]

Vallee argues that any collectivity has limited resources and energy and cannot spend them on maintaining ethnic-specific institutions and at the same time prepare its members for achievement in the larger society of which it is a part.

Both Canada and the United States have been experiencing a revival of ethnicity. Although the causes are no doubt multiple, one important force in Canada has been the assertion of Quebec nationalism, and in the United States the demands of non-white power groups particularly at the community level.

In Canada when the Royal Commission on Bilingualism and Biculturalism was established in response to the strength of French nationalism in Quebec, the government felt compelled to include in the commission's terms of reference "the contribution made by the other ethnic groups to the cultural enrichment of Canada and the measures that should be taken to safeguard that contribution."[5] An entire volume was to be devoted to the matter of the other ethnic groups.[6] Since that time there have been numerous conferences on the subject as well as a great deal of promotion of the idea of multiculturalism.

Now there is a federal government policy on the subject and as well some provincial governments are following along. There is much political rhetoric on the subject by leaders of all parties. Here is a recent example by Mr. Yaremko, the Ontario provincial secretary and minister of citizenship, in announcing the multicultural conference "Heritage Ontario":

> No other part of the globe, no other country, can claim a more culturally diversified society than we have here in this province. . . . But does everyone really grasp that Ontario has more Canadians of German origin than Bonn, more of Italian origin than Florence, that Toronto has more Canadians of Greek origin than Sparta. That we have in our midst, fifty-four ethno-cultural groups, speaking a total of seventy-two languages. . . . Just a hundred years ago the Canadian identity was moulded in the crucible of nationalism, it is now being tempered by the dynamics of multiculturalism.[7]

Mr. Yaremko also touched upon another cause of the current revival of ethnicity and that is the large non-British component of postwar immigration. He then went on to make the common mistake of seeing this component, made up of people from such a variety of countries, and being in some way homogeneous:

> There are generally speaking four demographic groups among us — Indians, Anglo- and Franco-Ontarian, and members of the third element. . . . One effect of the post-war boom in third element immigration has been to bolster ethnocultural groups, some of which have been here through four generations. The government has welcomed and encouraged this immigration. We have recognized and helped foster all our constituent cultural communities. Is it then any

> wonder that these communities have heightened expectations in many areas?[8]

In the bolstering of ethnocultural groups, as Mr. Yaremko puts it, the postwar immigrants have played an important leadership role because of their long association with nationalist political struggles in their European homelands. They have continued their activities often ideological as well as national, aimed at keeping alive in Canada the culture they believe is being obliterated abroad. This leadership has managed in some cases to shift the focus of activity of their national organizations from the problem of integration within Canadian society to the problem of cultural survival either in Europe or in Canada as a locus for cultures in exile.[9]

There is much confusion in the current discussion of multi-ethnicity and multiculturalism. This confusion does not attach to bilingualism or multilingualism. Recently Canadians have appeared more willing to accept bilingualism as an acknowledgment of their history. The main difference between a bilingual and a multilingual society is that the latter would be more costly or difficult to administer. While bilingualism is possible and multilingualism is difficult, I am not able fully to understand how biculturalism and multiculturalism have any meaning in the post-industrial world into which we are moving. Those who read government pronouncements and royal commission documents on the subject might agree that attempts to deal with these concepts and the related one of ethnicity in recent years have generated some of the most complex sophistry ever written. Most of it is aimed at avoiding the conclusion that ethnic groups are descent groups — when they are not also statistical artefacts, as I shall try to argue shortly.

It seems to me that making descent groups of such importance because they are the carriers of culture borders on racism with all the confused and emotional reactions that that term brings. If races have been evaluated as inferior and superior, so can cultures be. In fact the very laudable objective of making all ethnic groups and their cultures of equal importance and making all groups proud of their heritage is to overcome individious judgments about culture, which in their social effects at least can be as far-reaching as invidious judgments about race. Both racism and "culturism" stem from the fact that both are linked to the maintenance of descent group solidarity and endogamy.

Because of history and territorial distribution and claims, Canada can certainly be called a bi-ethnic, bicultural, and bilingual society. As social and cultural change takes place and Quebec too enters the post-industrial world we may end up being no more than bilingual. It is difficult to see how multiculturalism can survive without locality in urban environments and a post-industrial culture of science and technology. It is pointless to obscure these facts with the laborious webs of pseudo-anthropology that characterize government reports and political speeches on the subject. In the confused rationalization of multiculturalism in Canada it is possible to distinguish two major themes: culture as history and culture as a way of living. The former involves the continuation of historical cultures (say of Canadian immigrant groups) in the face of social change or their suppression in their countries of origin. The latter involves the desirability of multiculturalism in the face of the homogenizing trend of technology and bureaucracy. As well, the development of pride in ancestry is thought to be an important compensation for deprived status. I want to examine these alleged values of the multi-ethnic society.

Among the purposes of a multi-ethnic, multicultural Canadian society, it is said, are the transmitting and safeguarding of the various cultures from which Canada's immigrant groups have come. No academic would seriously dispute the desirability and responsibility of preserving culture, particularly in its expressive forms, but also in the behavioural sense of culture, because we want to know how people lived at different times and places.

There seem to be two ways in which this responsibility for preserving culture can be met. One is through the cultural association and the other through the ethnic group. Presumably if some people were interested in keeping alive some knowledge of past ways of doing things they could band together to form an association to do so. Clearly some people find the culture of ancient Egypt fascinating and rewarding to study. But if the culture of ancient Egypt is of value the various groups that promote it — archeologists who acquire money to investigate it and amateur Egyptologists who make it a hobby — must recuit new members to carry on their interests. One way, assuming they had managed to maintain the necessary age and sex distribution, would be to require as a condition of membership that members marry within the Egyptology group and, given the traditional right of parents to use their children as objects of cultural aggression, thus ensure the survival of the culture of ancient Egypt through the generations. Alternatively, they can do as they always have done and that is to recruit members by persuading them that studying and keeping alive this particular culture is a good thing. Governments or philanthropists might well be persuaded to subsidize such activities. All nations can be multicultural if they encourage such associational transmission of culture. A society of multicultured individuals is one in which people can be exposed to a wide variety of human expression, and so become liberated from whatever narrow cultural confines into which they might have been born.

The transmission and safeguarding of culture through ethnic groups may appear a more efficient mechanism, because ethnic groups are biological descent groups. Recruits are always available if the groups have succeeded in imposing rules of endogamy on their members. If they do not they will lose the primordial link with tribe or nation and the exclusive ethnic claims on culture will be eroded. Endogamy is a process of exclusion. There was a time when lowering rates of endogamy could be taken as an index of lessening prejudice, an indication that people of all groups would indeed allow their daughters or sisters to "marry one." In the current return to ethnicity the opposite judgment seems to be being made. It is better to exclude than to include. The metal of endogamy is more attractive because it is unmeltable.

It would appear, however, that because of urbanization and high levels of industrialization the prospects for rates of endogamy sufficiently high for survival are not good. The alternative is for groups to develop new associational forms of cultural survival. The prospects for this method of transmission are not good either because the ethnic bases of existing associations tend to exclude the outsider. As one observer of ethnic group activity in Toronto has noted:

> Even those organizations which are not by policy "closed" to outsiders do not usually make special efforts to attract outsiders and make them welcome. Most ethnic groups provide an active cultural life for their members. . . . However, each of these sets of activities is separated from the others by an opaque curtain partially but not wholly caused by language problems. Certainly very few outsiders are aware of this great variety of activity going on constantly in the metropolitan area.[10]

Such exclusiveness does not make much of a contribution to a multicultural Canada.

The survival of historical cultures is only one of the expressed purposes of multi-ethnicity. The second major theme in the discussions of multiculturalism involves cultures as different ways of living in the contemporary world. A society with a number of different cultures in which the members of relatively exclusive groups behave alike is said to be heterogeneous or diverse rather than homogeneous and uniform. (Since all are observing their own cultural norms it would seem that such diversity is more enjoyed by the beholder — whatever Olympus he might be viewing it from — than any of the actors within their enclaves.) Be that as it may, a strong case can be made for ethnic group affiliation for its role in solving problems of personal identity in the impersonal and shifting world of modern bureaucracy and technology. There are two social contexts within which this psychic shelter function of ethnic affiliation merits discussion. One is that of recently arrived immigrants, and the other is the continued ethnic identifications for the Canadian-born of second and subsequent generations (and that really means all of us), two distinct groups which are counted together in mich of the current usage of the concept of ethnic origin, particularly in Canada. For the immigrant the transition to a new social environment can be fraught with psychic hazards, particularly if he comes from the Azores or the Abruzzi to metropolitan Toronto. The question from the point of view of general social goals is whether the useful staging camp role of the ethnic community becomes permanent, or whether some dispersion into the wider community of various immigrant groups is more desirable. A suggestion that such dispersion is desirable now brings the cry of "liberal assimilationist."

For the rest of us it really seems questionable to me that we seek our psychic shelters through ethnic identification. There is no doubt that ethnic groupings can play this role, but at the cost of perpetuating ethnic stratification. Identities and psychic shelters can be found in other forms of association and interest groups which are not based on descent, for it is this aspect of the ethnic group which is the source of irrational, invidious comparison.

One of the most compelling arguments for the maintenance of strong ethnic affiliations is to enhance the self-concept of members of low status groups. When compensation for low status can be derived from "taking pride in one's culture or one's origin" programs can be devised to ensure that all cultures are treated as "worthy" despite the varying degrees of inequality which their members experience, and so there is less need for programs aimed at the inequality which is associated with ethnic differentiation.

However, there is some evidence that pride in one's own group does enhance one's view of oneself and this improved self-image is likely to make a firmer base from which to achieve. But there are contradictions here. Many cultures do not emphasize individual achievement, nor do they provide the appropriate skills for it. From the point of view of the Indians and Métis, does the promoting of their own culture help them toward equality in post-industrial society? The same question may be asked of some immigrant cultures. The answer lies to some extent in language rather than culture. Identification with and the use of their own language, particularly in education, may be an important facilitator of mobility for very low status groups.

For example, the use of an immigrant language, say Italian or Portuguese, combined with English in school may help a child in overcoming learning impediments that arise from speaking one language at school and another at home. He acquires some self-confidence because his language is not despised. But such use of language is quite different from the goal of ethnic communities as permanent and "worthy" to compensate for low status, or as psychic shelters in the urban, industrial world. We would hope for a society in which the compensatory role of the ethnic community is not necessary, and, as I have suggested, the development of ethnic communities as psychic shelters can perpetuate ethnic stratification.

Earlier, I suggested that in Canada ethnicity may be a statistical artifact arising from census definitions and procedures. The Canadian census insists on classifying one's ethnic origin by one's ancestor who first arrived in North America traced through the male line only (there is something for women's lib). That procedure excludes both American and Canadian as acceptable ethnic origins. Even after four generations one one cannot have a Canadian ethnicity — despite the fact that one might have lost the threads of one's male ancestry. And this is not because large numbers of the 84 per cent of the Canadian-born population in 1961 did not see themselves as being Canadian in origin; otherwise the officials would not have had to instruct enumerators what to do with that sizable number of people who could be expected to so respond. However, if people insisted on reporting Canadian as origin after these attempts to dissuade them the enumerators might accept it. Since none of the census tabulations tells us anything about these people it must be assumed they are included under "other" or "not stated."[11]

There was, it may be recalled, some considerable public discussion of the ethnic question before the 1961 census, but the matter never seems to have been raised publicly with respect to the 1971 census. This is in itself an indication of the new saliency that ethnicity had acquired in Canadian society, and of the political sensitivity produced by the increasing immigration from European countries, other than Britain, by the new ethnic leadership to which Mr. Yaremko referred, and by the publication of the bilingualism and biculturalism reports. Among the census takers themselves, however, there seems to have been some considerable disagreement, as they report in a working document on the preparation for the 1971 census.[12]

Arguments for and against the inclusion of each question were made. On the ethnic question this document reports: "this question has given rise in the past to emotional feelings on the part of respondents but while its inclusion is sometimes criticized *there is a heavier demand for data on ethnicity than on most other items.*"[13] The statement reflects a significant contradiction in Canadian society. Some are obviously repelled that anything should be made of one's biological descent group, but on the other hand it is about these groups that more information is demanded than any other. This contradiction is further reflected in the reasons given for including the question. Among these is "great use is made of census data on ethnicity by national and cultural organizations who are anxious to retain their identity." But also among the supporting reasons is: "a cross-classification of ethnic groups with mother tongue or language now spoken provides a good measure of the degree of assimilation of different groups." For data which can serve the needs of measuring both assimilation and ethnic identity one would have expected that the census takers would have given consideration to improving their recording instrument, for among the reasons against including the question is: "there is a relatively high degree of reporting error since respondents may not know their ethnic background."

One awaits with interest the 1971 census data on ethnicity. They are based on self-enumeration.

The hesitancy of census officials on the ethnic question no doubt reflects a lack of consensus on the part of the Canadian public. For some, and probably for still another minority, the problem of Canadian nationalism is more important than that of European or other nationalisms, but much of the resistance to the ethnic question is because many of us can remember that, because of the racialism of the interwar years, making much of one's descent group, or trying to discover and make something of another's, was thought to be morally improper, much as it is thought by some to ask such questions about faculty in Canadian universities today. In the preface to his extensive 1961 census monograph on immigration and ethnicity, Warren E. Kalbach refers to his distinguished predecessor at this task, W. Burton Hurd, whose monograph on the 1941 census, *Ethnic Origin and Nativity of the Canadian People,* was published for limited circulation in 1965, Kalbach says:

> Circumstances surrounding the delayed publication of Professor Hurd's last work attest, in part, to the sensitivity of the ethnic origin issue during the immediate post-war period. The debate concerning the propriety of asking questions about ethnic or racial background and the struggle to eliminate ethnic and racial distinctions from official records of vital events and decennial censuses continues. . . .[14]

The dilemma of the liberal social scientist on this matter is clear enough. On the one hand he might want to see the end of this preoccupation with biological descent groups for its atavistic, genetic, and racial overtones and the uses to which ethnic and racial categories can be put. He would prefer to see individuals as humans. On the other hand he finds such data an important indicator of prejudice and discrimination.

The census, however, is not an appropriate instrument for the analysis of such phenomena compared to, say, carefully designed sample surveys. In my view we would be well served if the question were abandoned, and the artifactual character of ethnicity removed.

Ethnicity quite obviously has a saliency apart from the census. Official documents refer to ethnic organizations as evidence of a group's "collective will to exist." Even the terminology is reminiscent of what Ernest Cassirer called mythical thinking.[15]

By an ironic twist, ethnicity has become a good thing. Now all are encouraged to have an ethnicity, other than Canadian, and ethnic communities should flourish, and all should identify with their descent groups.

The old liberal position is now pejoratively referred to as "liberal assimilationist," it is said to be overly rational, secular, and universalistic or "an over-hasty and naive apostasy of a naively held scientific faith."[16] The liberal assimilationist ignores the primordial attachment of human beings and so he has "betrayed a profound misunderstanding of the human condition."[17] These are views expressed by Andrew Greeley, an American sociologist, who is a very active supporter of Irish nationalism in particular and ethnic diversity in general. He is widely read and praised by the multiculturalists in Canada.

In seeking to choose between the ethnic stratification that results from ethnic diversity and the greater possibilities for equality that result from the reduction of ethnicity as a salient feature of a modern society I have quite obviously chosen an assimilationist position, and in seeking to choose between the atavistic responses that can arise from descent group identification and the more liberal view that descent group membership is irrelevant to human interaction I have chosen the latter.

Notes

1. (Ottawa, 1971), 70ff.
2. In the context of minority representation in a professional organization see Pierre L. van den Berghe, "The Benign Quota: Panacea or Pandora's Box," *The American Sociologist* (June, 1971).
3. *The Rise of Meritocracy* (London: Thames and Hudson, 1958).
4. Frank G. Vallee and Norman Shulman, "The Viability of French Groupings outside Quebec," in *Regionalism in the Canadian Community, 1867–1967*, ed. Mason Wade, (Toronto: University of Toronto Press, 1969), p. 95.
5. Royal Commission on Bilingualism and Biculturalism, *Report*, Book I, XXVI.

6. Ibid., *Book* IV.
7. Press release of address at the Canadian Club, Toronto, 20 March 1972.
8. Ibid.
9. Elizabeth Wangenheim, "The Ukrainians: A Case Study of the 'Third Force'," in *Canadian Society: Sociological Perspectives,* ed. B.R. Blishen *et al.* (Toronto: Macmillan, 1968), p. 658. See also Judith A. Nagata, "Adaptation and Integration of Greek Working Class Immigrants in the City of Toronto, Canada: A Situation Approach," and Clifford J. Jansen, "Leadership in the Toronto Italian Ethnic Group," in *The International Migration Review*, 4, no. 1 (1969), pp. 25–69.
10. Jansen, "Leadership in the Toronto Italian Ethnic Group," p. 660.
11. See Joel Smith, "Melting Pot-Mosaic: Considerations for a Prognosis," *Minorities North and South,* Proceedings of the Third Annual Inter-Collegiate Conference on Canadian and American Relations, Michigan State University, 1968, for an interesting comparison with the United States.
12. "The 1971 Census of Population and Housing: Development of Subject Matter Content" (Ottawa: DBS, 1969), p. 13.
13. Ibid.
14. *The Impact of Immigration on Canada's Population* (Ottawa: DBS, 1970), V.
15. *The Myth of the State* (New York: Doubleday, 1955).
16. Andrew Greeley, "The Rediscovery of Diversity," *The Antioch Review* (Fall 1971), p. 349.
17. Ibid.; see also Andrew Greeley, "The New Ethnicity and Blue Collars," *Dissent,* (Winter 1972).

Part Two

EDUCATION AND CULTURAL DIVERSITY

The role of the school in a culturally diverse society such as Canada is complex and problematical. This is particularly true, as this section demonstrates, with respect to issues of equality, federal-provincial relations in education, schooling in the official languages, instruction in the non-official languages and matters of educational autonomy and control.

The Royal Commission on Bilingualism and Biculturalism (1963) took the position that the school "is the basic agency for maintaining language and culture, and without this essential resource neither can remain strong." Legislation supportive of this position was not enough, however. Citing the failure of the British North America Act (1867) to protect English and French as languages of instruction, the commissioners noted the great disparity between the use of these languages in the nation's school systems, and observed that — almost without exception — it had been impossible for French-speaking students outside Quebec to complete their education in French through the elementary and secondary levels of schooling. The sources of this inequality, according to the commissioners, were not to be found in organizational difficulties. Rather they lay with English-Canadian attitudes and this was unacceptable. Canadian parents had a right to have their children educated in the official language of their choice.

The commissioners adopted a similar position on the school's role in transmitting culture. While it might help safeguard the contribution of other cultures, they argued nevertheless that "since those of British and French origin are the main groups in Canada, it is appropriate that British and French cultures dominate in the public schools."

The National Indian Brotherhood, on the other hand, categorically rejected this position. Their policy paper, "Indian Control of Indian Education," emphasized that the school's primary responsibility towards native children was to reinforce their cultural identity. Native children needed to learn their own history, values, customs and language, if they were to take pride in that identity. To achieve this end, moreover, control over native schooling must rest not in the hands of the dominant white majority but in those of the native peoples.

Great concern was also expressed in Quebec over the threat posed to their language and culture by the pervasive influences of the English-speaking community and its institutions, especially the attraction its schools held for immigrants. These influences were so great, a Commission of Inquiry into the State of the French Language and Linguistic Rights in Quebec observed, that since the 1930s the province's English-language minority schools had enrolled a vastly disproportionate number of immigrant children compared to the schools of the French-speaking majority. Such a situation was not to be tolerated. Moreover, the Commission declared it was not irreversible. Change could and would occur if the provincial government showed greater enterprise and initiative in legislating language use.

The Official Languages and Education

ROYAL COMMISSION ON BILINGUALISM AND BICULTURALISM

In this first Book we are concerned with a comparison of the status and use of Canada's two official languages as evinced by their protection through laws, statutes, and customs. This is a first step towards examining the possibility of a more equal partnership between those who speak the two languages. A similar examination of the institutions of the two communities will be the subject of succeeding Books. However, the opportunities to use a language are of little significance unless there exist at the same time opportunities to learn it and retain it — opportunities for an adequate education in the language. We therefore believe it is imperative, when we are suggesting the language regimes appropriate at various levels in Canada, to indicate some of the changes required in the educational systems within each level. At this point our comments will be very general, but a full discussion of the implications of new language regimes for education will follow in the Book on education.

The failure of the B.N.A. Act to protect English and French as languages of instruction in Canada has resulted in a great disparity in the use of these languages in our school systems and grave inequalities in the opportunities for the French-speaking minorities to have an education in their mother tongue. In Quebec, both languages were placed on an equal footing, and the principle establishing the right of both English-speaking and French-speaking children to be taught in their mother tongue was enshrined in the educational system of the province, in spite of the fact that it was not required by law. Because this linguistic equality was not firmly guaranteed for the country as a whole, however, the French-speaking minorities have been largely deprived of the right to an education in their mother tongue.

This inequality and its consequences were the subject of many

---

SOURCE: Canada, Report of the Royal Commission on Bilingualism and Biculturalism, "Education", Ch. VI, Book 1, *The Official Languages* (Ottawa: Information Canada, 1967), pp. 121–31. Reproduced by permission of the Minister of Supply and Services, Canada.

briefs presented to the Commission by Canadians of both language groups. The school is the basic agency for maintaining language and culture, and without this essential resource neither can remain strong. Of course the situation varies from province to province, but the fact remains that many francophones outside Quebec have been steadily losing their language.

Where the French-Canadian population is scattered, it is obviously not easy to provide a suitable program of education in French. But the real stumbling block has been not so much this as the unwillingness of the English-speaking majority to recognize the right of French-speaking parents to educate their children in French. In Quebec, where the right to equal access to an education in either official language has been respected, even remote and numerically insignificant English-speaking communities have been provided with reasonable opportunities for schooling in English. In most of the other provinces, until very recently, such teaching in French as was permitted was intended simply as a means of transition to the English language. Parents who wanted their children educated in their language and their culture had to bear the costs of a private education while still having to contribute to the English-language public school system.

Even in the provinces where they constitute a sizable minority — for example, 425,000 in Ontario and 35 per cent of the population in New Brunswick — the situation of French-speaking Canadians has suffered seriously by comparison with that of the English mother tongue minority of 13 per cent in Quebec. Almost without exception, it has been impossible for a French-speaking student outside Quebec to complete his education in French through the elementary and secondary public schools. But in Quebec, anglophones have access to a complete education in English through the public schools of the province — elementary, secondary, and university. Even English-speaking Roman Catholics have enjoyed a large measure of autonomy within the Catholic system. As a result, their language has never been in danger and they have been able to concentrate on improving curriculum and administration.

In most of the English-speaking provinces there has recently been evidence of modifications in the restrictions against French as a language of instruction. In some cases these changes represent little more than slight improvements on the status quo; in other provinces a real attempt is being made to redesign the French-language program to be more nearly comparable to the English-language program. It is fair to say that, in general, French-language education outside Quebec has suffered principally from two weaknesses. First, it has been largely achieved through the struggles of French-speaking

Canadians despite the resistance of the English-speaking majority. The toll in efficiency and vitality is readily appreciated. Second, it has not constituted a "system." There have been serious gaps and dislocations in the sequence from one educational level to another; essentials such as teacher-training, guidance, and so on, have left a great deal to be desired; a technical or scientific education has been largely unavailable. As a consequence, even where conditions have been most favourable, French-speaking children have been seriously handicapped in their education, with the result that often they were deficient in both languages. Not only has there been injustice in human terms, but these Canadian citizens have not been able to make their potential contribution to society. Therefore, any serious reforms will need to deal realistically with these two situations.

We believe that equal partnership in a bilingual Canada implies the fullest development and expression of both official languages compatible with regional circumstances. We interpret this to mean that it must be accepted as normal that children of both linguistic groups will have access to schools in which their own language is the language of instruction. Therefore, **we recommend that the right of Canadian parents to have their children educated in the official language of their choice be recognized in the educational systems, the degree of implementation to depend on the concentration of the minority population.** This is our only recommendation in this volume in respect to education. More specific recommendations and more detailed information will be forthcoming in the Book on education. We believe this recommendation is basic to any future changes. In practical terms, it will mean extending French-speaking Canadians' opportunities for schooling in the French language, since the English-speaking residents of Quebec already have the opportunities we are recommending.

We shall now indicate, again in general terms, how we consider the schools will be affected by this principle in the bilingual provinces, the bilingual districts, and in large urban centres which have a substantial official-language minority.

A. IN BILINGUAL PROVINCES

The principle of equal partnership implies comparable educational regimes for the minorities in the three officially bilingual provinces. This will make it possible for many francophones to live more completely in their own language. In New Brunswick and Ontario, the desirability of classroom instruction in the child's maternal language is already recognized and the right of parents to have their children educated in either French or English has been conceded in principle.[1] There is considerable disparity, however, in the ways this principle is applied in the three provinces. As we have seen, in Quebec instruction at all levels is available to the English-speaking minority in its own language. The situation of French-speaking Canadians in the other two provinces varies from that standard. We suggest that it would be advantageous for the three officially bilingual provinces to agree jointly upon the norms to be established for minority education. In Ontario and New Brunswick it is a matter of officially recognizing what is now unofficial practice, of extending this recognition to all levels, of adopting standard procedures for establishing these schools throughout the province. Equivalent educational facilities and academic standards must be ensured and maintained, whether the language of instruction is English or French; the appropriate administrative framework must be established and the necessary officials appointed. Compulsory education already obliges the provincial government to provide schools for all children. This will be extended to include the provision of French-language schools wherever there are enough French-speaking children to populate them. The provincial government of Quebec already fulfils the obligation to provide English-language schools wherever there are sufficient numbers of English-speaking children. In the officially bilingual provinces, then, there will be complete and parallel systems of education in French and English, from the elementary schools through the institutions of higher learning.

B. IN BILINGUAL DISTRICTS

Educational facilities represent a vital part of the regime for the language minority in the bilingual districts. (We must note once again that we are considering now the French-speaking minorities, since anglophones in Quebec already have these facilities.) It is in the bilingual districts that we can expect to find enough French-speaking children to populate schools in which the language of instruction is French. A local school, however, cannot exist in isolation; it must be seen as only a part of a complex educational system. Teachers must be trained, curricula must be planned, textbooks and teachers' guides must be developed, and inspection and guidance must be provided to maintain uniform academic standards. The minority schools will be no exception. They too must be part of an educational system which provides these essential services. What then will be the organization and administration of schools for the minority in bilingual districts?

C. ADMINISTRATION OF MINORITY SCHOOLS — ROLE OF FEDERAL AND PROVINCIAL GOVERNMENTS

Among the suggestions considered by the Commission was a proposal that the federal government should accept responsibility for minority schools. A federal system would have the advantage of ensuring a uniform curriculum and uniform standards for minority French-language schools. However — apart from the fact that, in the present Canadian constitution, education is a provincial responsibility — there are considerations which count against this solution. Local schools must be adapted to the needs of the community they serve — technical and commercial programs, for example, should complement the regional economy — and the advantage of a uniform curriculum from coast to coast would have to be sacrificed to some extent to the need for regional adaptation. Therefore we do not suggest a transfer of educational responsibility for minorities from provincial to federal jurisdiction, although we foresee a role for the federal government in helping to meet certain additional provincial costs. This is an example of what should become a new dimension in the role of the federal government as the only political institution shared by all Canadians.

Provincial administrations have a special knowledge of the educational needs of their provinces. It is obviously easier for an existing department of education to draw on its knowledge and experience and adapt its program to the needs of the provincial minority than it would be to duplicate this administrative competence in a federal department. The argument is even more convincing because the language of instruction has no bearing on so many administrative decisions, and existing provincial regulations on school construction, school equipment, transportation, and health services will be equally applicable to minority-language schools.

Through provincial administration, uniform academic standards can be maintained for all the children in the province. Schools providing instruction in the language of the minority without maintaining high academic standards would be a handicap rather than a privilege. In every province teacher-training programs and elaborate certification procedures have been developed to ensure a competent teaching staff. Textbooks, equipment, examinations, and departmental supervision have all been integrated into an educational system designed to achieve the highest possible standards. Only by establishing an equivalent system adapted to their own needs can there be any assurance that students attending the minority-language schools will receive an education equivalent to that provided for other children in the province.

The adaptation of the existing provincial school systems to bilingual education will require careful planning. Teachers will have to be specially qualified. Not only must they have the qualifications required for teaching in the provincial schools but they must also be able to teach in the language of the minority. There are many French-speaking teachers now, especially in Ontario and New Brunswick, but more will be needed. Adequate supervisory services must be provided. It is obvious that these various measures will increase the costs of education. We accept as a principle the responsibility of the federal government to contribute to the additional costs involved. The way in which this principle can be applied without interfering with provincial autonomy in education, and other aspects of the administration of minority-language schools, will be discussed in a subsequent study.

As we have seen in the preceding chapters, bilingual districts may be created in all provinces, whether officially bilingual or not. The basic assumption is that there is a public responsibility for education in French as in English. The extent of the services offered will be governed only by considerations of educational and economic practicality. In the provinces other than Ontario, Quebec, and New Brunswick, however, to establish French-language schools where they have not hitherto been provided will create a new situation and certain attendant problems. In the three officially bilingual provinces, for instance, the minority population is large enough that we can expect necessary administrative measures and services to be provided within the province. In other provinces, where there will be few minority-language schools, it will not be feasible for each provincial department to undertake the necessary curriculum development and teacher training for these schools, and interprovincial cooperation will be necessary. However, such interprovincial planning in education is already beginning. For the designated bilingual districts outside Ontario, Quebec, and New Brunswick, therefore, the same principle applies as for the designated regions within those three provinces. Parents will have the right to have their children educated in the official language of their choice.

D. OUTSIDE THE BILINGUAL DISTRICTS

The plan of developing services in both official languages in areas where there are appropriate numbers of French-speaking or English-speaking Canadians is intended to guarantee certain basic rights to these minorities. But members of such linguistic groups living outside these areas should not be excluded from similar opportunities to be served in their maternal language. Programs for such minorities must range from a minimum to a maximum service according to population concentration, but will still proceed from the acknowledged right of parents to have their children educated in the official language of their choice.

For most English-speaking citizens of Quebec and for most French-speaking citizens in the other provinces, this right will be established through the bilingual districts. But whether these districts are located in an officially bilingual province or not, there are settlements of provincial minorities outside these designated regions, and their need for teaching in their mother tongue is at least as important. Indeed, in view of their linguistic isolation, their need is probably much greater. Here, however, the right to an education in the minority language needs to be qualified by other considerations. In practice a school can only provide the normal options or maintain the required academic standards if the student body is large enough to warrant the necessary specialist teachers and equipment. The minority-language group is large enough in some communities outside these designated areas for a minority-language school, but in other communities it will be too small. The problem is to establish the right to an education in the minority language when it is feasible, without imposing an obligation on the provincial governments when it is impracticable.

The fact that minority-language schools already exist shows that such schools are feasible. However, controversy has arisen in the past when a request by the minority for a French-language school was rejected by the local school board. A formal procedure is required, by which the minority can assert its right to such a school. Provincial departments of education can decide from their experience the minimum number of students for either an elementary or a secondary school. It is proposed, therefore, that the departments of education formally state the requirements and the procedures by which a minority group outside the designated areas can establish its right to a minority-language school at either the elementary or the secondary level. Further, the basis upon which minority-language schools are made available should be such as to provide the maximum opportunity, rather than merely improving on the present situation. Hence, minority-language schools will not be restricted to bilingual districts but will be provided wherever the minority group in a community is large enough, in the judgement of the provincial authorities, to warrant a school.

Isolated families and scattered groups will not qualify for minority-language schools by the above terms. In some cases it will be possible to provide an elementary but not a secondary school; in other cases not even an elementary school would be feasible. For these children a variety of solutions is possible. Within the school, separate classes might be provided with the mother tongue used as the language of instruction in some subjects, although for other subjects the student would have to study in the language of the majority. For parents who want their children to follow a complete minority-language program, other possibilities exist, such as boarding schools or television teaching. Departmental regulations or at least departmental guidelines would help clarify the rights of the minority in these special situations.

E. IN LARGE URBAN CENTRES

One of the objectives which led to the Commission's recommendations on bilingual regions was the creation or consolidation of a network of bilingual areas across Canada, to provide services to francophones in those regions and to give the actual image of the dual nature of Canadian society. In this plan, as we noted above, the large urban centres have a major role to play, as poles of attraction for all Canadians. For reasons of mobility if for no other, it is essential that educational opportunities in the French language be provided in these centres for francophones who, without assurance that they can preserve their children's language, may rightly be reluctant to leave Quebec. In major urban centres where the number of French-speaking residents will not automatically ensure the existence of French-language schools, we propose basically the same arrangements as for bilingual districts, with certain additional administrative arrangements, such as transportation facilities. Students will have the opportunity to be educated in French, although they will often have to accept the inconvenience of travelling farther to school than English-speaking children. In this way, there will be — depending on local circumstances — separate French-language education in separate classrooms or in a separate school.

Moreover, the school might be considered as part of a French-language cultural complex. For the urban area as a whole, the cost of special administrative arrangements will be compensated for by the provision of facilities which will help to attract and retain French-speaking citizens who might otherwise never come. Such facilities will also be a stimulus and encouragement to the anglophones of those areas who are interested in the French language and culture. The interest which many anglophones have recently shown in learning French[2] and in having their children learn French, has been frequently frustrated by the lack of opportunity in many areas of the country to practise the language or to be adequately taught. Apart from the importance of fostering communication and understanding between the two language groups, the need for bilingual Canadians will increase as activities involving both groups become more common, and as the trend towards larger administrative structures in business, government, and social organization increases the contacts between francophones and anglophones. The Commission was expressly charged in its terms of reference with the responsibility of recommending procedures which will enable Canadians to become more bilingual. We intend to discuss fully the important question of second-language learning in our Book on education. Here we wish simply to point out that, because Canada will need more bilingual citizens in the future than it has in the past, a minimum objective must be for all students to receive a basic introduction to both official languages so that they may become bilingual if the need or the opportunity should arise. Indirectly, of course, the designation of the necessary services within bilingual districts will have the effect of stimulating greater individual bilingualism.[3]

F. CHARACTERISTICS OF FRENCH-LANGUAGE SCHOOLS

French-speaking children may be educated in a variety of situations, including schools where the instruction is entirely in the minority language and others where its teaching is limited to a few hours. Without attempting to lay down a fixed pattern for such schools, there are certain general characteristics to bear in mind.

Since the principal objective is to enable French-speaking children to expand their knowledge and enjoyment of their native language and culture, the quality of the teaching is tremendously important. The precise, sensitive command of one's own language is the essential and inestimable foundation of thought and communication. Lacking an adequate command of his language the child suffers the handicap of confused thinking and limited means of expression. Top priority therefore must be given to the teaching of the mother tongue, and the need for specially trained teachers and high quality texts cannot be over-emphasized. This is true of any language in any situation, but where the mother tongue is under the constant influence of a second language, much greater care has to be exercised to make the native language secure.

At the same time, students in the minority-language schools need to acquire an adequate command of the language of the majority. In the English-speaking provinces a knowledge of English is seen as an economic and social necessity. We were often told that "this is an English-speaking province," or even that "this is an English-speaking continent," and that a citizen was seriously handicapped in his career or his life in the community unless he knew the language. The English-speaking minority in the province of Quebec has not in the past been as conscious of the importance of learning the language of the majority, and has consequently lived rather apart from the French-speaking community. French-speaking residents of Quebec, while recognizing that a knowledge of English was an asset, would frequently say that "this is a French-speaking province," and the implication was that a resident of Quebec who did not know French was not fulfilling his responsibilities toward his community. In both cases, it is obvious that the minority is expected to learn the language of the majority. Again, the school is usually seen as the institution where this language should be learned.

Fortunately, learning the language of the majority presents few problems in these circumstances. Students can learn to speak two languages and, for children who belong to a linguistic minority, the learning situation is ready-made. The key factors in language learning are the desire and the opportunity to practise. Given motivation and opportunity, there is no reason to fear that the minority will not learn the language of the majority. Nonetheless, special curricula must be developed for language instruction in the minority-language schools. It is not enough to teach English to French-speaking students from textbooks and course outlines designed for English-speaking children, although this is the pattern today in most English-speaking provinces. Special programs are required to meet the special needs of the minority.

But language, important as it is, is not the only distinguishing feature of minority schools. The courses of study for English and French will obviously be different and the language of instruction for other subjects will vary. We shall later consider to what extent the program and content of studies should also be different because they must reflect the cultural character of the minority.

For French-speaking minorities especially, cultural identity has in the past been intimately linked with the confessional character of the schools. However, there appears to be an increasing tendency within French-Canadian communities across Canada to separate the question of language from religious objectives. Although we plan to come back to this complex question in a later Book, we wish to state here that what we consider essential under our terms of reference is to promote the establishment of French-language schools for the French-speaking minorities independently of religious consideration.

G. CONCLUSION

In the foregoing pages we have insisted on the right of parents to have their children educated in the official language of their choice, but at the same time we have suggested considerable flexibility as to how this right is exercised. We are convinced that it is important for Canada to maintain strong and vigorous links in the chain of French language and culture across the whole country. We believe furthermore that "equal partnership" for francophones necessitates a change of policy, from offering the minimum of education in their mother tongue to offering the maximum.

Notes

1. The Premier of Ontario, the Honourable John Robarts, in an address to the Association canadienne des éducateurs de langue française on August 24, 1967, said, "It is a fundamental necessity of 1967 that the Franco-Ontarians be enabled to experience the full benefits of our educational system. Encompassed in this recognition of necessity is the proposal to extend what now is being done to provide, within the public school system of Ontario, secondary schools in which the language of instruction is French. . . . It is only practical that such French-language secondary schools and classes can be established wherever the numbers of French-speaking students are great enough to warrant instruction in French. As far as possible, they should provide for French-speaking Ontarians the counterpart of the existing English-language educational programme. . . . In doing so, we would be meeting the needs of our French-speaking Ontarians for equal education opportunities at all levels of education, elementary, secondary and university. . . ."
2. Canadians seem to favour individual bilingualism in principle. The Social Research Group asked the following general question in a survey made for the Commission: "Do you think that it would be a good thing if everyone in Canada spoke both French and English?" Of the people interviewed, 77 per cent said "Yes", while 15 per cent said "No." This opinion favouring individual bilingualism is not equally shared by persons of different ethnic origins. Of those of British origin, 71 per cent answered "Yes," compared with 96 per cent of those of French origin. Opinions also varied between regions; 80 per cent of those of British origin in Quebec and the Atlantic Provinces were favourable to individual bilingualism, 72 per cent in Ontario, and 58 per cent in the four western provinces.
3. In reply to the question: "Do you think that in Canada, English-speaking children should learn French in primary school?", 79 per cent of all the people interviewed across Canada in the Social Research Group survey said "Yes," 15 per cent said "No," and 6 per cent either qualified their answer ("It depends") or had no opinion. Although the proportions varied between regions and between different ethnic groups, the great majority of people supported the proposition. For example, among English Canadians three-quarters were in favour, less than a fifth against, and 5 per cent were uncertain; among French Canadians there was hardly any division, with almost 95 per cent in favour; among Canadians of ethnic origins other than English or French, more than two-thirds also supported the idea. It is interesting to note that in the Prairie Provinces and British Columbia, two-thirds said "Yes" and slightly less than 30 per cent voted "No." On the related question: "Do you think that in Canada, French-speaking children should learn English in primary school?", the degree of support on the average was even higher. Ninety-two per cent of all Canadians said they were in favour of the idea and only 5 per cent were opposed. English Canadians and other ethnic groups across the country replied "Yes" 90 per cent, "No" 6 per cent; French Canadians themselves supported the idea that their children should learn English in primary school to almost exactly the same extent (95 per cent) as they supported the idea that English-speaking children should learn French in elementary school; only 4 per cent were opposed.

Education: The Cultural Contribution of the Other Ethnic Groups

ROYAL COMMISSION ON BILINGUALISM AND BICULTURALISM

Schools are the formal means by which a society transmits its knowledge, skills, languages, and culture from one generation to the next. Canada's public school systems are primarily concerned with the transmission of knowledge that is essential to all citizens, including knowledge about Canadian institutions, the traditions and circumstances that have shaped them, and the two official languages. Since those of British and French ethnic origin are the main groups in Canada, it is appropriate that the British and French cultures dominate in the public schools. But public schools can also provide an instrument for safeguarding the contribution of other cultures.

Because of the interdependence of language and culture we must consider the teaching of languages other than English and French in the educational system as an important aspect of any program to perserve the cultures of those of non-British, non-French origin. Such teaching can have the additional benefit of increasing the country's linguistic resources — resources important to any modern country and especially to one that wishes to play a role in the international community.

There are two aspects to the question of teaching languages other than the two official languages in Canada. On the one hand, there is the need to preserve the languages and cultures of those who have been in Canada for many generations. On the other hand, there is the need to preserve the languages and cultures of new immigrants while also integrating them into Canadian society. Obviously these two aspects require different techniques. Programs that would be appropriate for teaching languages to the children of those who have

---

SOURCE: Canada, Report of the Royal Commission on Bilingualism and Biculturalism, "Education," Ch. VI, Book IV, *The Cultural Contributions of the Other Ethnic Groups* (Ottawa: Information Canada, 1970), pp. 137–169. Reproduced by permission of the Minister of Supply and Services, Canada.

been here for many generations would not be suitable for immigrants' children, who must also learn one of the official languages as their working language, as well as the other official language.

The public education system is the first concern in this chapter. In this system, it is important to make a distinction between learning the official languages and opportunities for learning other languages and the cultural subjects related to them. We have already recommended in our Book on education a systematic development of full educational opportunities in both the official languages wherever population concentrations permit. We have also recommended the development of a systematic approach to teaching the second official language to members of both the major linguistic communities. We do not recommend the same degree of development for the teaching of other languages in Canada; rather, we recommend that there be opportunities to study many languages within the context of the public education system.

In Canada there are also private schools established by non-British, non-French cultural groups who want their children to share in the cultural heritage of their ancestors as well as in their Canadian heritage. In the second section of this chapter we describe the part played by these private schools in the maintenance of languages and cultures and suggest possible ways of helping these groups to continue this important work.

We have already stressed in our Book on education the need for an articulated and continuous approach in the provision of official-language minority higher education. The same approach should be followed in considering opportunities for other languages and their related cultural subjects. The third part of this chapter discusses higher education, and the need for integration among all three levels of the educational system insofar as other languages and cultures are concerned. The chapter concludes with a brief discussion of adult, or continuing, education.

In considering the question of educational policy we have been guided by three general principles. First, members of non-British, non-French cultural groups should have opportunities to maintain their own languages and cultures within the educational system if they indicate sufficient interest in doing so. Of course, population concentration, continuing immigration, and the different historical background of the various groups, both in their homelands and in Canada, all raise important practical considerations in the application of this principle. Second, where public support is concerned, the question of language and cultural maintenance must be seen within the broader context of the question of bilingualism and biculturalism in Canada as a whole; for example, the learning of third languages should not be carried on at the expense of public support for learning the second official language. Third, since the elementary school years are the most vital ones for the purpose of maintaining languages, the most extensive effort should be made at this level.

In earlier times in Canada, when people originally settled among other members of their cultural group, and when they could expect to be born, live, and die in one particular community, the local school could be conducted in the language of the community. This way of life is no longer possible. As we stated in Book II of our *Report,* "The modern school is a complex institution and is a part of an intricate and highly specialized system. Any kind of minority-language schools must be fitted into this school system" (paragraph 19). The principle of the right of parents to have their children educated in the official language of their choice was elaborated in detail in our Book on education where we discussed the practical implication of this principle and reviewed the complex question of languages of instruction in the modern education system. Our conclusion was that, in our mobile and changing society, with the increasing scope, sophistication, and complexity of modern educational facilities and curricula, it is not feasible for Canada's public education systems to employ languages other than English and French extensively as languages of instruction. While our recommendations below will propose substantial educational opportunities for languages other than English and French where sufficient demand exists, the aim of improving educational opportunities in the official languages must be maintained as the primary objective.

To a large extent, the study of a language or culture will gain a place in elementary school curricula if it involves basic knowledge and skills useful for life in Canadian society. It will gain entry to the curricula of the secondary schools if it is seen as a means of intellectual or vocational preparation. Although the operative languages in Canada will continue to be French and English the use of other languages and opportunities to learn them can be an important asset to all Canadians. Moreover, Canada has been and remains a country with a high level of immigration and this fact increases the viability and usefulness of other languages. For these reasons, and also because many Canadians of ethnic origin other than British or French wish to see their children provided with educational opportunities in their own languages, we recommend certain ways to develop the teaching of other languages and cultures in the public schools.

The perspective of those who wish educational opportunites in other languages for their children is a most important consideration. Where parents regard such opportunities as of primary importance, we feel that governments should offer as much assistance as possible.

All the factors discussed in this chapter must be carefully weighed, taking into consideration the overriding goal of ensuring that all children have the best possible education as preparation for a productive adult life. The most effective assistance can be offered by providing through the public schools optional instruction in other languages and related cultural subjects, wherever sufficient demand exists. Our Commission's research indicates that requests for such instruction would not be too extensive. A high level of education is assuming more and more importance for the individual in our society. Parents who choose to have their children instructed in a language that is not useful in the work world or in our institutions make a choice; in effect, they may be choosing for their children a knowledge of the language and culture of their own cultural group at the expense of instruction in other fields which are perhaps more relevant to Canadian society. Even so, the principle of parental choice remains valid and, in cases where Canadian citizens attach great importance to their linguistic and cultural heritage, opportunities for instruction in these areas should be available.

A. Public Schools[1]

1. THE TEACHING OF LANGUAGES OTHER THAN ENGLISH AND FRENCH IN ELEMENTARY SCHOOLS

All provinces authorize the teaching of a second language in elementary schools, and in some provinces (Manitoba, New Brunswick, Prince Edward Island, and Quebec) instruction in a second language is compulsory. French is almost invariably the second language for anglophone pupils and English for francophone pupils, which is to be expected in bilingual country where these are the two official languages. In two provinces, other languages are authorized beginning in Grade VII. During the 1966–67 school year, 2,100 Grade VII and VIII pupils in Manitoba were studying German. In Saskatchewan, three school districts offered Ukrainian as an option in Grades VII and VIII, and a six-year sequence of Ukrainian study from Grade VII to Grade XII, with the first two years stressing facility in conversation and comprehension. Otherwise, the study of modern languages other than French and English in public elementary and junior high schools has only been on a local, rather than a provincial, basis. German has been taught in a junior high school in New Germany, Nova Scotia; Spanish in Montreal; Russian in Toronto; and no doubt other languages have been taught elsewhere experimentally, either as an option or as part of a program of enrichment. However, the number of teachers and pupils involved has not been large. In all cases the courses are offered as preparation for high school programs.

Modern languages other than English and French have therefore won only a small place in the curricula of the public elementary and junior high schools in Canada. There are many communities where there is a concentration of people who share a particular ancestral language but where the language is not taught before secondary school, if it is taught at all. Yet the years between five and 14 are considered crucial for the retention of a language, and children need a firm grasp of their mother tongue before leaving elementary school if they are to retain it in later years.

a. Maintenance of languages and cultures

Briefs to the Commission have advocated the teaching of languages other than English and French as subjects at the elementary level in all the publicly controlled schools in areas where there is a strong concentration of a particualr group desiring such instruction. We believe that, where a demand on the part of parents exists, public education systems should provide courses that will assist the various cultural groups in the maintenance of their languages and cultures. They should do so in order to safeguard the contribution these languages and cultures can make to the quality of Canadian life. Therefore, **we recommend that the teaching of languages other than English and French, and cultural subjects related to them, be incorporated as options in the public elementary school program, where there is sufficient demand for such classes.**

Since education lies within the jurisdiction of the provinces, the provincial educational authorities, after consultation with representatives of the appropriate cultural groups and scholars in the relevant disciplines, must decide what constitutes a sufficient demand. It will be necessary when doing the planning for these classes to consider other demands on the school system (including the need to teach English or French to immigrant children), the number of languages that would be involved, possible difficulties in developing curricula and textbooks, and the problem of recruiting and training teachers. Where demand is sufficient and resources permit, it may also prove feasible that some instruction in the related cultural subjects can be offered using the appropriate language as the language of instruction. We also feel it is essential that eligibility for these classes not be based exclusively on ethnic origin or cultural background. We have often stated our conviction that ethnicity should not be a governing principle in Canadian life. Eligibility for such classes should be based on interest and ability. However, it is obvious that the children most interested will be those from homes where the language spoken corresponds with the language offered.

The introduction of such classes within the regular school program may present difficulties because of the priority that must be given to initiating courses in the other official language. We have already recommended that the study of the other official language should be obligatory for all students in Canadian schools. In addition, at the elementary level the curriculum provides relatively little flexibility for introducing optional subjects, since the teaching of basic knowledge and skills requires most if not all the school day. At this level, the teaching of languages other than French and English might mean eliminating some aspects of the basic curriculum, and would therefore entail a deliberate choice by parents and school authorities.

Nevertheless, the provision of these classes will affirm Canada's determination to maintain its linguistic resources. They will provide members of other cultural groups with the educational means of retaining their languages in any area where they are sufficiently numerous and concerned. The children will be taught their ancestral language during their most receptive years, and where it proves possible their language will be used as the language of instruction in teaching related cultural subjects. If the classes are carefully arranged to avoid interfering with the regular school program, they will neither deprive the children of association with members of other cultural groups nor interfere with the teaching of the two official languages. They will also provide opportunities for children to go beyond a knowledge of the two official languages to an acquaintance with other languages and cultures, an appropriate objective in our contemporary world.

b. Immigrants and the official languages

Immigrants and the children of immigrants present a particular educational problem and responsibility in a country such as Canada. The public schools must accept the task of teaching English or French to those who enter school with an inadequate knowledge of the official language which is being used as the language of instruction. This situation requires special smaller classes of ten to fifteen pupils, and teachers trained in the techniques of teaching a second language. Where possible, the schools should also provide special facilities for such classes and continuing evaluation of the courses offered. We have already recommended the establishment by provincial authorities of French- and English-language centres for the training of second-language teachers. Since the basic problems of second-language teaching are universal, these centres could also prepare teachers for these special classes.

The teaching of the appropriate official language is part of the process of integrating immigrant children into Canadian society as a whole: they are becoming Canadians and part of their education for citizenship is language education. The benefits of immigration and of linguistic diversity accrue to Canadian society at large. Therefore the federal government as the government of the country as a whole, rather than provincial or local governments, should be responsible for providing the funds required for the teaching of English or French to children entering the public school system without an adequate knowledge of either of the official languages. However, it should provide only those funds required over and above the cost of teaching any child in the school system. Therefore, **we recommend that special instruction in the appropriate official language be provided for children who enter the public school system with an inadequate knowledge of that language: that provincial authorities specify the terms and conditions of financial assistance for such special instruction; and that the federal authorities assist the provinces in mutually acceptable ways through grants for the additional cost incurred.**

These special classes should also be open to the children of Canadian-born parents who wish their children to learn another language. If such classes were available more Canadian-born members of the non-French, non-British cultural groups would be likely to teach their mother tongues to their children at home during the children's early years.

A phased introduction of the appropriate official language as the language of instruction may be the most effective method for such classes. Where there are sufficient numbers and resources instruction might be given in a language other than French or English in Grade I, with the appropriate official language being introduced gradully up to Grade V and the mother tongue concurrently reduced. After Grade V special instruction should no longer be necessary.

We are keenly aware of the problem presented by the choice of English-language or bilingual schools rather than French-language schools by immigrant parents in the Province of Quebec. However, we believe, that we must maintain the principle of the right of parents to choose between the official languages for the schooling of their children. At the same time, we are aware of the threat to the survival of the French language in Quebec. Because the issues inherent in this question are so profound, touching on the very nature of the country, we intend to deal with them in the concluding section of our *Report*.

2. THE TEACHING OF LANGUAGES OTHER THAN ENGLISH OR FRENCH IN SECONDARY SCHOOLS

A total of five modern languages other than French and English are authorized and taught in public high schools in Canada: German, Spanish, Italian, Russian, and Ukrainian. But no modern language is taught to anything like the same extent as French in the English-language high schools of Canada or English in the French-language high schools. Latin is the language second to French in many provinces, although it is nowhere compulsory except for francophones in Quebec's classical colleges. Latin and Greek were compulsory in Quebec's classical colleges until recently. Now one of Greek, Spanish, or German is compulsory.

Only German, and in the three Prairie Provinces, Ukrainian, can be said to have sizable enrolments. German owes its position in part to the number and long history of the German cultural group in Canada and in part to its status as a world language. The teaching of Ukrainian in the Prairie Provinces is clearly the result of the presence of large numbers of people of Ukrainian ethnic origin, many of them with a strong interest in maintaining their ancestral language. Spanish, Italian, and Russian all have some place in high school curricula as world languages. Italian has more students in Ontario, where the bulk of the large number of Italian immigrants are concentrated, than in other provinces. In recent years the number of students taking the Grade XIII examinations in Italian in Ontario has been considerably higher than the number taking the Grade XII examinations. This strongly suggests the presence of students fluent enough in Italian to attempt the senior matriculation examination without formal instruction in the language in earlier grades.

There appears to be a slight trend towards widening the range of modern languages offered in the high schools and lengthening the program in some of them. There is also some indication that teaching methods are changing to stress conversation and comprehension rather than grammar and literature. These changes have been helped by such innovations as television, language laboratories, and tape recorders, and by an increasing number of teachers fluent in the language they are teaching. Universities that in the past refused admission credits for certain modern languages are now broadening their language admission requirements.

At the secondary level any changes in language courses should be seen in relation to what is being done in the elementary schools. Language classes for elementary and junior high school children might well produce secondary school students having a knowledge of any one of many languages. Provincial education authorities should therefore investigate the possibility of providing more advanced work in secondary schools in certain languages spoken in Canada, and also in related cultural subjects. If the numbers are sufficient, advanced classes are desirable for students who already have some knowledge of a language. Classes for beginners would be continued as well unless demand declined. Provincial education authorities should also consider widening the range of language options authorized and taught, wherever sufficient demand exists. Therefore, **we recommend that more advanced instruction and a wider range of options in languages other than English and French, and in cultural subjects related to them, be provided in public high schools, where there is sufficient demand for such classes.**

This implies, of course, the development of curricula for these courses and the recruitment and training of teachers fluent in the languages to be taught. Sufficient demand must be defined by provincial educational authorities acting in consultation with representatives of the appropriate cultural group and scholars in the relevant disciplines. We do not underestimate either the difficulties involved, because of other demands on our school systems, nor the time that will be required to develop such courses. However, it is still important, in the Canadian context, that additional modern language programs be established and that this be done as rapidly as possible.

Another possibility at the secondary level would be the development of high schools in which a language other than French or English would be the main language of instruction. In addition to serving a particular cultural group, such schools would have the additional benefit of providing opportunities for intensive education in another language for students of all ethnic origins. Because such a development would have to be carefully weighed against other demands for educational resources, particularly that of developing official-language minority schools, we have not made this a recommendation. However, it is a development that might be possible in the future, and one which could provide a powerful instrument for safeguarding the language and culture of a particular group.

3. THE TEACHING OF CANADIAN HISTORY

For many cultural groups, it is as important that their contribution to the development of Canada be generally recognized as that their mother tongue be taught in the public schools. They feel that such recognition is necessary if their children are to take pride in their heritage and be respected by other Canadians. Many cultural groups feel that their contribution to Canadian life has not been adequately treated in textbooks or courses in Canadian history in the public elementary and high schools. For example, a brief presented to the Commission by the Ukrainian Canadian Committee recommended that:

> An extensive revision of school textbooks for public schools should take

> place in which the Ministers of Citizenship and Immigration together with provincial Ministers of Education examine their contents and exclude discriminatory material and give the students an unbiased social studies material, referring to the different ethnic groups, their origin, history, culture, literature and their accomplishments for the benefit of this country.

Commenting on the announcement that a study of Canadian history textbooks was to be undertaken for the Commission[2] a German-language newspaper wrote:

> It is to be hoped that these two historians will take the trouble to examine the historical contributions of "other ethnic groups" as well. Among these, the Dutch and the Germans have been established in the country for as long as the British themselves. This desire does not express a yearning for "history with feeling" but rather the demand that at long last Canadian history do justice to all ethnic groups in Canada and not only to those of British or French origin.[3]

What little information there is about the treatment of cultural groups other than the British and French in Canadian history courses and textbooks suggests that they have been virtually ignored. The courses of study in Canadian history for junior and senior high schools in the ten provinces were analysed almost fifteen years ago. Some thirty-six objectives of teaching Canadian history were given in the courses of study set out by the provincial departments of education, but few had to do with promoting understanding among the different cultural groups in the population. For example, the Ontario objectives included engendering "Tolerance, Respect and Goodwill," and those in Saskatchewan knowledge of "modes of life elsewhere." But none of the eighty-one topics into which the field of Canadian history was divided dealt specifically with cultural groups other than the British or French. Topics that might deal with such groups, such as the Manitoba schools question, population trends in Canada, immigration and emigration, social development in Canada, and urban-rural development received little class time. Immigration and emigration, for example, received an average of 50 minutes of class time in junior high schools during the school year, and the same amount of time in senior high schools.[4]

The Commission's study of the textbooks in Canadian history used in elementary and secondary schools did not deal specifically with cultural groups other than the British and French. None of the themes in the teaching of Canadian history selected for study dealt with other cultural groups. However, in treating themes of particular interest to the Commission the authors referred to the stress on the assimilation of languages and cultures other than French and English in English-language textbooks — a stress that did not necessarily preclude support of the notion of ethnic diversity in Canada.[5]

Evidence available from this and other studies not explicitly concerned with ethnic relations is slight but it concurs with our impression that almost no attention has been paid to cultural groups other than the British and French in Canadian history courses and textbooks in the past, and that little attention is paid to them at present.

In our Book on education, we examined this question from the perspective of the francophone and anglophone societies. There we noted:

> With two dominant themes of French Canadian survival and the survival of Canada as a political union, it comes as no surprise that Canadians of ethnic origins other than French or British are almost ignored. Their presence in Canada is usually overlooked and the scattered references to them suggest that they will become good Canadians when they have submerged their ethnic identity (Book II, paragraph 763).

While this attitude may not be surprising, we feel that it is unjustified. Available information suggests that there are grounds for the complaints about cultural bias in courses and textbooks. This bias results mainly from the selection of material but to some extent from probably unconscious misrepresentation.

Those of British and French origin have played the major roles in Canada's history, and Canadian institutions have been modelled chiefly on British or French institutions. It is natural, therefore, that the British and French heritages should be stressed in our public schools. They have become part of our Canadian heritage and as such must be understood by all Canadians. However, Canadian society does not consist of "a kind of hereditary aristocracy composed of two founding peoples, perpetuating itself from father to son, and a lower order of other ethnic groups, forever excluded from spheres of influence." The remarks we made on this subject in our Book on education are also pertinent:

> Students are taught history because societies believe that it provides a desirable and necessary training for future citizens.
>
> . . . students must learn from experience directly relevant to an understanding of their own society. History, it is assumed, can convey this knowledge by showing the problems and the challenges our predecessors faced, by showing the origins and development of our social institutions, by instilling a respect for our heritage (Book II, paragraphs 765–76).

Our public schools should give due weight to the role of those of all ethnic origins in our country's development and to the cultures and languages of all Canadians. All Canadian children can benefit from an awareness of our country's cultural diversity and a better knowledge of the contributions of the different cultural groups to Canada's growth.

Throughout elementary and secondary school, all courses that are directly concerned with Canadian development, and particularly courses in Canadian history and geography, should make explicit the essential part that people of many origins have played and are playing in Canadian life. We are conscious here, as in our earlier discussion on this subject in Book II, of the dangers of interfering with the work of those responsible for history texts and programs of study. Yet we feel strongly that the interpretation given to the role of those of non-British, non-French origin should be one of the criteria used to assess Canadian history as it is taught in our schools. Certainly all disparaging and prejudicial implications must be eliminated. We therefore extend the remarks on history and other textbooks which we made in our Book on Education to the treatment of the role played by Canadians of other than British or French origin, (paragraphs 764–73) and urge that the part played by all the cultural groups in Canada be included among the criteria outlined there.

B. Private Schools

Many cultural groups, feeling that neither Canadian society as a whole nor the Canadian public schools have provided adequate means for transmitting their languages and cultures to succeeding generations, have set up private schools to supplement or replace the public schools for their children. These private ethnic schools, whose existence is unknown to many Canadians, have been the object of very little research; yet they have played an important part in the maintenance of the languages and cultures of the non-British, non-French cultural groups.

In 1965 Commission researchers conducted a survey of 20 cultural groups in Canada, selected on the basis of their size and involvement in ethnic education. Questionnaires were sent to coordinating ethnic organizations where they existed (for example, the Canadian Polish Congress and the Canadian Jewish Congress), to ethnic associations, churches, and individual schools. Fairly complete information was received from the questionnaires and supplementary sources for twelve groups,[6] and partial information for four others.[7] The groups included in the survey made up over 90 per cent of the population of those of other ethnic origin.

Two types of ethnic private schools are operated in Canada, part-time schools and full-time schools. The two types differ markedly in their formal structure and in the intensity of their educational program.[8] Part-time schools teach language and cultural courses to children who receive their general education through the public school system. These schools usually operate for a few hours a week. Full-time schools are expected to cover the complete curriculum of the appropriate Department of Education and in addition to teach special language and culture courses.

1. PART-TIME SCHOOLS

For two reasons, we neither expect nor intend that existing part-time ethnic schools would be eliminated by the provision of optional language classes in the public school system. First, the new classes will teach language and culture as specific subjects within the basic curriculum. Part-time ethnic schools also teach language and culture, but at the same time they attempt to pass on to the students the total cultural heritage of their parents and to do so in as much detail as is possible in a society where everyday life is conducted in another language. This heritage may include particular religions or social traditions and economic or political ideology, and possibly even a dialect of the language. Since the public schools cannot and should not transmit such knowledge, there is little doubt that ethnic associations will continue to organize their own schools. Second, some cultural groups, because of their small size and lack of geographic concentration, will not have access to classes in their ancestral language in the public school system. Such groups may be equally concerned about the maintenance of their language and culture and may therefore wish to operate part-time schools.

The number and location of the part-time schools of sixteen cultural groups are shown in Table 1. Over 500 schools were reported to be operating during the 1965–66 school year, one-half in Ontario, one-third in the Prairie Provinces, and one-fifth distributed between Quebec and British Columbia. Three cultural groups — German, Ukrainian, and Polish — account for three-quarters of all Canada's part-time ethnic schools.

The significance of the number of schools can only be assessed when considered along with their enrolment, which varies from one dozen to several hundred students. In 1965 the total enrolment in the German, Ukrainian, and Jewish schools made up about 65 per cent of all students in ethnic schools, as shown in Table 2.

TABLE 1: Number of part-time ethnic schools for selected ethnic origin categories, Canada and six provinces, 1965

Ethnic origin	*Total*	*Quebec*	*Ontario*	*Manitoba*	*Saskatchewan*	*Alberta*	*British Columbia*
Total	*507*	*68*	*254*	*64*	*21*	*74*	*20*
Ukrainian	170	9	94	19	12	35	1
German	157*	4	66	36	8	32	11
Polish	57	10	38	5	0	2	2
Jewish	24†	15	–	–	–	–	3
Italian	22	12	9	–	–	1	–
Lithuanian	15	2	10	1	0	1	1
Hungarian	14	3	5	1	1	3	1
Latvian	14	1	12	1	0	0	0
Estonian	10	1	8	0	0	0	1
Greek	8	3	5	0	0	0	0
Slovene	5	1	3	1	–	–	–
Armenian	3	2	1	0	0	0	0
Portuguese	3	3	0	0	0	0	0
Dutch	2	–	2	–	–	–	–
Japanese	2	1	1	–	–	–	–
Chinese	1	1	–	–	–	–	–

Source: Based on Krukowski and McKellar, "The Other Ethnic Groups and Education."
*Excludes Mennonite schools.
†Excludes six schools in the Atlantic Provinces.
–data not available.

A significant indication of the intensity of a particular cultural group's interest in preserving their ancestral traditions can be obtained by comparing the total enrolment in ethnic schools with the total number in the corresponding ethnic origin category. On this basis the Baltic cultural groups — Lithuanians, Latvians, and Estonians — were at the top of the list, and some of the largest ethnic origin categories, such as the Polish and Italian, were at the bottom. The Jewish cultural group had a considerably higher proportion of children in such schools than the German or Ukrainian cultural groups. The Dutch, the fourth-largest ethnic origin category in the 1961 census, showed little interest in formal, part-time education aimed at the preservation of the Dutch language.[9]

A vast majority of part-time schools are at the elementary school level, for children from 7 to 12 years of age. The remainder are for the 13 to 16 age bracket, and rarely go beyond this level.

Partly because of tradition, and partly because of the private character of part-time ethnic schools, an overwhelming proportion of

TABLE 2: Number of students in part-time ethnic schools for selected ethnic origin categories, Canada and six provinces, 1965

Ethnic origin	*Total*	*Quebec*	*Ontario*	*Manitoba*	*Saskatchewan*	*Alberta*	*British Columbia*
Total	*39,833*	*10,397*	*16,224*	*3,529*	*1,054*	*4,084*	*4,545*
German	12,623	250	4,752	2,166	325	1,630	3,500
Ukrainian	8,702	1,106	3,896	879	682	2,101	38
Jewish	5,038	4,443	–	–	–	–	595
Polish	4,000	760	2,400	300	0	200	310
Italian	2,887	2,040	822	0	0	25	0
Greek	1,750	850	900	0	0	0	0
Lithuanian	1,520	120	1,360	40	0	0	0
Latvian	992	40	850	45	0	20	37
Estonian	685	60	600	0	0	0	25
Hungarian	601	198	190	18	47	108	40
Slovene	335	53	231	51	–	–	–
Armenian	328	216	112	–	–	–	–
Japanese	156	45	111	–	–	–	–
Chinese	120	120	–	–	–	–	–
Portuguese	96	96	0	0	0	0	0
Dutch	–	–	–	–	–	–	–

Source: Based on Krukowski and McKellar, "The Other Ethnic Groups and Education."
– data not available.

the classes are held on the premises of the sponsoring association, usually in a parish hall or club room. There is no definite pattern for the type and quality of classrooms. On the whole, the Jewish schools are the best equipped, and suitable premises and other facilities are also found among the Chinese, Ukrainian, and German part-time schools. As might be expected, the least suitable quarters are usually found among the smaller and more dispersed cultural groups.

The question of using public school buildings for part-time ethnic schools has received attention in ethnic publications, in briefs submitted to us, and at our public hearings. Public school boards were invariably criticized for their reluctance to permit use of their buildings and other facilities for part-time ethnic schools. In answer to this, school representatives have pointed out that most buildings are already overtaxed with extra-curricular activities, that opening the school to one group would inevitably lead to similar demands from other groups, and that the school budget could not bear the additional expense. However, some cultural groups in various parts of the country have made arrangements with local school authorities, and the number of part-time classes held in public school buildings by members of non-British, non-French cultural groups has been increasing. In the Toronto area, the German cultural group paid one local school board $5,000 as yearly rental for several classrooms in three public schools and in another case, $600 for two classrooms for one school year. In Montreal almost all part-time classes, except those sponsored by Jewish or Protestant groups, are held in schools operated by the Montreal Catholic School Commission.

The average school year of the part-time schools is shorter than that of regular public schools. Most schools offer between 25 and 30 periods of instruction which result in three hours or less of instruction per week. The curricula of these schools are similar in several respects. All include such humanist subjects as literature, history, and geography. The ancestral language of the sponsoring group is the focus of the program; indeed it is frequently the *raison d'être* of the school. Religious instruction given in the schools is usually under the direct control of a church, although this practice has been declining as a growing number of part-time programs have been designed to serve students of various religious affiliations.

An analysis of school curricula and other school activities leads to their division into two broad but distinct types on the basis of their formal design, the number of subjects offered, and related activities. In terms of these criteria we can made a distinction between "high" and "low" ethnicity programs. A "high" ethnicity school program contains several subjects — literature, geography, history, the arts — distributed over three to five consecutive grades. This program is frequently expanded to include music, dancing, folk-art, sports, scouting, and drama. These schools also issue report cards and organize graduation ceremonies and other aspects of school life. Clearly, high ethnicity school programs aim at immersing the children in the group's culture and are sponsored by groups determined to retain their cultural identity. They are found mainly among those of Jewish, Ukrainian, Chinese, and Greek ethnic origin.

The "low" ethnicity programs consist of a few hours of conversation weekly, about the native land carried on in the mother tongue. Students are taught to read and write the language and much of the program is left up to the individual teacher. Cultural activities, as well as other facilities available in up to date educational establishments, are often scarce or absent.

In general, English and French are neither taught as subjects nor employed as the language of instruction in the programs of part-time schools. Except in the Jewish schools, English is employed only sparingly as a supplementary medium of communication for students with limited facility in the ancestral language. The French language is not taught in the part-time schools in the predominantly anglophone provinces. In Quebec, part-time schools supported by the Catholic School Commission of Montreal offer one period of French per week to fulfil the condition for receiving the support. Recently, Jewish private schools in Quebec have made a concerted effort to include French language courses in their programs.

Textbooks are printed in the language of the sponsoring cultural group, and in many instances combine literature, history, and geography. The quantity, quality, and range of the subject-matter in these texts is a serious problem for part-time ethnic schools. Books are usually in short supply or on a limited range of subjects. Because the demand is insufficient to cover the cost of publishing new textbooks, older works tend to be reprinted. As a result, many of the textbooks now in use are becoming more and more out of date for educational purposes. Textbooks written and published in Canada and reflecting Canadian situations are rare, although some have been issued by Polish and Ukrainian organizations. The bulk of books used come either from the countries of origin or from the United States. Some foreign governments publish textbooks especially designed for schools abroad.

In 1961 there were over 1,000 part-time or full-time teachers in ethnic schools as shown in Table 3. Schools with small enrolments

TABLE 3: Number of teachers in part-time ethnic schools for selected ethnic origin categories, by sex, Canada, 1965

Ethnic origin	*Total*	*Male*	*Female*
Total	*1,241*	*301*	*626*
German	280	–	–
Jewish	246	79	167
Polish	142	25	117
Italian	113	48	65
Latvian	110	33	77
Ukrainian	109	38	71
Lithuanian	60	20	40
Greek	42	20	22
Hungarian	40	9	31
Estonian	34	–	–
Slovene	32	14	18
Armenian	12	6	6
Japanese	12	6	6
Portuguese	5	3	2
Chinese	4	0	4
Dutch	–	–	–

Source: Based on Krukowski and McKellar, "The Other Ethnic Groups and Education."
–data not available.

tend to have higher teacher-student ratios than those with large enrolments. This tendency is partly due to the smaller schools having a greater number of teachers engaged on a temporary basis for part of a school year. Full-time teachers constitute a small percentage of the total teaching staff and are usually in schools operated by Jewish, German, and Ukrainian groups. Teachers assigned to teach ethnic subjects at full-time schools often teach in part-time classes as well.

Teachers' qualifications vary widely. About half the teachers have limited training and experience or none at all. Many of the other half hold certificates from Canadian teachers' colleges and some also teach in the public schools. A relatively high proportion of the teachers are foreign-born and acquired their professional training in their country of origin. Fluency in the language and knowledge of the culture of a particular cultural group are the main prerequisites for a teaching position. Jewish, German, and Ukrainian schools seem to have the best qualified teaching staffs. Various cultural groups try to improve the level of teacher competence in their schools by offering special seminars, summer and weekend training courses, and literature on teaching methods. Some cultural groups sponsor their teachers' attendance at colleges in the United States or Canada.

However, the lack of qualified teaching personnel is an acute and perennial problem even for groups with well-established schools. Groups with a long history in Canada — the Germans, Mennonites, Jews, and to an extent the Ukrainians — can rely on members of their cultural group who teach in the public schools. Some recently established cultural groups whose countries of origin are outside the Soviet orbit recruit teachers from overseas.

Although most teachers are paid for their services, it is usually only a token payment rather than reasonable remuneration for the time and effort involved. On the average, teachers in part-time ethnic schools receive between $4.00 and $6.00 for each session. This scale of pay only enables them to earn from $120 to $180 each during the entire school year.

Many of the problems of part-time ethnic schools — in particular, their lack of suitable classrooms and other facilities, deficiencies in the textbooks available, and the shortage of qualified teachers — reflect the financial difficulties faced by almost all of these schools. There are two main sources of funds, fees paid by students and subsidies from sponsoring organizations. These sources usually do not provide enough money to meet the needs of the schools.

School fees are relatively low, from $1.00 to $5.00 per month per student; and payment may not be strictly enforced. Sometimes no fee is imposed, especially in schools with a small body of students. Often free tuition is provided for needy or promising students.

The sponsoring organizations or cultural groups provide support for part-time schools through regular yearly subsidies, irregular donations, or endowments. The organizations collect school funds through periodic campaigns or social events. Other sources of support for ethnic schools are sometimes found in the homeland of the sponsoring group or through its diplomatic representative in Canada.

Some ethnic schools operate on a sounder financial basis; their fees are much higher and the sources of funds more abundant. However, even these institutions lead a precarious financial existence and are always searching for new sources of money.

Some cultural groups have tried to overcome their financial difficulties by amalgamating with other groups and developing joint school programs. Schools of this type are now in operation in some cities. The main difficulty in developing such schools seems to be the division of the various sponsors into religious, ideological, and even generational camps, each unwilling to give up control of the school's budget or to eliminate divisive elements from their school programs. Many cultural groups have consolidated their educational activities with those of other groups over the past decade but it appears unlikely that this process will ever be complete.

One solution to the financial problem of the part-time schools is the policy of subsidization adopted by the Catholic School Commission of Montreal. For the last twelve years, this body has given financial support to part-time ethnic schools for Catholic cultural groups on condition that the program includes one period of instruction in the French language each week. The Commission provides accommodation in public school buildings, janitorial services, and pays the teachers' salaries, at a rate of $10.00 for a period of instruction lasting about three hours. The cultural groups are responsible for forming classes, which must have about twenty students, supplying textbooks, and finding teachers (who must be approved by the Commission). The sponsoring groups must also submit reports on attendance and agree to inspection from time to time by the Commission's representative, usually a school inspector. In 1965-66, nine cultural groups participated in the program; 4,600 students were enrolled; and there were 173 teachers in 189 classes, usually held on Saturday mornings. The cost of the program to the Commission was $71,000. The obligation to devote part of the short weekly session to French, which means recruiting teachers able and willing to teach French, is considered onerous by some cultural groups and has sometimes been only perfunctorily fulfilled. The Commission has taken action to improve the French instruction, in one case by supplying the textbooks for the teaching of French, in another by increasing the amount of time to be alloted to French and assuming control of the appointment of teachers of French. On the whole the program has been successful. It is one factor in the relatively high enrolment in part-time ethnic schools in Montreal, and it demonstrates that with some support from the public system, these schools are viable institutions.

We endorse this approach. Part-time ethnic schools have played an important part in the maintenance of languages and cultures. Support from local authorities, where it is possible, is the most appropriate form of assistance because of the variety of situations and factors that must be considered. It is encouraging that local arrangements have proven possible and successful, and we do not feel recommendations for action by either the provincial or federal levels of government are warranted.

2. FULL-TIME SCHOOLS

Private ethnic full-time schools offer a dual program. Their students follow the regular curriculum of the province in which the school is located, and in addition a program of linguistic, religious, and cultural courses. They are subject to inspection by educational representatives of the provinces, and their grades and diplomas are recognized by the provincial departments of education.

There are ethnic full-time schools in all the provinces except the Atlantic Provinces, and their total enrolment is close to 9,000. The Mennonites and the Jewish, Ukrainian, and Greek cultural groups operate such schools. The Mennonite religious community, approximately 150,000 strong, is one of the major supporters of full-time schools. It operates ten schools at the high school level with a total enrolment of about 1,300 students, and six Bible schools with an enrolment of about 400. There are also about 400 students in three Bible colleges primarily concerned with training prospective ministers and missionaries. In all, Mennonite communities across Canada operate nineteen educational institutions at the secondary and college levels.

Most Jewish schools are at the elementary level. It has been estimated that approximately 4,500 students are enrolled in twenty-six Jewish full-time schools, thirteen of them in Montreal. Some are maintained by local congregations, ranging from ultra-orthodox to reform in their religious practices. Others are run by lay bodies, and the teaching in these schools tends to stress the history and culture of the Jewish people.

Like the Mennonites, the Ukrainians have concentrated their efforts mostly at the secondary level. Their schools have been organized and maintained mainly by the two Ukrainian national churches. In the Prairie Provinces, the Ukrainian Catholic Church operates at least five full-time schools with about 2,000 students. The Greek group is the latest to establish a full-time school; in 1963 it opened an elementary school in Montreal, now attended by approximately 500 students. Other groups that once maintained such schools have closed them. Whether the total enrolment in full-time ethnic schools has declined is difficult to estimate, since the number and size of the schools operated by the active groups have been growing.

The distinctive feature of a private ethnic full-time school is that it brings together children of the same cultural group not only to study but also to engage in recreational activities. The children attending full-time schools also participate as a body in ceremonial events within the cultural group and represent it in ceremonies in the community. They are often spoken of and addressed as future leaders of their cultural group. The segregation of the children from children of other cultural groups, and the emphasis on their potential for leadership, seem designed to reinforce their sense of ethnic identity and their loyalty to the group's values.

The formal ethnic programs of these schools are usually provided for by a slight extension of school hours. The program may be spread over more grades and more days of the week than in the part-time school because teachers and classrooms are always available. However, full-time schools are not necessarily more effective than part-time schools in maintaining a cultural group's language and culture. Research in the United States resulted in the conclusion that "by every available index the All Day School is far less embedded in ethnicity and, therefore, far less concerned with language maintenance than any other type of ethnically affiliated school."[10]

Like other private schools, ethnic full-time schools are usually unable to provide as elaborate facilities and equipment as the public schools, or as wide a range of subjects and programs. In part this is a matter of size and organization; in part it is a matter of funds. It raises the question of whether or not these schools prepare their students as well as the public schools for full participation in Canadian society.

The tuition fee at full-time schools is usually $200 or $300 a year. Scholarships are frequently offered in order to maintain enrolment and attract outstanding students. If the schools are residential, free room and board are also offered in some cases.

The financial burden involved in the running of a full-time school is probably the major deterrent to the proliferation of such schools. The cost of building and maintaining schools is high and it is increasing rapidly. So are the costs of facilities and supplies and of teaching and supervisory staff. Churches have been the initiators and main supporters of full-time schools, but they have had to make heavy demands upon the whole cultural group for the funds required. The existence of such schools seems to be precarious, except within the Jewish community. Only in the Province of Quebec do ethnic private full-time schools receive provincial support.

In the future the financial burden may become an insurmountable problem for ethnic full-time schools, as the costs of providing an education adequate for full participation in modern society continue to increase. If they must compete with other schools for students, they are likely to do so by weakening the ethnic component in their programs. In the United States research indicates that such schools are tending to discontinue instruction in the mother tongue and to enroll ethnically "inappropriate" students.[11] If such schools raise their fees, they are likely to base their enrolment on economic factors rather than cultural origin. The grave concern of some of the Canadian ethnic full-time schools about funds, even at a time of heavy immigration and general affluence, seems to indicate pressures that may lead them in this same direction.

We have considered with care the proposal made in briefs that public financial support be provided for these schools but reject it because there are serious difficulties. These include the present heavy demands on all our educational resources, the need to provide all children with equal opportunities in terms of programs and services, the practical problems of teachers, textbooks, and space, and the question of public control over educational facilities supported by public funds. Our research and analysis lead us to conclude that even with some public aid, the smaller cultural groups could not afford to support a separate network of full-time schools that could maintain standards and facilities comparable to the public system, particularly in the range of their curriculum and special services. There is also a danger that the public school system would suffer in many communities if several cultural groups were to set up their own schools supported by taxes; the size of the constituency supporting the public schools would be reduced while at the same time the new full-time schools would not have open enrolment. We do not consider this potential impairment of the public system acceptable; the result could be detrimental to all children concerned.

As with part-time ethnic schools, local arrangements seem the most appropriate form of support. Private ethnic schools should receive the same treatment from provincial educational authorities as other private schools. We have no recommendations to make concerning these schools although we feel it important to record the part they play in the maintenance of the languages and cultures of those of other than British or French ethnic origin.

C. Colleges and Universities

1. THE TEACHING OF MODERN LANGUAGES

In 1965–66, as Table 4 shows, twenty-seven different modern languages other than English and French were taught at one or more of thirty-six Canadian universities and colleges. German, Spanish, or Russian were taught at many institutions; thirteen taught Italian, seven Ukrainian, and six Polish.

A number of the languages currently spoken in Canada were not offered at any of the universities or colleges studied; these included Swedish, Danish, Finnish, Estonian, Hungarian, and Dutch. No university or college taught any of the Eskimo tongues, and of the native Indian languages only Cree was offered as a subject for linguistic analysis, at the University of Alberta.

There is some correlation between ethnic concentrations and the language programs offered by local colleges or universities. At the University of Manitoba an honours program in Icelandic, orginally endowed with $250,000 by the Icelandic community, offered ten courses. The University of Manitoba also offered two courses in Yiddish and Hebrew through an endowment from the Jewish community. In Alberta, where there is a concentration of people of Scandinavian origin, courses in Norwegian are available. However, it appears that the total enrolment in various language classes owes more to the prestige of the language than to an interest on the part of the students in maintaining their ancestral languages.

One factor influencing the development of language courses at universities is the entrance requirements regarding languages, including how many languages are required. Entrance requirements are changing rapidly with changes in the high schools and with the establishment of new universities. Credits in modern languages are generally not demanded for entrance into faculties of engineering or applied science, although they may be used to fill one of the optional requirements and although students in honours course normally must pass a reading examination in a language useful in their research. Credits in modern languages usually are required for entry into other faculties of arts and science at most, although not all, Canadian universities. The requirements for twenty-three English-language universities in 1965–66 are listed in Table 5. The French-language universities had no specific language entrance requirement, because a knowledge of English was assumed.

It should be noted that, although some universities accept any approved language for credit on entering the institution, the vast majority of students in fact present English, French, German, or

TABLE 4: Courses in modern languages other than English and French offered in 36 universities and colleges, Canada 1965–66

Universities and colleges		*Romance languages*				*Slavic languages*						*Germanic languages*			*Other European languages*			*Asiatic languages*										*Other language*
	Total	*Catalan*	*Italian*	*Portuguese*	*Spanish*	*Czech*	*Polish*	*Russian*	*Serbo-Croat*	*Slovak*	*Ukrainian*	*German*	*Icelandic*	*Norwegian*	*Gaelic*	*Modern Greek*	*Yiddish*	*Arabic*	*Chinese*	*Japanese*	*Malay*	*Pali*	*Persian*	*Sanskrit*	*Tibetan*	*Turkish*	*Urdu*	*Cree*
Total		*1*	*13*	*3*	*33*	*1*	*6*	*23*	*2*	*1*	*7*	*34*	*1*	*1*	*1*	*1*	*1*	*3*	*2*	*2*	*1*	*1*	*2*	*2*	*1*	*2*	*2*	*1*
Acadia	1											x																
Alberta	8		x		x		x	x			x	x		x														x
Bishop's	3				x			x				x																
British Columbia	8		x	x	x		x	x				x							x	x								
Carleton	3				x			x				x																
Dalhousie	4				x			x				x						x										
Laurentian	4		x		x			x				x																
Laval	5		x	x	x			x				x																
Loyola	2		–		x							x																
McGill	10		x		x			x				x				x		x		x		x				x	x	
McMaster	4		x		x			x				x																
Manitoba	6						x	x			x	x	x				x											

Table 4 (cont.)

Marianopolis	2				x							x											
Memorial	3				x			x				x											
Moncton	2				x							x											
Montreal	9		x		x	x	x	x	x	x	x	x											
Mount Allison	2				x							x											
Mount St. Vincent	1				x																		
New Brunswick	3		x		x							x											
Notre Dame	2				x							x											
Ottawa	6		x		x		x	x			x	x											
Queen's	4		x		x			x				x											
R.M.C. (Kingston)	1											x											
Saskatchewan	6				x			x			x	x								x	x		
Sir George Williams	3				x			x				x											
St. Dunstan's	1				x																		
St. Francis Xavier	4				x			x				x	x										
St. Mary's	2				x							x											
St. Patrick's	2				x							x											
Toronto	17	x	x	x	x		x	x	x		x	x		x	x	x		x	x	x		x	x
Trent	2				x							x											
Victoria	3				x			x				x											
Waterloo	4				x			x			x	x											
Western Ontario	4		x		x			x				x											
Windsor	4		x		x			x				x											
York	3				x			x				x											

Source: Krukowski and McKellar, "The Other Ethnic Groups and Education."

Spanish. The right to offer any modern language for entrance credit is rarely utilized, partly because of the absence of a wide range of language courses in high school. In the three prairie provinces, the option of presenting Ukrainian as an entrance credit at local colleges

TABLE 5: Number of modern languages required or optional for admission to the faculties of art and science of 23 universities and colleges, Canada, 1965–66

	Arts		*Science*	
Universities and colleges	*Number of compulsory languages*	*Number of optional languages*[1]	*Number of compulsory languages*	
Acadia		1*	1	1*
Alberta		1†	1	1†
Bishop's		1‡	3	
Carleton		1*	1	1*
British Columbia		1*	2	1*
Dalhousie			1**	
Loyola		1††	1	1††
McGill		1*	1	1*
McMaster		1†	2	1†
Manitoba		1†	1	1†
Mount Allison		1*	2	1*
Ottawa		2††	1	1††
Queen's		1*	2	1*
Saskatchewan		1*	1	1*
St. Dunstan's		1*		1*
St. Francis Xavier		1*	1	1*
St. Mary's		1*	1	1*
Toronto		1†	1	1†
Trent			3	
Waterloo		1*	1	
Western Ontario			1	
Windsor		1†	2	1†
York		1*	2	1*

Source: Krukowski and McKellar, "The Other Ethnic Groups and Education."
[1] Number of modern languages student may present for credit.
* At the student's choice, with approval.
† Must be one of a specified list.
‡ French is required for students from Quebec.
**French or German is required.
†† French is required.

and universities encourages students to enroll in high school courses in the language, although to date it has not encouraged large numbers of students to continue their study of the Ukrainian language at university.

Many universities will have changed their entrance requirements since our survey, but because these entrance requirements exert a considerable influence on the choice of languages by students at the secondary level, and we feel they have been and may still be unduly restrictive in certain cases, therefore, **we recommend that Canadian universities broaden their practices in giving standing or credits for studies in modern languages other than French and English both for admission and for degrees.** This action would serve the interests of students and would also mean that Canada could gain greater advantage from the languages currently spoken here. It would be particularly appropriate for universities situated in areas where the languages in question are spoken by substantial numbers of people. As language teaching at the elementary and secondary school levels is improved the language capabilities of future university students will also improve. Colleges and universities should study the possibility of expanding their curricula in the fields of the humanities, particularly languages and literature, and the social sciences, to take advantage of the linguistic potential of their students.

2. AREA STUDY PROGRAMS

When a university or college offers courses in languages other than the two official languages, it may do so as part of an area study program. Such program consist of courses and research projects all related to a clearly defined area of the world, and emphasizing not only languages but also other fields in the humanities and social sciences, such as anthropology, economics, geography, history, linguistics, literature, philosophy, political science, and sociology. The area under study may be a specific country, or a region. There appears to be little relationship between the areas of the world singled out for study at Canadian universities and the areas from which large numbers of the Canadian population of other than British or French origin have originally come. The programs are generally not specifically concerned with the maintenance of the linguistic and cultural heritages of those represented in our population.

a. Soviet and Eastern European Studies

A survey of university calendars for 1965–66 indicated that the emphasis in area study programs was then focused almost entirely on Russian and Slavic studies, both at the undergraduate and graduate levels. Ten Canadian universities offered undergraduate programs in

TABLE 6: Number of courses in Soviet and East European studies offered at selected Canadian universities, Canada, 1965–66

Subjects	*Alberta*	*British Columbia*	*Carleton*	*McGill*	*Manitoba*	*Montreal*	*Ottawa*	*Saskatchewan*	*Toronto (undergraduate)*[1]	*Toronto (graduate)*	*Total*
Russian literature	9	7	6	8	4	5	25	5	8	8	85
Russian language[2]	9	7	4	9	4	9	25*	5	6	3	81
Ukrainian literature	5				2	1	15	2		2	27
Ukrainian language	7				4	1	7	2	3		24
East European history	2–H†	4	1–H	2–H	1–H		6½		1–H		17½
Polish language	3	2	1‡		3	1	3	1	3		17
Russian history	3–H	3	1–H	1–H	1–H		4	1–H	2–H	1–H	17
Polish literature	1	2			1	2	8			2	16
Russian geography	1–G	1	1–G	1–G	1	½–G	1–G	1–G	1–G	1–G	9½
Russian economy	2–E		2–E	1–E				1–E	1–E	1–E	8
Russian politics	2–P	1–P	1–P	½–P			1–P		1–P	1–P	7½
Marxist philosophy	1–P	1	½–P	½–P				1–P	1–P	1–P	6

Table 6 (cont.)

Russian culture and philosophy				1			1	2	1		5
Serbo-Croat language			1‡			1			3		5
East European culture and philosophy		1					1½				2½
Russian foreign policy		1–P	1–P								2
Serbo-Croat literature						2					2
East European geography				1–G		½–G					1½
East European economies	1–E										1
East European politics	1–P										1
East European relations		1									1
Czech literature						½					½
Slovak literature						½					½
Total	47	31	19½	25	21	24	98	21	31	20	337½

Source: Krukowski and McKellar, "The Other Ethnic Groups and Education."

[1] Except for the University of Toronto, no distinction is made between undergraduate and graduate courses.

[2] Language courses include grammar, composition, and other aspects of linguistics.

* Includes five courses in Slavic philology and linguistics.

† As many area study programs are interdepartmental, courses available to area study students but given within a department are indicated as follows: H-history, P-political science; E-economics; G-geography.

‡ A requirement for students selecting intensive study on Poland and Yugoslavia, not regularly offered and non-credit.

this field with the subject matter of the courses offered spread widely throughout the humanities and social sciences and including a variety of language courses.

Programs offered at the graduate level were generally closely related to undergraduate courses. For example, the University of British Columbia offered a master's degree in Slavic studies with seminars covering the same general areas as its undergraduate courses. Master of arts programs in Slavic languages and literature were widely available. McMaster University had a program devoted entirely to the Russian language and literature. The degree of doctor of philosophy was offered at the University of Ottawa and the University of Toronto, with the emphasis almost exclusively on language (plus linguistics and philology) and literature. A similar doctorate was also awarded at the University of Montreal until 1965 when the course was changed to conclude with the *diplôme d'études supérieures*. The University of Toronto also permitted a minor concentration in Polish, Ukrainian, or a Serbo-Croat language. Although there is no area study program as such at the University of Alberta, it was possible to take a doctorate in political science or history with specialization in the area of Eastern Europe or the USSR.

Table 6 is a summary of the courses in Soviet and East European studies available in 1965–66. Language and literature courses dominated at most universities. Only the Russian language was offered by all the Canadian universities having Slavic area study programs. A minimum of four and an average of more than six Russian courses were available at each of these universities. Ukrainian was taught mainly on the prairies. Although Polish language courses were available at more universities than Ukrainian, usually only one course was offered in Polish and nowhere were there more than three; even fewer courses were provided in Polish literature.

The University of Montreal was the only French-language institution offering a formal program in Soviet or East European studies, and no institution in the Atlantic Provinces offered a program in this area, although the Russian language was taught at Dalhousie University.

Several specific factors seem to influence the existence of Soviet or Slavic study programs. The size of an institution is important as well as the availability of source materials. The University of Toronto and the University of British Columbia offer a wide variety of courses in many subjects because of their size and resources; work on Eastern Europe is only one segment of this, although an important one. Course offerings also depend upon the presence of qualified professors. To a considerable extent the arrival of university-educated immigrants to Canada since 1945 has stimulated Soviet and

Slavic studies. The position of the USSR in the world today is unquestionably another powerful stimulant to Slavic studies in Canada.

b. Far Eastern Studies

Studies of the Far East were restricted to a very few institutions in 1965–66. The University of Toronto had separate graduate and undergraduate programs. A student could specialize in either Japanese or Chinese, which included classical Chinese and modern Mandarin. There were also courses on the literature of China and Japan, East Asian fine arts, the history of Asia and its major constituent nations, Asian philosophies, East and South Asian archaeology, and Pali and Sanskrit language and literature. The master of arts degree program consisted of language, literature, and philosophy.

The University of British Columbia's bachelor of arts course in Asian studies began with courses in modern Chinese and Japanese for two years, then classical Chinese. No other languages were offered. In addition to literature, philosophy, fine arts, and history courses, courses in Asian international relations were available. These same subject areas were also available in the graduate program leading to the degree of master of arts. A department of Far Eastern studies have existed at Saskatchewan since 1964, but the courses offered were limited.

c. Other Eastern Studies

In 1965–66, language and literature courses were also offered in Arabic, Malay (Indonesian), Persian, Turkish, and Urdu. Courses and seminars encompassed a variety of subjects and were divided according to region, rather than discipline. McGill University was explicitly concerned with the economic development of the Muslim nations, and graduate work could be carried out in the departments of political science, history, economics, and philosophy, oriented toward problems of the Near East, in conjunction with the Institute of Islamic Studies. McGill's program, founded in 1952, operated at the graduate level only. Doctoral candidates were required to have two years residence in the Muslim world.

At the University of Toronto, honours bachelor of arts, masters, and doctoral degrees were available in Islamic as well as ancient Near Eastern studies. Except for three interdepartmental courses each split among history, geography, and culture, the undergraduate program at Toronto dealt exclusively with Arabic, Persian, and Turkish language and literature. Graduate courses included area studies of Islam in North Africa and Spain, Islamic philosophy, the history of

Muslim civilization and Arabic, Persian, Turkish, and Urdu language and literature. Sanskrit and Pali were taught in the Far Eastern studies department; political and economic issues of Muslim India and Pakistan were also dealt with.

d. Other Programs

In 1965 the University of Toronto initiated a Latin American studies department, joining Laval University, the pioneer in this field. In 1965–66 only thirteen and twelve courses were offered at Toronto and Laval respectively so neither program could be regarded as intensive.

In Nova Scotia, St. Francis Xavier University conducted a Celtic studies program with four courses in Gaelic language and literature and two in history. The honours Icelandic degree at the University of Manitoba was purely literary and linguistic. Acadia University sponsored three West Indian studies courses within its political science department. There was a single course in Hungarian and Estonian literature within the graduate program at the University of Montreal, for which competence in these languages was a prerequisite and which was not given every year.

No Canadian university had formal area studies dealing with Western Europe or any country within it, such as France, Germany, or Italy. However, most courses in the humanities and social sciences dealt with Western Europe or its constituent countries. Regulations regarding the selection of courses might permit an individual to work out a specialized program concentrating on one or more Western European countries.

3. EXPANDING UNIVERSITY PROGRAMS

We have indicated above that we feel universities should study the possibility of expanding their curricula in the fields of the humanities, particularly languages and literature, and social sciences relating to particular areas. Much of this expansion could take place through area study programs. These programs would serve the national interest and facilitate Canada's international role. Such programs are complex and costly; they should probably be concentrated in relatively few universities, where high standards could be achieved with the resources available. There are many factors to be considered in determining which university should institute a particular program. One important factor might well be a concentration of people, in the region where the university is located, whose ethnic origin corresponds to the area of study. We feel that this question should be studied at once by the Association of Universities and Colleges of Canada, or by another inter-university body, in the interest of the most effective utilization of educational resources. Therefore, **we recommend that Canadian universities expand their studies in the fields of the humanities and the social sciences relating to particular areas other than those related to the English and French languages.**

4. ETHNIC COLLEGES AND UNIVERSITIES

We considered the case for a separate, federated university in western Canada, made up of ethnically based colleges, such as a Ukrainian college and a German college. We concluded that we could make no recommendation concerning the creation of such an institution. We note the formation of colleges serving particular cultural groups and employing the languages of those groups in addition to English, French, or both the official languages. For example, in Manitoba a Ukrainian Orthodox college (St. Andrew's) is part of the University of Manitoba; a Ukrainian Catholic college (St. Vladimir's) intends to become a degree-granting institution; and a research institute (the Ukrainian Free Academy of Sciences) has an adult education programme in Ukrainian studies. Such institutions could form a federated university and they should be free to do so. Probably, for both academic and financial reasons, they would prefer to be part of one of the larger, existing universities.

D. Adult Education

Various cultural groups in Canada carry out programs in the field of adult, or continuing, education. In Book II we pointed out that "the term continuing education at the present time is poorly defined, encompassing as it does a complex and widely differing range of agencies and programs" and noted the need for "a thorough study of the desirable organization and structures required to encourage discussion and further study among adults on Canadian affairs. . ." (paragraph 789). This remains true, but adult education is of special importance in the context of this Book. Programs conducted by the non-British, non-French cultural groups can play an important part in maintaining the cultural heritage of these groups.

In many cases the existing programs consist of courses on different cultures where the appropriate language is used as the language of instruction. Although varying quantitatively and qualitatively from group to group, their main objective is to raise the standard of education and knowledge of the group's members. Some are refresher courses; some are classes designed to up-date specialized advanced study; some are forums for the consideration of questions of daily life. Some inform group members about current cultural affairs or about the results of recent research on a particular culture. Some are courses in the language, literature, or history of a particular cultural group.

Although the Commission did not undertake a survey of such programs, there are a number of institutions which offer these types of courses such as the Polish Research Institutes in Montreal and Toronto, and the B'nai B'rith Foundation in larger centres; German cultural and educational organizations, such as Goethe Houses, the Ukrainian Prosvita Institutes, and Italian societies such as the Dante Alighieri groups. In 1966 the Polish Canadian Research Institute in Toronto organized a cycle of lectures "in order to acquaint the Polish society with the Problems that are dealt with by the Institute, and to bring the individuals interested in the activities of the Institute into contact with it. . . . Subjects of the lectures are within the orbit of the Institute's interests."[12] The Ukrainian Free Academy of Sciences in Winnipeg in 1968–69 offered adult education courses in Ukrainian language, literature, and history. Various Mennonite schools in Canada are involved in adult education for the German cultural group. These lectures and programs are geared to the level of education of the adult members of the relevant cultural group. They supplement the work of extension divisions of universities and school boards, which usually offer extension programs in adult education in either English or French.

Programs in the field of adult, or continuing, education for members of the non-British, non-French cultural groups emphasize particular cultures and languages. They play an important role in emphasizing the contribution made by these cultural groups in Canada, and thus contribute to the country as a whole. We feel, therefore, that they merit the interest and support of such educational authorities as the extension departments of school boards in relation to informational programs and the Citizenship Branch in regard to cultural programs. Such support could include assistance in providing suitable premises for courses and educational facilities such as materials and audio-visual aids.

Finally, we feel it most important that the special dimension of programs in various cultures and languages other than English and French be carefully considered whenever continuing education is studied or planned. When the thorough study of continuing education suggested in Book II is undertaken, the special contribution and needs of the non-British, non-French cultural groups should be given particular attention.

Notes

1. Data in sections A, B, and C is taken primarily from T. Krukowski and P. McKellar, "The Other Ethnic Groups and Education," a study prepared for the B.&B. Commission.
2. Marcel Trudel and Geneviève Jain, *Canadian History Textbooks: A Comparative Study,* Studies of the B.&B. Commission, No. 5 (English translation in preparation).
3. *Montrealer Zeitung,* April 21, 1966.
4. Joseph Katz, *The Teaching of Canadian History in Canada* (Winnipeg, 1953), 16.
5. Trudel and Jain, *Canadian History Textbooks*.
6. Armenian, Dutch, Estonian, German, Greek, Hungarian, Italian, Latvian, Lithuanian, Polish, Portuguese, and Slovenian.
7. Chinese, Japanese, Jewish, and Ukrainian.
8. A study of ethnic schools in the United States makes a distinction between schools on weekday afternoons, weekend schools, and all day schools. See Joshua A. Fishman and Vladimir C. Nathirny, "The Ethnic Group School and Mother Tongue Maintenance," in Joshua A. Fishman, ed., *Language Loyalty in the United States* (The Hague, 1966), pp. 92–126.
9. No enrolment figures were obtained for Dutch schools. Other sources, including a survey of voluntary associations done for the Commission, indicate little interest among the Dutch in ethnic schools for maintaining the Dutch language. However, there is considerable interest in religious schools among those of Dutch origin.
10. Fishman and Nathirny, "The Ethnic Group School and Mother Tongue Maintenance," p. 95.
11. Ibid., p. 100.
12. T. Krychowski, *The Polish Canadian Research Institute: Its Aims and Achievements* (Toronto, 1967), pp. 6–7.

Indian Control of Indian Education

NATIONAL INDIAN BROTHERHOOD

Statement of the Indian Philosophy of Education

In Indian tradition each adult is personally responsible for each child, to see that he learns all he needs to know in order to live a good life. As our fathers had a clear idea of what made a good man and a good life in their society, so we modern Indians, want our children to learn that happiness and satisfaction come from:

- pride in one's self;
- understanding one's fellowmen; and,
- living in harmony with nature.

These are lessons which are necessary for survival in this twentieth century.

- Pride encourages us to recognize and use our talents, as well as to master the skills needed to make a living.
- Understanding our fellowmen will enable us to meet other Canadians on an equal footing, respecting cultural differences while pooling resources for the common good.
- Living in harmony with nature will ensure preservation of the balance between man and his environment which is necessary for the future of our planet, as well as for fostering the climate in which Indian wisdom has always flourished.

We want education to give our children the knowledge to understand and be proud of themselves and the knowledge to understand the world around them.

SOURCE: National Indian Brotherhood, "Indian Control of Indian Education," Policy Paper presented to the Minister of Indian Affairs and Northern Development (Ottawa: National Indian Brotherhood, 1972), pp. 1–26. Reprinted by permission of the National Indian Brotherhood.

STATEMENT OF VALUES

We want education to provide the setting in which our children can develop the fundamental attitudes and values which have an honoured place in Indian tradition and culture. The values which we want to pass on to our children, values which make our people a great race, are not written in any book. They are found in our history, in our legends and in the culture. We believe that if an Indian child is fully aware of the important Indian values he will have reason to be proud of our race and of himself as an Indian.

We want the behaviour of our children to be shaped by those values which are most esteemed in our culture. When our children come to school they have already developed certain attitudes and habits which are based on experiences in the family. School programs which are influenced by these values respect cultural priority and are an extension of the education which parents give children from their first years. These early lessons emphasize attitudes of:

- self-reliance;
- respect for personal freedom;
- generosity;
- respect for nature; and
- wisdom.

All of these have a special place in the Indian way of life. While these values can be understood and interpreted in different ways by different cultures, it is very important that Indian children have a chance to develop a value system which is compatible with Indian culture.

The gap between our people and those who have chosen, often gladly, to join us as residents of this beautiful and bountiful country, is vast when it comes to mutual understanding and appreciation of differences. To overcome this, it is essential that Canadian children of every racial origin have the opportunity during their school days to learn about the history, customs and culture of this country's original inhabitants and first citizens. We propose that education authorities, especially those in provincial Departments of Education, should provide for this in the curricula and texts which are chosen for use in Canadian schools.

THE ROLE OF PARENTS IN SETTING GOALS

If we are to avoid the conflict of values which in the past has led to withdrawal and failure, Indian parents must have control of education with the responsibility of setting goals. What we want for our children can be summarized very briefly: to reinforce their Indian identity; and to provide the training necessary for making a good living in modern society. We are the best judges of the kind of school programs which can contribute to these goals without causing damage to the child.

We must, therefore, reclaim our rights to direct the education of our children. Based on two education principles recognized in Canadian society, *parental responsibility* and *local control of education*, Indian parents seek participation and partnership with the federal government, whose legal responsibility for Indian education is set by the treaties and the Indian Act. While we assert that only Indian people can develop a suitable philosophy of education based on Indian values adapted to modern living, we also strongly maintain that it is the financial responsibility of the federal government to provide education of all types and all levels to all status Indian people, whether living on or off reserves. It will be essential to the realization of this objective that representatives of the Indian people, in close cooperation with officials of the Department of Indian Affairs, establish the needs and priorities of local communities in relation to the funds which may be available through government sources.

The time has come for a radical change in Indian education. Our aim is to make education relevant to the philosophy and needs of the Indian people. We want education to give our children a strong sense of identity, with confidence in their personal worth and ability. We believe in education:

- as a preparation for total living;
- as a means of free choice of where to live and work; and
- as a means of enabling us to participate fully in our own social, economic, political and educational advancement.

We do not regard the educational process as an "either-or" operation. We must have the freedom to choose among many options and alternatives. Decisions on specific issues can be made only in the context of local control of education. We uphold the right of the Indian bands to make these specific decisions and to exercise their full responsibility in providing the best possible education for our children.

Our concern for education is directed to four areas which require attention and improvement: i.e., responsibility, programs, teachers and facilities. The following pages will offer in an objective way, the general principles and guidelines which can be applied to specific problems in these areas.

Responsibility

JURISDICTIONAL QUESTION OF RESPONSIBILITY FOR INDIAN EDUCATION

The federal government has legal responsibility for Indian education as defined by the treaties and the Indian Act. Any transfer of jurisdiction for Indian education can only be from the federal government to Indian bands. Whatever responsibility belongs to the provinces is derived from the contracts for educational services negotiated between band councils, provincial school jurisdictions, and the federal government.

Parties in future joint agreements will be: Indian bands, local provincial school jurisdictions, and the federal government. These contracts must recognize the right of Indians to a free education, funded by the Government of Canada.

The Indian people concerned, together with officials of the Department of Indian Affairs, must review all existing agreements for the purpose of making specific recommendations for their revision, termination or continuance.

In addition to the usual school services provided under joint agreements, attention must be given to local needs for teacher orientation, day nurseries, remedial courses, tutoring, Indian guidance counsellors, etc. Where bands want to form a school district under the federal system, necessary provision should be made in order that it has the recognition of provincial education authorities.

Master agreements between federal and provincial governments violate the principle of local control and parental responsibility if these agreements are made without consulting and involving the Indian parents whose children are affected. Since these children are often from many widely separated bands, it may be necessary to provide for Indian participation through the provincial Indian associations. In every case, however, parental responsibility must be respected and the local band will maintain the right to review and approve the conditions of the agreement.

LOCAL CONTROL

The past practice of using the school committee as an advisory body with limited influence, in restricted areas of the school program, must give way to an education authority with the control of funds and consequent authority which are necessary for an effective decision-making body. The federal government must take the required steps to transfer to local bands the authority and the funds which are allotted for Indian education.

The band itself will determine the relationship which should exist between the band council and the school committee: or more properly, the band education authority. The respective roles of the band council and the education authority will have to be clearly defined by the band, with terms of reference to ensure the closest cooperation so that local control will become a reality.

The local band education authority would be responsible for:

- budgeting, spending and establishing priorities;
- determining the types of school facilities required to meet local needs: e.g., day school, residence, group home, nursery, kindergarten, high school;
- directing staff hiring and curriculum development with special concern for Indian languages and culture;
- administering the physical plant;
- developing adult education and upgrading courses;
- negotiating agreements with provincial or separate school jurisdictions for the kind of services necessary for local requirements;
- cooperation and evaluation of education programs both on and off the reserve;
- providing counselling services.

Training must be made available to those reserves desiring local control of education. This training must include every aspect of educational administration. It is important that bands moving towards local control have the opportunity to prepare themselves for the move. Once the parents have control of a local school, continuing guidance during the operational phase is equally important and necessary.

REPRESENTATION ON PROVINCIAL SCHOOL BOARDS

There must be adequate Indian representation on provincial school boards which have Indian pupils attending schools in their district or division. If integration for Indians is to have any positive meaning, it must be related to the opportunity for parental participation in the educational decision-making process.

Recalling that 60 per cent of Indian children are enrolled in provincial schools, there is urgent need to provide for proper representation on all local provincial school boards. Since this issue must be resolved by provincial legislation, all provinces should pass effective laws which will insure Indian representation on all provincial school boards in proportion to the number of children attending provincial schools, with provision for at least one Indian representative in place where the enrolment is miminal. Laws already on the books are not always effective and should be re-examined. Neither is permissive legislation enough, nor legislation which has conditions attached.

A band education authority which is recognized as the responsible bargaining agent with financial control of education funds, will be in a strong position to negotiate for proper representation on a school board which is providing educational services to the Indian community.

There is an urgent need for laws which will make possible *responsible representation and full participation* by all parents of children attending provincial schools.

Indian organizations and the federal government should do whatever is necessary to conduct an effective public relations program for the purpose of explaining their role and that of the local band education authorities to the provincial ministers of education, to Department of Education officials and to school board members.

Programs

CURRICULUM AND INDIAN VALUES

Unless a child learns about the forces which shape him; the history of his people, their values and customs, their language, he will never really know himself or his potential as a human being. Indian culture and values have a unique place in the history of mankind. The Indian child who learns about his heritage will be proud of it. The lessons he learns in school, his whole school experience, should reinforce and contribute to the image he has of himself as an Indian.

The present school system is culturally alien to native students. Where the Indian contribution is not entirely ignored, it is often cast in an unfavourable light. School curricula in federal and provincial schools should recognize Indian culture, values, customs, languages and the Indian contribution to Canadian development. Courses in Indian history and culture should promote pride in the Indian child, and respect in the non-Indian student.

A curriculum is not an archaic, inert vehicle for transmitting knowledge. It is a precise instrument which can and should be shaped to exact specifications for a particular purpose. It can be changed and it can be improved. Using curriculum as a means to achieve their educational goals, Indian parents want to develop a program which will maintain balance and relevancy between academic/skill subjects and Indian cultural subjects.

To develop an Indian oriented curriculum for schools which enroll native children, there must be full scale cooperation between federal, provincial and Indian education people:

(1) In the federal Indian school system, funds must be made available for Indian people to work with professional curriculum planners. Together they will work out and test ideas for a relevant curriculum, utilizing the best from both cultures.

(2) In the provincial school system, this same kind of curriculum development must be pursued by the Department of Education with the involvement of the Indian people and the support of federal and provincial funding.

Some other measures for improving the quality of instruction for all students, both Indian and non-Indian, are recommended to provincial and private school systems:

(a) appointment of native people to curriculum staff for the purpose of supervising the production and distribution of Indian-oriented curriculum materials for provincial schools, complete with the manpower and other resources to accomplish this task;
(b) removal of textbooks or other teaching materials which are negative, biased or inaccurate in what concerns Indian history and culture;
(c) augmenting Indian content in curriculum to include Indian contributions to Canadian life through supplementary courses in: economics, science, medicine, agriculture, geography, etc., as well as special courses in Indian culture, music, art, dance, handicraft, language;
(d) cooperating with Indian people in developing Indian studies programs at all levels;
(e) eliminating the use of I.Q. and standardized tests for Indian children. It has been shown that these tests do not truly reflect the intelligence of children belonging to minority, ethnic or other cultural backgrounds.

Textbooks are needed which emphasize the importance of the Indian's role in Canadian history. Material for reading classes must be developed: material which is relevant to the experience of the Indian child living in isolated or northern areas. Federal and provincial governments must be ready to respond to the native people and support their legitimate wishes for improved texts. Indian people should be commissioned to work with historians and educators for the development of proper textbook material.

All Indian people, young and old alike, must be given a wide variety of educational opportunities. Specific problems in many Indian communities must be met by improved education. Much needed programs include: nursery and kindergarten education, junior and senior high school opportunity, vocational training, adult education, post-secondary education, and alcohol and drug abuse education.

Nursery Schools and Kindergartens

Financial support for nursery schools and kindergartens should be the special concern of governments. These programs should be designated as priority programs in every respect.

Many communities will view this pre-school experience as an opportunity for the children to learn the second language in which school subjects will be taught. Other communities will emphasize cultural content, for the purpose of reinforcing the child's image of himself as an Indian. This is the decision of the local parents and they alone are responsible for decisions on location, operation, curriculum and teacher hiring.

Junior and Senior High Schools

In places where junior and senior high school classes once operated, the children have been transferred to provincial schools. Alarmed by the increasing number of teenagers who are dropping out of school, Indian parents are looking for alternatives to the high school education which their children are now receiving in provincial schools. If Indian parents had control of high school education, they could combat conditions which cause failures by:

- adopting clearly defined educational objectives compatible with Indian values;
- providing a relevant educational program;
- making education a total experience: recognizing Indian language, life and customs, inviting the participation of Indian parents in shaping the program;
- providing more counselling by Indians for Indians.

The needs of children and the desire of parents would indicate that in some areas high schools and/or vocational schools should be established on certain reserves to serve students of surrounding communities. These schools would be operated and maintained by a representative education authority.

Serious planning must be directed to developing flexible, realistic and relevant high school programs to meet the specific needs of Indian students who have dropped out and desire to resume their high school studies.

Vocational Training

A new approach to qualifications for many jobs is needed, as well as a change in academic/vocational courses to meet new requirements. In many cases where these jobs are within the Indian community, job specifications should be set by the Indian people, and the training itself should be supervised by the local education authority, which is established and/or recognized by the band or bands involved. Some of these positions might include teachers, counsellors, social workers, probation officers, parole officers, community development workers.

On a wider scale, responsible efforts must be made to encourage business and industry to open up jobs for Indian people. Job training should correspond to job opportunity and the economic reality.

The local band education authority should be in a position to deal directly with Canada Manpower and other training institutions. When necessary, several education authorities might join together to plan programs for a particular region.

Adult Education

Adult education programs, properly conducted, can be a means for many Indians to find economic security and self-fulfillment.

If the native language is spoken in the community, then native instructors should be trained and employed to teach these adult courses. Grade advancement classes should be offered on and off the reserves, as well as basic literacy courses for those desiring to speak, read and write English. Basic oral English programs are also needed. Other adult programs which should be provided as the need demands, might include: business management, consumer-education, leadership training, administration, human relations, family education, health, budgeting, cooking, sewing, crafts, Indian art and culture, etc.

These programs should be carried out under the control and direction of the band education authority, on a short term or continuing basis, according to the local needs.

Post-Secondary Education

Considering the great need there is for professional people in Indian communities, every effort should be made to encourage and assist Indian students to succeed in post-secondary studies.

Encouragement should take the form of recruiting programs directed to providing information to students desiring to enter professions such as: nursing, teaching, counselling, law, medicine, engineering, etc. Entrance requirements, pre-university programs, counselling and tutoring services, course requirements, are some factors which influence how far a student can progress. He would be further encouraged if the Indian language is recognized for the second language requirement and a native studies program has a respected place in the curriculum.

Considering the tremendous educational disadvantages of Indian people, present rigid entrance requirements to universities, colleges, etc., must be adjusted to allow for entrance on the basis of ability, aptitude, intelligence, diligence and maturity.

Assistance should take the form of generous federal financial support eliminating the difficulty and uncertainty which now accompanies a student's decision to continue on for higher education. Indian students should be able to attend any recognized educational institution of their choice. Those who have the motivation and talent to do post-graduate studies, should receive total financial assistance. Since it will be many years before the number of candidates for professional training exceeds the demand for trained professionals, each request for financial assistance to do post-secondary or post-graduate studies should be judged on its own merits, and not by general administrative directives.

Indian people should seek representation on the governing bodies of institutions of higher learning. This includes university senates and boards of governors, as well as the governing councils of colleges, community colleges and technical schools.

Alcohol and Drug Education

There is immediate need for educational programs of a preventative and rehabilitative nature, designed and operated by Indians to meet the threat of alcohol and drug addiction which plagues both young and old alike. Whatever funds and means are necessary to operate these programs should be made available at the earliest possible date.

Some recommendations proposed by Indian provincial organizations for implementing these programs are:

(a) Training native people as social animators to initiate programs of group dynamics at the community level. In this way there would be community participation in decision-making which affects the community. Through the acquisition of knowledge about problems and services, combined with reality-oriented group discussions leading to community action, the solution of the socio-medical ills can be placed in the context of the community.

(b) Governments, federal and provincial, should encourage special seminars and study groups for teachers, parents and students, as well as making available the best audio-visual aids, in order to bring those concerned up to date on all that can be done to combat addiction.

(c) These programs should be directed not only to the victims of addiction but also to the communities, professions and institutions that necessarily become involved in the circle of human relationships which are affected by addiction.

LANGUAGE OF INSTRUCTION

Language is the outward expression of an accumulation of learning and experience shared by a group of people over centuries of development. It is not simply a vocal symbol; it is a dynamic force which shapes the way a man looks at the world, his thinking about the world and his philosophy of life. Knowing his maternal language helps a man to know himself; being proud of his language helps a man to be proud of himself.

The Indian people are expressing growing concern that the native languages are being lost; that the younger generations can no longer speak or understand their mother tongue. If the Indian identity is to be preserved, steps must be taken to reverse this trend.

While much can be done by parents in the home and by the community on the reserve to foster facility in speaking and understanding, there is a great need for formal instruction in the language. There are two aspects to this language instruction: (1) teaching in the native language, and (2) teaching the native language.

It is generally accepted that pre-school and primary school classes should be taught in the language of the community. Transition to English or French as a second language should be introduced only after the child has a strong grasp of his own language. The time schedule for this language program has been determined to be from four to five years duration. Following this time span, adjustment and adaptation to other languages and unfamiliar cultural milieux are greatly enhanced.

The need for teachers who are fluent in the local language is dramatically underlined by this concern for the preservation of Indian identity through language instruction. Realization of this goal can be achieved in several ways:

- have teacher-aides specialize in Indian languages;
- have local language-resource aides to assist professional teachers;
- waive rigid teaching requirements to enable Indian people who are fluent in Indian languages, to become full-fledged teachers.

Funds and personnel are needed to develop language programs which will identify the structures of the language; i.e., syntax, grammar, morphology, vocabulary. This is essential, not only to preserve the language, but to encourage its use in literary expression.

Serious studies are needed to adapt traditional oral languages to written forms for instructional and literary purposes.

In places where it is not feasible to have full instruction in the native language, school authorities should provide that Indian children and others wishing it, will have formal instruction in the local native language as part of the curriculum and with full academic credit.

While governments are reluctant to invest in any but the two official languages, funds given for studies in native languages and for the development of teaching tools and instructional materials will have both short and long term benefits.

CULTURAL EDUCATION CENTRES

The purpose of a cultural education centre is to provide for the personal development necessary for social and economic achievement in today's society. This personal development is achieved when an individual knows himself fully: his personal identity, dignity and potential. The cultural education centre will promote this through studies of Indian history, culture, language and values.

By learning ways to apply traditional beliefs, values and skills to survival in modern society, and by learning modern skills and behaviours needed to participate in the benefits of economic and social development, the Indian will gain self-confidence and independence. The cultural education centre will be designed to meet these needs and to make up for deficiencies in other educational programs. Considering the vital role that these centres could play in cultural, social and economic development, it is imperative that all decisions concerning their evolution (goals, structure, location, operation, etc.) be the sole perogative of the Indian people.

Funds for these centres should be available with a minimum of regulations. These latter should be the result of discussion and agreement between the government and the Indian people.

The Indian people will welcome the participation of other departments of government, of provincial or local governments, or business or industry, of churches or foundations in securing sufficient and continuing funds for the cultural education centres. These centres must be Indian controlled and operated, in view of the fact that they are established for Indian purposes and use.

Teachers

TRAINING PROGRAMS FOR TEACHERS AND COUNSELLORS

If progress is going to be made in improving educational opportunity for native children, it is basic that teacher and counsellor training programs be redesigned to meet the needs. The need for native teachers and counsellors is critical and urgent; the need for specially trained non-Indian teachers and counsellors is also very great.

Native Teachers and Counsellors

It is evident that the federal government must take the initiative in providing opportunities for Indian people to train as teachers and counsellors. Efforts in this direction require experimental approaches and flexible structures to accommodate the native person who has talent and interest, but lacks minimum academic qualifications. Provincial involvement is also needed in this venture to introduce special teacher and counsellor training programs which will allow native people to advance their academic standing at the same time as they are receiving professional training. Because of the importance to the Indian community, these training programs must be developed in collaboration with the Indian people and their representatives in the national and provincial organizations. The national and provincial organizations have a major role to play in evolving and implementing the training programs and in encouraging native young people to enter the education field.

Native teachers and counsellors who have an intimate understanding of Indian traditions, psychology, way of life and language, are best able to create the learning environment suited to the habits and interests of the Indian child.

There is urgent need for more Indian counsellors to work with students both on and off the reserves. If the need is to be met, many more training centres must be opened immediately. The few which are now operating can never supply enough trained counsellors for the job that has to be done.

Non-Indian Teachers and Counsellors

The training of non-Indian teachers for teaching native children, either in federal or provincial schools, is a matter of grave concern to the Indian people. The role which teachers play in determining the success or failure of many young Indians is a force to be reckoned with. In most cases, the teacher is simply not prepared to understand or cope with cultural differences. Both the child and the teacher are forced into intolerable positions.

The training of non-Indian counsellors who work with Indian children in either the federal or provincial systems, is also of grave concern to Indian parents. Counsellors must have a thorough understanding of the values and cultural relevancies which shape the young Indian's self-identity. In order to cope with another cultural group the self-image of the child must be enhanced and not allowed to disintegrate. It is generally agreed that present counselling services are not only ineffective for students living away from home, but often are a contributing factor to their failure in school. It is the opinion of parents that counselling services should be the responsibility of the band education authority.

Federal and provincial authorities are urged to use the strongest measures necessary to improve the qualifications of teachers and counsellors of Indian children. During initial training programs there should be compulsory courses in inter-cultural education, native languages (oral facility and comparative analysis), and teaching English as a second language. Orientation courses and in-service training are needed in all regions. Assistance should be available for teachers in adapting curriculum and teaching techniques to the needs of local children. Teachers and counsellors should be given the opportunity to improve themselves through specialized summer courses in acculturation problems, anthropology, Indian history, language and culture.

Primary teachers in federal or provincial schools should have some knowledge of the maternal language of the children they teach.

Until such time as bands assume total responsibility for schools, there must be full consultation with the band education authority regarding the appointment of teachers and counsellors. As part of its involvement, the community should also take the initiative in helping the teachers and counsellors to learn the culture, language and history of the local community.

INDIAN PARA-PROFESSIONALS

More Indian teacher-aides and more Indian counsellor-aides are urgently needed throughout the school systems where Indian children are taught. These para-professionals can play an important role in helping the young child or the adolescent to adjust to unfamiliar and often overwhelming situations during their school experience.

Job requirements and the personal qualities needed by para-professionals working with Indian children will be set by the education authority of the band. Instead of operating on the fringe at some clerical or irrelevant task, Indian para-professionals will be delegated by the parents to work with the children at the level of greatest need. The importance of this work warrants that the para-professional receive proper training and be given responsibilities in line with the position. These positions should serve as a training ground for professional advancement.

Performance and effectiveness rather than degrees and certificates should be the criteria used in hiring and in establishing salaries and benefits. For the protection of those who are qualified by experience rather than by academic standing, it is essential that the status of para-professionals be determined by their responsibility and function. On this basis they will be assured of parity in salaries and benefits with professionals doing the same job.

It should be the aim of the para-professional program to encourage young people to continue their commitment to Indian education.

To operate a good school, many types of jobs must be filled. There should be adequate funding to insure that Indian schools are adequately staffed, not only with professionals, but with well-trained para-professionals, including recreation assistants and specialist-aides.

Facilities and Services

SUB-STANDARD EDUCATIONAL FACILITIES

All unsafe or obsolete school buildings, equipment and teacherages on reserves should be replaced with modern, functional units. Where Indian communities wish to maintain educational services on their reserves, the reserve school facilities must be brought up to the same standards as those in the outside communities. To provide for all the improvements necessary, band councils must make long-term plans for building construction. If the Department of Indian Affairs cannot handle the financing under its usual annual budgeting scheme, other alternatives must be considered. One of these would be a basic change in the department's long-term building policy. Also, through the intermediary of the department, other agencies could become the source of long-term funding for Indian building programs.

NEW EDUCATIONAL FACILITIES

It shall be within the power of the band education authority to plan for and provide the school facilities needed for community educational programs: e.g., education of children, parental involvement in education, adult education, cultural activities, training sessions, etc.

EDUCATIONAL INSTITUTIONS

There is no single type of educational institution which will meet all of the needs of Indian children. Facilities and services must be many and varied to suit particular kinds of circumstances.

Residences

No general statement can be made on residences because of varying needs across the country. In many places the need still exists for this type of accommodation. However, many parents object to sending their children long distances and want accommodations provided at the village level. In all cases, the federal government is advised to consult all parents with children in residences, in order to determine their wishes on keeping or closing residences, and to examine alternative accommodations.

Admission criteria for student residences will be formulated by the people concerned: parents, band councils and administrators. The latter will reflect fiscal considerations.

Indian bands wishing to take over administrative responsibility and financial control of student residences should be given full assistance to do so. This will require changes in present department procedures for the operation of residences, as well as training Indian candidates for administrative positions.

Where a residence is in operation, there should be an active parent's council, representative of the student enrollment. This council will act with the responsible residence authority on matters of policy and program.

Programs must be implemented for bettering the qualifications of present staff members and assisting unqualified persons to meet job requirements. Residences should be staffed as far as possible by Indian personnel.

Where conditions warrant the closing of a residence, the land and buildings should revert to the use of the band or bands, with a preference for educational purposes.

Day Schools

The need for good schools in Indian communities is becoming more urgent. These schools should have two goals: (a) providing adequate and appropriate educational opportunity, where skills to cope effectively with the challenge of modern life can be acquired; and (b) creating the environment where Indian identity and culture will flourish.

In working toward these goals, the reserve school would be a major factor in eliminating the conditions which lead to dropouts: negative parental attitudes and student alienation.

To provide these facilities an increased financial and human investment must be made in the Indian community. Complete modern buildings, classrooms, equipment, gymnasiums and staff quarters are needed.

These reserve schools will be the vehicle by which Indian parents gain knowledge, experience and confidence in fulfilling their obligation and responsibility in the education of their children.

All school facilities should be available to the community for adult education, cultural activities and training sessions.

To facilitate the transition of students from reserve schools to others, it is essential that the provincial departments of education recognize Indian day schools as accredited educational centres. This presupposes that academic quality will improve, that federal Indian schools will become "models of excellence," recognized and imitated by provincial schools. If an Indian-oriented curriculum differs from that of the provincial system, steps should be taken by provincial authorities to develop appropriate criteria for grading and accrediting purposes.

Group Homes, Hostels

There is a need among students living off the reserve for familiar, homelike accommodations. These could be provided in the small hostel or group home setting. When administered and staffed by Indian people, these homes could give the young person the security and comfort of an Indian family while he or she is adjusting to a new way of life.

In northern communities there is a great need for this kind of home to replace the very large and often far distant residence. Located centrally in every village and operated by an Indian couple, the group home would provide long and short term care, i.e., food, shelter, recreation and companionship for all in the village who need it. This would include children whose parents were absent for hunting and trapping, and old people who might be left alone for the same reasons. The concept of this kind of home is derived directly from Indian culture, and if allowed to take form would contribute to a healthy Indian community.

Denominational Schools

As in all other areas of education, the parents have the right to determine the religious status of the local school. In as far as possible, there should be an attempt to satisfy the preference of everyone.

STAFF

Where there are Indian people in attendance at a school, the number of Indian staff hired, including professional, para-professional, clerical and janitorial, should be based on a minimum ratio of one Indian staff person to every twenty Indian students. This procedure should be observed in residences, reserve day schools and provincial integrated schools.

Professionals, para-professionals and community resource people are all needed to operate a good reserve school. In addition to teachers and teacher-aides, reserve schools must have good counsellors and counsellor-aides. Consultants with knowledge of curriculum development and curriculum adaptation are necessary. A recreation director has a special role to play. Where it is not economically possible to have a recreation director on the school staff, the community recreational program must be designed to include the requirements of the school curriculum.

Whenever possible these positions should be filled by native people. Consultants and specialists in Indian language, history, crafts, customs, dances, legends will be drawn from the local community.

RESEARCH

There is increasing need for factual and scientific information on which to base planning and decisions. The Indian people advocate that research be under the direction and control of Indian people. Monies labelled for research shall be channelled to research programs identified by band councils and Indian organizations in relation to their priorities and programs. Academics who are engaged to conduct research projects will be responsible to the Indian community, local or regional.

It is equally important that the Indian people have the direction and control of experimental programs conducted in their name by universities, academic centres or research bodies.

Problems of Integration

Integration in the past twenty years has simply meant the closing down of Indian schools and transferring Indian students to schools away from their reserves, often against the wishes of the Indian parents. The acceleration with which this program has developed has not taken into account the fact that neither Indian parents and children, nor the white community: parents, children and schools, were prepared for integration, or able to cope with the many problems which were created.

Integration is a broad concept of human development which provides for growth through mingling the best elements of a wide range of human differences. Integrated educational programs must respect the reality of racial and cultural differences by providing a curriculum which blends the best from the Indian and the non-Indian traditions.

Integration viewed as a one-way process is not integration, and will fail. In the past, it has been the Indian student who was asked to integrate: to give up his identity, to adopt new values and a new way of life. This restricted interpretation of integration must be radically altered if future education programs are to benefit Indian children. The success of integration hinges on these factors: parents, teachers, pupils (both Indian and white) and curriculum.

On the side of the Indian people, much more preparation and orientation is needed to enable parents to make informed decisions and to assist their children to adjust and to succeed. Indian parents must have the opportunity through full representation to participate responsibly in the education of their children.

The Indian child also needs preparation and orientation before being thrust into a new and strange environment. In handling the conflict of values, he will need the continuing support of his parents and Indian counsellors. Inferiority, alienation, rejection, hostility, depression, frustration, are some of the personal adjustment problems which characterize the Indian child's experience with integration. These are also factors in the academic failure of Indian children in integrated schools.

Indian children will continue to be strangers in Canadian classrooms until the curriculum recognizes Indian customs and values, Indian languages, and the contributions which the Indian people have made to Canadian history. Steps can be taken to remedy this situation by providing in provincial schools special auxiliary services in cultural development, curriculum development, vocational guidance, counselling, inservice training of teachers, tutoring and recreation. Evidently many of these services can be provided under the regular school program. However, if services are introduced especially for the Indian children, the school board should have financial support from the federal government.

The success of integration is not the responsibility of Indians alone. Non-Indians must be ready to recognize the value of another way of life; to learn about Indian history, customs and language; and to modify, if necessary, some of their own ideas and practices.

Education for Immigrants

COMMISSION OF INQUIRY ON THE POSITION OF THE FRENCH LANGUAGE AND ON LANGUAGE RIGHTS

This article deals with the role which has been or could be played by education for immigrants, or the importance of the school with regard to the position, the enhancement and development of the French language in Quebec. In other words, as far as Quebec is concerned, is the school the principal means for integrating the immigrant into the French-speaking community?

Working on the assumption that the position of the French language is threatened, can we expect to rectify the situation through measures to provide special education for immigrants? What sort of measures should be taken? Should we proceed by coercive or persuasive means? To which groups should the measures apply? The facts and figures will provide our answer. . . .

Conditions and Experience of Immigration in Quebec

If the concept of immigrant integration was slow to develop in Canada, it took even longer to register in the Province of Quebec where a Department of Immigration has only recently been created.

In Quebec, as throughout Canada, demographic and economic factors apart, little attention was paid to education or instruction as a means of integrating immigrants.

The first indications of attention given by the French-speaking group to immigrant integration through education barely go back to 1947–48 and even then, the several steps taken came to nothing.

The minutes of a meeting held on April 2, 1947 by a subcommittee in charge of studying the problem of the New Canadians mentioned a resolution in which His Excellency the Archbishop of Montreal, seconded by J.A. Savoie, notary, proposed that a highly qualified

---

SOURCE: Quebec, Commission of Inquiry on The Position of The French Language and on Language Rights. Quebec: Official Editor of Quebec, 1972, Chapter 2, pp. 193–194 and 200–236. Reproduced by permission of l'Editeur Officiel du Québec.

person be named by the Provincial Government to inquire into the situation of new immigrants throughout the Province, to see to the organization of such courses as they might need and to ensure that they have pleasant and profitable recreational possibilities.[1]

The same subcommittee recalled the gravity of the problem to the Roman Catholic Committee. In December 1954 and on December 6, 1956 the Académie canadienne-française pointed out the "scandalous situation" of the anglicization of immigrant children to the Department of Public Instruction.[2]

In its many interventions, the Académie canadienne-française makes a direct connection between the instruction of immigrant children and the breakdown of the bio-ethnic balance in Canada.

The report of a subcommittee of specialists, dated April 11, 1967, establishes at 69.4 per cent the percentage of New Canadian pupils in the English Catholic schools of the public sector in 1955–56, the percentage having increased by 24.5 per cent between 1931 and 1955.[3]

1. ACADEMIC INTEGRATION AND LANGUAGE CONCERNS

Only recently has a language threat become apparent in the school sector. It coincides with French Canadians' awareness of their position as a distinct majority in Quebec. At the same time, figures given in the Parent Report reveal a trend on the part of ethnic groups towards English Catholic schools. The figures show, for instance, that in 1962–63, 25.2 per cent of the children of Italian immigrants went to French-language schools while 74.8 per cent went to the English Catholic schools of the Montreal Catholic School Commission.[4] This situation was considered alarming as compared to that prevailing in 1930–31 when 52.2 per cent enrolled in French schools and 46.8 per cent in English schools. There was never an in-depth study, however, to discover the causes of this situation and whether it was simply the choice made by the parents of non-French and non-British children which led to the 1971–72 situation in which only 10.7 per cent of the children were enrolled in French classes and 89.3 per cent in English classes.

No one questioned sufficiently the causes of this situation; no one asked why enrollment in French-language schools fell from 52 per cent to 34.3 per cent and increased from 46.8 per cent to 65.7 per cent in English-language schools between 1930–31 and 1950–51 at which time there was no immigration because of the economic crisis. Yet it was during the economic crises and continental isolationism that the great migration towards English schools took place.

Historian Michel Brunet urges a study of the causes of this situation in order to achieve a better understanding of the present state and so be in a position to take the appropriate steps to combat deficiencies in the future. To this end he reminds us that impatience solves no problems. Only an objective knowledge of the past can suggest more efficient means of facing the problems of the present and the challenges of the future.[5]

In his opinion, the major cause is the anti-state attitude preached in the name of religion by the leaders of the community to protect the status quo:

> They opposed compulsory education, the standardization of school textbooks, the creation of the École des hautes études commerciales, the centralization of schools in cities, the abolition of rural schools, the creation of specialized schools directed by the state, the improved organization of the teaching profession, the reform of the Department of Public Instruction, and so forth. To recall these exhausting and sterile debates is to underline the recent causes for delayed progress in education in French Canada. These were added to those of the last century. It is difficult to evaluate the disastrous consequences. One even wonders whether the French Canadian community will ever manage to catch up in the field of education. That there be some doubt is understandable.[6]

Since the tragic lack of a large well-trained teaching body is considered to be one of the disastrous consequences of the opting out of the state, the author concludes that "*the entire educational system of the French Canadian community is two generations behind and this is an optimistic evaluation.*"[7]

The report of April 11, 1957

A report prepared in 1965 by René Gauthier mentions a secret report submitted to the Superintendent of Roman Catholic Schools on April 11, 1957 by a seven-member subcommittee responsible for an in-depth study of the school problem of New Canadians. This report reveals that around the year 1930, ethnic groups welcomed English-speaking American priests to serve in their parishes. These priests invited non-British and non-French parents to send their children to English Catholic schools. More serious yet, the report in question reveals that the French Catholic school commissioners were in the habit of sending all non-French, non-British children to English-language schools.[8]

At this point, mention should be made of the confessional character of Quebec schools and it should be stressed that, since the beginning of the century, Jews had by law been assimilated into the Protestant group and were naturally sent to English-language schools. Later, Orthodox and non-Catholic children were usually sent to Protestant schools. Since the school boards in question had never been asked to set up a French Protestant section, all the above-mentioned children were educated in English.

Between 1950 and 1960, however, the Catholic Church made praiseworthy efforts as regards the reception and entertainment of ethnic groups but this was done primarily through Christian charity and in order to preserve Catholicism. The contribution these ethnic groups might make was never taken into consideration, and the language problem was first mentioned by the Académie canadienne-française only in December 1954.

The Gauthier Report, dated January 27, 1967, noted that adult classes were organized by the MCSC between 1948 and 1964, without emphasizing the immigrant himself or his problems. The goal was to have immigrants learn French and to give this language priority in the curriculum. However, Montreal, which had a real language problem, spent $100,000 a year on adult education while Toronto allocated $1,723,000 for this purpose!

The same report recommended that a non-confessional French-language system be set up as well as special bilingual schools for New Canadians only.[9]

The allogenes, who wanted bilingual schools, influenced the thinking of school authorities, who proposed, in 1957, that such institutions be set up for the children coming from ethnic groups. The issue was dodged until May 17, 1961, and, when the Roman Catholic Committee of the Council of Education decided, in May 1962, to proceed with the project, English-speaking people opposed it; the French-language press and French-speaking Quebecers remained silent. Yet 165 parents had already enrolled their children in the bilingual classes which were to begin in eastern Montreal. Minister René Lévesque was the only one to defend bilingual schools before the Quebec Législature.[10]

A bilingual school was opened by the St. Leonard School Board after 1963. However, as we have already noted, the same teachers often taught French and English and, as many of them had not perfectly mastered their native language, the results were mediocre. These classes were abolished in 1968, an action which led to the St. Leonard crisis, then to Bill 63, adopted by the Legislative Assembly on November 28, 1969.

Turning back to the 1950s, we can observe another reason for the defection from French-language schools by the children of ethnic group members: confessional differences within groups of the same language. Thus the Germans, Ukrainians, Hungarians, Swiss, Dutch, and so forth, were sent to English- or French-language schools depending on whether they were Protestant, Orthodox or Catholic.

Even if the language choice had worked to the advantage of

French-language schools, the academic structure of the time would have exerted little attraction.

To this must be added the fact that sponsored immigrants were reunited with members of their families who already attended English-language schools. They would naturally do likewise. This group represented approximately 30 per cent of the immigrants.

2. THE PARENT REPORT

The Parent Report mentioned other causes leading to the precarious situation of education in the French-language schools. The Commission which drew up this report was itself the result of a sudden awareness of the weaknesses of the French Catholic school system.

The structures of French-language public schools, as we now know them, are recent, and obligatory school attendance only dates back to 1943.[11]

The Parent Commission revealed the cultural pluralism created by the arrival of groups of immigrants after the war and by modern society.[12] Among other things, its Report revealed that French-language teachers in Quebec had formed professional associations 75 years after their Protestant colleagues.[13] It pointed out the poor quality of textbooks.

> Elementary grade teachers and their pupils have suffered the consequences; many minds remain scarred by bad taste, by banality of expression, by empty religiosity, by dessicated and inadequate knowledge.[14]

The Report emphasized that in the French-language schools the teaching of English was: "... a painful, boring obligation, drudgery for both teacher and pupils."[15]

It requested that parents be given a certain freedom of choice as regards the teaching of this subject[16] and proposed that optional courses be offered for the study of other living languages which might interest certain students.[17] The Report also emphasized that: "One of the most pressing needs is the thorough screening of textbooks now in use, the short-coming of which contribute to the poor language habits of the pupils."[18]

The Report comments on the difficulties involved in confessional education and suggests that non-confessional courses be provided whenever a sufficient number of parents request it. It opts for the choice of schooling by the parents but requests an annual census to enable them to choose freely, after sufficient reflection, and thus provide the school board with an essential tool for rational planning.[19]

As regards New Canadians, the Report deplores the fact that the minority situation, the economic inferiority and attitude of French

Canadians, the absence of an adequate reception system, and defense reflexes have discouraged the necessary rapprochement of the two:

> It should not be forgotten that often an immigrant has been attracted to Canada, where certain of his relations and friends had already been living for several years, because of a personal interchange of information and opinion. The more welcome New Canadians feel in Quebec, especially among French-speaking citizens, the more will they make this known in their native lands, and the better will they prepare prospective immigrants to consider the possibility of casting their lot with the French-speaking majority, as, in the natural course of events, a considerable number should be expected to do.[20]

The same report added:

> In the preceding section of this chapter, we have indicated how urgent is the need to institute reform on all fronts so that French-language public education may reach a level comparable to that of public education in the English Protestant schools. It is not surprising that, when they see such differences in services and in quality, New Canadians should have been inclined to choose the better equipped schools, in which the teachers are ordinarily better prepared. For a certain number of New Canadians, the problem of choice between a French or an English school will be settled the moment French-language public education is of unquestionable quality and gives access to all university faculties. Only then is it reasonable to think that they are truly free to make a choice between French and English public schools of comparable merit.[21]

Lastly, the Report, while demanding a broader reception policy, particularly in Montreal, asks that a good quality of teaching of the second language be considered the primary means of attracting immigrants towards French-language studies.

> One of the reasons which induce immigrants to place their children in the English-language schools is that there they will learn the language spoken throughout most of North America. It is likely that if the teaching of English in the French schools were promptly improved, especially at the level of studies where this teaching could not enter into conflict with a thorough knowledge of the mother tongue of French-speaking students, there would be fewer parents, not originally English-speaking, who would be inclined to enrol (sic) their children in English language schools.[22]

Certain ethnic groups submitted briefs to the Parent Commission. All were unanimous in requesting bilingual schools for their children, including Jews from North Africa, who were of the French culture and who declared that French was a moral necessity for them.[23] However, since no effect was given to the recommendations of the

Parent Report with regard to the social and educational integration of immigrants, many were disappointed in their expectations.

It was not until 1971 that the Maisonneuve Regional School Board took the initiative of allowing Jewish students from the Laval area to attend its secondary schools, while offering them courses in the Hebrew language and culture.

Moreover, it was only at the end of November, 1972 that the Department of Education accepted the request of the Sephardic and French-speaking Jews to open a private French-language school:[24] 20 per cent of the cost is assumed by the parents.

3. SUBSEQUENT POLICIES

The Quebec Government's inactivity continued until 1968, when reception centres were set up following the St. Leonard crisis. It created a Department of Immigration and appointed the Commission of Inquiry on the Position of the French Language and on Language rights in Quebec in 1968, organized the immigrant orientation and training centres (COFI), was instrumental in having Bill 63 assented to in 1969, and obliged English-language schools to begin teaching French in the first year of elementary school. Bill 64, which was adopted in December 1970, allowed many professional associations to accept candidates having a working knowledge of French, thus enabling them to practice the profession for which they were qualified, regardless of their citizenship, on condition that they request Canadian citizenship after having completed the legally required period of time in the country. For the past two years record of the language spoken at home has been kept in student files.

The setting up of introductory classes, the Private Education Act and the agreement of May 18, 1971 between the provincial Department of Immigration and the federal Department of Manpower and Immigration with a view to improving information are some of the means recently instituted to help immigrants. Moreover, these same means facilitate the application of a policy for enhancing and developing the French language in Quebec.

CONCLUSION

Even though we can find only a distant analogy between the situations in various countries as regards immigration, an analogy still more distant where Quebec is concerned, a certain constant emerges from general observations.

Indeed, whatever the degree of importance given to the school system in the immigrant's adaptation to any milieu, the results, for all practical purposes, depend on other factors which, while not directly related to the school system are equally determining.

For example, a certain precondition seems necessary to any consideration of the role of the school in the integration of one language group into another; this precondition is the objective of a country or a state as regards immigration, as well as the knowledge and understanding of the content of this objective.

Every study on education or the school as a means of integration assumes that the immigrant feels wanted or needed by the community of which he hopes to become a part. The problem of the integration of the immigrant largely surpasses the role of the school and becomes fundamentally a question of motivation, as various studies have revealed.

These include works done by Morrison,[25] the United States Department of Health, Education and Welfare, Joti Bhatnagar, who carried out a masterly study[26] in England, in which he states that "The social acceptability of immigrant children appears to be reflecting the general state of race relations in the country", and R.A. Taft in Australia.[27]

Three dimensions of motivation are involved here:

(a) that of the host country where motivation is the result of a consciousness of its immigration objectives (need, suitability, goal), which become tangible in the form of adequate recruiting, welcoming, supporting and orientation measures;
(b) that of the host population which is sufficiently informed of the reasons for and benefits of immigration to accept and integrate the new arrivals;
(c) that of the new arrivals who have sufficient prior knowledge of the social conditions of the country to understand and accept reactions.

Any concept of motivation presupposes that in Quebec a knowledge of the French language is desired.

The question then becomes one of methodology. How can the objective, in this case acquiring the French language, be made attractive? How can its advantages be pointed out to those we wish to interest? How can the educational system assume a share of this role in Quebec and how is this being done at the moment?

These considerations must seem fairly abstract, particularly since in practice the situation seems to have been quite different. It is the immigration policy itself which must determine the measures to be taken but, in fact, we have generally been forced to take measures in the absence of any policy. Moreover, internal circumstances peculiar to each country determine policy. In short, only a thorough knowledge of the specific conditions of the country can inspire the proper measures to be taken.

It is vitally important for Quebec to determine its particular circumstances *vis-à-vis* immigration.

Quebec's Demo-Linguistic Situation in a Historical Context

If the problem of immigrant assimilation is considered on the provincial level, it can be seen that the immigrant population in Quebec has increased in large part because of the numbers of English-speaking people who began to arrive as far back as the Seven Years' War.

Even though official statistics are not available before 1851, it appears that large groups of English-speaking people were concentrated in Montreal, the Eastern Townships and the Outaouais Valley region. During this same period, according to historian Jean Hamelin,[28] Montreal had an English-speaking majority of 54.9 per cent, English-speaking people made up 41.7 per cent of the population of Quebec City[29] and 83.7 per cent of that of Sherbrooke.

It is evident that prior to 1760,[30] the settlement of New France, at least in the beginning, was accomplished only through immigration. Whether it be judged as "directed" or not, this immigration involved mostly French Catholics, thus conforming to the commitments of the companies which controlled it. The relatively small group of other immigrants that were noted included fugitive and Protestant Englishmen, French Huguenots, some black slaves, and a few citizens of Hamburg, all of whom the Quebec population assimilated well. The social and language picture at the time of the conquest was thus entirely French.

Immediately after the English takeover, immigration began from two sources, the Loyalists fleeing the American Revolution who were obviously English-speaking, and people from the British Isles. Toward 1830 Ireland provided more English-speaking immigrants.

Haldimand estimated the number of British settled in the colony to be 2,000 in 1780, or 1.6 per cent of the population.[31] In 1784 there were 25,000 inhabitants of Anglo-Saxon origin in Quebec resulting from Loyalist immigration, which was itself surpassed by immigration from the British Isles, according to the same author.

Between 1815 and 1823 the total of arrivals in Quebec City from English-language countries represented 21 per cent of the population of Lower Canada. However, French Canadians maintained their numerical superiority by reason of their birthrate and their concentration in the province of Quebec, and because of a circumstantial diversion of immigration from Britain to the United States. After 1848 the arrivals primarily increased the number of English-speaking people.[32] The figures regarding immigrants entering Quebec according to their last country of residence up to 1961, and to ethnic origin after 1961, bear witness to this.

Language Pattern of Groups Arriving in Quebec

It seems that generally speaking, from 1948 on, a large proportion of the immigrants who arrived were, because of their geographic or ethnic origins, English-speaking. In addition, some immigrants may have been attracted to the English-speaking group because they already had a knowledge of English as second language. . . . Professor Jacques Brossard, writing on the Canadian situation, emphasizes that

> as a whole, immigration has scarcely served the interests of French Canada. A very small proportion of the immigrants when they arrive are assimilated more easily by the French-speaking than by the English-speaking population. From 1945 to 1964, a third of the immigrants were actually of British origin, and about a quarter belonged to other related ethnic groups, such as the German, Dutch and Scandinavian; an even greater proportion of new citizens during this period were of Anglo-Saxon origin.[33]

And, adds the same author, "Even in Quebec, about 65 per cent of the British, Germans, Dutch, Scandinavians, Poles and Jews, as well as 60 per cent of the Russians and Ukrainians know only English."

If other indices are consulted, such as those provided by the statistical studies on the census of immigrant households in Quebec, according to the ethnic origin of the head of the household before 1946 and from 1946 to 1961, the predominance of the English-speaking immigrant group compared with the French-speaking immigrants appears even more marked.

In fact, 41,692 families in which the head of the household was of English origin had immigrated to Quebec before 1946 and from 1946 to 1961, that is 28,806 before 1946 and 12,886 from 1946 to 1961. By contrast, of the 20,329 families in which the head of the household was of French origin, 13,129 immigrated to Quebec before 1946 and 7,200 from 1946 to 1961.

The same statistical tables show figures on the number of ethnic households other than French and British which immigrated to Quebec during the same period and already spoke English as their second language, or were more naturally inclined to join the English-speaking group.

Thus, 28,093 households, in theory English-speaking, as well as

41,692 that are actually British, that is an overall total of 69,785 households using the English language, entered Quebec prior to 1961. This does not include the 47,176 households uncertain of their language allegiance, which proved to be mainly English-speaking, with the exception of the Italians. Such figures indicate a marked trend toward the English-speaking group.

Lastly, the figures quoted by Joy,[34] show that before 1946, 141,000 immigrants entered Quebec, and from 1946 to 1961, 248,000, of whom 55 per cent spoke only English before 1946 and 46 per cent after 1946.

On the other hand, the calculations of the provincial Immigration Office concerning the numbers of immigrants coming to Quebec from French-language and English-language countries, as compared with the overall immigration numbers, indicate that immigrants coming from English-language countries predominated over those arriving from French-language countries between 1964 and 1971.

The following numbers of immigrants arrived in Quebec from French-language countries:

in 1964, 5,851, or 22.5% of the total immigrant population;
in 1965, 6,424, or 21.2%
in 1966, 8,883, or 22.7%
in 1967, 11,729, or 25.7%
in 1968, 9,821, or 27.7%
in 1969, 5,859, or 20.8%
in 1970, 4,595, or 19.9%

The last countries of residence considered as being French-language are Algeria, Morocco, Tunisia, St-Pierre and Miquelon, Belgium, Luxembourg, Switzerland, France and Lebanon.

The following numbers of immigrants arrived from English-language countries:

in 1964, 6,362, or 24.5% of the total immigrant population;
in 1965, 8,188, or 27%
in 1966, 11,142, or 28.4%
in 1967, 12,067, or 26.4%
in 1968, 8,692, or 24.5%
in 1969, 9,457, or 33.5%
in 1970, 7,940, or 34.1%

Countries considered as English-speaking are Great Britain, Ireland, the United States, British Guiana, Jamaica, Trinidad and Tobago, Bermuda, Barbados, the rest of the British West Indies, Australia, New Zealand, India, Pakistan, Kenya, the Republic of South Africa and Ceylon.

The Immigration Office does not take into consideration the immigrants coming from other countries such as Scandinavia, Germany, Greece, Russia, Poland, the Ukraine, etc., among whom defection from their mother tongue to the advantage of English or French was shown to favor the English-speaking group in proportions ranging from 56.9 per cent to 21.3 per cent respectively as at the 1961 census.

A report from the Immigration Branch to the Department of Cultural Affairs, prepared for a Quebec immigration policy, states that

> twice as many British as French arrive, even though their numbers account for only 10 per cent of the total Quebec population. Moreover, if we consider that, theoretically, certain ethnic groups, such as the Germans, Austrians, Dutch and a great many of the immigrants coming from the United States, almost naturally integrate with the English-speaking group, the inevitable conclusion is that at least 50 per cent of the immigrants electing Quebec residence are already familiar with the English language and culture.[35]

The report also adds: "By language and cultural affinities, the English population of Quebec can count on "natural allies" such as the Germans, Dutch, Scandinavians, etc."

It is indisputable — and perhaps this is one of the major reasons for the fact that immigrants enter the English-language sector — that this population already established has, by force of circumstances, exercised and continues to exercise a power of attraction over immigrants, who are neither British nor French by origin, to an extent which is difficult to assess.

There is nothing particularly surprising in this predominantly English-speaking population's selecting the English-language sector of the educational system in force, offered them for the education of their children.

What is the extent of the school age population represented by this demographic increase? Where is it? Which educational system did it enter?

Because of the very definition of "mother tongue" as the "language spoken in childhood and still understood," statistics on persons less than twenty years of age have a greater validity. To the extent that mother tongue may be defined as the language generally used in the home, the children's mother tongue becomes a better indication of the parent's language preference. Therefore, we shall describe this immigrant population under twenty as compared with the whole population, the under-twenty population of Quebec, as well as the whole immigrant population. It is self-evident that such data does not take deaths, departures or returns to the country of origin into account. However, they are indicative of the proportion of the under-twenty newcomers to Quebec and the advantage they represent for the group to which they have chosen to belong.

The Demo-Linguistic Educational Situation

When the question is more closely examined, we discover that the newly arrived under-twenty population constitutes only a very small proportion of the total population of the Province of Quebec, that is, for the census period 1951 to 1961, it accounted for 1.15 per cent of the total population. It also represents a very small portion of the under-twenty group, that is, for the same period, 2.28 per cent of the population under-twenty. For the 1961–1971 census period, it represented 1.46 per cent of the total population of the Province of Quebec and 3.34 per cent of the under-twenty population.

According to the 1961 census, the total population of Quebec was 5,259,211, of whom 2,330,821 were under twenty and 60,320 were immigrants under twenty. According to the 1971 census, the total population of Quebec was 6,027,765, of whom 2,406,827 were under twenty and 81,645 were immigrants under twenty.[36] The number of children of immigrants in the under-twenty age group who arrived in Quebec in 1971 was 5,034, about half of them of school age. Most of them were English-speaking.

If we refer to the data given by the provincial Department of Immigration in Montreal, the proportion of the under-twenty immigrant group for each of the years 1958 to 1970 inclusive, compared with the total population under twenty in Quebec, is somewhere between 0.2 per cent and 0.5 per cent. However, since the vast majority of Quebecers of other ethnic origins settle with their children in the Montreal area and its suburbs, the presence of these children in the school system becomes a legitimate question of concern.

It is quite obvious that the city of Montreal is the preferred place of residence for most of the people arriving in Quebec; therefore, the figures, to the extent that they seem similar in the various reports, remain quite a conclusive indication of the newcomers' school option.

Quebec City is in seventh place as regards the number of children of immigrants enrolled in school. Integration of children of immigrants into the school situation takes place naturally; the few English-speaking families who settle here generally enroll their children in the English-language schools, in particular at St. Patrick's and Holland schools. The same is true for French-speaking persons who wish to take advantage of the opportunity to learn a second language.

Statistics on the choice of New Canadian parents of a school for their children's education are complicated and incomplete. The only available statistics concerning the distribution of the children of immigrants among French and English classes in the Montreal Catholic School Commission show that before 1934, the French section attracted more Canadians of other ethnic origins than the English section. After 1935, the roles were reversed; although the change was slow, it was steady. Since 1961, this trend has become more noticeable and is reaching alarming proportions.

We have attempted to complete the statistics supplied to the Commission by the Montreal Catholic School Commission with figures subsequently supplied by the Montreal Catholic School Commission and the Department of Education. However, considering the limitations of these statistics, the most that can be gained from them are general indications. Under these circumstances, it is almost impossible to describe the demo-linguistic school situation either in general or in detail. The best that can be suggested is that uniform accurate statistics be kept and compiled over a sufficient length of time so as to obtain a clear idea of the position. As long as such statistics are lacking, there is a serious risk that in legislating for the minorities either the majority or the minorities will be discriminated against.

The number of New Canadian children in the French section of the MCSC has been steadily decreasing; the number of non-British, non-French children in the English schools of the MCSC has been steadily increasing. In 1955–56 the non-British, non-French children already equaled the number of children of British origin in the English Catholic School section in Montreal. This is demonstrated in the following figures:

pupils of British origin: 8,992 or 40.9%
pupils of other ethnic origins: 8,886 or 40.4%
pupils of French origin; 4,112 or 18.7%

Immigrants alone are not responsible for the increase in the number of pupils in the English-language schools because according to R. Joy[37] the number of English-speaking children in the Province of Quebec have themselves increased in number. From 1931 to 1961, there was an increase in the size of the English-speaking family. The English-speaking school-age population has more than doubled since 1931, while the number of children from French-speaking families has only increased by 80 per cent.

It seems that in the MCSC English classes alone, the children multiplied three-fold between 1931 and 1963. Italians, Spanish and Portuguese are generally considered, because of their cultural affinity, to gravitate towards the French language, but they enroll their children to a great extent in the English sector of the MCSC.

It would be vain to close our eyes to the implications of the data set forth below:

1. the general tendency of New Canadians to choose for their children the English-language educational system, although in the Catholic sector;
2. the statement of quite a number of pupils, in the elementary and secondary levels of the English system, that French is the language usually spoken at home;
3. the marked trend during the past few years of the Italian group to enroll in the English language schools of the Catholic sector;
4. the heavy concentration of pupils of Italian origin in B region of the English sector of the MCSC, where they constitute the majority in 16 elementary and 3 secondary schools.

Here we must stress the difficulty in finding comparable statistics on school enrollment according to ethnic origin and language. For the future, as already mentioned, a permanent inventory according to uniform variables of these enrollments is essential if we wish to obtain an adequate view of the situation.

For example, there does not exist, or it was impossible to obtain from the Protestant schools of Montreal, statistics on the distribution of school enrollments according to ethnic origin comparable or even similar to those supplied by the MCSC for the years prior to 1970. The Protestant School Board of Greater Montreal and that of Greater Quebec have not taken such variables into consideration.

Other statistics emanating from the Department of Education confirm the state of affairs for 1970. They describe the school population of the Montreal administrative region according to language spoken at home, and according to religion in the French and English Catholic public schools, in the French and English Protestant public schools and in the private Catholic and Protestant schools.[38] The only variables considered are: the language spoken at home, English, French or other languages; religion, Catholic, Protestant or others.

The Catholic public sector

In 1970, the pupil enrollment in the MCSC schools of the Montreal region, (which totalled 222,964) was divided according to the language spoken at home in the following manner:

In the French schools, out of a total enrollment of 179,663,

— 175,535 pupils state they speak French at home, that is 97.7%;

— 1,282 pupils state they speak English at home, that is 0.72%;
— 2,846 pupils state they speak a language other than French or English, that is 1.58% of the total.

In English schools, out of a total enrollment of 42,810.

— 3,675 pupils state they speak French at home, that is 8.58%;
— 15,566 pupils state they speak English at home, that is 36.3%;
— 23,569 pupils state they speak a language other than French or English, that is 55.02% of the total.

In bilingual schools, out of 491 pupils,

— 475 state they speak French at home;
— 16 state they speak English;
— none state they speak a different language.

In the MCSC schools, the pupils who state they speak a language other than French or English at home account for 11.8 per cent of the total enrollment of 222,964. However, the percentage of pupils who state that they speak a language other than French or English at home, compared with the enrollment in the English Catholic schools, is 55 per cent.

The Protestant public sector

In 1970, the pupil population in the public Protestant sector of the Montreal region were divided according to the language spoken at home in the following manner:

In the French schools, out of a total enrollment of 327 pupils all speak French at home.

In English schools, out of a total of 60,698 pupils

— 2,654 state they speak French at home, that is 4.37%;
— 46,889 state they speak English at home, that is 77.24%;
— 11,155 speak a language other than French or English at home, that is 18.38% of the total enrollment.

In bilingual schools, out of a total of 2,682 pupils,

— 991 state they speak French at home, that is 37.3%;
— 1,108 state they speak English at home, that is 41.3%;
— 583 state that they speak a language other than French or English at home, that is 21.4% of the total.

This means that, out of a total enrollment of 63,707 students in the public Protestant sector of the Montreal region, 21.4 per cent speak a language other than English or French at home.

The private Catholic sector

As shown in the table of the pupil enrollment in the private Catholic sector of the Montreal region for 1970:

out of a total of 40,133 pupils in the French schools of the private Catholic sector:

— 38,973 give French as the language spoken at home;
— 696 give English as the language spoken at home;
— 464 give a language other than French or English as the language spoken at home, that is, 464/40,133 = 1.15%.

In the English schools, out of a total of 4,139 pupils:

— 839 give French as the language spoken at home;
— 2,870 give English as the language spoken at home;
— 430 give a language other than French or English as the language spoken at home, that is 10.4% or 430 out of 4,139.

The private Protestant sector

As indicated in the table of the pupil enrollment of the private Protestant sector in the Montreal region, for 1970:

out of a total of 15 enrolled in a French school registered as part of the private Protestant sector:

— 2 give French as the language spoken at home;
— 10 give English as the language spoken at home;
— 3 give a language other than French or English as the language spoken at home, that is 3 out of 15 or 20%.[39]

In the English schools, out of a total of 3,954 pupils:

— 148 give French as the language spoken at home;
— 3,661 give English as the language spoken at home;
— 145 give a language other than French or English as the language spoken at home, that is 145 out of 3,954 or 3.7%.

In the bilingual schools, out of a total of 1,999 pupils:

— 1,317 give French as the language spoken at home;
— 577 give English as the language spoken at home;
— 105 give a language other than English or French as the language spoken at home, that is 105 out of 1,999 = 5.02%.

"Other" schools

In the "other" French schools, out of a total of 305 pupils enrolled, 305 speak French at home.[40]

In the "other" English schools, out of a total of 4,326 pupils enrolled:

- — 360 give French as the language spoken at home;
- — 2,012 give English as the language spoken at home;
- — 1,954 give languages other than English or French as the language spoken at home, that is 1,954 out of 4,326, or 45.2%.

It is not possible to sort out Quebecers of other ethnic origins from among the persons included in these data; however, we can easily consider as such those who say they speak a language other than English or French at home, that is 2,634 compared with the total enrollment in the private sector, which is 54,871, constituting 4.83 per cent.

CONCLUSION

Once again, these figures, although fairly precise, do not enable us to define accurately, or comparatively, the actual number or geographic location of children of the third group in the schools of the Montreal Catholic School Commission, the Protestant School Board of Greater Montreal and the private education sector.

The enrollments do not cover the same areas, they are not differentiated as regards ethnic origin or even the true status of the immigrant. If we study them as they are presented however, restricting ourselves to those who say they speak a language other than French or English at home and are obviously of other ethnic origins, recent or distant, we see that only the English schools of the public Catholic sector have an appreciable proportion of New Canadian pupils: (55.02 per cent).

Into which Educational System in Quebec Will the Immigrant Integrate?

Obviously, the immigrant who comes to a bilingual country and settles in a province with a French majority faces a different situation from that he would encounter in a province with a large English-speaking majority.

Generally, no one disputes the fact that school legislation in the Province of Quebec has accepted this duality which recognizes that differences exist, that the ethnic and religious personality of the two founding peoples must develop normally and that each cultural heritage must be set off to advantage.

In any case, the school system developed gradually and legislative text followed upon legislative text until the 1941 office consolidation of school laws and the Education Department Act of 1964 came into being.

It seems worthwhile to recall certain historical highlights which might have had some effect on the instruction given immigrants of all races and religions.

(a) *Historical landmarks*

The 1801 proclamation of the Royal Institution establishing a system of free non-confessional English schools, the only ones to be subsidized, gave rise to opposition and the creation of a Catholic school system.

The first act pertaining to schools, voted in 1801, was entitled An Act for the Establishment of Free Schools and the Advancement of Learning in this Province. This Act contained the seed of a non-confessional system. It naturally had many opponents among the Quebec clergy but was passed at the third reading, thanks to the support of certain French-Canadian members. In 1824, an act known as the Fabrique Schools Act was passed to make the parish the basis of the school organization. In 1829, an Act for the Encouragement of Elementary Education was passed to reinforce and make more effective the first two.

An act repealing the above-mentioned laws was passed in 1841 to create and maintain public schools in the province. It established the principle of confessional schools. According to some documents, the Protestant groups were in the main responsible for requesting that the separation of Catholics and Protestants in the school system be written into the 1841 act.[41]

At last, in 1856, the basic school system act, Bill 9, Victoria, ch. 27, created the Council of Public Instruction and finally resulted in the confessional school duality of today which still remains a controversial subject:

1 — a Protestant public sector and a Catholic public sector divided yet again into English, French, bilingual and "other" schools;

2 — a Catholic private sector including both English and French schools, a Protestant private sector with English, French and bilingual schools and other schools belonging to no denomination in particular but with either French or English as the language of instruction.

The distinction between English and French schools in Catholic School Commissions is a response to the force of numbers but it is also an answer to the need to give English-speaking pupils in the Catholic system an English cultural education. Separation by religion was confirmed at Confederation by section 93 of the British North America Act which guaranteed the education rights of religious minorities.

Although not stated in so many words, the protection of the pupils' mother tongue was in a certain manner ensured since Catholics were considered as being French-speaking and Protestants English-speaking. Protection was therefore "de facto" rather than "de jure." This lack of precision as regards language majorities and minorities has always been maintained and has led to situations in which language sometimes gave way to religion and religion sometimes gave way to language, but misunderstandings and latent conflicts have always been entangled with the question of religion.

Between 1900 and 1960, the two religions each had their own complete education system financed by elementary and secondary school taxes[42] under the auspices of a Council of Education which heads two all-powerful committees, the Roman Catholic Committee and the Protestant Committee.

The Parent Commission recommended that all educational services be united within the framework of one department. This was acted upon only in 1964 and at present the principle of Protestant and Catholic confessional schools, both French and English, public and private is maintained. Only since 1969, has it become possible, at least in theory, to cross religious and language lines in the school system.

> From now on, Department legislation and regulations, standards and procedures apply equally to Catholics and Protestants, to English-speaking and French-speaking citizens, that is, to the entire student population of Quebec.[43]

The Quebec education system has thus been developed in terms of a liberal, secular respect for the rights of the English-speaking minority.

It is into such a system that the immigrant has been required to integrate, at least since 1867. It is not surprising that the majority of immigrants, largely English-speaking, have been drawn toward the English schools with the majority ending up in the English Catholic or Protestant sector of the Quebec education system, especially since, through negligence, indifference, inertia, ignorance of the situation and perhaps even powerlessness, the French-speaking group does not seem to have done anything until two years ago to encourage immigrants to send their children to French schools.

(b) Bill 63

The Act to promote the French language in Quebec (Bill 63), assented to on November 28, 1969, confirms the exclusive right of French-speaking and English-speaking parents to choose their children's schools. This provision frees certain non-Catholic ethnic groups from the obligation to register their children in English-language Protestant schools.

(c) Effects

It is hardly possible to evaluate the effect of Bill 63 on the behaviour of immigrants as regards schools because of the lack of perspective and of comparable information, the great cultural and language diversity of the subjects, the unreliability of available statistics and so forth.

Moreover, it is impossible to say with any precision, how many children of immigrants took advantage of Bill 63 to go over to the English-language system, since in all probability such transfers were being carried out even before the bill was passed and, more particularly, since there is no way of telling how many of the 1,075 children who went over to the English-language system between 1969 and 1970 were Canadian-born French-speaking children and how many were really immigrants.

Student records for 1970 mention on one form the child's language of instruction for the years 1969 and 1970 and, by this very fact, deal with the same group of students. All preceding statistics when there are any, deal with a different group of students, and consequently population variations cannot be interpreted comparatively. Moreover, the language of instruction given in earlier records is sometimes the language of the school and sometimes the language of the child. Finally, these statistics are not available in all school boards.

The only valid figures on the transfer of children from one language of instruction to another, in this case from French to English, also have their limitations since the records were useful for only 72 per cent of the enrolled pupil population. It should also be specified that the records make use of factors which clearly distinguish the pupils whose language is neither English nor French and who can thus be considered as immigrants; but they do not distinguish immigrants within the English-speaking or the French-speaking groups.

Once these limits have been defined, the fact remains that, considering only the distribution of Quebec pupils whose mother tongue is neither French nor English in kindergarten, in elementary and secondary schools or in schools for exceptional children, in the private and public sectors, it will be noted that:

— between 1969 and 1970 the French education sector lost 414 students from all levels combined, or 0.69% of its "other" student population;
— the "other" education sector during the same period, experienced a drop of 661 students, or 1.10% of the "other" student population at the same levels.

These two sectors lost 1,075 "other language" pupils to the English-language education sector, or 1.79 per cent of the "other" student population estimated to be 60,111 students at the levels in question.[44]

According to a survey carried out for the Department of Education by Sorecom Inc. on April 1, 1971,[45] 1,920 of the pupils who transferred (70.7 per cent) chose English schools, while 796 (29.3 per cent) chose French schools. A total of 2,716 pupils were involved, a tiny fraction of the 2,406,827 pupils in Quebec in 1971. Mrs. V. Neal, chairman of the French Committee of the Quebec Federation of Home and School Associations believes that the Sorecom survey failed to take into consideration the French immersion programs set up by the Protestant schools in which 5,253 pupils are enrolled at present.[46]

Bill 63's effect was the removal of religion as an obstacle which had limited the choice of parents as regards language. It was to be hoped that this would result in a more pronounced preference for French-language schools, but this was not the case. It is not difficult to attribute their hesitation to the economic and social insecurity, the threat of possible coercion, the quality of instruction or any other cause.

As already mentioned, it would be premature and practically impossible to assess the effects of Bill 63 on the behaviour of immigrants as regards schools and to make value judgments. At the most, the statistics provided give a few general indications which suggest that extreme caution be used in the methods chosen to deal with the situation. There is no doubt that extended observation and a very careful interpretation of the results of such observation would be required to avoid adopting measures which would shift the emphasis with regard to the problem without solving it.

The problems undoubtedly lie in the causes, not in the symptoms, and involve the immigrant at the moment of exposure to the causes, that is to say, long before he faces the school problem, and above and beyond this problem, which is but one episode in his integration. The welcome received and the importance of English in professional activities and for social mobility are two of the causes and these exert major pressures which affect the choice of school.

Finally, it must be remembered that Bill 63 also requires the Department of Immigration, in conjunction with the Department of

Education, to take the necessary steps enabling immigrant applicants to acquire a knowledge of the French language before they even arrive in Quebec; no action has as yet been taken in this direction.

These same departments should take measures to have immigrants learn French and to have their children taught in schools where classes are given in French. The recently created introductory classes fulfill the hopes placed in them since the great majority of the 500 pupils received annually continue their studies in French.

It must now be considered whether everything possible has been done to encourage immigrants and their children to learn French. Some steps taken to facilitate the integration of immigrant children into the French-speaking sector and to help the adults learn French will be described in the following paragraphs. One conclusion can be drawn even before the quality and quantity of these measures is presented, a conclusion identical to that concerning school transfers: it is too soon to judge objectively the extent of favorable results or to make reliable appraisals.

Various Barriers to Choosing French-Language Schools

The demo-linguistic situation in schools shows that English is the mother tongue or second language of most of the children of immigrants in Quebec. This is a major obstacle to the choice of French-language schools. Other obstacles also affect this choice, be they economic, religious, or purely academic such as the quality of instruction or the qualifications and attitudes of the teachers and pupils.

(a) ECONOMIC IMPERATIVES

The post-1929 economic crisis brought immigration into Canada and Quebec to an abrupt halt. The restrictive American immigration laws and the very negative effects of the depression throughout the North American continent prevented a new population "drain." During the forties, however, the decision was made to begin teaching English in French schools only in Grade six (the equivalent of Grade five today) instead of in Grade two (the equivalent of Grade three today) as had previously been the case. These changes were very badly timed. Surprising as it may seem, a major landslide towards English-language schools took place during the depression between the two world wars. This move coincided, moreover, with the decline of French as the world's first international language.

The depression which began in 1929 thus had deplorable effects on the school situation. This is a factor which is too often forgotten when the enhancement and development of the French language are studied.

The effects of school transfers between the two world wars extended beyond that period, for after 1946, immigrant parents who were neither French nor British and who were able to choose schools followed the established pattern and sent their children to English-language schools. Moreover, the economic, political and language influence of the United States was such that it was difficult to ignore the absolute necessity to know English, the new international language. This need was also felt by the French Canadians who set the example in Montreal and made extensive use of English as the language of communication at work.

(b) THE CONFESSIONAL SYSTEM

The distinction between Protestant and Catholic schools systems prevented many parents from making a free choice. European immigrants in particular considered the system an anachronism since they were accustomed to non-confessional schools. Restrictions resulted from official regulations as well as from current practice. Jewish children, for example, were directed towards the Protestant and consequently the English-speaking sector as a result of the 1903 act, 3 Ed VIII, ch. 16, sec. 6. Also, as already seen, local Catholic school authorities, directors and even teachers refused to admit non-Catholic pupils, or those professing no religion, and the French-speaking sector thus lost a number of Orthodox Christian, French-speaking Jewish and other non-Catholic immigrants, usually because of religious zeal or a desire to avoid complications. This isolationist trend did not favour close relations between the ethnic groups and the Quebec majority group.

(c) THE QUALITY OF EDUCATION

In the past, the Government of Quebec showed little interest in public education. The education budget in 1946, for instance, was about $9 million. It increased to $107 million in 1960 and to $701 million in 1969, to climb to over a billion dollars in 1972.

As already mentioned, public education became compulsory only in 1943 and was considered lacking on many points as compared to that provided by the English schools.

The ethnic groups have always called for non-confessional bilingual schools or French-language schools where a satisfactory amount of English would be taught. They requested that, where the number of pupils and the interest warranted it, other languages be taught for a few hours each week. The failure of efforts to create such classes has been pointed out in another section. The Parent Report recommendations on this point and similar recommendations by the Interdepartmental Committee in 1967 remained dead letters.

More recently, in the briefs submitted to the Commission by various ethnic groups and during seminars organized by the Commission, adequate English instruction was again requested as a prerequisite to the choice of French-language schools. It was not only the representatives of the ethnic groups who called for an improvement in the teaching of English. The MCSC, in a brief submitted to the Commission in September 1969, deplored the poor quality of second-language instruction. Surveys and inquiries among both French-speaking and English-speaking parents brought the same concerns to light.

The opinion of the MCSC

In its brief, the MCSC described as follows the situation which already existed in 1958:

> English is taught in our schools from the fifth to the twelfth grade inclusively, to over 100,000 children. The timetable allows for four half-hour classes, or two hours each week in grades 5, 6, and 7 and, in secondary school, five 45 minute periods. This would be sufficient under ideal teaching conditions but, as shall be shown further on, the real situation is quite different.[47]

The brief goes on to say that

> in spite of the efforts made, particularly in elementary classes, results remain debatable. The lack of competent teachers is the main reason for this partial failure. This is also the opinion of the Association for the teaching of English in Quebec which stated in a report on teacher training: "There are very few experts in TESL in the Province and practically no resources for training the people who now teach ESL."
>
> ......
>
> The following are additional observations which account for the relative failure of the steps taken:
>
> — the time provided for in the timetable is not always respected;
> — English is sometimes actually omitted from the timetable and the allotted time granted to other subjects;
> — pupils are less and less motivated since English is not included in the general average on report cards;
> — some teachers attribute little importance to this subject.[48]

Studies and surveys

In March 1971, the Public Relations Department of the MCSC carried out a survey among the members of the MCSC's Consultative Committee on the teaching of second languages in French-language and English-language schools. At the time of the survey, English schools began teaching French in Grade three. Of the French-speaking parents, 63.38 per cent asked that English schools begin teaching French at an earlier period and 75.2 per cent of the English-speaking parents were in agreement. The survey was also carried out in French-language schools where English courses are at present begun in Grade 5. Of the French-speaking parents, 78.4 per cent asked that English courses be introduced in a lower grade and the majority of English-speaking parents (91.6 per cent) made the same request.[49]

Another inquiry resulted in a general statement by the parents of their desire to see increased French instruction in the elementary schools of the PSBGM. Thirty-six per cent of the 25,830 replies received (representing 59 per cent of the population consulted) would like to see the time devoted to French doubled, 7 per cent want their children to receive half their instruction in French, 6 per cent call for a completely French curriculum, 17 per cent suggest that the amount of French be increased without any change in the present curriculum and 33 per cent are satisfied with the present arrangement.[50]

(d) TECHNICAL DOCUMENTATION

In view of the influence and scientific importance English is expected to have throughout the world during the next ten or fifteen years, insufficient instruction in English in the French-language schools is prejudicial to the children's education. Research carried out by the Commission supports this statement.[51]

In a typical year it is estimated that about two million documents and articles, 26,000 journals and 30,000 books on scientific and technical topics are published in a wide range of languages. A study of the contents of six major English-language abstracting publications results in the table of scientific literature by language of publication shown on page 176.

(e) TEACHING SECOND LANGUAGES

Second-language instruction must be improved: French, because it is the language of the majority and is bound to become the common language of use in Quebec; English, because of its world-wide importance in the scientific field and because it is a prerequisite for the educational development of the child and an important factor in the choice of French-language schools by the children of non-French and non-British parents.

Immigrants who wanted to improve the employment prospects of their children by having them acquire a knowledge of English experienced difficulty in finding French schools offering English

Breakdown by language of publication of literature indexed in six major English-language abstracting and indexing publications

	Journals					
Language	*Chemical Abstracts*	*Biological Abstracts*	*Physics Abstracts*	*Engineering Index*	*Index Medicus*	*Mathematical Reviews*
	%	%	%	%	%	%
English	50.3	75	73	82.3	51.2	54.8
Russian	23.4	10	17	3.9	5.6	21.4
German	6.4	3	4	8.6	17.2	8.7
French	7.3	3	4	2.4	8.6	7.8
Japanese	3.6	1	0.5	0.1	0.9	0.7
Chinese	0.5	1	0.1	0	0.4	0.2
Other	8.5	7	14	2.7	16.1	5.4

Source: Science Council of Canada, Report No. 6, September 1969.

instruction corresponding to their expectations. As we have already seen, the teaching of English started in the second grade (today's third grade) during the first third of the century but since the beginning of the 1940s it has started with the sixth grade (the present fifth grade), averaging two hours' instruction per week at most, and the teachers often being French-speaking.

Hence, at present, in most French schools, the teaching of English begins with the fifth grade in the public sector and in the third grade in schools in the private sector. The Commission's Research Service made a survey of the qualifications of teachers of English as a second language in the Catholic public sector of the Montreal administrative region (where most of the immigrant population is concentrated), and found that only one teacher has a master's degree in English. In the private sector, the highest qualifications of teachers of English do not exceed a general master's degree in Education, held by only six of the teachers in this category.

Some immigrants turned to the so-called bilingual schools. These schools were rather few; however, in 1970, three teachers of English holding a doctorate in English were teaching in these schools in the No. 6 administrative region of Montreal. Therefore, as regards the teaching of the second language both in schools of the Catholic School Commissions as well as in those of the PSBGM, the considerable efforts to train teachers and improve methods proved unequal to the task.

Conclusion

Considering the ethnic origin of the newcomers to Quebec since the country was surrendered to England, the immigrating population's adhesion to the English-speaking group was a foregone conclusion. Over all those years, Quebec's population was not particularly alarmed at this. For a long time, language considerations were put aside and demographic factors were the only ones taken into account, as Canada was in an initial stage of its development.

Demographic and economic factors apart, little attention was devoted to education or teaching as a means of integrating the immigrant. It is true that there was no need to be alarmed. One has only to consider the school-age group of children attending Quebec's schools whose language is neither French nor English to realize that the size of this group is small in comparison with that of the total under-twenty age group in Quebec's population. Even in Montreal where that particular group is concentrated and sometimes even exceeds the minority of British origin and the English-speaking majority in certain sectors, it would still be proportionately small if it had been distributed throughout the entire school-age population of the Montreal administrative region.

Consequently, it is quite clear that the problem of the integration of immigrants stems from causes quite beyond the mere fact that immigrant's children attend English-speaking schools. It is much more closely linked to the attitudes of the majority group, economic and denominational pressures, or the quality of the education dispensed, all of which are causes that have been and still constitute obstacles to the harmonious integration of immigrants' children into the schools.

Notes

1. Minutes of the meeting of the Roman Catholic Committee of the Council of Public Instruction, May 5, 1948, cf. René Gauthier, "Intégration éducationnelle et scolaire de l'immigrant au Québec," 1965, p. 20 (Educational and academic integration of the immigrant in Quebec).
2. "Rapport du Comité interministériel sur l'enseignement des langues aux Néo-Canadiens" (Report of the interdepartmental committee on language instruction to New Canadians) submitted to the Ministers of Education and Cultural Affairs on January 27, 1967, p. 30.
3. Gauthier, "Integration. . .", pp. 23–24.
4. *Parent Report,* Part Three, ch. III, sec. IV, par. 186.
5. Michel Brunet, *Québec Canada anglais,* p. 17.
6. Ibid., pp. 87–88.
7. Ibid., p. 97.
8. Gauthier, "Intégration," p. 24.
9. Gauthier, "Rapport," p. 43.
10. Gauthier, "Intégration," p. 33.
11. *Parent Report,* Part I, chap. I, sec. V, para. 35.
12. Ibid., Part II, chap. I, para. 3 and chap. I, sec. I, para. 4.
13. Ibid., chap. IV, sec. I, para. 155.
14. Ibid., chap. IV, sec. I, para. 161.
15. Ibid., chap. XIII, sec. III, para. 686.
16. Ibid., chap. XI, sec. III, para. 700.
17. Ibid., chap. XIII, sec. V, para. 214.
18. Ibid., chap. XII, sec. II, para. 616. See also Chalvin, Solange and Michel, *Comment on abrutit nos enfants,* "La bétise en 23 manuels scolaires" (How we degrade our children, the nonsense found in 23 textbooks) (Ottawa: Les Editions du Jour, 1962).
19. *Parent Report,* Part III, chap. II, sec. III, para. 189.
20. Ibid., chap. III, sec. IV, para. 190.
21. Ibid.
22. Ibid., para. 193.
23. Gauthier, "Intégration. . .", pp. 26–27.
24. L'école Maimonide (see *La Presse*, December 4, 1972), p. 8). This school had been requested for the past ten years in briefs to both the Parent Commission and to the Quebec Government.
25. J.C., Morrison, *Puerto Rican Study* (New York: New York Board of Education, 1953–1957).

26. Joti, Bhatnagar, *Immigrants at School* (London: Cornmarket Press) p. 156.
27. R.A. Taft, *Opinion Convergence in the Assimilation of Immigrants,* 1962.
28. Jean, Hamelin, "La dimension historique du problème linguistique," (Historical dimensions of the language problem), p. 27. Study prepared at the Commission's request.
29. R. Maheu states that in 1851 English-speaking people made up 35 per cent of the population, Cf. Matheu, *op. cit.,* doc. 416, p. 2.
30. G.D. Guay, "Immigration sous le régime français" (Immigration during the French regime), doc. 270/E, p. 1.
31. Taken from Fernand Ouellet, *Histoire économique et sociale du Québec 1760–1780, Structures et conjonctures* (Economic and social history of Québec from 1760 to 1780: structures and circumstances) (Montréal, 1968), p. 13.
32. From 1843 to 1847, of an annual immigration rate of 37,911, 33 per cent came from England, 57 per cent from Ireland, and 7 per cent from Scotland. From 1848 to 1852, of an annual immigration rate of 35,875, 24 per cent came from England, 53 per cent from Ireland, and 13 per cent from Scotland, Cf. Ouellet "Histoire économique. . .", p. 472.
33. Jacques Brossard, *L'immigration* (Montréal: Les Presses de l'université de Montréal, 1967), pp. 17–19.
34. Richard Joy, *Languages in Conflict, The Canadian Experience* (Toronto: McClelland and Stewart, 1972), pp. 62 and 58.
35. Report of January 30, 1967, p. 27 and ff.
36. Provincial Immigration Office, Population of Quebec, censuses of 1961 and 1971.
37. Joy, *Languages in Conflict,* p. 41.
38. The following data were compiled by the Research Service of the Commission, according to the Statistics of the Data-Processing Service of the Department of Education of Quebec (SIMEQ).
39. It is obvious that the data from the Quebec Bureau of Statistics on this matter are incomplete. The school in question is called "Cours privé L. Farmer", of Montréal.
40. "Other" designates certain schools which operate on a non-confessional basis.
41. Lionel Groulx, *Histoire du Canada français,* IV (Montreal, 1952), p. 63.
42. Pierre de Grandpré, "Bilinguisme et système d'éducation au Québec face au Rapport sur le Bilinguisme et le Biculturalisme" (Bilingualism and the education system in Québec in view of the Report on Bilingualism and Biculturalism). Conference held on December 13, 1970, p. 3.
43. Excerpt from an address given by Mrs. Thérèse Baron, Deputy Minister of Education, during a seminar on Quebec culture and society ("Culture et société québécoise"), organized by the *Centre québécois des relations internationales* in Quebec City on October 3, 1972.
44. Information provided by the Department of Education (Commission doc. 1650 CXL).
45. Étude de l'orientation linguistique de quelques groups dans la région de Montréal.
46. Québec Bill 63 Statistics Misleading — H&S, *The Gazette,* October 24, 1972, p. 3.
47. Resolution XXV, Regular session of May 6, 1958, p. 27 of the brief.
48. Ibid., p. 29.
49. The results of the survey were submitted to the Parliamentary Committee on Education in November 1971.

50. Quebec Federation of Home and School Associations, "Report re French instruction in Elementary Schools of the PSBGM", March, 1970.
51. "Évolution des exigences linguistiques des familles de fonctions dans les entreprises québécoises pour les quinze prochaines années" (Development of linguistic requirements of job categories in Quebec enterprises for the next fifteen years), Ducharme, Déom et Associés, Ins., August 30, 1971.

Part Three

LANGUAGE, CULTURE AND SCHOOLING

This section, as its title suggests, is devoted to a consideration of the close and controversial nature of the relationship between language, culture and schooling. Particular attention is paid to the language of instruction, the role of the school in the maintenance and promotion of native languages, the results of the non-official languages study, and the cognitive and social benefits to be gained from being at ease in two languages and cultures.

The controversial nature of language and language policy is highlighted by the Parti Québécois government's flat rejection of French-English bilingualism in the province. Quebec's Charter of the French Language declared it to be the sole official language of Quebec and legislation in the form of Bill 101 was quickly enacted to this effect in 1977.

Four principles underlie Quebec's Charter of the French Language. The first states that, in Quebec, the French language is not just a means of expression, but a medium for living as well. The second speaks of the necessity for respect for minorities (including the English-speaking minority), their languages and cultures. The third emphasizes the importance of learning languages other than French. The fourth observes that the status of the French language in Quebec is a question of social justice. These principles illustrate the Quebec government's strong belief in the interdependence of language and culture. Its language policy is aimed at "protecting the existence of an original culture and developing it to its fullness — a mode of being, thinking, writing, establishing relations between groups and individuals, and even carrying on business."

Native language education is the subject of Barbara Burnaby's paper. Here she discusses, within the broader context of native culture, a variety of language policies that have been adopted in the education of native students. Problems abound. Tensions, for example, exist between the three agencies involved in administering native education: the federal and provincial governments and local Indian bands. Governments, she points out, have as their primary aim the production of "citizens with adequate skills in language and culture to compete as equals in majority Canadian society." Conversely, the native peoples, while not denying the merits of this objective, insist that schools also reinforce the student's Indian identity. Yet the traditional approach to language education for native students has been one of assimilation with total immersion in the English language. Searching for alternatives, Burnaby describes several innovative approaches that have been adopted or proposed, including programs designed to teach native children in their ancestral language.

That public school systems might profitably pay greater attention to instruction in the mother tongue is a theme taken up in the extract from "The Non-Official Languages Study: A Review of the Principle Results." Funded by the Secretary of State's office, the study examined the main patterns of non-official language knowledge and use in Canada. Its aim: to determine the extent to which support existed for the retention of the non-official languages as viable sources of cultural identity and preservation. Acknowledging that the crux of their study, and the philosophy of multiculturalism which gave rise to it, turns on the desire of Canada's non-English or non-French residents to retain their ancestral heritage, the authors found support to be strong and widespread.

The study's findings not only revealed the existence of extensive knowledge of the non-official languages, but also that such knowledge was being almost lost within a single generation. Fluency, for example, was reported by only one in ten in the second generation, and had disappeared entirely in the third and subsequent generations. Unless, the authors concluded, "direct intervention aimed at language preservation is undertaken as early as the second generation, a lack of opportunity and justification for continued use of the ancestral tongue will rapidly reduce and eventually extinguish non-official language knowledge in the descendents of Canada's residents of non-English or non-French origin." It is the public school, moreover, not the ethnic school, that is seen as the most appropriate societal institution to carry out this work. Very strong and clear support exists among Canada's non-official language groups for inclusion of their languages in public systems of schooling as languages of instruction, especially in the elementary schools.

Wallace Lambert's presentation on "Culture and Language as Factors in Learning and Education" opens with a discussion of two key propositions: that the similarities shared by ethnolinguistic groups are more important than the differences between them; and that cultural and linguistic backgrounds do not affect basic structures of thought and personality. He suggests that a very persuasive argument can now be advanced that bilingual children have a very definite advantage over monolingual children in the domain of cognitive flexibility. Moreover, there exists no empirical basis for the belief that becoming bilingual or bicultural necessarily means a loss or dissolution of one's identity. On the contrary, "there is accumulating evidence that children can very easily become comfortably bicultural and bilingual, and that from this base they can enhance that sense of personal well-being, their sense of social justice, and their tolerance and appreciation of human diversity." He therefore adopts the position that ethnolinguistic groups should be encouraged "from as many sources as possible" to maintain their linguistic and cultural heritage.

Principles for a Language Policy

CAMILLE LAURIN

There is no doubt that the situation of the French language in Quebec justifies vigilance and intervention by the government. A refusal to accept the absolute urgency of the matter would be a denial of unquestionable facts. The question is how to define the standards by which vigilance and intervention are to be guided. Certainly, remedies cannot be arbitrarily applied on the pretext that the situation is serious; there are inherent requirements, criteria of justice and equality, and legal rules in any normal society, and these are at stake.

Such principles are briefly described in this article.

The first principle: in Quebec, the French language is not just a means for expression, but a medium for living as well

Speaking French rather than some other language which has equal prestige in the world is not merely one aspect among many of personal and social existence. Because of their common language, people realize that they are part of the same group and that their feelings are similar to those of others; language shapes both dialogue and argument. Language, therefore, is a real and concrete medium, and not just a means of communication. Awareness of the state of a language, care for its health and its precision, as well as work to develop it, are actions which follow from the consideration of language as one of the principal ingredients of the "quality of life."

There is more. If a way of life is at stake, the unquestioned importance of a predominant language for any human society must be recognized. While a multiplicity of means of expression in a territory is useful and productive, it requires that a common language unite people. Without this, the cohesion and consensus essential to the development of any people will be lacking. In stating that everyone

SOURCE: Chapter II, *Quebec's Policy on the French Language*, Presented to the National Assembly and the People of Quebec by Camille Laurin, Minister of State for Cultural Affairs, March 1977, pp. 28–49. Reprinted by permission of l'Editeur Officiel du Québec.

must know French in a society like Quebec, the government does not mean to prevent the learning and speaking of other languages as well. It wishes merely to ensure that there is a communal language base similar to that found in all other normal societies, such as the rest of Canada where English is the primary instrument of communication.

The government thus satisfies a desire which the French-speaking population here has had from its beginnings. For a long time, the French nation in America has had neither the need nor the occasion to express this feeling in laws it passed itself. It had adopted it, as time passed, in daily conversation, in the joys of festivals and in the griefs of trials. The "miracle of survival" was evoked. The expression exaggerates. It is none the less true that this nation does not speak French by chance, because it has done so from the beginning. If we speak French, whether well or badly, this is not simply a reminder of the long confinement of our people to the rural scene. Our forebears tried to transpose the language to the city and to industry, where, in spite of compromises and adjustments imposed by a foreign language, the old language was preserved. The French of America, especially in Quebec, have gone further. They have founded schools and universities, and created a literature in French. Our society has not only lived in French; it has fostered French institutions.

In addition, it has officially had the right to speak French for a long time. Although the nation was conquered early, the English conquerors consented to the survival of the French language. Long before the recent Canadian act respecting the status of the official languages of Canada, and sometimes more explicitly, the British Empire recognized us as a particular people speaking a particular language. In 1774, a special status was granted to us among the American possessions of the Empire: the Quebec Act recognized that Quebec was a French country, preserving the customs of a French country, its own civil law, and its language.

The problem of the French language in North America cannot be reduced to a trivial question, namely the right of each individual to express himself in that idiom when he addresses governmental bodies, school administrations, his wife and his children. Here, the French language coincides with a society through a historic heritage, which one may regret or exult in, but which is a fact.

In presenting as a priority item a bill on the rights and use of the French language, the Government of Quebec does not claim to start from scratch in dealing with a problem that has been present in the history of our society from its beginnings. It starts from a historical fact which nobody can dispute. From an assured position in history and in law, the Government of Quebec seeks to draw conclusions and plan the future. Is this not, in this matter as in all others, the prime duty of the legislator? The role of government is not limited to ensuring efficient operation of certain aspects of social life; it is also concerned with the quality of the habitat, of which language is a major component.

The aim of a language policy in Quebec is within the context of a search for maturity. What the French-speaking people want has nothing to do with "translated from the English" which policies on bilingualism wish to guarantee. It is a matter of protecting the existence of an original culture and developing it to its fullness — a mode of being, thinking, writing, creating, meeting, establishing relations between groups and individuals, and even of carrying on business. This requirement, which has many implications, goes beyond the technical processes of translation: it cannot be achieved by the simple fact that French terminology has condescendingly been granted for realities which remain culturally foreign or hostile. If we say "hot dog" and "banana split" this is a sign not of a linguistic problem but of a cultural one. For if we must limit ourselves to requiring slavish translation of a foreign mode of life into French words, who could become interested or oppose it?

On the contrary, Quebeckers since 1960 have participated with growing hope in a marvellous cultural flowering in the realm of the arts, poetry, films and the *chanson* — a joyous explosion of talent and creativeness marked the indisputable aspiration of a culture to maturity. Think, in passing, of the impressive number of magazines and periodicals in English, which, until now, have had to content themselves with translating their original content word for word when they addressed their Quebec clientele. To adapt to the new requirements of today's Quebec reader, these same publications have had to provide themselves with entirely French-speaking teams of writers capable of discussing today's problems in Quebec's own cultural terms. All these manifestations are signs, with many others, that French in Quebec is the expression of a creative *milieu*.

Second principle: there must be respect for the minorities, their language, and their culture

French must become the common language of all Quebeckers. This first principle leads to a second, which is no way a giving in, still less any sort of Machiavellian concession: respect for minorities.

Any vital society must look upon the contributions made to it, by reason of its own diversity, as an indispensable source of enrichment; one need only consider what the culture of our first inhabitants, the Amerindians, has given us and which Quebeckers have integrated into their own lives without, unfortunately, always realizing its source. The same must be said of the culture of the English, the Italians, the

Jews, the Greeks and many other ethnic groups which affect the lives of all Quebeckers. Although Quebec wishes to be a French society, it has never been, nor would it wish to be, what some call a *tribe*.

In this respect, as in others, Quebec must not be merely tolerant; it must expect and invite from the other cultures which constitute it the essential vitality inherent in them.

In effect, the fact that Quebec is exercising its right to be French in no way prevents groups and individuals from knowing and speaking another language or even several other languages. The "minority groups" (this ambiguous expression must be used not only because it is in common usage but also because nothing better has yet been found) will of course be able to preserve their language and pass it on to their children. English in particular will always hold an important place in Quebec, not only because it is *the* language of communication in North America, as we hear repeatedly, but also because it is part of the cultural heritage of Quebeckers. Nevertheless, in a Quebec which lives in French it is natural that all its citizens, whatever their ethnic and cultural origin, should be capable of expressing themselves in French, participating fully in a French society, and conceding that French is the common language of all Quebeckers.

The government recognizes that an English population and an English culture exist in Quebec. Even though they have for too long been isolated in a network of institutions separate from but parallel to those of the French, this population and this culture constitute an irreducible component of our society.

Moreover, the status of this population and culture poses several questions which it would be naive and wrong to disregard.

Firstly, by the very force of its numbers, this minority controls important decision-making powers which affect the majority of French-speaking Canadians. There is nothing surprising in this; many other societies in the world are in a similar situation. In this particular phenomenon, the wealth of the one group and the poverty of the other are the decisive factors. Another factor, already emphasized, is language. A higher percentage of French-speaking persons in decision-making circles would not only have assured a more equitable division of powers but would also have made possible exchanges of a more concrete and authentic nature between the English-speaking minority and the French-speaking majority. The soundness of our collective existence as a society would have gained by it.

But there are legal factors to be considered which could reinforce the barrier whose existence we so regret. It might be wise to dwell on these for a moment.

The "acquired rights" of the English language in Quebec might appear to have the effect of limiting *a priori* all desire to extend the use of French in English circles.

First, if we are going to consider things in a strictly legal light, it must be said that the concept of "acquired rights" is ambiguous and debatable in our British parliamentary system. All laws are intended to grant certain rights and restrict others. Since parliaments are sovereign bodies, there is nothing to prevent them from introducing into a law special prescriptions which give that law a basic character, by stipulating for example that no incompatible provision of another law is valid unless it explicitly amends the original law. This procedure was used, for example, in the case of declarations of human rights. It has never been applied to language rights. The very adoption of Bill 22 was evidence of the irrelevancy of the concept of acquired rights with regard to language questions in Quebec. By repealing Bill 63, Bill 22 changed a legal situation and eliminated rights which might have been considered acquired. This statute was nevertheless judged constitutional by the courts.

In addition, a study of the texts reveals that there is no constitutional guarantee for the English language in Quebec.

Section 133 of the British North America Act does of course allow the use of both English and French in the National Assembly and in the courts, and requires that the statutes be published in both languages. However, paragraph 1 of section 92 of the same act authorizes the provinces to amend their internal constitutions except as regards the office of the Lieutenant-Governor. Most jurists, particularly during the consultations which took place at the time of the Gendron Commission, have expressed the opinion that when applied to Quebec, section 133 forms part of the internal constitution of the province and may be amended by the National Assembly.

The situation is even clearer with regard to school rights. The constitutional guarantees provided for in section 93 of the B.N.A. Act apply to denominational instruction and not to the language of instruction. There is no constitutional provision which protects instruction in the English language and even less the existence of an English-language school system.

Therefore, to consider the English minority and the English language in Quebec in strictly legal terms leads to an impasse. Rather, we are dealing here with a reality whose continued existence depends on the respect that the Quebec community has always shown for, and which it has no intention of withdrawing from, this largest of its minority groups, the individuals who compose it, or their cultural values. Without such an attitude, any legal guarantee would be precarious. English-speaking Quebeckers must preserve their language, their culture and their way of life. The government not only does not object to this but acknowledges the fact as part of our common history. The government certainly does not envisage as an ideal for either group the coexistence of two closed societies.

Other minorities, many of them large, have settled in Quebec more recently. These comprise individuals and groups as to whose originality and vitality there can be no doubt. In its determination to revive in Quebec a social life in which French is the common language, the government has not the slightest desire to belittle the contribution of these ethnic cultures.

The need for French-speaking Quebeckers to concern themselves constantly with their cultural survival, and their own inferior economic and political position, has resulted in their neglecting the efforts made by their Italian, Jewish, Greek and other compatriots in the minority groups to preserve their own mother tongue and cultural values. Fortunately, the "melting pot" policy of the United States is being increasingly questioned today. Immediate assimilation of all new immigrants, to the point that in one or two generations they have lost all feeling for their countries of origin, is hardly a desirable objective. A society which allows its minorities to preserve their language and culture is all the richer for it and probably more stable. This could be the case in Quebec.

There could not of course be any question of granting privileges to minority languages and cultures at the cost of endangering the integration of these groups into Quebec's French-language society. It should be stressed once again, however, that this type of problem does not arise in a stable society. When the national language and culture are not threatened, the existence of vigorous and active cultural minorities can only be a source of enrichment, provided the individuals concerned have sufficient knowledge of the national language to enable them to integrate into the society.

It is to be deplored that the support offered to date by the Quebec Government to our compatriots of various ethnic origins in their efforts to preserve their own language and culturre has been so weak. This is particularly true with respect to the larger groups, such as the Quebeckers of Italian, Jewish and Greek origin. Their individual and common endeavours to retain their cultural values merit greater encouragement on the part of the government, for the whole of Quebec society will benefit from their success.

If this principle holds true for Quebeckers of foreign origin, it is doubly true for the Eskimos and Indians of Quebec. Certain steps have already been taken to this end, notably with regard to the language of instruction in the territory of the New Quebec School

Board. Increased Quebec Government aid, however, is necessary to safeguard and promote the languages and cultures of our first inhabitants.

Third principle: it is important to learn languages other than French

At this time, a problem should be emphasized which has been a subject of debate for the past two centuries: it concerns what we refer to by that ambiguous expression "a second language." It affects the whole of Quebec society, French-speaking, English-speaking and others. To repeat a well-worn idea, we live in America, a continent where English is the language of the majority. To ignore this fact is to join the company of the blind. We must approach the problem logically.

Although English is the language of communication in the vast worlds of science and of the economy in North America, it is still not necessary, either for the economy or for science, that everyone use English in his daily life. In Quebec as in Mexico a waitress in a restaurant or a mechanic in a garage is not required to know immediately how to answer customers in their own tongue. Nor is there any reason for the members of the management staff of a company to speak English simply because one of them is unilingual, speaking only English, in the province of Quebec. In the absence of legislation, good manners should long ago have taken care of such a situation.

A principle is in question here, one which was stressed at the outset: whether we like it or not, the fact remains that in Quebec the French language is more than a transitory mode of expression; it is an institution, a way of life, a manner of conceiving one's existence. It is not acceptable to confine this language to private life or to subordinate it to a bilingual collective life; the result would be to reduce it to the level of folklore. The history of our people has willed otherwise and it is understandable that we, today, have no intention of contradicting our history.

That being said, we do not deny that it is essential for certain French-speaking Quebeckers to speak English. This is irrefutable. There are two main conditions, however: the learning of English must not be imposed so early on that it constitutes a danger to the required basic technical and cultural training which in any coutnry must remain a fundamental human concern, and the learning of another language must not be inconsistent with the need to play a full part in one's own culture.

The political and cultural environment of Quebec and the constant threat which it represents for French-speaking Quebeckers puts the whole question of the teaching of a second language in a false light. In any society, learning a language other than his own is an important acquisition for an individual; no one would dream of considering this a threat to the native tongue. The education system of any modern state should provide citizens with the opportunity of acquiring a good knowledge of a second and even a third language. Such a situation already exists in several industrialized nations of Europe. In a world which is shrinking daily, multilingualism is always an advantage and is becoming more and more of a necessity. However, the fact remains that in the Quebec context, as in many others, it is necessary to reconcile the teaching of a second language with the destiny of the first. Improvement in the teaching of a language other than French is a necessity for Quebec and must not be considered an impediment to the increased use of French. Only when the survival of the French language is assured, however, will second-language teaching programs be seen in their proper light and become truly effective.

Although we cannot escape the fact that because of our geographical situation English will predominate with respect to the teaching of second languages, the teaching of other languages should not be neglected.

French-speaking Quebeckers will therefore have to re-examine, coolly and calmly, the learning of languages other than their own. As long as the language of social and economic promotion was English, unilingual French Quebeckers (61 per cent) were for the most part obliged to work in subordinate positions. For this category of worker, chronically underpriviledged, there was no question of any "second language" other than English; it was the key to promotion. This restrictive concept will certainly change once every Quebecker is in a position to demand to be allowed to work in his own language. When this comes about, we can be fairly certain that Quebeckers, according to their occupation or personal interests, will be far more inclined to learn about other major cultures through the medium of a second or third language.

It is equally hoped that, the day the English language ceases to be, in the eyes of many, the pervasive symbol of perpetual economic and cultural domination, the lack of interest in and even downright aversion toward the learning of that language on the part of the Quebec student body will give way to a much more constructive attitude.

In a word, the question of "second language," automatically equated with "English language," has for too long been presented to Quebeckers in an abstract context. Let us suppose — and this is mere theorizing — that from the strict point of view of psychological attitudes, French-speaking pupils could learn English from a very early age. In addition, it would be necessary to take into consideration the socio-political context in which such a program was carried out. An experiment which would have remarkable success in a school in a Paris suburb would doubtless be a fiasco, because of the deterioration of the French mother tongue, if carried out, without the necessary adaptation, in a French-language school in Montreal's West Island where the almost completely English environment already threatens daily to assimilate the French-speaking students.

Fourth principle: the status of the French language in Quebec is a question of social justice

The government's three major language principles are the following: there must be a common language in Quebec; the existence of this common language does not exclude the enriching presence of other languages and cultures; the learning of one or more languages other than French is something to be desired and encouraged. There is a fourth principle, which results from the extensive examination of the position of the French language in Quebec, and which has already become more than merely apparent. Economic inequality is a source of injustice, and the same can be said of cultural inequality. The Government of Quebec intends to concern itself with both of these factors as part of its principal objectives. It does not conceive of a language policy as something quite different and separate from sectors more easily recognized as relating to the just distribution of wealth and freedom.

For a very long time French-speaking workers in Quebec have been in underprivileged positions in far too many business firms, because the language of work, in varying degrees, has been English. This priority was the result of many factors: with regard to technical terminology, no attempt was made to find good French equivalents; the administration, with its requirements which were sometimes justified, sometimes not, added to the problem; there was a tendency to ensure that the English, as members of an "exclusive club," had the best jobs and positions, by retaining English as a necessity and as a barrier. The use of English was part of "the order of things" which had a tendency to perpetuate itself but which must be changed.

In numerous cases, this situation imposes on the French-speaking workers an oppressive working condition: the obligation, whether tacit or express, to speak a language which is not their own in order to obtain a certain job, attain a certain promotion, or aspire to a certain career program. This obligation lays them open to refusal on the pretext, often quite unfounded, that their knowledge of English is inadequate. It also has the effect of raising unduly the level of qualifications required by adding knowledge of a language which is not the employee's own. This obligation tends to keep the mass of

French-speaking workers in an inferior position and furthermore works in favour of the promotion of another group which already has the best positions, higher pay, and a certain degree of power and prestige.

The resulting requirements are not always justified by the objective needs of the enterprises themselves.

Moreover, if the cultural and linguistic disintegration of French-speaking Quebeckers were to worsen, the consequences would be particularly serious for the workers. Among conquered minorities, those relegated to the bottom of the heap — and there are several examples of these in the world — the working people follow the fate of the unfortunate community to which they belong; they become last among the last.

There is little choice: what Quebec's French-speaking majority must do is reassume the power which is its by right, not in order to dominate, but to regain the status and latitude proper to its size and importance. To guarantee the free use of its own language is part of the task of this majority, a task which consists in establishing a people historically in such a manner that there will no longer be any danger of disintegration, or of a poverty which would be an injustice committed by that people's own hand.

Language in Native Education

BARBARA BURNABY

Introduction

The subject of this paper is language in Native education in Canada.[1] The theme is what is known and what is yet to be learned about it. By way of introduction, a brief description of the present Native population is given with emphasis on the areas of language and culture. Next, the structure of administration for Native education is outlined. In this section particular attention is paid to the roles and objectives of the various agencies involved. Then, language programs and policies for Native education are discussed. The final section is a summary of the main points. Throughout the paper it may seem that an unnecessarily large amount of space is devoted to aspects of Native education and Native society which are not obviously related to language in Native education. In the discussion of programs and policies, however, it will become clear that the issues are complex and can only be satisfactorily evaluated in the context of structures and events outside the walls of the classroom.

THE NATIVE POPULATION

Canadians of Native ancestry are a highly varied group. There are more than 280,000 status Indians in the country — that is, Native people who are individually recognized by the government to have certain rights under the Indian Act and individual treaties. In addition, there are approximately 18,500 Inuit people. Since 1939 most Inuit people have had more or less the same relationship to the federal government as status Indians. And there are approximately 750,000 Métis and non-status Indian people. These people have no special legal relationship to the government, but are often similar genetically and culturally to the status Indian people in the areas in which they live.[2]

SOURCE: *Canadian Society for the Study of Education Yearbook,* 3 (1976), *Bilingualism in Canadian Education,* pp. 62–85. Reprinted by permission of the author and the Canadian Society for the Study of Education.

NATIVE LANGUAGES AND CULTURES

Among Native Canadians there are eleven different language families, each subsuming a number of different languages, and dialects within languages. There were no forms of literacy other than a few disputed pictographic systems for any of these languages before the time of contact with Europeans. Writing systems have been and are being developed for many of the Native languages today. A few of these systems have gained some currency in their respective Native societies. None has developed a large literature, however. For historical and geographic reasons, traditional cultural practices and language use are not necessarily coextensive among Native groups. Therefore, some people who speak the same or closely related languages may have quite different traditional cultures. On the other hand, peoples who share a common cultural tradition may come from several different language or even language family backgrounds.[3]

Native Languages

Between the time of first contact with Europeans and the present many linguistic and cultural changes have taken place. One of the clearer pictures of present-day language use by Native peoples is provided in census data. The figures given do not necessarily match those quoted above because the methods of obtaining them were different. In the 1971 Canadian census 312,765 people were reported to be of Native Indian or Inuit origin (1.4 per cent of the total Canadian population). 179,820 people or .8 per cent of the total Canadian population reported that their mother tongue was a Native Indian or Inuit language, and 137,285 said that a Native Indian or Inuit language was most often spoken in their homes. Among those who were reported to have a Native Indian or Inuit language as their mother tongue, 61,845 were between the ages of 0 and 14 and are therefore mostly in the present school population. Of those who were reported to be of Native Indian or Inuit origin, 250,870 said they spoke English only, 12,080 said French only, 11,085 said they spoke both English and French, and 38,725 said they spoke neither English nor French.

Native Cultures

An economic and cultural picture of Canada's Native people is difficult to draw. There are still people who live year round in tents, who depend mainly on hunting and fishing for their food and who are nomadic in their way of life. There are others whose lifestyle is comparable to that of the upper middle class in Canada's largest urban areas. But these are extremes. The Canadian Association in Support of the Native Peoples describes the majority of Native peoples as "the most economically deprived groups in Canada and far behind other Canadians in every respect."[4]

Even in the most remote areas and among people who still know how to live off the land in the manner of the traditional Native economies, subsistence is becoming impossible. And for the majority of Native people for whom the nineteenth century Native economic systems and the material aspects of the cultures of their ancestors are things of the past, cultural conflicts, lack of educational qualifications, isolation and discrimination still bar the way to entry into the economic life of Canada's cultural majority. And even if the majority culture is willing to accept them, they very often face a critical personal conflict between retaining traditional cultural ways and accepting aspects of the majority culture.

But we are being narrow-minded if we think that the only alternatives left to Native people are endemic deprivation because of economic pressures or total assimilation to the majority culture. The positive and creative attitude that many Native people have toward their future as an ethnically and economically viable entity has been described by R. Palmer Patterson.

> In this situation (1876-c. 1950) [the Canadian Native people] had lost control of the political shaping of their lives. They were encouraged or coerced into continuing social and ideological change as well. And it was at this point that they appeared to be either dying out as a biological entity or as a cultural entity or both. Many Europeans, including Indian affairs administrators, missionaries, and teachers on reserves, spoke of the Indian as undergoing the transition, in isolation and on reduced land, to Westernization. What they did not see was the cohesiveness and tenacity of the Indian community and in most cases the capacity of the Indian to adapt without loss of identity. Because individuals assimilated to Canadian society and because Indian culture was clearly not what it had been at earliest European contact, non-Indians assumed that Indians were being assimilated. This understanding of the situation served to underscore the prevalent view of Indian culture as static, and encouraged a tendency to interpret all change as evolution toward assimilation rather than as the creation of a new synthesis which continued to be Indian culture.[5]

Cultural information is essential to the planning and development of language programs for Native education. It is not quantifiable in the way that much linguistic data is. Researchers and educators often do not know what to look for until they have found it. There is a fair amount of information about Native cultures available. The problem for educators generally is that social scientists have tended to look for the exotic aspects rather than concentrate, as Patterson has, on mechanisms in Native cultures for adaptation and change. More study of the effects of schooling in all types of Native societies would be valuable.

The Administration of Native Education

Because of the provisions of the British North America Act and the Indian Act, the federal government is responsible for the education of status Indians. It is also responsible for the administration of the Territories, including the provision of education for the residents, many of whom are Inuit and non-status Indians. In this way the federal government is responsible for the education of the majority of Canada's Native people. According to the British North America Act, however, education is normally the responsibility of the provinces and the federal government does not really want to be involved in the education business. In the Territories, local governments have now been established which function much like provincial governments and which have their own education departments.

For status Indians who live in the provinces, the federal government has made a variety of arrangements over the years. Until about 1950, it contracted out the job of educating status Indians to religious organizations. Curriculum or staff certification policies were not dictated in these contracts. In the late 1940s, the federal government formulated a new Indian policy. The move was to be from the old approach of paternalism and isolationism to integration with the rest of Canadian society. The federal government took over direct control of Indian education. It decided that all teachers in Indian schools should be certified to teach in the province in which the school was located. And the Indian schools were to follow the curriculums of the respective provinces. The aim was to make the education of Native children as much like that of all other Canadian children as possible. In line with this policy, the government attempted to turn over as much of the direct administration of Indian schooling as possible to the provinces. Joint agreements were made between local school boards and the Department of Indian Affairs for Indian children to attend provincial schools. These agreements stated that Indian children were to receive precisely the same education as the other children in the school.[6] From the federal point of view the ideal would have been to make agreements for all of the administration of Indian education. But many Native people live in remote areas far from any provincial schools. The federal government has been building and administering schools so that Native children can get at least the first few years of schooling in their home communities.

In 1969 Jean Chrétien, then the Minister of Indian Affairs and Northern Development, brought out a policy on Indian affairs which stated that the federal government was prepared to divest itself of all administrative responsibility for Native people. It would continue the same services for status Indian people, but the administration would be in the hands of whatever government agency would normally be responsible — for example the provincial education authorities would take over the administration of all Indian education.[7] Native reaction to this policy was mainly in the area of education. Native people, who up until that time had not been very vociferous or coordinated in their criticisms of the government, were adamant and virtually unanimous in their disapproval. They felt that this change would mean the end to any hope they might have of getting special attention paid to their particular problems as a group. In 1972 the National Indian Brotherhood published a policy statement called *Indian Control of Indian Education* in which it demanded that Native people be given direct control over the education of their children. Since 1973 the federal government has accepted the positions expressed in *Indian Control of Indian Education* as its basic policy in Indian education. Different degrees of control over education are gradually being given to bands as they want and are ready to accept them. And Native people are slowly getting seats on provincial school boards which administer schools their children attend.[8]

In the reaction to Chrétien's policy statement, one of the points made was that some provincial school situations discriminated against Native children and were not sensitive to their needs.[9] In 1971/72, 61 per cent of status Indian students were attending non-federal schools.[10] Since the federal government accepted Indian control as its policy, some bands have persuaded the government to provide federal schooling for their children even though the band was covered by an agreement with a provincial school board. At present, slightly less than half of the status Indian students attend provincial schools.

POLICIES AND OUTLOOKS OF THE THREE AGENCIES ON LANGUAGE AND CULTURE

The *federal government* has a definite national policy on language and culture. Through the Official Languages Act it pledges to do business with any citizen in either French or English. And it supports linguistic and cultural diversity in the country through its multiculturalism policy. The Canadian Bill of Rights also protects speakers of any language in the course of certain official transactions through a provision for interpreters. But there is a difference between the kind of support given to bilingualism and to multiculturalism. The government takes the initiative and the responsibility to provide services in English and French. For support of multicultural and non-official language matters, however, the initiative must come from those who want it. The government only supplies the financial support. It is particularly cautious when such support is called for to use in schools, since education is a provincial matter.

But the federal government is directly involved in Native education. And it has a particular responsibility toward Native citizens. The question that then arises is how far the federal government is responsible for supporting or maintaining the languages and cultures of Native people as opposed to its responsibility to other citizens with particular ethnic interests. To the extent that the linguistic and cultural attributes of Native people make the administration of Indian affairs unique, it behooves the government to be sensitive to them. But the manner in which it perceives and interprets such attributes is usually specific to particular situations and issues.

The *provincial governments* have taken over a great deal of the federal government's responsibility for Native education by agreement. In the areas of curriculum development and teacher certification (those areas most affecting Indian education) it is this writer's view that the main objective of the provinces is to produce citizens with adequate skills in language and culture to compete as equals in majority Canadian society. Although ten different sets of legislation and policy in education are involved, it is possible to generalize from them that the provinces consider English (or French in the case of Quebec), to be the normal language of instruction, that few legal provisions are made to help those children who come to school speaking neither official language, and that special arrangements must be made for instruction through the medium of the other official language for native speakers of that language.

But the schools become deeply concerned when the conflict between the language and culture of the school and of the child means that the school does not succeed in its aims. As in the case of the federal government, the provincial governments are forced to be sensitive to ethnic concerns if these concerns are standing in the way of educational success as the provinces define it. The provinces have been reluctant to grant major educational concessions to ethnic groups mainly because of the problem of grant-it-to-one-grant-it-to-all. Status Indian children, since they have the dubious distinction of being one of the greatest educational problems and of being legally marked by their status, have received special educational treatment from some provincial governments.

In describing *the point of view of the bands,* I will take the liberty of using the positions expressed in *Indian Control of Indian Education* to represent it. In many cases this is not entirely fair to the diversity of opinion among Native people, but it is the most general and visible statement available. *Indian Control of Indian Education* states that:

> What we want for our children can be summarized very briefly:
> ..... to reinforce their Indian identity,
> ..... to provide the training necessary for making a good living in modern society.[11]

Native people are mostly in agreement with the provincial governments' objective for Native education (which presumably is the same as the second objective quoted above) but they want more than this. They want this education to be carried out in such a way that the identity of the Native child is not damaged — indeed that it is reinforced. Among the ways to fulfill these objectives, the National Indian Brotherhood includes local control of education (which, as has already been pointed out, bands are getting to some degree), more Native and Native-sensitive content in the curriculum (which is being developed and implemented in some federal and provincial schools), more Native teachers (the Department of Indian Affairs now claims to employ about 20 per cent Native teachers) and vernacular transition or Native as a second language programs (there were 208 Native language programs involving 23 languages in federal and provincial schools in 1974/75: five of these were vernacular transition programs).[12]

The net effect of this is that the federal government and the provincial governments take as their responsibility to educate Native children to become economically viable citizens. From the educators' point of view this involves the child's learning to control skills and habits of at least some areas of the majority culture. Native people are not in basic disagreement with this approach. Also, both governments are willing to consider accommodating their methods of education to particular Native language and cultural needs if this accommodation will improve the chances of success in meeting the basic educational goal. And finally, the federal government is willing to give some financial support to Native efforts to maintain their languages and cultures as long as the initiative comes from the people themselves. A great deal of rhetoric in support of these policies and objectives has been committed to paper.

But this agreement in principle is of no value unless the precise areas of contrast between the essential aspects of Native cultures and identity on the one hand and the attitudes and skills necessary to give the Native child an equal opportunity in the majority system on the other are identified and agreed upon. The Native solution to this issue is that Native children be given an education that prepares them to make informed choices in their lives. The National Indian Brotherhood says:

> We do not regard the educational process as "either-or" operation. We must have the freedom to choose among many options and alternatives.[13]

In the remainder of this paper, some methods of providing Native children with the freedom to choose between languages will be explored.

OBJECTIVES FOR NATIVE EDUCATION

From the outlooks and policies outlined above, of the various agencies involved in Native education we can distill three possible objectives for the implementation of any program or policy. One is that the program or policy would give the Native child an opportunity to learn the skills and attitudes that he would need in order to operate as an equal in the majority culture. The second is that the program or policy would improve the Native child's learning environment in such a way that he would achieve significantly more in his learning of the regular (majority culture oriented) curriculum work. The third is that the program or policy would contribute to the reinforcement of the Native child's sense of identity as a Native person. It is in the light of such objectives that language programs and policies in Native education should be evaluated.

Programs and Policies

Now, finally, let us look at some actual or proposed language programs and policies. Most of those described here are designed for use with children who come to school speaking only or predominantly a Native language. Two are for Native children who speak little or no Native language. It is important to keep in mind the diversity of situations to which any of these could be applied. The descriptions below are intended to point out the potential of the programs and policies in relation to the objectives outlined above. The choice of a program or policy for a school would depend on the actual objectives of the school and on the many local factors that could affect that potential.

THE IMMERSION POLICY

The first item could be called the "immersion policy." It has to be considered a policy since there is no specific curriculum, other than any regular provincial curriculum, associated with it. It occurs in federal and provincial school situations in which the Native children come to school speaking only or predominantly a Native language. The policy is that English (or French in some areas) will be the medium of instruction and that the children will earn that language by constant contact through the school's regular program. The main objective of this policy is to promote the learning of regular curriculum work. The second objective is to teach the Native child a skill, namely the control of the English language. This second objective is valuable because English in itself is useful and since, under this policy, there is no option but to have the regular curriculum presented in any medium other than English.

This policy has been in force in the majority of Native schools for Native-speaking children since the beginnings of Native education in Canada. It was and is used partly because educators believed that it was the best policy and partly because no other options were possible or were entertained. Since Indian schools started to use the provincial curriculums and hire only provincially certified teachers, and since federal policy has been to make Native education as much like that for all other Canadian children, it has been the basic language policy for Native education. Any of the other language programs and policies discussed later are considered to be extras — special additions to the basic format that this policy entails. Because it is considered basic, it is difficult to judge the extent to which this policy, unadulterated, is used in schools for Native-speaking children. One can only assume that it is still relatively widely used.

Native-speaking children who receive their schooling under this policy do not do as well in their regular curriculum work as the majority of Canadian children. This statement and every other comparative comment on school achievement that will be made in this paper must be qualified by the fact that there is very little information available on the school achievement of Native children. Statistics on school achievement broken down by the various school subject areas or by the mother tongue of the pupil are not published. And formal, controlled evaluations of specific Canadian Native education programs are not in the literature on education. Therefore, while it is fairly safe to make the general statement above, it is not known how well Native-speaking children do in the specific area of English language learning, particularly in relation to other groups of children. From the information given above, then, one can say that the immersion policy is limited in its success in meeting its main objective, and probably succeeds to some degree in meeting its second objective.

It is possible to look at the results of the immersion policy in two different ways. One is that it is surprising that Native-speaking children learn as much as they do. Certainly Native-speaking children do not learn as much of the regular curriculum work and possibly as much of the language as most other children in school, but that could be considered to be entirely understandable since they have the extra burden of having to learn the medium of instruction first. UNESCO has called it axiomatic that it is better for children to have their first few years of schooling through the medium of the vernacular language.[14] Alternatively, one could say that it is surprising that Native-speaking children learn as little as they do. There are impressive attestations to the effectiveness of French immersion programs in teaching the French language and the regular curriculum work under apparently very similar educational conditions. Obviously there must be some critical differences in the two situations to account for the fact that Native-speaking children do not achieve as much, at least in the area of regular curriculum work, as the French immersion pupils do.

When comparing the usual French immersion program conditions with the immersion policy in Native education, it becomes apparent that the relative assumptions of the programs are importantly different. French immersion programs are designed to give children a special educational opportunity — to give them control of an additional language over and above the usual school achievement in regular curriculum work. The immersion policy is built on the assumption that a certain minimal standard (fluency in English) must be met before regular education can proceed.[15] If this latter comment seems unfair one has to remember the lack of opportunity the Native schools had in the past to develop alternative solutions. The French immersion programs are an educational experiment to meet a highly approved educational and political goal. The immersion policy is the result of public ignorance or neglect and local impotence with respect to a complex and difficult educational problem. One of its main goals is a considerable degree of assimilation to the majority culture. Anything more than an appreciation of French ways is not considered necessary in a French immersion program. In the French immersion situation the parents have considerable control over the education system through the normal political channels, and they voluntarily choose whether or not to place their children in such a program. In the Native case, however, parents are still not often satisfied with their control over education policies and have no choice about the type of program to which to send their children.

Other areas in which contrast can be seen between the two are the kinds of teachers, materials, pupils and languages which are usually involved. Although the Department of Indian Affairs is able to boast that almost 20 per cent of its teachers are Native people, it still remains true that certified Native teachers are the exception in Native schools. The relationship between the number of Native teachers and the number of bilingual official language–vernacular language teachers to this 20 per cent figure is a very complicated one. More will be said about this later in the paper. Certified teachers are hired and sometimes given a short orientation course, then are sent into Native schools to do what they can with the skills and experience they have gained from the majority culture. The teaching experience and retention rate of teachers in the Native schools are lower than in regular majority culture schools because the cultural pressure and often the isolation put heavy strains on them. The teachers in the French immersion programs are all bilingual in English and French and live in desirable locations. Both languages involved in the French immersion programs are official languages — standardized, literate and internationally recognized. It can safely be said that the differences between French and majority English-Canadian cultures are not as great as to cause serious conflict with respect to educational goals and methods. Therefore the French immersion programs can obtain French curriculum materials that can be adapted to the French immersion programs without massive alteration. The French immersion teachers allow the children to respond in their first language for the first year or so, and can use that language in case of necessity or important misunderstanding. And they can communicate with the children's parents and community as social equals.

The children who are placed in French immersion programs are usually, although not always[16] from middle class families. They come from areas in which good school achievement is expected and valued. Their parents appear to risk sending them to such an experimental program because they are likely to be good in school anyhow.[17] The Native children, on the other hand, are less likely to be good school achievers than almost any group in Canada. Despite the fact that good school achievement is often valued by their community, it is not a common experience on the part of their parents or peers. And their mother tongue is not valued in the country as a whole. They come from a language community which is under attack from majority language pressures. The French immersion children can be secure in the fact that their native language is a safe and valued part of the culture of the country. After a few years of French immersion, they receive instruction in and about English. Even if the pressures of the French immersion experiment prove too great, they can still retreat to English-medium schooling with no loss to their educational status or eventual viability in their home community. In sum, it is easy, from this comparison, to see why Native and non-Native educators call the immersion policy not immersion but *sub*mersion.[18]

MODIFICATIONS TO THE IMMERSION POLICY

One cannot avoid the conclusion that it is not the immersion policy itself that is to blame for the failure of Native-speaking children to achieve as well as other Canadian children in regular curriculum work. If their teachers could make their earliest school experiences more comfortable for them by permitting them to speak in their first language for the first year or so, if they had the feeling that they were being given a special opportunity to learn English — not just that they were expected to do so — if their mother tongue held a valued place to which they could resort if necessary in the country at large, and if their home cultural experience involved more experience with good school achievement, then perhaps the results of the immersion policy would be more like those of the French immersion programs. Other factors such as parental control over education, community-school relations, and culturally compatible concepts of curriculum and education in general may also be important.

These factors have all been recognized by educators of Native children and Native people themselves. Attempts have been made to equalize Native-speaking children's educational opportunities by providing ameliorations to the immersion policy. One feature of the French immersion programs is that, at the beginning, the child can express himself in his first language. Even if the teacher rarely uses it, the child is free to resort to it and can expect to be understood.[19] To reproduce this situation exactly in schools for Native-speaking children, bilingual certified teachers would have to be hired. Such people are rare indeed. Not many Native people choose to become teachers. In 1971, 83,325 status Indians were being supported by the federal government in all levels of education. Of these 14.6 per cent were receiving post-secondary training. Among that 14.6 per cent only .1 per cent were in teacher training.[20] To become a teacher one has to become an ambassador for the majority culture. Those who receive teacher certification are likely to be among the most assimilated, are less likely to speak a Native language and do not necessarily want to go to teach in a Native community, particularly one in which a Native language is the main medium of communication.

Nevertheless, the National Indian Brotherhood in *Indian Control of Indian Education* called for more government support for teacher training for Native people.[21] The Department of Indian Affairs *Annual Report 1974/75* announced that eight universities or teacher training institutions offer teacher training programs designed specifically for Indians.[22] These programs usually feature special Native language and cultural content and emphasize off-campus work in Native communities. Although there is a high rate of attrition from these programs, and many of the graduates do not end up teaching in regular Native schools, the number of Native teachers in

Native schools is growing. How many of these teachers speak a Native language at all or speak the same Native language as that of the community in which they teach is not known. One other way to get bilingual teachers is to train English monolingual Native or non-Native teachers to speak the language of the community. The Native teacher training programs often have short courses in one or two Native languages. And some teachers in communities in which a Native language is predominant learn enough of the language to use it for some purposes in the classroom.

But there are other ways to introduce the Native-speaking child's first language into an English-medium classroom. Even if the teacher is not bilingual, bilingual paraprofessionals can mediate between the teacher and thc children. This solution is common in Native schools. There are approximately 1,300 Native paraprofessionals employed in Native schools as teacher assistants, social counsellors, counsellor technicians, home and school corrdinators, etc.[23] Most of these people are employed in the school in their home community. Again, the number of these who speak a Native language is not known, but if the community children do not speak English the chance that a local adult will speak the child's language is very good. There is no consistent way in which bilingual paraprofessionals are used in Native classrooms. Practices range from having the paraprofessional act more or less as the teacher's secretary, to having him or her do a good deal of the actual teaching, particularly in the early grades. One of the greatest difficulties in these situations is to establish the duties, training and pay scale for paraprofessionals without antagonizing provincial teachers' organizations.[24]

Does the provision of bilingual personnel mean more success in reaching any of the objectives of Native schooling? No formal evaluations have been done in Canada to ascertain if the presence of bilingual personnel contributes directly to improved achievement in English-language learning or in any other area of curriculum work. We also have no empirical evidence that this recognition of the child's first language in the school contributes to an improvement in his sense of identity as a Native person. If French immersion programs work and this change makes the Native immersion policy more like the French immersion programs, then one can hope that it will help. Also, many Native people and educators of Native children *think* it helps. And finally Nancy Modiano, in her study of Indian children in Mexico, felt that the employment of bilingual Native teachers, rather than teachers from other cultural backgrounds, was an important factor in the relative success of the programs she studies.[25] Canadian Native people, educators of Native children and Modiano agree that the reason that bilingual personnel are likely to contribute to improved school achievement is that they can work in many ways to soften the contrast between the school and the community environments. But the actual relationship between the presence of the Native bilinguals in Canadian Native schools and changes in school achievement or the child's sense of identity cannot be ascertained from the data we have at present.

Schools for Native-speaking children can also emulate the French immersion situation by taking particular account of the fact that Native-speaking children are different from most other children in Canadian schools in that they do not natively speak the language of instruction. Even if the Native children do not have any choice in the medium of instruction for their schooling, the school can take a positive attitude to the teaching of English as part of its responsibility towards its pupils. In the past fifteen years or so Canadian educators have been instituting English as a second language (ESL) programs for non-official-language-speaking children. This movement has had an effect on Native education. Although there are still not many sources of teacher training in ESL methods, Native schools are now getting some teachers with backgrounds in the area of ESL. Most of the curriculum materials available are designed for urban children from immigrant families, but Native schools are adapting these or creating new materials to suit their own needs. The degree to which ESL has affected schools for Native-speaking children in terms of the number of teachers with ESL training, or actual changes from the basic immersion policy cannot be ascertained from the information available. But there is no reason to believe that using ESL methods and materials is anything but an advantage in schools for Native-speaking children. Whatever policies or programs are undertaken with regards to the use of Native languages in the school, the ESL approach can still be used in the English language program.

We now come to the consideration of the role of the child's mother tongue in the school and in society. In the discussion above, it was noted that bilingual personnel could be used in the hopes of reducing the conflict between the home and the school environments. This measure appears to be sufficient for the transition of the French immersion pupils from their English home environment to their French-medium school. But is it enough for Native-speaking children? It has been pointed out that the Native languages are under pressure from the official languages and appear to be losing ground. The French immersion pupils are native speakers of the most powerful language in the country. They receive English language arts instruction from about Grade 2 on. And the French immersion pupils can be expected, from their background, to be good school achievers. The Native-speaking pupils cannot. Can programs or policies involving more use of the Native child's mother tongue be expected to reduce the effects of such differences in Native schools?

Today two types of programs are popular in the education of Native-speaking children. One is the provision of Native language enrichment and/or literacy programs. These programs are taught by local Native people, some of whom have been trained and some not. The children generally receive a few hours a week of education in some aspect of their first language — literacy, oral practice or Native folklore.

The other type of program is more projected than in practice. To this writer's knowledge Ontario, Quebec, Manitoba, Saskatchewan, the government of the Northwest Territories and the National Indian Brotherhood[26] have all recognized in one way or another the need for bilingual transition programs for Native-speaking children. The format proposed for these programs (and implemented in five schools in Manitoba in the past few years) is Native language medium instruction for Native-speaking children from kindergarten to about Grade 3. During this time the proportion of Native language medium instruction is to be decreased until it is used about 10 per cent of the time in Native language enrichment programs from Grade 4 on. English is to be taught as a second language from kindergarten on and slowly introduced as a medium of instruction in other areas of the curriculum. Literacy is to be first introduced in the Native language.[27]

The objectives of the Native language enrichment and literacy programs are improved sense of Native identity on the part of the children, and maintenance of the use of the Native language in the community and in the lives of the children. The objectives of the vernacular transition programs include the above two objectives and add the expectation that such a program will improve the child's chances of achieving more in the regular school curriculum work through the medium of his mother tongue.

Are these objectives likely to be met by such programs? All the problems of getting suitable bilingual teachers or paraprofessionals cited above are equally relevant here. And the problems of creating curriculum materials for the many Native languages, dialects and cultures involved are great. Majority-culture certified teachers are often hesitant to go into ordinary classrooms without the support of curriculum materials that have been devised, tested and standardized by recognized educational authorities. Can we expect new or even untrained Native personnel to venture (with virtually no curriculum materials) into classrooms to persuade children who are notoriously poor school achievers to save their endangered languages from extinction? The fact that most of the languages have to have orthographies developed for them in order to establish a literacy program is one of the many complicating factors in Native curriculum development. It is only fair to ask why one should expect a Native literacy program to improve a Native child's sense of identity as a Native person by creating something — namely literacy — which has never existed in his home culture before. These and other problems notwithstanding, the Department of Indian Affairs is not pessimistic and provides approximately $2 million annually to support Native curriculum development projects for curriculum enrichment (not necessarily in a Native language) and Native language programs. There are now 52 local curriculum committees which have been organized to advise the schools on cultural content and the development of curriculum materials. Many of these are directly involved in producing Native language curriculum materials.[28]

Patricia Lee Engle, in her paper "The Use of Vernacular Languages in Education," compares studies from all over the world on what she terms "the direct approach" — which is comparable to the immersion policy[29] described here — and the "native languages approach" — which is comparable to the Native vernacular transition programs described here. In brief, her conclusions are that the empirical evidence available on the efficacy of the two approaches is insufficient to support a definite choice between the two. The linguistic, sociological, political and educational factors behind the 24 reports she reviews are so varied that it is hard to even find among them situations that would be satisfactorily parallel to the Canadian Native circumstances for direct comparison. Also, Canadian Native conditions vary widely enough among themselves as to make such comparisions even more risky. Engle agrees with Bernard Spolsky[30] that a wide range of local factors must be taken into consideration before a decision is made on the effectiveness or potential effectiveness of any particular course of action. Spolsky describes six main areas outside of directly educational concerns which must be considered before and while action is taken. There are linguistic, psychological, sociological, economic, political and religiocultural factors. Engle suggests that the following 12 points need to be taken into account if further research (and presumably program) designs in the area of bilingual education are undertaken:

1. The lingusitic relationship between the two languages;
2. the functions of the two languages in the broader community, and the possible uses of literacy in each language;
3. the cultural context of learning in the community;
4. the relationship of the two ethnolinguistic groups in the larger society;

5. the initial linguistic status of the child;
6. the period of the child's development in which the second language is introduced;
7. instructional methods and materials used;
8. the ethnic group membership of the teacher;
9. the training and linguistic knowledge of the teacher;
10. the length of time necessary to observe an effect;
11. the specific subject matter under consideration;
12. the appropriateness of the assessment devices for both languages.[31]

Since no formal evaluations have been published on the effects of Canadian Native language enrichment or vernacular transition programs, little more can be said except that educators and Native people are generally enthusiastic about the results of the potential for such programs in schools for Native-speaking children.

NATIVE AS A SECOND LANGUAGE PROGRAMS

The 1971 Canadian census figures quoted above suggest that at least half of the ethnically Native population sends it children to school speaking only an official language. It would be easy to assume that such children would adjust much more easily to school than their Native-speaking counterparts because they do not have the same language barrier to overcome. The figures available to this writer on the achievement of Native children in school are not broken down by the mother tongue of the pupils. Therefore, it is impossible to ascertain if, in fact, the official language-speaking children do better. From purely personal experience and subjective reports from educators in Native schools, it appears to me that while official language-speaking Native children generally achieve more in school than Native-speaking children, they still do not do as well as the majority of Canadian children. On rather shaky grounds, since the milieu of Native-speaking children is usually somewhat different from that of the official language-speaking Native children, it can be suggested that language is not the central factor in the difference in school achievement between Native children in general and the rest of the Canadian school population.

The National Indian Brotherhood has proposed that the appropriate Native language should be taught to the Native children who do not speak or are in danger of losing their ancestral language. The objectives of such programs would be to reinforce the child's identity as a Native person, to revive or maintain the language in Native society and possibly to improve the child's recognition of the value of his ancestral language in a school setting. Many Native as a second language programs are now given in schools for Native children — some in federal and some in provincial schools. The usual format for such programs is that a Native person from the community, chosen by the band, comes into each class for a few hours each week to teach a Native language as a subject of instruction. Often literacy in this language is introduced after some oral work has been covered.

The same problems in teaching training, acceptance of teacher qualifications by certifying agencies and curriculum development are experienced by those involved in programs for official language-speaking Native children as those for Native-speaking children. And again, the lack of formal evaluation of the effects of these programs leaves us in doubt as to whether they are able to achieve any of the objectives set for them. In addition, there are two other problems that affect the Native as a second language programs.

The first of these problems arises from the fact that the majority of the official language-speaking Native children come from communities in which the Native language is seldom or never used by adults. Fishman reports in his international study of bilingual education schooling that school use of a language is not enough. A language must be supported by institutions outside the school in order for the school program to be effective in producing bilingual students.[32] Since the language situation in the home communities of the offical language-speaking children is widely varied, the relevance of Fishman's observation may be different from community to community. But it is very often the case that the school is the only institution in which the Native language has any place — however artificial. Under such circumstances, however, the initiation of Native as a second language programs has sometimes produced impressive side effects. The fact that such a program has been introduced into the school has created such an interest in the community that other Native language related activities, such as story telling, Native language newsletters, as well as second language learning and literacy courses for adults have been started.

The other problem is that official language-speaking Native children are more likely to attend the provincial elementary schools than Native-speaking children. In the provincial schools they attend classes with, and follow exactly the same curriculum, as the non-Native children. What is the effect on Native children's self-concept if they study their ancestral language in a provincial classroom with non-Native children? It is often the case that non-Native children are better school achievers in all subject areas. Under such circumstances it is likely that the Native child's self-concept will suffer more than it gains if the non-Native children prove to be better at learning his ancestral language than he is. For this and other reasons some Native communities have decided that school is not the appropriate place for their children to learn a Native language.

One second-language program deserves particular mention. Influenced in part by the French immersion model, although it is really an extension of the Native language instruction programs, the school at West Bay on Manitoulin Island in Ontario has introduced an Ojibwa immersion program. Although Native people on Manitoulin Island have effectively maintained the use of their Native language for a long time, many of the present generation of elementary school children speak only English. The principles of the French immersion programs are used in the West Bay school, but the timing is from the transition model. In other words, although the children are taught only through the medium of Ojibwa in junior kindergarten, kindergarten and Grade 1, and are first introduced to literacy in Ojibwa in Grade 1, the proportion of time the Ojibwa medium is used is reduced year by year from Grade 2 to Grade 4. From Grade 5 on, one content subject is continued in Ojibwa while the rest of the curriculum is presented in English.[33] No formal evaluation has been done of this program.

Summary and Conclusions

The descriptions of the language programs and policies for Native education can be summarized in terms of the first language of the children and the language of instruction. Figure 1 shows four cells, each of which represents a possible educational alternative.

Figure 1: Educational alternatives

	English medium instruction	Native medium instruction
Native-speaking children	A English immersion (± Native language enrichment)	B vernacular program (ESL)
English-speaking children	C regular program (± NASL)	D Native immersion (English language enrichment)

Cell A represents the immersion policy with all its modifications. Cell B represents the vernacular programs such as those in Manitoba. In Cell C would fall all the Native as second-language programs except for the Manitoulin Island immersion program which would be Cell D. The A and C types are the most common because they are the easiest. No new curriculum materials or special teachers are required for the basic programs. And they are identical or close to the normal form of schooling in Canada. While there are a few programs of the B type and one of the D type, these are less common. They require radical changes in the regular education program involving special teachers and curriculum development.

In order for a school or agency to decide on a program or policy, a certain amount of background information is necessary. This information could be arranged under the headings — present situation, objectives and evaluation. It is obvious that some kinds of information are not readily available.

The heading, "present situation," covers such topics as the languages used by the prospective students, their parents and their communities, the kinds of literacy present and required, Native and majority cultural factors which might affect the school program, etc. At the level of an individual school, it is not difficult to collect such information providing that there is good communication between the school and the community. But for a decision at the level of a provincial or federal government, enough information has not been collected or exploited to give a comprehensive picture of the situation. This problem is particularly great when Inuit, Métis or non-status people are involved. Information in this area would be critical in decisions between A and B type programs over C and D types. It would also affect the institution, content and form of Native as a second-language programs.

It is essential that program and policy decisions at all levels be made in relation to clear objectives for education. The objectives used in the discussion above are only *possible* objectives. Not all of them would necessarily be appropriate for all situations. Other objectives might be included or modifications made to those stated here. It is not easy to discern from most government publications on Native education what the governments' precise objective are. *Indian Control of Indian Education* does not necessarily represent the views of all Native groups or individuals. More forthrightness and precision in stating objectives on the part of government agencies is necessary. And sources of information on Native opinions on education should be exploited. A lack of clear objectives would compromise decision-making for any type of program, but it is particularly important in decisions on Native as a second language programs, Native language enrichment programs and on changes in the medium of instruction (A and C over B and D).

The greatest problem in program and policy decisions is evaluation. Even if adequate information about the present situation is available, and if clear objectives have been set, there is not enough data on the effects of different language programs to predict the effectiveness of any program with satisfactory accuracy. A certain amount of guesswork is involved in instituting any new educational change. And each school, community and province has its unique aspects. But educational decision-makers should have available to them information on the effects of various language programs and policies used with different populations. They should also have detailed data on the effects of the programs which are in use in their schools at the time a change is contemplated. And they should have the time, funds and expert advice necessary to evaluate the effects of any innovations that are made. Without such background information, decisions between A and C type programs over B and D types are more or less shots in the dark. Any change in education usually involves expense, the time and energy of educators, and the lives of students. It is critical that decisions are made on the basis of adequate information.

Notes

1. In this paper "Native" will be used to refer to the people who were living in North America before 1500 and their descendants. "Native language" will refer to any of the languages spoken by Native people before 1500 and the languages and dialects that have subsequently developed from them.
2. Canadian Association in Support of the Native Peoples, *And What About Canada's Native Peoples?* (Ottawa: Canadian Association in Support of the Native Peoples, 1976), pp. 1–4.
3. Canada, Department of Indian Affairs and Northern Development, *Linguistic and Cultural Affiliations of Canadian Indian Bands* (Ottawa: Queen's Printer, 1970), p. 2.
4. Canadian Association in Support of the Native Peoples, *Native Peoples,* pp. 8–9.
5. E. Palmer Patterson II, *The Canadian Indian: A History Since 1500* (Don Mills, Ontario: Collier-Macmillan Canada Ltd., 1972), p. 40.
6. H.B. Hawthorn, *A Survey of the Contemporary Indians of Canada, Vol. II: Economic, Political, Educational Needs and Policies* (Ottawa: Indian Affairs Branch, 1967), p. 35.
7. Canada, *Statement of the Government of Canada on Indian Policy* (Ottawa: Queen's Printer, 1969).
8. Canada, Department of Indian and Northern Affairs, *Indian Education: Curriculum Development, Native Languages and Native Studies* (Ottawa: Indian and Northern Affairs, 1975), p. 3.
9. Indian Chiefs of Alberta, *Citizens Plus* (Edmonton: Indian Association of Alberta, 1970).
10. Canada, Department of Indian and Northern Affairs, *Indian Education Program* (Ottawa: Indian Affairs and Northern Development, 1972), p. 17.
11. National Indian Brotherhood, *Indian Control of Indian Education* (Ottawa: National Indian Brotherhood, 1972), p. 3.

12. Department of Indian and Northern Affairs, *Indian Education: Curriculum Development,* p. 10.
13. National Indian Brotherhood, *Indian Control,* p. 4.
14. UNESCO, *The Use of Vernacular Languages in Education*, Monograph on Fundamental Education, 8, (Paris: UNESCO, 1958), p. 11.
15. It should also be noted that Bernard Spolsky and Merrill Swain (personal communication) feel that there is another important difference between the French immersion programs and programs for minority groups. The minority group pupils are *expected* to achieve native speaker-like fluency in English and are penalized if they do not. The French immersion pupils are *not expected* to achieve native speaker-like fluency in French, and any achievement in French they demonstrate is considered an educational plus.
16. G.R. Tucker, W.E. Lambert and A. d'Anglejan, "Are French Immersion Programs for Working Class Children? A Pilot Investigation," *Language Sciences*, 25 (1973), pp. 19–26.
17. Barbara Burnaby and Merrill Swain, "Draft Report on the Analysis of a Personality Measure in Relation to Language Achievement Scores of Young Children Learning French" (Toronto: Ontario Institute for Studies in Education, 1976) (mimeo).
18. Ida Wasacase, "Native Bilingual-Bicultural Programs" (Ottawa: Department of Indian Affairs and Northern Development, 1976), p. 7, (mimeo); Andrew D. Cohen and Merrill Swain, "Bilingual Education: The 'Immersion' Model in the North American Context," *TESOL Quarterly*, 10:1 (1976), pp. 45–53.
19. Merrill Swain, "More About Primary French Immersion Classes," *Orbit,* 27 (1975), pp. 13–15.
20. Canada, Statistics Canada, *Perspective Canada* (Ottawa: Statistics Canada, 1974), p. 251.
21. National Indian Brotherhood, *Indian Control*, pp. 18–20.
22. Department of Indian and Northern Affairs, *Annual Report 1974–1975,* p. 32.
23. Department of Indian and Northern Affairs, *Indian Education: Curriculum Development,* p. 3.
24. Bernard Spolsky, Joanna B. Green and John Read, *A Model for the Description, Analysis and Perhaps Evaluation of Bilingual Education,* Navajo Reading Study Progress Report No. 23 (Albuquerque, New Mexico: University of New Mexico, 1974), p. 19.
25. Nancy Modiano, *Indian Education in the Chiapas Highlands* (New York: Holt, Rinehart and Winston, 1973).
26. Ontario, Ministry of Education, *People of Native Ancestry: A Resource Guide for the Primary and Junior Divisions* (Toronto: Ministry of Education, 1975); *North American Indian Languages,* Martin, p. 7; Ida Wasacase, "Manitoba Native Bilingual Program" (Ottawa: Department of Indian Affairs and Northern Development, 1975), (mimeo); Ida McLeod, Department of Indian Affairs and Northern Development, Saskatoon, Saskatchewan (personal communication); Northwest Territories, Department of Education, *Elementary Education in the Northwest Territories: A Handbook for Curriculum Development* (Yellowknife, N.W.T.: Government of the Northwest Territories, 1972); and National Indian Brotherhood, *Indian Control,* pp. 15–16.
27. Ida Wasacase, "Manitoba Native Bilingual Program."

28. Department of Indian and Northern Affairs, *Indian Education: Curriculum Development,* p. 3.
29. Patricia Lee Engle, "The Use of Vernacular Languages in Education," *Review of Educational Research,* 45:2 (1975), pp. 283–325.
30. Spolsky, Green and Read, *Political Education.*
31. Engle, "Vernacular Languages," p. 316.
32. Joshua Fishman, "The Sociology of Bilingual Education," *Etudes de Linguistique Appliquee,* Nouvelle Serie 15, Multilinguisme et Multiculturalisme en Amerique du Nord (Juillet-Septembre, 1974), pp. 112–24.
33. Ida Wasacase, "Bilingual 'Immersion' Native Language Ojibwa Pilot Project, West Bay, Ontario" (Ottawa: Department of Indian Affairs and Northern Development) (mimeo).

The Non-Official Languages Study

K.G. O'BRYAN, O. KUPLOWSKA and J.G. REITZ

The Non-Official Languages Survey was conducted to examine the main patterns of non-official language knowledge and use in Canada, and to ascertain whether there is a real desire to support the retention of such languages as a viable source of cultural identity and preservation among members of groups whose ancestral language is other than English or French. The survey accomplished this objective, and at the same time has created a very rich and unique data bank on Canadian ethnic groups. . . .

In assessing and interpreting the results of the study, it is important to remember that it dealt only with large metropolitan samples and the reader should bear in mind that the other segments of each group, small-urban and rural, may differ perhaps markedly.

Overall, we found that substantial group-by-group differences exist on nearly all variables included in the study. Moreover, the group differences did not always follow the same pattern. Quite clearly, it is erroneous to speak of Canada's residents of other than French or English ancestry as through they are a homogeneous "group." They certainly have in common the fact that their origins are different from those of the French or English, but it does not follow that they all stand in the same attitudinal relation to the French and the English. Some have become assimilated and seem to have lost or discarded altogether the heritage of their ancestry. Other are vigorously aware of their origin. Therefore, total group data are often without meaning until broken down on a group-by-group basis. Indeed, the total group data cannot be taken to reflect accurately each specific group's points of view, nor level of knowledge, use or support for the language.

Therefore, we believe that policy-making and research would be ill-founded if based on a presupposition that the non-official language groups constitute a homogeneous entity. Nevertheless, it is

---

SOURCE: *Multiculturalism as State Policy*, Second Canadian Conference on Multiculturalism, Ottawa, 13–15 February 1976, pp. 131–48. Reproduced by permission of the Minister of Supply and Services, Canada.

clear that for many groups, ethnic heritage survival, and especially language survival, is a key concern which has very substantial social and emotional impact. This was well illustrated in the data that we collected and analysed, and it leads us to conclude that both the principle and practice of multiculturalism are most valid and desirable when they are applied in the recognition of specific ethnic group aspirations. These aspirations are often powerfully expressed and illustrate the degree to which some groups in various ways view themselves as representatives of Canadians whose origins are other then English or French. But, it is clear in our data that some members of Canada's "cultural mosaic" seek to reflect their cultural origins more brightly than do others.

Non-Official Language Knowledge

The extent of current knowledge of the non-official languages is basic to an assessment of group support of language retention in relation to multiculturalism. Since we were unable to administer any actual tests of language knowledge, our findings are based entirely on self-report and are, consequently, liable to some error. Nevertheless, self-reported fluency is itself a valid variable and our results clearly indicate that there currently exists quite extensive knowledge of non-official languages in Canada. This can be considered an immense cultural resource. It is, however, almost lost in a single generation. In a number of groups fluency may be lost even more quickly. Indeed, only seven in ten immigrants overall reported retention of full fluency. Some of this loss may be attributable to a "never was" condition since reading and writing skills were included in our fluency criteria. In any case, fluency was reported by only one in ten in the second generation, and had disappeared entirely in third and subsequent generations. Its fading was accompanied by a general loss of even partial knowledge of the language.

Some group differences in generation-specific rates of language retention were found, but these were actually rather minor differences. As matters now stand, the generational transition is a powerful force in language loss, even among those groups possessing the higher retention rates. We were able to present clear evidence that by the third generation the question is not one of retention but of reacquisition and primary acquisition. Despite the vast reservoir of language knowledge held in Canada by first-generation settlers, without direct and possibly substantial assistance, the non-official language skills will attenuate quickly in their children, and their grandchildren will know little if anything of their linguistic heritage.

It becomes obvious, from the data obtained on this variable, that under current conditions, language knowledge is not generally transmitted from immigrant parent to Canadian-born child in a fully fluent and permanent form and is inevitably lost to almost all in the natural order of generational succession.

Language knowledge is greater in the two larger of the five cities. One reason for this is the tendency of new immigrants to gather and settle in the bigger metropolitan areas. Another possible explanation may be related to the facilities available for language exercise such as ethnic newspapers, movies and radio programs. Higher concentrations of people in predominately unitary ethnic areas such as is the case with Greeks, Chinese and Italians are also likely to contribute to the quite substantial differentials found between the larger and smaller cities. Again, language knowledge is highly related to certain specific groups. As a result, where large concentrations of Greeks, Chinese, Italians and — in some cases — Ukrainians are present, overall language knowledge is greater. Toronto and Montreal do possess high concentrations of these groups and they also reflect a higher reported fluency rate. By contrast, the Scandinavians and the Dutch consistently tended to depress the overall city statistic on language fluency wherever they were concentrated.

From previous studies it had been expected that education and income differences might be significantly, and negatively, related to current levels of knowledge of language. However, there seems to be only a slight relationship between income and language retention in any of the generational classifications, suggesting that economic success, on a whole group basis, is important neither as a cause nor a consequence of language retention.

The picture is somewhat different when education is considered. Fluency is less among better-educated respondents who are, in the most part, of the second and third generation, and who would, based on the data, be expected to have such deficits in retention occurring. But even within generational groups, there is some tendency for respondents having more formal education to have lost knowledge of their ancestral language. The reason is evidently unrelated to the greater economic success of well-educated persons, since income was not related to language knowledge. Perhaps those who know the ethnic language seek job opportunities which are not tied to education. There is also the possibility that persons with different educational experiences may use different criteria to assess their own language knowledge. The more well-educated may apply a more rigorous standard and give themselves a lower rating as a result.

Education in Canadian schools may itself tend to militate against language acquisition. The time, and energy and social experience required to proceed to a university degree may divert attention away from the family and the ethnic community, and may undermine opportunities to retain language fluency. The educational institutions themselves currently make only minor attempts to develop and support interest in ethnic attachments. Lack of opportunity to study and use the language during the high school and university years when the child is further removed from parental contact may reduce interest in the ethnic language and the motivation to retain it.

The evidence of a negative relation between education and language retention needs to be considered when policy or research questions are asked, since it implies that those possessing greater communication skills or, perhaps, social and political awareness, are likely to be less conversant with the language of origin than the less formally educated persons in the same ethnic groups. This may, in some groups, lead to a greater degree of negativism towards language retention from those potentially best able to express their point of view. On the other hand, it should be noted that expressed *support* for language retention tended to decline as years of education increased in some groups, while a reverse relation existed in others. Moreover, in the second and third generations, which may be more important in the long-term perspective, education is sometimes positively associated with support for language retention.

Non-Official Language Use

Of those who know their ancestral language at least to some degree, more than half use the language at least once every day, and less than one in ten rarely or never use the language. This clearly substantiates the view that the languages in question are in active and viable usage in Canadian cities. Nevertheless, language use falls often in the second and third generations even more rapidly than does language knowledge. It would seem that opportunity and motivation, as usual in most human endeavour, are critical to continued ancestral language use.

Non-official languages are used every day or often by more than three-quarters of Montreal respondents and by nearly as many of Toronto's sample. By contrast, less than half the respondents in the other cities regularly make use of their ancestral language. That the question is more complex than the effect of size of the city is obvious and such variables as generational status, group characteristics, opportunity for use of the language, family, religious and attitudinal patterns, and access to media are, again, involved.

The city-by-city differences found and reported in the study indicate the importance of provision of opportunities for language use and for active language instruction if the language is to survive the natural erosion accompanying the generational transition.

We devoted considerable attention to the social context of non-official language use because such contexts were believed to help define the domains of ethnic salience, as well as the part played by the languages in Canadian life. We found that almost all of the fluent respondents use the ancestral language in whole or in large part in communication with their families, while almost exactly three-quarters used it regularly among close friends. Nearly half of the respondents made *exclusive* use of the ethnic tongue with at least one member of the family, while more than one-third did so with close friends from the same ethnic origin. Language use falls off rapidly as one moves away from the informal and relatively intimate context of family and friends.

The significant exception to the general pattern for some ethnic groups is the use of the language in the context of religion. Overall, more than half spoke with clergy in the ancestral tongue, and the ethnic language is used exclusively with clergy by four out of every ten fluent respondents. This proportion is very similar to the exclusive-use figures for family members and it illustrates the importance of religion in language use and retention.

Use of the ancestral tongue in other contexts is less frequent but approximately one-quarter of the fluent respondents made some use of the language among classmates or in their dealing with their tradesmen or professionals. The use of the non-official language outside the family is, of course, dependent upon the availability of people with whom it may be used, and might be expected to increase should there be greater opportunity and support, both financial and moral, for such use.

Among respondents possessing only some knowledge of the language, a substantially similar pattern of language use occurred but with considerably lower frequencies across all variables.

There is good reason to suppose that reduced opportunities to use the language would seriously affect its rate of retention. Where there are strong ethnic communities with a high number of first-generation residents, and in which there are professional, trades and religious personnel able to use the non-official language, it can be expected that frequency of retention rates will be high and that essential viability of the language will be maintained. If language use is primarily in the home, as our data tend to indicate is the case, its longevity will be dependent almost exclusively upon its usefulness for familial communication. When all members of the family become fluent in the official language the need, in the narrow sense of family use diminishes, and fluency vanishes. Where, however, there are other real outlets, for example in day-to-day communication with the providers of goods and services, the potential for language use is substantially improved.

For a true picture of language use, it is necessary to turn to each set of group respondents rather than rely on total sample statistics. This is particularly the case in the matter of language use. We have seen that variation between the groups is most marked. As one example, we noted that more than six in ten Greeks used only Greek with family members compared with two in ten Dutch respondents making similar exclusive use. There can be no real justification therefore in treating Greek and Dutch responses in the aggregate as representing combined patterns of non-official language use in the two groups. Nevertheless, the data often reflect substantial similarities among groups. This is especially so between Greeks and Italians who are regularly joined in their viewpoints by the Portuguese, the Chinese and Ukrainians, occasionally by the Poles, rarely by the Hungarians and Germans, and almost never by the Dutch and Scandinavians. But all do share a common trait — knowledge and frequency of use of the language decline together and generational differences are closely linked to this decline. Therefore, we believe that for all groups (whatever their aspirations concerning language retention), unless direct intervention aimed at language preservation is undertaken as early as the second generation, a lack of opportunity and justification for continued use of the ancestral tongue will rapidly reduce and eventually extinguish non-official language knowledge in the descendants of Canada's residents of non-English or French origin.

There is no doubt that success for the organizers and producers of the non-official language media is currently very much determined by levels of language knowledge which, as we have seen, is highly related to generation. Thus, there is a potential interaction present between language retention and the effect and success of non-official language media. On the one hand, the media are dependent on retention and, on the other, they can serve as an agent in retention. Fluent respondents do use the ethnic press a great deal: almost three-quarters of them over all groups read non-official language newspapers. This readership was quite evenly spread through all groups. Furthermore, it is strong among groups who have been a long time in Canada while the Portuguese, who are largely a recently arrived group, indicated the least proportion of regular users. The Portuguese experience may be partly a matter of literacy rates, or the lack of a variety of well-established Portuguese language papers. In any case, there is clear evidence that the press is substantially used by a very large proportion of fluent first generation respondents from all groups and as such, represents a powerful agent for potential exploitation in language retention programs should these be desired.

The use of the language by audiences of ethnic television and radio programs was more difficult to measure because of the scattered availability of such programs. However, those who knew of available programs and who reported fluency, or at least some knowledge of the ethnic language, were asked to report the frequency with which they watched or listened. In spite of the scarcity of ethnic television programming, a large group of fluent respondents report regular viewing of known programs and nearly one-quarter watch sometimes. Almost identical results were obtained amongst respondents reporting some knowledge of the language. Ukrainians appeared to be very regular viewers of programs in their language; Italians and Greeks also indicated regular patterns of viewing. The difficulty of the measurement became clear when the statistics for Dutch and Scandinavians were examined. Programming availability was very limited for these respondents and this is clearly an important determinant of viewing frequency. It will always be a very difficult task to accurately interpret patterns of viewing until more programs become available.

Television programming was reportedly much less accessible to respondents than was radio. No more than six in every ten knew of ancestral language television programs broadcast in their area.

The situation with respect to attitudes toward the media is not clear cut. Of respondents who were not aware of any available television programs, a little less than one-third expressed strong interest in the provision of non-official language television while a similar number was somewhat interested. But approximately one-third was not. Very strong support for television programming was shown by Chinese of whom five respondents expressed interest for every one not interested. There were somewhat similar findings for Ukrainians who returned a ratio of approximately four to one, as did Hungarians and Portuguese. By contrast, the Dutch, Germans, Scandinavians and Greeks were almost equally divided.

It is one thing to express a general desire for newspapers or for radio and television programming to be made available and another to actually watch it were it to be provided. It can be said, however, that a substantial number of respondents do read the ethnic press and have, thereby, given evidence of their interest in using the non-official language. These same people would likely be prepared to watch, at least once, programs for television made in the ancestral language. Thereafter, it becomes a question of relative production quality and interest levels. It is a truism that people will watch only what they like in television, and therefore, if an attempt is to be made to develop non-official language programming, that programming will have to be at least as compelling as its competition if it is to be successful.

The Greeks, Italians and Portuguese were the most aware of radio programs in their local areas. The programs themselves were well supported with almost one-quarter of all respondents listening to them regularly. More than one-third of our sample among groups for whom radio programs were readily available made extensive use of them and the medium is doubtlessly an important source of language exercise among the first-generation respondents.

Apparently the Chinese and Hungarians are not well served with radio in their respective languages. For the Chinese this may be a fairly complex problem altogether, since there will probably be a variety of languages involved. Nevertheless, both groups reported marked interest in having such programs broadcast.

The radio program appears to be the most flexible current means of providing real-life exercise in language retention. The high degree of its acceptance apparent in our findings indicates that it could play a very important role in efforts designed to maintain non-official language fluency and general use in Canada.

If linguistic diversity is to become a permanent and integrated feature of Canadian society, it may indeed be necessary to encourage the electronic media to provide high-quality productions in the various languages. The media have, clearly, a potential following of sufficient number to make them commercially viable if they are qualitatively competitive. It would (in our estimation) be a definite loss to ignore the contribution they might make to the frequency of language use among those who are currently able to do so, and for those who may wish to retain or regain that ability.

The crux of the study, and of the philosophy of multiculturalism which gave rise to it, turns on the desire of Canada's non-English or French residents to retain their ancestral heritage. In the particular instance of this research, the key variable was expressed support for language retention, and we turn now to an examination of our findings in this issue.

Support for Non-Official Language Retention

Support for retention of the non-official language is very widespread among Canada's metropolitan ethnic groups, However one defines support, whether in terms of absolute numbers, proportions or intensity, the data very clearly show it to be substantial. In the sampled cities and groups alone, nearly a million persons — almost one-twentieth of Canada's entire population — support the concept of non-official language retention. Moreover, an estimated 400,000 members of ten ethnic groups in five major cities across the country *strongly* support the concept of language retention. Over 150,000 Italians, 66,500 Germans and 54,000 Ukrainians (the three largest ethnic groups sampled) strongly supported language retention, while substantially more in each of these groups were in *general* favour of such a position. An estimated 118,000 persons from the ten groups in the five cities were unfavourably disposed towards language retention, while the remaining 270,000 were indifferent. Overall, 70 per cent of the respondents support language retention, and in each group, there is majority agreement that language retention is desirable. Overall, less than one in ten of all respondents were reported to find the concept of support for language retention either somewhat or very undesirable.

Were this a soft voice, or a "motherhood" vote, we might have expected a greater degree of general indifference to have appeared, but there is a most marked consistency in the data that indicates a high degree of reliability in the responses. Our evidence specifically on the intensity of support is consistent with this interpretation. Overall, language loss was mentioned most often as the most serious problem facing the ethnic group, by contrast with problems such as job discrimination or educational opportunities. Almost all of those who support language retention gave specific reasons for their position, but many in the small opposed group gave no reason at all.

The lack of serious opposition to the principle is striking. It is very strong evidence that our residents of other than French or English origin view their language as an important factor which can and should exist in conjunction with the official languages. We found very little to suggest even a moderate urge to suppress the language of origin in favour of the official languages. Furthermore, there are some very powerful group-by-group statistics which force the conclusion that language retention is a key issue among Greeks, Italians, Chinese and Ukrainians. It occupied much less prominence among Hungarians, Scandinavians and Dutch, but even among these groups there was fairly widespread support for language retention.

We believe our data are quite powerful on the issue of support for language retention, and that they clearly point to the need for programs to be developed to meet the expressed views of the respondents concerned. Our data contain also very detailed information on opinions about types of programs which need to be developed, and how they should be financed. On this point there are a number of conflicting views, and it is not possible for all suggestions to be implemented. But it is important to know that opinions do exist on these detailed questions, and should be taken into account in decision-making.

Support for language retention does decline somewhat in the second and third generations, but this decline is much less marked than the decline in actual language knowledge and use. This indicates that current rates of language loss are viewed as unsatisfactory not only by the immigrants, but also by their children and grandchildren. Our data show that highest levels of very favourable views on support were found among first-generation respondents while the highest reported indifference and unfavourability were found among second-generation and older family respondents. One in five first-generation respondents were very favourable towards support, twice as many somewhat favourable, a quarter were indifferent and less than 10 per cent unfavourable. Among the other generation respondents, a majority were in favour, and most of the rest were indifferent, rather than opposed.

Much of the support for language retention occurs among those respondents who already possess a substantial degree of knowledge of the tongue concerned. But this was by no means confined to such people only. Many who reported total loss of the ancestral language expressed firmly positive views on supporting its preservation. In other words, there is general support for language preservation by those who have lost it as well as language retention by those who still possess it.

The group-by-group support for language retention across all levels of current language knowledge is formidable evidence that a strongly felt need has been expressed and is worthy of recognition.

On a group-by-group analysis, it was clear that among first-generation respondents, Greeks, Ukrainians and Italians expressed the highest percentage favourably disposed towards language retention. Very similar but lower positive intensity results were obtained in groups with sufficient representation for other generations.

Support for language retention does not appear to adopt a curvilinear mode as some scholars have suggested. That is to say, there is no evidence that a decline for support occurs for the second generation followed by a reawakening of interest among the third and older generation respondents. In fact, the data indicate a more linear relationship with a levelling-off effect as generation increases. That a very important relationship between generation and support exists has been demonstrated by the study and this should be taken into account when multicultural policy decisions are being formulated.

Perhaps the greatest significance of the analyses linking generation to support lies in their reflection of the importance that language viability holds for the new settlers in Canada. While there is a reduction of this perceived importance for their children, there is little doubt that official recognition of both a substantive and moral nature would be well appreciated by the majority of Canada's non-official language residents and is actively sought after by several specific groups. We suggest that the data point quite clearly to the areas of greatest receptivity for active government support of preservation of non-official languages and that such support would be generally well received across all generations but primarily in the first and second.

One of our major interests was to see how retention is related to the persistence of ethnic self-identification, that is, whether a person of Italian origin defines himself as "Italian-Canadian," "Canadian of Italian origin" or simply as a "Canadian." Almost half of those defining themselves with a simple ethnic label see language retention as *highly* desirable. Very few found such retention undesirable. Of respondents identifying themselves generally as ethnic-Canadians or as Canadians of ethnic origin, one-third considered retention highly desirable and only one in twenty claimed it to be undesirable. These two groups do differ strongly from respondents who identified themselves as Canadians. But even in this latter group, a majority expressed general support for language retention.

On a group-by-group basis, among those describing themselves using an ethnic label, degree of demand for retention was highest among Greeks, Italians and Chinese and lowest among Scandinavians and Dutch. Scandinavians reported the highest percentage of respondents considering language retention undesirable, but Hungarians, Chinese and Portuguese were also relatively high in this regard.

The pattern is relatively clear-cut: self-identification — which was closely related to generation — is a guide to support for language retention. While the strongest support is definitely located among those who see themselves as still primarily attached to the ancestral country there was, nevertheless, no substantial overall opposition to language retention among most of those who identify as Canadians. Thus, it is suggested that a policy designed to preserve the languages of origin would be popular among non-French and non-English Canadians whether they identify themselves as Canadians or otherwise.

Issues in Language Retention

As was mentioned earlier, the groups exhibited a generally consistent pattern in which loss of language was represented as the prime cause of a major, usually *the* major, problem facing the group. This is a particularly interesting finding in the context of the study since, overall, almost one-third more respondents listed loss of language over job discrimination in the most serious problem category. That such a finding should appear is very significant indeed, in that it shows clearly the importance placed on language above the more economically related problem of job discrimination. Furthermore, language loss was considered a more pressing problem than a generalized fading of customs and tradition.

Every group but the newly arrived Portuguese listed language as the main problem. While it is clear from the data that the mass of respondents were not overly concerned with a multiplicity of issues and that even language loss itself was not considered an overriding concern, there is little doubt that the variable is a key to successful efforts in multicultural preservation.

In specific group terms, it should be noted that Chinese respondents reported the highest level of perceived job discrimination and that members of this group were also concerned about the fragmentation of their communities. We suggest that this latter problem may be a result of changes in the nature of the Chinese sections in the downtown areas of Vancouver and Toronto, where the cohesion of the Chinatowns has been threatened by development and rapidly rising taxes. Certainly it is a problem of significance for the Chinese and it is very difficult to offer suggestions for a possible solution.

Some of our most intriguing findings concerned the reasons given by respondents for supporting language retention. Very large percentages of respondents expressed reasons related to intra-group use and to direct cultural retention. These data, when combined, show that very large numbers mention two qualities of the non-official language, that of permitting communication between group members and assisting the group to maintain its own integrity and cultural viability.

Of those in favour of support who were asked for reasons why language retention might be undesirable, approximately 10 per cent felt that it may prevent mixing between group members and other Canadians. A sensitivity to the possible negative effects of the use of the language on the user's relationship with other Canadians may be present. This might reflect only an awareness of the possibility that others may become uncomfortable when they cannot understand a conversation, or it may indicate a by no means general concern that continued retention of the language directly inhibits relationships with others not of that ancestral language. Should the latter possibility be true, it could imply a disadvantage of such support. A similar trend was evident in responses drawn from those who regarded themselves as indifferent towards language retention and, as might be expected, a large percentage of respondents among those expressing opposition to language retention suggested that non-official language preservation may prevent mixing with other Canadians.

It seems that the mixing question is most prominent as the problem inherent in language retention. We suggest this to be a relevant finding of the study, since it documents a concern of some members of non-official language groups opposed to language retention. Their views are important since any decisions arising out of the study should also take into account possible effects on Canadians of ethnic origin who may be opposed to language retention.

In this study, those respondents negative to support were generally in a very small minority and were not completely related to a particular generation or to a single non-official language group. There is powerful evidence that positive reasons for the support of language retention are held by the vast majority of respondents and it is reasonable to assume that policy directions aimed at supporting non-official language would be very well received by the groups involved.

The study examined questions concerning several types of ethnic organizations which might contribute to language retention. Our data showed that participation in organized clubs and groups, other than churches, by members of the sample was not markedly high. While it was not possible to suggest that groups and organizations are not presently factors in ethnic groups' activities in the cities studied, it would certainly seem that the various clubs and such are not dominant in the social structure of the respondents' lives in Canada and that they currently should not be overestimated as sources of cultural and linguistic retention. It should be pointed out, however, that without such clubs, cultural and linguistic viability might be further impaired. Moreover, the club leaders may have some potential to mobilize political support for their points of view. Nevertheless, only one in ten respondents was engaged in an ethnic club or organization. To estimate *relative* importance of ethnic clubs, etc., compared with similar French or English organizations, we would require a study of, or figures concerning, the latter.

On the other hand, there may be a factor of cultural retention potential among the organizations used by the low retention support groups, such as Scandinavians and Dutch. In short, the possibility exists that cultural factors, other than linguistic, can be preserved by ethnic clubs, particularly those which deal with sports, arts, and social facets of ethnic relevance.

The relationship of the church to language retention was of considerable interest. It is very clear that there is a relationship between language preference in church and support for language retention. There are hazards in drawing conclusions of a causative nature from correlational data, but we did consider it likely that the church plays some role in language maintenance. Quite possibly, like the media and language support, the roles are interactive and the church might, in some instances, be strongly sustained should language be preserved. On a group-by-group basis, the relevance of the church becomes even more notable. Its importance in the case of the Greek language is most marked. This is in sharp contract to its very low relevance in the preservation of the Dutch language where almost all services were conducted in the official languages. It may be that a continuation of the trend towards use of the dominant local language in some churches will diminish the viability of the non-official language concerned and possibly erode its basis of support among those concerned in religious factors.

We investigated a number of other organizations and activities which might encourage the retention of the non-official language. These included the question of more visits to the old country, the establishment of summer camps for children, the establishment of group cultural centres and the provision of more books in the ancestral language. Each of these was examined in the context of language knowledge by groups and the data obtained illustrated the close relationship that existed between knowledge of the language and support for its retention. Generally, these organizations do not currently play a very substantial role in language retention, but they may well be developed to do so. Currently, they received most support from those who already have some knowledge of the ancestral tongue and least from those whose linguistic retention is very small or has vanished.

Ethnic Schools and Language Retention

At present perhaps the most direct attempt made at language retention is through instruction in group-supported schools. Since the schools are intended for the instruction of children, they are a direct expression of parents' interest in providing for language retention. Where parents are concerned, language retention is almost universally considered to be a good thing for their children whose time could be readily made available by parents for learning the non-official language. Whether this would be the case if there were to be conflicts with other activities considered essential for the child's education was not ascertained. In any case, there is very clear evidence that the ethnic schools are an active force in language retention.

The schools were found to be in widespread use for most groups interested in language retention. Nearly one-quarter of our respondents would have supported increasing their number and improving their quality. However, at least one-third considered such schools relatively unimportant in language retention. In short, our respondents are divided on the issue to a marked degree.

Again the pattern changes when group-by-group results are considered. There is strong support for group schools found among Greeks, Ukrainians, Italians and Chinese compared with minor interest among the Dutch and the Scandinavians. The split is very much apparent in these data and among results bearing on the best type of school to provide instruction in non-official languages.

In general, our respondents indicated that it is *not* the ethnic school which is most favoured as the source of language retention but the public school, and especially the lower grades of the public school. There is very strong and clear support among many members of Canada's ethnic minority groups for inclusion of the non-official languages in the courses of instruction and as vehicles of instruction in the public schools and especially in the elementary schools. This point should not be missed since it reflects a high degree of concern expressed by many parents for the teaching of the ancestral language to their children. Indeed, many said they would insist on their children taking the courses and almost all would encourage them to do so. The degree of intensity was closely related to generation, however, and we should point out that there was a substantial lessening of insistence and a greater degree of indifference recorded as generation increased.

Not surprisingly, a large number of respondents felt the primary responsibility for the teaching of cultural and linguistic retention lay with parents, but our data on loss-by-generation indicate this task is not being successfully borne by parents. Actually, the job of preserving language is quite possibly beyond them and we feel this is illustrated by the number (more than or close to half in all but the older families group) who nominated the schools as the prime agent of retention.

These data have substantial importance for multicultural policy development at all levels and we suggest that very detailed cross-tabulations of the current data and further studies by educational researchers be commissioned. The roles of educational agencies are difficult to interpret because of the cross-jurisdictional problems involved. However, it is very obvious that, for whatever they are worth, the ethnic schools are not seen by members of their groups as the best agency to shoulder the burden of language and heritage retention. There is a strongly expressed view that the best place to achieve their aim is in the public school system. There is mixed feeling, however, as to who should foot the bill. While more than one-third of all respondents in every generational group would call on the Canadian taxpayer to cover the cost of the provision of courses in, of and about the non-official language and culture, almost as many would place it directly on the parents and a substantial number would place it on the specific groups involved. In short, there are very mixed views on the costing of the teaching of the non-official language and culture and we suspect that there would be a strong demand for shared responsibility if programs involving these issues were to be promoted, whether in formal or informal educational institutions. . . .

Having arrived at the end of our report, we must note that in terms of study of the problems of language and culture in the context of Canadian multiculturalism, we are in fact at the beginning. This statement is more than a clichéd turn of phrase, because what we believe to be the most important fact of our research is that it has *provided* a beginning. We have, for the first time in this country, a wealth, almost an abundance, of information on our citizens and residents of origins of other than French or English. We have data that will fuel research, both theoretical and applied, for several years and we have a base against which change and effect can be measured.

Culture and Language as Factors in Learning and Education

WALLACE E. LAMBERT

It is difficult to dislodge deep-seated beliefs. The one I would like at least to loosen somewhat is the belief that culture and language have profound influences on cognitive processes. The trouble is that it makes awfully good common sense to say that people from different cultural or linguistic backgrounds think differently, and it even makes fairly good social-scientific sense. For instance, some time ago the anthropologist Lévy-Bruhl (1926) presented a certain type of evidence to support the idea that the thinking of "primitive peoples" differed in substance and structure from that of more "civilized" man. Although this thesis has been thoroughly criticized over the years, especially by other anthropologists, it has been difficult to devise decisive empirical counter-demonstrations so as to eradicate its influence within the behavioural sciences (cf. Cole, Gay, Glick and Sharp, 1971). In the case of language, the ethnolinguists Sapir (1921) and Whorf (1941) presented an equally attractive argument for language's influence on thought, and although disputed by many, it has also proved resistant to empirical counter-proofs (cf. Carroll and Casagrande, 1958).

Over and above the difficulties we all have in defining culture, language and thought, I have come to question the notion that culture (or language) affects cognitive structures and the related notion that culture affects the structure of personality. I was impressed early in my training with Kroeber's (1948) principle of the "psychic unity" of mankind, so much so that now I am persuaded that similarities among ethnolinguistic groups are much more prominent than differences; that cultural and linguistic backgrounds do not reach down to the basic structures of thought or personality; that variations of thought and personality within cultural or national groups (as reflected, for

SOURCE: *Education of Immigrant Students: Issues and Answers,* Aaron Wolfgang, Editor, Symposium Series/5, Toronto: The Ontario Institute for Studies in Education, 1975. Reprinted by permission of the author and OISE.

example, in socio-economic background differences) are much greater than between-group variations; and that few if any modal personality or modal cognitive profiles of any substance are likely to turn up in cross-cultural or cross-national research.

This statement of the matter is perhaps too enthusiastic and too strong in view of the important debates on the subject that are just getting under way. To be fair, it must be said that there actually are no good grounds yet available for deciding one way or the other. In the domain of language, for example, the Piaget school argues for the independence of language and thought while the Vygotsky school argues for an interdependence. In the domain of culture's influence, there is a socially significant debate going on between those who argue that certain cultural or linguistic groups are "deficient" relative to others and those who hold that it is a question of "differences" rather than "deficiencies." And now both of these points of view are challenged by a third that questions whether there are any real deficiencies *or* differences (Cole and Bruner, 1971; Cole, Gay, Glick and Sharp, 1971). Hopefully these debates will stimulate research that will in time help us to grapple better with the issues involved if we regard with a robust skepticism any claims about cultural or linguistic influences on the basic structures of thought or personality. There is, of course, no debate about the influence of culture and language on the *content* of thought or the *expression* of personality, but these are much less captivating than the one we are concerned with here.

My own early skepticism has been strengthened by personal research experiences where cultural and linguistic contrasts were expected to emerge, but didn't. It started with a large-scale, cross-national study Otto Klineberg and I conducted some years ago on children's conceptions of foreign peoples (Lambert and Klineberg, 1967). Anthropologists helped us select ten world settings that would likely provide cultural contrasts in the ways children view themselves, their own national or ethnic group, and foreign groups. For example, through interviews we solicited the views of large numbers of children in such supposedly diverse settings as Japan, Brazil, Israel, South Africa, Turkey, France, Canada and the United States. Instead of cultural or national contrasts, what emerged from this study was a large and consistent set of age changes in children's conceptions of the world, and these were essentially the same from one setting to another. There were some differences that appeared to be cultural in nature, but it would have been very difficult in our investigation to disentangle the influences of social class, types and amounts of schooling, amounts of travel experience, and the like from what seemed to be differences attributable solely to cultural setting. In this instance, then, we were expecting cultural differences; we gave them ample opportunity to show through; but few if any unambiguous ones did.

It happened again when I tried to investigate cultural differences between Canada's two main ethnic groups, the French and English Canadians (Lambert, 1970). Here the research involved between-group comparisons of attitudes, various aspects of social perception, indices of achievement motivation and competitiveness, and values associated with child training. Again, the major outcome was a pattern of similarities between the two ethnic groups, and the few contrasts that did turn up, as in the case of child training values (Lambert, Yackley and Hein, 1971), cannot be attributed to cultural factors in any simple direct way. They could, in fact, be due as much to differences in social class, education, religion and the like as to ethnic background. At McGill University we are still probing for reliable and unambiguous cultural differences among ethnic groups in Canada, and there is much work yet to do, particularly in making sure that we select comparison groups and testing procedures that will permit real cultural differences to show through. Nonetheless, when a serious attempt was made to find cultural differences where they might most be expected in the Canadian setting, few if any have as yet turned up.

One further research experience impressed me, this one conducted by my brother and Leigh Minturn (Minturn and W.W. Lambert, 1964), who were interested in the varieties of ways mothers bring up children and how upbringing affects personality. In collaboration with anthropologists they chose six cultural settings that, according to the anthropological literature, would likely provide the maximum in contrasts. Their investigation called for one- to two-year residences in each of the six cultural settings during which time detailed observations and interviews were carried out. The major outcome in this study was also unanticipated: they found very few instances of unambiguous cultural differences in styles of mothering. Instead the styles of mothering that did emerge seemed to depend on conditions such as the number of persons living within a particular space, the amount of time available, after required work, to be with children, and so forth. What struck me was that mothers from such diverse settings as southern India, the Philippines, Mexico and the United States could be so much alike in their associations with their children when account is taken of the environmental exigencies placed on them as parents, exigencies that can be found in all cultural settings.

These, then, are some personal experiences that have probably enhanced the bias in my thinking. Bias or not, it was nonetheless reassuring to read a recent article by Michael Cole and Jerome Bruner (1971), who support a very similar point of view. As they examined the claim that children of minority groups suffer from some sort of intellectual deficit, they were far from convinced. In fact, they argued that the theory as well as the data now available "casts doubt on the conclusion that a deficit exists in minority group children, and even raises doubts as to whether any nonsuperficial *differences* exist among different cultural groups" (p. 868; italics in original). A similar idea has recently come from a less technical and less academic source: Richard Hoggart, the Assistant Director-General of UNESCO, from his own experiences has developed a faith in cross-cultural communication and understanding because of the "common qualities, the ribs of the universal human grammar" that link all men, and because of "common experience" and "common sorrows which above all link us" (Hoggart, 1972).

There are thus the beginnings of an argument to be made against cultural or linguistic differences and their putative impingement on the structures of personality and cognition, and in time the argument may become convincing enough to disturb deep-seated beliefs to the contrary. But until that time arrives, the argument for most people will remain academic. It is this dilemma that intrigues me: namely, that people's beliefs can become so pervasive and so deeply rooted that no attention is given to evidence that might either support or contradict the beliefs held. A researcher confronted with this inconsistency might be well advised to drop the topic and move on to other research matters. But I feel that it is more productive to study the beliefs themselves and to try to understand their workings — in this case, to examine people's beliefs about the influence of culture and language and try to understand how such beliefs affect the lives of both ethnic majority and ethnic minority groups. Perhaps with our focus on belief systems we can better understand the practical importance of cultural and linguistic backgrounds in learning and education and see more clearly ways of ameliorating the learning experiences of young people from "different" backgrounds.

Let us start, then, with the working hypothesis that most people believe that cultures differ in basic ways and that cultural and linguistic backgrounds shape our personalities and our modes of thought. Beliefs of this sort are rooted in the early socialization of children. For instance, our own cross-national research on children's views of foreign peoples (Lambert and Klineberg, 1967) indicates that, from infancy on, young children are puzzled about who they are, where the limits of their own family or community or nation lie, and what criteria should be used to differentiate in-groups from out-groups. Parents, it turns out, become the crucial teachers of children in providing answers to these questions, and what parents typically do (regardless of their "cultural" background) is to draw contrasts for the child between the child's own ethnic group and various other, usually quite distinctive, foreign peoples. This parental training in contrasts among ethnic groups uses the own group as a reference point, and typically the own group is stereotyped and presented in a better-than, more favourable light than the comparison groups. Through early education in group contrasts, then, children are likely to pick up the idea that other peoples are different, strange and generally less good and less dependable. Through schooling, these early-developed beliefs are usually strengthened by training in civics, history and social studies to the extent that this aspect of education draws contrasts of own nation and own social system in comparison with distinctive others in foreign settings, and does so with an ethnocentric bias. Thus education within the family and within the school typically contributes to a belief that one's own national or cultural group is special, and this is done with the best of aims — socializing the child, or preparing him to take on constructive roles in his own community and society.

The perception of cultural differences is enhanced as well by people's tendencies to link cultures with specific languages or dialects, these linguistic differences being concrete and real. To the extent that cultural or national differences are more apparent than real, the language associated with particular ethnic groups take on all the more social significance, as though the language differences are used in people's thinking to verify the belief in cultural differences. The tendency to reify the link between a culture and a particular use of language is as characteristic of those who judge speakers of a foreign language as it is of those so judged. It is not difficult, therefore, to understand why linguistic minority groups often demand and fight for the right to use their own language as a working or learning language instead of a national or international language that might well be of more practical or utilitarian value. In my view this becomes a powerful emotional issue because the group's identity is associated with its distinctive language, and this linguistic distinctiveness becomes an enormously precious personal characteristic that dominates that group's system of beliefs. Because culture and language become linked in people's thinking, the more one questions the reality of differences in culture, the more important the distinctiveness of the language becomes.

We can start then with the proposition that linguistic distinctiveness is a basic component of personal identity for members of an ethnic group; ethnicity and language become associated in the thinking of those outside a particular ethnic group as well as those within the group. With these assumptions about people's belief systems as a reference point, I would like to discuss certain socially relevant questions that some of us at McGill are trying to answer. The questions are:

1. Do people's beliefs about a particular ethnolinguistic group affect the efficiency of learning that group's language?
2. Is there any basis to the belief that in becoming bilingual or bicultural one dulls his cognitive powers and dilutes his identity?
3. Should minority groups try to maintain their ethnolinguistic identities and heritages in the North American setting?

These questions are interdependent. The first suggests a way of testing whether beliefs are really important for the learning process — specifically, whether attitudes toward a particular cultural group affect the efficiency of learning that group's language. Similarly, one wonders if beliefs about an ethnic group are contagious enough to affect the desire of members of the ethnic group itself to maintain the language. In other words, the first question explores the way beliefs about a cultural group get associated with the language that group speaks and thereby affect the language-learning process. The second question examines the sacredness of the language–culture link by exploring the not uncommon belief that in becoming bilingual and bicultural (that is, violating the "one-language–one-culture" rule), one deteriorates his cognitive powers and the clarity of his cultural identity. The third question depends on the answers to the other two. Depending on the truth or falsity of the belief that bilingualism and biculturalism are debilitators, and on the importance of such a belief for the learning process, we would approach the adjustment problems of ethnolinguistic minority groups in quite different ways. Our major goal, then, is to suggest appropriate ways of helping ethnolinguistic minority groups who may become victims of other people's belief systems as well as their own.

Do beliefs about a particular ethnolinguistic group affect the efficiency of learning that group's language?

Robert Gardner and I first became interested in people's beliefs about foreign groups in the context of learning and teaching foreign languages (Gardner and Lambert, 1972). How is it, we asked ourselves, that some people can learn a second or foreign language so easily and so well while others, given what seem to be the same opportunities to learn, find it almost impossible? With this as a start, we began to wonder about the more general question of what it is to have a knack for languages. To say that one has to have "an ear for languages" is to give an excuse rather than an answer, since it is too easy to transfer mysteries to biology as the source of either linguistic difficulties or linguistic genius. Perhaps the knack for languages lies in a profile of abilities or aptitudes that develop differently from person to person, some profiles favouring the language-learning process more than others.

This idea makes good sense, but there is likely something more to it than aptitudes. Everyone or almost everyone learns his native language painlessly; so why would not everyone have at least a minimally adequate aptitude profile? And history makes it clear that when societies want to keep two or more languages alive, and learning more than one is taken for granted, everyone seems to learn two or more as a matter of course.

As social psychologists we believed that there was something more involved. We expected that success in mastering a foreign language would depend not only on intellectual capacity and language aptitude but also on the learner's perceptions of and beliefs about the other ethnolinguistic group, his attitudes toward representatives of that group, and his willingness to identify enough to adopt the distinctive aspects of the behaviour, linguistic and nonlinguistic, that characterizes that other group. The learner's motivation for language study, it follows, would be determined by his attitudes and readiness to identify and by his orientation to the whole process of learning a foreign language.

We saw many possible forms the student's orientation could take, two of which we looked at in some detail: an "instrumental" outlook, reflecting the practical value and advantages of learning a new language, and an "integrative" outlook, reflecting a sincere and personal interest in the people and culture represented by the other group. It was our hunch that an integrative orientation would sustain better the long-term motivation needed for the very demanding task of second-language learning, and here we had in mind students in North American contexts studying the popular European languages. For the serious student who in time really masters the foreign language, we saw the possibility of a conflict of identity or alienation (we used the term *anomie*) arising as he became skilled enough to become an accepted member of a new cultural group. His knowledge of the language and the people involved would both prepare him for membership and serve as a symptom to members of the other group of his interests and affection. Thus the development of skill in the language could lead the language student ever closer to a point where adjustments in allegiances would be called for.

In our early studies with English-speaking Canadians in Montreal, we found support for such a theory: achievement in French, studied as a second language at the high school level, was dependent upon linguistic aptitude and verbal intelligence on the one hand, and, quite independent of aptitude, upon a sympathic set of beliefs toward French people and the French way of life. It was this integrative orientation that apparently provided a strong motivation to learn the other group's language. In the Montreal setting, students with an integrative orientation were more successful in second-language learning than those who were instrumentally oriented.

A follow-up study (Gardner, 1960) confirmed and extended these findings, using a larger sample of English-Canadian students and incorporating various measures of French achievement. In this case it was difficult to dissociate aptitude from motivational variables since they emerged in a common factor that included not only French skills stressed in standard academic courses but also those skills developed through active use of the language in communication. Apparently, in the Montreal context, the intelligent and linguistically gifted student of French is more likely to be integratively oriented, and hence more probably capable of becoming outstanding in all aspects of French proficiency. Still in the same study, the measures of orientation and desire to learn French emerged as separate factors, independent of language aptitude, and in these instances it was evident that they play an important role on their own, especially in the development of expressive skills in French. Further evidence from the intercorrelations indicated that this integrative motive was the converse of an authoritarian ideological syndrome; and this finding opens the possibility that basic personality dispositions may be involved in language-learning efficiency. The integrative motive, incidentally, is not simply the result of having more experience with French at home. Rather it seems to depend on the family-wide attitudinal disposition.

The same ideas were tested out in three American settings (communities in Louisiana, Maine and Connecticut) with English-speaking American high school students learning French. Although each community has its own interesting patterns of results, the role played by attitudes toward one's own group and toward foreign groups emerged again as an important influence on the learning process.

Attitudes of this sort also affect the language learning of French-American young people in these same settings, for it affects the ways they adjust to the bicultural demands made on them. For example, it became evident in our investigation that the attitudes of French-American adolescents toward their own ethnolinguistic group and toward the American way of life can influence their development of linguistic skills in French and English: in some instances there may be a dominance of French over English, in other instances a dominance of English over French, and in still others a bilingual competence. The outcome seems to be determined, in part at least, by the way the young French-American handles the conflicts of allegiances he is bound to encounter. For instance, we found in Louisiana that positive attitudes of French-American teenagers toward the French-American culture, coupled with favourable stereotypes of the European-French, were highly correlated with expressive skills in French. Other types of outlook, however, seem to restrict the potential development of these young people. Thus, a very strong pro-French attitudinal bias or an exceptionally strong motivation and drive to learn French does not automatically promote outstanding competence in the French language. Nor does a strong pro-American outlook assure proficiency in English.

Certain modes of adjustment were especially instructive in the sense that they provide the young French-American with models of how best to capitalize on his bicultural heritage. In Louisiana, for example, students who had very favourable attitudes toward their own cultural group and who also had a good competence in English were outstanding on various measures of proficiency in French. This pattern suggests that French-Americans who are content and comfortable with both facets of their cultural and linguistic heritage are psychologically free to become full bilinguals. In Maine we noted a somewhat different type of adjustment, one of equal interest: French-American students who have a strong instrumental orientation toward French study, and who receive parental encouragement to do well in French, demonstrate outstanding skills in various aspects of French and feel assured of their competence in both French and English. While "instrumental" has a quite different meaning for students learning their own language, this family-supported instrumental approach offers the French-American a real chance of being both French and American.

To test further these notions, we wondered whether they would apply in more foreign settings. This led us to the Philippines, where a foreign language (English) has become not only a second national language but also the medium of instruction from the early grades on and an essential language for economic advancement and success. For the Philippine study we had to rework the content of many of our measures and change our expectations about student reactions, for in this case the language being offered has enormous instrumental value. The results of this investigation brought to light certain cross-nationally stable relationships and certain others that are tied to particular cultural contexts. For example, we found that Filipino students who approach the study of English with an instrumental orientation and who receive parental support for this outlook were clearly successful in developing proficiency in the language. Thus, it seems that in settings where there is an urgency about mastering a second language — as there is in the Philippines, and in North America for members of linguistic minority groups — the instrumental approach to language study is extremely effective. Nevertheless, for another subgroup of Filipino students, an integrative orientation toward the study of English had a striking effect on proficiency, especially the audiolingual aspects. This cross-cultural support for the importance of motivational and attitudinal dispositions strengthens greatly our confidence in the basic notions we started with.

But still the Philippine investigation changed our perspective on the instrumental–integrative contrast. We see now that the typical student of *foreign* languages in North America will profit more if he is helped to develop an integrative outlook toward the group whose language is being offered. For him, an instrumental approach has little significance and little motive force. However, for members of ethnic minority groups in North America, as for peoples of nations that have imported prestigious world languages and made them important national languages, the picture changes. Learning a second language of national or worldwide significance is then indispensable, and both instrumental and integrative orientations toward the learning task must be developed. The challenge for these minority groups or those who import languages is to keep their own linguistic and cultural identity alive while mastering the second language, and in this regard various findings indicate that becoming bilingual does not mean losing identity. In fact, we are now convinced that striving for a comfortable place in two cultural systems may be the best motivational basis for becoming bilingual and in turn is one's best guarantee for really belonging to both cultures.

These investigations make it very clear that beliefs about foreign peoples and about one's own ethnicity are powerful factors in the learning of another group's language and in the maintenance of one's own language.

Is there any basis to the belief that in becoming bilingual or bicultural one dulls his cognitive powers and dissipates his identity?

EFFECTS ON COGNITION

The technical literature on the consequences of becoming bilingual or bicultural stretches back to the turn of the century and is still growing. In the early literature (1920s and 1930s) we find a generally pessimistic outlook on the effects of bilingualism, but since the 1960s there is a much more optimistic picture emerging. Bilingualism and biculturalism, as one might expect, generate much emotional and political steam, which often clouds whatever facts are available. In general, the researchers in the early period expected to find all sorts of problems, and they usually did: bilingual children, relative to monolinguals, were behind in school, retarded in measured intelligence, and socially adrift. One trouble with most of the early studies was that little care was taken to check out the essentials before comparing monolingual and bilingual subjects. Thus, social-class backgrounds, educational opportunities, and the like were not controlled, nor was much attention given to determining *how* bilingual or monolingual the comparison groups actually were. But even though there were grounds to worry about the adequacy of many of these studies, there was nonetheless an overwhelming trend in the outcomes: the largest proportion of these investigations concluded that bilingualism has a detrimental effect on intellectual functioning, a smaller number found little or no relation between bilingualism and intelligence, and only two suggested that bilingualism might have favourable consequences on cognition.

With this picture as background, Elizabeth Anisfeld and I started an investigation on the bilingual–monolingual topic in 1962 in the Canadian setting. We, of course, had strong expectations of finding a bilingual deficit as the literature suggested, but we wanted to pinpoint what the intellectual components of the deficit were in order to develop compensatory education programs. We argued that a large proportion of the world's population is, by the exigencies of life, bound to be bilingual, and it seemed to us appropriate to help them if possible.

We were able in our first investigation to profit from most of the shortcomings of earlier research, and thus felt relatively confident about the results (see Lambert and Anisfeld, 1969). What surprised us, though, was that French-English bilingual children in the Montreal setting scored significantly ahead of carefully matched monolinguals both on verbal and nonverbal measures of intelligence. Furthermore, the patterns of test results suggested to us that the bilinguals had a more diversified structure of intelligence, as measured, and more flexibility in thought.

For someone who doesn't really believe that language influences thought, these results — suggesting the possibility that a double-language experience might affect the structure and flexibility of thought — came as a double-barrelled surprise. But one investigation rarely has enough weight to change the course of events, even though an important follow-up study (Anisfeld, 1964) confirmed the 1962 conclusions. What was needed was confirmation from other settings and from studies with different approaches.

Since then confirmations have started to emerge from carefully conducted research around the world: from Singapore (Torrance,

Gowan, Wu and Aliotti, 1970), from Switzerland (Balkan, 1970), from South Africa (Ianco-Worrall, 1972), from Israel and New York (Ben-Zeev, 1972), from Western Canada (Cummins and Gulutsan, 1973), and, using a quite different approach, from Montreal (Scott, 1973). All of these studies (and we have found no others in the recent literature to contradict them) indicate the bilingual children, relative to monolingual controls, show a definite advantage on measures of "cognitive flexibility," "creativity," or "divergent thought." Sandra Ben-Zeev's study, for example, involved Hebrew-English bilingual children in New York and Israel, and the results strongly support the conclusion that bilinguals have greater "cognitive flexibility." In this case the term means that bilinguals have greater "skill at auditory reorganization" of verbal material and a much more "flexible manipulation of the linguistic code," and are more advanced in "concrete operational thinking," as these were measured in her investigation. Anita Ianco-Worrall's study involving Afrikaans-English bilingual children in Pretoria, South Africa, lends equally strong support for a somewhat different form of cognitive flexibility — an advantage over monolingual controls in separating word meaning from word sound. The conclusion is drawn that the bilinguals were between two and three years advanced in this feature of cognitive development. Ianco-Worrall also found good support for a bilingual precocity in realizing the arbitrary assignment of names to referents, a feature of thinking that Vygotsky (1962) believed reflected insight and sophistication.

The recent study by Sheridan Scott (1973), involving French-English bilinguals in Montreal is perhaps the most persuasive. She worked with data collected over a seven-year period from two groups of English-Canadian children. One group had become functionally bilingual in French during the time period because they had attended experimental classes where most of the instruction was in French. The other group had followed a conventional English-language education program. At the grade 1 level, the two groups had been equated for measured intelligence, socioeconomic background, and parental attitudes toward French people. In fact, had the opportunity been presented to them, it is likely that most the parents in the control group would have enrolled their children in the experimental French program, but no such opportunity was available since it was decided in advance to start only one experimental class per year (see Lambert and Tucker, 1972).

Scott was interested in the effect becoming bilingual would have on the cognitive development of the children — in particular, what effect it would have on the children's "divergent thinking," a special type of cognitive flexibility. The term was apparently introduced by Guilford

(1950, 1956) to characterize a cognitive style that contrasts with "convergent thinking." Convergent thinking is measured by tests that provide a number of pieces of information that the subject must synthesize to arrive at a correct answer; thus, the information provided will funnel in or converge on a correct solution. Divergent thinking provides a starting-point for thought — "Think of a paper clip" — and asks the subject to generate a whole series of permissible solutions — "and tell me all the things one could do with it." Some researchers have considered divergent thinking as an index of creativity (e.g., Getzels and Jackson, 1962), while others suggest that until more is known it is best viewed as a distinctive cognitive style reflecting a rich imagination and an ability to scan rapidly a host of possible solutions.

Scott was interested, among other things, in whether bilingualism promotes divergent thinking. Her results, based on a multivariate analysis, show a substantial advantage for the bilingual over the monolingual children on the divergent thinking tests, and in this investigation one can examine the year-by-year development of the advantage. Her study opens up many interesting possibilities for more in-depth analysis of the bilingual's thought processes.

There is, then, an impressive array of evidence accumulating that argues plainly against the commonsense notion that becoming bilingual — having two strings to one's bow, or two linguistic systems within one's brain — naturally divides a person's cognitive resources and reduces his efficiency of thought. Instead we can now put forth a very persuasive argument that there is a definite cognitive advantage for bilingual over monolingual children in the domain of cognitive flexibility. Only further research will tell us how this advantage, assuming it is a reliable phenomenon, actually works: whether it is based on a better storage of information by bilinguals, whether the separation of linguistic symbols from their referents or the ability to separate word meaning from word sound is the key factor, whether contrast of two linguistic systems aids in the development of general conceptual thought, or whatever. In any case, this new trend in research should give second thoughts to those who have used the notion of bilingual deficit as an argument for melting down ethnic groups. Hopefully, too, it will provide a new insight to those ethnolinguistic groups who may also have been led to believe in that notion.

One feature of the studies just reviewed merits special attention: all the cases reported (in Singapore, South Africa, Switzerland, Israel, New York and Montreal) dealt with bilinguals using two languages both of which have social value and respect in their respective settings. Thus, to know Afrikaans and English in South Africa, Hebrew and

English in New York and Israel, or French and English in Montreal would in each case be to add a second socially relevant language to one's repertoire of skills. In no case would the learning of the second language portend the dropping or the replacement of the other; the development of high-level skills in English among French-Canadians or Spanish-Americans does not imply a corresponding loss of French or Spanish.

We might refer to these examples of an *additive* form of bilingualism and contrast that with a more *subtractive* form experienced by many ethnic minority groups who, because of national education policies and social pressures of various sorts, are forced to put aside their ethnic language for a national language. Their degree of bilinguality at any point in time would likely reflect some stage in the subtraction of the ethnic language and its replacement with another. The important educational task of the future, it seems to me, is to transform the pressures on ethnic groups so that they can profit from an *additive* form of bilingualism, and, as we'll see in the final section, this project runs up against beliefs and attitudes again.

EFFECTS ON IDENTITY

What about the notion that becoming bilingual and bicultural subtracts, through division, from one's sense of personal identity? Here, too, there are signs in the recent literature of interest in this topic, but there are still only a few studies to draw on. Three, however, do bear on the issue of the identity of bilinguals, and all three are encouraging in their outcomes.

The first is the study, mentioned earlier, of French-Americans in communities in New England and Louisiana (Gardner and Lambert, 1972) and their ways of coping with a dual heritage. Some oriented themselves definitely toward their French background and tried to ignore their American roots; others were tugged more toward the American pole at the expense of their Frenchness; and still others apparently tried not to think in ethnic terms, as though they did not consider themselves as being either French or American. These three types of reactions parallel closely those of Italian-American adolescents studied earlier by Child (1943). To me these ways of coping characterize the anguish of members of ethnic groups when caught up in a subtractive form of biculturalism — that is, where social pressures are exerted on them to give up one aspect of their dual identity for the sake of blending into a national scene. We will return to these three reaction styles later when we can contrast them with a fourth sytle, which reflects an additive form of biculturalism, that also turned up in our study of French-Americans. The important point here is that identities are fragile and they can, through social pressures, be easily tipped off balance.

Identities need not be so disturbed, though, as the study of Aellen and Lambert (1969) showed. In this case we were interested in the adjustments made by adolescent children of English-French mixed marriages in the Montreal setting. We examined the degree and direction of the offspring's ethnic identifications as well as a selected set of their attitudes, values and personality characteristics.

The children of these mixed marriages come in contact with and are usually expected to learn the distinctive social and behavioural characteristics of the two cultures represented in their families. The question is whether the demands made on them necessarily generate conflicts, whether the experience with two cultures possibly broadens and liberalizes them, or whether some combination of both outcomes is typical. In addition to the cultural demands made on them, the children of mixed-ethnic marriages may face other difficulties to the extent that their parents, as suggested by Gordon (1964) and Saucier (1965), may have married outside their ethnic group because of personal instability and immaturity. Much of the previous research suggests that persons who intermarry in this way often have relatively strong feelings of alienation, self-hatred and worthlessness, and are disorganized and demoralized. Mixed-ethnic children might well find it difficult to identify with their parents if these characteristics are typical or representative. Still, the children could develop understanding and sympathy for parents with such an outlook. On the other hand, people may intermarry in many instances because they have developed essentially healthy attitudes and orientations that are nonetheless inappropriate within their own ethnic group, a situation that could make intermarriage with a sympathetic outsider particularly attractive. They may have become like Park's marginal man, "the individual with the wider horizon, the keener intelligence, the more detached and rational viewpoint . . . always relatively the more civilized human being" (Park, 1950, p. 376). In that case, their children might be particularly well trained in tolerance and openmindedness, especially since the children themselves are likely to feel that they, unlike their parents, are automatically members of *both* ethnic groups. The purpose of this investigation was to examine both these possibilities as objectively as possible by comparing groups of adolescent boys of mixed French-English parentage with others of homogeneous background, either French or English. All groups in the comparison were similar with respect to age, socioeconomic class, intelligence and number of siblings.

It was found that the profile of characteristics of the boys with mixed-ethnic parentage is a healthy one in every respect when comparisons are made with groups from homogeneous ethnic backgrounds. They identify with their parents, especially with their fathers, as well as the comparison groups do; they relate themselves to and identify with both ethnic reference groups, particularly those in a French academic environment; they show no signs of personality disturbances, social alienation or anxiety; nor do their self-concepts deviate from those of the comparison subjects. They see their parents as giving them relatively more attention and personal interest, and their attitudes toward parents are as favourable as those of the comparison groups. They seek out distinctively affectionate relationships with peers. Their general attitudinal orientations are similar to those of the comparison groups, while their specific attitudes toward both English and French Canadians are relatively unbiased. Their values show the influence of both ethnic backgrounds, as do their achievement orientations, which are less extreme than those of the comparison groups. Rather than developing a divided allegiance or repressing one or both aspects of their backgrounds, as has been noted among the offspring of certain immigrant groups (e.g., Child, 1943), they apparently have developed a dual allegiance that permits them to identify with both their parents, and to feel that they themselves are wanted as family members. One of the mixed-ethnic boys summed up this finding by saying: "I respect both my parents, and I respect their origins." One might argue that the concern of the parents of these adolescents to "include" their children is exaggerated, a symptom of tension and value conflict; but such an interpretation is negated by the apparent success the parents have had in passing on a sense of being wanted. There are, however, many features of this pattern of results that need further study.

This profile sketch is more pronounced for the mixed-ethnic subjects who are part of the French-Canadian high school environment. These young people may be more susceptible to the English-Canadian culture than those attending English-Canadian schools would be to French-Canadian culture, because of the Canadian cultural tug-of-war that seems (at least until recently) to be controlled by the more powerful and prestigious English-Canadian communities (see Lambert, 1967).

Two general modes of adjustment to a mixed ethnic background became apparent. In one case, the children incorporate both ethnic streams of influence, which are either modified by the parents before they are passed on to their children or are tempered by the children themselves, so that they are less extreme than those represented by either of the major reference groups. A tendency to amalgamate both cultural streams of influence is suggested by the contrasts noted between the mixed-ethnic groups and the homogeneous groups: for example, the unbiased ethnic identifications of the former, their perceptions of parents as being inclusive, their favourable attitudes toward both English and French Canadians, and their less extreme achievement values. In the other case, they tend to adapt their views to the predominant features of the academic and cultural environment in which they find themselves. This form of adjustment is suggested by the tendency of the mixed-ethnic groups to line up with the respective homogeneous groups with whom they attend high school, such as in their choices of the values they hope to pass on to their own children, the personality traits they see as undesirable, and their judgments of the relative attractiveness of English-Canadian or French-Canadian girls.

This illustration provides hope for biculturality in the sense that offspring of mixed-ethnic marriages appear to profit from the dual cultural influences found in their families. Rather than cultural conflicts, we find well-adjusted young people with broad perspectives who are comfortable in the role of representing both of their cultural backgrounds. We also have here an illustration of the additive form of biculturalism; the boys studied were caught in the flow of two cultural streams and were apparently happy to be part of both streams.

There is a similar outcome in the investigation, mentioned earlier, conducted by Richard Tucker and myself (Lambert and Tucker, 1972) concerning the English-Canadian children who took the greater part of their elementary schooling via French, and who after grades 5 and 6 had become functionally bilingual. Here we were able to measure on a yearly basis their self-conceptions and their attitudes toward English-Canadian, French-Canadian, and European-French ways of life. The attitude profiles of the children in the experimental French program indicate that by grade 5 important affective changes have occurred during the course of the project. The children state that they enjoy the form of education they are receiving and want to stay with it; their feelings toward French people have become decidedly more favourable; and they now think of themselves as being both French and English Canadian in personal makeup.

It is this apparent identification with French people — those from Canada and those from Europe — that raises the question of biculturalism. Has the program made the children more bicultural? It is difficult to answer this question because the meaning of bicultural is so vague. It is certain that the children now feel they can be at ease in both French and English-Canadian social settings, and that they are becoming both French and English in certain regards; but they are not becoming less English as a consequence. It is certain too they have learned that in classes with European-French teachers they should stand when a visitor enters, while they need not stand in classes that are conducted by English-Canadian or French-Canadian teachers. We wonder how much more there is to being bicultural beyond knowing thoroughly the languages involved, feeling personally aligned with both groups, and knowing how to behave in the two atmospheres. Are there any deeper personal aspects to cultural differences? That is, does culture actually affect personality all that much, or is it perhaps a more superficial and thinner wrapping than many social scientists have suggested?

The attitudes of the parents at the start of the project were basically friendly and favourable, although marked with very little knowledge about the French-Canadian people around them. These parents wanted their children to learn French for essentially integrative reasons — getting to know the other ethnic group and their distinctive ways — but they did not want them to go so far as to think and feel as French Canadians do — in other words, to lose their English-Canadian identity. How will they interpret the attitudes of their children who by grade 5 come to think of themselves as being both English and French Canadian in disposition and outlook? Some may see this as a worrisome sign of identity loss, but we believe they will come to interpret their children's enjoyment in having both English and French Canadian friends and both types of outlooks as a valuable addition, not a subtraction or cancellation of identities. As we see it, the children are acquiring a second social over-coat that seems to increase their interest in dressing up and reduces the wear and tear placed on either coat alone. Our guess is that the children are beginning to convince any worried parents that the experience is, in fact, enriching and worthwhile.

Of course, the parents cannot share fully their children's experience or their development of a dual identity. Nevertheless, in the few noticeable cases where the divergence of views between parents and children has become very apparent, even those parents give the impression that they are pleased that their children are being prepared to take their place in a new type of multilingual and multicultural society and help shape its development. As parents, they can easily take pride in the fact that they have gone out of their way to help in this special type of preparation.

These studies suggest to us that there is no basis in reality for the belief that becoming bilingual or bicultural necessarily means a loss or dissolution of identity. We are aware of the possible pressures that can surround members of ethnolinguistic minority groups and make them hesitant to become full-fledged members of two cultural communities. At the same time, though, we see how easy and rewarding it can be for those who are able to capitalize on a dual heritage. The question of most interest, then, is how in modern societies these possibilities can be extended to ethnolinguistic minority groups, and this is the major issue of the section to follow.

Should minority groups try to maintain their ethnolinguistic identity and heritage in the North American setting?

In order to suggest an answer to this question, it seems to me that we need first to examine in more detail the types of conflicts ethnolinguistic groups in North America can encounter in their attempts to adjust to the bicultural demands made on them. Hopefully through this explanation we will be able to discern which factors in the society lead to crises of allegiances and which provide opportunities for a comfortable bicultural identity. To this end, we will start with the case of French Canadians and their continuing struggle to survive as an ethnic group. Perhaps through a brief survey of Canadian research we can get a perspective on the general problems faced by ethnic minorities.

A series of investigations was started in 1958 with French-Canadian (FC) and English-Canadian (EC) residents of Montreal, a setting with a long history of inter-ethnic group tensions. The research technique employed in these studies, referred to as the "matched-guise" procedure, has groups of subjects drawn from various age and social-class levels of the EC and FC communities give their impressions or evaluations of the personality characteristics of speakers who represent their own and the other ethnic groups. Thus, groups of EC and FC subjects are asked to estimate or judge the probable personality traints of a number of speakers — say, twelve — presented to them on tape. Half of the speakers use French and half use English in reading a standard translation-equivalent passage. Listeners are kept in the dark about the fact that they are hearing not twelve speakers but rather six balanced French-English bilinguals, and the reactions elicited by each speaker's two linguistic guises are later matched up and compared statistically (see Lambert, 1967; Giles, 1971a). The procedure has proven instructive and useful as a means of investigating social tensions in bicultural or multi-ethnic settings such as Quebec (see Lambert, 1970), Israel (Lambert, M., Anisfeld and Yeni-Komshian, 1965), and Great Britain (Giles, 1971b).

The early research showed that EC college students evaluate the personality of speakers more favourably when the speakers use their EC rather than their FC linguistic guise. Furthermore, and somewhat surprising, FC students showed the same tendency in a more exaggerated form; that is, they too rated the EC guises much more favourably than the FC guises (Lambert, 1967). Apparently, then, both English and French Canadians attribute different status and different degrees of respect to those who represent the two communities in French Canada.

But there are in Quebec various forms of French currently in use, and each of these is also given its own position in the status hierarchy. For example, Chiasson-Lavoie and Laberge (1971) recently found evidence of a linguistic insecurity among working-class French Canadians in Montreal. D'Anglejan and Tucker (1973) also reported on a similar type of language sensitivity, which shows itself in an over-attention to correctness of speech among working-class French Canadians and a marked preference for European-style French by French Canadians of various regional and occupational backgrounds. Thus French Canadians tend to react, as minority groups often do, by downgrading their own characteristic modes of behaviour, including speech.

These sociolinguistic phenomena also affect the fate and durability of social contacts between members of various ethnic and linguistic groups. For instance, the status relations and role expectations of the two or more people involved in social interaction are likely coloured by the inferences each person makes of the others — inferences that are based to an important extent on speech styles (Giles, 1971c; 1972).

The dilemmas are not merely those of college-age people in the French-Canadian community, for youngsters also get involved, and in this case too there are no signs of amelioration when 1960s and 1970s research is compared. In 1962 Elizabeth Anisfeld and I (Anisfeld and Lambert, 1964) examined the reactions of ten-year-old French-Canadian children to the matched guises of bilingual youngsters of their own age reading French and English versions of a standard passage and found that the FC guises of the speakers were rated more favourably than the EC guises on a whole series of traits. One decade later, Sylvie Lambert (1973) took a further and more extensive look at ten-year-old French Canadians' self-views. Her results, collected in 1972, suggest that these children now downgrade representatives of their own ethnolinguistic group to a marked degree in comparison with representatives of the European-French (EF) community; and on a selection of traits related to social attractiveness (such as interestingness, amusingness, sureness of self), they evaluate their own group less favourably than ECs. What is particularly instructive about this study is that it included the views of French-Canadian school teachers, and it was found that elementary school teachers have essentially the same profiles of stereotypes as the ten-year-olds. The social implications of these trends and the changes noted over a ten-year period are enormous.

All told, these research findings indicate that little has been done in

North America to help ethnolinguistic minority groups maintain respect in their linguistic and cultural heritage so that they could become full-fledged bicultural members of their national society. There are, however, several recent developments in the American society that hold out a new and exciting type of hope. These developments, in fact, constitute another instance where the United States has an opportunity to set an outstanding example of what can be done for ethnic minority groups. The first development is a new perspective, generated it seems by the critical self-analysis of college activists in the 1960s, on what it means to be American. It was American college students who demanded national respect for minority groups of every variety, including Afro-Americans and American Indians. As a nation, these young people argued, we have no right to wash out distinctive traditions of any minority group since their ways of life, relative to the so-called American way of life, are in many respects admirable.

The second development, which may have stemmed from the first, takes the form of a national willingness to help minority groups. One way this willingness manifests itself is in new education laws that provide extensive schooling in Spanish for Spanish-Americans in the large centres, in the passage of the Bilingual Education Act, and in new laws passed in states such as Massachusetts that provide schooling in any number of home languages whenever a group of parents requests it.

The third development is a new direction in psycholinguistic research, which, although only now getting under way, indicates that the hyphenated American can perhaps most easily become fully and comfortably American if the Spanish, the Polish, the Navajo or the French prefix is given unlimited opportunity to flourish. For example, the research of Padilla and Long (1969; see also Long and Padilla, 1970) indicates that Spanish-American children and adolescents can learn English better and adjust more comfortably to American if their linguistic and cultural ties with the Spanish-speaking world are kept alive and active from infancy on. Peal [Anisfeld] and Lambert (1962) came to a similar conclusion when they found that French-Canadian young people who are given opportunities to become bilingual are more likely than monolinguals to be advanced in their schooling in French schools, to develop a diversified and flexible intelligence, and to develop attitudes that are as charitable toward the other major Canadian cultural group as toward their own. A similar conclusion is drawn from more recent work of Lambert and Tucker (1972), where English-Canadian youngsters are given most of their elementary training via French. These children too seem to be advanced, relatively, in their cognitive development, their appreciation for French people and French ways of life, and their own sense of breadth and depth as Canadians.

In view of these sympathetic and supportive new developments, is it now possible to help the hyphenated Canadian or American to become fully and comfortably bilingual and bicultural? Is it now possible to counteract and change the reactions of ethnically different children in North America so that they will no longer feel different, peculiar and inferior whenever they take on their Spanish, Portuguese, Polish, Navajo, or French styles of life as a temporary replacement for the North American style?

Asking ourselves these questions prompted us to start a community-based study in Northern Maine (Lambert, Giles and Picard, 1973). The setting for the investigations was Maine's St. John Valley area, an American peninsula that protrudes into Quebec and New Brunswick. The closest Anglo community is nearly fifty miles to the south of Madawaska, centre of the St. John Valley. On a personal, social and cultural level the ties are much closer with French New Brunswick and Quebec than with the rest of the state of Maine. The total valley region is made up of approximately 70 to 75 per cent French-Canadian descendants, with the local language still a strong part of the way of life.

The research questions that shaped the investigation took the following form:

1. How do America's ethnolinguistic groups adjust to the bicultural demands made on them? It is typical for French-Americans in New England, for example, to reject their ethnolinguistic affiliations and identify more closely with the majority English-speaking culture? What is the developmental nature of changes that take place in their ethnic identity? In psycholinguistic terms, would the typical French-American evaluate speakers of English more favourably than speakers of one of the various forms of French?
2. Does participation in a bilingual education program influence children's attitudes toward the various forms of French, and if so, in what direction?

To provide at least partial answers to these questions, different subgroups of people living in Maine, some from the Valley region and some from outside, some French-American and others not, were asked to listen and give their subjective reactions to a variety of speech styles as presented by adult native speakers of one or another of the styles. The speech styles decided on were European-French (EF), middle-class French-Canadian (mcFC), lower-class French-Canadian (lcFC), middle-class Madawaskan French (mcMF), lower-class Madawaskan French (lcMF), middle-class Madawaskan English (mcME), and middle-class non-regional English (nrE).

Three groups of listeners were decided on so that we could examine age changes in the reactions of native French-Americans. In the first study, attention was directed to the evaluative reactions of two groups of college students, one comprising French-Americans and the other comprising non-French-Americans who live outside the St. John Valley. In the second study, our focus was on French-American high school students from the Valley region, and in the third study on French-American ten-year-olds, some of whom had had schooling in French for four years under the Title VII Bilingual Program and other who had not.

The listeners in the three studies were required to evaluate each speaker separately by rating him or her on bipolar adjectival trait scales (good/bad, wise/foolish, and so on). The traits finally used were selected after a preliminary testing in the Valley schools and colleges that permitted us to identify those personality qualities seen as valuable and worthwhile by each age group. The details of these investigations are available elsewhere (Lambert, Giles and Picard, 1973), but the general outcomes are particularly pertinent.

Do French-American young people typically reject their French affiliation and identity more closely with the majority English-speaking culture?

If we consider the findings of all three studies, we can examine this matter developmentally. There is substantial evidence to suggest that at the age of ten, the typical French-American youngster from Maine's Valley region who follows a conventional all-English curriculum in public school rejects his French ethnicity and orients himself to the English-sepaking American as a model. The ethnic allegiances that he does have are apparently limited to his own ethnolinguistic group — the lower-class local French community — but even in this instance his affiliations are ambivalent and potentially self-effacing. The influence of European-French as a model appears to be minimal at this age, although the EF speakers are perceived more favourably than are French Canadians.

By adolescence, however, a different ethnic orientation seems to develop. The thirteen to seventeen-year-old French Americans from the Valley also appear to orient themselves toward the English-speaking American model, but other factors come into play that tend to reduce this model's impact. For instance, European-French people are seen to be as competent (intelligent, determined, confident, etc.) and as attractive socially as American, judging from the reception given to nonregional and middle-class Madawaskan English speakers. Also, in the eyes of the adolescent, the middle-class version of the local French dialect (mcMF) has assumed an advantage over the working-class counterpart (lcMF) in the sense that is is judged as favourably as the English models or EF in terms of social attractiveness.

College students in the Valley region appear to have equally sympathetic attitudes toward European and local forms of French and toward English. That is, English no longer has a pre-eminent position in the hierarchy. This finding is of special interest because it could mean that the French-American elite who go on to college have developed an understanding and appreciation for both aspects of their biculturality. This possibility will be checked out carefully with follow-up research, as it has both theoretical and social importance (see Gardner and Lambert, 1972). At any rate, we find that college students judge speakers of the European and middle-class Madawaskan styles of French to be as competent as speakers of the various English styles. Stated otherwise, these styles of French are considered by the French-American college students to be as appropriate and respected media of social interaction as English.

These results contradict the commonly held belief that with time members of America's ethnic minority groups become assimilated, a process often taken to mean forgetting about the old country and old-country ways (including language) and becoming "American." In this community we have evidence of an increase through the age levels in appreciation for old-country ways in the sense that European and local versions of French are given the same degree of respect as English by college students. It could be that for these young people being "American" implies being French or being ethnic, no matter what variety. We are aware, of course, that in these studies we have not systematically controlled for the social class and educational potential of the three age groups brought into comparison (the ten-year-olds, the adolescents and the college students). Replications of these studies should therefore include young adults in the community who have not had the opportunity of college training to determine if this favourable outlook toward French is general. It would also be valuable to compare the St. John Valley region with other French-American communities to determine if these outlooks are shared.

How do non-French-Americans from Northern Maine react to the various styles of French, particularly the local variety?

Unfortunately, we have only the actions of the college sample to draw on for an answer. Limited as this base is, the results show clearly that college students living in Northern Maine who are not part of the

French-American community also indicate that the mcMF and EF speech styles of French are as acceptable and valuable in their eyes as are the two styles of English. This subgroup of informants was sensitive to social-class differences and showed this by downgrading the lower-class variety of local French. The fact that members of the greater "American" culture share the evaluative norms of the French-American population of Northern Maine must be seen as a most favourable and optimistic sign, one that makes it all the more necessary that this finding be verified through replications of the same type of study with other than college students and in various regions of New England.

Does experience in a bilingual education program influence French-American children's attitudes toward the French and English languages?

The findings from our third study certainly suggest that substantive changes are made by French instruction in the children's attitudes toward their two languages. It was found that the English-taught children were strongly Anglo-oriented in their evaluative reactions, whereas the children with experience in the bilingual education program were, in contrast, much more favourably disposed toward French. Indeed, the bilingual program children's outlook toward French was much more like the older age groups studied, except that they did not rate mcMF as favourably as the high school and college students did and they had a more favourable orientation toward Canadian-style French than did the older age groups. Judging from the attitudes of the older subjects, one might anticipate that in time the mcMF style would naturally attain more prestige for these children. Of course, the natural development of favourable attitudes toward the local version of French could be jeopardized if the bilingual program in any way belittled the local variety in comparison with the two imported styles — the European and the Canadian. The point is that the planners of bilingual programs should keep prevailing adult preferences in mind, and our evidence is that this community favours European and the educated form of local French.

The results of the third study also suggest that the bilingual program children may have been made overenthusiastic and slightly biased toward French, in contrast to the more balanced bicultural outlook of the college group investigated. But we have to keep in mind that there is a major difference in the educational experiences of the two groups. The ten-year-olds in the bilingual program are being schooled in part through French, and the value of being French is unmistakably introduced to the children via the program. The older students have never had such an experience; they followed a conventional all-English program of schooling designed for "American" students, and it is much less likely that they would be literate in French. We can, then, easily understand the enthusiasm of the bilingual program children.

Nevertheless, those responsible for such programs must keep overall goals clearly in mind and aid the children in ultimately making a two-language and two-culture adjustment. My own bias is that a bilingual education program, to be helpful and constructive, should attempt to develop the full potential of ethnolinguistic minority groups so that members can become fully American or Canadian at the same time as they remain fully French, Polish, or whatever. There is accumulating evidence that children can very easily become comfortably bicultural and bilingual, and that from this base they can enhance their sense of personal well-being, their sense of social justice, and their tolerance and appreciation of human diversity (see Gardner and Lambert, 1972, and Lambert and Tucker, 1972).

The results of these pilot studies should, then, be heartening to all those involved in the local bilingual education program, since it seems clear that such programs can have a powerful influence on the fate of the cultural and linguistic identities of young members of ethnolinguistic minority groups. Equally satisfying is the realization that the St. John Valley community as a whole, even those who are not French-American, react as favourably to the educated version of local French as they do to the European version; both forms of French are as respectable media of communication as English.

Encouraging as these studies are, they are only a start, and we are currently redoing this type of research in other New England communities. But in my mind there are grounds enough here to answer the last question above in the following way. North American ethnolinguistic groups should be encouraged from as many sources as possible to maintain their dual heritage. Not only are they North America's richest human resource, but now that we are beginning to see where conflicts of allegiances are likely to arise and how these groups can be helped to attain a comfortable bilingual and bicultural way of life by being themselves, their potential value to the nation is all the greater. In my mind, there is no other way for them to be comfortable, for to subtract one of their heritages would be to spoil their chances of adjustment. In other words, I don't think they will be able to be fully North American unless they are given every possibility of being fully French, Portuguese, Spanish, or whatever as well.

References

Aellen, C., and Lambert, W.E. Ethnic identification and personality adjustments of Canadian adolescents of mixed English-French parentage. *Canadian Journal of Behavioural Science,* 1, (1969), pp. 69–86.

Anisfeld, E. A comparison of the cognitive functioning of monolinguals and bilinguals. Unpublished doctoral dissertation, McGill University, 1964.

Anisfeld, E., and Lambert, W.E. Evaluational reactions of bilingual and monolingual children to spoken languages. *Journal of Abnormal and Social Psychology,* 69, (1964), pp. 89–97.

Balkan, L. *Les effets du bilinguisme français-anglais sur les aptitudes intellectuelles.* Brussels: Aimar, 1970.

Ben-Zeev, S. The influence of bilingualism on cognitive development and cognitive strategy. Unpublished doctoral dissertation, University of Chicago, 1972.

Carroll, J.B., and Casagrande, J.B. The function of language classifications in behaviour. In E.E. Maccoby, T.M. Newcomb, and E.L. Hartley, eds. *Readings in social psychology.* (3rd ed.) New York: Holt, Rinehart & Winston, 1958, pp. 18–31.

Chiasson-Lavoie, M., and Laberge, S. Attitudes face au français parlé à Montréal et degrès de conscience de variables linguistiques. In R. Darnell, ed. *Linguistic diversity in Canadian society.* Edmonton: Linguistic Research, 1971, pp. 89–126.

Child, I.L. *Italian or American? The second generation in conflict.* New Haven: Yale University Press, 1943.

Cole, M., and Bruner, J.S. Cultural differences and inferences about psychological processes, *American Psychologist,* 26, (1971), pp. 867–76.

Cole, M., Gay, J., Glick, J.A., and Sharp, D.W. *The cultural context of learning and thinking.* New York: Basic Books, 1971.

Cummins, J., and Gulutsan, M. Some effects of bilingualism on cognitive functioning. Unpublished manuscript, University of Alberta, Edmonton, 1973.

d'Anglejan, A., and Tucker, G.R. Sociolinguistic correlates of speech styles in Quebec. In R. Shuy (Ed.), *Social and ethnic diversity.* Washington, D.C.: Georgetown University Press, 1973.

Gardner, R.C. Motivational variables in second-language acquisition. Unpublished doctoral dissertation, McGill University, 1960.

Gardner, R.C., and Lambert, W.E. *Attitudes and motivation in second-language learning.* Rowley, Mass.: Newbury House, 1972.

Getzels, J.W., and Jackson, P.W. *Creativity and intelligence.* New York: Wiley, 1962.

Giles, H. Our reactions to accent. *New Society,* 18, (1971), pp. 713–15. (a)

Giles, H. Patterns of evaluation to R.P., South Welsh and Somerset accented speech, *British Journal of Social and Clinical Psychology,* 10 (1971), pp. 280–81. (b)

Giles, H. A study of speech patterns in social interaction: Accent evaluation and accent change. Unpublished doctoral dissertation, University of Bristol, 1971. (c)

Giles, H. Communicative effectiveness as a function of accented speech. Unpublished manuscript, University College, Cardiff, Wales, 1972.

Gordon, A.I. *Intermarriage: Interfaith, interracial, interethnic.* Boston: Beacon Press, 1964.

Guilford, J.P. Creativity. *The American Psychologist,* 5, (1950), pp. 444–54.

Guilford, J.P. The structure of intellect. *Psychological Bulletin*, 53, (1956), pp. 267–293.

Hoggart, R. *On culture and communication.* New York: Oxford, 1972.

Ianco-Worrall, A.D. Bilingualism and cognitive development. *Child Development,* 43, (1972), pp. 1390–1400.

Kroeber, A.L. *Anthropology.* (Rev. ed.) New York: Harcourt Brace, 1948.

Lambert, S. The role of speech in forming evaluations: A study of children and teachers. Unpublished master's thesis, Tufts University, 1973.

Lambert, W.E. A social psychology of bilingualism. *Journal of Social Issues, 23(2) (1967), pp. 91*–109.

Lambert, W.E. What are they like, these Canadians? *The Canadian Psychologist,* 11 (1970), pp. 303–33.

Lambert, W.E., and Anisfeld, E. A note on the relationship of bilingualism and intelligence. *Canadian Journal of Behavioural Science*, 1 (1969), pp. 123–28.

Lambert, W.E., Anisfeld, M., and Yeni-Komshian, G. Evaluational reactions of Jewish and Arab adolescents to dialect and language variations. *Journal of Personality and Social Psychology,* 2 (1965), pp. 84–90.

Lambert, W.E., Giles, H., and Picard, O. Language attitudes in a French-American community. Unpublished manuscript, McGill University, 1973.

Lambert, W.E., and Klineberg, O. *Children's views of foreign peoples.* New York: Appleton-Century-Crofts, 1967.

Lambert, W.E., and Tucker, G.R. *Bilingual education of children: The St. Lambert experiment.* Rowley, Mass.: Newbury House, 1972.

Lambert, W.E., Yackley, A., and Hein, R.N. Child training values of English Canadian and French Canadian parents. *Canadian Journal of Behavioural Science,* 3 (1971), pp. 217–36.

Leopold, W.F. *Speech development of a bilingual child.* 4 vols. Evanston, Ill.: Northwestern University Press, 1939–49.

Lévy-Bruhl, L. *How natives think.* London: Allen & Unwin, 1926. (Republished, New York: Washington Square Press, 1966.)

Long, K.K., and Padilla, A.M. Evidence for bilingual antecedents of academic success in a group of Spanish-American college students. Unpublished manuscript, Western Washington State College, 1970.

Minturn, L., and Lambert, W.W. *Mothers of six cultures.* New York: Wiley, 1964.

Padilla, A.M., and Long, K.K. An assessment of successful Spanish-American students at the University of New Mexico. *College Student Personnel Abstracts, 5 (1969), pp. 109*–10.

Park, R.E. Introduction. In E.V. Stonequist, *The marginal man.* New York: Scribner, 1937, pp. xiii-xviii. (Republished in R.E. Park, *Race and culture.* Glencoe, Ill.: The Free Press, 1950, pp. 372–76.)

Peal, E., and Lambert, W.E. The relation of bilingualism to intelligence. *Psychological Monographs,* 76 (1962), (27, Whole No. 546).

Sapir, E. *Language.* New York: Harcourt Brace, 1921.

Saucier, J.F. Psychiatric aspects of interethnic marriages. Unpublished manuscript, McGill University, 1965.

Scott, S. The relation of divergent thinking to bilingualism: Cause or effect. Unpublished manuscript, McGill University, 1973.

Torrance, E.P., Gowan, J.C., Wu, J.J., and Aliotti, N.C. Creative functioning of monolingual and bilingual children in Singapore. *Journal of Educational Psychology,* 61 (1970), pp. 72–75.

Whorf, B.L. The relation of habitual throught to behavior and to language. In L. Spier, A.I. Hallowell, and Newman, eds. *Language, culture and personality.* Menasha, Wis.: Sapir Memorial Publication Fund, 1941.

Vygotsky, L.S. *Thought and language.* Cambridge: Massachusetts Institute of Technology Press, 1962.

Part Four

CURRICULUM AND TEXTBOOKS

The purpose of this section is to examine the extent to which in the recent past the school curriculum has served to help Canadian students understand and appreciate the culturally and racially diverse nature of their society.

In their examination of prescribed social studies curricula across Canada, Ted Aoki and his colleagues draw attention to the fact that minority ethnic groups, when they were discussed at all, were generally interpreted in terms of either one or both of the dominant British or French communities. They also discovered that ethnic studies at the elementary school level focused largely upon material aspects of culture and emphasized the unique, the static and the exotic; the approach to culture at the secondary school level, on the other hand, was more often than not conceived in historical or heritage terms. Students, moreover, were encouraged to romanticize their heritage, rather than grapple with problems of cultural pluralism, language conflict and aboriginal rights. Rarely was attention given to the cognitive aspects of culture or issues of contemporary cultural change. This approach to curriculum development, in which the developers adopt a unidimensional cultural viewpoint, develop programs on the basis of taken for granted perspectives, and pass them on uncritically to their youthful consumers is, the authors maintain, demonstrably at odds with the contemporary and historical realities of Canadian society. It should be replaced by an approach to curriculum development which involves minorities as "co-producers" and in which the locus of decision-making is shared with teachers, students and the local community.

In somewhat similar vein, David Pratt argues that both non-white and white ethnic minority groups have been accorded little space in Canadian school textbooks. The actual ethnic model of Canadian society that they convey is in fact a very far cry from the normative model of cultural pluralism so widely espoused in social and educational policy. What they present is a consensus, non-controversial, conventional view of society; culture conflict is not considered seriously and for the most part students are exposed to a single, unitary view of Canadian society.

Paul Robinson also sees the schools as agents for the promotion of Anglo or French conformity. Taking the education of native peoples as his starting point, he argues that if Canadians are to take contemporary cultural diversity seriously, then a fundamental redefinition of the total school curriculum is required. Basic to such a redefinition are: (a) the use of the student's mother tongue as the language of instruction in the initial years of schooling and the gradual introduction of English or French as a second language; (b) the need for classroom programs to reflect an evaluation of different cultures on an equal basis; (c) the importance of each student enjoying freedom of choice between differing cultural lifestyles; (d) the eradication of systematic segregation of pupils on biased and arbitrary measures of competence; and (e) that communication — the essential link within the curriculum — be defined as broadly as possible.

Thomas Symons concludes this section by emphasizing the importance of Canadian Studies and advocating self-knowledge as the ultimate goal of all education. Ethnicity, he believes, pervades almost every aspect of Canadian life and, to a large extent, it is the particular features of this cultural diversity which give Canada its distinctiveness as a society. This central fact of Canadian life, however, is seriously under-represented in the curriculum at all educational levels, including our colleges and universities.

Whose Culture? Whose Heritage? Ethnicity Within Canadian Social Studies Curricula

T. AOKI, W. WERNER, J. DAHLIE and B. CONNORS

Ethnicity is evidenced within social studies curricula simply because social studies is about people. It interprets their cultures and heritages, their histories and lifestyles, and their beliefs and values within the Canadian mosaic. It is a market place not only for cross-cultural contacts, but also for shaping biases and stereotypes. As for the child who is of an ethnic minority, social studies is one more place where he meets the values and perspectives of the dominant culture. More importantly, he meets himself in the image of minorities presented to him within curricula. As navigators watch the bias of their instruments, so educators need to be aware of cultural bias in order to make corrections.

This article has grown out of a look at ethnic and multicultural content in prescribed elementary and secondary curricula used across Canada during the 1974-75 school year. We make no claims for the current status of ethnic studies, nor does it represent classroom activity in any part of Canàda. Judgments, conclusions and interpretations are inferential and are intended only to reflect a national status. It is not to be construed as picturing individual provinces or territories; nor is it a comparison of the stances taken by departments of education. Presented is a global and interpretative picture of patterns and trends within the curricula of social education. No value neutrality is claimed for the generalizations made in this article. It is biased. It is written from a particular perspective and represents only one interpretation of social studies programs. Interpretations which differ from the ones made here are certainly possible.

SOURCE: This article is adapted from a booklet entitled *Whose Culture? Whose Heritage? Ethnicity within Canadian Social Studies Curricula* published in 1974 by the Centre for the Study of Curriculum and Instruction, Faculty of Education, University of British Columbia and is reprinted here by permission of CSCI.

ACROSS THE PROVINCES

Examination of ethnic and multicultural studies in prescribed social studies curricula across Canada raises an important question for social educators. Whose culture and whose heritage are represented by social studies?

Differences in ethnic studies are evident when provincial and territorial curricula are compared. The degree of commitment and the approach taken toward ethnic studies, the interpretation of multiculturalism, the amount of energy expended in developing materials, and the role of ethnics in program development differ markedly. Some departments of education claim to have done quite a bit of work in the area of cross-cultural studies, but as yet have not produced to any significant degree curriculum materials for publication and distribution. A few departments in Canada have not even embarked upon much work nor have they given high priority to this area. Where topics have been developed within curricula to focus explicity on multiculturalism, the differing approaches reflect a diversity of interpretations of Canadian pluralism.

There is a range in terms of the number of ethnic groups mentioned within curricula. The number selected for study ranges from four to sixteen. Although the British, French, Inuit and Native Indian remain the four basic groups studies throughout Canada, some departments of education are introducing to the curriculum four times as many ethnic groups as other departments. Why are there such differences among departments of education?

Those provinces and territories with the greatest percentage of language other than English or French spoken as mother tongue tend to stress a greater number of ethnic groups within social studies curricula. Where there is an overwhelming English and French linguistic composition within a province or territory (over 85 per cent), the curriculum tends toward the monocultural orientation of these dominant groups and manifests generally a neglect of ethnics who are not Native Indian, Inuit, British or French. This is in contrast to those provinces and territories where over 15 per cent of the population speak languages other than English and French as mother tongue. Their curricula tend to stress more diversity of minority groups. For example, in the Northwest Territories linguistic diversity seems to be related to a concern for developing curricula which evidence cross-cultural understanding, community involvement and linguistic equality. The greater the linguistic diversity, the greater the orientation towards multi-ethnic studies within social education.

There is also some correlation between the manner in which a department of education has defined social education and the number of ethnic groups introduced within curricula. For example, as we move from social studies with a heritage emphasis to one emphasizing a social issues and interdisciplinary approach to cross-cultural studies, there is a tendency towards inclusion of a larger number of ethnic groups for study.

Some curricula are open in the sense that they allow for various degrees of input at the classroom level from teacher, student and community. Within those programs where the teacher is given some freedom to select not only methodology but content for study, there tends to be inclusion of a greater number of ethnic groups. For example, some departments of education leave open from one-fifth to one-third of the curricula, thereby allowing programs to reflect concerns of the community. The greater the flexibility to accommodate teacher choice and student interest, the greater the orientation towards cross-cultural studies.

THE ILLUSION OF NEUTRALITY

If we all wore the same blue-coloured spectacles, our observations would lead us to conclude that our world is blue. In a metaphorical sense each one of us has his own spectacles which colour what we see. In this sense any view of an object remains a product of the perspective which we adopt. We obtain different profiles of the object when we see it from varying distances, angles and elevations, when we see it under changing lighting effects, contextual conditions and time periods, and when we see it through our selected interests, feelings and experiences.

There is no such thing as neutrality concerning multiculturalism and ethnic pluralism within social studies. Bias is inevitable because curriculum development is a social process. People have to write the program. Individuals and groups are involved in specifying goals, selecting materials for study, and defining activities to be carried out in classrooms. They are all born somewhere and are all influenced by the situations of their lives. Inevitably their expectations and beliefs are shaped by experiences within some social and geographical location and their own ethnic affiliations. Each brings to social studies a viewpoint on what it means to be ethnic within a multicultural society. This perspective serves as a basis for developing and teaching social studies. Invariably, any curriculum must reflect someone's point of view which embodies biases created by a set of underlying values, beliefs and experiences. At the same time this persepctive will affect the student's observations, interpretations and consequent actions within the Canadian mosaic.

Although most departments of education do express an interest in relating multiculturalism to schooling, the shape of this interest differs within curricula. The particular ethnic content selected, the emphasis and the slant given to it, and the time provided to issues of pluralism betray not only the relative importance given to ethnic studies by departments of education, but also, and more fundamentally, a conception and interpretation of what is Canadian multiculturalism.

Within Canadian curricula two general perspectives tend to predominate, the monocultural and the multicultural.

MONOCULTURAL PERSPECTIVE

Most social studies curricula reflect on overwhelming monocultural orientation, that of the dominant British-French group. The ideal of equality, distinctiveness, mutual respect and interaction between these two ethnic populations is certainly commendable. However, by initiating students to the British and the French perspectives on the Canadian experience, multiculturalism tends to be viewed as monoculturalism. Emphasis upon European cultural content to the exclusion of nearly all non-European influence within Canada is evident. Our society is shown to be derived from European traditions, art, literature, music and personalities. Classical antiquity becomes exclusively that of the Greeks and Romans rather than that of the Chinese and West Coast Indians. The history of Britain and France overshadows all other histories. The boundaries and centre of world geography are defined by the empires of these two groups. In this manner all students, regardless of their cultural backgrounds, are provided with the same cultural tradition and values. Homogeneity rather than diversity becomes the acceptable norm.

Minorities are interpreted in terms of the goals, values and history of the dominant groups. Ethnic studies tend to become an examination of the "problems" minorities encounter as they fit into the dominant cultural frame of reference. Issues become defined in terms of assimilation, minority-majority relations and conflict. Such an orientation obviously destroys any uniqueness which may adhere in the minority viewpoints. They are reduced to the artifacts of material culture for students to look at and to interpret or evaluate in terms of similarities and differences with the dominant culture.

A monocultural orientation makes curriculum developers selective in their interpreting of multiculturalism. The focal criterion of selectivity is ethnocentricity. For example, almost without exception within elementary school curricula the cultural bias toward the dominant ethnic groups is ascertained through the holidays regarded as most suitable for study. Emphasis is placed almost exclusively upon Easter, Christmas Day, St. Valentine's Day, Halloween, Hannukah and Thanksgiving. No mention is made of non-European cultural and religious holidays which many Canadians may recognize. This

Christian-Judaic religious bias of the dominant group is discriminatory against minorities because students are subtly taught that for all Canadians some holidays are more legitimate than others. Or to take another example, a stated objective for high school students may be that they formulate and clarify their own personal philosophical position on man, freedom and values. They are to do this through comparisons of various philosophies. However, the content of the curriculum becomes ethnocentric because only prominent Western-European philosophies are provided for student examination. Thales, Anaximander, Anaximenes, Pythagoras, Heraclitus, Xenophanes, Parmenides, Zeno, Empedocles, Anaxagoras, Leucippus, Democritus, Socrates, Plato, Aristotle, Aquinas, Russell and Moore are considered to be legitimate alternatives. Contemporary non-Western ideas influential in Canadian society appear to be ignored. Why? Does multiculturalism imply that our philosophical and religious roots are, or should be, the same? Although objectives within curricula may sound admirable, the underlying and hidden curricula may be ethnocentric. Ethnocentric selection within curricula implicity reduces to homogeneity the diversity of lifestyles, cultures and philosophies which define multiculturalism.

MULTICULTURAL PERSPECTIVE

Adoption of a policy of multiculturalism by the government of Canada reflects its concern that ethnic groups be recognized and that they be provided opportunities to participate in the definition of Canadianism. Underlying multiculturalism is a pluralistic notion of equality. In pluralistic society, groups have the right to develop their own identities, lifestyles and languages, as well as to preserve their own cultural heritages, on a basis of equality with the British-French tradition; no one group has cultural superiority; each ethnic experience is recognized as being equally Canadian, and, therefore, a valuable and integral part of the total Canadian experience rather than recognized as a "problem to overcome."

So, too, heterogeneity is considered desirable, and harmony is possible even within diversity. Further, implied in heterogeneity and equality is mutual respect for different languages, different reality views, different conceptions of social issues, and an exchange of different ideas. Unity is not to be found in forcing homogeneity of cultural ideas and experiences, but in an understanding and acceptance of diversity.

When an individual is allowed to respect his own cultural background, the resulting security allows him to honour what is different in his neighbour. By reflecting upon his own ethnicity he may come to understand that every Canadian is reared in some social group, and that he must live in some geographical and cultural milieu, from which his values are shaped and his perspectives are meaningful. A multicultural orientation transcends any one ethnic superiority by seeing that there are many avenues whereby Canadians can interpret their society as meaningful.

Illustrative of a multicultural perspective is the social studies curriculum of the Northwest Territories. Their multicultural orientation to social education is committed to using the cultural contexts served by the schools for determining in part the aims, content and values within curriculum. This means that the primary world of the student — including his language and ethnic experiences, as well as the issues and values of his community is accepted and incorporated. The objective is to utilize the local diversity that exists, to build upon various interpretive frameworks and learning styles, and thereby to avoid a negative self and ethnic image for students whose background is different from that of the dominant cultural group. There is no total imposition of the dominant cultural perspective upon him, nor is he forced to integrate and to adopt the mores and attitudes of other groups. Differences which the student may bring to the program are recognized, understood and respected by the content, aims and activities of that curriculum. As he sees that his own ethnic and linguistic background has equal worth with other backgrounds, and that he does not have to be like other groups, he can respect and operate within the mosaic of communities in the larger society. Once he is secure in this acceptance, a foundation has been established from which greater cross-cultural understanding can be developed.

Curricula with a multicultural orientation must have flexibility for local input. Rather than a central or one-goal system, program development must incorporate community goals and concerns, on the principle that social education must be reflective of heterogeneous cultural goals. Encouragement should be provided for ethnic groups to define their own experience, both for themselves and for the larger society of which they are a part, by incorporating parental, student, and community involvement in the defining and controlling of curriculum development. The locus of power in curriculum development shifts, then, from one group to many groups. A pluralistic notion of equality in social education not only must stress respect for the diversity of ethnic experiences, but also must influence equality of access to program development for all groups. It is not just equality in terms of access to a single provincial or territorial program, but rather equality of access to power in defining the attitudes and perspectives expressed therein. This may well mean that the social studies curriculum within a province or territory should become multifaceted as it relates to and emerges from local linguistic concerns, values, and goals rather than from one centralized group of social studies experts.

Admittedly, there is little consensus on a single notion of multicultural social education among the various departments of education. Interpretations, as evidenced by curricula orientations, differ considerably. However, monocultural perspectives towards ethnic groups and multicultural issues tend to predominate. Where there is a multicultural orientation of some kind, there is a concern evidenced for equality of diversity within curricula.

MARGINAL AND HYPHENATED CANADIANS

According to most social studies curricula, non-white groups play a minor role in Canadian history. Note how the movers of history have in the main British or French names. This means that linguistic and cultural minority groups are relegated to being marginal actors, hyphenated Canadians who have little importance in shaping Canada's character. Their significance comes insofar as they help (or hinder) the dominant white apostles of civilization spread their religion, further their trade routes, paddle their canoes and build their railroads.

Minorities are examined and interpreted largely as they relate negatively or positively to the expansion and history of the dominant group. Thus, whether Native peoples are viewed as either "enemies" or "allies," or as either "saints" or "foes" depends on the aims of fur companies and settlers. Métis become notorious because of "rebellion" against the majority culture. A description of the Iroquois as a "menace" to New France not only provides students with the dominant group's point of view, but also with a value position on the Iroquois.

Where minorities are given a place in the study of Canadian history, they are typically interpreted in terms of "contributions" *to* the dominant society. They are mere contributors. A grade three student is asked to prepare a report on the contributions of some ethnic group to Canada, whereas a grade eight pupil is asked to list the contributions to Canada made by French culture. Inevitably, students come to understand and appreciate the many worthy contributions made by marginal minority Canadians who have been or are presently being integrated into present-day Canadian life.

Not only are minority groups seen to contribute to the dominant society, in general they are also the "beneficiaries." The British and French are seen as the "benefactors" to such an extent that paternalism becomes evident within many social studies programs. In the first place, this paternalism is manifested by the stated desire to instil in minorities an appreciation of their own values and lifestyles.

For instance, students of Native ancestry are assisted to appreciate their own history and heritage, to be given a sense of pride in their own background and cultural values. It is interesting, though, that representatives of the ethnic groups are not brought into the school to assist in achieving this objective. The interpretation of their own culture which Native students are given is that of the dominant group. An outsider selects that with which the student is to be instilled.

This paternalism is also evidence in the oft-stated aim that schooling is to assist minorities to enter into the educational, social and economic life of the dominant Canadian society. These marginal Canadians must be taught to "cope" within the alien society, and this entails being given appropriate traits, social customs and attitudes of the majority culture. For example, teachers may be admonished to have considerable patience and tact in dealing with the parents and students of a particular ethnic group, for the cultural differences are viewed as problems which need "to be appreciated and closely studied" in order to arrive at an understanding of the "basic causes" and "reasonable solutions." The problem is that it is impossible for certain grade one, two, and three pupils to have daily baths because they come from homes not equipped with modern plumbing. The solution is that the school must teach the value and practice of cleanliness. It is suggested that students be shown and constantly supervised in "the washing of face and hands," "the brushing of teeth regularly with inexpensive dentrifices such as salt or baking soda," and "the blowing of noses with Kleenex." Further, stress is to be placed upon the beautification of the yard with flowers and trees, the growing of vegetables, the wise use of money, the care of the home through the use of screens and cleanliness, the washing of dishes, the sewing of buttons, the learning of acceptable eating manners, and the care of clothing not only at school but also at home. Why the beautification of the yard at home? And in whose aesthetic system? The underlying value system is that of the dominant white (and even middle class) culture. Ideas, skills and attitudes acceptable to the majority group are to be stressed. Lines are clearly drawn between the "benefactors" and the "beneficiaries."

The difficulty with viewing minorities as marginal Canadians who have contributed, yet remain largely the "beneficiaries" of the dominant culture, is that one culture becomes the standard for social education, and all other groups are interpreted in terms of that culture's frame of reference. Subtly, Canadian ethnic diversity is placed within a hierarchy of cultures. Whenever a curriculum is developed within the perspective of one group alone, the implicit curriculum underlying the program is one of cultural superiority for *one* value framework and *one* history used to define the Canadian experience and identity. Generally, this hierarchy remains taken-for-granted within programs. Yet there it is in the bias evident in what is selected and what is omitted for study.

Neglect of many minorities in social studies may provide students with a value framework concerning the nature of multiculturalism. Some groups would appear to be important and other groups of little significance merely through the emphasis, the lack of emphasis and the time accorded them. And lifestyles, languages and cultural experiences are treated equally only rarely, for the standard of judging worth and development is naturally the achievements and world view of the dominant society. Differences may even be viewed as evidence of *backwardness* in relation to the dominant culture, rather than as evidences of *different* belief systems. For example, when viewed from the monocultural orientation of many programs, minorities are interpreted and evaluated in terms of their "becoming like us." A grade three student may learn that the homes of Native Indians are becoming more and more like his, that they generally have electricity and water just like his does, and that dirt and disease are lessening as these people rediscover hygiene. And students representing the dominant culture are to appreciate and respect the contributions of the minorities and their attempts to integrate into the majority lifestyle.

The hidden curriculum underlying much of Canadian social education betrays multiculturalism within a hierarchy rather than within an equality of cultures. This is evidenced in the image of minorities as marginal Canadians, as the contributors, as the beneficiaries of majority paternalism, and as those who are attempting to integrate into the mainstream lifestyle. For the minority group child, social studies may be a place where he learns insecurity in his own cultural background.

THE INSIDERS AND THE OUTSIDERS

Images of minorities are generally from the dominant, and thereby the outsider's viewpoint. Rarely are ethnic groups allowed to speak for themselves, to present the insider's point of view on issues which may affect them or the larger society in general, or to give their interpretations of Canadian history. Social and historical issues are examined primarily through the perspective of the program developer who typically ignores the values, attitudes and contexts of other groups. To ignore the variety of views involved in a particular issue or event is to understand only partially the event or issue. This does not seem to matter to many curriculum developers. Minority viewpoints are not considered to be important. Stripped of their own history, interpretations, values and beliefs, minority peoples are reduced to artifacts for students to look at, to the frames of reference of the dominant group, and to the classification schemes and images imposed upon them.

Few programs encourage or even provide room for students to define their own ethnic experience both for themselves and for other students. Personal ethnicity is often ignored. In those rare instances where their own cultural background is emphasized, students may be asked to write an essay on this background to investigate the ethnic origins of families within the community, to interview members of various groups, and to reconstruct accounts of journeys from countries of origin to Canada. Activities which help students clarify their own values, biases and feelings about their own ethnicity and that of other groups are not explicitly stated.

Further, there is little instructional material suggested or provided which is written from the insider's point of view. Most of the print resources appear to be an interpretation of ethnic experiences as perceived by outside non-group members. Few programs stress the use of first-person accounts, poetry, novels, film and student involvement with materials which encourage cross-cultural communication and understanding within different communities. The implication for ethnic studies is obvious: what students study (as well as how they study it) is limited to the extent that a variety of teachable and quality resources are available for presenting *both* insider and outsider viewpoints. For example, at the present, Canadian history is told largely from the European point of view. That Canadian history begins in the fifteenth century when the Europeans were searching for routes to India, as well as white interpretations of Native Indian–white relations throughout subsequent history, are well known to social studies students. But non-white interpretations of these interactions and relations are becoming available. There is a trend towards development of resource material by ethnic groups themselves.[1] Such activities are scattered across Canada and do involve co-actively communities, universities and both the federal and provincial governments. To this time, however, the primary emphasis of this community-directed activity which presents the insider's viewpoint has been related to Native Indian groups.

Surprisingly, the necessity of the insider's perspective in social studies is not stated explicitly within curricula. That the student's perception is dependent largely upon his own cultural context is so basic to social education that it appears to be taken for granted. Information about other peoples is previewed within the framework of his own cultural group. Unless shown otherwise, he will translate and interpret the perspectives of other groups within his own outsider's standpoint. He simply brings his own cultural values and experience to bear upon the situation.

What appears to be lacking in social studies curricula are explicit rationales and strategies to help the student as much as possible understand the insider's experience and view. As students are allowed to encounter various cultural standpoints which make up the Canadian mosaic, they may begin to see that their own views are also to some extent culturally influenced. They have a mirror for making themselves aware of their own ethnicity, the ethnicity of others and the difficult concept of ethnicity within Canadian multiculturalism.

In short, curricula often appear to be affectively sterile in their images of ethnics. The human element of ethnicity is lost if ethnic experiences are not portrayed in life and blood terms, and through the insider's viewpoint.

THE ORGANIZATION OF ETHNIC STUDIES

No curricula are designed to deal in depth only with multiculturalism and issues related to the Canadian mosaic. Cross-cultural topics are dealt with on a limited basis. Underlying these topics are particular approaches for understanding people and for organizing ethnic studies.

Approaches to Organizing Ethnic Studies

	Gr. 1–3	*Gr. 4–6*	*Gr. 7–9*	*Gr. 10–13*
Museum Approach				
Heritage Approach				
Discipline Approach				
Issues Approach				

The approach used for organizing ethnic studies is important, for in accordance with it content is selected and structured, and what teachers and students do within classrooms is influenced in part by it. The approaches used in social education for understanding people are not neutral. They convey values and assumptions, and may contribute to the development of the student's attitude towards ethnic groups and issues.

Museum Approach

Many programs have units or topics of study which may well be described as "A Student's Manual to the Canadian National Ethnic

Museum." Student understanding of ethnic groups and issues is organized around artifacts and interesting "facts" through which he is taken as a tourist and immersed within a cultural smorgasbord of things and anecdotes. The student colours teepees, draws igloos, eats curried rice, makes models of villages, bakes Hutterite bread, listens to ethnic songs. He learns isolated details about how a minority group lives, random lists of dress and food, and highly visible objects of some culture. Unfortunately, this approach tends to make objects of people, to focus upon the material aspects of culture, to emphasize trivial differences among groups, and to perpetuate stereotypes. Most important, this approach to people tends to ignore the conceptual understandings, issues and cultural meanings which underlie the objects students look at.

The museum approach is strongest within curricula for grades one to seven and is popular with Departments of Education. It tends to predominate where there is no stated rationale within curricula for teaching about multiculturalism, and where the orientation is monocultural. Since this approach becomes often the pupil's first exposure within school to ethnic groups, it may well be the most undesirable for fostering cross-cultural understanding. Its effects upon student attitudes, its perpetuation of stereotypes and its neglect of conceptual understanding of the Canadian mosaic all need to be considered.

Heritage Approach

The heritage approach emphasizes the historical Anglo-French roots of the dominant culture. Certain institutions, personalities, places and values tend to be romanticized, and culture is defined in terms of a static view of traditions and the past.

A heritage approach tends to be ethnocentric and paternalistic. If non-European groups are mentioned, the emphasis is upon what the dominant heritage has done *for* them, whether via missionaries, the fur trade, law and order, or the amenities of civilization. And different heritages are implicitly ordered hierarchically by the amount of time and depth accorded to them in curricula. In pursuing a topic such as "A British subject I was born," a student must define his heritage from a monocultural orientation; it is the British and French heritages which are made important to Canadian life, regardless of who the student is. A Canadian history course which starts with British geography and traditions alone, without even a mention of other possible sources, presents an explicit bias of what is Canadian and of whose cultural heritage should be the norm. Other minority groups are the contributors and beneficiaries of the unquestioned heritage.

Although the heritage approach is used in varying degree by most Departments of Education, it appears to be the counterpart of the museum approach. Whereas younger students are to define ethnicity through artifacts and stereotypes, older students are enculturated with a romantic and ethnocentric heritage.

Discipline Approach

A common approach to ethnic studies from grades seven to thirteen is via a history framework (not heritage) or through social science disciplines offered as regular or optional courses for students. Understanding of multicultural issues is obtained within the concepts, generalizations, methods and organization of history and the social sciences. Indeed, a treatment of such issues is restricted by the conceptual and inquiry framework of the disciplines. Whereas history curricula tend to concentrate upon the British and French factor, the introduction of such courses as anthropology, sociology and psychology has led to the examination of a wider range of minorities. This would suggest that the trend towards disciplinary electives at the secondary school level offers promise for increased multicultural learning activities. Unfortunately, the people studied most often are the highly visible groups.

The discipline approach tends to place the student in a detached relationship to ethnicity. He is encouraged to objectify various groups under social science labels (e.g., integrated, acculturated, assimilated, alienated, adapted), to look at groups as if they were objects in a laboratory, and to obscure the life goals, attitudes and interpretations which group members have of themselves. Multicultural issues are thereby made safe emotionally. Personal ethnicity is neutralized in favour of theoretical considerations. As an example, the stated objectives of a geography curriculum may be to develop positive attitudes in relation to the interdependence of peoples, to develop respect for similarities and differences of peoples and to clarify values regarding other value systems. However, the curriculum does not make it clear how mapping the spatial distribution of ethnic groups is to fulfill the affective objective of respect and value clarification. It is assumed that this will somehow take place by using the discipline mode of inquiry and conceptual framework.

One of the obvious strengths of this approach is the conceptual breadth and depth brought to ethnic studies. Although at present none of these curricula are developed primarily around the concept of multiculturalism, they do deal with it at the topic level with far greater sophistication than do the museum and heritage approaches. For instance, an anthropology or sociology curriculum's objective to provide students with a better understanding of their own society and culture is carried out systematically within a well-defined conceptual and inquiry framework. Patterns of ethnic relations are developed through such notions as annihilation, expulsion, partition, segregation, discrimination, integration, pluralism, amalgamation, submissive manipulation, marginal adaptation, withdrawal, oppression, nativism, violence, reform, group self-hatred, coercive and enacted change, and community behaviour. Unless the teacher has the theoretical background to make sense of these notions, the discipline approach to minority groups may become a conceptual jungle of isolated terminology for students to write in their notebooks.

Issues Approach

An interdisciplinary issues (problems and values) approach to multiculturalism is associated usually with a social studies rather than a social science view of social education. Such studies begin from a contemporary topic or value problem facing Canadian society. History, geography and the other social sciences are then drawn upon for appropriate concepts, methods and understandings which are relevant to the topic. The student is encouraged to consider alternative actions and possible consequences, to make value decisions and to take a stand on multicultural issues. For example, after researching a question concerning what problems face Native peoples today, he is then asked not only to suggest possible solutions, but whether there is anything he can do personally. He is asked to clarify his own value position on what it means to be a Canadian, whether Canada should be a melting pot or a cultural mosaic, whether Canada should strive to be a multilingual, bilingual or unilingual nation, or whether Canada should cultivate explicitly a unique "Canadian culture."

It would appear that this interdisciplinary issues approach to ethnic studies requires students to think about the conflicting interpretations, contemporary values and trends underlying multiculturalism. Rather than just drawing maps, colouring pictures of ethnics and generally stereotyping some highly visible group, the student is required to apply the social sciences to social problems, to have an understanding of history (and even an appreciation of heritage) underlying social issues, and to make decisions on problems which have contemporary political import. Values clarification is one way to get at a greater understanding of bias, to clarify attitudes to personal ethnicity and to encourage decision making on political issues. There is a danger, however, that a student may come to view minorities as simply problems to which social solutions need to be found.

THE WHY OF ETHNIC STUDIES

A desirable objective of social education within a society like Canada might well be a deeper understanding of ethnic pluralism and a tolerance for diverse lifestyles. Departments of Education could be expected to formulate clearly rationales for relating schooling to the multicultural status of our country. As evidenced by the provincial curricula we examined, this is not the case in general. Apart from the Northwest Territories, there was little evidence of explicit rationales on ethnic studies within social studies curricula. Why students should study the ethnic mosaic, what they should know or be able to do about it, or how the topic should be approached are questions which are rarely justified. Either rationales are in developmental stages, or else they are not of particular interest to most Departments of Education.

The general lack of explicitly stated rationales leaves serious questions unanswered concerning how social studies educators are to define the relationship between multiculturalism and schooling. What is multiculturalism within social education? What are the relationships between national policies of multiculturalism and the goals of departments of education? How are the interests and relevances of ethnic groups related to curricula? Why should social studies reflect the diversity of Canadian pluralism? What should the role of local community personnel be in program development?

What rationale is in evidence are of three types. The first two are explicitly stated within some curricula, whereas the third tends to be alluded to in general and ambiguous statements concerning multiculturalism.

1. Rationale for Increasing Integration

There appears to be a trend towards supplemental programs, primarily for Native Indians, Métis and Inuit, and secondarily for minority French groups. Supplemental is here used in the sense of an extension to the existing regular programs designed primarily for the majority. Some minority groups are thereby accorded special status on the assumption that they need remedial treatment. In-service activities and curriculum materials are developed specifically in the hope that these will improve the schooling of minorities.

When supplemental or remedial programs are designed for Native students, the rationale is, in some cases, explicitly that of integration. In these cases educators are to assist students to overcome the difficulties they face when attempting to enter the economic, social and political life of the majority society. Education is viewed as the most effective means through which minorities can be integrated into the dominant lifestyle. The underlying premise of such curricula is that students must enter the economic mainstream of Canadian society. They have no choice. To be isolated from this majority society leaves students at a disadvantage economically. And in order to cope successfully with employment, they need to understand and adopt the values, customs and attitudes of the larger group within which they must live and work. Having thus defined the problem of the minorities as integration, curriculum developers can justify supplemental social studies programs. Though this view of integration may be a goal of the Departments of Education, little evidence is provided within the curricula that this is necessarily defined as a goal, or even a problem, by the minorities themselves. At face value, therefore, such programs appear rather paternalistic. A relation of multiculturalism to social education is interpreted as increasing homogeneity of skills and values deemed necessary by program developers for economic viability. Becoming like the majority culture is equated with economic security, and difficulties facing minority groups are rectified to the degree that integration successfully occurs.

2. Rationale for Maintaining Diversity

A contrasting rationale is found in the curriculum of the Northwest Territories which clearly states the relation of schooling to multiculturalism for all the subjects and grade levels. According to this rationale, social education is not to deny any student his ethnic self-worth, nor is it to be construed by the student as a turning aside from his people. He is not expected to embrace the dominant British-French history and perspectives as his own. Pride in his own historical background, cultural traditions, and linguistic community are to be respected.

To accomplish such goals, curricula have been developed on stated premises concerning the role of minorities within the larger mosaic, the role of language in schooling, the role of local community needs and interests in program development, and the anticipated difficulties related to assimilatory pressures students will encounter within schooling situations. Recognition of Canadian diversity implies that curricula must reflect equality in the emphasis and the time accorded to the study of various cultures and groups. Certain peoples and histories are not more important, and therefore deserving of more emphasis and time. There is no hierarchy of cultural backgrounds. Token and supplemental approaches to minorities are rejected, and aspects of local culture and history are not introduced into the program for a few minutes each week. Rather, curricula are developed from multicultural and multilingual perspectives, and are committed to equality, heterogeneity and a broad base of community involvement. Such programs are not so much *about* multiculturalism, but rather are cross-cultural in their orientations, concepts, resources and activities. Schooling is multicultural in outlook, emphasis and content. This represents an explicit interpretation of what multiculturalism is in relation to education.

3. Rationale for Encouraging Awareness

Increasing visibility for ethnic issues appears to be a trend for many Departments of Education. The social studies are beginning to place more stress on education about minority groups — especially information about Native peoples — than has been placed there in the past. Concern is expressed for eliminating stereotyping within curricula and for updating materials and resources. Although its impact is just beginning to be felt, legislation and regulations with respect to second-language education has stimulated in some measure this increased concern for larger questions related to ethnic studies and minority rights.

Where Departments of Education have stated commitments to increasing ethnic and multicultural studies, the trend in program development appears to be the compensating of existing programs with ethnic units or issues. Attempts are made to incorporate ethnic content and objectives for increased awareness of multiculturalism in existing courses of studies, and not by creating additional separate courses and subjects. For example, extra units of study may be predefined and prescribed for some grade level, ethnic groups and issues may be suggested, multicultural resources and concepts may be listed, or bibliographies may be provided for teachers and students. The objective in expanding and improving existing programs is to make students more aware of pluralism and diversity within Canada.

However, infusion into existing programs does not imply necessarily that new rationales and orientations are being developed. These additive activities may detract from the rethinking which Departments of Education may need to direct to what multiculturalism means for social education. In some cases, it would appear that the perspective of present curricula needs to occasion a shift rather than merely incorporating additional ethnic content to a conceptual framework which mitigates against pluralism. A reorganization of existing curricula may be required rather than a supplementing of them with a compensating bias in an attempt to ameliorate previously neglected elements.

4. A General Lack of Rationales

It may be surprising that some social studies programs neither have explicitly stated rationales on multiculturalism (whether for integration, diversity or awareness), nor display much evidence in the prescribed content and goals of even an implicit rationale. In such cases, the notion of multiculturalism does not appear to be an important organizing idea for the study of Canadian society. The idea is not a starting point for defining what social education should be or should do.

Whereas some curricula seem to be based upon an implicit assumption that ethnic groups should be studied, there is little explanation as to why or how this is to be done. General aims are stated concerning an appreciation of heritage, an understanding of contributions, and a development of some respect for minorities. Aims related to "appreciation" and "understanding" tend to be expressed rather vaguely and with considerable ambiguity. For example, a curriculum may state that students should grasp the diversity and versatility of mankind in order that students may become more sensitive to the spiritual and material aspects of their own majority ethnic group. Little indication is given as to how or why this is to occur in the classroom, nor do the content and activities of the curriculum relate to the student's own ethnicity within a multicultural society. Further, the appreciation which is to occur is usually from the dominant perspective. Thus a grade three student is taught to appreciate the bravery and courage of Native Indians, to respect their adjustments and worthy contributions. And minorities are to be instilled with an appreciation of their own values, a pride in their own heritage, and interpretation of their own history.

Associated with a lack of explicit rationale is a random approach to ethnic studies. Guidelines are not evident as to why certain minorities are selected and emphasized, or why certain issues are of concern. Small and visible groups are stressed and made objects of study, their cultures are viewed as if they were static and material, and the past is emphasized in terms of tradition or heritage. Such programs remain biased toward monocultural perspectives. The selectivity of ethnic content is related at times to subtle stereotypes. It would seem that some Departments of Education need to define what Canadian multiculturalism means and what its relation to schooling should be. Explicit rationales are the starting point for ethnic studies.

A MATTER OF POWER AND CONTROL

Curriculum development is a political act. Those groups (whether ethnic, occupational or special interest) who have access to program development have power to define social reality and to impose these definitions upon other groups. This means that certain individuals and groups have the power to control the thinking of students and teachers by shaping conceptions of the society in which they live. In this way program developers become the gatekeepers of reality definitions. They select, classify and evaluate viewpoints and knowledge for inclusion within programs. Certain perspectives are legitimized to the exclusion of other points of view. Such gatekeeping represents an unequal distribution of power among groups within schooling contexts because everyone does not have equal power to

Models of Curriculum Development

	Minorities as consumers	*Minorities as advisors*	*Minorities as co-producers*
Locus of power in decision-making	Curriculum experts	Curriculum experts	Shared with experts & various groups
Direction of control in decision-making	Unidirectional & hierarchical	Unidirectional & hierarchical	Mutual & horizontal
Role of ethnics in decision-making	Consumers	Advisors; ad hoc committees; consumers	Co-producers; broad base at grass-roots
Major concern in decision-making	Efficiency; maintenance of power & control	Legitimization of decisions	Curricula which have meaning in local situations

control the content of curricula and in part the attitudes and activities of students.

Social studies curricula transmit and distribute selected interpretations of ethnic groups and social issues. Implications of this power and control for social education are not simple within a pluralistic society such as Canada. Though schools are in general a meeting place of diverse ethnic experiences and views on social issues, it appears that the experiences and views of only certain ethnic groups are selected and transmitted within programs. The exclusion of many minorities is evident and the very choice of groups to be studied does not reflect the character of Canadian multiculturalism. Coverage of Native Indians, Inuit, and small yet visible minorities as the Hutterite or Doukhobor, is done from the point of view of the British and French majority. Numerically significant groups are conspicuously absent, and a host of minorities are neglected totally. Majority views and experiences are established as the legitimate interpretations of Canadian history and issues.

This distribution of power among ethnic groups can be traced to the particular models of curriculum development used within the provinces and territories. These models can be differentiated on the basis of who has the power to make decisions in social studies program development.

Minorities as Consumers

The locus of power in decision-making rests with the social studies expert, usually defined by his government or university affiliation. These curriculum experts select and order the goals, content and activities which they consider relevant to ethnic studies. Power is not shared with teachers, students, community or minority groups. As a consequence, social studies programs are developed "outside," apart from the concerns and interests of local situations, and are handed down as products to consumers in a unidirectional and an hierarchical fashion. Decision-making moves from the top downwards, with the ethnic groups under study having little control over what is studied about them, how it is studied and from whose points of view. The legitimate frame of reference used in social education is defined by the experts alone.

A major interest underlying this model is *efficiency* in decision-making and *control* of the knowledge and perspectives students are to be given concerning ethnic groups and issues. Images and conclusions concerning ethnicity are unidirectionally shaped for and transmitted to the student and teacher, who in turn are expected to legitimate these values and interpretations. They are not encouraged to encounter actively various ethnic groups apart from the curriculum, to find out how minorities interpret Canadian issues, to test ideas and stereotypes about groups, or to follow up particular interests related to community affairs. It is the curriculum which dispenses the proper information about multiculturalism and the legitimate images about ethnics for the student and for his community.

Of the curricula examined, all except that of the Northwest Territories and, to some extent, Manitoba, appear to have been developed in varying degree on this model. This producer-consumer approach is especially evident in those programs which tend to have a strong monocultural orientation. Information about minorities is cast within the dominant history, values, and interpretation of the world, thereby making other groups marginal or hyphenated Canadians. Such curricula may lack relevance and honesty for students, teachers and community members who do not represent the dominant culture. Images and knowledge transmitted to them may not reflect their own ethnic experiences and views; the relationship between curriculum experts and community is such that the goals and reality of the expert are placed upon all for whom the curriculum is designed. The result is cultural homogeneity. The hidden curriculum is integrative, moving the program consumers toward the values, biases, and lifestyles represented and interpreted by the program developer. Those groups who are not represented in the monocultural stance of the curriculum may come to distrust and suspect the design and purposes of the curriculum expert. The only way that diverse groups can enhance their particular interests and goals within curricula is to gain and maintain power within program development. This fosters competition and not harmony within the Canadian mosaic as minorities attempt to gain influence for their position. As such, this model of curriculum development may be incompatible with a multicultural view of social education.

Minorities as Advisors

Some Departments of Education express an interest in sharing limited power in decision-making with the ethnic authorities. The locus of power in decision-making concerning the content and aims of ethnic studies still rests with the experts, although community personnel may be invited to cooperate with the department in an advisory fashion. Power is distributed to selected representatives of minorities. For example, curricula for Native Indian and Métis students may be developed by a committee of experts, and then the completed program is presented to such organizations as the Métis Federation, the Indian Brotherhood, the Department of Indian Affairs and Northern Development, and various friendship centres for their criticisms and appraisals. Although this may represent a small degree of decentralization of power in decision-making, the locus of control in deciding what should be taught still rests with the experts. The role of minority group personnel is advisory and on an ad hoc basis. A major interest underlying this model is that of legitimization: a degree of consensus achieved with selected ethnic representatives gives their approval to the program, and it is thereby legitimized as a reasonable interpretation of the minorities under study. However, it is important to note that this cooperation does not represent a shift in the decision-making base for the role of ethnics is strictly advisory. It is a political move on the part of the experts to gain increased legitimization for their product. Once this cooperation results in legitimization, the curriculum is transmitted undirectionally and hierarchically to the consumers.

Minorities as Co-producers

Curricula for the Northwest Territories are based upon a recognized need for continuous program development through the mutual efforts of those affected at the local community and classroom levels. The locus of power is shared to some extent with teachers, students, community personnel and minority groups. Although control ultimately lies with the Department of Education, there is an attempt to gain a broad base and degree of involvement in program development. The process is towards the devolution of power and the decentralization of control. Decision-making is shared with all those who are interested in social education. Since the locus of power is shared with community personnel, their relation with curriculum experts tends toward mutual influence and understanding rather than majority dominance and hierarchical decision-making. Ends are not established totally apart from community interests, but emerge out of concerns and needs of both the Department of Education and the community. This means that an entire province or territory is not treated as a homogeneous group which should accept the same goals, values, and interpretations made by experts. Flexibility and freedom within curriculum development allows for and encourages heterogeneity because decision-making is shared and has a broad base. The result is a curriculum which has meaning in local situations and which is relevant to the various ethnic experiences and views of Canadian issues. Interest underlying this model is in a social education which has meaning in local situations. Meaning comes when ethnic realities are portrayed honestly, when there is opportunity for more than one interpretation of Canadian history and issues, and when local linguistic and cultural characteristics can be incorporated to some extent within programs. Cross-cultural understanding is facilitated because the various minorities involved within curriculum development must interact and understand one another to a greater extent than in possible under the other two models discussed. They must work together. In this manner the diversity of cultures and the various lifestyles extant in Canadian society have a chance to be incorporated within programs which become multicultural in their orientation and content.

Just as Canadian multiculturalism is an ongoing and changing mosaic, so curricula are not to be thought of as finished products to be disseminated throughout classrooms. In varying degree programs must allow for continuous community input of local resources, ideas, and perspectives. Providing teachers and students with freedom and flexibility to accommodate local interests and conditions is a necessary provision to achieve equality of minority viewpoints. As such, students can explore their own linguistic, cultural and community roots, as well as those of others, rather than just the dominant British-French frame of reference. Students are encouraged to reflect upon their own ethnicity from their own cultural perspective rather than through the stereotypes and bias of the outsider's point of view. Instead of transmitting a static and unchanging heritage to all Canadians, programs which allow for local freedom and for diversity of input reflect the changes constantly occurring within our social mosaic.

CONCLUSION

There is an overwhelming British and French cultural perspective within most curricula. Other ethnic groups are interpreted in terms of one or both of these dominant groups. Typically, the choice of ethnic groups to be studied does not reflect the character of Canadian multiculturalism. At the elementary school level there is almost exclusive coverage of Native Indians, Inuit and small yet visible minorities as the Hutterite or Doukhobor; at the secondary school level, concern is focused on those two groups who represent the majority. Numerically significant groups such as the German, Italian and Ukrainian are neglected. From examining curricula, one would conclude that Canada's population consists primarily of Indians, Inuit, British and French. Those minorities which represent one-quarter of Canada's population are conspicuously absent.

The notions of culture and ethnicity are defined generally at the elementary school level as material things, with an emphasis upon that which is unique, static and different. Ethnic studies thus become like a trip to a museum or an art gallery. At the secondary school level these notions may be conceived historically as heritage. There is little emphasis upon cognitive culture or contemporary cultural change. Students are encouraged to look at material details relative to ethnic groups or to romanticize about a heritage more often than to grapple with such issues as pluralism, cross-cultural communication, governmental policy, language and aboriginal rights and value conflicts. This emphasis upon material culture and heritage tends to perpetuate an implicit hierarchy of ethnic groups. Our Canadian "heritage" becomes exclusively British and French, with the host of minorities portrayed as marginal actors on the stage of history. Cross-ethnic relations may be placed within a conflict framework in which the minorities are the problems for the majority culture.

Curriculum developers appear to be culturally monopolarized at times, developing programs from their own taken for granted perspectives. As such, students are not encouraged to see from more than one cultural perspective, and their frame of reference becomes ethnocentric and paternalistic when interpreting those who are ethnically different. Little attempt has been made to involve representatives of ethnic groups in program development, nor has there been much encouragement for local community involvement in jointly developing such programs with governmental and university personnel. Ethnic issues within curricula have been defined and interpreted by educational experts for students. Flexibility and freedom to incorporate community concerns are not evident generally. Curricula are treated as completed products which pass unidirectionally from the producers to the consumers. The cultural biases, stereotypes and perspectives of the group who has the power to control program development thereby become legitimized as the proper interpretive schemes for Canadian history and for contemporary issues.

Curricula provide virtually no suggestions for preservice and inservice training of personnel using, preparing to use, or assisting in the developing of ethnic and multicultural studies. Methods and suggestions concerning how teachers and students are to understand the values and outlooks of other groups are essential in order to control cultural bias and circumvent the fallacy of interpreting and judging another value and belief system in terms of the standards of one taken for granted lifestyle. Clearly stated rationales concerning the relation of multiculturalism to social education are rarely evident, and though terms such as pluralism and mosaic are introduced, programs do not reflect in general the meaning of these terms within the prescribed content and activities.

Underlying the generalizations of this article is a call for ethnic studies which are truly ethnic in name, content and perspective. This concern is important because of possible consequences which images and stereotypes in social studies have for students. If people act on the basis of their beliefs, then what students believe concerning multiculturalism, about certain groups and about their own ethnic background is significant because of the human capacity for self-fulfilling outlooks. The perspectives they hold of themselves and of their society contribute to what they become, to the society they construct and live within and to the manner in which they treat and interpret their neighbour. Only by examining the underlying and unquestioned perspectives they adopt can students, teachers and curriculum developers reflect critically upon the nature of their own biases and liberate themselves from the encapsulating power of their own ideas and prejudices. Whose culture and whose heritage are portrayed in social education, as well as how these are portrayed, are questions of central importance because of their implications for educational practice and for interpretations of fellow Canadians within social studies curricula.

Note

1. Curricula have been developed in cooperation with various agencies such as federal and provincial governments, universities and ethnic groups. Projects at Morley, Hobbema and Blue Quills are illustrative within Alberta of community-based development of curriculum material which reflects ethnic viewpoints more honestly. For examples of local development of resource material related to ethnic studies, see the following: T. Aoki, "Toward Devolution in the Control of Education on a Native Reserve in Alberta," *Council of Anthropology and Education Newsletter,* 5, no. 4 (November 1973); P. Robinson, "Curriculum Development," *Canadian Native Schools in Transition: Yearbook of Canadian Society for the Study of Education,* 5, no. 1 (1974); J. Wyatt, "Self-Determination Through Education: A Canadian Indian Example", *Phi Delta Kappan,* 5, no. 58 (January 1977).

The Social Role of School Textbooks in Canada

DAVID PRATT

Textbooks and the School Context

Public schools exist primarily for the purpose of socializing the young. The child's basic political and social orientation is established during his years in elementary school; thereafter his ideology may change in complexity, but rarely in its general direction (Sullivan, Byrne, and Stager, 1970). From these and similar findings, such researchers as Hess and Torney (1967) have concluded that "the public school appears to be the most important and effective instrument of political socialization," but, as critics have pointed out, this conclusion does not necessarily follow (Sears, 1968). The actual effect of the school as compared to the effects on attitudinal development of such other socializing agencies as the family, the media, and the peer group has yet to be exactly determined. And while a continuity of attitudinal development in children is apparent, more research is needed before it can be known to what extent adult behaviour is determined by attitudes developed in early life. This cautious approach to the role of the school, however, does not affect the initial premise: that what distinguishes the school from other socializers is that it is the agency through which society makes its most deliberate attempt to structure socialization.

The school socializes in many ways. Haller and Thorson have argued that the group-teaching pattern that prevails in schools develops in children ideas of universalism and equality before the law (1970). The hierarchy of power in a school and the sex distribution of teachers at different grade and authority levels provide important sex and political models for children and adolescents. Grading and streaming practices not only determine a student's academic cohorts, but also influence his choice of peers outside the classroom. Sports

SOURCE: E. Zureik and R. Pike, eds., *Socialization and Values in Canadian Society, Vol. 1* (Toronto: McClelland and Stewart, 1975), pp. 100–25. Reprinted by permission of Carleton University Press.

and extracurricular activities provide quasi-formal socializing experiences. Even apparently trivial policies are capable of having important affective results. The arrangement of desks in a classroom reflects certain conceptions of human relationships. The choice of norm-referenced over criterion-referenced grading implies a belief in the relationship between competition and achievement. The effect of such elements will vary with such factors as the size of the school and its social and economic setting.

But society makes its most conscious attempt at developing students' attitudes and beliefs through the school curriculum. Curriculum guidelines issued by provincial Departments of Education endeavour to outline the knowledges, skills, and values which should be inculcated, and the experiences to which students should be exposed in the classroom. Such guidelines, however, can do no more than give general directions, which will be interpreted variously by different schools and different teachers. The degree of influence over the curriculum as it affects the student is in inverse relation to distance from the classroom. In Western educational systems, accordingly, the classroom teacher is normally the most important modifier of the curriculum, his or her influence, however, being subject to three potential constraints.

The first constraint is a powerful inspectorate, which enforces adherence to a single interpretation of the official curriculum. This constraint exists in few present-day Canadian jurisdictions. The second is a system of external examinations, such as prevails in England and prevailed in Ontario for grade thirteen until 1967, which obliges teachers to follow a common curriculum. The third constraint on the teacher's curricular autonomy is the limitation of his or her choice of textbooks to an officially authorized list. This constraint is the only one of the three that currently prevails in all provinces of Canada.

Hodgetts' study of the teaching of Canadian studies in 847 Canadian classrooms in 1966-1967 clearly demonstrated that teachers of history and civics allow the content of the textbook to determine to a great extent the content of instruction. Hodgetts' researchers found that in studying controversial issues:

> Eighty-nine per cent of the classes we observed unquestioningly followed the gray, consensus version of the textbook. . . . In twenty-five per cent of the Canadian history classes we visited, the students were engaged in learning and recording in their notebooks. . . . the "ready made verdicts of the textbooks". . . . The lowest category in our scale of methods was reserved for classes in which . . . the content was obviously a mere recitation of the prescribed textbook. Twenty-one per cent of all classes included in our survey fell into this lowest category.[1]

To the influence of the teacher over the content of instruction, then, must be added the influence of those who write, edit, and authorize textbooks. While the textbook influences students indirectly, by influencing instruction, it also has the potential to affect students' attitudes directly. It has long been established that written communications can affect the attitudes of readers (Tannenbaum, 1953; Watts, 1967). It has further been shown that school children's attitudes toward social issues, and especially toward minority groups, can be influenced by certain kinds of textbook and other reading material (Fisher, 1968; Lichter and Johnson, 1969). There are a number of reasons why this should be so.

For many children, textbooks constitute the bulk of the reading material that they encounter, particularly throughout the formative elementary grades. Moreover, the textbook is not simply *any* book; it is an *official* book, authorized by the government, promoted by the school, acknowledged by the teacher. Textbooks, particularly those in such social studies as history, civics, and geography, will provide students with their first introduction to many social issues. For some social and cultural questions, the influence of the textbook may remain decisive. Only in the later years of their schooling do students reach the Piagetian stage of formal operational thought, at which a mature critical attitude toward what is read may emerge (Hallam, 1967; Sullivan, 1967). When this biologically-determined uncritical attitude toward textbooks is reinforced by institutional policy, the potential influence of a textbook becomes immense. Furthermore, research on the dogmatic and authoritarian personality has indicated that students who make high scores on scales on authoritarianism tend to treat teachers and textbooks as sources of ultimate truth (Gladstein, 1960); this tendency, one suspects, applies to some extent to the majority of students, especially in elementary school.

The attitudinal content of school textbooks is therefore a matter of interest. There is now a growing body of knowledge concerning the attitudes and ideologies propounded in school textbooks. This article focuses attention on the attitudes expressed in textbooks toward questions of social and political diversity, culture conflict, and cultural pluralism.

Attitudes in Canadian textbooks

Treatment of cultural differences in textbooks has been a subject of research in Europe and North America since the early part of the century. The European work, largely conducted under the aegis of such organizations as the League of Nations, the Council of Europe, and UNESCO, has tended to concentrate on treatment of other nations in history and geography textbooks. The postwar influx of non-white immigrants into Britain has resulted in attention being paid more recently in that country ot the racial attitudes of textbooks. In the United States, where most of the work has been done within universities, studies of textbook treatment of the American Negro have predominated, with more recent work on treatment of Indians and other ethnic minorities. The amount of textbook analysis completed in Canada has been relatively small, and it has concentrated mainly on treatment of French Canadians and Indians; nevertheless, the accumulated evidence is now sufficient to allow some general conclusions to be drawn concerning evaluative treatment of various social and cultural issues in Canadian textbooks.

Two limitations need to be borne in mind in the ensuing discussion of Canadian textbooks. First, most of the textbook analysis in Canada has used Ontario texts for its data. However, it is probably legitimate to generalize from these findings to Canadian textbooks as a whole. More than one-third of Canadian school pupils are found in the public and separate schools of Ontario. Many of the texts used in Ontario are also used in other provinces (Pratt, 1969). The official list of textbooks authorized for use in Ontario schools includes both English texts and French texts written by French Canadian authors and intended for students in francophone or bilingual schools in Ontario. Finally, the findings of studies of textbook treatment of most social issues have been remarkably consistent across different provinces, and, for that matter, throughout the English-speaking world. A second limitation on the textbook studies is in terms of subject. Research has shown that evaluative treatment of social and cultural topics is largely found in social studies texts, especially history. Where the subject of the texts studied in the research cited in the following pages is indicated as social studies, this term is used to comprehend history, geography, civics, economics, politics, sociology, and law as they are taught at the pre-university level.

TREATMENT OF RACIAL GROUPS

Non-white racial groups receive relatively little attention in Canadian textbooks, but as a function of the history of Canada, the Canadian Indian is the non-white group most visible in social studies textbooks, and reference to this group probably outnumber those to all other non-white racial groups. This is particularly the case in the later elementary grades, where the history of Canada is a common subject of study. The nature of the treatment this group receives in textbooks is now fairly well established.

In 1963 Leduc, Belanger and Juneau completed a study of history texts used in Protestant and Catholic elementary schools in Quebec.

The study was the first in Canada to use quantitative techniques for textbook analysis, employing a word-count of the favourable terms applied to different groups. The study indicated that while the English and French texts differed reciprocally in their treatment of English and French Canadians, they concurred in the small number of favourable terms they applied to Indians. In the following year, the Indian and Métis Conference of Manitoba studied the textbooks used in that province and reported that the texts were contemptuous of Indian religious beliefs, concentrated on Indian faults but ignored Indian virtues, glossed over the negative results of the white man's impact, ignored Indian contributions to Canada's development, and represented drinking, gambling, and fighting as specifically Indian habits. During the next few years, this particular subject became a popular area of study: research was conducted by federal and provincial departments, by community organizations and individuals. The reports of the Royal Commission on Bilingualism and Biculturalism and the Ontario Committee on Aims and Objectives of Education (1968) commented on the inadequate treatment of Indians in school texts. The federal Department of Indian Affairs conducted its own study of textbooks used in its schools (usually those used in the province in which the schools were located) and reported a lack of information on Indian contributions to Canadian culture, use of perjorative terms to describe Indians, stereotyping, anachronism, lack of balance, and inappropriate illustrations. According to this study, "the history books in general use in Quebec would appear to require a complete review."[2] The press and television became interested in the subject (*Globe Mail*, 1967; *Telegram*, 1968; *Toronto Daily Star*, 1968; CHCH Television, 1969), particularly after the Ontario Human Rights Commission, following numerous complaints it had received concerning textbooks, commissioned a major study of the treatment of minorities in Ontario textbooks. This study by McDiarmid and Pratt (1971) of 143 Ontario social studies textbooks, and a subsequent study of 69 history textbooks by Pratt (1971), reviewed treatment of various racial, ethnic, religious, and political minorities and out-groups. A technique was developed for analysis, using the ratio of favourable to unfavourable evaluative terms, which made it possible to plot the evaluative treatment of subjects in a text as points on an interval scale. Figure 1 shows the mean positions of French Canadians, Arabs, Indians and Negroes in Ontario history textbooks authorized for 1968-1969 (Pratt, 1971). The scale indicates that whereas approximately four out of every five evaluative terms applied to French Canadians in the texts were favourable, only one out of every three terms applied to Indians and Negroes was favourable. A frequency count was made of the evaluative terms applied to the four groups.

Figure 1: Location of Four Groups on a Favourable-Unfavourable Continuum in Ontario History Textbooks

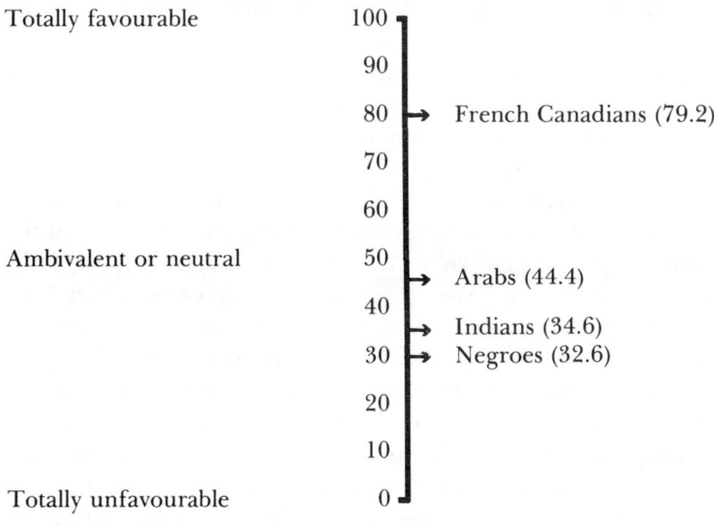

Table 1 shows the percentage of all evaluative references to each group accounted for by each of the ten terms most frequently applied to the group. The high frequency of the word "savage" associated with Indians is due to the tendency of texts to use this word as a synonym for Indian, particularly in the case of French textbooks ("sauvage").

The illustrations in social studies textbooks were also analysed, the

Table 1: Relative Frequency of Application of 10 Terms Most Frequently Applied to 4 Groups in 69 Ontario History Textbooks

Arabs	*%*	*Fr. Canadians*	*%*	*Indians*	*%*	*Negroes*	*%*
great	3.9	great	4.2	savage	10.1	friendly	9.2
cruel	2.1	brave	3.9	friendly	6.1	unfriendly	5.0
feuding	2.1	courageous	3.6	massacre	4.9	savage	4.2
kind	2.1	skillful	3.3	skillful	4.0	faithful	3.4
pagan	2.1	heroic	2.7	hostile	3.8	kind	3.4
brilliant	1.6	determined	2.0	fierce	3.1	fierce	2.9
dictator	1.6	proud	1.7	great	2.3	primitive	2.6
fierce	1.6	devoted	1.6	murder	2.1	murder	2.4
friendly	1.6	famous	1.6	unfriendly	1.7	violent	2.4
resentful	1.6	daring	1.4	thief	1.6	backward	2.4

main results of the analysis being shown in Table 2. As the table indicates, the stereotype of Indians which prevails normally shows them half naked or in native dress, with feathers in their hair, and frequently in some aggressive posture.

These studies also provided clear evidence of the tendency of textbooks to ignore important aspects of the history of non-white racial groups as well as their contemporary situation, and to minimize interracial conflict except where the non-white race could be unequivocally cast in the role of aggressor. Thus it was discovered that the extermination of the Beothuk Indians of Newfoundland and the status of the modern Canadian Indian were both largely ignored by texts; the history of the American Negro was characterized by blandness and superficiality where it was not ignored altogether; treatment of the Japanese Canadians in the Second World War was rarely discussed in textbooks dealing with the period; and the racial policies of the Nazis were omitted or glossed over in a manner that was surprising even to hardened textbook analysts. Less surprising was the finding that the treatment of the concept of race was marked by omission, confusion, inaccuracy and outright ignorance in nearly all textbooks. Of the thirty-four history and geography textbooks which the researchers expected to treat this topic, only four were classified as "good," the best two of these being French geography texts published in Paris.

Table 2: Depiction of Four Groups in Illustrations in Ontario Social Studies Textbooks

	White Canadians	*Asians*	*American Indians*	*Africans*
	%	%	%	%
Clothing				
Naked, half-naked	0	11	42	39
Native costume	0	66	53	41
Western dress	100	23	5	20
Aggression				
Fighting	0	2	12	2
Weapon in hand	6	5	20	13
Non-agressive	94	93	68	85
Decoration				
Feathers			86	
No Feathers			14	

A few quotations from textbooks may serve to summarize the issue of treatment of racial groups:

> Champlain spent the winter with the Hurons, living in a long house swarming with Indians, mice, fleas, and lice (Creighton [1962] p. 77).
>
> The Jesuits fought bravely against the rude beliefs of the Indians. It was hard to make them understand the white man's God. Gentleness and kindness were signs of weakness to the savages (Chatterton, Holmes, and Kuska [1966], p. 112).
>
> Slaves on the southern plantations were seldom badly treated. It was in their master's interest to keep them healthy and content to work in the tobacco fields (Tait [1960], p. 338).
>
> In Britain, before the war, there was hardly any coloured population and therefore no problem. Of late, however, immigrants have begun to pour into Britain from Jamaica and elsewhere in the West Indies. They were used to a low standard of living and soon turned several areas of London and other cities into coloured slums (Ricker, Saywell, and Rose [1960], p. 373).
>
> The nations of the West have all outstripped the other world, which economically, politically, and socially, stopped centuries ago. . . . The ruling aristocracy in their luxury must bear a large part of the blame for the poverty, sloth, and backwardness of much of the Asian continent. . . . In many ways Asia must blame herself for her backwardness (Innis [1965], p. 24.)

The results of the survey of Ontario social studies textbooks were published in a book entitled *Teaching Prejudice,* which provoked considerable comment in the press and in the provincial legislature. The Minister of Education countered by citing evidence from his department's own study of textbooks, the results of which, however, were not published at that time.

TREATMENT OF ETHNIC GROUPS

Studies of treatment of ethnic groups have concentrated largely on the relative treatment of English and French Canadians. As early as 1945, a committee of the Canada and Newfoundland Education Association discovered that two histories were being taught in Canada: in French schools, a history that focused on the glories of New France and saw the post-conquest history of Canada largely as the struggle for "la survivance"; in English schools, a political and constitutional history of English Canada, with French Canada providing occasional local colour (Committee for the Study of Canadian History Textbooks, 1945). These findings were confirmed by a succession of studies (Quebec: Royal Commission of Inquiry on Education in the Province of Quebec, 1965; Sevigny, 1966; Wilson,

1966), and both French- and English-Canadian historians have deplored the chauvinistic nature of history teaching in French and English Canada (Adair, 1943; Brunet, 1954, 1968). The Royal Commission on Bilingualism and Biculturalism summarized the results of a study conducted for it by Trudel and Jain with the comment that, "After studying Canadian history from a textbook, a student may well conclude that only French- and English-speaking Canadians count for anything — and that only the attitudes and actions of his own language group can be justified."[3]

It is to be expected that authors approaching Canadian history from different cultural perspectives will produce essentially different histories. But despite the attention it has received, it seems probable that the French-English issue is more fairly treated in Canadian textbooks than most other subjects in the area of intercultural relations. The research of Leduc, Belanger and Juneau showed that French texts reserve their praise largely for French Canadians, and English texts largely for English Canadians; other than that study, there is a lack of quantitative comparative evidence on treatment of English Canadians in English and French texts. But the findings that emerge from study of treatment of French Canadians in English and French texts used in Ontario suggest that the difference is not between favourable and unfavourable treatment, but between favourable and very favourable. A comparison by Pratt of evaluative terms used to describe French Canadians in twenty-six English texts and seven French texts used in Ontario showed that an average of seventy-seven per cent of the terms were favourable in the English texts and eighty-seven per cent in the French texts (difference significant at .05) (1969, 131). Of the eleven "critical issues" whose treatment was studied by McDiarmid and Pratt, the two issues in English-French relations (the expulsion of the Acadians and the conscription crisis in World War I) were the most adequately dealt with in Ontario social studies texts. The major criticism to be made of treatment of French Canadians in English texts is not of negative treatment but, as Table 1 suggests, of an unconvincing stereotype.

White ethnic groups other than English and French Canadians are accorded little space in Canadian textbooks. The nineteenth-century immigrants to Canada are admired because "they were hardy peasants and were not afraid of work" (Peart and Shaffter, 1961), and because "they stuck it out to become respected and valuable Canadian citizens" (Hodgetts, 1960). They were a "problem" only insofar as they were slow to assimilate: "they would have become Canadian more quickly if they had associated with English-speaking Canadians from the first" (Garland, 1961). The definition of a Canadian in Anglo-Saxon terms precludes recognition of the contribution of immigrants in adding a dimension to the Canadian ethnic mosaic. The cosmopolitan influence of the million non-British European immigrants to Canada since 1945 is similarly overlooked, as is the entire question of economic exploitation of immigrant groups.

In sum, the ethnic model of Canadian society conveyed in the texts is a far cry from a position of cultural pluralism, and if it does not exactly fit the melting-pot metaphor, then the appropriate image is perhaps that of a double-boiler.

TREATMENT OF RELIGIOUS GROUPS

Where religious issues arise, Canadian textbooks normally adopt a Christian viewpoint. "David and Susan Go to Church" in the second-grade social studies text (Holmes, 1958); "Your father puts money on the collection plate at church each Sunday morning" in the history book (Deyell, 1958). Some French texts adopt an avowedly confessional point of view. "On a big sheet of paper," instructs an exercise in an elementary history text written by two religious, "write in large letters the invocation: Holy Canadian Martyrs, pray for us" (Charles and Léon, 1960). A number of such texts express their regrets over the Reformation, while one categorizes the Spanish Civil War as "essentially a war of religion between Catholicism and Communism" (Brault, 1965).

McDiarmid and Pratt compared the treatment of Christians, Jews and Moslems in Ontario social studies texts, and found that treatment of all three was favourable, with Christians and Jews significantly more favourably treated than Moslems. Christians were typically "devoted," "zealous," and "martyrs"; Jews "great," "faithful," and "just"; while Moslems were "infidels" and "fanatics," but also "great," "devout," and "tolerant." While the development of Christianity is a major theme of history textbooks up to the Reformation, other religions rarely obtain more than a two- or three-page synopsis.

TREATMENT OF SOCIAL CLASSES

It is a truism that a middle-class stereotype prevails in school textbooks. It would be unrealistic to expect that the school, a middle-class institution par excellence, should reinforce any but middle-class mores. Studies by Sobel (1954) and Meyers (1968) provided empirical evidence of the class bias in American textbooks, but little research has been done into this aspect of Canadian texts. Poverty, unemployment and economic disparity rarely feature in textbook accounts of the contemporary Canadian scene. Hard work, respectability, ambition, and the deferment of gratification are seen as the means to success, which is measured in terms of property and financial affluence. This much is revealed by a superficial reading of the texts. The study conducted for the Ontario Human Rights Commission reviewed the treatment in Ontario history texts of the Canadian labour movement; the findings throw some light on the class assumptions of textbook writers. Textbook accounts of strikes usually associate them with violence and bloodshed, without indicating which parties were responsible (McDiarmid and Pratt, 1971). The labour relations policies of governments and corporations in the 1920s are praised; the practices of Henry Ford in this area are cited by one text as "typical of a new concern by businessmen for their employees' welfare" (Nicholson, Boyd, Rannie and Hobbs, 1962). Treatment of the Winnipeg General Strike, the watershed of Canadian union history, is marked by inaccuracy and hostile insinuation — Woodsworth, Dixon and Heaps, on trial for seditious conspiracy, "put up such a brilliant defence that they were acquitted" (Hodgetts, 1960). There tend to be few references to the Canadian labour movement since 1920, but McDiarmid and Pratt cite the following passage from an intermediate level textbook as indicative of a patrician approach to the subject:

> The appearance of an organization like the Canadian Labour Congress, with a membership of well over one million workers, and the recent exposure of criminal leadership in some of the American unions, raises the question of whether trade unions are in danger of becoming too strong. Many Canadians feel that new laws are required to control the unions, while others advocate that they should be forced to sever their connection with the American labour movement. Whatever the outcome of these suggestions may be, it is certainly true that the workmen of Canada should be more determined than ever before to elect trade-union officials capable of wielding their power with a deep sense of responsibility to society as a whole as well as for the benefit of their own members. Otherwise, there is the danger that an overly agressive, irresponsible labour movement could kill the goose that lays the golden egg.[4]

It is, however, significant that within the past few years two well-balanced texts specifically on the Winnipeg General Strike have been authorized for use in Ontario in secondary school history courses (Balawyder, 1967; Magder, 1960).

TREATMENT OF POLITICAL GROUPS

The political viewpoint espoused by textbooks is of major interest because of the role of the school in political socialization; yet of all aspects of textbooks, this has been among the least studied.

Canadian school textbooks identify "democracy" with the North American way of life. Democracy, however, is never defined; rather, it is used as a synonym for a general political good. A middle-of-the-road political position is usually promoted implicitly and occasionally made explicit. In one Ontario text, for example, a cartoon illustrates the caption, "Moderates who stand near the centre are usually those who think over a problem calmly and carefully" (Deyell, 1958).

It is impossible to say whether the generally cautious treatment of political topics in Canadian texts is voluntary on the part of authors or the result of pressure from publishers or governments. Such pressure has been known to exist elsewhere. In Mississippi, a Senate Education Committee recommended in 1940 that civics texts for Negro schools be void of references to voting, elections, civic responsibility, or democracy (Bierstedt, 1955). The writer has been unable to verify the legend that in the 1940s a committee was appointed by the Department of Education in British Columbia to comb school textbooks for references to the CCF and to expunge them. What is obvious from a reading of the textbooks is the contrast between the lack of critical discussion of North American political institutions and the no-holds-barred treatment of Communist countries. "The problem of peace: The Soviet menace" is a chapter heading in a Grade 10 history text (Ricker, Saywell, and Rose, 1960). A textbook authorized for use in the Ontario World Politics program, and written by a Canadian political scientist, reads like a primer for the Cold War: "Chapter 6: The Iron Fist — Nazism and Fascism . . . Chapter 7: The Iron Mind — Communism" (Fox, 1965). One text, published in 1954, but still authorized for use in Ontario in 1971-1972, includes a cartoon depicting election day in the Soviet Union, complete with bus labelled "Salt Mine Special" — "A special bus for ungrateful comrades who do not vote for George" (Brown, Careless, Craig, and Ray, 1954).

While texts expatiate on the "spying, secret arrests, torture, Siberian exile, forced labour camps, and individual and mass executions" (Ricker, Saywell and Rose, 1960) in the Soviet Union, treatment of right-wing totalitarian states receives rather cursory coverage. McDiarmid and Pratt found that of nineteen Ontario textbooks dealing with twentieth-century history, eight did not mention Nazi treatment of minorities, and none was rated higher than "fair" in their discussion of this topic.

In order to determine more exactly the political complexion of Canadian textbooks, an analysis was conducted by the writer on six textbooks authorized for the study of history at the intermediate level (Grades 7-10) in Ontario for 1971-72. The six texts were the following:

1. Brown, Careless, Craig and Ray. *Canada and the World.* 1954.
2. Hodgetts. *Decisive Decades.* 1960.
3. Lambert. *The Twentieth Century.* 1960.

4. Ricker, Saywell and Rose. *The Modern Era.* 1960.
5. Peart and Schaffter. *The Winds of Change.* 1961.
6. Nicholson, Boyd, Rannie and Hobbs. *Three Nations.* 1962, revised 1969.

The sample represented all the English-language texts for that level that dealt with the twentieth-century history of North America and Europe. The study aimed to assess the relative treatment of various political individuals and groups from the political "left," "centre," and "right." Three hypotheses were proposed: 1) that the textbooks would favour the political right over the political left; 2) that the textbooks would favour the political centre over the political extremes; and 3) that the political viewpoints of history textbooks and of history teachers would be similar. The instrument used to analyse the texts was ECO Analysis. This is a quantitative content analysis technique which has been described fully elsewhere (Pratt, 1971a); it produces a "Coefficient of Evaluation" representing the percentage of the value judgments expressed about a subject in a source which are favourable. Thus a Coefficient of zero indicates a totally unfavourable affective treatment of a subject, and a Coefficient of 100 totally favourable.

Table 3: Evaluation of 21 Political Subjects in 6 History Textbooks

Rank	*Subject*	*Coefficient of Evaluation*	*N of Evaluative References*
1	Sir John A. Macdonald	95.2	21
2	J.S. Woodsworth	88.0	25
3	President Herbert Hoover	70.6	34
4	President Woodrow Wilson	69.9	113
5	President Franklin D. Roosevelt	69.9	83
6	Sir Wilfrid Laurier	67.7	89
7	Sir Robert Borden	57.8	45
8	CCF-NDP	50.0	18
9	Karl Marx	45.0	27
10	Socialists	33.9	59
11	Nicolai Lenin	33.3	30
12	John Foster Dulles	31.3	13
13	Richard B. Bennett	30.0	20
14	Bolsheviks	27.0	36
15	Communists	24.5	380
16	Benito Mussolini	24.1	108
17	Fascists	21.8	78
18	Nazis	21.4	143
19	Adolf Hitler	18.8	307
20	Ku Klux Klan	10.3	29
21	Senator Joseph McCarthy	4.3	46

A minimum of ten evaluative assertions concerning a subject is necessary to calculate the Coefficient of Evaluation. As five of the twenty-six subjects originally chosen (Duplessis, Anarchists, Castro, Franco, Chiang Kai-shek) received less than ten evaluative references, these subjects were not included in the analysis. The Coefficients achieved by the other subjects are shown in Table 3.

The unit of analysis in the study was the six textbooks as a whole. To determine whether grouping of the results in this way obscured differences among the texts, scores were determined for each subject in each text, where sufficient references could be found. The Coefficients for those subjects for which Coefficients could be determined in four or more texts are shown in Table 4, which reveals a high degree of consistency among the texts.

Having determined the evaluation of the political subjects in the texts, the next stage was to investigate the relationship between evaluation of the subjects and their location on the political spectrum. The ranking of the twenty-one subjects on the left-wing–right-wing continuum is largely self-evident, but to avoid the unreliability of a single judgment, practising history teachers were asked to rate each subject on a scale of 0 (extreme left) to 100 (extreme right). The teachers (N = 35, median age = 30.7 years, median teaching experience = 5.5 years) were engaged in an in-service training program at Queen's University during the summer of 1972.

Table 4: Evaluation of 8 Political Subjects in 6 History Textbooks

	Text					
Subject	*Canada & the World* 1	*Decisive Decades* 2	*The 20th Century* 3	*The Modern Era* 4	*The Winds of Change* 5	*Three Nations* 6
Wilson	—	64.7	60.0	86.7	73.1	70.0
Roosevelt	—	76.0	66.7	68.8	66.7	—
Laurier	—	65.4	—	76.2	65.2	70.0
Communists	19.3	22.6	34.0	30.8	25.5	18.2
Mussolini	—	29.4	19.0	23.1	25.0	26.7
Fascists	12.5	31.7	8.3	—	46.2	—
Nazis	—	23.4	4.5	11.8	37.5	20.0
Hitler	14.3	17.5	22.0	14.0	19.3	20.0

Table 5 shows the median judgments of the thirty-five teachers regarding political location of the subjects, compared to the evaluation of the subjects in the textbooks. Correlation of the two sets of scores yielded a correlation coefficient of −.320. The first hypothesis was therefore not sustained. Instead of favouring the right-wing subjects, the texts showed a slight and not statistically significant tendency to evaluate right-wing subjects less favourably than left-wing subjects. (No immediate relationship between political orientation and age was established for the teachers. The correlation between teacher age and evaluation score accorded by teachers to Socialists was .075.)

Table 5: Evaluation of Political Subjects by Texts Compared to Location on Political Spectrum

Subject	*Coefficient in Texts*	*Evaluative Rank in Texts*	*Right-left score by teachers*	*Right-left rank by teachers*
Macdonald	95.2	1	60.7	11
Woodsworth	88.0	2	35.5	16
Hoover	70.6	3	70.9	8
Wilson	69.9	4	55.2	12
Roosevelt	69.9	5	50.5	14
Laurier	67.7	6	52.0	13
Borden	57.8	7	70.7	9
CCF-NDP	50.0	8	32.5	17
Marx	45.0	9	10.2	21
Socialists	33.9	10	35.6	15
Lenin	33.3	11	10.9	18
Dulles	31.3	12	78.0	7
Bennett	30.0	13	62.5	10
Bolsheviks	27.0	14	10.8	20
Communists	24.5	15	10.9	18
Mussolini	24.1	16	85.8	6
Fascists	21.8	17	90.3	3
Nazis	21.4	18	90.6	1
Hitler	18.8	19	90.4	2
Ku Klux Klan	10.3	20	90.1	4
McCarthy	4.3	21	88.0	5

An "index of extremeness" was next derived by measuring the distance of the median "right-left score" as judged by teachers from the theoretical mid-point of fifty. These data are summarized in Table 6. The observed correlation between the columns in Table 6 was −.772 (sig. at .01). The second hypothesis was therefore sustained: the evaluation of political subjects in textbooks is related to the distance of the subject from the political centre.

Table 6: Political Extremeness and Evaluation of Political Subjects by Texts

Subject	*Coefficient in Texts*	*Evaluative Rank in Texts*	*Extremeness Index*	*Extremeness Rank*
Macdonald	95.2	1	10.7	18
Woodsworth	88.0	2	14.5	15
Hoover	70.6	3	20.9	12
Wilson	69.9	4	5.2	19
Roosevelt	69.9	5	0.5	21
Laurier	67.7	6	2.0	20
Borden	57.8	7	20.7	13
CCF-NDP	50.0	8	17.5	14
Marx	45.0	9	39.8	5
Socialists	33.9	10	14.4	16
Lenin	33.3	11	39.1	7
Dulles	31.3	12	28.0	11
Bennett	30.0	13	12.5	17
Bolsheviks	27.0	14	39.2	6
Communists	24.5	15	39.1	7
Mussolini	24.1	16	35.8	10
Fascists	21.8	17	40.3	3
Nazis	21.4	18	40.6	1
Hitler	18.8	19	40.4	2
Ku Klux Klan	10.3	20	40.1	4
McCarthy	4.3	21	38.0	9

Finally, a comparison was made between evaluation of political subjects by the textbooks and by history teachers. the history teachers mentioned above were asked to rate each subject on a scale of 0-100, representing their evaluative opinion of each subject. The order of this and the previous question were scrambled to counteract the reaction of one question with the other. Subsequent discussion with the teachers revealed that some of the thirty-six teachers completing the questionnaire misinterpreted the instructions to "evaluate the subjects" as being intended to elicit their opinion as to how interesting the topics were as school subjects. Favourable evaluation of both Communists and Hitler (at sixty or over) was taken as *prima facie* evidence of this misinterpretation. Eleven papers were rejected for this reason, leaving a sample of twenty-five (median age 30.5, median years experience 5.5). The median evaluations of the political subjects by this group is shown in Table 7. The similarities in rank, and in some cases in score, between the textbooks and the teachers are remarkable, and amongst other things further validate the instrument used in text analysis. Only three subjects are evaluated much differently by teachers than by texts; textbooks evaluate Hoover more favourably than do teachers, while teachers are more favourably inclined toward Scoialists and Lenin than are texts. The observed correlation between the scores in Table 7 was .797 (sig. at .01). The third hypothesis was thus sustained: the political viewpoints of teachers and textbooks reinforce one another.

Table 7: Evaluation of Political Subjects by Textbooks and by Teachers

Subject	*Coefficient in Texts*	*Evaluative Rank in Texts*	*Evaluation by teachers*	*Evaluative rank by teachers*
Macdonald	95.2	1	74.9	1
Woodsworth	88.0	2	60.0	5
Hoover	70.6	3	35.0	13
Wilson	69.9	4	69.9	4
Roosevelt	69.9	5	70.3	3
Laurier	67.7	6	70.4	2
Borden	57.8	7	49.8	10
CCF-NDP	50.0	8	50.3	9
Marx	45.0	9	59.6	8
Socialists	33.9	10	60.0	5
Lenin	33.3	11	60.0	5
Dulles	31.3	12	35.0	13
Bennett	30.0	13	45.0	11
Bolsheviks	27.0	14	40.0	12
Communists	24.5	15	30.2	15
Mussolini	24.1	16	19.6	16
Fascists	21.8	17	14.8	17
Nazis	21.4	18	10.4	19
Hitler	18.8	19	10.2	20
Ku Klux Klan	10.3	20	0.4	21
McCarthy	4.3	21	14.0	18

A final indication of the nature of the value judgments of political subjects by textbooks was provided by a frequency count of the evaluative terms used in texts about political subjects. The five or six terms most frequently used in evaluative assertions concerning six of the subjects are shown in Table 8. It should be borne in mind that terms such as "just" and "idealist" in the list comprehend such words as "justice" and "ideals" or "idealism" in the sources. The table illustrates the somewhat stereotyped and repetitive treatment of political extremes by textbooks.

Table 8: Relative Frequency of Application of Terms Most Frequently Applied to 6 Subjects in 6 History Textbooks

Wilson	%	*Laurier*	%	*Communists*	%
just	7.1	eloquent	5.6	dictatorship	8.2
idealist	5.3	great	4.5	threat	3.9
peace	5.3	bitter	4.5	strong	3.4
failure	5.3	determined	3.4	fear	3.2
freedom	3.5	remarkable	3.4	force	2.6
great	3.5				
Mussolini	%	*Nazis*	%	*Hitler*	%
dictatorship	27.8	aggressive	7.0	dictatorship	8.8
aggressive	4.6	tyranny	6.3	aggressive	5.2
threat	3.7	menace	3.5	threat	4.2
ruthless	2.8	dictatorship	3.5	force	2.6
failure	2.8	threat	2.8	ruthless	2.3
glory	2.8			strong	2.3

Conclusions and Implications

The content analysis studies show that Canadian school textbooks do not represent or support a culturally pluralist model of society. They do support a consensus, non-controversial, conventional view of society. A number of reasons may be suggested for this.

School textbook authors themselves represent a narrow segment of the population. Much more source analysis is needed in this area, but the general delineation is clear. Authors are typically successful teachers in their thirties or forties who have risen in the administrative hierarchy of the schools to department head, principal, or teachers' college instructor. Often a university academic is included as co-author or consultant, but textbook authors are not as a rule academics. The books are written ten or twenty years after the authors' academic training. The similarity of treatment of topics among different textbooks suggests use of common secondary sources rather than original research. Almost inevitably, these middle-class, middle-aged, middle-income, middle-status authors share common social and political ideologies: they are middle Canada.

The centripetal tendency of the authors' output is compounded by the existence of official authorization committees. A textbook that fails to obtain authorization may not even pay for the cost of its publication; but a text which achieves authorization and retains it for a decade or more can reap enormous profits. It is therefore in the interest of publishing houses to ensure that textbook content is acceptable to authorizing committees, and this common sieve through which textbooks pass probably serves to eliminate expressions of divergent opinion on social issues.

A further conformist pressure subsists in the nature of the textbook itself. If a text is designed as a compendium or condensation of knowledge in a social area, sometimes compressing the history of three centuries or the geography of a dozen countries into three hundred pages, then it is most likely that the text will concentrate on common features and ignore diversity. In consequence of these factors, the advantage of authorities providing a choice of alternative textbooks and encouraging teachers to use multiple textbooks for a given grade level and subject are illusory.

Conformity goes hand in hand with blandness. Culture conflict is not a serious issue in many textbooks. Where it exists, it is recorded in terms of savage natives who unsuccessfully opposed the inexorable march of progress, represented by the white man. Deliberate pains are taken to minimize well-known episodes of conflict. The Canadian Indian perpetrates, but is rarely the object, of massacres; he simply fades quietly out of the textbooks in the later nineteenth century. Life was rosy in the ante-bellum South, except for the "extremists known as Abolitionists" (Rogers and Harris, 1967). Joe Hill, Sacco and Vanzetti, Norman Bethune, and the Rosenbergs do not appear in school texts. Little or no coverage is given to movements suggesting alternative patterns of social organization. The labour and civil rights movements are seen only as the struggle of certain groups to become more, not less, typically North American. The Canadian Bill of Rights, a rarely enforceable showpiece statute, is invariably cited in civics textbooks; mention of enforceable provincial legislation against discrimination is conspicuous by its absence.

In sum, the school textbook introduces students to a unitary view of society. Official pronouncements in favour of cultural pluralism find no counterpart in Canadian school textbooks. Social and ideological divergence provide occasional interesting episodes and anecdotes, but are not considered part of the mainstream of Canadian life. Canada is viewed as a white, Christian, homogeneous, middle-class country where liberal democracy and free enterprise have combined to produce the ideal society. That society may not remain static, but may be transformed, does not concern the textbooks, for none of the subjects taught in school consider the future a legitimate part of their subject matter. Students whose aspirations and opinions differ from the monolithic model are likely to be considered, and to consider themselves, misfits.

But there are signs of the beginning of change. The academic writing of Canadian history is itself changing, so that the history of Canada is no longer written as the view from the Commons' press gallery. Mealing's criticism of Canadian historians, issued in 1965,

> Our shortcoming has been to ignore rather than to deny the class structure of society. . . . The greater number of historians have taken their agenda from dead politicians[5]

has since become less valid. It would be unlikely that one of Canada's leading historians could today, as Creighton did in 1957, publish a "history of Canada" that made no mention of the Winnipeg General Strike. Admittedly a time-lag of about two decades exists between the leading edge of academic thought and school textbooks. But textbooks authorized for use in Ontario in the last two years include at least ten texts on Canadian Indians, and several on such topics as immigration, student unrest, Americanization, Progressivism and Socialism, and particular episodes of culture conflict such as the Conscription crises, the Riel affair, and the Acadian deportation. The great majority of these texts are collections of readings, which increases the diversity of viewpoints represented. (On the other hand, some of them perpetuate the deficiencies of the traditional textbook; in one reader on Canadian Indians (Sheffe, 1970), made up almost entirely of newspaper articles, less than a quarter of the items are actually written by Indians.) New courses of study, such as the Ontario programs in World Religions, Man, Science, and Technology, and People and Politics, provide a vehicle, and in fact call for, a close look at questions of cultural diversity and social dissent. In the long run, these changes may have little effect on students' attitudes, partly because it is easier to change texts and programs than to change teachers, and partly because students' social beliefs are largely determined in the elementary school, where little change in textbooks and programs is evident.

We return, therefore, to the original proposition of this paper, that the school reflects society, and reflects most accurately the stratum of society which controls education by providing the civil servants, board members, and teachers whose decisions largely determine the nature of schooling. If society changes radically enough to alter the complexion of this middle stratum, then schools and textbooks will alter with it, as educational decision-makers begin to co-opt as teachers, administrators, or textbook authors, individuals who at present would be classified as dissenters, and this in turn will socialize school children into varied or different social ideologies. Such changes are already visible on a minute scale. On any major scale, they remain in the distant future.

Notes

1. A.B. Hodgetts, *What Culture? What Heritage? A Study of Civic Education in Canada* (Toronto: Ontario Institute for Studies in Education, 1968), p. 24, 26–27, 45.
2. Canada, Department of Indian Affairs and Northern Development, *Report on Textbooks* (n.d. Received February 1969), p. 7.
3. Canada, Royal Commission on Bilingualism and Biculturalism, *Report*, Vol. 2, Education (Ottawa: Queen's Printer, 1968), p. 282.
4. Hodgetts, *"What Culture? What Heritage?"* p. 537.
5. S.R. Mealing, "The Concept of Social Class and the Interpretation of Canadian History," *Canadian Historical Review,* Vol. 46 (1965), p. 202.

References

Adair, E.R. "The Canadian Contribution to Historical Science," *Culture*, Vol. 4 (1943), p. 63–83.

Balawyder, A. *The Winnipeg General Strike.* Toronto: Copp Clark, 1967.

Bierstedt, R. "The Writers of Textbooks," in L.J. Cronbach *et al., Text Materials in Modern Education.* Urbana, Ill.: University of Illinois Press, 1955, pp. 96–128.

Brault, L. *Le Canada au XXe siècle.* Toronto: Nelson, 1965.

Brown, G.W., Careless, J.M.S., Craig, G.M. and Ray, E. *Canada and the World.* Toronto: Dent, 1954.

Brunet, M. "Histoire et Historiens," in M. Brunet, *Canadians et Canadiens.* Montreal: Fides, 1954, pp. 32–46.

Brunet, M. "La Recherche et l'Enseignment de l'Histoire," in M. Brunet, *Quebec-Canada Anglais: Deux itineraires, un affrontement*. Montreal: Editions H.M.H., 1968, pp. 43–58.

Canada. Department of Indian Affairs and Northern Development. *Report on Textbooks.* Mimeographed (n.d. Received February 1969).

Canada. Dominion Bureau of Statistics. *Canada Yearbook 1971.* Ottawa: Queen's Printer, 1971.

Canada. Royal Commission on Bilingualism and Biculturalism. *Report,* Vol. 2. *Education*. Ottawa: Queen's Printer, 1968.

Charles, Frère, and Léon, Frère. *La nouvelle France.* Toronto: Nelson, 1960.

Chatterton, W.G., Holmes, M.W., and Kuska, A. *New World Social Studies*. Toronto: Holt, Rinehart, Winston, 1966.

CHCH Television, Hamilton, Ontario. Program on the Treatment of Indians in School Textbooks (First broadcast 18 February 1969. C. Screen Gems, Toronto).

Committee for the Study of Canadian History Textbooks. "Report," *Canadian Education,* Vol. 1 (1945), p. 2–34.

Creighton, D. *Dominion of the North: A History of Canada*. Rev. ed. Toronto: Macmillan, 1957.

Creighton, L.B. *Canada: The Struggle for Empire.* Rev. ed. Toronto: Dent, 1962.

Deyell, E. *Canada: A New Land.* Toronto: Gage, 1958.

______. *Canada: The New Nation.* Toronto: Gage, 1958.

Fisher, F.L. "Influences of Reading and Discussion on the Attitudes of Fifth Graders towards American Indians," *Journal of Educational Research,* Vol. 62 (1968), pp. 130–34.

Fox, P. *Battlefront: The Fight for Liberty.* Toronto: Holt, Rinehart, Winston, 1965.

Garland, A. *Canada, Our Country: Part 2.* Toronto: Macmillan, 1961.

Gladstein, G.A. "Study Behavior of Gifted Stereotyped and Nonstereotyped College Students" *Personnel Guidance Journal,* Vol. 38 (1960), pp. 470–74.

Globe and Mail. "Human rights: Insulting references sought in textbooks," November 28, 1967.

Hallam, R.N. "Logical Thinking in History," *Educational Review*, Vol. 19 (1967), p. 182–202.

Haller, E.J. and Thorson, S.J. "The Political Socialization of Children and the Structure of the Elementary School," *Interchange,* Vol. 1, No. 3 (1970), pp. 45–55.

Hess, R.D. and Torney, J.V. *The Development of Political Attitudes in Children.* Chicago: Aldine, 1967.

Hodgetts, A.B. *Decisive Decades.* Toronto: Nelson, 1960.

______. *What Culture? What Heritage? A Study of Civic Education in Canada.* Toronto: Ontario Institute for Studies in Education, 1968.

Holmes, M.W. *We live in Greenwood Village.* Toronto: Dent, 1958.

Indian and Métis Conference, Committee of the Community Welfare Planning Council. *Survey of Canadian History Textbooks: Submission to the Curriculum Revision Committee, Manitoba Department of Education*, Mimeographed. Winnipeg, 1964.

Innis, H. *History of Civilization.* Rev. ed. Toronto: McGraw Hill, 1965.

Lambert, R.S. *The Twentieth Century.* Toronto: Grant, 1960.

Leduc, A., Belanger, P.W., and Juneau, A. *Les Manuels d'histoire du Canada.* Mimeographed (Quebec City: Laval University, 1963).

Lichter, J.H., and Johnson, D.W. "Changes in Attitude of White Elementary School Students after Use of Multiethnic Readers," *Journal of Educational Psychology,* Vol. 60 (1969), p. 148–52.

Magder, B. *The Winnipeg General Strike: Management Labour Relations.* Toronto: Maclean-Hunter, 1969.

McDiarmid, G.L. and Pratt, D. *Teaching Prejudice.* Toronto: Ontario Institute for Studies in Education, 1971.

Mealing, S.R. "The Concept of Social Class and the Interpretation of Canadian History," *Canadian Historical Review,* Vol. 46 (1965), pp. 201–18.

Meyers, H.W. "An Analysis of Selected Elementary Textbooks to Determine the Extent of Expression of Certain Social Class Values," *Dissertation Abstracts,* Vol. 28 (1968), p. 4537-A.

Nicholson, G.W.L., Boyd, H.H., Rannie, R.J., and Hobbs, A.E. *Three Nations.* Toronto: McClelland and Stewart, 1962.

Ontario. Provincial Committee on Aims and Objectives of Education in the Schools of Ontario. *Living and Learning: Report.* Toronto: Ontario Department of Education, 1968.

Peart, H.W. and Schaffter, J. *The Winds of Change.* Toronto: Ryerson, 1961.

Pratt, D. "An Instrument for Measuring Evaluative Assertions concerning Minority Groups and Its Application in an Analysis of History Textbooks Approved for Ontario Schools." Ph.D. dissertation, University of Toronto, 1969.

______. "Value Judgments in Textbooks: The Coefficient of Evaluation as a Quantitative Measure," *Interchange*, Vol. 2, No. 3 (1971), pp. 1–14.

______. *How to find and measure bias in textbooks.* Englewood Cliffs, N.J.: Educational Technology Press, 1971.

Quebec: Royal Commission of Inquiry on Education in the Province of Quebec. *Report.* Vol. 3. *L'Administration de l'enseignment*. Quebec City, 1965.

Ricker, J.C., Saywell, J.T., and Rose, E.E. *The Modern Era.* Toronto: Clarke Irwin, 1960.

Rogers, S.J. and Harris, D.F. *Nation of the North.* Toronto: Clarke Irwin, 1967.

Sears, D.O. Review of *The Development of Political Attitudes in Children* by R.D. Hess and J.V. Torney, *Harvard Education Review,* Vol. 38 (1968), pp. 571–77.

Sevigny, R. "Analyze de contenu de manuels d'histoire du Canada." M.A. thesis, Université Laval, Quebec City, 1966.

Sheffe, N. *Issues for the Seventies: Canada's Indians.* Toronto: McGraw-Hill, 1970.

Sobel, M.J. "An Analysis of Social Studies Textbooks in regard to their Treatment of Four Areas of Human Relations," *Dissertation Abstracts*, Vol. 14 (1954), p. 950.

Sullivan, E.V. *Piaget and the School Curriculum: A Critical Appraisal*. Toronto: Ontario Institute for Studies in Education, 1967.

Sullivan, E.V., Byrne, N., and Stager, M. "The Development of Canadian Students' Political Conceptions," *Interchange,* Vol. 1, No. 3 (1970), pp. 56–67.

Tait, G.E. *Fair Domain.* Toronto: Ryerson, 1960.

Tannenbaum, P.H. "Attitudes Towards Source and Concept as Factors in Attitude Change through Communications," *Dissertation Abstracts*, Vo.. 13 (1953), p. 1288.

Toronto Telegram. "Bias as history," (editorial, Dec. 13, 1968), p. 6.

Toronto Daily Star. "Tell it the way it was," (Editorial, Oct. 15, 1968), p. 6.

Watts, W.A. "Relative Persistence of Opinion Change Induced by Active compared to Passive Participation," *Journal of Personality and Social Psychology,* Vol. 5 (1967), pp. 4–15.

Wilson, R.D. "An Inquiry into the Interpretation of Canadian History in the Elementary and Secondary School Textbooks of English and French Canada." M.A. thesis, McGill University, 1966.

Curriculum Development

PAUL ROBINSON

Introduction

In the past the ethnically pluralistic nature of Canadian society has not been adequately accounted for in curriculum development for schools. This statement does not constitute a charge of omission, but instead, taking into account demographic data respecting ethnicity in this country, particularly since the 1890s, reflects a premise about the nature and function of the schooling process: schools have been seen primarily as agents of socialization for Anglo- or Franco-conformity.

As undefinable as the term "national consciousness" might be, it is probably the best descriptive term of a recent reorientation, in fields as diverse as literary criticism and politics, to the celebration of the sociological fact that Canada is, to echo the political cliche "a pluralistic society existing within a bicultural framework."

The implications for curriculum development are revolutionary. Educationists cannot simply append the concept to the existing corpus. This article makes an attempt to demonstrate, with reference to a specific (itself heterogenous) population, the Native groups of Canada, that (a) curriculum developers must define this pluralism in more incisive terms than heretofore; and (b) that this redefinition dictates a recategorization and reintegration of the components of curriculum development; with the outcome that (c) previously held notions about objectives, content, implementation, and teaching and resource personnel must be radically altered.

A definition of culture. To include such culture-specific curriculum components as snow-shoe making, and the teaching of syllabics, and to champion such curriculum changes with the modifiers "cross-cultural," "culturally inclusive" and "multicultural" is misleading. The origin of this tokenism is the definition of culture as a collection of traits. Culture, thought of in this way, is more easily manipulated by non-native curriculum developers, but when the artifacts of this

---

SOURCE: *Canadian Society for the Study of Education Yearbook,* 1 (1974), *Canadian Native Schools in Transition,* pp. 35–46. Reprinted by permission of the author and the Canadian Society for the Study of Education.

definition are manifest in schools, they are often simply inappropriate, perceived as incongruities by the community to which they were meant to speak.

Cross-cultural understanding. This poses a rhetorical question: Can an individual of one culture ever fully understand a culture different from his own? The qualified answer that concerns us is that one can try to achieve an increasing competence in analytical and intuitive understanding of that other culture.

As people involved in the development of potential learning experiences for individuals representing a variety of cultures, it is incumbent upon curriculum developers to be as sensitive as possible to culture differences and similarities. Such sensitivity must exceed the obvious. Curriculum developers must realize that such practices as including some "first" language teaching, some trapping and other out-of-doors experiences, and some legends and story-telling are, at best, initial and limited steps in developing a truly multicultural education program. It would be misleading to suggest that this is all that is required. Until such time as people can see their group's attitudes and values reflected in the total learning experience which schools provide, there is no justification for complacency.

Reciprocity. Cross-cultural understanding, by definition, presupposes reciprocity between cultural groups. In Canada, the Euro-Canadian society has been slow to recognize that it has much to learn from the Indian and Inuit peoples. For example, of increasing concern in the dominant Canadian society is the relationship of man to his environment. Typically, the non-native establishment seeks answers through reliance on science and technology. Pollution control measures are enacted; controlled growth or even no growth policies are advocated; research studies become the "name of the game." The paradox of this search is that the non-native society looks everywhere for solutions except right on its own doorstep: over several centuries the "first citizens" of the North American continent have developed an efficacious value system respecting man's place in nature. It is reasonable to suggest that in this and other areas representatives of non-native cultures could learn from their Indian and Inuit counterparts if they would but recognize that cultural understanding is a shared proposition, and that native cultures incorporate values worthy of emulation. Unfortunately, non-native peoples rarely admit that their cultures do not have all the answers.

From the sociological realities of Canadian society, an imperative is derived: that curriculum development for native students be approached on a more nearly comprehensive basis in order that every aspect of the learning experience be integrated and be addressed to the attitudes, values, customs, and traditions of young learners. In order to realize this goal a number of principles for curriculum development have been isolated. Note that no claim is made that these are the only principles worthy of consideration. Realistically, the following can be considered only as starting points.

PRINCIPLES OF MULTICULTURAL CURRICULUM DEVELOPMENT

a) The multicultural curriculum envisaged here originates from the point of view that learning experiences are best provided when they are built upon the strengths the child brings with him to the school. The implication is that the teacher will diagnose and determine the child's strengths prior to developing the learning program. Building upon the strong attributes of the child, the learning program can attempt to build the bridges necessary to lead to development in terms of the weaker learning areas.
b) One of the most important strengths the Indian/Inuit child may bring to the classroom setting is his capability in terms of his mother tongue. In those localities where the mother tongue is the language of common currency, the learning program in the first three or four years should be carried on in the mother tongue with English or French being introduced gradually, and taught specifically as a second language.
c) The pluralistic character of Canadian society implies that classroom programs must reflect an evaluation of various cultures on an equal basis. There can be no implicit or explicit hierarchy of cultures that suggest that non-native cultures are more important and therefore automatically deserving of greater emphasis. It is imperative that school programs ensure a kind of parity in scheduling of the manifestly "cultural" aspects of any program, course offering, or classroom activity.
d) Closely related to language and cultural considerations is the principle of freedom of choice on the part of the individual student. The school must provide those learning experiences which will afford the child an opportunity to develop the lifestyle that is compatible with his needs and interests. In this respect, education must make it possible for the individual to choose between and among such possible life patterns as: the wage-earning economy; trapping, fishing, hunting economy; guaranteed annual income economy; and leisure-oriented social living. The emphasis must be open-ended so that the developing individual is free to make his choice rather than having his future predetermined by the educational system.

e) Rigid confinement of curriculum content to particular grade levels is obsolete. A thirteen (K-12) year continuum of learning experiences must be regarded as being internally fluid in character. The child must have the opportunity to develop at his unique rate of growth and in keeping with his abilities, needs and interests.

f) The organization of learning material is based on the assumption that there will be no systematic segregation of pupils on the arbitrary and biased basis of evaluation of competence. There is ample evidence to indicate that homogeneous grouping procedures do affect the expectations that teachers set for particular groups. Moreover, ability grouping procedures tend to deprive the child who is experiencing learning difficulties of the stimulation and motivation that he might be expected to receive from members of his peer group.

g) The various disciplines, as these are defined in the composite curriculum, should be viewed as categorical aids in the pupils' quest for skills, understanding and emerging attitudes, and not as discrete bodies of content to be mastered, nor as organizing criteria for such things as timetables, evaluation and, in general, administrative and teacher convenience. It should be acknowledged that subject fields, and their adjuncts, textbooks and the like, are useful primarily as resources and not as ends in themselves. The emphasis is thus placed on the all-embracing nature of the learning experience and not on discrete subject areas.

h) The tie that binds the curriculum is communication, broadly defined. Conventionally, communication is thought of in terms of the language arts: listening, speaking, reading and writing. This interpretation is too narrow in that it excludes communication via art, music, drama, mathematics, science experimentation, physical education and recreation; and, indeed, any activity through which the individual conveys meaning without the necessity of resorting to verbalization. Given the difficulties created by the fact that the national language is the second language of many students, it is emphasized that a variety of avenues of communication should be explored and utilized. The child who has problems communicating through the spoken and/or written word may find the medium of art to be more suited to his needs. Pantomine, cuisenaire rods, jigsaw puzzles, creative dance — all are ways and means of communication that have a legitimate place in the classroom. Moreover, there is little reason, save tradition itself, for the continuing emphasis that is placed on print as the one effective communication tool. Certainly, it is apparent that film in its many forms, tapes, records and transparencies are often not used sufficiently. Reiterated in stronger terms, a successfully enunciated curriculum will be amenable to mediation via the widest range of possible communication models.

Curriculum Implementation

Utilizing the aforementioned principles as a framework within which the actual writing of the curriculum can take place, it is necessary to examine certain specific multicultural education variables. It is probable that the degree of sensitivity to these variables will predetermine the success or failure of any attempted curriculum implementation. The primary area of concern may be stated in terms of attitudes and values.

Young people today live in a society characterized by ever-shifting patterns of attitudes and values. Recognition of this has become apparent through the growing awareness of the multiplicity of value systems found in diverse cultural groups, and by the identification of conflicting attitudes and values which have evolved within cultural entities. In specific instances the emerging conflicts strike very close to the foundation upon which North American society is built. In helping young people to prepare themselves for living in the latter part of the twentieth century, the educator will ignore these conflicts at his peril. Here are some examples to consider:

a) The motivational forces that determine much of the activity taking place in a school are essentially middle class in derivation. The WASP atmosphere of the average classroom can be very real. Such alleged virtues as hard work, minimum play, competition, striving, acquisition of material goods, applying oneself to a task in the hope of future rewards, can be said to be ingrained in the Euro-Canadian society. There is research suggesting that educators, disproportionately representing the low-middle income group, are not immune to value systems characterized by the aforementioned values. In fact, participation in the teaching profession is for many upwardly mobile individuals open acknowledgement of the acceptance and worth of this complex of values. In Indian/Inuit societies, middle class values can be meaningless. The following examples may be useful in demonstrating the conflicts which can occur.

Euro-Canadian	*Indian-Inuit*
All men should strive to climb the ladder of success. In this sense success can be measured by a wide range of superlatives: *first, the most, the best, etc.*	The influence of one's elders is important. Young people lack maturity and experience. A man seeks perfection within himself not in comparison with others.
People should save for the future: "a penny saved is a penny earned," "take care of the pennies and the dollars will look after themselves."	Share freely what you have. One of the greatest virtues is giving. "He who has plenty while others are in need is shamed."
It is necessary to be aggressive and competitive in order to get ahead.	It is preferable to remain submerged within the group until such time as one's specific skills and/or assistance is called for. There is no need overtly to seek to lead or to attempt to dominate.

b) "Searching for alternatives" typified the attitude of many people. Implicit in this attitude is a dissatisfaction with the perceived sterility of the assembly-line, mass production society. Few individuals are prepared to accept the notion that man is born to exist as a neatly processed product in a packaged-like consumer society. Practical alternatives to this approach to life can include "returning to the land," communal living and, in extreme cases, individual withdrawal from society itself. Where native people have been relegated to a ghetto-type existence in large urban areas, this movement away from "civilization" can be observed with increasing regularity.

c) Closely allied to this "people movement" has been the growth in interest in the "old ways" with particular emphasis given to religious understanding and expression. Among Indian and Inuit peoples there is a renewed awareness of the strength to be found in pre-Christian traditional beliefs. The age of religious replacement is ended. The quest is now for a combination of elements of the old and the new, in the hope of expressing adequately a philosophy that has meaning for the individual.

For those who are involved in planning learning experiences, these and other attitudinal changes imply a need for re-evaluating the role of the school as it affects the lives of people. The school has to become open in its attitude toward making it possible for young people to question and analyse alternatives. Moreover, the scope of the investigation has to be sufficiently broad to insure that ways of thinking which may be quite at odds with the purely scientific method are not summarily dismissed or belittled. Schools must be places where young people can "find themselves" and come to know and appreciate the unique, as well as the similar, qualities that characterize the human family.

Among a dozen or more other multicultural variables worthy of consideration by curriculum developers, the question of survival must be discussed. If learning experiences are to have effective meaning in the lives of people, these experiences must provide the understanding and skills that are basic to surviving in a hierarchy of social organizations of increasing complexity. The question is: "How does John Q. Citizen sort out and come to understand the multiplicity of agencies that have come to influence, even to dominate, his existence?" At the community level, at the area and/or regional level, at the level of Territorial or provincial government, at the national level, the individual is confronted with a complex and often confusing assortment of officials, offices, policies and programs all of which impinge in some way upon his life. To find just who is responsible for what under these circumstances can be far from simple. How much more difficult is it to "know what is going on" if you come from a background where English is not your native tongue; where, in your culture, the asking of incessant questions in order to find answers is not the way things are done; where you are quite unaware of what the trappings of status in bureaucracy mean? Schools have been ineffective because they have failed to provide information about how the system can be made to work in the interests of people from the native cultures. The health, mental and physical, of people depends in large measure on being able to tolerate the stresses and strains that organized society imposes. Not only do people need to know how to cope with the present, but perhaps more importantly, there is the necessity of being prepared to contend with the unforeseen, the improbable, the unpredictable; in a word, the future.

Survival in an urbanized location poses its own peculiar problems. The change from having living space "on the land," to apartment, row housing, and plywood boxes squeezed into community streets constitutes a traumatic discontinuity in the living habits of people. These factors, combined with the ready availability of alcohol and drugs and the potential spread of communicable diseases, add up to a social atmosphere bordering on the chaotic, if not the catastrophic.

The school simply cannot ignore these realities. The facts of life today for Indian and Inuit peoples suggest strongly that unless people are given life skills to enable them to survive in the present and the future, the traditional learning program will be of esoteric value only;

and then only to the middle class child who is relatively less dependent upon the formal schooling process for the achievement of control of his destiny.

Multicultural Learning Materials

Curricula may be and are being prepared which reflect an attempt to take these factors into consideration. (e.g. *Elementary Education in the Northwest Territories: A Handbook for Curriculum Development; Learning in the Middle Years: A Handbook for Curriculum Development*.)[1] But in fact these sources tell but one side of the story. They are simply handbooks prepared for teacher use. The quality of multicultural learning materials made available to the young learner deserves more attention since such, materials are crucial in the learning experiences that are provided. With this in mind, the question of learning materials can be examined from two perspectives: the adaptation of existing material, or the creation of totally new material.

Obviously, the range of commercially available items can be evaluated. Two criteria loom large in this respect. Sins of commission are common and readily apparent. The use of "loaded" terminology is a case in point. "Savage," "pagan," "massacre," "redskins," "primitives," are well known examples. Allied to this problem is the indoctrination and preparation of stereotypes. The original Canadians, be they Indian or Inuit, are dealt with as non-entities and, be it noted, nearly all Canadian historians convey this point to the reader in no uncertain terms. One can only hazard a guess as to the damage that is done in terms of human understanding by placing one race (white) on a pedestal, while non-white people appear in the pages of Canadian history as so much "comic relief" or "end-men" on a stage dominated by the apostles of "civilization." Book burning, of course, is not the answer to the problem. If all the prejudicial material were to be summarily destroyed not much would be left. Teacher awareness and discretion in utilizing material of this nature is of utmost importance.

Sins of omission are equally common but may be less apparent. A general practice in Canadian historical writing is to ignore native peoples, particularly in the post Louis Riel era down to the present day. In a real sense, once the white man established a foothold throughout the country, the native peoples were written out of the pages of Canadian development. Current observation seems to indicate that this situation is being rectified on the part of publishing firms. However, the social studies teacher, in particular, is obliged to provide the full panorama of native history and not to confine his attention merely to the Jacques Cartier–Samuel de Champlain–Indian wars period. The fact that native traditions and cultures have survived the onslaught of white attempts at assimilation and probable destruction of native culture surely is demonstrable evidence of their viability. Learning programs must give full recognition to the strength so clearly demonstrated by the cultures.

The other, and indeed more exciting, approach to multicultural learning materials is to consider the preparation and publication of Canadian materials for Canadian children on a local basis. The key to this process is simple: curriculum authorities must make it possible for Indian, Inuit (and other cultural minority groups) to become involved in the collection, translation and illustration of materials which meet their needs and interests and which are based on their customs and traditions. Undoubtedly, problems will be encountered at the outset. The reason for these problems is straightforward. For literally decades the Indian and Inuit peoples have been "ripped-off," to use the vernacular, by itinerant anthropologists, sociologists, missionaries, educators and others of similar ilk who have written, taped and otherwise taken the stories and legends of the people to use for their own pecuniary or self-serving interests. It is little wonder, therefore, that considerable suspicion has been aroused in the minds of native peoples when yet another individual or group comes along and suggests that "this time the material is going to be used in the learning programs of your children." There is no easy solution for overcoming these justifiable feelings. The only possible approach is one based on mutual trust and respect. If, for example, a history series of the Chipewyan people is to be written, then the curriculum developers must insure that the authenticity of the material as provided by old and mature native people is maintained. Similarly, if the legends of the Copper Inuit are to be published it is imperative that the legends be left intact. Too frequently supposedly authentic legends have been altered by editors who have assumed that a "Hollywood" type ending will somehow improve the literary, if not the commercial, value of the end product.

In similar fashion, the utilization of Indian or Inuit illustrations should be incorporated with as little alteration as possible. The emphasis must be on making it possible for people to create those things that have meaning for themselves and their children. It can happen that the insensitive observer of this type of local materials preparation will reject books, picture sets, magazines, and filmstrips, because "they do not meet the standards of the learning materials industry which is oriented toward the middle class." Surely this sort of criticism contradicts the basic premises of the multicultural curriculum. If we, as educators, are sincere in our attempts to develop multicultural learning environments, then we shall make it possible for people from whatever backgrounds and from whatever ethnic groups to become actively involved in creating those learning items that convey their attitudes, values, customs and traditions. To do less is to perpetuate the conventional farce: "you can participate in the education of your child as long as it is on my terms, because I am the professional educator!"

The bibliography at the end of this chapter will demonstrate that it is possible to begin to right the balance in terms of people involvement in curriculum development. It would be regrettable if the reader were left with the impression that the amassing of a diversity of culturally relevant materials was the primary objective of this aspect of curriculum development. The encouragement and support that this approach can give to people who heretofore have been conditioned to seeing themselves as having little of value to contribute to the formalized educational process is much more important. The reinforcement of feelings of self-worth and pride in one's identity and heritage have to become the focal point of the energies of everyone involved in the field of multicultural education.

Note

1. Activity in this area is Canada-wide and reflects involvement at a variety of institutional levels: governmental (federal and provincial), academic, private and community. Examples of this are found in the projects supported by the University of Quebec at Chicoutimi; in provincially operated schools for Inuit in Nouveau Quebec; at the Department of Indian and Northern Education at the University of Saskatchewan, Saskatoon; the B.C. Indian Languages Project, based in Victoria; such independent on-reserve curriculum projects as those at Hobbema and Blue Quills, in Alberta; projects sponsored by Indian cultural centres (e.g., those at Assumption and Cold Lake, coordinated by the Alberta Indian Education Centre); and material produced, particularly in language learning by religious organizations. Several provincial departments of education and subsidiary school jurisdictions produce curriculum materials that reflect this orientation. A model project, combining involvement of nearly all these institutional levels in what is a manifestly community-directed enterprise is the Stoney Cultural Education Project at Morley, Alberta.

Bibliography

Multicultural and learning materials researched, written, illustrated and published by:

Programme Development Division
Department of Education
Yellowknife, N.W.T.
(1969-1974)

1. Elementary Education in the Northwest Territories: a Handbook for Curriculum Development, 1972.
2. Learning In the Middle Years: a Handbook for Curriculum Development, 1973.
3. Tendi Readers: 8 books with teacher's manual, 1972 (English and Dogrib)
4. Johnny Readers: 9 books with teacher's manual, 1972.
5. Dogrib Legends: 6 books with teacher's manual, 1972.
6. Chipewyan History: 13 books, 1973.
7. Whale Cove Series: 5 books in English and 5 books in Inuktitut, 1974.
8. On the Land: 1 book in Inuktitut and 3 books in English, 1972.
9. Tales From the Igloo: Copper Inuit legends, 1972.
10. Northern Games Charts: 20 traditional games of the Mackenzie Delta people, 1971.
11. Dechinta — In the Bush Picture Series: 35 full colour 18″ × 22″ pictures of life on a caribou hunt; with teacher's resource book, 1973.
12. Nanaptinni: a social studies unit written in Inuktitut and English based on life in the high Arctic, 1971.
13. PIK — A northern Magazine for Children: issued approximately quarterly, 1973–74.
14. Have You Ever Seen A Walrus: an alphabet book written in Inuktitut and English, 1973.
15. Olympiada: an inter-school activity book, 1971.
16. Art, N.W.T.: an idea book for teachers, 1971.
17. Dictionary & Grammar of the Tukudh Language: a reprint of a 1911 edition, 1972.
18. Dogrib Legends Multi-Media Kit: 6 filmstrips in colour with accompanying cassette tapes in English and Dogrib, 1973.
19. Exhah Nat'á — Raven Fools Himself: a legend written in the Slavey language with illustrations for the children to colour, 1974.
20. Flora & Fauna of the North: a package of illustrated cards with text on reverse side, 1974.
21. How Kabloona Became and Other Legends of the Inuit: a collection of illustrated stories and recollections of the people of Eskimo Point, 1974.
22. Leather: a craft handbook for teachers, 1971.
23. Arcturus: a periodical for people interested in Northern education, 1970–1974.
24. Piksaaq: a packet of illustrated cards depicting traditional Inuit artifacts with accompanying text, 1974.
25. Eskimo Games: the traditional games of the Eastern Arctic written in Inuktitut and English, 1973.
26. Syllabics books from: Spence Bay, Baker Lake, Grise Fiord, 1973–1974.

The Rationale for Canadian Studies

T.H.B. SYMONS

Throughout the course of its inquiry, this Commission has been forced to confront a fundamental question: why be concerned with Canadian studies? Many people with whom the Commission communicated took for granted the value of Canadian studies. But others were either uncertain as to whether such studies merit scholarly attention or were openly hostile to any suggestion that these studies have a legitimate place in the university. It is, therefore, essential that an answer be provided to the question: why be concerned with Canadian studies? Moreover, it is essential that this answer be given at the outset of the *Report* for at least two reasons. First, it is likely that the assumptions that have shaped the Commission's investigations will determine, in large measure, the nature of its observations and recommendations. Secondly, a failure to clarify those assumptions may lead to confusion and misunderstanding.

THE CONCEPT OF CANADIAN IDENTITY

Many persons concerned with Canadian studies bring to their concern a range of presuppositions, which often carry a strong emotional charge. A significant body of these presuppositions may be grouped under the general rubric "Identity" — a concept that requires some attention here.

For a large number of interested Canadians, whatever their mother tongue, the concept of "Canadian studies" is inseparable from the concept of "Canadian identity". As one francophone correspondent put it, "en dernière analyse, votre recherche porte sur la question fondamentale de l'identité canadienne." Many others appear to share this basic assumption and its various corollaries. Some believe that the nature of the Canadian identity is not known, and that it is the principal purpose of Canadian studies to discover it and then to

SOURCE: Excerpt from T.H.B. Symons, Report of the Commission on Canadian Studies, *To Know Ourselves,* pp. 11–20 and 81–83. Reprinted by permission of the publisher, Association of Universities and Colleges of Canada, 151 Slater Street, Ottawa.

encourage, indeed even to inculcate, an acceptance of the definition thus derived. Others hold that the nature of the Canadian identity is known and that the primary purpose of Canadian studies is to make it known to others. Many members of both these groups agree that the Canadian identity, whether known or not, is threatened by certain forces, some external, some internal; thus, they argue, the ultimate purpose of Canadian studies is to combat these forces, be they forces of imperialism, continentalism, regionalism, centralization, federalism, or whatever. Often, those who start by expressing concern about Canadian studies finish by voicing alarm about Canadian sovereignty. They wish to enlist Canadian studies in a campaign to protect what they perceive to be a fragile and threatened political, economic, cultural or academic sovereignty.

Such assumptions about the purpose and proper role of Canadian studies — often ones most vigorously attacked by critics of Canadian studies — should be understood; but they are not the assumptions adopted by this Commission as the primary rationale for Canadian studies, however tempting they might appear on first examination. It might, for example, have been convenient to rely upon the strong feelings of nationalism obviously abroad in the land to mobilize opinion in support of the recommendations of this *Report*. But for pragmatic reasons, and for reasons of principle, the Commission was determined to resist this temptation. Patriotic appeals to preserve and develop Canadian identity do not constitute, in practice or in principle, an adequate rationale for Canadian studies at any level of education. For instance, while a large number of Canadians are undoubtedly concerned about national identity, few agree upon what that identity is. In fact, many are locked in strong, occasionally violent, disagreement about its nature. Nor are the strongest differences of opinion always between Quebec nationalists and English-speaking Canadian nationalists, as is so often suggested. Equally passionate disagreements about the question of identity exist between many other groups of Canadians, for example, among Francophone Québecois themselves, between Acadiens and Québecois, between Maritimers and "Upper Canadians," and between "Easterners" and "Westerners." Hence, on purely pragmatic grounds, belief in the possibility of indoctrination in any narrow nationalistic, ideological, or political sense would indeed be a shaky foundation upon which to base an inquiry of this nature or recommendations of the kind proposed in this *Report*. It simply would not be possible to achieve a consensus across Canada on any one perception of the Canadian identity that could serve as the springboard for Canadian studies.

Beyond these pragmatic objections lie deeper objections of principle. The function of the university is to train the critical intellect, not to inculcate belief. It would be a betrayal of the essential function of universities for them to purvey or promote a particular perception of the Canadian reality to the exclusion of any other. If Canadian studies were to proceed from the assumption that a particular perception of the Canadian identity is the right one, the only one, and that this perception must be instilled into the consciousness of every Canadian, such studies would not merit a place at any university. The university must be a centre in which the critical intellect is left free to arrive at whatever conclusions the evidence and its own logic may require. Hence no perception of the Canadian reality may automatically be excluded as a viewpoint deserving examination.

Although the inculcation of one particular perception of Canadian identity is not, therefore, the purpose or justification of Canadian studies, the concept of identity remains, nevertheless, an important consideration in the rationale for the scholarly study of Canada. In the Commission's view, however, the most valid rationale for Canadian studies is not any relationship that such studies may have to the preservation or the promotion of national identity, or national unity, or national sovereignty, or anything of the kind. The most valid and compelling argument for Canadian studies is the importance of self-knowledge, the need to know and to understand ourselves: who we are; where we are in time and space; where we have been; where we are going; what we possess; what our responsibilities are to ourselves and to others.

But before the quest for such knowledge can begin, an individual or a collectivity must first be conscious of being Canadian. Unless Canadians recognize their distinctiveness in time and place, and are sufficiently interested in themselves and in their society and country, what motivation is there for self-study? The perception of Canadian identity may differ markedly from one person to another, from one language or cultural group to another, and from one part of the country to another. But an awareness of being Canadian, and an interest in the nature of that condition, is necessary for the achievement of self-knowledge; for what is self-knowledge, as far as a Canadian is concerned, if not the knowledge of one's identity? If one considers identity in terms of those qualities, ideals, experiences and institutions that we have in common as Canadians and that distinguish us from non-Canadians, our identity will be made up of numberless components, about any one of which one may legitimately disagree. However, any contribution to our knowledge of these components, whether they be cultural, sociological or environmental, could be viewed as part of the search for the diverse elements that make up the total of Canadian identity. This search is, then, but an extension of our quest for self-knowledge and, as such, it is a legitimate avenue of scholarly inquiry.

It should be emphasized that we are distinctive as a people. Although we are a highly heterogeneous country — geographically, climatically, linguistically, culturally, economically and politically, the total constitutes a unique entity called Canada. Indeed, this diversity is one of the key elements in the country's distinctive character. It is true, as George Grant has noted, that the vast majority of Canadians are a product of western civilization and live within the forms and assumptions of that enterprise.[1] But in both dramatic and subtle ways we are distinguishable from other peoples who live within this civilization, including our American neighbours with whom we tend to be most closely identified by others and often by ourselves. In the case of Americans, for example, while we have much in common, our differences are many and diverse. Reference to even a few circumstances illustrates this point. Culturally, we face in Canada the large challenge of bilingualism and multiculturalism with the declared goal of cultivating these heritages, whereas the United States faces the different challenge and objectives of a melting pot society. Politically, the strengths and weaknesses of our form of federalism, and of our responsible parliamentary institutions, differ markedly from those of the United States with its written constitution, separation of powers and entrenched bill of rights. Our cities are generally of a younger industrial age than those in the United States, and there are significant differences in the nature and qualities of urban life in the two countries.

Certain physical characteristics, separately or in combination, are also more significant in the life of Canada than in the United States or most other countries. These include, for example, the vast tundra and forested areas, the impact of snow and ice, enormous fresh water resources, extensive coastlines on three oceans and the realities of long distances and low human population density. Geographical, geological and climate characteristics of this kind contribute to our distinctiveness, as do a variety of special social characteristics, including the linguistic and cultural diversity already mentioned, a unique historical development and the effect of proximity to a major metropolitan state combined with strong and valued ties to older civilizations in other lands.

Unless our programs of teaching and research in Canada pay reasonable attention to such realities, they are likely to be substantially irrelevant, or misleading, or grossly wrong. A curriculum in this country that does not help Canadians in some way to understand the physical and social environment that they live and work in, that affects so profoundly their daily lives and that in turn is affected by their actions, cannot be justified in either academic or practical terms. It is essential from the standpoint both of sound balanced scholarship and of practicality that studies of the Canadian situation occupy an appropriate place in the curriculum and research interests of every university in Canada. As the Commission argues in chapters on science and technology and on education for the professions, this requirement is by no means confined to disciplines in the humanities and social sciences: it applies, to a greater or lesser degree, to nearly every area of academic activity.

SELF-KNOWLEDGE

The need for self-knowledge, which is the soundest justification for Canadian studies, has been a principal theme of classical and western thought since Heraclitus summed up his philosophy with these words: "I have sought for myself." Canadian studies thus constitute one part of a long tradition of scholarly inquiry, and the questions addressed by Canadian studies are at once as ancient and as contemporary as philosophy itself.

The concept of self-knowledge has been so central to much of western thought, from Plato and Plotinus to Spinoza, Kant and Hegel, that its evolution requires no detailed review here. It is perhaps sufficient ot recall the words of the cultural historian Ernst Cassirer:

> That self-knowledge is the highest aim of philosophical inquiry appears to be generally acknowledged. In all conflicts between the different philosophical schools, this objective remained invariable and unshaken: it proved to be the Archimedean point, the fixed and immovable centre, of all thought.[2]

In our own century the progress and achievements of modern psychology since Freud and Jung have served only to broaden and to intensify the quest for self-knowledge, not merely as the highest aim of culture but as the indispensable condition for health and growth in the life of the mind.

An otherwise intellectually alert person who lacks self-knowledge will be constantly at odds with himself. He will be constantly tripping, as it were, over his own feet. Lacking self-knowledge, he will inevitably entertain a false conception of himself and must try to act, more or less adequately, in accord with that false conception. Moreover, his attempt to act in a certain manner to comply with that conception may change his nature just enough to add to the confusion. Success will appear to confirm the original misconception; failure may weaken his confidence. Thus, lack of self-knowledge will lead to a state of conflict within the self. There is perhaps nothing inherently dangerous in this state of discord. In fact, if the feeling of dissatisfaction that it produces leads to an attempt to resolve these contradictions, it can be the pre-condition to the search for a more adequate self-knowledge. Before one can seek such knowledge, he must be aware that he does not possess it and that it is indeed worth seeking. This is the beginning of true education. But if the conflict within the self is not resolved in this manner, it can lead to the disintegration of the personality.

If this is true of an individual, it is equally true of a society or nation. If, for example, the citizens of a country, which in reality is composed of many diverse regions and more than one culture, think of it as a homogeneous country that can and should be governed in a uniform manner through centralized institutions, this idea of the country will appear to receive confirmation from the fact that its leaders do attempt to govern in this manner. If the citizens are not alive to the contradictions inherent in this false image of the country, the conflicts within the country may be exacerbated rather than contained or ameliorated. To take another example: if a country looks upon a powerful neighbour as one that can protect its independence and integrity from potential external threats, the very idea of a community of interest will be self-confirming. But if, in fact, the greatest threat to that independence is posed by the same powerful neighbour, a country may unwittingly lose its independence in its uninformed attempt to defend it. To take a third example: if a nation invests faith, hope and capital in the development of a vast region within its own frontiers but lacks adequate empirical knowledge about the ecological system of that region, it runs the risk of damaging or destroying a large portion of its territory and of hurting its own future. This is self-destruction through lack of self-knowledge; for knowledge of the self includes knowledge of the space within which the self lives.

Self-knowledge of the individual cannot be divorced from knowledge of the society in which one lives. The two kinds of knowledge are not only mutually dependent, but are ultimately one and the same, as the main tradition of Western thought suggests. It was Plato who first stated clearly, above all in the *Republic*, that the fulfilment of the Delphic maxim "Know Thyself" could not be attained by and for an isolated individual, but rather that the individual mind is an inadequate focus and must be magnified, and that man is a social being and can only be known as a member of a society. While Socrates had first emphasized that man is a part of society, Plato set about a systematic formulation of this idea and its implications. The quest for self-knowledge, now as then, must embrace the study of culture and community.

Hence, if a Canadian is to seek the self-knowledge that is essential for both health and wisdom, he must have access to a wider self-knowledge of his historical community and its contemporary circumstances. That is the answer to the Commission's question: why be concerned with Canadian studies? And it is the source of the further question that underlies this *Report:* are the universities of Canada making an adequate and reasonable contribution to the quest for national self-knowledge, which is the indispensable condition of individual self-knowledge?

If Canadian studies are designed to advance self-knowledge rather than performed as an exercise in a narrow type of nationalism, some important implications follow. For one thing, the concept of self-knowledge (to use James Mavor's phrase) opens windows on the street of the world instead of shutting them.[3] It links Canadian scholarly activity to one of the main concerns of Western culture. But it does more. It makes a knowledge of other lands and other times essential to our understanding of our own land and ourselves. Just as an individual cannot hope to know himself without knowing his own society and culture, so a society or a culture cannot hope to know itself without knowing the other societies and cultures that share its world. As C.G. Jung has written:

> We always require an outside point to stand on, in order to apply the lever of criticism. . . . How, for example, can we become conscious of national peculiarities if we have never had the opportunity to regard our own nation from outside? Regarding it from outside means regarding it from the standpoint of another nation. To do so, we must acquire sufficient knowledge of the foreign collective psyche, and in the course of this process of assimilation we encounter all those incompatibilities which constitute the national bias and the national peculiarity. Everything that irritates us about others can lead us to an understanding of ourselves.[4]

Obviously, then, our quest for knowledge of ourselves cannot fully succeed if accompanied by an unthinking indifference or hostility to non-Canadian studies. Studies that do not relate to Canada in an immediate and obvious way may none the less be a prerequisite to self-knowledge. What is required is a reasonable balance of the two; and if the impetus for this Commission has been an intuition that the balance has not been reasonable, there is no justification for exaggeration in the opposite direction. The judicious spirit required has been well expressed in an essay by Desmond Pacey:

> There is a respectable body of literature which has spring from our land our own people, and what is more natural that that we should read it and enjoy it? To say this is not to suggest that it should supplant the study of English and American literature. . . . But the first duty of man

> is to know himself. To know oneself as a Canadian, of course, necessarily involves knowing something of the roots from which Canadians sprang, be they English, Irish, Scots, French, German, or Icelandic. But to know oneself as a Canadian also means knowing what the human imagination has been able to make of this huge sprawling land, with its violent extremes of climate and topography, and of the society which has evolved here. . . . What one hopes to see develop in our young people from the study of our literature, in other words, is not a narrow sense of relevance nor a parochial kind of nationalism but rather an enlarged awareness of themselves as another imperfect but nevertheless distinct segment of the human race.[5]

The Commission believes that such an attitude towards the study of Canadian literature ought to be extended to the entire range of Canadian studies.

Professor Pacey is right to speak of "roots," for the pursuit of self-knowledge implies a particular attitude towards the past. We cannot possess the world of our own culture except by a constant effort to recapture the past through historical recollection. If, then, we in Canada would seek self-knowledge in a way that is helpful both to ourselves and to the wider international community, we must heed the advice of the father of modern social science, Auguste Comte: "To know yourself, know history."[6] The Commission is convinced that further progress in our self-knowledge will depend to a large extent upon the historical dimension of Canadian studies at two levels: at the level of subject matter and at the level of the evolution of the disciplines themselves. That is, it is important to know not only what attention is being given, in both teaching and research, to Canadian economic history, Canadian legal history or Canadian historical sociology, for example, but also what attention is being given to the history of Canadian economic scholarship, of Canadian legal scholarship and of Canadian sociological scholarship. In other disciplines, such as physics or philosophy, where the subject matter may not be as distinctively Canadian, the second question becomes especially important. There is hardly a department or field of study in a Canadian university that can be exempted from such scrutiny — and certainly not the history departments themselves. There is, after all, the history of Canadian history.

THE UNIVERSITIES AND SOCIETY

If the concept of Canadian studies as self-knowledge implies a certain attitude to the past, it also implies an attitude to the present and to the future. Since full self-knowledge can be achieved only in conjunction with knowledge of community, and if Canadian studies are to become a major concern and responsibility of our universities, the universities will need to re-examine their relationships to their surrounding communities.

The Commission is, of course, well aware that there are as many dangers to be feared as there are benefits to be gained from an openness to the current concerns of society. A university must be sufficiently detached from its immediate community to be able to subject the values and institutions of that community to critical examination. A university too preoccupied with local or immediate interests and anxieties may not devote sufficient attention to questions of a more enduring nature. On the other hand, there is also a danger that, if a university becomes so absorbed by its own internally generated concerns or by those concerns defined by other academic communities, it may forget that it is a part of a living community. The university must therefore always remain alert to the fact that it draws much of its strength from its host community (be it a country, a province, a county, city or town), and that, in return, it owes to that community a measure of intellectual attention and service, both for its own good and for that of the community.

The truth is, the universities are becoming almost the chief institutions of society in terms of both cost and impact. While universities in Canada are provincially chartered institutions for which the provinces have carried a major responsibility, they are also institutions of national importance. They are, indeed, one of the country's greatest national assets and, as such, they have an important role to play in serving society at all levels. To fulfil such a role effectively, universities must constantly seek ways of relating their activities to the needs of the wider community. As J.A. Corry has noted, universities everywhere have been at their vital best when they were interpreting the felt needs of society in a discerning way. "They have been at their worst and their most sterile when they have neglected their trust and lost touch with the urgencies of their society."[7]

In addition, Canadian universities of course have special obligations to the international community because knowledge can never be confined to national borders. But a modern university must also serve its own community because a university grows and develops out of its community. Moreover, a university is financially supported by its community. In Canada's case, the total expenditures on university education by all levels of government and the private sector combined in 1975–1976 will amount to more than two and one-half billion dollars.[8] The social responsibilities of a university, which are entirely compatible with but not identical to its intellectual responsibilities, cannot reasonably be denied. This idea has long been accepted in practice by other nations. But, as the following chapters of the

Commission's *Report* attempt to document, the Canadian university has been slower than universities in many other countries to respond to its obligations to educate students, to undertake systematic research and to foster knowledge with the need of its own society specifically in mind.

Following extensive research and discussions with teachers, students and researchers in all parts of Canada, the Commission became convinced that the principal threat to the integrity of the universities arises not from too great a contact with the outside community but from too little. To the extent that Canadian universities study their own society they tend to do so as if they were, in the words of one brief, "a group of anthropologists, observing an Amazonian tribe in the very process of disappearing." They need to become more aware of what is going on in the community and world outside the university. That is why this *Report*, in almost every chapter, asks in what ways our universities are serving, and should serve, their communities, whether local, provincial, regional, national or international. There are many specific areas in which the universities can and should be involved in the affairs of their communities, for example, by serving as cultural and intellectual centres, as bases for advanced research into social and economic problems of particular relevance to Canada, as sources of expertise in a variety of areas, as storehouses of information, as training centres for manpower, as centres for continuing education and extension teaching and in many other ways. Each culture and community has its own needs, and it should be among the tasks of each university and college to identify what these are and to consider how they can best contribute towards them.

SELF-KNOWLEDGE AND PROBLEM-SOLVING

Intensive study and investigation of the Canadian physical, social and economic setting are essential elements in the search for self-knowledge. Though intrinsically valuable, self-knowledge is not sought solely for itself; a high level of knowledge and understanding of their society will help to ensure that Canadians respond effectively to practical problems and needs as they arise. It is simply a matter of prudent housekeeping, or good stewardship, for Canadians to attend in a conscientious, deliberate and thorough manner to teaching and research related to Canadian problems in whatever field. As the president-elect of the Canadian Sociology and Anthropology Association wrote in 1974, "a sociologist or anthropologist who is not concerned with the problems relevant to the setting in which he (or she) lives is hardly worth his salt".[9] This could also be said of academics in other disciplines.

Knowledge is essentially universal in character, but its application has strong and often differing implications for the culture and well-being of each community. There is an obligation to put knowledge to use in the service of man. In pursuing the obligation, Canadian universities should observe their particular responsibility to give service to the people of their own community by directing an appropriate amount of attention to the needs and problems of that community. Apart from the matter of social obligation, it is only reasonable to work on the nearby problems and the problems of one's own society before tackling those that are more remote. Who is in a better position to understand and to work on these problems than Canadians? And who will tackle them if we do not?

Subsequent chapters of the *Report* are replete with examples of problems and areas of study relating to Canada that are crying out for attention by Canadian scholars. Despite their importance to Canada, these problems have received inadequate study or have neglected altogether. In some cases we have also failed to develop innovative approaches and solutions appropriate to our own problems, preferring instead to employ so-called "comparative models," imported from other societies, from which we uncritically extract mediocre solutions with sometimes disastrous results.

The Commission is not suggesting that universities should become slaves to community needs or to short-term priorities at the expense of their primary function, which is to preserve, transmit and increase human knowledge. On the other hand, Canadians face problems and circumstances that in many instances are not at all identical to those of other countries. We simply cannot afford, in either academic or economic terms, to ignore these problems or to adopt findings and solutions based on research done outside Canada when, as so often happens, they are inappropriate here. This is as true of social questions as it is of scientific and technical matters. It would be a betrayal of both their social function and their intellectual function if Canadian universities failed to contribute substantially to an understanding and amelioration of Canada's distinctive problems.

SELF-KNOWLEDGE AND EFFECTIVE DECISION-MAKING

A knowledge of their total environment will not only tell individuals something of importance about themselves and enable them to understand their country better, it will also enable them to make more informed decisions about the significant issues facing the civic polity, of which they are members. Self-knowledge is, in fact, the strongest foundation for effective decision-making. Indeed, without a thorough understanding of the nature of his or her society and of its problems an individual is unqualified to make decisions affecting its welfare. A citizen's primary duty, Northrop Frye has suggested, is "to try to know what should be changed in his society and what conserved".[10] This responsibility cannot be discharged unless a citizen knows his country well.

In a moment of masterful understatement, Lord Haldane once urged on the British government that, in the sphere of public policy, "the duty of investigation and thought, as a preliminary to action, might with great advantage be more definitely recognized."[11] The findings of the Commission on Canadian Studies suggest that this observation might well be made of Canada today. This country faces enormous decisions in the coming decades that should require of its citizens a "duty of investigation and thought, as a preliminary to action." To help us to reach good decisions, Canadians must have available, and be able to rely upon, findings and assessments of those engaged in research in government, in industry and at the universities. Informed study, comment and criticism directed at Canadian conditions have an important role to play in the formation of public policy, in decision-making and then in effective problem-solving at all levels of government and in all sectors of society. As one scholar expressed the point to the Commission, "we cannot, as scholars, tell Canada what it ought to do; but as citizens informed by scholarship, we may seek to influence the nation."

Illustrations of the contribution that research in Canadian studies at the universities might be expected to make are identified throughout the *Report*. For example, the renewal of popular and scientific interest in the Canadian North is barely a few years old and yet the country is facing in the immediate future decisions of great consequence relating to northern petroleum and resources development. It is embarrassingly clear that we are not sufficiently informed about the economic, social and environmental implications of such public policy decisions. This is an area, surely, where the country might have been better served by the university community in anticipation of decisions requiring research based upon a lengthy period of investigation. Now, when there is a real and urgent need in Canada for well-researched information, provided by research programs, that are not under the thumb of government or industry, too little is available; nor can such information now be easily assembled, especially in a short period of time. Again, in the North and elsewhere, plans are being made for vast programs of water diversion and hydro-electric development. Not unexpectedly, the inadequacy of the information base on which decisions relating to such projects may be taken has led to questioning by concerned Canadians.

Extensive, well-researched information and a lengthy period of lead-time to digest and assess the implications of such information are essential elements in effective and responsible decision-making. Members of the university community have an opportunity to identify the long-term decisions that a society must make and to work toward an understanding of the issues involved in advance of the time for public decision.

CANADA'S OBLIGATIONS TO INTERNATIONAL SCHOLARSHIP

There is an additional rationale for Canadian studies, one closely connected with the contribution that universities can make to problem-solving and decision-making in Canada. Canadians have an obligation, which the rest of the world expects us to honour, to play the leading role in scholarship relating to Canada and to be especially zealous at academic work that Canadians may be able to do better, or more readily, than anyone else because it concerns the cultural or physical conditions of the country in which they live. Other countries have similar responsibilities relating to their own particular circumstances. Indeed, in many instances, if Canadians do not address the problems of knowledge relating to this country, a gap will be left in the knowledge available to the human community that no one else will fill. This would be a loss not only to Canadian scholarship and to Canadian self-understanding, but to international scholarship as well. Geographically, Canada is one of the largest countries in the world, occupying a vast area of the North American continent. What happens in the rest of the world will often influence Canada. But what is done in Canada may also have a profound and helpful influence elsewhere. By addressing Canadian problems and conditions in our research and study, we can help others to understand not only our country and ourselves but also their situation and themselves. The maxim "to know thyself one must know others" applies equally to all societies.

One letter to the Commission expressed the view that the simplest yet perhaps most valid justification for Canadian studies is that Canada exists. "Perhaps," the letter stated, "this is too like the climber's explanation of why he wants to scale a mountain, "because it is there." But, surely, such a rationale carries great force. Northrop Frye concluded his final review of Canadian poetry for "Letters in Canada" in the *University of Toronto Quarterly* in 1960 with the remark: "The centre of reality is wherever one happens to be, and its circumference is whatever one's imagination can make sense of." Canadians are here and our imagination starts here. While this imagination reaches out to encompass the heritage of other times and other places, it is only natural that Canadians should feel a particular interest in the study of their own community. And it is only natural that, in the words of Hugo McPherson, "we want to be recognized as a people who have something to say to ourselves, and something to say to the world. In sum, we are intelligent, imaginative people, and we want ourselves and the world to enjoy our experience."[12]

The ancient principle *bonum diffusum sui* is applicable to the Canadian experience as to any other.

Canada's experience is as fascinating and as legitimate an area for academic study as that of any other country. Canadian problems are, or should be, of interest to us because they are ours. But more than that, Canadian problems are of universal and philosophic importance, for, while Canada is a distinctive political and cultural entity, this country is also part of the historical mainstream and is subject to difficult social and political problems that are often similar to those faced by other countries. Thus it is likely that Canadian innovations, though perhaps developed in some cases to meet primarily internal requirements, will be of interest to people in other lands facing generally similar situations. For the same reason there is increasing cause for students abroad to examine the Canadian experience from their perspective. Canadian social and political problems are clearly of intrinsic interest for all students of parliamentary government, federalism, nationalism, cultural pluralism, political parties and modern movements, the international role of middle powers, the problems of American alliance, the multinational corporation, and national sovereignty, to mention only a few examples. The point is, the Canadian experience deserves scholarly attention not simply because it is Canadian but because it has value as a subject of intellectual examination. There are many areas of scholarly inquiry relating to Canada that offer great opportunity and challenge to the academic community. Canadian scholarship has, thus, a strong international obligation to direct appropriate energies to teaching and research about the problems and conditions of its own society.

THE GROWING INTERNATIONAL RECOGNITION OF THE ACADEMIC VALUE OF AREA STUDIES

Despite the intrinsic value of Canadian studies, academics in Canada have too often in the past viewed Canadian-oriented courses and research with scepticism if not with outright disdain. The irony is that many of these same people have accepted without question as valid courses and research projects relating to the culture or circumstances of other countries and areas, such as those dealing with American literature or the geography of the Sahara, or German idealistic philosophy or the lives of aborigines in New Guinea. Briefs to the Commission suggested that the fact that many staff members at Canadian universities are, or have been, non-Canadian or have been trained outside Canada has tended to strengthen this attitude. But there is abundant evidence that Canadian-born and Canadian-trained academics themselves are frequently least aware of the scholarly benefits and the valuable insights to be gained by studying the culture and history of their own society. By excluding Canada as a subject of study, often in the name of academic rigour, Canadian teachers and researchers in fact deny themselves and their students the opportunity both of knowledge and of a valuable learning experience. As has been pointed out, "the concept of culture is a lush, important one, perhaps the most germinal idea in 20th century scholarship in the social sciences and humanities."[13] The chapters of the Commission's *Report* dealing with science and the professions attempt to make clear the importance of culture as a concept in many other areas as well.

In recognition of the academic value of area studies, universities around the globe are developing courses on this basis. The Commission's investigations revealed, for example, that no fewer than twenty-nine universities in Great Britain now offer specific courses or programs in European studies, in addition to the substantial amount of work being done in the field of European studies within the confines of traditional departments. This burgeoning of European studies at British universities has also been paralleled at polytechnical institutions in the United Kingdom. In 1968 a University Association for Contemporoary European Studies was founded to bring together staff and students working in this area in Britain. In the United States almost three hundred universities (not including two-year colleges) now offer courses or programs in American studies. Bachelor's degrees in the field are offered by 180 of these institutions; master's degrees, by 33; and doctorates, by 14. The remainder offer courses or a concentration in American studies as part of their normal degree program.

There are active centres for American studies at a number of universities in Japan, including the University of Tokyo, and an American Studies Foundation has developed a wide-ranging program in that country. Moreover, a growing number of countries and private industries are contributing to higher education institutions abroad to further teaching and research about their society in other countries. The Krupp Foundation of West Germany, for example, has contributed two million dollars to Harvard University to establish a new chair in European studies and to support graduate students doing research into European problems. The West German government has established a $30 million dollar fund to promote European studies in the United States. The government of Japan and various Japanese companies have made a series of million dollar gifts to American and British universities as part of a program to promote

Japanese studies throughout the world. Extensive programs of Italian studies are being developed at various universities in Italy and of Scandinavian studies, in Sweden. Programs of African studies are being created in a dozen countries on that continent, and studies about Malaysia are being encouraged in the universities of that country. Many other examples of the growing recognition of the value of area studies outside Canada could be cited.

Why, then, should the value of Canadian studies be questioned? As one correspondent put it, "the reason for *not* having Canadian studies are much more curious than the rationale justifying them."

While it would be only natural for Canadians to want to encourage and support scholarly work about Canada abroad, indeed, in a separate chapter, the Commission argues for such support, we must always keep in mind that universities everywhere have limited resources and therefore cannot study everything. Foreign universities have their own special interests and priorities, which reflect their locations and their relationships to their own societies. Although it is hoped that they may devote appropriate attention to Canadian matters, foreign universities are unlikely to make the study of Canada a matter of top priority for themselves. Canadian universities have the primary responsibility for Canadian studies, for the same scholarly and practical reasons that American universities should be concerned with American studies or British universities with British studies. In many countries this assumption scarcely arises for discussion; it is so naturally taken for granted. The Commission believes that it is high time that we in Canada, too, recognized the common sense of this assumption.

STUDENT INTEREST IN CANADIAN STUDIES

While the Commission encountered indifference, and sometimes even open hostility, towards Canadian studies on the part of many university teachers and administrators in every part of Canada, this attitude was not as prevalent among the students. On the contrary, at public hearings, in briefs and letters, in personal interviews and in informal submissions to the Commission students at all educational levels demonstrated a genuine desire for more and better courses on Canadian matters. Our country is an enigma to many Canadians, and there is a growing wish to explore this enigma, especially among the young. This country appears to exist in spite of language, geography and economics, and thoughtful young people are curious to know how such a phenomenon came about and what the chances are of its survival — in fact whether its survival is even worth the effort that may be required. Their interest has, of course, been stimulated by the centennial celebrations of 1967, followed by those of Manitoba,

British Columbia and Prince Edward Island, as well as by events in Quebec and by the growing tensions between Eastern and Western Canada.

Canada provides a North American alternative to life under the government of the United States. Canadian studies provide students with an opportunity to examine the significance of this alternative and to assess its practical effects upon their lives. Many of them have a vague feeling of Canadian patriotism, but are almost completely uncertain as to whether or not the sentiment has a rational basis. They want an opportunity to think about it. They also want to understand, if possible, why other Canadians think differently — those who would prefer to be part of the United States and those who, while anxious not to be part of the United States, would prefer that their province or region should become sovereign rather than remain part of a federal union. Why is it that, as the power of the central government has increased in the United States, the power of the provinces has increased in Canada? What would be the effect of an effort either to reverse or to accelerate this trend? What part should Canada play in international affairs? What is the extent of our resources and should they be developed? What is the potential of this country? Fundamental questions of this sort, touching upon every aspect of the Canadian experience, are being asked by thousands of students across Canada.

In short, Canadian studies are needed because there is a strong and legitimate student interest in them. This demand is not being satisfactorily met at most educational institutions in Canada. Students at all levels of education told the Commission that they feel, as one put it, that they have been "short-changed," that they have not learned nor been helped to learn about themselves. Because of this, many think that the system has failed them in a fundamental area of education. They also feel that what there has been of Canadian studies "lacks guts," in the words of another. (Much more colourful language was sometimes used.) They are being urged, as they should be, to study about the United States, about countries in Europe, about the Soviet Union, and about Latin America — in fact, about almost every country and society but their own. However, they should be equally encouraged to study their own country. It is clear that a great number of students want a chance to satisfy their curiosity about this country and about their place in it. Canadian studies can satisfy that curiosity — not by the inculcation of nationalism or by encouraging a conception of Canada isolated from the rest of the world, but through an academically rigorous pursuit of self-knowledge. In wanting such an opportunity, Canadian students are giving contemporary expression to the need to know thyself. . . .

ETHNIC STUDIES AND CANADIAN CULTURAL PLURALISM

Canada is unique in the extent and nature of its ethnic diversity. Given the important role that cultural pluralism has played, and continues to play, in Canadian affairs, it should be clear that ethnic studies have a vital contribution to make to a knowledge and understanding of Canada. Yet, as the Royal Commission on Bilingualism and Biculturalism has observed, "the vast opportunities for research that our population provides have hardly been touched."[14] Similarly, the curriculum of our educational system, at all levels, still shows little recognition of the multicultural character of Canada.

As an area of academic work, ethnic studies encompasses diverse fields of inquiry and overflows the boundaries of traditional disciplines. Professor Cornelius Jaenen has pointed to the scope for such studies:

> I would include within the compass of ethnic studies such socially discernible and historically documented experiences as immigration history, inter-group relations, race relations, aboriginal history, as well as the study of individual ethnic groups. It flows over into the disciplines of sociology, political science, Slavic studies, linguistics, demography, psychology, human geography, ethnology, anthropology, law and the fine arts.[15]

Ethnic studies is indeed an integral part of Canadian studies and its implications pervade almost every aspect of the study of Canadian society. Ethnicity is a major theme in the history, literature, politics and sociology of our country. To a large extent it is the particular features of our cultural pluralism that give distinctive character to Canada. This point has been noted by Andrew Gregorovitch, the bibliographer of Canadian ethnic groups:

> A study of ethnic groups, where they settled and the characteristics they have contributed to that area, gives us a much clearer idea of what is Canadian. Our ethnic elements are somewhat similar to those of other nations, but our unique composition and the history of these ethnic elements sets our nation apart from the United States, Australia and Britain. As a distinctive Canadian culture grows, it is our distinctive ethnic composition, including our French heritage, which will continue to set us apart from the American nation.[16]

Ethnic studies are not only important to a knowledge and understanding of Canada. The insights gained from an examination of the role and relationships of cultural groups in this country can make a significant contribution to a wider understanding of inter-ethnic relations in the modern world. Ethnic studies is, therefore, an area in which the study of the Canadian experience may well yield something of value to the international community. The potential usefulness of comparative studies between ethnicity in Canada and in other societies, for example, the United States, was pointed out by the Royal Commission on Bilingualism and Biculturalism:

> Canadian society differs from American society in a number of respects that are of direct importance to immigrants and cultural groups. Among these are the greater social role of government, the existence of two linguistic communities, the idea of a cultural mosaic instead of a "melting pot," the fact that large-scale immigration to Canada continued after the United States' policy became restrictionist, the low density of our population, and Canada's proximity to a more populated and more highly developed country. By studying the effects of these factors, scholars could make distinctive contributions to social science, and also help to develop the understanding which must underlie sound social policy in Canada. Since Canada is one of the most technologically advanced of the highly pluralistic societies, research on the Canadian experience could also offer other countries more understanding of complex societies.[17]

Although ethnic studies were, until recently, a much neglected area of Canadian studies, there has been a considerable expansion in the academic and public interest in this field in the past half-dozen years. Building on the substantial pioneering contribution made to the study of multiculturalism in Canada by such collectors, writers and public administrators as John Murray Gibbon, Dr. Watson Kirkconnell and Dr. V.J. Kaye, a growing number of scholars are now teaching and researching in the field of ethnic studies. The Canadian Ethnic Studies Association, founded in 1971, is developing an active program and has drawn together many of those who share an interest in this area.[18] The broad range of their interests is reflected in the contents of *Canadian Ethnic Studies,* first published in 1969 as the bulletin of the Research Centre for Canadian Ethnic Studies at the University of Calgary and more recently expanded as the official journal of the Canadian Ethnic Studies Association.[19] Seeking "to promote singly and collectively the interests and aspirations of all ethnic groups comprising the Canadian cultural mosaic, and to help effect greater understanding on the part of these groups of the diverse problems and perspectives of each," the journal takes an interdisciplinary approach. Published biannually, it contains articles, reviews, translations from significant primary sources, oral histories in print and bibliographic information. In addition to the journal, the Canadian Ethnic Study Association publishes a quarterly *Bulletin*, in both official languages, from its office at the University of Ottawa in an effort to acquaint scholars with research in progress in the various discipline areas relating to ethnicity.

There have also been important developments in ethnic studies at the regional level in several parts of Canada. For example, the Canadian Plains Research Centre at the University of Regina is acting as a clearing house for information on ethnic studies in Western Canada to assist the newly formed western Canadian ethnic research association.

Both the federal government and several provincial governments have given substantial support to multicultural activities, including teaching and research. A major initiative in the field of Canadian ethnic studies was undertaken, for example, in the creation of the ethnic history series, following the Prime Minister's speech on the subject of multiculturalism to the House of Commons, 8 October 1971. Scholarly studies of some twenty ethnic groups have been commissioned by the Department of the Secretary of State. The writing of these volumes has, in most instances, been undertaken by individual academics. However, teams of researchers are also being assisted to cover a broad range of topics relating to each ethnic group, including the historical background, social origins, causes of immigration, settlement patterns, population growth, education, religion, values, associations, occupations, family, acculturation, recreation, arts and letters and the press and other media. In addition, scholarly attention is being devoted to the attitudes of each group toward inter-group relations, and developments in their original homeland, as well as to an examination of such special topics as political behaviour, economic circumstances, social mobility and culture retention.

Many other actions, although often still of a tentative or preliminary nature, have been undertaken by the federal government to support ethnic studies as a part of its multicultural program. Conferences and workshops have been sponsored, research and publications assisted and the formation or further development of societies encouraged. Through both its regular grants and awards, and by means of the Exploration Program, the Canada Council has given strong support to many aspects of ethnic studies. The National Museums of Canada have developed special collections and programs relating to our multicultural heritage. The Public Archives of Canada has established a National Ethnic Archives to encourage Canada's many cultural communities to record their heritage and to preserve all types of archival documents. The National Library is developing its own collections in this field and encouraging and assisting others to do so.

The activity of some of the provinces in support of ethnic studies also deserves comment. For example, Ontario, Manitoba and Alberta have each sponsored large conferences, as well as research and publication, in this field.

None the less, as the first annual report of the Canadian Consultative Council on Multiculturalism has emphasized, more support is needed for almost every aspect of ethnic studies, both to make up for past neglect and because of the pervasive importance of these studies to an understanding of historical and contemporary Canadian society.[20] Further research is required concerning every ethnic group in Canada. In some instances, indeed, such research has scarcely begun. The remarkable Celtic contribution to the life of this country, for example, has received little attention. The Commission comments elsewhere upon the neglect of studies relating to the Indian and Inuit peoples, and also upon the need for more studies dealing with the French-speaking minorities outside of Quebec, and with the English-speaking minority in that province, in addition to the other ethnic groups. The British or Anglo-Canadian heritage is in danger of being taken for granted and ignored by scholars who may fail to perceive that it, too, is a part of the Canadian cultural mosaic.

To help make available the results of scholarship, more support is needed for publication in the field of ethnic studies and for the translation of both source materials and academic writing. Few Canadian university libraries have as yet developed strong collections in ethnic studies. The Commission recommends that, given the importance of the subject to this country, every university library should build up a basic collection in this field and that appropriate universities in each region should develop special collections. Extensive bibliographical work is required. Bibliographics do not appear to have been prepared as yet even for such major groups as the Scottish, Irish, German, Dutch or Welsh, despite their long and substantial role in Canadian affairs. There is at present no complete guide to the ethnic periodical press in Canada. A vigorous program of archival collecting, in which universities can often play a useful part, is required to secure materials of value before they are lost or destroyed. There is also much work to be done in recording oral history, and there is urgency that this be done while those who could contribute to our knowledge in this way are still available for interview. To help support and coordinate these and other activities, it may be desirable to establish a National Institute for Canadian Ethnic Studies. The Commission recommends that this possibility be explored by the Department of the Secretary of State, in consultation with the Council of Ministers of Education, the Canadian Ethnic Studies Association, and the Association of Universities and Colleges of Canada.

The results of such activity in research and publication would bring necessary support to teaching in Canadian ethnic studies, and would make possible an enlargement of the place of ethnic studies in the university curriculum in keeping with the role of ethnicity and cultural pluralism in our society. Such an enlargement should occur both through the expansion of ethnic studies programs at selected institutions and through an increased awareness of the ethnic studies factor in the teaching of traditional disciplines. In addition, the Commission has argued elsewhere in this chapter the great value to Canada, as well as to the individuals concerned, of the many non-official languages that are spoken in this country, and has recommended that more effort and resources be devoted to the support of teaching and research in the non-official languages by the provincial and federal governments, by the universities and by other levels of the educational system. A recent study has indicated that in the five cities of Montreal, Toronto, Winnipeg, Edmonton and Vancouver nearly one million people amongst the ethnic groups surveyed support the concept of non-official language retention and would welcome expanded educational opportunities to assist those who wish to retain or develop their language skills.[21] The Commission has also noted elsewhere the need for interpreters and translators familiar with the non-official languages and has recommended that this need be borne in mind in the future development of schools of interpretation and translation at Canadian universities. The burgeoning growth of ethnic studies in the school systems of the country, too, will have implications for the universities with their responsibilities for teacher education.

Finally, the Commission notes the particular need for contemporary studies relating to current problems and circumstances involving Canadian cultural pluralism. Many questions of public policy — for example, in such areas as human rights, immigration, education, social welfare and external affairs — are closely related to the ethnic diversity of this country.

Notes

1. George Grant, "Canadian Fate and Imperialism," *The Evolution of Canadian Literature in English, 1945–1970,* ed. Paul Denham (Toronto and Montreal, 1973), p. 100.
2. Ernst Cassirer, *An Essay on Man* (New York, 1944), p. 1.
3. James Mavor, *My Windows on the Street of the World* (London, 1923).

4. C.G. Jung, *Memories, Dreams, Reflections* (revised edition, New York, 1973), pp. 246–47.
5. Desmond Pacey, "The Study of Canadian Literature," a submission to the Commission on Canadian Studies, subsequently published in the *Journal of Canadian Fiction* (Spring, 1973).
6. Auguste Comte, *Lettres à Valat,* p. 89.
7. J.A. Corry, "Universities Education: Prospect and Priorities," *Queen's Quarterly,* Vol. 74, No. 4 (Winter, 1967), p. 565.
8. *Advance Statistics of Education, 1974–75,* Statistics Canada, Catalogue 81-220 (Ottawa, 1974), p. 30.
9. Fred Elkin, *Bulletin,* Canadian Sociology and Anthropology Association, No. 34 (July 1974).
10. Northrop Frye, the Convocation Address delivered to engineering students at the University of Waterloo, June 1972.
11. Viscount Haldane *et al., Report to the Minister of Reconstruction of the Machinery of Government Committee,* HMSO Command Paper CMD 9230 (London, 1918), p. 6.
12. Hugo McPherson, "Why Read Canadian? Three Lectures and a Coda," a paper delivered to the Ontario Association of College and University Libraries in Toronto, 11 May 1973.
13. Jay Mechling *et al.,* American Culture Studies: The Discipline and the Curriculum," *American Quarterly,* Vol. 25, No. 4 (October 1973), p. 369.
14. *Science and The North* (Ottawa: Information Canada, 1973).
15. C.J. Jaenen, "Ethnic Studies — An Integral Part of Canadian Studies," Presidential Address to the National Conference on Ethnic Studies, Toronto, 27 October 1973.
16. Andrew Gregorovich, *Canadian Ethnic Groups Bibliography* (Toronto, 1972), p. vii.
17. Ibid., pp. 225–26.
18. Canadian Ethnic Studies Association, c/o Department of Sociology, University of Toronto, 563 Spadina Avenue, Toronto, Ontario, M5S 1A1.
19. *Canadian Ethnic Studies,* University of Calgary, Calgary, Alberta T2N 1N4.
20. *First Annual Report of the Canadian Consultative Council on Multiculturalism* (Ottawa, 1975).
21. K.G. O'Bryan, J.G. Reitz, O. Kuplowska, *Non-Official Languages: A Study in Canadian Multiculturalism* (Ottawa, 1975).

Part Five

COMMUNITY, SCHOOLS AND TEACHERS

Renewed interest in the relationship between communities and schools in Canada has coincided with the revitalization of interest in ethnicity. This has led minority communities to reassess the role of the school in transmitting and creating culture. They have also become more vocal and confident in expressing their educational needs and aspirations. For their part, educators are responding in varying ways depending upon context and setting.

Vandra Masemann's article deals with the response of the City of Toronto Board of Education to the educational needs and demands of a variety of concerned racial and ethnic groups. Throughout the 1950s and 1960s Toronto was the receiving area for large numbers of immigrants. By the early 1970s, the city's anglophone cultural base had declined to the point where it constituted a minority 47 per cent of the total population. The initial response of the Board of Education to this radical shift was to focus its efforts on helping immigrant pupils learn English as quickly as possible. Inevitably, however, more fundamental questions were raised which prompted the establishment of a system-wide evaluation of school programs. A Working Group on Multicultural Programs was formed in 1974 and solicited input from community groups, the school system and the public at large. Differences of opinion naturally surfaced within as well as between groups. Most striking, however, was that while briefs from the ethnic communities expressed strong support for a model of schooling consonant with linguistic and cultural pluralism, those emanating from within the educational system itself tended (with some important exceptions) to embrace a basically assimilationist role for the school.

In other cities, too, parents and community groups have actively sought schools more suited to their needs and aspirations. In Edmonton, for example, an experimental bilingual English-Ukrainian program was introduced into the city's public school system in 1974. Beginning in selected schools at the kindergarten and Grade 1 levels, and extending into higher grades in subsequent years, the language of instruction in these schools is divided equally between

English and Ukrainian. English-language arts, maths and science are taught in English; social studies, Ukrainian-language arts, music and art are taught in Ukrainian. Since the program's inception annual evaluations have been carried out. Their aim is to evaluate whether pupils in the program are achieving at or above grade level in English and mathematics, whether they are acquiring an appreciation of Ukrainian culture and developing skills in the language, and whether parents and children view the experience positively. As the study by Lamont and colleagues illustrates, the findings indicate that based on matched comparisons with pupils in the regular school program, achievement in regular curriculum areas have not been adversely affected, participants have made significant gains in appreciating the Ukrainian culture and learning the language, and support among parents, teachers and school administrators is growing.

Support for such programs among teachers is crucial if they are to be effective. Yet teachers may not possess the basic understandings and skills, as well as teaching-learning materials, essential to their successful performance in a culturally diverse classroom. The last two articles in this section, therefore, are devoted to a discussion of teacher education. The first, by June Wyatt, describes an attempt to establish a school-based teacher education program within a native community. At every step of the process community participation is emphasized as is the native culture and language which is central to the experience of student teachers enrolled in the program.

The second and concluding article to the section describes the need, as yet largely unfilled, for pre-service teacher preparation programs that deal centrally with the culturally diverse nature of Canadian society. Regardless of their subject specializations, teachers need to develop the attitudes, skills and knowledge to appreciate, understand and cope with cultural differences. Such training, moreover, should not be restricted to beginning teachers. Unless we are prepared to wait twenty or thirty years, the need for in-service programs along the lines described, we believe, are both self-evident and essential.

Multicultural Programs in Toronto Schools

VANDRA L. MASEMANN

The focus of this paper is a debate about multiculturalism and education in Toronto, a debate which has been waged for many years but which has intensified since 1974.[1] Moreover, this is not just a municipal debate, but a provincial and national debate, having implications for and being influenced by policy decisions by the federal cabinet in relation, for instance, to national language policy and immigration policy. It is a debate that has occurred and recurred in the more than one hundred years since Confederation.

In brief, this paper discusses the responses of the Toronto Board of Education over a period of some ten or more years to the facts of the cultural and linguistic diversity of its student population. First a brief summary of the history of immigration to Canada and to Toronto in particular is given, in order to demonstrate the very central position that Toronto now holds as a reception centre for immigrants. The next section of the paper considers the types of programs instituted in the schools to deal with a continuing influx of students from Hong Kong, the West Indies, Portugal, India, Greece, Italy, South American nations and other countries. Third, the shifts in emphasis and thinking of some educational administrators, teachers and concerned citizens in the last ten years are examined. Next the recent work of the Toronto Board of Education's Work Group on Multicultural Programs is discussed in detail, with reference to the present ethnic and linguistic composition of the Toronto student population, the role of community and educational groups in providing recommendations for a policy on multiculturalism, the philosophy and policies advocated in the Work Group's report, and finally public reaction and policy implementation. In conclusion, the nature of this debate — particularly over the response to cultural and linguistic diversity — is examined with reference to debates on

SOURCE: *Interchange*, 9, no. 1 (1978–79), pp. 29–44. Reprinted by permission of the author and the Ontario Institute for Studies in Education.

cultural pluralism generally and with special reference to the political, economic and legislative realities which lend support to myths, lead to their speedy demise, or create situations fraught with unresolvable paradoxes. Basically it is my intention to demonstrate to what extent it was possible to initiate positive action on multiculturalism in education within a city in which celebration of Anglo-conformity had been a way of life.

Immigration to Canada

An examination of census statistics reveals shifts in patterns of immigration of various groups in the years since Canadian Confederation in 1867. At that time the population (with the count excluding Newfoundland and the sparsely settled regions of the north and west) was 3,689,000. By 1971 the population had increased to 21,568,000 (Department of Manpower and Immigration, 1974, p. 5). Natural increase, of course, accounts in part for this growth, primarily among the earliest immigrants from Northern Europe — in particular the British Isles, France and Germany. However, heavy emigration to the United States in the late nineteenth and the early twentieth century also occurred primarily among those of the same origin (Palmer and Troper, 1973, p. 17). As this exodus halted with the closing of the American frontier, the government of Wilfrid Laurier waged a promotion campaign to attract immigrants into Ontario and the prairie provinces. Thus in the 1921 census, a considerable number of immigrants from Austria, Germany, Holland, Scandinavia, Poland, Russia and the Ukraine were identified (Department of Manpower and Immigration, 1974, pp. 9–10). Those from the first four sources were considered rather more desirable than those from the latter three. Although the federal government espoused a policy of immigration into rural areas, the influx of such immigrants from Italy, Macedonia, the Russian Pale, and other southern and eastern European countries created a demand for immigration restrictions on the basis of "race," a term which at that time referred to ethnic origin (Palmer and Troper, 1973, p. 18).

The impact of immigration in the 1920s and 1930s was felt primarily in the prairies, but also in the major urban centres of Toronto and Montreal (Harney and Troper, 1975, p. 27). After World War Two, however, the focus shifted almost completely away from the rural west; Toronto and nearby cities such as Hamilton, and to a lesser extent Vancouver and Montreal, became the main areas of immigrant reception. Clearly this pattern is related to overall patterns of rural–urban migration and to the arrival of urban-oriented southern Italians, Greeks, Portuguese, Hungarians and West Indian blacks (Palmer and Troper, 1973, p. 20).

What is particularly relevant for this discussion is the growth in the foreign-born population of Toronto from 30.9 per cent of the total in 1951 to 43.6 per cent in 1971. The national figure for foreign-born population during that period increased only from 20.7 per cent to 23.7 per cent (Department of Manpower and Immigration, 1974, p. 17). When one examines immigration statistics by province, it is also evident that Ontario continues to be the most desirable destination in absolute and relative terms. From 1946 to 1973, of 3,842,963 immigrants who entered Canada, 2,034,022 (or approximately 53 per cent of the total) expected to settle in Ontario (Department of Manpower and Immigration, 1974, p. 38). The implications for education of this continuing flow of immigrant children into the school system, of Toronto particularly, are the focus of later discussion.

The distribution of these immigrants in terms of country of last permanent residence shows that while Great Britain and the United States supplied the largest numbers of English-speaking immigrants (984,551 and 384,137 respectively), the ten sources of the largest numbers of non-English-speaking immigrants between 1946 and 1973 were the following: Italy (463,970); German Federal Republic (315,161); the Netherlands (177,612); Greece (115,837); Portugal (111,626); France (110,314); Poland (108,764); Hong Kong (71,781); Austria (67,000); and Hungary (55,335). When the figures are examined in five-yearly breakdowns, it is apparent that the ethnic composition of immigrants altered somewhat during this period. The years 1963–1967 were a period of high Italian (121,802), Greek (32,616), and Portuguese (32,473) immigration, but in subsequent years immigrants from various West Indian, Asian, and South American countries arrived in similarly large numbers. For the years 1968–73, the countries supplying the largest number of non-English-speakers or dialect speakers of English were as follows: Italy (156,984); Portugal (54,199); Hong Kong (45,377); Greece (35,621); India (33,859); Jamaica (27,792); France (27,437); German Federal Republic (25,903); Trinidad/Tobago (24,866); and the Philippines (23,802) (Department of Manpower and Immigration, 1974, pp. 33–37).

The resulting fact of life for the Toronto school system has been

> a change in the city's cultural base so that the dominant cultural base finds itself represented in a forty-seven per cent minority of the total population . . . the fifty-three per cent majority represents a conglomerate of some fifty extra Anglo-Canadian minority groups. (Draft Report of the Work Group on Multicultural Programs, 1974, p. 5)[2]

In addition, the new immigrants differed from the previous ones in two respects. Large numbers of the Asian and black West Indian immigrants spoke not a foreign language but a dialect of English that was not that spoken by English Canadians and were racially different from the predominantly white population. Although the focus of the later discussion will be on non-English-speaking immigrants, the Work Group took full cognizance of the educational needs of dialect speakers of English and of problems of racism in its reports.

Education of Immigrants in Toronto Schools until 1970

It is evident from this brief review of immigration to Canada, and to Toronto in particular, that large numbers of non-English-speaking children have been entering the schools over a period of many years. If the emphasis in this paper appears to be on English or the lack thereof, it is because there is a marked preference on the part of immigrants for that language vis-à-vis French. Since 1941, the English language has been "gaining ground" in Canada. "While 30 per cent of immigrants already speak English when they reach Canada, about 95 per cent of those who are not of British or French origin adopt English as their home language, and their descendants take it as their mother tongue" (Henripin, 1974, p. 37).

However, one might look at the situation from another perspective. Recognizing that most immigrants who come to Canada settle in Ontario, and that most of those Ontario-bound immigrants settle in Toronto, one should then examine how the school system responds in curriculum and language teaching to the needs of students. Historically the efforts of the Toronto Board of Education have been directed towards educating the child to be fluent in reading, writing and speaking English. Thus what happens in the Toronto education system is of much greater impact than merely municipal. The debate over the future of multiculturalism in Toronto is, in a sense, a national debate. Even the mere numbers can be convincing: Metropolitan Toronto has a population today greater than that of any province in Canada except Quebec (and, of course, Ontario).

Palmer and Troper (1973, p. 18) described the prevailing ideology in Canada prior to World War Two as "Anglo-conformity," an ideology based on "the desirability of sustaining British institutions and norms as the established bases for building Canadian society." Such "desirability" was to all intents and purposes unquestioned in the education of immigrants. In Toronto particularly, this attitude was also expressed in relation to the subordinate position of French language and culture.

However, after World War Two, with the increasing numbers of non-English-speaking children entering the schools, attention did shift to the provision of English specifically for immigrants. I recall from my own childhood in Toronto in the early 1950s the great effort on the part of teachers to convince children to call the new arrivals from Europe not D.P.s (Displaced Persons) but New Canadians. This appellation is still visible in the name of the New Canadian Programs Department of the Toronto Board. The response to the "language problem" in the 1950s and early 1960s was to organize special English classes for children in the schools and evening English classes for adults. In its most general terms, it was phrased in the common parlance that Toronto had an "immigrant problem" and that basically the problem was one of language, which could be solved by teaching English to New Canadians as quickly as possible.

However, during the 1960s immigration soared; and new solutions to the "language problem" were discussed and adopted. In 1965 a school was established in Toronto's east end, known as the Main Street School (an interesting choice of name, although it did happen to be on Main Street, a rather unassuming thoroughfare). It has since been demolished, and its function is now served by Greenwood School, still in the city's east end, where there is a high immigrant population. The philosophy behind Main Street School was "cultural immersion," Anglo-Canadian style. New Canadian students of all ethnic backgrounds attended the school in a program which had as its goal facilitating the acquisition of skill in reading, writing and speaking English through an immersion in the Anglo-Canadian culture.

It was considered to be a reception program, in which students were exposed to the many diverse aspects of living in a large metropolitan Canadian city, through field trips, visual materials, and so on. A publication of the Toronto Board notes that the Board "attempts to set the teaching of English as a second language into a philosophical context" (Toronto Board of Education, 1969, p. 6).

> The field trip is an immersion strategy for involving the immigrant student in the cultural pattern of our society. This immersion affords the child the opportunity of working his way into a community of strangers. . . . The deep workings of this entire process by which language arises through a commitment to integrate oneself in the new cultural fabric becomes visible. . . .

Some trenchant criticisms have been levelled at the approach taken to education for immigrants in the 1960s in Toronto. Until 1970, all of the programs for immigrant children were directed toward the goal of initiating the child into the dominant Anglo-Canadian culture.

As Loren Lind (1974, pp. 106–107) points out, "without ill will, almost coincidentally, immigrants became defined as problems. Their potential bilingualism became a stigma rather than an asset . . . The New Canadian approach bulldozed all the alien languages into one unrecognizable heap."

The implications of seeing the entire problem of immigrant adaptation as a language problem were that undue emphasis was laid on the teaching of the English language itself, with almost no appreciation of the cultural cost to the immigrant or to the greater Canadian society. Barr Greenfield (1976, p. 112) discusses this approach:

> Second language and cultural programs in our schools thus illustrate a malaise which is common to Canadian society generally. We approach them technocratically, with little concern for what they are to do as long as we can convince ourselves that the programs are "effective", acceptable to taxpayers, and good for children. Whether the programs meet any of these criteria is seldom known, for they rarely receive searching analysis in terms of their relationship to the language and cultural questions which so obviously beset Canadian society.

In addition, such emphasis on the teaching of English alone, with no reference to the child's mother tongue, may in fact be a less efficient method pedagogically than teaching in two languages (Greenfield, 1976, p. 118). This question, however, is outside the scope of the present discussion.

Another place one could look to assess the impact of the New Canadian program is the immigrants' own perceptions of how well it fulfilled their needs. As Lind (1974, p. 115) points out, "How much it hurts a child to have his own language ignored in a class of strangers probably never will be measured by the social scientists." However, a study of occupational graduates' perceptions of their schooling was carried out in Ontario in the early 1970s; the sample included immigrants who had attended Toronto schools in the 1960s (Harvey and Masemann, 1975). The entire sample responded to a telephone questionnaire, and a sub-sample were subsequently interviewed personally. A summary of their experiences is as follows:

> When discussing their school experiences, they mentioned how they came to school soon after arrival in Canada, and how they sat and listened to the teacher speaking and did not understand one word. They recounted the various solutions to this situation. In some cases a fellow pupil who was bilingual would be assigned to clarify matters for them, or the teacher would give them individual attention. Other students were transferred to the English immersion program for immigrants, and still others to special classes for 'slow learners' with children with other kinds of learning difficulties.

> The stories respondents told had two kinds of outcomes: success or failure. On the one hand, the student might learn English rapidly enough to be transferred back to a regular classroom and catch up with the other students. On the other hand, the student might never acquire facility in English and would feel himself slipping farther and farther behind in his academic work. In either event, if his grade 8 work had not reached the requisite standard, he was advised to transfer to the occupational program. (Masemann, 1975, pp. 112–13)

As is intimated in this excerpt, the most important result educationally for immigrant students of their "language problem" was that disproportionately large numbers of them were unable to enter the academic stream in high school and instead ended up in the technically oriented occupational program, which did not necessarily lead to even a high school graduation diploma. Interviews with the graduates clearly revealed that the realization of their plight dawned only in high school or at work. "They bear the scars of having been taunted by their Anglo classmates for not being proficient in spoken English, and finish with the stigma of having attended a school that 'slow learners' also attend" (Masemann, 1975, p. 120).

Thus the narrow definition of the immigrants' problems as language alone resulted in psychological, cultural, pedagogical and economic costs. By the early 1970s, these costs were becoming evident, not only to immigrants but also to some teachers, principals, and members of the Board of Education. The scene was set for a rethinking of policy concerning education for immigrants.

Toronto's Response to Multiculturalism since 1970

The publication of the Royal Commission on Bilingualism and Biculturalism's report in the mid-1960s led to passage of the Official Languages Act in 1969, which conferred on both French and English "equal status as official languages of the Parliament and Government of Canada" (Innis, 1973). Centennial celebrations and the public hearings held before the Commission also generated a great deal of interest by ethnic minorities in their own particular place in Canadian society. Moreover, the federal government thereafter adopted an official policy of multiculturalism within a bilingual framework in response to volume 4 (*The Cultural Contribution of the Other Ethnic Groups*) of the Commission's report. Prime Minister Trudeau's official pronouncement was as follows:

> First, resources permitting, the government will seek to assist all Canadian cultural groups that have demonstrated a desire and effort to continue to develop a capacity to grow and contribute to Canada, and a

> clear need for assistance, the small and weak groups no less than the strong and highly organized.
>
> Second, the government will assist members of all cultural groups to overcome cultural barriers to full participation in Canadian society.
>
> Third, the government will promote creative encounters and interchange among all Canadian cultural groups in the interest of national unity.
>
> Fourth, the government will continue to assist immigrants to acquire at least one of Canada's official languages in order to become full participants in Canadian society. (Canada, House of Commons, *Debates*, 1971, p. 8546)

At this time, Canadians considered multiculturalism to be a new policy, although "until the 1960s the mosaic, which John Porter (1965) described as Canada's most cherished value, was regularly lauded by prominent politicans" (Burnet, 1975, p. 206). It is indeed one of the myths from which Canadians derive considerable self-satisfaction in comparing themselves with the United States. And yet although the phrase "the cultural mosaic" was often heard, it was not translated in any concrete sense into educational programs that actively encouraged the maintenance or development of the immigrant languages and cultures.

However, the results of this very major shift in thinking and in federal government policy did eventually lead to several dramatic changes in pronouncements on local educational policy in the 1970s. Since 1971, the Toronto Board of Education has introduced programs for kindergarten children in which Italian is used as the transitional language to English (the Grande proposal). Evaluation of this program showed that the children in Italian transition kindergarten were "learning the English language at a rate equal to that of children in regular programs" (Purbhoo & Shapson, 1975, p. 44). In addition, bilingual/bicultural classes for Chinese students, funded by the efforts of the Chinese communities, were established in 1974 at Orde Street and Ogden public schools; Chinese children participate in about a half-hour's instruction per day during school time in Chinese culture and language. Similar classes for Greek children were set up at Franklin and Jackman Avenue public schools on an after-school basis. The Italian community has had an after-school program for several years, organized by the Dante Society with the support of the Italian government; they choose and pay their own teachers, but receive free space in the public school. One other experimental program, conducted in the Catholic schools for both Italian and Portuguese children by Henderson and Silverman of OISE, used bilingual instruction in regular class time (Lind, 1974, p. 113).

At the same time, the Toronto Board has continued with its regular

English as a Second Language classes for children and adults. The "reception" function is still performed by Greenwood School. Reception classes are defined as "special classes designed to provide non-English-speaking immigrant students with an opportunity to develop a basic working facility in English which will permit them to participate in regular school programs at the earliest possible time. These classes normally occupy the full school day" (Draft Report, p. 138).

In addition, instruction in English as a Second Language and in other curriculum subjects is offered in transition classes. Students who have achieved a basic working competence in English and who have left the reception class are withdrawn daily from their regular class for additional help. Thus these classes are "transition" classes with English the language of transition from reception class to the regular school program.

In the policy formulation area, the most visible response of the Toronto Board of Education to this shift in federal thinking was the appointment in 1974 of the Work Group on Multicultural Programs. The subsequent work of this group and the community response to it form the substance of the following discussion.

The Work Group on Multicultural Programs

The Work Group was established in May 1974, and consisted of a group of elected Board of Education Trustees[3] whose terms of reference were defined as follows:

- i) To investigate and explore the philosophy and programs related to the City's multicultural population. This must include consultation and involvement with staff, students, parents and the community at large.
- ii) To examine current practices related to the operation of the Board's multicultural programs.
- iii) a) To recommend to the Board long-range policy-related philosophy and programs.
  - b) To recommend to the Board implementation procedures for the above.
  - c) To consider the financing and structural needs determined by the proposed policy. (Draft Report, p. 10)

The Work Group was an Advisory Committee which had to have its recommendations voted on by the Board as a whole. The views of the Work Group as reflected in the draft and final reports were thus not to be construed as official Board policy.

Consistent with the first of its terms of reference, the Work Group proceeded in 1974 to contact representatives of ethnic communities, teachers, school principals, community groups, and Education Centre (of the Toronto Board) staff in order to solicit briefs and presentations relating to education and multiculturalism. Its members held formal and informal discussions with school personnel and other interested persons. In addition they contacted officials in other provinces, in Britain, and in the United States. In October 1974 they visited New York City, a visit which occasioned some criticism:

> The Work Group . . . made the predictable visit to New York City where its members were impressed by the programs developed to serve the linguistic and racial groups which live under ghetto conditions in that city. On its return, the Work Group wrote a report which regretted that Toronto does not have ghettos like New York and that the American solution will not work here. (Greenfield, 1976, p. 111)

Members of the appropriate ministries of the federal and Ontario governments were also contacted. Letters containing information and a questionnaire on multiculturalism were sent to Members of Parliament representing Toronto constituencies in the Ontario Legislature and the federal Parliament.

In early 1975, the Work Group continued to accept briefs and oral presentations from interested individuals, schools, and community groups. They consulted with officials of the federal government's Multicultural Program, continued correspondence and meetings with federal and provincial officials, and continued consultation with ethnic groups and Education Centre staff. They also attended meetings of specific ethnic minority groups as observers to "listen in" on discussions of multiculturalism from the ethnic point of view. By April 23, 1975, they had received a total of 133 briefs in their first round of activity. Of these, 35 were from elementary schools, 22 from secondary schools, 28 from central departments of the Board of Education, 29 from ethnic organizations, and 13 from community groups.[4]

CONTENT OF THE BRIEFS

In the most general terms, there seemed to be four main trends of opinion in briefs from school and community representatives. One trend, evident especially among some principals and teachers in Toronto schools, reflected the ideas of an Anglo-conformist model: since immigrants had voluntarily chosen to move to Canada, they should accept education here as it exists. This same opinion was also reiterated by some individuals of non-Anglo descent who had lived in Canada for some years and who felt that since they had adapted positively to life in Canada, so could the new immigrants also. The second trend could be termed the "sympathetic English as a Second Language model." This opinion was expressed by very well-meaning citizens, teachers, and principals who made many useful recommendations on how English teaching and reception services to New Canadians could be improved. These briefs were generally very explicit in policy recommendations regarding staffing, pupil/teacher ratios, teaching English as a Second Language (hereafter referred to as ESL), teacher qualifications, and so on. The underlying assumption here was very much the assimilationist view, but rendered humane. The third trend in opinion was that of representatives of ethnic groups whose children were presently attending school. In general members of these groups were strongly in favour of the school's playing a role in the maintenance and development of the child's ethnic language and culture. Finally, the fourth trend reflected the "pragmatist" view, which cross-cut the other three views. This view was tied very solidly to the practical realities of fiscal and legislative restraints on the implementation of new programs for immigrants. Basically summarized, in the words of one brief, it suggested that "every ethnic community should be made aware of how budgetary constraints affect the Board's ability to offer all services and programs requested by the New Canadian communities."

The relative strength of each of these views was not equal, as became clear in the public reaction to the recommendations of the Draft Report. In terms of the briefs themselves, the "sympathetic ESL model" was probably most strongly represented among members of the education system, and the Anglo-conformity model was less popular among teachers or principals who were directly concerned with immigrant children. The third trend (emphasis on original language and culture) found its strongest support in the ethnic community, although a vociferous minority of educators, among them some members of the Work Group itself, supported it. The "pragmatic model" held strong sway among most sympathizers of Anglo-conformity and improved ESL teaching, but seemed less evident in the briefs of the "original language and culture" sympathizers. In the ensuing community response, these four strands of thought formed the core of the debate on the future of multiculturalism in Toronto schools.

When the Work Group's recommendations were published in the Draft Report, in May 1975, they appeared to respond to all of these diverse opinions. Very specific recommendations were made with reference to (1) improvement in recruitment and training of ESL teachers, (2) withdrawal of students for special classes, (3) improvement in reception and transition programs, (4) a New Canadian summer program, (5) full secondary school English credits for summer ESL study, (6) improvements in adult ESL classes, (7) provision of child care for offspring of adult ESL students, (8) increase in the number of New Canadian consultants, (9) numerous recommendations regarding the New Canadian Programs Department, and (10) the development of a new Reception Centre in the city's Area 6 (North Toronto). These recommendations appeared to respond to many of the requests of those in the education system.

However, other far more "radical" recommendations were made which addressed the central belief on which the entire Report was based — namely, that the school system had become unresponsive to the cultural base of Toronto society. The Work Group recommended, therefore, that (1) the Toronto Board of Education's Language Study Centre develop programs relating to the teaching of English as a Second Dialect (for West Indian immigrants); (2) the bilingual/bicultural programs be expanded and funded by provincial and federal government ministries; (3) the Toronto Board of Education request the Ontario Ministry of Education to amend the Ontario Education Act to permit a language other than English or French to be used in teaching, and to be taught as a subject at primary level; (4) the Board endorse in principle bilingual transition programs of the type presently in existence at General Mercer Public School (transition kindergarten), and the establishment of other such programs; and (5) the Board continue to be responsive to requests for the institution of third-language (i.e., other than English or French) subject credit programs at the secondary school level.

There were several other recommendations relating to (1) multicultural content in all subject areas of the general curriculum; (2) system sensitivity (particularly in the qualifications and training of New Canadian teachers); (3) the establishment of School–Community Relations Department; (4) improvement of communications to the community, making visible the schools' commitment to multiculturalism; (5) greater involvement of guidance personnel in responsibility for immigrant students; (6) amplification of the role of social workers and interpreter counsellors; and (7) greatly increased involvement of senior government levels in providing financial assistance, counselling for immigrants before immigration, and cultural curriculum materials for schools. All of these recommendations were aimed at relating the multicultural reality of the community to the multicultural reality of the school. The resources to achieve these goals were requested from the federal government, through the Secretary of State responsible for multiculturalism, and from the Ontario Government for areas related to curriculum and education (Draft Report, p. 165).

In summary, all the recommendations addressed themselves to the four sets of concerns raised in the school and community briefs. The ESL and New Canadian recommendations responded to the expressed concerns of school staff who were involved in teaching English to immigrants. However, they were also acceptable to Anglo-conformists and others who supported the inevitable primacy of English. The implications of such recommendations did nothing to threaten the English basis of education in Toronto and were based squarely on a model of cultural assimilation. On the other hand, the recommendations supporting the maintenance and development of the child's original language and culture, which responded primarily to the briefs from ethnic communities, implied a reorientation of the school system toward the language and culture of immigrants.

Public response to the recommendations reflected exactly these differences in implications. Letters to the editor of the Toronto *Globe and Mail* expressed very strong opinions on behalf of either side. The debate was narrowed to a discussion of the role of the school in maintaining immigrant language and culture. The view opposing the Work Group's stand is summarized in one letter as follows:

> For many years, Japanese, Ukrainian, Estonian and Jewish people have cared enought about their languages and cultures to keep them alive, *at their own expense* [original emphasis]. Irish and Scottish people have cared enough about their music and dances to provide lessons to their children at the parents' expense.
>
> Let the Italian, Greek, Chinese, Pakistani, West Indian, Hindu, Polish and Portuguese pay their own expenses, *if* they care enough to preserve their language and culture, and after — not during — school hours. (*Globe and Mail,* May 10, 1975, p. 6)

Certain sections of the Draft Report were considered much less problematic than the language and culture question, and thus in June 1975 the Board approved the recommendations concerning the improvement of ESL programs, the establishment of subject upgrading programs, and the development of closer school–community contacts. In relation to the remaining issues, the Work Group once again undertook the task of eliciting school and public response. They distributed summaries of the recommendations in seven languages,[5] attended public meetings, held hearings, and received oral and written submissions. Moreover, they consulted with educators and government officials[6] in Vancouver, Winnipeg and Montreal, and with federal and Ontario government officials.

The 114 briefs which were received in this second round naturally reflected a more specific concern with points raised in the Draft Report. It is pointed out in the Final Report (p. 23) that "during the consultative period preceding the distribution of the Draft Report, there existed broad and specific majority community support for Issues 3, 4, 5" (maintenance of original culture and language, the use of third language as a language and subject for instruction, and increased multicultural content in the general curriculum).

Although the Work Group had originally perceived strong community (usually ethnic community) support for the maintenance and development of immigrants' language and culture, they point out that the publication of the Draft Report aroused "newly participating groups in opposition to certain "ideas" contained in the report" (Final Report, pp. 23–24):

> 1. The school system's new responsiveness to "ethnic demands" in the area of language and culture will create ghettos. People must assimilate to the "Canadian way of life".
> 2. The system cannot afford [financially] to be responsive to the ethnic minority groups.
> 3. It is the responsibility of "these people" to adjust since they chose to come to this country. it is not the school system's responsibility to adjust to them.
> 4. Culture and language development is the responsibility of the home. The school's responsibility is education.
> 5. Language maintenance or development programs in the schools, other than French or English, will retard the English language development of ethnic minority children, and they will impede English language development of the ethnic minority community themselves.
> 6. Responsiveness to ethnic minority wishes in the areas of original language and cultural development or maintenance is impractical [financially and culturally].

These views produced a community counter-response from the original supporters of these issues and others on (1) concern for the immigrant students' loss of identity, (2) apprehension at growing indications of prejudice and racism, (3) demands for programs which would recognize and reflect the immigrant students' cultural and racial integrity, and (4) concern for the rights of parents.

Although the opposition to the maintenance of immigrants' language and culture was "a significant minority opinion" in terms of the briefs submitted to the Work Group (Final Report, p. 24), it was aligned with two powerful facts of existence for the Toronto Board of Education. The first fact was that the Ontario government did not appear to be planning to amend the Education Act so as to allow the use of a third language, and the second was the reality of fiscal constraints. Thus the "significant minority opinion" had in fact the force of a "majority opinion" financially and legislatively. Therefore, the Work Group announced publicly its intention of dropping the recommendations in these three contentious areas (*Globe and Mail*,

February 14, 1976). The Work Group concentrated the rest of its efforts on elucidating and amplifying its recommendations on system sensitivity, school–community relations, and the role of senior governments.

THE NATURE OF THE DEBATE

The nature of this three-year debate concerning multiculturalism and the Toronto school system reveals, indeed, to what extent Anglo-conformity still prevails as a mode of thought. It demonstrates that the shift in sentiment since World War Two has not been such as to call into question the predominantly Anglo cultural basis of the schools. Ultimately the Work Group, which had espoused a multicultural approach, was forced by the weight of that portion of public opinion which was aligned with legislative and fiscal constraints to conclude, so limply, "The Work Group considers it unwise to recommend the establishment of third language programs at the elementary level" (Final Report, p. 28). While this fundamental shift has not occurred, however, it is noteworthy how many recommendations were made and accepted for improvements in programs for immigrants generally.

This debate in Toronto cannot be dissociated from two other debates, both of which make it a part of a Canadian national debate on social policy. The first is the French–English debate in Canada generally, and the second a comparative debate on definitions of the nature of social equality and the place of ethnic diversity.

The status of French as an official language in Canada renders the question of teaching immigrants to Canada in their own language a rather more complicated one than the question, for example, of teaching Mexican immigrants to the United States in Spanish. The Work Group were cognizant of this difficulty, as can be seen in their response to the Work Group on Implementation of French Programs (Draft Report, Appendix G). They agreed that the "day of unilingualism and splendid isolation is over" and that all Canadians should enjoy "the opportunity to educate their children in the official language of their choice and that children have the opportunity to learn as a second language, the other official language of their country" (Draft Report, pp. 208–209). However, they strongly disagreed that the French core program be made compulsory for all students in Toronto elementary schools because of the difficulties it would pose for children with neither French nor English. They considered that this proposal would place these children in the position of learning a "second, second language" (Draft Report, p. 210).

This reasoning appears to coincide, although paradoxically, with language policy of the Ontario government in its unwillingness to amend the Ontario Education Act. While the intent of the Act is clearly assimilationist, in offering education in English or education in French, its terms have the effect of removing the dilemma of educating the immigrant child in three languages. The Act is consonant with the federal government's bilingualism policy and is in that sense in accord with political realities, although not the cultural realities of the immigrants' lives.

Guy Rocher discusses this relationship between culture and politics from the point of view of a francophone commentator on multiculturalism. He points out that while from a sociological standpoint Canada may be seen as a multicultural nation (as are many others), it is not so politically. In his view,

> Canada is a country defined by a twofold culture, Anglophone and Francophone, and it is the interplay of political forces between these two great "societies" . . . that will determine the future of this country. . . . To the Francophone Quebecker, therefore, multiculturalism appears as another way of referring to the Canadian Anglophone community. . . . Multiculturalism may thus be said to exist outside the Quebec Francophone community. Worse, it is a threat to the survival and political power of the latter. (Rocher, 1976, pp. 48–49)

Although very little was said in the Draft Report about the place of French as the other official language, it can be seen as the element which renders the debate totally different from such debates in large American cities with substantial ethnic populations. In a sense, the criticisms of the Work Group's "predictable visit to New York" were valid ones. The cultural argument in favour of bilingual education in the immigrants' language in the end was not able to compete with the political realities of Canada's two official languages and their place in the Ontario Education Act, which ensures Anglo dominance.

In a more general sense, one can examine what models of multiculturalism were being propounded and why certain models were found far more acceptable than others. Margaret Gibson in a recent symposium outlined five conceptual approaches to multicultural education which are relevant in an examination of the Work Group's task. In brief, these approaches are named (1) Education of the Culturally Different or Benevolent Multiculturalism, (2) Education about Cultural Differences or Cultural Understanding, (3) Education for Cultural Pluralism, (4) Bicultural Education, and (5) Multicultural Education as the Normal Human Experience (Gibson, 1976, p. 7). I shall summarize the assumptions behind these approaches and delineate to what extent each is applicable in the Toronto setting.

The first approach has as its purpose the equalizing of educational opportunity for students who are culturally different from the dominant Anglo culture. These children are considered to have unique learning handicaps in schools dominated by mainstream values, and to remedy this situation multicultural education programs must be devised to increase home/school compatibility. These new programs will in turn increase students' academic success. Gibson criticizes this approach on two counts: first, there is no empirical evidence that minority students' achievement is improved, and second, it is still conceived of as a special program for a special group of students. Finally, she considers it paternalistic and agrees with Freire that "pedagogy which begins with the egoistic interests of the oppressors . . . and makes of the oppressed the objects of its humanitarianism, itself maintains and embodies oppression" (Gibson, pp. 8–9).

The second approach, education about cultural differences, is directed to all students. It teaches students to value cultural differences, to understand the meaning of culture, and to accept others' right to be different. It is the basic assumption of this approach that schools be oriented to the cultural enrichment of all students, and that these programs will in turn decrease racism and prejudice. Gibson's criticisms of this approach are concerned with the danger of teachers' becoming cultural relativists to the point that they overemphasize cultural differences, and with its assumption that the existing social order can be changed via the school system.

The third approach, education for cultural pluralism, is based on a rejection of cultural assimilation and the "melting pot." The programs are intended to serve the needs of the ethnic community which proposes them, and to decrease the power of the majority to oppress the minority. Gibson (p. 12) points out that "for cultural pluralism to exist in a complex society . . ., structural pluralism must also exist."

The goal of the fourth approach, bicultural education, is to produce learners who can operate successfully in two different cultures. It is based on the assumptions that a student's ability to function in the native (original) culture and the mainstream culture will be enhanced, and that the student will acquire competencies in the second culture without rejection of the original culture. Ideally, it is aimed at all students rather than the non-mainstream.

The fifth approach, multicultural education as the normal human experience, is derived from anthropological definitions of education, whereas the previous four are drawn from the educational literature on bicultural and multicultural education. It is defined as "a process whereby a person develops competencies in multiple systems of standards for perceiving, evaluating, believing, and doing" (p. 15). As

Gibson describes it, multicultural education in this sense appears to provide a student with a mixed bag of cultural tools, which he/she may draw upon to use in the appropriate situation.

In the Toronto case, and in the Canadian case generally, Gibson's categories find themselves exemplified to varying degrees. In fact, the debates on the pages of the two Work Group reports, in the multitudinous briefs, and in the local press do reflect a conflict among these five models and the extent to which various segments of the community accepted their basic assumptions or their goals.

First and foremost, the argument on bicultural/bilingual education (approach four) has been played out on the national scene and has been enshrined in the wording of the Ontario Education Act. The force of the argument for bilingual/bicultural competence appears to have been spent on the English/French question in Ontario; and arguments in favour of English/Italian, English/Greek, or English/Chinese competence were not favourably received by non-members of these ethnic groups.

Likewise, the argument in favour of general multicultural competence can be seen as having a national context in Canada which makes it a highly unlikely solution. As Guy Rocher stated, such a patchwork approach can be seen primarily as associated with anglophone interests and thus unacceptable to francophones.

We are left, then, with the other three approaches which formed the core of the debate. Probably the least contentious model was that of education about cultural differences. Numerous recommendations were made in the Draft Report concerning improved multicultural content in the curriculum, increased visibility of ethnic festivals in the schools, and so on. The Work Group's concern with racism and intolerance was clearly stated, and these recommendations were aimed specifically at alleviating intercultural misunderstanding. There was no strong opposition to these sections of the Draft Report, as long as they were not seen as directed at maintenance of the immigrants' original language and culture.

The two approaches which formed the core of the debate in Toronto were benevolent multiculturalism and cultural pluralism. These are referred to in the analysis of briefs as the "sympathetic ESL" model and the "original language and culture" model. In essence, the immigrant community's requests for programs responsive to their language and culture, which clearly would have resulted in the diminution of the force of Anglo-Canadian culture in the school system, were rejected by vociferous community members, by some teaching personnel, and by the Ontario government. However, the "benevolent multiculturalism" response tended to blur the lines of contention somewhat, since it had about it an aura of concern and goodwill. In the end, the immigrants' cause lost to the realities of an official federal bilingual policy and benevolent Anglo-conformity.

It is very difficult to foresee what the long-term implications of the outcome of this debate will be, since they seem to be clearly associated with the fate of multiculturalism as a goal of Canadian social policy generally. In the short term, some of the less contentious recommendations will serve to alleviate some of the more mundane problems of students' lives. One thinks of improved counselling procedures and increased multicultural content in the curriculum. However, problems of racism still loom large and will not be stilled by surface acknowledgment of symptoms rather than causes. Even in the more than two years since the Draft Report was written, there does not seem to be an improved climate of community responsiveness to immigrants. In a very cynical vein, one could even argue that the short-term concessions granted by a benevolent multiculturalism have not been enough, on the one hand, to "buy off" the immigrants nor, on the other hand, to quiet the fears of those who see cultural differences as a threat to a united social fabric.

The long-term fate of cultural pluralism as a goal in this country will not be settled in the schools of Toronto! The result of the November 1976 Quebec election and the subsequent national debates concerning French–English relations will once again shift the argument from multicultural to bicultural concerns; the outcome of any debate on third-language teaching must await the resolution of the political debate on the place of the first two languages. Subsequent language policy in the Ontario Education Act will reflect this outcome and will in the future, as now, define to what extent ethnic minorities can make any claims to a policy of structural pluralism in this province. The schooling offered to immigrants in the Toronto school system will reflect, as now, the resolution of these political questions.

Notes

1. Grateful acknowledgment is made to Mel LaFountaine and Ceta Ramkhalawansingh for their assistance and helpful discussion of the work of the Toronto Board of Education's Work Group on Multicultural Programs, and to David Wilson, Garnet McDiarmid, and Jocelyn Desroches for their comments. This is a revision of a paper presented at the Annual Meeting of the Comparative and International Education Society, Toronto, February 1976. Any errors are the author's.
2. Hereafter referred to in references as "Draft Report." The Work Group's Final Report will also be referenced in the text simply as "Final Report.
3. Trustees Atkinson, Cressy, Leckie, Lister, Meagher, and Ross participated in 1974; in 1975 the composition changed to Trustees Leckie (Chairman), Atkinson, Chumak, Major, Meagher, and Nagle (representing Separate School electors).

4. In terms of representations from ethnic/racial and community groups: Black 3, Chinese 5, East Indian 1, Greek 4, Italian 1, Japanese 2, Lithuanian 1, Native People 1, Polish 5, Portuguese 3, Serbian 1, Slovakian 1, Ukrainian 1, School–Community organizations 3, Opportunities for Youth 5, Others (individuals) 6.
5. Chinese, English, Greek, Italian, Polish, Portuguese, Spanish.
6. Whether these were municipal or provincial government officials is not specified (Final Report, p. 2).

References

Burnet, J."The policy of multiculturalism within a bilingual framework: An interpretation", in A. Wolfgang, ed. *Education of Immigrant Students.* Toronto: Ontario Institute for Studies in Education, Symposium Series/5, 1975.

Canada. House of Commons, *Debates.* 28th Parliament, 3rd Session, Vol. 8, 1971.

Department of Manpower and Immigration. *Immigration and Population Statistics.* Ottawa: Information Canada, 1974.

Gibson, M. "Approaches to multicultural education in the United States. Some concepts and assumptions." *Anthropology and Education Quarterly*, 7(4), (1976), pp. 7–18.

Globe and Mail, May 10, 1975, p. 6; February 14, 1976, pp. 11, 15.

Greenfield, T.B. "Bilingualism, multiculturalism, and the crisis of purpose." *Canadian Society for the Study of Education Yearbook,* 3 (1976), pp. 107–36.

Harney, R.F., and Troper, H. *Immigrants. A Portrait of the Urban Experience, 1890–1930.* Toronto: Van Nostrand Reinhold, 1975.

Harvey, E.B., and Masemann, V.L. *Occupational Graduates and the Labour Force.* Toronto: Ontario Ministry of Education, 1975.

Henripin, J. *Immigration and Language Imbalance.* Ottawa: Information Canada, Department of Manpower and Immigration, 1974.

Innis, H.R. *Bilingualism and Biculturalism.* Toronto: McClelland and Stewart and Information Canada, 1973.

Lind, L. "New Canadianism: Melting the ethnics in Toronto schools," in George Martell, ed. *The Politics of the Canadian Public School.* Toronto: James Lewis & Samuel, 1974.

Masemann, V.L. "Immigrant students' perceptions of occupational programs," in A. Wolfgang, ed. *Education of Immigrant Students.* Toronto: Ontario Institute for Studies in Education, Symposium Series/5, 1975.

Palmer, H., and Troper, H. "Canadian ethnic studies: Historical perspectives and contemporary implications," *Interchange,* 4, no. 4 (1973), pp. 15–23.

Porter, J. *The Vertical Mosaic.* Toronto: University of Toronto Press, 1968.

Purbhoo, M., and Shapson, S. *Transition from Italian.* Toronto: Board of Education, Research Report No. 133, October, 1975.

Rocher, G. "Multiculturalism: The doubts of a francophone," in *Multiculturalism as State Policy.* Conference Report, Second Canadian Conference on Multiculturalism. Ottawa: Canadian Consultative Council on Multiculturalism, 1976.

Special Joint Committee on Immigration Policy. *Minutes of Proceedings and Evidence Respecting the Green Paper on Immigration Policy.* 30th Parliament, 1st Session, Issue No. 34. Ottawa: Queen's Printer, June 11, 1975.
Toronto Board of Education. *English as a Second Language.* Toronto, 1969.
Toronto Board of Education. *The Bias of Culture: An Issue Paper on Multiculturalism.* Toronto, October 25, 1974 (revised April, 1975).
Work Group on Multicultural Programs. *Draft Report*. Toronto: Board of Education, May 20, 1975.
Work Group on Multicultural Programs. *Final Report*. Toronto: Board of Education, February 12, 1976.

Evaluation of the Second Year of a Bilingual (English-Ukrainian) Program

D. LAMONT, W. PENNER, T. BLOWER, H. MOSYCHUK AND J. JONES

A bilingual (English-Ukrainian) program was introduced at the kindergarten and grade one levels by the Edmonton Public School System in September 1974. The following year the bilingual program was expanded to include grade two with an extension of the program to grade three planned for September 1976.

In its second year of operation four Edmonton Public Schools offered the program to grades one and two. At both grade levels the program is designed so that 50 per cent of instructional time is conducted in Ukrainian, the other 50 per cent in English. Arithmetic, English-language arts and science are taught in English, whereas social studies, physical education, Ukrainian language-arts, art and music are taught in Ukrainian. Ukrainian culture and language receive equal emphasis.

The specified objectives for the bilingual program in both grades one and two were as follows:

1. The pupils will follow the English language curriculum in language arts, mathematics and science and will achieve at or above the average for their grade level in each of these areas.
2. In grade one the pupils will learn oral Ukrainian through the presentation of language arts, social studies, music, art and physical education programs in the Ukrainian language. In grade two the pupils' listening and speaking skills in Ukrainian will be further developed and Ukrainian reading and writing skills will be introduced.
3. Pupils will develop a greater appreciation of the Ukrainian culture.
4. The pupils and their parents will have positive feelings about the participation of the pupils in the program.

SOURCE: *The Canadian Modern Language Review/La Revue canadienne des langues vivantes,* 34, no. 2 (January 1975) pp. 175–85. Reprinted by permission of the Editor.

In order to assess the program, the Research and Evaluation Department of the Edmonton Public School Board, began a three-year evaluation in September 1974. This report covers the second year of the ongoing evaluation and was designed to assess the extent to which the program's four objectives were achieved in grades one and two.[1]

Specifically, the evaluation procedures were addressed to the following four questions:

1. Are the pupils in the program achieving at or above their grade level in the English language arts and mathematics?
2. To what extent are the pupils acquiring skills in the Ukrainian language?
3. Are the students developing an appreciation of the Ukrainian culture?
4. What are the attitudes and perceptions of the pupils, their parents, their teachers and their school administrators toward the program?

Method

SUBJECTS

Information relevant to the evaluation of the bilingual program was obtained from the following:

1. Students in grades one and two of the bilingual program (62 — grade one, 54 — grade two);
2. All students in regular grade one and two classes in schools which offered the program (223 — grade one, 244 — grade two);
3. Parents of children in the program (116);
4. Parents with a Ukrainian surname who had children in the regular grade one program at the bilingual program schools (16);
5. Teachers of children in the bilingual program (2 — grade one, 2 — grade two; 2 — combined grades one and two);
6. Principals (4) and assistant principals (4) of the schools which offered the bilingual program.

The scholastic readiness, socio-economic status, linguistic background and ethnic origin of the grade one bilingual program students is given in tables 1, 2 and 3. Generally the grade one students were of average scholastic ability (as ascertained from Metorpolitan Readiness Test Scores) and came from homes in which the majority of their parents had some knowledge of the Ukrainian language and had also some Ukrainian ancestry.

Table 1: Description of Grade One Students in the Bilingual Program

Variable	*Range*	*Mean*	*Standard Deviation*
Age as of Sept. 1, 1975	5 yrs. 6 mo. 6 yrs. 5 mo.	6 yrs. 1 mo.	
Socio-economic Status[a]	7-87	46.0	15.5
Metropolitan Readiness Test (raw score)	15-87	66.3	12.1

[a] The SES was determined on the basis of the Occupational Prestige scores by occupational classes developed by P. Pineo and J. Porter.[3] Any occupations not included on the Pineo-Porter scale were rated by two independent judges using the Pineo-Porter scale as a reference. The average of the two ratings was considered the SES value for a particular occupation. The possible range of scores is 1 to 100.

Table 2: Language Background of Grade One Bilingual Program Students

Language Characteristic		*Percentage*
1) Parents have some knowledge of Ukrainian[a]		
– the mother only	11	18.0
– the father only	9	14.8
– both parents	32	52.5
– neither parent	9	14.8
2) Parents speak Ukrainian fluently[b]		
– the mother only	9	14.8
– the father only	10	16.4
– both parents	24	39.2
– neither parents	18	29.5
3) Parents speak Ukrainian with the child		
– the mother only	13	21.3
– the father only	7	11.5
– both parents	21	34.4
– neither parent	20	32.8

Note: The information on language background was obtained by telephone interview. Of the 62 Grade One program parents, 61 could be contacted.

[a] A parent was considered to have some knowledge of the Ukrainian language if he/she obtained a score of >5 on the questions pertaining to the reading, speaking, or understanding of Ukrainian and the degree to which he/she spoke the language in the home (maximum possible 16).

[b] A parent was considered fluent in Ukrainian if he/she obtained a score of ≥ 8 on the questions pertaining to the speaking and comprehension of Ukrainian (maximum possible 10).

Since information on the age, socio-economic status, scholastic readiness, IQ and linguistic background of the grade two program students had been gathered the previous year [Bilingual Program

(English-Ukrainian) Evaluation, 1975] only the ethnic origin of these students was investigated in the second year. Like the grade one students, the majority were of Ukrainian descent.

In both grades the program students were compared to all the students in the same grade of the regular program on the basis of reading and mathematics achievement test results. The pupils in the regular program receive instruction through the medium of English only and have no Ukrainian instruction.

Table 3: Ethnic Origin of Grade One Bilingual Program Students

Ethnic Origin	*Number*	*Percentage*
Both parents are of Ukrainian origin	20	40.8
Mother is of Ukrainian descent, father is either of partial Ukrainian descent or has no Ukrainian background	8	16.3
Father is of Ukrainian descent, mother is either of partial Ukrainian descent or has no Ukrainian background	12	24.5
Either one or both parents are of partial Ukrainian descent	6	12.2
Neither parent is of Ukrainian origin	3	6.1

Note: The statistics for Table 3 are from the May, 1976, parent questionnaire. Forty-nine of the 62 grade one parents responded.

Table 4: Ethnic Origin of Grade Two Bilingual Program Students

Ethnic Origin	*Number*	*Percentage*
Both parents are of Ukrainian origin	24	54.5
Mother is of Ukrainian descent, father is either of partial Ukrainian descent or has no Ukrainian background	6	13.6
Father is of Ukrainian descent, mother is either of partial Ukrainian descent or has no Ukrainian background	9	20.5
Either one or both parents are of partial Ukrainian descent	2	4.5
Neither parent is of Ukrainian origin	3	6.8

Note: The statistics for Table 4 are from the May, 1976, parent questionnaire. Forty-four of the 54 grade two parents responded.

In order to assess progress in the Ukrainian language skills, a control group of regular grade one students identified as having Ukrainian surnames and who attended the program schools was established. These sixteen students were matched with sixteen bilingual program students on the basis of sex, their parents' familiarity with the Ukrainian language and Metropolitan Readiness scores.

INSTRUMENTS AND PROCEDURES

The instruments and procedures used are discussed in terms of the four major questions to which the study is addressed.

Are the pupils in the program achieving at or above their grade level in the English language arts and mathematics?

In May 1976, the Stanford Achievement Test and the Elementary School Mathematics Survey were administered to all the grade one and two students in the program schools. In order to compare the achievement of the regular students and the bilingual program students in the same grade, t-tests for independent samples were performed on the raw scores.

The grade one students were also compared on the basis of Metropolitan Readiness scores (administered in September 1975).

Since the sample sizes were so discrepant, an F test of the sample variances was performed. If the variances differed significantly a t value based on the separate variance estimate for $\frac{\sigma}{D}^2$ was used. If the variances were not significantly different, a t value based on the pooled variance estimate for $\frac{\sigma}{D}^2$ was used.[2]

To what extent are the pupils acquiring skills in the Ukrainian language?

In September 1975, and again in May 1976 the Ukrainian Language Skills Test was administered to all grade one and two bilingual program students. This test, developed by personnel from the Edmonton Public and Edmonton Catholic School Boards was based upon the intended content of the Ukrainian language curriculum for each grade. The grade one test measured listening comprehension, expressive vocabulary, and ability to follow instructions. In grade two listening comprehension, expressive vocabulary, oral conversation, oral reading, writing and silent reading comprehension were tested.

A t-test for dependent samples was used to compare pre- and post-test results.

In addition, parents of grade one bilingual program pupils and of grade one pupils with Ukrainian surnames who attended the program schools were interviewed in January 1976, to obtain biographic data. The Biographic parent Interview Format, which consisted of seventeen questions, was designed to provide information on:

a) mother's fluency in Ukrainian;

b) father's fluency in Ukrainian;
c) amount of Ukrainian spoken to the child in the home;
d) mother's educational level;
e) father's educational level;
f) occupation of the major wage-earner; and (for nonprogram parents only)
g) awareness of the bilingual program.

The grade one Ukrainian Language Skills Test Part One was administered to fourteen of the sixteen control students in the spring. (The other two children were unavailable for testing.)

Are the students developing an appreciation of the Ukrainian culture?

Questionnaires developed by the Edmonton Public School Board Research and Evaluation Department were sent to bilingual program personnel and all program parents in the spring. Both teachers and parents were asked to assess pupils' appreciation of Ukrainian culture.

What are the attitudes and perceptions of the pupils, their parents, their teachers and their school administrators toward the program?

In the spring questionnaires were sent to the principals and assistant principals of the bilingual program schools, program teachers and all parents who had children in the program.

The teacher questionnaire, the administrator questionnaire and the parent questionnaire were designed to obtain information regarding program personnel, program objectives, overall program operation, attitudes toward and perceptions of the program.

Results

ACHIEVEMENT IN THE ENGLISH LANGUAGE CURRICULUM: GRADE ONE STUDENTS

The results of the regular and bilingual grade one students in the spring achievement tests are shown in Table 5.

There were no significant differences between the regular and the bilingual program grade one students on the paragraph meaning and vocabulary subtests of the Stanford Achievement Test. Bilingual program students were significantly higher ($p < .05$) on the word reading and word study skills subtests.

The bilingual program students scored significantly lower ($p < .05$) on the Elementary Mathematics Survey than the regular grade one pupils. However, further examination of the results suggest that only one of the four bilingual program classes accounted for this

Table 5: Comparison of Grade One Students in the Regular and Bilingual Programs on Reading and Mathematics Achievement Tests

Variable	*EPSB System 1976*		*Bilingual Program*		*Regular Program*		*Difference Between Regular and Bilingual Program*	
	Mean	*S.D.*	*Mean*	*S.D.*	*Mean*	*S.D.*	*df*	*t value*
Metropolitan Readiness	64.0	14.7	66.3	12.1	66.6	14.9	251	−0.16
Stanford — Word Meaning	23.5	7.2	26.3	6.9	24.4	6.7	283	2.05*
Stanford — Paragraph Meaning	21.4	9.7	25.3	8.8	22.9	8.6	283	1.91
Stanford — Vocabulary	21.1	6.5	21.9	7.2	21.6	6.3	283	.39
Stanford Word Study Skills	39.4	10.2	43.5	11.0	39.5	11.0	283	2.53*
Elementary Mathematics Survey	43.4	7.1	40.2	11.6	43.5	7.7	76.7	−2.10*

*$p < .05$

Table 6: Comparison of Grade Two Students in the Regular and Bilingual Programs on Reading and Mathematics Achievement Tests

Variable	EPSB System 1976		Bilingual Program		Regular Program		Difference Between Regular and Bilingual Program	
	Mean	*S.D.*	*Mean*	*S.D.*	*Mean*	*S.D.*	*df*	*t value*
Stanford — Word Reading	19.8	7.5	21.8	10.5	19.5	8.0	67.3	1.52†
Stanford — Paragraph Meaning	31.4	12.6	33.6	12.2	31.0	13.6	296	1.32†
Stanford — Word Study Skills	40.4	21.0	46.4	11.4	40.3	12.4	296	3.33*
Elementary Mathematics Survey	39.9	7.2	41.4	6.5	37.7	10.2	118.4	3.35*

*$p < .001$
†$p > .05$

difference. The other three classes were not significantly lower than the regular grade one classes.

There was no significant difference between the two groups on Metropolitan Readiness Test scores.

ACHIEVEMENT IN THE ENGLISH LANGUAGE CURRICULUM: GRADE TWO STUDENTS

Table 6 shows the results of the grade two students on the Stanford Achievement Test and Elementary Mathematics Survey.

No significant differences were found between students in the bilingual and regular programs on either the Stanford word reading or paragraph meaning subtests. The bilingual program students scored significantly higher on the Stanford word study skills subtest ($p < .001$) and also on the Elementary Mathematics Survey ($p < .001$).

ACHIEVEMENT IN UKRAINIAN LANGUAGE SKILLS

The bilingual program students in both grades one and two showed significant improvement on the Ukrainian Language Skills Test from the fall pretest to the spring post-test ($p < .001$) (see Table 7). The mean score increased by 28.1 marks for the grade one students and 65.3 for the grade two students.

The gains in Ukrainian language skills may reflect classroom learning or they could be a factor of other variables which operate independently of the classroom bilingual experience. Variables, such as school readiness skills, mother's fluency in Ukrainian and father's fluency in Ukrainian, which could have an effect on second language learning were examined as possible predictors of the grade one post-test scores.

Table 7: Comparison of Pre- and Post-test Scores on the Ukrainian Language Skills Test

Grade	*Pre-test Mean*	*Post-test Mean*	*Maximum Possible Score*	*df*	*t value*
One	45.0	73.1	90	61	13.25*
Two	35.1	100.4	125	53	26.44*

*$p < .001$

Only Metropolitan Readiness scores were found to be significantly correlated ($p < .05$) with post-test scores of the Ukrainian Language Skills Test grade one. Neither the mother's or father's knowledge of Ukrainian were a significant factor (see Table 8).

Table 8: Correlations of Grade One Ukrainian Language Skills Test Results With Variables Related to Second-Language Learning

Related Variable	*Pearson r*	*df*	*t value*
Metropolitan Readiness Test Scores	.28	59	2.24*
Mother's fluency in Ukrainian	.12	58	.94
Father's fluency in Ukrainian	.25	58	1.98

*$p < .05$

Also the effect of previous attendance by the pupils in a Ukrainian kindergarten was examined using a t-test for independent samples. Although on the average the grade one students who had attended the Ukrainian kindergarten achieved higher scores on the grade one Ukrainian Language Skills post-test, the difference between those who had attended and those who had not was not statistically significant (see Table 9).

Table 9: Comparison of Pupils Who Attended Ukrainian Kindergarten to Pupils Who Did Not on the Grade One Ukrainian Language Skills Post-test

Type of Pupil	*Mean*	*n*	*S.D.*	*df*	*t value*
Attended Ukrainian Kindergarten	74.4	41	12.6	58	1.1
Did Not Attend Ukrainian Kindergarten	70.0	19	14.6		

No statistical comparison could be made between the fourteen grade one bilingual program and control students since the control students had not been pretested in the fall and both the pre- and post-test results for the bilingual program subjects were much higher than the spring testing results for the controls.

APPRECIATION OF THE UKRAINIAN CULTURE

The majority of grade one bilingual program parents (91.8 per cent) reported a positive change in their child's appreciation of Ukrainian culture. The parents of grade two children were not asked to assess the development of their child's attitudes toward the culture.

In both grades, 75 per cent of the program teachers felt that their pupils increased their appreciation of the culture.

In both grades the majority of parents (53.1 per cent of grade one, 63.6 per cent of grade two) thought that the program had placed equal emphasis on the learning of Ukrainian culture and Ukrainian language skills. The majority of teachers reported that they had indeed given equal emphasis to both.

Most parents (61.2 per cent of grade one, 63.6 per cent of grade two) wanted equal emphasis to be given to both language and culture. Of those who did not, one person thought culture deserved higher priority and the others (30.6 per cent of grade one, 31.8 per cent of grade two) felt the emphasis should be given to Ukrainian language development.

When the parents of children in both grades of the program were asked what topics they felt should be taught as Ukrainian culture the results were mixed. There was some consensus that Ukrainian religious traditions, crafts, singing and dancing should be covered. There was also some agreement that information on famous Ukrainian people be given low priority. The parents were of divided opinion on the history of Ukrainian settlers in Canada and the culture of present-day Ukraine. Some felt the topics deserved high priority, others felt they deserved minimal coverage, and some felt they should not be taught at all.

ATTITUDES CONCERNING THE BILINGUAL PROGRAM

All program parents, teachers and administrators were asked to complete questionnaires on their perceptions of the program. All of the teachers and administrators, forty of the sixty-two grade one parents (79.0 per cent) and forty-four of the fifty-four grade two parents (81.5 per cent) returned their questionnaires.

Parents' attitudes. When questioned on specific issues related to the success of the program the majority of parents of children in both grades of the program reported that they were satisfied with the special activities offered to program students, the amount of Ukrainian materials brought home and the home-school communication. The parent's bulletin issued four times during the year was considered helpful and interesting. Courses in conversational Ukrainian had been offered to the parents and nine of the ten who took the classes wished to see such courses continue.

In general, 95 per cent of the parents in both grades reported that they were happy or very happy with their child's participation in the program and the majority (100 per cent in grade one and 95.5 per cent in grade two) wished to see the program continue as is or with slight changes.

Pupils' attitudes. All the teachers and the majority of the parents (89.5 per cent in grade one and 92.7 per cent in grade two) felt that the pupils had enjoyed the program.

Attitudes of Edmonton Public School System personnel. The majority of program teachers and administrators thought that the program objectives were being achieved, felt the bilingual classes were an integral part of the school and considered the program a success. All the teachers and school administrators wished to see the bilingual program continue as is or with only minor modifications.

Discussion

The findings from the second year of the evaluation of the bilingual (English-Ukrainian) program are quite consistent with the results from the previous year.

In the 1974–1975 evaluation of the grade one bilingual program, students had equivalent scores to those of their matched controls on the mathematics achievement test and three of the Stanford reading subtests. Although the bilingual program students were statistically lower on the fourth subtest, word study skills, only one of the four program classes accounted for the difference.

In the second year, the bilingual program students in both grades one and two achieved at or above average for their grade level in all the reading tests. The grade two bilingual program students were also above average in mathematics. Although one of the grade one program classes was weak in mathematics, the other grade one bilingual program students performed as well as the regular students in this subject. Thus, in both the first and second year it was found that, for the most part, participation in the bilingual program had not adversely affected pupil achievement in regular curriculum areas.

In terms of their achievement in the Ukrainian language, students in the bilingual program in both grades were found to have made significant progress during the school year. Results from the first year showed that school readiness skills, the mother's use of Ukrainian and the child's previous attendance in a Ukrainian-language program were positively correlated to the final Ukrainian Language Skills Test results and could therefore be considered as possible contributors to the improved language skills. The second year the results indicated that only school readiness skills were significantly related to the grade one Ukrainian language post-test scores. The difference between the first and second year is probably due to the different grade one students each year. However, whatever the other possible factors in addition to classroom experience that could be contributing to the acquisition of the Ukrainian language, the results show that in both years the students in the bilingual program have learned a significant amount of Ukrainian.

With regard to the third aspect of the evaluation, the majority of both parents and teachers perceived a positive change in the students' appreciation of the Ukrainian culture.

Finally, parents and personnel involved with the bilingual program were pleased with it, considered it successful and wished to see it continue.

Notes

1. For a report on the evaluation of the first year, see L. Muller, W. Penner, T. Blowers, J. Jones, and H. Mosychuk, "Evaluation of A Bilingual (English-Ukrainian) Program," *The Canadian Modern Language Review,* 33, no. 4 (March 1977), pp. 476–85; "Bilingual Program (English-Ukrainian) Evaluation," 1975 (available from the Department of Research and Evaluation, Edmonton Public School board, 10010-107A Avenue, Edmonton, Alberta T5H 0Z8).
2. H. Nie, H. Hull, J. Jenkins, K. Steinbrenner, and D. Brent, *Statistical Package for the Social Sciences* (Toronto: McGraw-Hill, 1975).
3. P. Pineo and J. Porter, "Occupational Prestige in Canada," *The Canadian Review of Sociology and Anthropology,* 4 no. 1 (1967), pp. 21–40.

Native Teacher Education in a Community Setting: The Mt. Currie Program

JUNE WYATT

Introduction

One of many changes in the field of native education is the development of native teacher training programs. The National Indian Brotherhood position paper, "Indian Control of Indian Education",[1] a paper presented to the Minister of Indian Affairs and Northern Development in 1972 and the basis for present DIAND educational policy, outlines the need for native teachers, along with proposals for change in all phases of native education. Uniting the guidelines for development is the suggestion that involvement of native people is crucial to the promotion of successful educational experiences for native children. Specifically, needs exist for local control of educational financing and increased local authority in decision-making. In addition to increased administrative autonomy, Indian-oriented curriculum materials, and native teachers and counsellors who "have an intimate understanding of Indian ways of life . . . are required" (p. 18).

Since the early 1970s teacher-education programs for native people have begun in several places in Canada. Published information on these programs is, however, scanty. The purpose of this paper is to describe the Mt. Currie Native Teacher Education Program, based in this small reserve community one hundred miles from Vancouver. Other programs mentioned give an indication of the variety of approaches being taken and of issues common to all. My experience as director of the Mt. Currie program and data available on other programs[2] suggest there are five basic issues involved in the development of native teacher education programs:

1. community involvement at the local level;
2. incorporation of native language and culture;
3. decentralization;

SOURCE: *The Canadian Journal of Education*, 2, no. 3 (1977), pp. 1–14. Reprinted by permission of the Canadian Society for the Study of Education.

4. entrance requirements and paraprofessional training; and
5. program quality.

Community Involvement

Alienation of native communities from schools is in most instances deeply rooted. In the past, schools have had the job of divesting native people of their language and culture. Administration by federal and provincial authorities has helped to widen the gap between community and school. Native teachers who participate fully in the activities of both the community and the school are a potential link between the two. Administration that is in the hands of native people is also a means of reducing alienation.

Community involvement is the hallmark of the Mt. Currie program. Events in the development of the all-native Mt. Currie Education Advisory Board and of the Mt. Currie Community Based Native Teacher Education Program illustrate steps taken to integrate the school and the native community. Until February 1973 the Mt. Currie School was administered by the Department of Indian Affairs. Then, under the terms set out in the policy paper "Indian Control of Indian Education," the Education Advisory Board composed of eight members chosen by the band council, took over administration of the school. This gave them the authority to hire staff, draw up the education budget, determine curriculum and make long-range plans for the school's development. In September 1973 the Board approached the Faculty of Education at Simon Fraser University for assistance in preparing native teacher aides to become qualified teachers. In all phases of program development the principle of local native involvement guided action. I worked with Board members in drawing up a program proposal, choosing the site for the program, interviewing and selecting student teachers and program staff and in making decisions about program content. Student teachers were involved in each of these processes except, naturally, their own selection for the program.

PROGRAM PROPOSAL

The following objectives, set out in the program proposal, reflect the importance of native involvement:

1. to provide all practice teaching and academic course work *in the community;*
2. to insure the Board plays an on-going role in program development: e.g. student, staff, and course selection;
3. to adapt the program to the unique resources of the community;

4. to provide for entry for native teacher aides who might not have the usual university entrance requirements but who demonstrate potential for becoming successful teachers; and
5. to maintain program standards.

COMMUNITY SITE

The Mt. Currie community and school were chosen as the site for the program to insure the maintenance of close contact with the community. One of the goals of the Board is to bring parents into the life of the school. All staff members are expected to make home visits to parents and encourage parents to come to the school as resource persons teaching cultural activities, or simply as visitors. At present one-third of the staff is non-native. Participation in community sports and social gatherings provide additional avenues for contact and are easily within the reach of native student teachers. Casual dissemination of information by student teachers about their work and the school has partially increased parental attendance at school meetings where curriculum, discipline, grading systems, expenditures for field trips and values conveyed in the school are discussed.

INTERVIEWING AND SELECTION OF CANDIDATES

Applicants to the program were accepted or rejected after being interviewed at Mt. Currie by Board members and representatives of the Faculty of Education admissions committee — myself included. Each candidate had a minimum of two months of experience as a teacher aide (a prerequisite for entry) and was asked to tell the selection committee about work done in lesson preparation and implementation and classroom management. Candidates were also asked to comment on their reasons for working in and wanting to pursue a career in the Mt. Currie Community School. Previous academic experiences in high school or university were not ignored but neither were they given a high priority — a third of those accepted had not completed high school. Letters of reference were solicited from classroom teachers who had supervised the applicant's work. As well, a supervisor from the Faculty of Education documented and assessed the work of the applicants. Board members were able to provide background information on the growth, maturity and commitment of applicants. The decision to accept an applicant carried with it a commitment on the part of the Board and the university to support the individual in strengthening professional skills. Detailed outlines of strengths and weaknesses provided check points for future assessments of improvement. Early diagnosis of problem areas (lateness, inadequate preparation, heavy handedness with children) let candidates know clearly what was acceptable behaviour. Twelve individuals applied for the program and eight entered. Applicants who did not enter the program did not lose their jobs as aides. A number decided they wanted to continue as aides but did not want the extra responsibilities of being a student teacher. Others were judged not sufficiently prepared for admittance.[3] Each applicant accepted is employed by the school as an intern and each has made a commitment to working for two years at the school after completing certification. The internship has eased financial difficulties normally experienced by students in other programs.[4]

The interview and discussion process was not only a procedure for assessing applicants, it provided Board members with an opportunity to develop their relationships with applicants and to broaden their knowledge of school activities. Establishing a close working relationship between Board and trainees provides a unique opportunity for developing long-term programming that is well integrated with community needs.

CHOOSING COURSES AND INSTRUCTORS

The Simon Fraser University teacher education program is a one-year program consisting of one-and-a-half semesters of practicum, half a semester of curriculum workshops, and one semester of upper-level course work chosen from arts, science, or education. At Mt. Currie this program is supplemented with additional academic course work necessary for certification. Student teachers and Board members at Mt. Currie selected the courses to complement the practicum. The program started in July 1975 with an introductory English composition course and a linguistic course dealing with the fundamentals of reading and writing the native language. Subsequent courses included a more advanced course in the native language, Canadian literature and poetry, introduction to psychology, and curriculum studies. The five instructors for those courses were approved by the Board and student teachers as well as by the university. Every candidate visited Mt. Currie for an interview with students and the Board whose concern was to screen out individuals who wanted to "help the Indians" and to select those who showed initiative in adapting course material to the resources available in Mt. Currie. Ability to relate easily and informally to students was also highly valued.

Involvement can, in spite of its strong points, entail a number of difficulties. University administrators were concerned that giving too much control to the local school board in the selection of candidates could result in nepotism — that weaknesses would be overlooked where relatives were involved. Given the close and pervasive kinship ties in reserve communities it is virtually impossible to avoid situations where relatives make important decisions about each other. Board members' judgments were considered along with those of sponsor teachers and university supervisors; nonetheless, their opinions were striking for their forthrightness. While an individual might hesitate to point out the shortcomings of another's relatives, he was quite candid in constructive criticism of his own.

Other difficulties in community involvement have arisen. First, native people often show hesitancy in supporting their own people in positions of responsibility. Student teachers just completing their training find that many of the people in the community have scoffed at the idea of their being teachers. They have for so long identified the role as one that is and ought to be occupied by non-Indians from outside the community that it is difficult for them now to believe that their own people are good enough. The Board had initially hoped that student teachers would be influential in drawing parents into the school. In some cases this has happened — increased attendance at school meetings is one sign of it. The Board will, however, have to do more to assure parents of native teachers' competence before the native teachers can in turn involve parents more in the school.

A second factor hampering community involvement in the school is that it is structured according to conventional patterns where classroom rather than community learning experiences are given priority. Parents are skeptical about activities which diverge from past patterns — as much as they may be dissatisfied with the results of these — and teachers have not had the appropriate preparation to make full use of community resources in constructing learning activities. The teacher education program provides an avenue for the development of community-oriented education but innovations are undertaken only after careful preparation. Since student teachers are operating in a classroom context largely defined by their classroom teachers and reinforced by community views, this context dominates their experience. Excessive pressure for them to introduce radical innovations would thrust them directly into a conflict situation. Nonetheless, innovations such as curriculum development oriented to community resources are proceeding.

DEVELOPMENTS IN OTHER PROGRAMS

The emphasis given to community involvement in Mt. Currie is similar to what is being done in the Alaska Rural Teacher Training Corps (ARTTC), which strongly emphasizes involvement of interns in the village community. The program attempts "to establish a system in which community citizens participate in the governance of the project and function as resources to project development to the extent of their interest and willingness."[5] Thus, at the very least, community people recommend candidates for the program — a characteristic of programs at Lakehead University, the universities of Alberta, British Columbia, Calgary, Manitoba, Saskatchewan and Quebec. In addition, in ARTTC "teams [of students] in each community provide within their ability, educational opportunities and activities which the citizens of the communities state a need for, outside of the formal school program."[6] Similarly the Lakehead Program identifies, as a major concern, community-oriented school programs in which an exchange of resources occurs between school and community. Aside from these instances of community involvement no indications are given in other program descriptions of well-defined, on-going roles for native advisory groups at the local community level. The advisory boards of most programs are made up of native people drawn from a number of different communities and/or associations, reflecting the fact that these programs serve many native communities. The Mt. Currie program, which involves only one community, provides for greater direct involvement of a local advisory group.

Incorporation of Native Language and Culture

Placing native teachers in classrooms has the value of providing native children with positive role models, but the rationale for preparing native teachers extends beyond this. Native teachers are in a far better position than non-natives to bring native linguistic and cultural resources into the classroom. Incorporation of these is seen by native people and educators across North America as critical in reducing native students' alienation from school and in building positive self-images and educational success.

In spite of the high value placed on bringing native culture into the classroom there is concern that young native people — who are frequently those most interested in teaching — are not in the best position to draw on these resources. The assertion is frequently made that native people, particularly members of the younger generation, have lost their culture. This assertion arises when native culture is identified as traditional culture. Native culture of course includes traditional life, but it encompasses contemporary adaptive patterns as well. Thus, cultural materials for classroom use can be drawn from the present as well as the past and are well within the experience of young native teachers. Analysis of native literature and of contemporary political and social issues and discussion of personal experiences assist student teachers in identifying their concerns and values. This identification is a step in the process of defining contemporary cultural patterns. Student teachers can in turn guide their students through a similar process. In addition, through contacts with older relatives student teachers have access to traditional cultural resources and can integrate these into classroom experiences.

Because Board members and student teachers have strong feelings that native language and culture should form an integral part of the school curriculum, one of the earliest decisions made in planning the teacher education program was to include course work in the native (Lillooet) language and to adapt other university courses to cultural resources available at Mt. Currie. In the view of the Board (and of many others in education) feelings of pride and self-worth essential to educational success can be partially built on understanding, knowledge and respect for native culture. Instead of rejecting the lifestyle of parents and grandparents, that lifestyle can be valued as a unique culture adaptation. It is not the intent of the Board to completely resurrect traditional culture and turn the school and the community into a "living museum," but to present such facets of native life more positively than has been the case in the public schools. Additionally, the Board and student teachers want to promote the development of contemporary native culture. This entails identifying resources in the present-day community and incorporating these resources into daily educational experiences. Steps were followed to implement these ideas.

All student teachers have completed two linguistic courses in which they developed skills in reading and writing and their native language (Lillooet), and some are developing a graded language program for the school.

Student teachers have also completed a course in English composition and one in Canadian literature. In the former, their own experiences — going to residential school, fishing, berry picking, attending potlatches, participating in road blocks and protest movements — provided the raw material for writing. In the literature course the vision of native life presented by native writers (Sarain Stump, Johnny Tetso, etc.) was contrasted with that of non-natives who write about native life (Christie Harris, George Ryga). Poems about Canadian rural life by non-native poets were contrasted with students' own views of their environment. In conjunction with both courses, student teachers carried over what they had learned into their own classrooms. Puppets in the elementary grades and VTR in the upper ones help to dramatize literary works. The fact that both courses and practice teaching take place in Mt. Currie and are scheduled concurrently facilitates this type of follow-up.

In addition to university course work providing material for a native language and culture curriculum, student teachers have themselves or with resource people initiated sessions in story telling, music and dance, fishing, basket-making and snowshoe manufacturing. These activities involve learning skills which are part of the contemporary culture of Mt. Currie. Children's discussion of and writing about these activities provide practice in literacy and communication skills — a central concern of the school.

Developing knowledge of and familiarity with traditional and contemporary culture is not intended to be pursued to the exclusion of developing skills necessary for survival in contemporary western society. The Board feels both are necessary. But they are operating on the principle that children will learn best when they are learning in and through a familiar context. They can then build outward to familiarity with other contexts.

This approach has not always operated smoothly. While student teachers in the program (ages 19–40) do not consider themselves thoroughly knowledgeable in native language and culture, they have shown a sincere interest in learning. But a number of their students, particularly the older ones (junior and senior secondary) have not shown the same interest. On occasion they have been rude and inattentive to resource people who have visited the school. As well, a number have found the idea of learning to speak the native language laughable or boring.[7] Such reactions are a serious challenge to the school's operating principles. The solutions to these dilemmas begin to emerge when the situation is viewed in historical perspective. Adolescents who attended public schools (as did most of the secondary school students enrolled at Mt. Currie) have been alternatively ridiculed and ignored because they are native, and most have internalized a negative view of themselves. Native student teachers who have had similar experiences in their own schooling are doing an excellent job of helping students sort out their feelings about their identity as natives. They are also recognizing that conventional teaching strategies do not have this effect.

One step being taken to change strategies is to take students out into the community rather than bringing resource people to the school, where they are ill at ease.

Resource people who had lost interest in coming to classrooms are eager to work with students who come to their homes or accompany them on field trips. Students are beginning to take note of the fact that people in their community are knowledgeable and speak with authority. Two years ago they laughed at the idea of learning native songs; now singing and drumming initiated by the students are extremely popular.

Other changes are being made in teaching strategies. In the native language program, emphasis is given to oral rather than written activities, and efforts are bring made to make native language a part of social studies and science rather than an isolated linguistic exercise. Such changes, together with student counselling, are slowly leading students to a more positive view of native culture. They are beginning to see that native culture is not just what happened one hundred years ago — it is also the contemporary way of life of the community, *their* way of life as well as that of their parents. Recognition of this by students and teachers provides a wide spectrum of activities and knowledge which is constantly being added to and will serve as a source of materials for program development.

OTHER PROGRAMS

Virtually all native teacher education programs in Canada contain course work on native language and culture. The major difficulty which most encounter is that the age group most interested in teaching is least knowledgeable about traditional culture. Access to cultural resources poses significant difficulties. Adapting the resources for classroom use (curriculum development) is a major area of concern. Beginning teachers who are not yet fully comfortable in their new roles frequently do not have the time, skills, or access to resources necessary to develop curriculum. A number of solutions to these difficulties have emerged. At the University of Calgary the Indian Students University Program proposed the development of a curriculum centre where individuals would practise the skills required to adapt information about their culture for classroom use. A centre of this type has been established by the Federation of Saskatchewan Indians. A standard part of the University of British Columbia's NITEP is a course in curriculum development focussing on native cultural resources. In the Northwest Territories, excellent locally developed curriculum materials serve as a model for on-going developments by native teachers. In the ARTTC, interns take course work that trains them to gather resource data from community sources.

Access to and continuity in the development of local resource materials is facilitated at Mt. Currie by the fact that the program operates entirely in the community. Instructors are committed to orienting their courses to the local context, and when student teachers feel they do not have necessary skills it is relatively easy to find someone in the community who does.

Decentralization

Rural areas of Canada, Indian reserves in particular, have always had to bear the brunt of teacher shortages and mobility. Urban-bred teachers frequently see non-urban schools as temporary diversions in a career path that leads to the city. On the other hand, potential teachers from reserves are often frustrated in their career plans because they are unable to move families and homes to metropolitan university centres, and in some cases are unable to adapt to the conditions of big city life. Frequently those who do make the move experience difficulties in readapting to their home environments; reserve and city life styles conflict with each other. Decentralization provides a mechanism for circumventing these problems.

Students at Mt. Currie were not able to attend a teacher education program on an urban university campus — physical and psychological adjustments as well as financial considerations made this extremely difficult. A number had attended programs in Vancouver and found them unsatisfactory. Among the younger members of the groups, considerable shyness and apprehension were expressed about going to the city.

The Mt. Currie program bridges the gap between the reserve and the city. Students work on the reserve and educational resources are brought into a milieu where the student teachers feel at home. One of the added advantages of holding the program in Mt. Currie is that internship arrangements with the Board have eased financial difficulties.

Curriculum workshops held every other week by visiting members of the Faculty of Education and classes in linguistics, English and psychology held on a weekly basis have provided considerable variety; support from individuals instructing in these courses has been excellent. Organization of and follow-up on workshops by the resident faculty associate, who also supervises day-to-day practice teaching, has done a great deal to maximize the value of these sessions. The faculty associate is able to spend time co-ordinating these activities because he is responsible for supervising eight student teachers — half the usual assignment. Because library and audiovisual resources are difficult to arrange and student teachers have increasingly felt the need to see the way other schools operate, visits to schools in Vancouver are being arranged. When trips of this type were suggested by program staff earlier in the program, interest was low. Growth in interest can be interpreted as a reflection of growth of self-confidence and understanding of the teaching process.

OTHER PROGRAMS

Decentralization is an integral part of the operation of the program at the University of British Columbia, Brandon University, the University of Alaska and the Northwest Territories Program as well as a number of others. It is generally recognized that to expect potential reserve teachers to take their training in urban schools is self-defeating.

The programs mentioned above, with the exception of Mt. Currie, involve short-term summer orientations, and in some cases a full year of course work at the university centre. In the Mt. Currie program it is possible to complete the requirements for a British Columbia Teaching Licence (one semester of academic course work and three semesters of teacher preparation) entirely at Mt. Currie. Additional work towards the next levels of certification may be completed at Mt. Currie or the university — formal plans for this stage of training are now in process and will depend on the extent of financial support available from the university and the Department of Indian Affairs.

Entrance Requirements and Paraprofessional Training

There are growing numbers of native people in Canada who are working effectively in educational settings but who have not completed high school or entered university. Special grants from the Department of Indian Affairs and Canada Manpower create jobs for teacher aides, cultural resource personnel, language teachers and counsellors. Thus, there is a pool of potential teachers whose practical experience can serve as an alternate criterion for university entrance and as a basis for granting advanced standing in teacher education programs. At Mt. Currie and in other native teacher education programs paraprofessional training is recognized as an alternative to strictly academic entrance criteria.

Entry to the Simon Fraser University teacher education program requires two years of university work with a C+ average. Entry to the Mt. Currie program requires demonstrated teaching ability developed through experience as a classroom aide — it is not necessary that the applicant have completed high school or be twenty-three years of age (university mature-student entry age). A minimum of eight weeks of experience as an aide is credited as one-third of the total practicum experience. Academic course work which is ordinarily a prerequisite for entry is taken concurrently with and after completion of the practicum. Commitment to and aptitude for teaching, rather than prior academic success, are being considered as predictors of success in teaching. Observations of aides by university personnel and thorough selection procedures, described earlier, make this admissions procedure a viable one.

All of the native teacher training programs in Canada admit students through mature-student entry clauses, and a number have mechanisms for granting advanced standing. This procedure raises the issues of reverse discrimination. Similar procedures (e.g., mature-student entry directly into teacher training programs) are generally not applicable to non-native students. Many of the developers of native education programs feel, however, that as long as overall program quality is not affected, adapting entry requirements is the only way to insure that the inequalities present in education are levelled. The dropout rate among native people in public schools is approximately 95 per cent. If successful high school completion and two years of university are maintained as requirements it will be very difficult to increase the number of native teachers — a vital step in insuring educational success for native children. Using alternative criteria provides a needed avenue for entry. It also helps to maintain program quality.

Program Quality

It is often asked whether program quality is sacrificed where there is community involvement, native language and culture, decentralization, and entry based on paraprofessional experience. Community involvement may be criticized because it engages non-professionals in critical educational decision making. Incorporation of native language and culture can be seen as expending energy on activities that have no survival value in the modern world. Decentralization makes it difficult to deliver resources, and adapting entry requirements may be seen as lowering standards.

Contrary to these views, community involvement is not simply a matter of throwing responsibility for decision making to people without providing the requisite knowledge for decision making; it can serve as an educational process for non-professionals to learn about options in education. Similarly, concentration on native language and culture is not a suicidal attempt to drown in the past. In all discussions by native people of their educational futures, they have stated that they and their children must have the skills necessary to function in modern society. Decentralization does pose difficulties in the delivery of services, but rural non-natives as well as native communities are demanding that these difficulties be overcome. University extension programs, use of video, and programmed course materials are beginning to meet the needs of non-urban areas. Furthermore, adapting entrance criteria to respond to the special talents of a group of students is not the same as lowering criteria; it is recognition of the fact that expertise can be acquired and expressed in a variety of ways.

The Mt. Currie program suggests ways for native teacher education programs to differ from standard models without loss of quality. Community involvement in program planning provides an opportunity for non-professionals to study a variety of teacher education models before deciding what would be best for their community. It gives them the additional experience of learning how to interview and assess the work of native aides. Integration of course work on native language and culture with work focusing on contemporary skills such as literacy and curriculum planning is occurring without jeopardizing achievements in either area. Grades for courses in native language and English literature show a normal distribution. Competency in classroom teaching is developing at a regular pace. Program participants unanimously reject the idea of being coddled or given a water-down education because they are native. Some were concerned that program decentralization and modified entrance requirements would adversely affect program quality. Staff from the university teaching at Mt. Currie indicate that students work as hard as students in other programs. The differences they note are greater cautiousness about becoming involved in new activities, and in the case of some individuals (a minority) considerable difficulty with academic skill development. Assistance from the faculty associate and individualized instruction by university personnel allows individuals to develop academic skills while engaged in course work and practice teaching. Consequently students are, in a number of instances, carrying a heavier workload than would normally be the case. Recommendations by university staff and supervising classroom teachers indicate that the work of students in the Mt. Currie program qualifies them for the same provincial teaching credentials received by student teachers in other programs.[8]

Like the Mt. Currie program, all other native teacher education programs in Canada are dealing with the issues of community involvement, native language and culture, decentralization, and entrance requirements and the way in which these affect program quality. All programs, as in Mt. Currie, grant standard teaching credentials to their students, indicating that provincial departments of education across Canada are recognizing the validity of these alternative programs. A comprehensive evaluation of the Mt. Currie program is not yet available, nor to my knowledge are comparable evaluations available for other programs. The purpose of this article is to explore the major issues raised by these programs rather than to do a comprehensive evaluation of their effectiveness. Assessments of program quality at Mt. Currie made here cannot and should not go beyond the data currently available. Long-term effects on the educational achievements of children at Mt. Currie are not yet known.

Conclusions

Native teacher education programs across Canada (and the United States) reflect a variety of approaches. Although community involvement, incorporation of native language and culture, decentralization, entrance requirements and paraprofessional training and program quality are issues of concern to all programs, the programs are far from identical.

The hallmark of the Mt. Currie program is community involvement. Other aspects of the program follow from community involvement. First, native language and culture are easier to incorporate in a community-run school than in, for example, a provincial school. Second, the Mt. Currie program illustrates that community involvement can lessen the problems of decentralization for students. Although decentralization is part of other native teacher education programs, decentralization in and of itself does not necessarily solve the problems native students experience in urban centres. Often decentralization means that native student teachers work away from urban university centres but also away from their home communities. Alienation from a small (but foreign) rural community may thus be substituted for alienation from an urban setting. The Mt. Currie student teachers are working in their own community at their own school. Community involvement here makes for successful decentralization; but decentralization does not guarantee community involvement. Finally, community involvement in the school and the teacher education program means that potentially successful teachers can be spotted by a community board personally familiar with a candidate's strengths and weaknesses. This, coupled with the community's support of student teachers throughout their education, means that program quality is not sacrificed.

The Mt. Currie program has come about because the Mt. Currie Board is convinced that educational success for native people is closely linked with their gaining control in education. The program developed as a response to the needs of a particular community; in no other instance has the development of a native teacher education program been so closely articulated with the development of a native community school.[9] Over a three- to four-year period it will prepare eighteen teachers, all of whom intend to continue working in the community school. When their education is complete the program will be dissolved — native teachers for other native communities or for the provincial schools are not being trained at Mt. Currie, nor will they be.

The Mt. Currie program is one model for native teacher education, one in which community involvement is the key ingredient. Repeating the program elsewhere depends on the extent to which community involvement in education can be stimulated and the degree of government and university support for native community education. This type of program is not possible everywhere. Mt. Currie has the largest population (1,200) of all bands in British Columbia; enrolment in the community school (formerly a Federal Indian Day school) is about 300, and the school has programs for students from nursery to grade 12. The size of the community and the school has made it possible to run the school independently. Smaller communities and day schools have been more readily absorbed by the provincial school system; many lack the educational facilities and number of potential teachers needed to support a community-based teacher education program. Moreover, an increasing number of status Indians live off reserve, and they, like non-status Indians, may not be part of a geographically distinct Indian community. Although "Indian control of Indian education" is the official policy of DIA (the Department of Indian Affairs) there are only about a dozen Indian-run schools in Canada. Because 60 per cent of native children attend provincial schools, most native teachers will be trained in this setting, which does not as yet allow for the degree of native involvement that is possible where the school is located on the reserve and is under the control of a local native Board.

Small programs catering to single communities are not typically part of university commitments, and universities may be reluctant to support many such programs. For all these reasons Mt. Currie cannot serve as a model for the training of all native teachers. Community involvement, however, carries with it many benefits and is a worthy goal of any program.

The creation of native teacher education programs has been a step forward in developing equal educational opportunities for native people. Future positive developments depend on increasing the educational options open to communities and individuals. Diversity in programming, rather than uniformity, must be encouraged.

Notes

1. National Indian Brotherhood, "Indian Control of Indian Education," Policy paper presented to the Minister of Indian Affairs and Northern Development (Ottawa, 1972).
2. Third Annual Conference on Canadian Indian Teacher Education Programs, Banff, April 1976. M. Aldous, D. Barnett and C. King, eds., *Teacher education programs for native people* (Saskatoon, Sask.: University of Saskatchewan, College of Education, Research Resources Centre, 1974).

3. These individuals were admitted to the program one year later.
4. Internship salaries and tuition are paid by the band with funds received from the Department of Indian Affairs. All other program costs are paid by the Faculty of Education, SFU.
5. D.M. Murphy, *Opinionnaire: Selected teacher corps programs* (Anchorage, Alaska, 1973), p. 1.
6. Ibid.
7. Most children in Mt. Currie understand but do not speak the native language when they enter school. By the time they reach grade 2 or 3 they have forgotten most of what they knew. There are still a large number of adults in the community who speak the language.
8. The first group of eight student teachers admitted to the program in July 1975 all completed licences by December 1976. The second group of ten admitted in July 1976 will complete licences by December 1977.
9. At the band-controlled school in Fort Alexander, Manitoba, native student teachers in the IMPACTE Program (Brandon University) do part of their practicum in this school; however, not all of these individuals are from or plan to remain in Fort Alexander. Neither has the development of the school been so centred on the development of the IMPACTE program.

Teacher Education for a Multicultural Society

JOHN R. MALLEA AND JONATHAN C. YOUNG

> There is nothing new in asking teachers and teacher trainers to re-examine their work in the light of social change. What is new, however, is the urgent challenge presented by the recent emergence of a society which contains not only the seeds of racial disharmony but also the potential for immense cultural and human enrichment. This is the situation which schools and colleges have to face. Far too many teachers are inadequately prepared to cope with it (Community Relations Committee, 1974, p. 45).

Introduction

In recent years the nature of Canadian society has undergone considerable scrutiny and evaluation, especially with respect to the role of Canada's ethnic and cultural minorities. Not surprisingly, the school, one of society's most important formal agencies of socialization, has inevitably found itself at the centre of the debate. Thus, while the above assertion is made by a British educator, it could serve equally well as a succinct and pertinent commentary on the situation currently facing teachers and teacher education in Canada.

As the arguments over multiculturalism continue, Canada's teachers (the carriers and disseminators, the prime agents of socialization) have tried to secure a firm base from which to carry on their work. Naturally enough, if society changes its image of itself and recognizes a new reality, then teachers at all levels will need assistance in interpreting and reshaping its efforts. To help them do so is essential. If we are to ask them to perform new functions, different from those for which they have been prepared, then this should be

SOURCE: This article is an edited version of a paper presented at a symposium on Intercultural Education and Community Development held at the Faculty of Education, University of Toronto, June 1978, and published in *Teacher Education* (14 April 1979), pp. 28–38. Reprinted by permission of the Editor.

reflected in all levels of teacher preparation. This paper attempts to contribute to the process by examining what is required if teachers are to function effectively in a multicultural society.

MULTICULTURALISM

Canada and its people are increasingly rejecting the assimilation approach to social cohesion and cultural nationalism. For example, the Royal Commission on Bilingualism and Biculturalism (established in 1963) recognized and validated the aspirations of Canada's ethnic minorities. The Commission agreed that measures should be taken to safeguard their important contribution to Canada's cultural enrichment. Such recommendations were followed by the Prime Minister's announcement of the federal government's policy of "Multiculturalism within a Bilingual Framework," in October 1971. In this policy statement Mr. Trudeau declared that the time was overdue for Canadians to become more aware of their rich tradition of cultural diversity, that his new policy aimed at ensuring the continuation of that tradition, and that it sought to enhance the appreciation of the contribution of the many ethno-cultural groups in Canadian society. In the words of Gérard Pelletier, then Secretary of State, the policy called into being a new vision of society: one which refused to sacrifice diversity in the name of unity, and which placed the cultures of Canada's many groups on an equal footing.

Ontario, along with several other provinces, moved quickly to endorse the federal government's policy. Task forces have since been appointed, reports have been published, findings promulgated, and a whole series of recommendations have been advanced. Efforts are now being made to implement these findings, and many seminars and workshops have been held. Not surprisingly, the school as the formal agency for the transmission of culture is seen as having a central role to play in these efforts.

SCHOOLING IN A PLURAL SOCIETY

Along with increased recognition of the contribution of ethno-cultural groups to Canadian society has come a vigorous attack on the school as an agency of assimilation. Canadian schools, their critics declare, have not only failed to meet the needs of minority students, they have also fallen short in their efforts to prepare all students for life in a multicultural society.

What these critics fail to recognize sufficiently, perhaps, is that Canadian society traditionally viewed the school as the major agency of assimilation of its minorities. Moreover, as has been pointed out, "The public educational system in the postwar period has generally remained as dedicated to the Anglo-conformist model as it had been before the war, although socialization was increasingly tempered with large doses of democratic liberalism" (Palmer and Troper, 1973, p. 21). Society's leaders deliberately charged the school with direct responsibility for the systematic transmission of mainstream (some would say anglophone) culture from one generation to the next. The school was expected to imbue its young citizens with a system of values that stressed the modern and the universal, and downplayed the traditional and the unique. Teachers were seen as cautious managers of change as well as guardians of all that was moral and valued. In this sense, then, teachers and schools responded appropriately to the responsibility that society laid at their doors. Language and values associated with ethno-cultural heritages had no place in the classroom; adjustment and adaption to mainstream norms were considered all-important.[1]

Such assumptions are currently the source of extensive international debate. Increased ethnic awareness has assumed the hallmarks of a global trend. In its wake, the role of teachers and schools is changing. Over the last decade a great deal has been written in Canada on the failings of the school. Curriculum, textbooks and teachers have been criticized for failing to prepare students for life in a multicultural society, where cultural pluralism is not merely a demographic fact but a valued part of Canadian social reality. Hodgetts, in his pioneering book, *What Culture? What Heritage?* reminded us that although we laughed and believed things were different, in actual fact we were continuing to "teach a white, Anglo-Saxon, Protestant, political history of Canada" (Hodgetts, 1968, p. 20). His timely reminder was reinforced by McDiarmid and Pratt (1971), who found that school textbooks did *not* portray a pluralist model of Canadian culture, but continued to present a consensus, non-controversial view of society. Other studies followed, and their findings only underlined what many educators were hesitantly beginning to accept: materials, programs, classrooms and schools were not adequately reflecting the ethno-cultural mix of contemporary Canada.

Similarly, teachers and teacher training institutions paid scant attention to the implications of teaching in and preparing for a society whose cultural mosaic was undergoing considerable change. Not surprisingly, therefore, when our society addressed itself to the challenge of translating a policy of multiculturalism within a bilingual framework into practice, teachers were ill prepared to cope. Indeed, their very success in responding to the promptings of assimilation made it all the more difficult to respond to the new political reality.

In the rest of this paper we shall attempt to develop some aspects of the training of teachers which we consider fundamental if the policy articulated for Canadian society by the Prime Minister is to be reflected in our schools.[2]

Teacher Education

Two fundamental assumptions which underlie our thinking on the subject of teacher education need to be emphasized. First, we believe that teacher education has to be a career-long process of professional development in which academic studies, preservice training, induction, and subsequent inservice work are considered separate but indispensable parts of the process. Secondly, we believe that Canada is a multicultural society and that teacher education programs need to prepare *all* of our teachers with this in mind. Therefore, to argue that certain teachers who have certain specializations, or who intend to teach in certain areas, will never interact with children from a variety of cultural backgrounds, is to miss the point: all teachers need to prepare themselves and their students for life in a multi-ethnic, multiracial Canada.

Operating on the basis of these two assumptions, we wish to propose and examine interrelated questions facing anyone involved in teacher education, these three in particular:

1. What ideal characteristics would we wish the well prepared Canadian teacher to possess?
2. Given the importance of a sound knowledge base, what might it consist of and how might it be established?
3. What sort of pedagogical principles, skills and competencies should be covered, and in what settings, in order to prepare an individual to teach in a plural society?

PROGRAM CONTENT

Tomàs Arciniega suggests that the first step in preparing teachers to teach in a culturally plural society is to identify the skills and expertise required of the successful teacher, and to work back from there to define ways in which they may be actualized. Adopting his approach, we can pose the question: "What does the ideal teacher in a system committed to multiculturalism look like?" And, in attempting to answer the question we can further draw on the work of Professor Arciniega by taking his three dimensional teacher profile and placing it in a Canadian setting (Arciniega, 1977).

A. Personal Characteristics

(1) The belief in cultural pluralism as a worthy goal of Canadian society, and a commitment to that goal.

(2) A recognition that, in the past, minority cultures such as Canada's Native people have generally been regarded as inferior to the dominant culture, and that this has contributed to a negative self-image in many minority children.

(3) A commitment to enhance the minority child's positive self-image.

(4) A respect for the culturally different child and the culture that he or she brings to the school.

(5) The conviction that the culture a minority child brings to school is worth preserving and enriching.

(6) An awareness that cultural and linguistic differences are positive, individual differences.

(7) A confidence in culturally different minority children and their ability to learn.

(8) A belief in his or her ability to contribute to a multicultural program.

(9) A willingness to learn more about multicultural education.

(10) Flexibility in human relations and an ability to contribute and share ideas.

B. Professional Characteristics

(1) Effective experience in a multicultural school environment.

(2) A knowledge of areas such as English or French as a second language related to bilingual and multicultural education.

(3) Literacy in the minority language or dialect of the target population.

(4) An awareness of the implications of culture to learning.

(5) An interest in continuing to seek out better ways to "reach" culturally different students in the school.

(6) The ability to adapt materials to make them culturally relevant and to design relevant curricula.

(7) A knowledge of the research in multicultural education and its relevance.

(8) A commitment to the objectives of the program.

(9) A facility in applying modern approaches to the teaching of concepts, skills, and performances.

(10) A readiness to participate in team-teaching and other innovative staffing patterns, and to cooperate with other adults in a classroom setting. (i.e., teachers, aides, parents, community resource people).

C. Community Orientation Characteristics

(1) A recognition of the legitimate role of parents in the educative process.

(2) A readiness to participate in a variety of minority community activities.

(3) A desire to involve minority parents and community residents in school-community programs.

(4) An understanding of the dynamics of the minority community.

(5) A willingness to receive guidance and support from members of the minority community regarding the special needs of their children.

(6) Organizational abilities in sponsoring community service projects and programs to benefit the target community.

(7) A genuine sensitivity to the desires and needs of the minority communities which his or her school serves.

Having prepared a list of what we consider desired qualities for the well-prepared teacher, the next question becomes, "How can these characteristics best be developed?"

THE DEVELOPMENT OF A SOUND KNOWLEDGE BASE

We believe strongly that one basic requirement for all teachers is the possession of a sound knowledge base. And here we are reminded that Symons, in *To Know Ourselves* (Volume 1), specifically refers to the inadequate job being done for students at all levels of education in developing a knowledge of Canadian society. His report contains, for instance, the following scathing criticism of the effects of teacher education programs: "The product of our high schools in the whole area of Canadian Studies is most disappointing, and the principal reason is the inadequate job being done across the country in training teachers as to their responsibility in this area. Many, many teachers don't know, and have not been encouraged to care" (Symons, 1975, pp. 195–6).

Assuming that these criticisms are valid, how might teacher education institutions approach their responsibilities in this area? What would such a knowledge base consist of and how might it be developed? We would suggest that the following components might mark a beginning:

(1) Preservice and inservice teachers should be afforded the opportunity to rigorously study their own ethno-cultural heritage, or that of a local community, in order to identify and develop appropriate themes, organizing principles, conceptual knowledge and relevant theories.

(2) In much the same way they could observe and analyse various manifestations of racism, prejudice and discrimination as they are found in the everyday life and history of Canadian society.

(3) Efforts to respond positively to the presence of cultural diversity, both at home and abroad, could also be studied so as to reinforce the fact that cultural diversity, not homogeneity, is the chief characteristic of human settlement. Issues of regionalism, federalism and a variety of approaches to social cohesion (assimilation, adsorption, integration, multiculturalism) lend themselves equally well to examination.

(4) The study of the formation of new societies, Canada's immigration patterns and policies, together with their impact on schooling, would bring further valuable insights and understandings.

(5) Even more specifically, the changing role of the school as it tried to respond to the demands of an expanding Canada would provide excellent opportunities to study the manner in which mainstream society dealt with its minorities.

We believe, then, that students should be encouraged to develop a conceptual framework that enables them to test ideas and practices with a view to determining their worth for a society that seeks equality and cherishes diversity. But this in itself is not enough. Canadian teachers must also possess such important attributes as cultural awareness and sensitivity; for as we have pointed out, our "ideal" teacher is not produced merely by the acquisition of knowledge. To attain this sensitivity, every effort needs to be made to involve student teachers personally, so that they may confront their own prejudices and discuss them without feeling threatened or inhibited. This involvement might include the vicarious experience afforded by literature, films and drama. Nothing, however, seems quite as effective as personal interaction with members of minority groups.

THE CLINICAL EXPERIENCE

Personal involvement and immersion is a *sine qua non* if teachers are to identify and critically examine their own attitudes towards other ethnic and cultural groups, and increase their insights into the situations facing many minority students in our schools. However, as we have learnt to our cost, exposure to the community life of other ethnocultural groups does not automatically create understanding. Indeed, exposure in the absence of prior preparation or after-the-fact examination is just as likely to reinforce barriers as it is to erode them.

If the "clinical experience" is to be effective, it must be carefully planned, monitored and assessed. Of assistance here are Hunter's six components of a valid clinical experience in multicultural education: (a) that feedback be provided on student performance; (b) that students experience multicultural class situations; (c) that there is cultural diversity within the student population; (d) that the program staff are culturally diverse, and have demonstrated an ability to operate effectively in this environment; (e) that students have access to culturally diverse communities; (f) that their multicultural experiences take place over a prolonged period of time. (Hunter, 1974, p. 36)

PEDAGOGICAL SKILLS AND COMPETENCIES

Several areas of competencies seem particularly relevant for teachers in a plural society. They include curriculum analysis and design, language teaching skills, and test analysis and construction. As noted earlier, it is particularly important that teachers be able to recognize cultural bias and discrimination as it exists in the school curriculum. Moreover, they should also be skilled in the techniques of curriculum design so as to be able to modify or redesign existing curricula.

In preparing teachers for classrooms in a multi-ethnic society, attention needs to be given to the language skills necessary to assist children whose mother tongue is not English/French, or who may not speak "standard" English/French. Today, such skills are possessed only by specialists. Tomorrow, however, might bring the recognition that while Canada has two official languages, many children first learn the language of the home and this can often be neither of these two languages. To take an extreme example, 46 per cent of the Toronto school population in 1975 had a language other than English as their mother tongue (Murray, 1977, p. 33).

In any event, teacher preparation programs might include coverage of the following; (i) the importance of a positive acceptance of the child's own language; (ii) how the child's own language can be developed into a more versatile tool, in particular a tool for education; (iii) the definition of specific targets in teaching patterns of "standard" English and a consideration of dialect differences in relation to the teaching of reading and writing; (iv) an understanding of the potential sources of bias (for linguistically and culturally diverse students) existing in tests of intelligence, language and concept development.

Conclusion

For the purposes of organizational clarity, we have separated the development of knowledge, pedagogical skills and clinical experience, but in reality they must be carefully interwoven and mutually supportive activities. Implicit in the approaches that we have suggested in this paper is the realization that teacher education is a career-long process. It is not something that is restricted to preservice training. There can be at least three "cycles" in teacher education: preservice, induction and in-service. Most of our suggestions can easily be translated into action in the first and third of these "cycles."

But the second of these, induction, might well be used more extensively in Canada than it is at present. In the first two years of probationary teaching, for example, a beginning teacher might be required to teach only four out of five school days. The fifth day might then be for continued preparation and training. Such an arrangement would provide an excellent opportunity for them to obtain specialized assistance relevant to the teaching situation in which they found themselves. Such specialized assistance, moreover, would differ from region to region, community to community, group to group.

In these and other ways, the aspirations and needs of Native peoples, the official language minorities, and a multiplicity of ethno-cultural groups could find expression and realization. In a society that claims cultural diversity as an enduring and enriching value, nothing less will suffice.

Unless we are prepared to wait twenty or thirty years, the importance of the third cycle, inservice training, becomes self-evident. Here a number of the criticisms we have made of preservice training are equally appropriate, perhaps more so. All too often, continued professional development has been sparse, spasmodic and unrelated. Even today, for example, after thirty years of heavy immigration, thousands of Canadian teachers try to help children whose mother tongue differs from either of our two official languages. Thousands lack the skills to do so. The upshot is that both teachers and students experience frustration and failure. It is painfully clear, for example, that stop-gap English or French in second language courses, while useful, are totally inadequate to meet the needs of the teachers, the province, or the nation.

Regardless of their subject specializations, teachers will need to develop the skill to both understand and cope with cultural differences. Teacher educators, for their part, should not attempt to help them develop those skills in isolation. Nor should they assume that pre-service training is either adequate or unconnected with what should follow. Induction, in-service, and graduate studies should be of a piece. That they have not been to date is obvious. What is required, if we are to meet the demands of the present and prepare outselves for the future, is a radical reshaping of the substantive core of the three 'cycles' of teacher education.

Notes

1. See J. S. Wordsworth, *Strangers Within Our Gates*, as an illustration of early efforts to implement the Anglo-conformist model.
2. While space does not permit a survey of existing teacher education programs, we believe that attention to cultural diversity is usually sporadic, and is confined to specific students and specific minorities.

References

Arciniega, T.A. "Planning and Organizational Issues in Operationalizing the Multicultural Education Standard," a paper presented to the AACTE Leadership Training Institute on Multicultural Teacher Education, Washington, 1977.

Community Relations Commission. *Teacher Education for a Multicultural Society:* The Report of a Joint Working Party of the Community Relations Commission and Association of Teachers in Colleges and Departments of Education. London, 1974.

Hodgetts, A.B. *What Culture? What Heritage?* Toronto: O.I.S.E. 1968.

Hunter, W.A., ed. *Multicultural Teacher Education Through Competency Based Education*. Washington: A.A.C.T.E., 1974.

McDiarmid, G. and Pratt, D. *Teaching Prejudice*. Toronto: O.I.S.E. 1971.

Murray, J. *Toronto Educational Governance/Multiculturalism Case Study*. Toronto: O.I.S.E., 1977.

Palmer, H. and Troper, H., "Canadian Ethnic Studies: Historical Perspectives and Contemporary Duplications," *Interchange,* 4, no. 4 (1973).

The Royal Commission on Bilingualism and Biculturalism. Book IV: *The Cultural Contribution of the Other Ethnic Groups*. Ottawa: Information Canada, 1970.

Symons, T.H.B. *To Know Ourselves,* Report of the Commission on Canadian Studies, Vols. I and II. Ottawa: Association of Universities and Colleges of Canada, 1975.

Part Six

ISSUES AND INNOVATIONS IN THEORY AND PRACTICE

The contents of the previous five sections underline the considerable spread of opinion as to the significance of ethnic pluralism in Canada, its implications for educational policy and the diversity of responses it has brought forth. Our concluding section reinforces these points by focusing on key issues and innovations in policy and practice. These include the lack of consensus on the nature of Candian pluralism and the role of formal education in its expression, the implications of changing educational achievement standings among minority groups for social and ethnic stratification patterns, the remarkable success of French immersion programs, and, finally, and perhaps most controversially, the extent to which non-official languages are to be introduced into the regular school program.

Jon Young's article stresses the close links that exist between Canadian schools and the society in which they are located. The sub-title of this article, "What Sort of Education? What Sort of Society?" is deliberately provocative. He suggests, for example, that Canadians still have to make up their minds as to which model of cultural pluralism they wish to embrace. As long as these larger questions remain unanswered, he implies, so will the question as to what sort of education is desired.

The second article in the section is suggestive in terms of both title and content. Edward Herberg's analysis of census data from 1951–1971 indicates that a considerable shift took place in the educational standings of thirteen ethno-racial-religious groups in five major Canadian cities over this period. Each group and each city, moreover, demonstrated different patterns of attainment, thereby helping support the importance of the theory of ethnic relativism for Canada. His analysis suggests that Canada's ethnic and social hierarchy is less rigid than may previously have been thought (see John Porter's article in Section One). Even more striking is his contention that, in 1971, the visible minorities, especially second-generation members of these groups, formed Canada's new educational elite. Whether these findings are supported by data from the

1981 census (currently being analysed) is of course unknown. The question is an important one, however, and no doubt researchers are eagerly awaiting its outcome.

David Stern surveys the development of French immersion programs, arguably Canada's most successful educational innovation in a decade. He makes the point that innovation in education "is hardly ever the result of critical analysis, research and purely rational decision-making; rather it is an expression of the hopes and aspirations of strong-minded people and their hunches, their determination, inventiveness and enthusiasm." To illustrate this he describes the origins and early impetus for French-language immersion which are to be found in the activities of a small group of English-speaking parents in St. Lambert, Quebec. Convinced of the importance of bilingualism for Canada's future, as well as that of their children in Quebec, they formed a Bilingual School Study Group which developed and implemented an innovative school immersion program in French.

The program subsequently served as a blueprint for similar programs across the country. A broad data base was formed permitting comparison (over the years) of the academic performance of children enrolled in experimental immersion programs with children taking regular French instruction classes. As early as 1973, Stern maintains, a definite pattern of results emerged. They indicated, that while the learning of French in the immersion programs improved beyond anything that could normally be expected from conventional French instruction, progress in the mother tongue and general educational achievement levels did not suffer. Such evidence proved persuasive and French-language immersion programs are now widely considered as positive intellectual challenges, particularly for younger children.

Traditionally, as we have seen, the primary objective of provincial school systems has been to strengthen the majority-language skills of children, often at the expense of their minority language. The underlying assumptions of this position have been subjected to serious re-scrutiny of late, however. Minority-language children, as Jim Cummins points out, do not constitute a homogeneous group and both research and experience suggests that considerable variation exists in the extent to which they benefit in a school environment which concentrates on the majority language and ignores the child's knowledge of his or her mother tongue. High levels of academic performance are achieved by some; others seem to benefit most from "language shelter" programs in their mother tongue. Neither approach, therefore, is appropriate for all minority language children. Given this, Cummins argues, what is needed is a flexible, open-minded approach to the question; an approach which takes account of the psycho-educational needs and potential strengths of minority children as well as the cultural aspirations of their parents. Whether his advice is likely to be heeded in the near future, however, is far from clear. There are already signs, for example, that the issue of incorporating instruction in the non-official languages into the formal school curriculum is capable of arousing considerable opposition and antagonism.

Education in a Multicultural Society: What Sort of Education? What Sort of Society?

JONATHAN C. YOUNG

Multiculturalism is a concept whose use is characterized by currency rather than consensus. In fact, so great is the ambiguity associated with the term that it has been suggested that it is ready for the "conceptual graveyard" (Stent, 1973). Since education itself has rarely been free from controversy, it is hardly surprising that the issue of multicultural education is both confused and contentious. Carlson (1976), commenting on this confusion, observed:

> Multicultural education (MCE), as described by many of its advocates, is a labyrinth of assertions and assumptions which need to be examined. To those who make the largest contributions to education — namely, individual teachers and students in specific communities — the assertions and assumptions often make little sense (p. 26).

Despite the ambiguities in terminology there appears to be little disagreement that Canada is a society characterized by ethnic and cultural diversity. However, differences arise from consideration of the appropriate responses to this diversity, by society in general and the school in particular. This paper endeavours to negotiate a path through the "labyrinth of assertions and assumptions" in order to clarify some of the concepts associated with multiculturalism and multicultural education.

The paper argues that issues in multicultural education inevitably pose questions of purpose in the wider society and that different images of Canadian society demand different responses from the school system. Several different visions of society are outlined and the paper attempts to examine the extent to which each is relevant to the Canadian context and congruent with a particular interpretation of multicultural education.

SOURCE: *The Canadian Journal of Education,* 4, no. 3 (1979), pp. 5–21. Reprinted by permission of the Editor.

ETHNICITY, CULTURE AND SOCIAL STRUCTURE

Because the terms "multicultural" and "multi-ethnic" are often used interchangeably in the literature, it is advisable at this stage to draw some distinctions between the terms "culture" and "ethnic group." Further, it seems useful to separate the concept of culture from that of social structure, although it is a distinction rarely made in educational literature.

Definitions of "ethnic group" differ considerably. A major source of difference is the extent to which membership is seen to be biologically defined or based upon self-identification. Vallee (1957), like Porter (1972), argues for the former, using the term to refer to a biological descent group sharing a common culture based on national origin, language, religion, or race, or any combination of these. Conversely, Enloe (1973) maintains that the primary emphasis of membership is not that of descent but of self-identification, and that ethnic groups share clusters of beliefs and values, expressed through associational forms, and are networks of regular communications and interactions. Further disagreement centres around the extent to which the term should be restricted to describing minority groups within a society or, as is more general in modern usage, may be applied to the dominant group or groups as well. This paper will use the term in the sense suggested by Schermerhorn (1970, p. 12) of describing "a collectivity within a larger society, having real or putative common ancestry, memories of a shared historical past, and a cultural focus on one or more symbolic elements defined as the epitome of their peoplehood." Examples of such symbolic elements might include kinship patterns, religious affiliations, language or dialect, nationality, phenotypical features, or any combination of them.

The term "culture" has likewise failed to achieve any generally accepted definition. Kroeber and Kluckholm (1963) report over three hundred different definitions. Banks (1977, p. 3) defines culture as "the behaviour patterns, symbols, institutions, values and other human-made components of society . . . the unique achievements of a human group that distinguishes it from other human groups." While it is in this broad sense that the term is usually applied to educational issues, Oliver (1977) and Schermerhorn draw an important distinction between culture and social structure. To Schermerhorn culture is "a pattern of fundamental beliefs and values differentiating right from wrong, defining rules for interactions, setting priorities, expectations, and goals." These "rules for life" he separates from social structure, which is used to refer to

> the set of crystallized relationships which its [society's] members have

> with each other which places them in groups, large or small, permanent or temporary, formally organized or unorganized, and which relates them to the major institutional activities of the society, such as economic and occupational life, religion, marriage and the family, education and government (p. 80).

While this separation is rarely made in educational literature — indeed, the term multicultural is usually used where multi-ethnic would be more appropriate — it does imply that a particular social structure may or may not be congruent with a particular culture, and raises the question to what extent the social structure represented in a school is congruent with the various cultures brought to it by its student population.

ETHNIC RELATIONS: ASSIMILATION AND PLURALISM

Wirth (1945) has suggested that ethnic minorities in a society are faced with a choice between four options: assimilation, the abandonment of cultural differences; pluralism, to seek tolerance of their differences by the majority group; secession, an independent existence; or militancy, to wrest power from the majority group. While it could be argued that each option has relevance to contemporary Canadian society, this paper will confine its attention to the first two.

Gordon (1964) offers a multidimensional model that provides a more specific instrument to help understand the process of assimilation. His seven dimensions are: cultural or behavioural assimilation, the absorption of the cultural or behavioural patterns of the "host" community; structural assimilation, entrance into the social cliques, organizations, institutional activities and general civic life of the host community; marital assimilation; identificational assimilation, the development of a sense of peoplehood based exclusively on the host community; attitude receptional assimilation, the absence of prejudice; behaviour receptional assimilation, the absence of discrimination; and civic assimilation, the absence of value or power conflict. Of the seven dimensions, the author suggests that the first two are the most potent, that in majority-minority group contact cultural assimilation is most likely to occur first, and that if it is accompanied by structural assimilation all other forms of assimilation will inevitably follow.

Recent years have witnessed a global questioning of assimilation as a worthwhile societal goal and instead an ideology has been promoted in which ethnic and cultural differences are either tolerated or actively supported. Such ideologies usually go under the title of "pluralism," "cultural pluralism," or "multiculturalism." The terms are used both as descriptive models — to explain what is — and as goals — as statements of what ought to be. To separate these two usages Schermerhorn suggests the use of the term "normative pluralism" to refer to the goal model — implying a general ideology that maintains the desirability of preserving cultural differences among different ehtnic groups. In the same way "normative multiculturalism" would apply to a similar ideology.

Used as a descriptive model, Schermerhorn goes on to distinguish between cultural and structural pluralism. Cultural pluralism is used to refer to a society in which one or more ethnic group has a language, religion, kinship form, tribal affiliation, and/or other traditional norms and values which are embodied in patterns and which set them off from other groups. Structural pluralism, on the other hand, is used to refer to societies in which the different cultures are segmented into "analogous, parallel, non-complementary, but distinguishable sets of institutions, at least in their most pronounced forms" (Schermerhorn, p. 124). The extent to which the two concepts are in reality separated would seem to be a critical issue in the nature of inter-group relations. Schermerhorn calls them "virtual Siamese twins" noting that cultural differences need to find expression in structural forms. The relationship between the two concepts is central to the issue of multicultural education, and poses important questions for those charged with the design and implementation of educational programs. As such it is a theme that will be returned to in this paper.

In translating the ideology of "normative multiculturalism" into practice a critical issue becomes the way in which access to societal rewards and resources is determined. Based on this, Gordon (1975) distinguishes between liberal and corporate pluralism. Liberal pluralism is characterized by the absence, even prohibition, of any legal or governmental recognition of racial, religious, language or national origin groups as corporate entities with standing in the legal or governmental process, and the prohibition of the use of ethnic criteria for any type of discrimination, or conversely any favoured treatment. In such a situation structural pluralism would exist only as an unofficial reality in communal life, as would some measure of cultural pluralism "at the will of the ethnic group members, and subject to the pressures towards conformity to general societal norms implicit in whatever degree of industrialization and urbanization was present in the society" (p. 106).

Corporate pluralism, on the other hand, implies that racial and ethnic groups are recognized as legally constituted entities with official standing in society. Economic and political rewards are allocated on a quota system based on some measure of the numerical strength of the group in the society. Structural pluralism is officially encouraged and, indeed, becomes the necessary setting for individual action, and cultural pluralism tends to be reinforced even in the urban, industrialized setting. The dilemma of the liberal pluralist stance is pointed to by Glazer and Moynihan (1975) in their description of the development of anti-discrimination legislation in the United States of America in the 1960s. They note:

> The Civil Rights Act of 1964 was the very embodiment of the liberal expectancy. Race, color, religion, sex, national origin; all such ascriptive categories were to be outlawed. No-one was to be classified in such primitive, offensive terms. In particular, government was to become color-blind. However, within hours of the enactment of the government statute, in order to enforce it, the federal government was, for the first time, beginning to require even more detailed accounting of subgroups of every description . . . in terms of race, color and sex. The expectancy that such things would not be known was instantly replaced by the requirement that they not only be known, but the fact as to distribution be justified. Skewed distributions would not do; quotas appeared in American society (p. 10).

CANADIAN APPROACHES TO ETHNIC RELATIONS

The ambiguous uses of terminology relating to ethnicity make all statistics at best open to question. Porter (1975) warns us that figures taken from the census are "artifacts of the census itself and result from the questions from which the data are derived" (p. 279). Based on the interrelation of language and culture, Ryder (1955) suggests that a more meaningful picture of the size and strength of Canada's ethnic minorities could be obtained from measures of retention of mother tongue. This, he maintains, would give a better measure of Canadian ethnic diversity than traditional census statistics on ethnic origin, and would also indicate the extent to which minorities were assimilating to either French or English cultures. Porter (1975) applied this approach to the 1971 census statistics to show that while non-English, non-French groups make up some 28 per cent of the population by ethnic origin, only approximately 12 per cent have the same mother tongue as their ethnic origin language, and only 6 per cent speak that language most often in their homes. While these figures give an indication of the different measures of ethnic diversity that can be obtained using different definitions of ethnicity, few people seem willing to argue that ethnic diversity is not a fundamental characteristic of contemporary Canadian society. Neither is this diversity a product of recent years; rather it predates Confederation, and has been the object of different policies and perspectives at different periods of Canadian history.

Despite the "myth of the mosaic," intergroup relations in Canada have traditionally been characterized by assimilation, and the school has been seen as a major instrument by which this was achieved. Murray (1977), discussing the introduction of free schooling to Toronto in 1871, documents the contemporary viewpoint that

> free schools would make the new arrivals [the Irish] into Canadians, through coercion if necessary. The immigrant child would have to be separated from the influences of its parents between the ages of roughly five and twelve, during which time he would be taught the values of an expanding mercantile society (p. 64).

Palmer (1976), while agreeing that intergroup relations in Canada have traditionally been characterized by assimilation, distinguishes between a prewar ideology, which he sees as predominantly one of Anglo-conformity, and the ideology of the "melting pot," which he suggests characterized the 1950s and 1960s.

However, the 1970s have seen Canadian society increasingly question the assimilationist response and instead move tentatively towards a position in which ethnic diversity has been seen as a positive element of Canadian society to be fostered (O'Bryan, 1976; Berry, 1977). Palmer (p. 101) suggest that the roots of this shift lie in the impact of French-Canadian nationalism and the Pearson government's establishment of the Royal Commission on Bilingualism and Biculturalism, an appreciation of the way in which ethnicity could provide a basis for personal identity in an impersonal mass society that was unsure of its values, the increasing awareness of the value of cultural diversity in an affluent and technological society, and the upsurgence of English-Canadian nationalism which sought to distinguish Canada from the United States by asserting the existence of the Canadian "mosaic" in contrast to the American "melting pot." The establishment in 1963 of the Royal Commission on Bilingualism and Biculturalism provided a focus for these different forces working to question traditional perspectives towards ethnic relations in Canada. Originally intended to concentrate on issues related to Anglo-French relations, the commission found itself confronted with other ethnic groups who successfully petitioned for a widening of its terms of reference to include the concerns of "other ethnic groups." To this end, *Book IV: The Cultural Contributions of the Other Ethnic Groups,* was included in the Report in 1970, and paved the way for the federal government's policy of multiculturalism within a bilingual framework announced by the Prime Minister in 1971.

The Prime Minister's announcement of the federal policy on October 8, 1971, contained the now familiar observation that the time was overdue for Canadians to become more aware of their rich tradition of cultural diversity, that his policy aimed to ensure the continuation of that tradition, and that it sought to enhance the appreciation of the contribution of the many ethno-cultural groups to Canadian society. In the words of the then Secretary of State Gerard Pelletier, the policy called into being a new vision of society; one which refused to sacrifice diversity in the name of unity and which placed the cultures of Canada's many groups on an equal footing (Pelletier, 1972).

The development of the federal policy has been subject to criticism from several directions. To Porter the pluralist vision of society contained in the policy which stressed group maintenance rather than individual self-development is regressive. It is a policy, he asserts, that serves to perpetuate in Canada a "vertical mosaic" in which class lines coincide with ethnic lines by preserving conservative values which he regards as detrimental to the social and economic mobility of individuals from minority groups. Rather he advances a position that he calls "liberal assimilation" in which ethnicity is acknowledged as a potentially valuable, temporary "staging post" or "psychic shelter" for recent immigrants, but is given no long-term formal or institutional recognition. A second line of criticism has been that the policy represents a distortion of the realities of Canadian life because there are two main cultures tied to two official languages (Rocher, 1976; Mallea, 1976). It is, from this perspective, contradictory to have a policy of official bilingualism alongside a policy of multiculturalism because language and culture are inseparable. To these critics the government's policy is not only sociologically mistaken; it is also politically dangerous because it detracts from the status of French-Canadians in Canada.

In applying the terms "liberal" or "corporate" pluralism to the Canadian approaches to ethnic diversity it is important to acknowledge that policies invariably represent a compromise of conflicting and often contradictory pressures — at both the federal and provincial levels — rather than a coherent and consistent response to clearly defined issues. Further, Canada's ethnic groups do not represent a homogeneous "third element" in the country's population, but rather, as is clearly shown by O'Bryan's 1976 national survey, consist of many different groups of differing size and internal cohesiveness and with different aspirations as to their place in Canadian society.

Given these constraints upon the validity of generalized conclusions, it might be argued that in recent years the federal response to francophone Canada and to the native people has been a predominantly corporate pluralist one, recognizing them as groups with official standing in the society and promoting separate, parallel sets of institutions.[1] Conversely, for most of the rest of Canada's other ethnic groups the predominant — although not exclusive — response of the federal government appears to be that of liberal pluralism.

As discussion of the appropriate responses to ethnic diversity continues at the societal level, the school is inevitably drawn into the debate. The confusion that has characterized discussions of multiculturalism has tended to become compounded with regard to multicultural education. However, the thesis of this paper is that differing perceptions of multicultural education are defined by different interpretations of the appropriate societal response to ethnic diversity, and the next section of the paper will be directed towards outlining several different conceptualizations of multicultural education and examining the degree to which each is congruent with one of the differing perceptions of multiculturalism outlined above.

MULTICULTURAL EDUCATION: A TYPOLOGY

In an attempt to reduce the ambiguity surrounding the concept of multicultural education Margaret Gibson (1976) suggests that it is possible to identify four different approaches with different objectives described in the literature on multicultural education. These she calls Education of the Culturally Different, Education about Cultural Differences, Education for Cultural Pluralism, and Bicultural Education. While recognizing that in reality these approaches will interrelate and overlap, she suggests that they may be considered in the ideal type as analytically distinct.

Education of the Culturally Different

To Gibson, "Education of the Culturally Different" or "Benevolent Multiculturalism" (Hilliard, 1974) is an attempt to equalize educational opportunities for "culturally atypical" students. The approach is based on evidence of lower academic achievement, higher dropout rates and restricted career aspirations among certain ethnic groups, and a rejection of cultural or genetic deficit models to explain these characteristics (Harvey and Masemann, 1973; Hawthorn, 1966; Grande, 1975; Gershman, 1976). Instead of a cultural deficit model the differential success rates are rationalized in terms of cultural discordance between the school and the minority student's home. Stated pointedly by Hunter (1974), "for the student who comes from cultural settings deviant from the assumed norm, schooling constitutes a threatening, low-win or no-win situation. Their differences are treated as handicaps, burdens, and short-comings to be overcome" (p. 36).

Hawthorn sees a similar conflict lying at the root of the failure of the formal school system to meet the needs of Canada's native people. He describes the process whereby an Indian student is placed at the centre of a battle for his cultural allegiance and its impact on the student's development as follows:

> The young Indian student is subjected to an informal educational system within his own society which enables him to become an Indian; formal education in the public school seldom overlaps the Indian educational process but it does make some inroads. At adolescence, about fifth to eighth grade, the antithetical position of the two cultures becomes crucial because it places the Indian youth in a dilemma he cannot resolve. In essence, it forces him to choose between being an Indian and being an Indian "White." This is clearly a decision which he cannot make simply because, whatever else he might be he is an Indian and others regard him as such. . . . By fifth grade he begins to realize the futility of his efforts to achieve socially and academically. He then withdraws from any participation in the learning process until he is legally of age, when he withdraws completely. Achievement, attendance, self-image, and level of aspiration drop markedly (pp. 126–27).

To the proponents of benevolent multiculturalism the solution lies in making the school adapt in order to reduce home/school discordance. This in turn, it is argued, will lead to improved self-image, motivation, and academic success.

Processes designed to sensitize the school to minority students and reduce cultural conflict include teacher education programs designed to prepare teachers to meet the needs of specific minority groups (Kirman, 1969); special materials prepared for practising teachers, along with inservice programs (Witzel, 1969); the recruitment of school-community liaison personnel (Toronto Board of Education, Workgroup on Multicultural Programs, 1975); and special programs designed for the culturally atypical students such as English as a Second Language or Transition Programs. In these programs teaching during the initial years of school is carried out in the student's mother-tongue as well as the majority language, in order to facilitate the student's overall progress regardless of his or her proficiency in the majority language and to reduce the student's initial culture shock (Grande, 1973; Murray, 1977).

As outlined above, the approach of Education of the Culturally Different describes a strategy congruent with the stance of the liberal assimilationist or the liberal pluralist. It is a perspective not based upon any specific concept of the value of cultural diversity, but rather at the pragmatic level it recognizes the existence of diversity and asserts that equal educational opportunity requires that the school pay attention to the student's cultural identity. Thus cultural diversity is seen as a social reality to be accommodated rather than a resource that has any intrinsic worth and which should be promoted by the school. In seeking to produce success in the "mainstream" culture without permanently modifying that culture the approach is compatible with Porter's (1975) stance of liberal assimilation. Also, to the extent that the approach is based upon a recognition of the social reality of ethnic and cultural diversity and seeks to reduce institutional discrimination and promote individual equality it is also compatible with Gordon's (1975) concept of liberal pluralism in which diversity is maintained at the will of the ethnic community and subject to the pressures towards uniformity of an industrialized and urbanized society.

Education about Cultural Differences or Cultural Understanding

Education about Cultural Differences or Cultural Understanding, as an approach to multicultural education, differs from the previous approach, according to Gibson, in that it has as its target population all students and seeks to promote in them an appreciation of the value of ethnic and cultural diversity and the right of others to be different. Given this perspective on the positive contribution of diversity it is suggested that the school as a major, formal institution of socialization has a responsibility to promote cultural understanding.

That the school has traditionally failed to do this has been well documented in recent years.[2] Hodgetts in his 1968 book *What Culture? What Heritage?* criticized the ethnocentricity of Canadian social studies programs and commented that "although we laugh at ourselves for doing so and perhaps have convinced each other that today things are different we are continuing to teach a white, Anglo-Saxon, Protestant, political and constitutional history of Canada" (p. 20). Similar studies have followed making similar criticisms (Symons, 1975; Aoki, 1976). Pratt (1975) extended this criticism to Canadian textbooks. He notes that the textbook is not simply any book: it is an official book, authorized by the government, promoted by the school, and acknowledged by the teacher. Following an extensive content analysis of Canadian textbooks, he concludes:

> Canadian school textbooks do not represent or support a culturally plural model of society. They do support a consensus, non-controversial, conventional view of society. . . . In sum, the school textbook introduces students to a unitary view of society (pp. 119–22).

Neither have teachers and teacher-training institutions escaped the criticism of ethnocentricism. The National Indian Brotherhood (1972), commenting on traditional approaches to teacher education, stated that "in most cases, the teacher is simply not prepared to understand or cope with cultural differences. Both the child and the teacher are forced into intolerable positions" (p. 19).

The reaction to this criticism has been to demand that the school become oriented towards the cultural development of *all* of its students by designing programs and creating environments that actively and positively endorse ethnic and cultural diversity. In Ontario such a perspective is advanced by the Ministry of Education's curriculum guidelines for primary and junior grades, *The Formative Years* (1975). These guidelines require that all students be given the opportunity to:

1. Develop and retain a personal identity by becoming acquainted with the historical roots of the community and culture of his or her origin, and by developing a sense of continuity with the past, and,
2. Begin to understand and appreciate the points of view of ethnic and cultural groups other than his or her own.

Further, the ministry through its Circular 14 — a listing of approved textbooks — is able to exclude extremes of ethnocentricism or cultural bias from school textbooks and to promote those books that are supportive of ethnic and cultural diversity in Canada. Locally, task forces and work groups have been established to review curricula materials, to generate new multicultural materials, and to ensure "ethnic visibility" throughout the school curriculum.

In the area of teacher preparation and professional development the perspective calls for a more comprehensive approach than that of education of the culturally different. Proponents argue that "to suggest that certain teachers who have certain specializations or who intend to teach in certain areas will never interact with children from a variety of backgrounds is to miss the point: teachers and students should be prepared for life in a multicultural society" (Mallea and Young, 1978). Such a perspective argues that some appreciation of and sensitivity towards ethnic diversity in Canada should be a part of all teachers' preparation and ongoing professional development.

The implications for the wider society stemming from this approach would seem to hinge upon the extent to which the term "cultural differences" is used strictly in the sense outlined earlier of "rules for life" or is taken to include both cultural and structural differences. An approach that focuses on cultural issues and seeks to eliminate discrimination and ethnocentricism from the school program is congruent with a liberal pluralist position. However, to the extent to which the approach stresses aspects of structural diversity and studies the institutions existing within the ethnic communities it may be seen as legitimizing ethno-cultural institutions and, as such, tending towards a more corporate pluralist vision of society.

Education for Cultural Pluralism

Advocates of this approach see its primary objective as the maintenance and extension of ethnic and cultural diversity in society. It is an approach that requires the structural recognition of cultural differences as a way of increasing the power of minority groups in the school system and thus creating a climate for academic success. Pachecio (1977) says of the approach: "More sensitive to the lack of parity in real life it attempts, through a variety of structural arrangements in the school, to aggressively support the right of a cultural group to maintain itself" (p. 20). The belief that the school should actively be involved in the maintenance of cultures separates the approach from the two previous perspectives and gives it the unique characteristic of attempting to reinforce cultural boundaries. In the extreme educational situation these boundaries would be physically defined by separate schools, as is common, for example, with the Hutterite Brethren (Oliver, 1977; MacDonald, 1977) or by separate school systems as illustrated by the Roman Catholic school boards. In other situations the approach takes the form of additional after-hours schooling to supplement or "offset" regular schooling within the public school system. Within the public school system proponents of this approach have advocated such strategies as cultural retention classes, instruction in the mother tongue, and quota systems for teachers and administrators in order for the school to reflect the ethnic and cultural make-up of the population that it serves.

The belief that the school should take an active role in cultural maintenance is clearly stated in the National Indian Brotherhood's 1972 policy paper *Indian Control of Indian Education,* which stated:

> Unless a child learns about the forces which shaped him, the history of his people, their values and customs, their language, he will never really know himself or his potential as a human being. . . . The lessons he learns in school, his whole school experience should reinforce and contribute to the image he has of himself as an Indian (p. 9).

Stressing the importance of control of the decision-making process, the policy paper maintained, "Indian parents must have control of education and the setting of goals. . . . We must therefore reclaim our right to direct the education of our children" (p. 3).

The establishment of separate schools or school systems has offered a powerful way of resisting what are seen as the forces of assimilation acting within the public school system. However, in recent years, looking at programs in Ontario, it is possible to point to developments in which both the provincial government and local school boards have moved to promote cultural retention within the public school system. The Heritage Language Program, announced in the Throne Speech to the Ontario legislature of March 29, 1977, may be seen as the most significant move in this direction.[3] It represents a move by the provincial government and some local school boards to become involved in teaching a language other than English or French in the elementary schools as well as the secondary schools. While these programs usually take place in after-school classes, some have been integrated into the regular school timetable. Although such programs fall short of what might be described as the ideal by proponents of Education for Cultural Pluralism — which might involve instruction in the students' mother tongues by teachers from the same ethnic backgrounds — they do represent a recognition of the legitimacy of ethnic and cultural diversity within the school system and a conscious attempt to maintain that diversity, thus separating the approach from the two previous ones.

While it could be argued that in its extreme the approach is more compatible with a secessionist stance than a pluralist one, in general advocates of Education for Cultural Pluralism appear to be advocates of a corporate vision of society. It is a position congruent with the corporate pluralist stance of requiring structural recognition of cultural differences as a way of obtaining equality, not at the individual level, but at the level of the group.

Stent (1972) suggests that cultural separation may be a necessary first step to equality in an open society, a position echoed by Stokely Carmichael (1973), who observed that "before a group can enter the open society it must first close ranks." Bryce (1970) articulates a similar point with regard to Canadian Indians who he suggests are saying: "By your treaties you have set us apart. You must now honour that setting apart. You must let us re-discover what it means to be an Indian. Once we know, then we can meet with your society, then we can be better Canadians."

Bicultural Education

The fourth, and most elusive, of Gibson's concepts of multicultural education is that of Bicultural Education. It is an approach designed to produce learners who have "competencies in, and can operate successfully in two different cultures" (p. 13). While recognizing that such an approach may combine elements of all of the three previous approaches, Gibson maintains that it is unique in that it is concerned with fostering biculturalism and in its emphasis on reciprocity. Proponents assert that one's native culture ought to be preserved and that the "mainstream" culture (if different from that of the native culture) ought to be acquired as an alternative or second culture.

Furthermore, supporters believe that students whose native culture is the mainstream culture will also profit from the acquisition of competencies in a second culture.

A fundamental issue in the concept of Bicultural Education is the meaning given to the stated objective of the acquisition of competencies in a second culture. To maintain that a person can be equally comfortable and committed to two different cultures is incompatible with the definition of culture used in this paper. If different cultures possess, and are distinguished by, different sets of fundamental beliefs and values then the acquisition of a second culture implies an inherent value conflict and makes little practical sense. However, if bicultural education does not seek to promote dual cultural membership, it can still be argued that it goes beyond the cultural understanding and general tolerance of cultural differences characteristic of education about cultural differences. Bicultural education programs invariably centre on bilingualism, for as Rocher (1976) has observed, "knowledge of the second language is a stepping-stone to better understanding of the other group's culture — its literature, theatre, mentality and ideas" (p. 51). In this the approach implies a deeper understanding of the second culture, and through language acquisition promotes participation in the institutions of the second culture, and cross-cultural interactions.

A second important distinction to be made is between individual biculturalism and institutional biculturalism. The Royal Commission on Bilingualism and Biculturalism recognized this distinction and focused on the latter. Commenting on the concept of Canadian biculturalism and its own role the commission observed that it was not

> in our view a suggestion that individuals should acquire the traits and peculiarities of two cultures. What we are mainly asked to do is to establish whether both cultures possess the institutions they need, whether they are properly represented within the principal common institutions, and whether persons who participate in each of them have the opportunity to conserve and express their own culture. (Royal Commission on Bilingualism and Biculturalism; Book I, p. xxviii).

As an approach that emphasizes individual bilingualism and reciprocity, examples within the Canadian context are few, and generally limited to English/French-Canadian biculturalism. Within English Canada there are programs that go beyond treating French as merely another subject option and instead seek to produce bilingual-bicultural students (Greenfield, 1976; Stern, 1976). Such programs usually involve either immersion programs (Swain, 1976), in which the entire course is conducted in the second language, or programs where part of the course is taught in the second language and part in the mother tongue.

A more radical interpretation of the concept was outlined by a Toronto workgroup in 1974 which proposed the establishment of a "Balanced Bilingual School" (Toronto Board of Education, Workgroup on French programs, 1974). The school was seen as providing the opportunity to create "a truly Canadian bilingual milieu and cultural centre" where a balanced program was offered in French and English, taught by bilingual staff, and offered to students from both English and French backgrounds.

Implicit in the concept of bilingual education is an appreciation of the benefits of cultural diversity and a commitment to a pluralist vision of society. Yet in its emphasis on cross-cultural interactions and on individual rather than institutional biculturalism some people argue that it will inevitably promote assimilation to the majority culture. As outlined above, the approach of bicultural education seems the most elusive of the four conceptualizations with regard to the Canadian context, and one that fits uneasily into a limited corporate vision of society to the extent that individual biculturalism inevitably demands structural and institutional recognition of ethnic diversity.

CONCLUSIONS

The purpose of this paper has been to argue that the term "multicultural education" has obtained no single, universally acceptable meaning. Instead it is possible to recognize several different interpretations of the concept each of which carries with it an explicit or implicit vision of Canadian society. In endeavouring to make these school and societal relationships explicit and to furnish practical illustrations of the different interpretations of multicultural education the paper has sought to reduce some of the ambiguities surrounding the term, and in addition to provide a framework for looking at the responses of different school systems to ethnic diversity. As such it may offer a way to distinguish political rhetoric from educational reality: the paper has argued that to espouse a particular vision of Canadian society carries with it specific implications for multicultural education, and it is perhaps in the extent to which students have access to these programs that school policy should be critically evaluated.

Notes

I wish to express my thanks to Roger I. Simon, John Mallea and Stephen B. Lawton for their helpful suggestions and comments on the various drafts of this article.

1. Such generalized conclusions are invariably subject to debate. For a critical attack on the federal practices towards native people as distinct from political statements, see Harold Cardinal's book *The Rebirth of Canada's Indians*.
2. It should be noted that this "failure" reflects the fact that Canadian society traditionally viewed the school as the major agency of assimilation of its minorities and in this sense teachers and schools responded appropriately to the change that society laid at its door.
3. It should be noted that the Heritage Language Program is provided under the Continuing Education Program of the province and as such is not subject to all of the regular requirements such as certification of instructors.

References

Aoki, T. *Towards devolution in the control of education on a native reserve in Alberta: The Hobbema story*. Paper presented at the meeting of the American Anthropological Association, Toronto, 1972.

Aoki, T., Werner, W., Dahlie, J., and Connors, B. *Whose culture? Whose heritage?* Vancouver: Centre for the Study of Curriculum and Instruction, Faculty of Education, University of British Columbia, 1974.

Banks, J.A. "Multicultural education," in Klassen, ed., *Pluralism and the American teacher*. Washington: AACTE, 1977.

Berry, J., Kalin, and Taylor. *Multiculturalism and Ethnic Attitudes in Canada*. Ottawa: The Queen's Printer, 1977.

Canada. Royal Commission on Bilingualism and Biculturalism. Report. Vol. I: *General Introduction: The Official Languages*. Ottawa: The Queen's Printer, 1967. Vol. 4: *The Cultural Contribution of the Other Ethnic Groups*. Ottawa: The Queen's Printer, 1969.

Canada. House of Commons, *Debates*. 28th Parliament, 3rd Session, Vol. 8, 1971, p. 8546.

Canadian Consultative Committee on Multiculturalism. *Multiculturalism as State Policy*. Ottawa: The Ministry of Supply and Services, 1976.

Cardinal, H. *The Unjust Society: The Tragedy of Canada's Indians*. Edmonton: Hurtig, 1969.

Cardinal, H. *The Rebirth of Canada's Indians*. Edmonton: Hurtig, 1977.

Carlson, P.E. "Towards a definition local-level multicultural education." *Anthropology and Education Quarterly*, 7, no. 4 (1976), pp. 26–30.

Carmichael, S. *Black Power*. New York: Random House, 1973.

Enloe, C. *Ethnic Conflict and Political Development*. Boston: Little Brown, 1973.

Gershman, J. *Background of Students in Special Education and New Canadian Programs*. Toronto: Board of Education for the City of Toronto. Research Report No. 141. 1976.

Gibson, M. "Approaches to multicultural education in the U.S.: Some concepts and assumptions." *Anthropology and Education Quarterly*, 7, no. 4 (1976), pp. 7–18.

Glazer, N., and Moynihan, D. *Ethnicity: Theory and Experience.* Cambridge: Harvard University Press, 1975.

Gordon, M. *Assimilation in American Life.* New York: Oxford University Press, 1964.

______. "Towards a theory of racial and ethnic group relations," in N. Glazer and D. Moynihan, eds. *Ethnicity: Theory and Experience.* Cambridge: Harvard University Press, 1975.

Grande, A. *A Transition Program for Young Children: Experimental Program.* Toronto: Board of Education for the City of Toronto, 1973.

______. "A transition program for young immigrant children," in A. Wolfgang, ed. *Education of Immigrant Students: Issues and Answers.* Toronto: Ontario Institute for Studies in Education, 1975.

Greenfield, T.B. "Bilingualism, multiculturalism, and the crisis in Canadian culture," in M. Swain, ed. *Bilingualism in Canadian Education.* Third Yearbook of the Canadian Society for the Study of Education. Edmonton: CSSE, 1976.

Harvey, E., and Masemann, V. *Occupation, Graduation and the Labour Force.* Toronto: Ontario Ministry of Education, 1973.

Hawthorn, H.B. *A Survey of the Contemporary Indian of Canada.* Ottawa: The Queen's Printer, 1966.

Hilliard, A.G. "Restructuring teacher education for multicultural imperatives," in W.A. Hunter, ed. *Multicultural Education Through Competency Based Teacher Education.* Washington: AACTE, 1974.

Hodgetts, A.B. *What Culture? What Heritage: A Study of Civic Education in Canada.* Toronto: Ontario Institute for Studies in Education, 1968.

Hunter, W.A., ed. *Multicultural Education Through Competency Based Teacher Education.* Washington: AACTE, 1974.

Kirman, J.M. "The university of Alberta's intercultural education program." *Peabody Journal of Education,* 47 (1969), p. 15.

Kroeber, A.L., and Kluckholm, C. *Culture: A Critical Review of Concepts and Definitions.* New York: Vintage Books, 1963.

MacDonald, R.J. "Hutterite education in Alberta: A test case of assimilation 1920–1970." *Canadian Ethnic Studies,* 8, no. 1 (1976), pp. 9–22.

Mallea, J.R. "Multiculturalism within a bilingual framework: A note on the Québécois response." *Multiculturalism,* 1, no. 2 (1977), pp. 3–5.

______. *Quebec's Language Policies: Background and Responses.* Québec: Presses de l'université Laval, 1977.

______. Young, J.C. "Teacher education in a culturally plural society." Paper presented at the Symposium on Intercultural Education and Community Development, Toronto, Faculty of Education, University of Toronto, June 1978.

Masemann, V.L. "Multicultural programs in Toronto schools." *Interchange,* 9, no. 1 (1978/79), pp. 29–44.

McDiarmid, G., and Pratt, D. *Teaching Prejudice.* Toronto: Ontario Institute for Studies in Education, 1971.

Murray, J. *Toronto Educational Governance/Multiculturalism: A Case Study.* Toronto: Ontario Institute for Studies in Education, 1977.

National Indian Brotherhood. *Indian Control of Indian Education.* Ottawa: The Brotherhood, 1972.

O'Bryan, Reily, and Kuplowska, P. *Non-official Languages: A Study in Canadian Multiculturalism.* Ottawa: Ministry of Supplies, 1976.

Oliver, D. *Education and Community.* Berkeley: McCutcheon, 1977.

Ontario Ministry of Education. *The Formative Years.* Toronto: Ministry of Education, 1975.

Pachecio, A. "Cultural pluralism: A philosophical analysis." *Journal of Teacher Education,* 28, no. 3 (1977), pp. 16–31.

Palmer, H. "Reluctant hosts: The Anglo-Canadian view of multiculturalism in the twentieth century," in *Multiculturalism as State Policy.* Ottawa: Canadian Consultative Committee on Multiculturalism, 1976.

Pelletier, G. Elements of a speech by the honorable Gerard Pelletier in Vancouver, March 6, 1972. Press Release, Department of the Secretary of State.

Porter, J. "Dilemmas and contradictions of a multi-ethnic society." *Transactions of the Royal Society of Canada,* 10, no. 4 (1972), pp. 193–205.

______. "Ethnic pluralism in Canada," in N. Glazer and D. Moynihan, eds. *Ethnicity: Theory and Experience.* Cambridge: Harvard University Press, 1975.

Pratt, D. "The social role of school textbooks in Canada," in E. Zureik and R. Pike, eds. *Socialization and Values in Canadian Society,* Vol. 1, Carleton Library, No. 84. Toronto: McClelland & Stewart, 1975, pp. 100–126.

Purbhoo, M., and Shapson, S. *Transition from Italian: The First Years.* Toronto: Board of Education for the City of Toronto. Research Report No. 126. 1974.

Rocher, G. "Multiculturalism — the doubts of a francophone," in *Multiculturalism as State Policy.* Ottawa: Canadian Consultative Committee on Multiculturalism, 1976.

Ryder, N. "The interpretation of origin statistics." *Canadian Journal of Economics and Political Science,* 21, no. 4 (1955), pp. 466–79.

Samuda, R., and Tinglin, W. "Can testing serve minority students?" *School Guidance Worker,* 33, no. 4 (1978), pp. 39–44.

Schermerhorn, R.A. *Comparative Ethnic Relations: A Framework for Theory and Research.* New York: Random House, 1970.

Stent, M.D., Hazard, W.R., and Rivline, S., eds. *Cultural Pluralism in Education.* New York: Appleton-Century and Crofts, 1973.

Stern, H.H. *French Programs: Some Major Issues.* Toronto: Ministry of Education, 1976.

Swain, M., ed. *Bilingual Schooling: Some Experiences in Canada and the United States.* Toronto: Ontario Institute for Studies in Education, 1972.

Symons, T.H.B. *To Know Ourselves: The Report of the Commission on Canadian Studies,* Vols. 1 and 2. Ottawa: Association of Universities and Colleges of Canada, 1975.

Toronto Board of Education. *Workgroup on French Programs.* Toronto: Author, 1974.

______. *The Bias of Culture.* Issue Paper of the Workgroup on Multicultural Programs. Toronto: Author, 1974.

______. *Draft Report of the Workgroup on Multicultural Programs.* Toronto: Author, 1975.

______. *Final Report of the Workgroup on Multicultural Programs.* Toronto: Author, 1976.

______. *Report on Every Student Survey, 1976. A Supplement to the Every Student Survey (1975). A Profile by Administrative Area.* Toronto: Author, 1976.

______. French programs. *Education Toronto,* No. 14. Toronto: Author, 1978.

Vallee, F.G., *et al.* "Ethnic assimilation and differences in Canada." *The Canadian Journal of Economics and Political Science,* 28, no. 4 (1975), pp. 540–49.

Wirth, L. "The problem of minority groups," in R. Linton, ed., *The Science of Man in the World Crisis.* New York: Columbia University Press, 1945.

Witzel, A. *A Critical Bibliography of Materials on China.* Toronto: The Board of Education for the City of Toronto, Research Report No. 65, 1969.

French Immersion in Canada: Achievements and Directions

H.H. STERN

A Glance into the Past: The Immersion Story

ORIGINS, SOURCES, EARLY IMPETUS

An educational innovation is hardly ever the result of critical analysis, research and purely rational decision-making; rather, it is an expression of the hopes and aspirations of strong-minded people and their hunches, their determination, inventiveness and enthusiasm. The immersion story is no exception. It is a happy story; but it is also an unusual one. We can learn a great deal from its short history.

The initiative did not come from the professionals — teachers, psychologists, administrators — but from parents' groups. Of crucial importance to this particular innovation was the work of a small group of English-speaking parents who were active between 1963 and 1966, or thereabouts, in St. Lambert and who clamoured for some form of bilingual education for their young children. They were prompted primarily by a belief in the importance of bilingualism for Canada and a knowledge of French for their own and their children's future in Quebec. They initiated out-of-school French classes for their young children; they read about language teaching experiments elsewhere; they went into the theoretical arguments for an early start and consulted with such authorities as Drs. Penfield and Lambert; they lobbied the local administrators and politicians to set up experimental early French language classes for anglophone children. Eventually, out of the different parent initiatives, one small group — the St. Lambert Bilingual School Study Group, under the chairmanship of Olga Melikoff — guided and gave strength to the development of early immersion. If today we want to show appreciation for the beginnings of immersion and other forms of bilingual education in Canada and want to acknowledge the originators of this movement, this honour, in my view, must go to the St. Lambert parents' groups and particularly the St. Lambert Bilingual School Study Group.[1]

SOURCE: *The Canadian Modern Language Review/La Revue canadienne des langues vivantes,* 34, no. 5 (May 1978), pp. 836–54. Reprinted by permission of the Editor.

The St. Lambert parents presented two briefs — the first to their school board and the second a year or so later to the Quebec Minister of Education. In these briefs, they formulated the curriculum pattern for early French immersion and for continuing bilingual education which would extend throughout their children's schooling. These parents' groups talked about immersion into a "language bath" — a term that had been coined around 1960 by American language educators. The conception of immersion education developed by the St. Lambert parents has formed the basis of early immersion programs almost everywhere in Canada during the past ten or twelve years.[2]

Why immersion? Why early immersion in kindergarten? The roots lie in the educational innovations of the sixties, the world-wide interest in second-language learning, in the persuasive message of Penfield, in the American FLES movement and other early-language teaching experiments of the fifties, in the international schools in Europe, in the example of the Toronto French School, in Lambert's counterblast against the Cassandras of bilingualism — all this provided fuel to fire the initiative of the St. Lambert group. This extraordinarily active body of parents was able to gain the support of a principal and the acquiescence of the Quebec Ministry of Education for an immersion experiment in a public school setting. In retrospect, it is amazing that it happened at all; but once it did, it was fortunate that immersion was experimented within a public school and was therefore potentially significant not just for a fee-paying elite but for the ordinary child in the ordinary schools of the country.

Not only did this parents' group provide the lead in formulating the broad lines of curriculum; they also had the good sense at an early stage of the experiment to look for systematic evaluation. From the beginning, immersion was scrutinized by evaluative research, and what made it doubly fortunate was that this research was carried out with the skill and mastery of Lambert, Macnamara, Tucker and others in the Department of Psychology at McGill. The evaluative research on the first two St. Lambert immersion classes by Professor Lambert and his colleagues became the model for most of the subsequent evaluations of immersion programs.

The research reports which, from 1969, began to come out of the St. Lambert studies greatly influenced the spread of immersion.[3] The impetus everywhere was the same: the interest of parents' groups and educators to improve and strengthen French instruction for anglophones in a more radical way than was possible through a twenty-minute oral French program. The recent setting up of a new Canada-wide association, "Canadian Parents for French," indicates that this early impetus has not spent itself.

A by now familiar sequence of events repeated itself in many places:

1. a school board decides to set up an immersion class or classes on the basis of parental, school board or administrative initiative;
2. an immersion class teacher is appointed; a curriculum is developed, or, at times, improvised and put into operation;
3. in some instances, a research team is found and given the task of evaluating the effects of the project.

This is what happened on a large scale in Ontario and was soon to happen also on a more restricted scale in other provinces.

SPREAD TO ONTARIO

An oral French program — radical by the standards of the sixties, but modest from today's point of view — was introduced in Ottawa as early as the late fifties and in other parts of Ontario in the mid-sixties. However, the hoped-for bilingualism did not materialize. By about 1969, particularly in Ottawa, disappointed parents and school board trustees began to attack the school board administrations for being timid and half-hearted about French. The improvement of French became a political issue. Here again parents took the lead in urging the boards, particularly in Ottawa, but later also elsewhere, to follow the example of St. Lambert after the first results on immersion reported in the articles by Dr. Lambert and his colleagues had become known around 1969. Since the reports were positive and promising, it was argued, why not try the same in Ottawa where the demand for effective bilingualism was just as great as in Montreal?

Around 1970, some school boards in the Ottawa region tried to respond to these pressures, but the board officials were worried about what they were letting themselves in for. They, therefore, turned to universities and research institutes such as the University of Ottawa and OISE to get some help in evaluating these innovative programs, just as St. Lambert had turned to Dr. Lambert and his colleagues at McGill.

The immersion efforts in Ontario were at first concentrated in the Ottawa area. In 1969, the Ottawa Roman Catholic Separate School Board decided to institute immersion classes and Dr. Henry Edwards, the Dean of the Faculty of Psychology in the University of Ottawa, was asked to evaluate the program in the school system year by year from 1970. The Ottawa and Carleton public school boards began their experiments in 1970 and systematic evaluation started in 1971. They invited the OISE Modern Language Centre to evaluate their experimental immersion programs.

Aware of the need for a research and development approach to help school boards with these experiments, the OISE Modern Language Centre began its Bilingual Education Project in 1970. One of the first steps of this project was to arrange a conference in 1971 which brought together all the available knowledge and experience in immersion and other forms of bilingual education from kindergarten to university in Canada and the United States. The proceedings of this meeting, published in 1972 under the title of *Bilingual Schooling*, were edited by Dr. Merrill Swain who had just joined the Bilingual Education Project and who soon became its leading figure and director. *Bilingual Schooling* well describes the state of the art around 1971. Together with Dr. Heni Barik, another researcher and a former student of Dr. Lambert, and the rest of the OISE Bilingual Education Project team, Merrill Swain has undertaken the evaluation of a number of different immersion projects in Ontario from 1972 until today. The publications of the McGill group and other researchers in Montreal, of the OISE Bilingual Education Project, of the Ottawa and Carleton research teams, and a few other research reports from British Columbia and the Maritimes, constitute a solid body of material on immersion ranging from the mid-sixties until today.[4]

THE EXPANSION OF IMMERSION

Immersion has not only advanced through the grades; it has also spread geographically throughout the provinces. In 1974, the Department of the Secretary of State organized a federal-provincial conference on immersion in Halifax. It showed that immersion extended from Coquitlam in British Columbia to Fredericton, New Brunswick. It also made it evident that immersion had become part of the educational scene in Ottawa and Montreal; it was no longer a tentative experiment. It was available now to a much wider range of pupils, not only to the children of a limited number of middle-class parents. Furthermore, different types of immersion programs, for example, a "partial immersion" or bilingual program from grade one in Elgin County, a "late immersion" program in grade seven established by the Protestant School Board of Greater Montreal, and a "late immersion" program in grade eight initiated in 1971 in Peel County, illustrate promising departures from the St. Lambert type of program.

Meanwhile, some school boards also instituted a less radical extension of French; they increased the time available for the language and included one or two subjects to be taught in French, the so-called extended or intensive French programs.

Already as early as 1973, a definite pattern of results of immersion education became clear. It confirmed the encouraging findings summarized in a book by Lambert and Tucker in 1972. The learning of French was improved beyond anything that could normally be expected from conventional French instruction; mother tongue as well as general educational progress did not suffer; and such findings were not based on superficial impressions, but on "hard data" in which experimental immersion and regular classes had been systematically compared over two or three years in the same way as Lambert and his colleagues and students had done in St. Lambert since the mid-sixties.

However, a number of people continued to have misgivings about the very success of the immersion program and were concerned about the enthusiasm and partisanship that was aroused by immersion.

1. Some people mistrusted the optimistic results in the research reports. They feared that the tests were too insensitive to capture the possibly negative effects of immersion on cognitive or affective development in children.
2. Others, particularly administrators, mistrusted the "bandwagon effect" and the excessive enthusiasm aroused by immersion. Questions about long-term results and about the possibility of negative side effects began to be raised.
3. The practical problem of creating a minor French educational system for anglophones within an English-speaking system had unknown implications for school administration, teacher recruitment, and for English-speaking teachers within that system.
4. In some quarters there was a strong fear of a "backlash" against French.

Administrators, around 1973, were therefore in a dilemma between a poorly working core program of twenty minutes of oral French a day, and a supposedly highly effective program with all kinds of question marks. At this point in time, two events occurred, both of which helped in coming to grips with this issue:

1. The Ontario Ministry of Education set up a committee (the Gillin Committee) charged to review the entire position of French in Ontario and to make recommendations about future policy.
2. About the same time (1973), the federal government — eager to develop bilingualism — gave to Ontario the sum of two million dollars for one year for experimentation in teaching French in Ottawa schools because Ottawa, as the seat of the federal government, was felt by the authorities to be of essential importance to bilingualism in Canadian schools. Another two

million dollars was made available the following year. These grants enabled the four Boards of Education in the Ottawa area, in 1974–75, to try a variety of experiments in the teaching of French which ranged from minor changes in the regular French program to immersion at various levels.

The Ontario Ministry of Education was anxious that these French curriculum experiments should be properly evaluated. At the instigation of the Ministry, the four Boards, therefore, set up independent research teams to undertake this task. At the same time, the Ministry invited a research team at OISE to make a synthesis and overview of the entire research effort in Ottawa. In addition, early in 1976, after the two-year study had been completed, the Ministry invited three outstanding "guest analysts" as external evaluators, J.B. Carroll, Clare Burstall and Wilga Rivers, to review the experiments, the research reports of the Board teams as well as the OISE synthesis. The research teams, evaluators and administrators eventually all met in a colloquium in April of that year and made presentations on which the three guest analysts commented. The taped deliberations have been published as a special issue of the *Canadian Modern Language Review.*[5]

Once more, after this thorough vetting, the findings were favourable to the immersion solution. The Gillin Report and the Ottawa research reached more or less the same conclusion: immersion was recommended as one among several options for providing French in anglophone school systems, perhaps as the most promising option for those who wanted to achieve the highest level of French in school.

REVIEW OF MAIN FINDINGS

It is appropriate at this point to indicate briefly some of the main findings of immersion research. These have been stated on several occasions elsewhere but it is useful to remind ourselves of them to substantiate the claim that immersion works. Immersion has by and large met four main criteria of educators and administrators. At the same time we must not ignore open questions and unresolved issues.

Criterion 1: Everyone wants the children in school to learn more French than they have in the past.

Without question, children in immersion programs learn more French than students in extended or core programs. From the point of view of French, immersion has undoubtedly proved the most effective program wherever it occurs in the school system. However, it would be unjustifiable to claim that immersion leads quickly and painlessly to full bilingualism.

Criterion 2: Everyone would like to see children gain a positive outlook on the French language and a desire to communicate with French speakers.

Students in immersion programs seem to gain a more positive outlook on French than students in other programs. However, if I interpret the limited findings available correctly, a fair number of students continue to regard French as something within the school unless special steps are taken by schools, parents or the students themselves to bring the students into contact with francophones.[6] Occasionally, one comes across pleasing instances where this has happened. But my cautious interpretation to date is that immersion by itself has not become the simple bridge between the two solitudes. More must be done to strengthen opportunities for direct communication.

Criterion 3: No one wants the increase in French to be bought at the price of a loss in English.

Here research reports have been positive. Most studies of early immersion indicate a slight temporary loss in editorial skills of English language arts, e.g., punctuation, spelling, capitalization. Generally speaking, no long-term negative effects of immersion programs on English language skills have been identified; in some instances, the comparison even favours the immersion group.

Criterion 4: No one wants the increase in French to entail (a) a loss in general education in other subjects or (b) in the personal development of students.

In these two areas, too, findings are reassuring. Nothing decidedly negative or positive has come to light. Thus, as far as content learning in other subjects is concerned, a large number of data relating to different subjects (maths, social studies, geography, history, etc.) at various levels in the elementary school were summarized in one study as follows: "Students learn subject material taught to them in French and demonstrate achievement levels comparable to students taught the same subjects in English."[7]

In a forthcoming paper, Swain has analysed in detail aspects of the treatment of content subjects at the secondary stage, such as history, geography, science, mathematics and has concluded that "Immersion students sometimes scored as well as, sometimes better, sometimes worse than the English-instructed comparison groups on achievement tests related to content taught them in French."[8]

None of the fears that have sometimes been expressed about personal identity, cognitive confusion or emotional insecurity as a result of the immersion experience have been substantiated. Far from damaging cognitive development, immersion has been considered an intellectual challenge, particularly for younger children with possible cognitive and social benefits.

TEACHERS AND ADMINISTRATORS

So far, nothing has been said about immersion class teachers. It is a reflection of the immersion story; we have thought of the parents' groups that gave the impetus to the immersion experiment; we have identified some of the researchers who have analysed and evaluated the effect of immersion on children. But we have hardly mentioned the teachers who made this experiment work in the classroom day-by-day and assured its success. They have remained anonymous. It is good to see that they are now coming together in this Association and can make their collective voice heard. They have played a key role in this pioneer effort.

Most of the teachers are native speakers of French. Many have come from Quebec and other parts of French Canada. A number have come from the European francophonie, others from North Africa or other areas of the world francophonie. Some have previously taught oral French in elementary schools. Others have taught general subjects to native speakers of French. In the immersion programs, all of them have been faced with a novel situation. For some of them, the anglophone educational systems of Canada were a new experience to become familiar with. Each of them, whatever their origin or educational background, has to learn to play a new dual role of second-language teacher and general educator in French to mainly anglophone children. Organized teacher training for this new task is of very recent origin. In some cases no clearly defined program of school activities has been provided for the immersion teacher. We talk about the children being immersed into a language bath. What about the teachers who are plunged into a very unfamiliar and largely unknown educational bath? Much has been learned over the last ten years. It is part of the function of this Association, as I see it, to bring to light and share this experience on a national scale.

I hope that in the title of the Association "Immersion Teachers" includes those on whom classroom teaching has depended but who are not themselves in the immersion classroom all the time: principals, supervisors, administrators and other officials. In the immersion story, as, for example, told by Olga Melikoff, administrators appear as somewhat reluctant partners. Their caution, however, has been justified since they have had to work out the administrative and budgetary implications of this experiment and would have had to face the public indignation if immersion had failed. They have acquired a great deal of valuable practical knowhow on how to provide for immersion in a school system. Not only should their role be acknowledged, but I am glad to see from the workshop program that it is the intention of the Association to include administrative and cost factors among the range of ACPI/CAIT activities and interests.

REVIEW

Where other language-teaching experiments started hopefully, then floundered, and were finally almost viciously demolished — I'm thinking particularly of the audiolingual method but there are many other instances — immersion education has been the exception. It has firmly established itself within Canadian education. It can almost be considered a model of how one would wish an educational innovation to be instituted. This is largely due to the fact that it began with a bold but well thought out and well substantiated idea: the St. Lambert parents were bright and determined but they also did their homework. The regular and continuous association of skillful research with this experiment has been a help. Last, the combination of local, provincial and federal participation in planning the experiment with the public support of parents has been fortunate. One might almost say that anyone concerned with other educational changes, for example in the field of sport education or education in the arts and music, could learn much from the ten years of the immersion experiment on how to initiate, implement and evaluate an educational innovation.

New Directions

I would now like to suggest four areas which, in my view, need the Association's attention if immersion is to continue to make a positive impact on the educational scene:

1. It must clarify the relationship of immersion to other forms of language teaching.
2. It must monitor the quality of the second language development of students in immersion programs.
3. It must establish its future research and development emphases.
4. It must press for special teacher training for immersion.

1. IMMERSION AND OTHER FORMS OF LANGUAGE TEACHING

The terms immersion, full immersion, partial immersion, submersion, brutal immersion, gentle immersion, language bath and modified language bath are watery kinds of analogies. They are "fluid" also in the figurative sense: the concept "immersion" is not always clearly understood. As a result, immersion has been interpreted in different, even contradictory ways. It is not unimportant for an association which has the term "Immersion" in its title to be clear what distinguishes immersion from other forms of language teaching.

I would like at this point to introduce two sets of terms which, I hope, will help us to remove the ambiguity: the distinction between *formal* and *functional* strategies of teaching and learning a language. What I have called "formal" strategy has been called "linguistic classroom" or "instructional approaches" by others; and what I have called "functional" has been referred to also as "communicative language learning," "informal language learning," "natural" or "free" learning.

Take a child with one francophone and one anglophone parent; assume that both languages are spoken in that home: this child is likely to grow up bilingual. This and other fascinating and enviable instances of free, functional learning have prompted the idea of re-creating the same or similar conditions in an ordinary school context through immersion.

We can contrast this free or functional language learning approach with methods of second or foreign language teaching in the classroom. Here, the focus of attention is one the language itself, language as a code, on words, sentences, pronunciation, grammar rules and practice, exercises and drill. Questions are asked and answered, not because one has anything to communicate but as a means of developing skills which later would come into use.

This, then, is the formal strategy. It comprises the different methods of classroom language teaching with which you may or may not be familiar. But whether we use the audiolingual, the audiovisual or the cognitive methods, or whatever other classroom technique you may think of, the object of such teaching is to provide the students with practice *in* the language or with knowledge *about* the language. Most language teaching in the past and present has used these mainly formal strategies. Since World War Two, it has become customary, particularly in the language training of soldiers, to depart from the time-honoured one-hour language class, the common period of instruction in high schools, and to institute intensive, all-day language learning programs so as to speed up the student's progress in the foreign language. Government language training programs in Canada have also largely relied on this intensive approach. Such intensive courses have also been referred to as "immersion" programs. But they are different from the immersion programs as we know them in school; for the so-called immersion course in army or government language programs uses a mainly formal strategy.[9]

The school systems that have set up immersion programs following the St. Lambert model have instituted immersion with a mainly functional strategy. That is, they have tried to create situations in which the language is largely acquired through use in learning other school subjects.

To sum up, if an immersion program is conducted as an intensive language course, the teacher employs a formal strategy. If, on the other hand, the focus in the immersion program is on the subject taught and not language, for example, on social studies, mathematics or geography, then the strategy is functional; here the learning of language becomes incidental to language use.

Some theorists in recent years have gone far in condemning the formal strategy of second-language learning. They regard formal strategies as ineffective and even as theoretically unsound and instead recommend more emphasis on functional use; that is on learning a language by using it in real acts of communication.

In my view, this conflict has been overstated. I visualize the distinction between the formal and functional strategies not as mutually exclusive dichotomies, but as a continuum. At the extremes, of course, there is on one side the formal language class, occupied with language study and practice and nothing else; and at the other end, the class is entirely given over to a general curriculum, e.g., kindergarten activities or to a subject, e.g., history, with language purely used as a vehicle of teaching and learning.

But there are many gradations between these extremes. Teaching a language in a formal language class as a subject may involve talk, reading and listening of interest to pupils and teachers, in other words, real communication; thus a formal language lesson can become functional. At the other end, using the second language as a medium of communication in an immersion program may involve stopping and considering words or expressions, correcting language errors and giving linguistic explanations. The mainly functional immersion class has its formal side.

French immersion, as we have come to know it since the first St. Lambert kindergarten classes in 1965, has certain features which distinguish it from other forms of language teaching: (a) a substantial amount of educational time — it may be up to 100 per cent — is given to French; and (b) a substantial amount of that French time is spent on educational activities conducted *in* French rather than on the study *of* French per se.

Immersion defined in this way always has this dual aspect: French language combined with other educational content. Immersion teachers are not merely or mainly French-language teachers; they are educators who teach through the medium of French as a second language. An immersion class teacher may of course use both formal and functional strategies; but if a program is to qualify as an immersion program, the functional use of French, that is, using French as a medium of instruction or communication, must predominate.

On the basis of this analysis, immersion can now be related in a constructive way to other language programs. For example, the so-called extended French program has the same ingredients as the immersion program. But the total amount of French time is reduced compared to full immersion and the proportions of formal versus functional activities may be different.

The regular or core program is by definition intended to teach the language as a subject, and the formal approach may well be predominant; but that is no reason why this program should not also contain functional activities in which French is used as a means of communication or instruction.

Immersion may be organized as a distinct alternative to the regular or core program; it may be offered as a separate pathway through the school system; it may even be offered in a different specially designed school, a bilingual or immersion school. But another possibility is that it appears as a functional component or ingredient of the ordinary French language class, the core program.

We have become familiar with a number of variants of the immersion theme: early or late immersion, full or partial immersion, or extended French. Moreover, the immersion principle need not be limited to the classroom. The school environment itself, including the office of the principal and the administration, can become part of the immersion setting. An immersion class is usually understood to be an anglophone class with a francophone teacher; but a different form of bilingual education may include a mix of French and English students. Moreover, there are other patterns of alternating or combining cultures and languages. For example, the binational German-American John F. Kennedy School in Berlin, or certain bilingual education experiments in Australia use a much freer mix of languages than we are accustomed to in immersion.[10] In other words, the St. Lambert model which has been widely adopted, admirable as it is, is only one of several ways of providing immersion or bilingual education. . . .

2. LANGUAGE DEVELOPMENT IN IMMERSION

Immersion programs were prompted by the hope and expectation that they would make children "bilingual," in any case that they would lead to a much more substantial knowledge of French than was achieved in conventional programs. This hope has been met. Ordinary classroom observation and extensive testing programs show that the immersed student knows more French than students in other types of programs.

Consider some tests of reading and listening comprehension that have recently been devised by the OISE Bilingual Education Project for grade six immersion students. The reading test includes, for example, French newspaper clippings of the kind that interest youngsters followed by multiple choice questions in French about these clippings. The listening test includes unaltered French radio recordings, for example, a newscast, a sportscast, a radio advertisement and a weather forecast, followed by questions asked in French. The result of these tests have not yet been completely worked out; but preliminary findings indicate that grade six immersion students can cope with these demanding tasks very adequately. We don't know yet how conventionally taught students at grade six level would perform on the same tests; my guess is that these tests would be very demanding for them and for a good many students, even at more advanced stages of schooling, they would be completely out of range.

These results on the receptive use of French are gratifying for the immersion approach; but they must be looked at in conjunction with other findings on the productive use of language at this stage.

Take some grade six French immersion children with six or seven years of French behind them and, as Spilka has done, show them a short silent film of approximately twenty minutes' duration and ask them to tell the story of the film to a French-speaking child of the same age; these immersion students can perform this task and convey meaning adequately to the francophone child, but their speech is relatively slow and halting and they make many mistakes: they are hampered in their speech by words and expressions they don't know.[11]

In a similar study, Harley and Swain have recently analysed the mastery of the French verb system by five immersion class children in their sixth year of French as it appeared in an interview situation and compared it with the verb system of francophone children of the same age interviewed in similar circumstances. The five immersion children, like the francophones, were able to sustain twenty to twenty-five minutes of conversation with a sympathetic francophone interviewer. This is indeed a positive result and corresponds to the achievement of Spilka's children who were able to explain a film to someone who had not seen it. Yet, their responses, although understandable to the interviewer, contained many errors, hesitations and, in some cases, English expressions. These results are in keeping with what one would expect from our general knowledge about language acquisition and second-language learning.

However, the question we should now ask is no longer: "How much better is immersion French than the French of students conventionally taught?," rather it should be: "What levels can reasonably be expected after one, two, three or more years of immersion?"; "Is the level of French reached after a given number of years of immersion the best that can be attained in this type of program, or could it be further improved?"; "For how long is the superior level of French reached maintained after the program has ceased?"; "What level of French in speech, reading, comprehension, and writing is adequate to undertake all the complex mental operations that are demanded by different school subjects taught in French?"[12] We must remember that students who have gone through an immersion program eventually should be able to receive part of their further schooling, professional or university education through the medium of French. Could they cope with it satisfactorily? If not, are there ways in which the immersion program can be strengthened so that it will meet these objectives?

It would be a disservice to immersion education if we looked at the language performance of immersion students through rose-coloured spectacles. Instead, we should give full support to the kinds of research on the language and cognitive development of the immersion student, illustrated by the studies I have referred to. We should carefully examine the findings of such studies and consider what they imply for the pedagogy of the immersion class. Such studies can also help us to define reasonable expectations. Furthermore, teaching experiments are needed exploring ways and means of helping immersion students to move on to, and maintain, levels of French proficiency which clearly meet the educational and communicative demands that are expected as the desirable outcome of immersion programs.

3. RESEARCH AND DEVELOPMENT EMPHASIS

The immersion experiment has been fortunate in arousing the interest of a number of linguists, psycholinguists and educational researchers and, as we have seen, it has been the subject of a good many research and evaluation studies. This has been valuable and has helped in the critical analysis of the immersion approach. It has given reassurance to parents, administrators, educators and politicians. It has played an important role in the spread of immersion. Indeed, it was vividly shown at the Research Conference on immersion in Montreal in November 1975 that new research questions are asked by the investigators, indicating that the research approach is alive and has not become a routine merely to allay the misgivings of administrators and the public.[13]

But while immersion has already been well served with research support, the financial and human resources that have gone into *curriculum development for immersion classes* have been much more modest. In many instances, immersion teachers have been left to their own devices; they've been abruptly plunged into the immersion-class "bath" and have had to improvise a curriculum without receiving sufficient resources or much help. There are, of course, exceptions to this rule. Here in Ottawa, for example, valuable work has been done in curriculum development. The list of materials in different subject areas, collected from the experience of a number of immersion experiments in Ottawa that the OISE team has been able to publish in 1976 as an appendix to the final report on the Ottawa evaluation of immersion, is impressive in size and scope.[14] A materials evaluation survey of the OISE Bilingual Education Project, recently published, provides further evidence of the strides that have been made in curriculum development.[15]

Much more, however, needs to be done systematically at all levels of education at which immersion or bilingual programs are offered, particularly so for late immersion programs which have so far received too little attention from the curriculum developers. If you agree with me in this, the Association would put a great deal of emphasis on curriculum research and development, program experimentation and formative curriculum evaluation.

This task has to my mind been underrated. If an immersion or bilingual education curriculum is to respond to the full potential of this type of education, it should be guided by at least four considerations:

1. The immersion curriculum must aim to be fully equivalent to its English counterpart; it must not be an impoverished pastiche. I am not implying that today's immersion courses are not equivalent. I am merely trying to indicate general principles to guide us. If mathematics or history are to be studied in French, the information content and the intellectual skills brought into play should be equal to the best corresponding programs in English.

2. However, a history course of studies in French immersion should not be merely a translation of the English history course. It should offer more than that: while the framework and overall objective may be the same as that covered by the English guideline, it should also be inspired by sources and resources taken from Francophone education in Canada, France, Belgium, Switzerland and other francophone countries. What is needed — subject by subject — is a reinterpretation of curricula and materials in Canadian terms, enriched by a French ingredient or a French

perspective. This may in many instances involve a lot of rethinking and rewriting of materials, or writing new materials altogether.

3. In the same way, it is not possible simply to take a textbook produced for French native speakers in France, Belgium or Quebec and to assume that it can be used without adaptation in an immersion setting.

4. Any curriculum preparation for immersion must further bear in mind that the learner is studying the subject matter in a second language, that he needs to acquire the use of language specific to the area of study. Much of the recent work that has been done on *languages for special purposes* (LSP), particularly in Europe, is relevant. The LSP approach is mainly intended for language use in the professions, e.g., engineering and medicine, but it has important lessons for the preparation of curriculum materials in French for immersion programs.[16]

If immersion is to be a truly alternative form of education and a genuine equivalent to schooling in English, curriculum development must be done at all levels, the kindergarten, the primary grades, junior and intermediate grades, and in selected subjects at senior high school level.

4. THE EDUCATION OF THE IMMERSION TEACHER

From what has been said about immersion, about language growth in immersion classes, and the curriculum of immersion programs, it should be clear that the immersion teacher has a demanding and very specialized task to fulfill. It is because of this specific role that, I believe, it is justified to create an Association for French immersion teachers.

As was already pointed out, a French immersion teacher is not simply a French language teacher. He or she is primarily an educator who teaches children at a given level of education, e.g., in kindergarten or grade one, two, and so on, or in a given subject area, e.g., mathematics or science. Since these teachers teach anglophone children, they must also possess the skills of second language teachers.

Since they must combine the qualities of general educators with those of second-language teachers, this combination will make special demands on the training of immersion class teachers. Ideally, a teacher should:

1. be a good practitioner at the educational level and in the subject area(s) for which he or she is responsible;

2. be bilingual, with a nativelike command of French but with sufficient knowledge of English to understand the language background and problems of the students, and an ability to speak

English in an emergency and to communicate with anglophone colleagues or parents;

3. be able to represent Francophone culture;
4. understand the culture and the educational methods of the system in which he or she works;
5. understand the language development of children and the specific nature of bilingual education.

The curriculum of teacher education for immersion and bilingual education follows from the above considerations. It should include the following components:

1. general educational studies and studies on the special problems of immersion students;
2. educational specialization for a level (e.g., kindergarten), or a subject (e.g., history, social studies, mathematics) and a study of the problems of teaching this specialization under conditions of immersion;
3. studies on language development, bilingualism and second-language learning and their relevance to immersion;
4. second-language methodology and immersion as a special approach to second-language learning.

It seems to me that immersion teacher training should be available as a form of preservice and inservice education in conjunction with other teacher training facilities. Ministries of education and teachers' colleges are increasingly conscious of this need. Since one essential condition of immersion education is a nativelike command of French, it is likely that most immersion teachers will be native speakers. But the opportunity should be offered to non-native speakers to improve their French so that they can also teach in immersion programs. Hence, the training itself should be an experience in immersion or bilingual education.

One excellent suggestion recently made to me is that high school teachers who teach French and a second subject, e.g., history, should be offered the opportunity to receive inservice training so that they can teach this second subject, history, in French. This would greatly strengthen the bilingual potential of high schools.

Conclusion

The experience of immersion has largely been gained over the past twelve years in French immersion in school settings. I regard it as one of the, perhaps *the* most significant, contribution that Canada has made in the field of second-language education.

The applications and implications of this experience are far-reaching. Immersion is not confined to kindergarten and the early years of schooling. I personally would like to see more immersion-type bilingual schooling at the high school level. Here it could be strengthened if incentives were offered, e.g., if additional credits were given to taking a subject successfully in the second language. Moreover, teachers who teach subjects other than French bilingually should qualify for a special bilingual allowance.

Equally, the opportunities for bilingual education in adult and higher education at universities, in business education, in engineering, theology, law, medicine, etc., are possibilities that have not yet been adequately explored. But they are needed if Canada is to continue to strengthen its French language capabilities and opportunities.

In this context, it would seem to me important for this new Association to make contact with bodies and associations, particularly at the national level, which promote different aspects of education and curriculum, e.g., early childhood education, the teaching of reading, or the teaching of different subjects, such as mathematics or history, as well as associations which promote the education of francophone minorities. In this way, immersion education will remain abreast of current thought and practice in education generally. Moreover, in national educational associations, immersion educators can form a valuable link between francophone and anglophone educators.

The immersion alternative has been developed as an approach to the learning of French by anglophones in Canada, and the tacit assumption of ACPI/CAIT is that we are concerned with French immersion for anglophones. However, the immersion message has also something to offer to other second-language situations. For example, in the early seventies, I made a recommendation to the Gendron Commission favouring a trilingual immersion type program as a solution for ethnic minority education in Quebec.[17] These minorities had recognized the need for learning French as the principal language in Quebec and English as the majority language of Canada and North America generally, and they wished simultaneously to maintain an ethnic language. The French immersion approach may have implications for the education of those French minorities in English-speaking parts of Canada where the mother tongue heritage has been weakened by prolonged contact with the anglophone majority language and culture. I am thinking, for example, of certain Franco-Ontarian and Franco-Manitoban districts. I am also convinced that eventually in Quebec, where at present the primary concern is the maintenance of French, the advantages of a dual language command will lead to an interest in English immersion programs for francophones. In many other countries which use a world language as a medium of instruction, or as a medium of national and international communication, English, French, Hindi, Arabic or Swahili, immersion programs or an immersion component might well be considered as a practical solution. There is no doubt that the immersion option as a form of bilingual education is gaining international recognition.

The field of activity for this Association, then, is considerable. Let me end on a note of caution. Immersion over the last twelve years has had an excellent record as an educational innovation and for its evaluative research. This is no reason to treat other approaches to language learning lightly. Some people have been so stunned by the success of immersion that they treat it as the ultimate answer to the entire language teaching problem, especially for Canada. For them, immersion is the only solution and traditional classroom teaching a relic of the past.

My conviction is that classroom language learning, especially if it is combined with short-term immersion-type experiences, can be very effective. If immersion demonstrates the effectiveness of a functional approach to language learning, this approach can become a valuable component in most forms of language teaching. It is all the more important that this association will seek to cooperate with other associations of language teachers. I know that such bodies as the Canadian Association of Second Language Teachers and the Ontario Modern Language Teachers' Association are sympathetic to immersion, provided immersion is not treated as the only valid approach to second-language learning.

It must be remembered that immersion, even partial immersion, demands fairly radical changes in educational provision, and not all educational systems are prepared to make them nor is it practical in all instances of second-language learning. It is a false dichotomy to think of immersion as right and successful and classroom language teaching as wrong and inevitably unsuccessful. All forms of language teaching in schools settings — immersion and non-immersion alike — are to a certain extent artificial and have their limitations; they all can be more or less successful; none has a monopoly of virtue; they all can involve both formal and functional strategies of teaching and learning. It is important to explore the most economical and most effective combinations of these strategies and this requires coordination of different approaches to language learning.

Once we adopt the immersion solution, it is important to make sure that it is well done; because if it is not, it is not only French that suffers but the entire education of the child. This association, I hope, will not only strive for immersion, but also for excellence in immersion.

Notes

The following members of the OISE Modern Language Centre team have helped me in the composition of this paper by their insightful comments and suggestions: Birgit Harley, Sharon Lapkin, Merrill Swain and Alice Weinrib. Henri Barik supplied me with recent data from the Bilingual Education Project testing program.

1. For an account of the early development of French immersion, see O. Melikoff's article, "Parents as Change Agents in Education: The St. Lambert Experiment," Appendix A in *Bilingual Education of Children*, W.E. Lambert and G.R. Tucker (Rowley, Mass: Newbury House Publishers, 1972), pp. 219–36. For some earlier international developments preceding the St. Lambert experiment, see H.H. Stern, *Foreign Languages in Primary Education: The Teaching of Foreign or Second Languages to Younger Children* (London: Oxford University Press, 1967) and H.H. Stern, ed., *Languages and the Young School Child* (London: Oxford University Press, 1969).
2. As Olga Melikoff has described it in her account of the beginnings of immersion: "the essence of the problem was how to increase the number of contact hours in French to attain fluency without sacrificing subject matter. The solution appeared to be sufficient exposure in the early grades to permit the teaching of any subject in either language in the higher grades.

   "It was felt that the skills required in learning to read and write were sufficiently similar in concept in both languages, so that learning them in French was essentially the same experience as learning them in English. Hence there was little or no hesitation in recommending French reading and writing before reading and writing in the mother tongue" (pp. 223–224).

   In their brief to the Quebec Minister of Education requesting a bilingual school in the city of St. Lambert, the study group outlines the now familiar pattern of immersion: "a bilingual curriculum (they argued) should be largely, if not totally, in the second language in the first few years to hasten the goal of a balanced bilingualism and take advantage of the special capacities of young children in language learning. Ideally, a nursery school and kindergarten should be entirely in the second language and Grades One and Two, largely in the second language . . .

   "After the primary cycle, when the second language should be at a fairly high level, teaching time could be balanced between the two languages. The subjects studied in each language could be rotated through the years in order to achieve a balanced vocabulary."
3. W.E. Lambert and J. Macnamara, "Some Cognitive Consequences of Following a First-Grade Curriculum in a Second Language," *Journal of Educational Psychology*, 60 (1969), pp. 86–96. See also Lambert and Tucker, *Bilingual Education*.
4. For reviews of the various projects and bibliographical references to numerous studies see three special issues of the *Canadian Modern Language Review:* A. Mollica, ed., "Bilingualism in Education," 31, no. 2 (1974); M. Swain and M. Bruck (Guest Editors) "Immersion Education for the Majority Child," 32, no. 5 (1976); B. Harley (Guest Editor),

"Alternative Programs for Teaching French as a Second Language in the Schools of the Carleton and Ottawa School Boards," 33, no. 2 (1976).

5. Ibid.
6. M. Bruck, W.E. Lambert and G.R. Tucker, "Assessing Functional Bilingualism Within a Bilingual Program: The St. Lambert Project at Grade Eight," mimeographed (Montreal: McGill University, 1975).
7. H.H. Stern et al., *Three Approaches to Teaching French: Evaluation and Overview Studies Related to the Federally-Funded Extensions of the Second Language Learning (French) Programs in the Carleton and Ottawa School Boards* (Toronto: Ontario Ministry of Education, 1976).
8. M. Swain, "L2 and Content Learning: A Canadian Bilingual Education Program at the Secondary Grade Levels," in *Language Development in a Bilingual Setting* ed. E. Brière. Los Angeles: National Dissemination and Assessment Centre, 1979, pp. 113–120.
9. For a discussion of some terms, e.g., bilingualism, bilingual education, immersion see H.H. Stern, *Study E7: Report on Bilingual Education* (Quebec: The Quebec Official Publisher, 1973).
10. W.F. Mackey, *Bilingual Education in a Binational School: A Study of Equal Language Maintenance Through Free Alternation* (Rowley, Mass.: Newbury House Publishers, 1972); M. Rado, ed., *Bilingual Education* (Bundoora, Victoria: Occasional Paper from the Centre for the Study of Teaching, La Trobe University School of Education, 1974).
11. I.V. Spilka, "Assessment of Second-Language Performance in Immersion Programs," in Swain and Bruck, "Immersion Education," pp. 543–61; B. Harley and M. Swain, "An Analysis of the Verb System Used by Young Learners of French," *Interlanguage Studies Bulletin 3,* 1 (1978).
12. J. Cummins, "Psycholinguistic evidence" in Bilingual Education: Current Perspectives (Vol. 4), Education (Arlington, Virginia: Centre for Applied Linguistics, 1977).
13. Swain and Bruck, "Immersion Education."
14. Stern *et al., Three Approaches to Teaching French*.
15. Enquiries about this survey should be addressed to the Bilingual Education Project, Modern Language Centre, The Ontario Institute for Studies in Education, 252 Bloor Street West, Toronto, Ontario, M5S 1V6.
16. For a helpful and comprehensive review on teaching languages for special purposes, see P. Strevens, "Special-Purpose Language Learning: A Perspective," *"Language Teaching and Linguistics: Abstracts,"* 10 (1977), 145–163.
17. H.H. Stern, *Study E7: Report on Bilingual Education* (Quebec: The Quebec Official Publisher, 1973).

References

Mackey, W.F. *Bilinguisme et Contact des Langues.* Paris: Editions Klincksieck, 1976.

Ontario Ministry of Education. *Report of the Ministerial Committee on the Teaching of French* (Gillin Report). Toronto: Ontario Ministry of Education, 1974.

Swain, M., ed. *Bilingual Schooling: Some Experiences in Canada and the United States.* Toronto: The Ontario Institute for Studies in Education, 1972.

The Vertical Mosaic in Flux: Ethnicity and Education in Urban Canada, 1951–1971

EDWARD N. HERBERG

There are a variety of factors, in part external to any ethnic group, that influence its pattern of cultural adaptation in the Canadian social milieu. These include the number of people in a geographic area that identify themselves, or are identified by others, with the ethnic group; the proportion that the group members made up of the entire areal population; the cultural and demographic histories of a group in the area; and the strength or cohesion of ethno-racial-religious bonds within a particular group at any time or geographic location.

Since education is generally considered to be an integrative force, providing youth and adults with "resources" for social and economic interaction in the arenas outside of the home and ethnic group, the nature of the linkage of education to the ethnic group becomes critical. Groups with high ethnocultural solidarity or low social acceptance by the majority/dominant ethnic group in the locale usually have been postulated to seek means other than formal education as entry mechanisms to attaining jobs, social relations, and such. It has also been postulated that groups with lower ethnocultural solidarity in a particular locale would readily seize a formal education as a means to assure their socio-economic success.

The other side of this conceptual coin is that inward-directed ethnicities with high cohesion have been postulated to have an antithetical relationship with formal education, especially higher education. This is because of the well-documented history of the public (including the separate) schools actively or implicitly "Canadianizing" their students, and even their students' parents. Even were this not actually the case in recent years, should members of minority ethno-racial-religious groups perceive the schools as a

SOURCE: This is a revised version of a paper presented at the Ninth Biennial Conference of the Canadian Ethnic Studies Association, Edmonton, Alberta, October 1981. Published by permission of the author.

source of de-ethnitizing influence — of having the result of tearing their children away from their cultural heritage and assimilating youth to "Canadian" values and practices — formal education of their children beyond basic literacy would still be eschewed, as a defensive mechanism in order to assure maintenance of the ethnic culture in later generations.

In addition, members of inward-directed Canadian ethnicities may not perceive any significant social-economic benefits to derive from education beyond basic literacy. Many members of these groups, pointing to their own economic success in Canada despite their meagre formal education, characterize the completion of secondary school and especially the attendance at post-secondary facilities as requiring years that could more profitably be expended in establishing youth in their future vocations and marriages. Such time in furthering education would be viewed, according to some, as withholding valuable social and economic production from the family and ethnic collectivity.

It is just this theorized relationship between the implicit or explicit orientation in a group's culture in Canada to formal education that Porter and others have suggested is the basis of social inequality, and comprises a stable social dynamic in Canada. The often-mentioned Jewish predilection for acquiring formal education and the frequent citation that the British group is the top of the educational (and socioeconomic) hierarchy are but two examples of this ethnic equation. Most, furthermore, assume that because of discrimination or ethnic predisposition, or both, visible minority groups in Canada are in the educational basement. Or, to put it another way, the "ethclass" theory as formulated by Porter (1965, 1979) and Isajiw (1975) predicts either that an ethnicity with high solidarity is almost immutably antithetical to achieving high formal education, or that the low level of schooling a group collectively possesses relegates them and their children to the lower steps in the socioeconomic hierarchy in Canada.

In contrast, however, the ethnic connection to formal education can be conceptualized as merely one dynamic among many that should be carefully inspected to ascertain exactly what is the pattern of ethno-racial-religious group adaptation to Canada over time, and to the changes Canadians have experienced. That is, one can transform the ethclass theorem into a hypothesis to be tested. For example, it can be hypothesized that the function formal education actually varies from group to group and even within the same group in different locales. Further, one can hypothesize that some groups possessing *high* ethnic solidarity will be positively oriented to formal education (for reasons unique to the group), while the majority of such groups will be negatively oriented to formal education. Adopting such a relativist perspective casts formal schooling within inward-directed ethnicities as less relevant to economic success than early entry into the economy combined with "hard work." Conversely, it can also be hypothesized that some outward-oriented groups with *low* ethnocultural solidarity may be little inclined to perceive formal education as the engine of social mobility, while the majority of such groups will conform to the more usual education-success equation.

The ethnic relativity conceptualization has more profound implications than this, however. What holds for an ethnic group in a particular locale and/or time may not hold for the same group in another time or place. Conditions, for example, both within and outside the groups may have varied in the past by locale and date and continue to do so in the present. Thus, the utilization of education by, say, Italians in Toronto may well be different than that of Italians in Vancouver or Halifax or Montreal. Likewise, the educational standing of one group in the Toronto of 1951 may well be different than that of the Toronto group in 1971 or 1981.

The relativity formulation also infers that each ethno-racial-religious group must be examined as an independent entity in itself rather than being seen in comparison with the so-called British or French charter groups — an approach that still comprises the central theme of ethnic studies today. In effect, therefore, the British (that is, the English, Irish, Scots and Welsh) group becomes just one (or more accurately four) among Canada's ethnocultural groups, each possessing a different history, tradition and set of ethnic group dynamics. This reformulation, moreover, would not only reduce or eliminate the practice of using the British or French groups as a standard against which other groups are measured, it would likewise mitigate the practice of aggregating many ethnic groups into a "non-charter" category and would encourage the view that each ethnic group possessed equal theoretical and empirical status with the British and French ethnic groups.

The multiple aspects of the relativistic principle discussed here may be characterized via the metaphor of the "ethnic looking-glass theory," as suggested by the following passage from Lewis Carroll's *Through the Looking-Glass:*

> . . . I'll tell you all my ideas about Looking-glass House. First, there's the room you can see through the glass — that's the same as our drawing-room, only the things go the other way. . . . I want so much to know whether they've a fire in the winter: you never *can* tell, you know, unless our fire smokes, and then smoke comes up in our room too — but that may be only pretence, just to make it look as if they had a fire. Well then, the books are something like our books, only the words go

> the wrong way. . . . You can just see, only you know it may be quite different beyond — how nice it would be if we could only get through into Looking-glass House! I'm sure it's got, oh! such beautiful things in it!

This article focuses (a) on the educational attainment of adults between 1951 and 1971[1] and (b) the educational attendance of youth -young adults in 1971 across thirteen ethno-racial-religious groups in *each* of five cities: Halifax, Montreal, Toronto, Winnipeg and Vancouver. The thirteen groups were selected because of the variations they represent in cultural, racial and religious dimensions as well as differing history and distribution across Canada. Similarly, the five cities represent quite different types of ethnic group mixture and numerical and social dominance, different sizes and geographic locations. Taken together, data on the thirteen groups in five cities offer an opportunity to examine many of the ethnic and urban variations that one might consider to influence either ethnic group dynamics or the historical-cultural meld in communities, and, in turn, educational statuses.

The data were drawn almost entirely from Canada census information: published reports from the 1951 through 1971 censuses, unpublished tabulations from these censuses, and special analyses conducted for me by Statistics Canada from the 1971 census. The relevant persons in 1971 are all those aged 20 years or older (adults) who were counted as residents of each city for the 1971 census, and all youth aged 15-24 years who were categorized as residing in their parental/guardian's home.[2] In total, data on 1,725,240 adults and 256,785 youth in the thirteen ethnicities in the five cities were analysed. The city as opposed to metropolitan levels of analysis was selected because it is generally the municipal level of government that has most impact on educational policies and practices.

Unfortunately for the purposes of the present study, Statistics Canada persists in refusing access to individual data from the censuses. Therefore, rather than using the Public Use Sample of the census with its much smaller number of cases (a 1 per cent sample which would overly constrain the depth of analysis desired), an analysis has been used based on the level of education and other characteristics in each of 650 "strata" of 13 ethnic groups x 2 genders x 5 generation-immigration categories x 5 cities. Though concern may be expressed over the use of collective data — the so-called ecological fallacy — recent evidence indicates that little, if any, misrepresentation of individually based patterns derives from the analysis of aggregate information (see Herberg, 1980, pp. 218 -25).

For the adults in the sample, the two sets of educational outcome measures are (a) the mean years of education within each group in each city, and (b) the percentage of the group possessing post-secondary education. For the youth–young adult population, educational outcome is defined as the percentage of the group's cohort attending an educational facility. By dint of the ages covered, 15 to 24 years, the schooling level to which this measure refers is from grade 9 through post-secondary programs.

Changes in Ethnic Adults' Educational Attainment

In this section, three analytical foci on shifts in the educational attainment of ethnic adults are followed. The first compares educational levels (average education or percentage with post-secondary) in 1951, 1961 and 1971, controlling for ethno-racial-religious group and city; the second examines the relative educational standing (rank) of each group in each city in 1951 and 1961 compared to 1971; and the third looks at the shifts as an index of change in education between 1951 and 1971.

Regardless of educational outcome, measure or analytic focus, three dominant patterns characterize ethnic group education in the period 1951–1971: there is wide variation between cities, even within the same group, there is equally wide variation between ethnicities, even within the same city; and remarkable shifts in the education of ethnic groups have occurred.

MEAN YEARS EDUCATION

Table 1 sets out the mean years of formal education attained by adults in each of the thirteen ethnic groups in the five cities from 1951 to 1971. Here we can see that the visible minority groups have made the largest gains, while the British and Italians have benefited least. In part, the small improvement by the British group can be explained by their relatively high 1951 level of schooling. However, as subsequent analysis will show, despite their high educational level in 1951, their performance over the next twenty years resulted in the attainment of the British group falling below that of several other groups in 1971.[3]

ETHNIC GROUP RANKINGS

The relative rank of each ethnic group's mean educational attainment by city and year is contained in Table 2. It is quite obvious that the two charter groups (British and French) and most of the long-resident white ethnicities (Germans, Scandinavians and Ukrainians, and probably Jews as well) occupied a much lower position on the educational ladder in 1971 than they did in 1951. Conversely, several

TABLE 1: Mean Years Educational Attainment in the Five Cities, by Ethno-racial-religious Group 1951 –1971

		Black	*British*	*Chinese*	*East Indian*	*French*	*German*	*Greek*	*Italian*	*Japanese*	*Jewish*	*Portuguese*	*Scandinavian*	*Ukrainian*	*Entire city*
Halifax:	1951	6.0	9.3	3.3	6.6#	8.0	9.0	*	8.8	6.6	10.0	*	9.1	9.7	9.1
	1961	6.7	8.3	5.2	6.8	7.2	8.3	*	6.4	6.9	9.1	*	8.3	8.3	8.1
	1971	9.7	11.0	10.6	15.4	10.0	11.3	9.4	9.9	13.9	12.9	10.9	11.8	12.2	10.9
Montreal:	1951	*	9.1	5.1	6.3	7.6	9.1	*	6.1	7.9	8.1	*	9.7	6.5	7.9
	1961	*	8.8	4.4	8.0	6.7	9.1	*	4.5	9.2	8.5	*	9.3	6.4	7.1
	1971	12.0	10.4	9.2	14.3	8.9	11.0	7.6	6.5	12.2	10.3	6.1	11.6	8.6	9.1
Toronto:	1951	*	9.5	4.5	7.9	8.4	9.4	*	6.7	7.7	7.5	*	9.6	7.0	9.0
	1961	*	8.4	4.4	8.6	6.9	8.2	*	4.1	8.3	7.2	*	8.7	6.6	7.5
	1971	11.3	11.4	9.8	14.5	10.0	11.8	7.7	6.3	11.7	12.2	5.7	12.2	9.1	10.3
Winnipeg:	1951	*	9.5	4.7	6.5	7.8	7.6	*	7.3	6.9	8.2	*	8.6	6.7	8.5
	1961	*	8.9	4.5	8.1	6.8	7.2	*	5.6	7.8	8.8	*	8.3	6.6	7.8
	1971	11.5	10.9	10.5	15.2	9.3	9.8	8.5	7.4	10.5	11.0	6.1	10.5	8.6	10.0
Vancouver:	1951	*	9.7	4.1	5.3	8.8	8.4	*	6.2	7.3	9.8	*	8.5	7.6	9.2
	1961	*	9.1	4.6	6.3	8.1	7.7	*	5.5	7.9	9.7	*	8.2	7.0	8.4
	1971	12.5	11.6	8.5	10.6	10.7	10.8	9.0	8.1	11.4	12.7	7.3	10.8	9.5	10.9

Notes: *No data.

#In the 1951 Halifax census data, East Indians and Japanese were subsumed under a generic category of "Other Asians."

of the non-white groups have moved much higher up the ladder in the same period: for example, Blacks, East Indians and Japanese possessed much higher 1971 rankings than in 1951 and had surpassed most other groups in terms of educational attainment.[4] Every group, as can be seen, experienced a change in relative educational standings. The British, French, Italian and Ukrainian groups experienced the greatest *relative* decline in educational attainment levels (the Germans and Jews tended to experience less of a shift), while those of the visible minorities increased.

Those white ethnic groups that had increased their numbers considerably via immigration since 1951 (Greek, Italian and Portuguese) occupied the lowest rungs of the educational ladder in 1971. Yet the visible minorities which also have increased their numbers greatly by immigration clustered around the top of the rankings. Blacks in Halifax and Toronto, Chinese in all five cities, and Vancouver East Indians are exceptions to this pattern.

Probably the most startling and deepest shift in educational status has been that experienced by the British group. In 1951 this group occupied the highest or second-highest ranking in three cities and never fell below third rank in any of the five. By 1971, however, only in Vancouver did the British place third — and even there being third represents a slight decline. East from Toronto, the average education of the British group tumbled while that of East Indians, Japanese, Jews (and in three of the five cities, Blacks) increased considerably. These shifts in the educational hierarchy, it is worth emphasizing, contrast sharply with the rankings Porter observed immediately following the Second World War. Also worthy of note is the strong regional basis of the British group's pattern of decline, which is greatest in the east and least in the west.

POST-SECONDARY EDUCATION

This measure of adult education, as Table 3 indicates, carries much sharper patterns of variation than either of the previous two measures. For example, differences both between ethnic groups in the same city and within them across the five cities are much greater in terms of the percentages possessing any amount of post-secondary education. Changes within and between groups from 1951 to 1971 are also accentuated more than they were for the average education data. Note, too, the immense increase in the percentage of every group (on which data exists), in every city between 1951 and 1971 possessing at least some higher education, and the impact of extensive immigration in the decade following 1951 in terms of a decline in rank position, in almost all instances, for Canada's "white ethnics" but not for the visible minorities. The latter, it can be seen, achieved slight

TABLE 2: Educational Rank of Ethno-Racial-Religious Group's Mean Educational Attainment

		Black	*British*	*Chinese*	*East Indian*	*French*	*German*	*Greek*	*Italian*	*Japanese*	*Jewish*	*Portuguese*	*Scandinavian*	*Ukrainian*
Halifax:	1951	10	3	11	8.5	7	5	*	6	8.5	1	*	4	2
	1961	9	3.5	11	8	6	3.5	*	10	7	1	*	3.5	3.5
	1971	11	7	9	1	10	6	13	12	2	3	8	5	4
Montreal:	1951	*	2.5	10	8	6	2.5	*	9	5	4	*	1	7
	1961	*	4	10	6	7	3	*	9	2	5	*	1	8
	1971	3	6	8	1	9	5	11	12	2	7	13	4	10
Toronto:	1951	*	2	10	5	4	3	*	9	6	7	*	1	8
	1961	*	3	9	2	7	5	*	10	4	6	*	1	8
	1971	7	6	9	1	8	4	11	12	5	2.5	13	2.5	10
Winnipeg:	1951	*	1	10	9	4	5	*	6	7	3	*	2	8
	1961	*	1	10	4	7	6	*	9	5	2	*	3	8
	1971	2	4	6	1	9	8	11	12	6	3	13	6	10
Vancouver:	1951	*	2	10	9	3	5	*	8	7	1	*	4	6
	1961	*	2	10	8	4	6	*	9	5	1	*	3	7
	1971	2	3	11	8	7	5.5	10	12	4	1	13	5.5	9

Notes: *No data.

Rank 1 = the highest rank; 11 (for 1951 and 1961) or 13 (for 1971), the lowest.

to marked increases in the share of their members with advanced schooling.

EDUCATIONAL RANK

The information contained in Table 4 on the post-secondary educational rank of each group powerfully substantiates the trends obtaining for average educational levels. With the sole exception of the Jewish group, the relative educational standings for all white ethnic groups in virtually every city dropped markedly, particularly between 1961 and 1971. On the other hand, for East Indians, the Japanese in cities other than Toronto and Winnipeg, and the Chinese outside of Montreal and Vancouver, the trend is upward mobility from middle or lower rankings to much higher and often the high positions. In addition, if we posit that in 1951 relatively few Blacks possessed post-secondary experience, then their position in 1971 also represents a considerable improvement, except in Halifax.

The British group, conversely, which possessed high amounts of post-secondary education in 1951 and 1961, had dropped to middle or even lower rankings by 1971. In some cities, the French and German groups experienced a similar loss in relative status. Significantly, it is in the cities where the British and French groups were numerically dominant in 1951 (Halifax, Toronto and Vancouver for the British and Montreal for the French) that they experienced the steepest declines. The decline was most precipitous in the eastern cities (including Toronto) where the British have formed the dominant group for well over two centuries, but was also reflected in Manitoba and British Columbia.

Clearly, a major cause of the British group's overall fall in the educational rankings is their great loss of position relative to other groups in the acquisition of post-secondary schooling. While the proportion of British, French and German groups with advanced training has increased at a relatively low rate, the visible minorities achieved at least a three fold increase in most cities. Thus to the extent that structural or institutional discrimination has been practised by the British majority group, it appears to have failed. Or alternatively, perhaps the British have not deemed it essential to retain their educational superiority. Whatever the explanation, the widening of educational opportunity since the 1950s has resulted in their possessing average or even inferior levels of education compared to a number of other ethnic groups, particularly the visible minority groups.

TABLE 3: Percentage with Post-secondary School Educational Attainment for the Five Cities, by Ethno-racial-religious Group, 1951 –1971

		Black	*British*	*Chinese*	*East Indian*	*French*	*German*	*Greek*	*Italian*	*Japanese*	*Jewish*	*Portuguese*	*Scandinavian*	*Ukrainian*	*Entire city*
Halifax:	1951	1	13	3	5#	6	10	*	11	5#	24	*	10	10	11
	1961	1	9	6	8	4	6	*	6	0	20	*	7	9	8
	1971	29	36	42	82	28	40	23	30	62	57	44	44	50	36
Montreal:	1951	*	12	6	5	6	16	*	3	8	9	*	18	5	7
	1961	*	10	5	13	4	10	*	1	18	12	*	15	6	5
	1971	44	31	28	73	19	39	12	10	46	32	7	46	24	21
Toronto:	1951	*	15	5	13	9	17	*	4	9	11	*	17	7	13
	1961	*	8	4	18	4	6	*	1	6	7	*	9	8	7
	1971	32	31	32	74	24	39	11	8	36	43	6	44	21	28
Winnipeg:	1951	*	11	3	3	5	4	*	4	5	12	*	8	3	8
	1961	*	10	3	17	4	4	*	2	7	19	*	7	4	7
	1971	41	29	42	56	19	24	15	12	25	40	7	28	17	25
Vancouver:	1951	*	13	3	8	9	7	*	5	6	20	*	7	4	12
	1961	*	10	4	9	7	6	*	2	7	22	*	7	4	7
	1971	47	32	24	40	28	33	19	14	34	49	10	28	21	31

Notes: 1951 statistics are for thirteen or more years education.

*No data.

#East Indian and Japanese were subsumed in the 1951 Halifax data under the generic category of "Other Asians".

TABLE 4: Educational Rank of Ethno-racial-religious Groups' Percentage with Post-Secondary Educational Attainment, by City of Residence and Year

		Black	*British*	*Chinese*	*East Indian*	*French*	*German*	*Greek*	*Italian*	*Japanese*	*Jewish*	*Portuguese*	*Scandinavian*	*Ukrainian*
Halifax:	1951	11	2	10	8.5	7	5	*	3	8.5	1	*	5	5
	1961	10	2.5	7	4	9	7	*	7	11	1	*	5	2.5
	1971	11	9	7	1	12	8	13	10	2	3	5.5	5.5	4
Montreal:	1951	*	3	6.5	8.5	6.5	2	*	10	5	4	*	1	8.5
	1961	*	5.5	8	3	9	5.5	*	10	1	4	*	2	7
	1971	4	7	8	1	10	5	11	12	2.5	6	13	2.5	9
Toronto:	1951	*	3	9	4	6.5	1.5	*	10	6.5	5	*	1.5	8
	1961	*	3.5	8.5	1	8.5	6.5	*	10	6.5	5	*	2	3.5
	1971	6.5	8	6.5	1	9	4	11	12	5	3	13	2	10
Winnipeg:	1951	*	2	9	9	4.5	6.5	*	6.5	4.5	1	*	3	9
	1961	*	3	9	2	7	7	*	10	4.5	1	*	4.5	7
	1971	3	5	2	1	9	8	11	12	7	4	13	6	10
Vancouver:	1951	*	2	10	4	3	5.5	*	8	7	1	*	5.5	9
	1961	*	2	8.5	3	5	7	*	10	5	1	*	5	8.5
	1971	2	6	9	3	7.5	5	11	12	4	1	13	7.5	10

Note: *No data.

Longitudinal Change, 1951–1971

Another way to examine changes in adults' education is by comparing their 1951 education to their 1971 average schooling. This is done in Table 5, where the ratio cited is the quotient of the 1971 education, divided by the 1951 figure, for both average ($\bar{x}$) years of education attained and percentage of the group possessing post-secondary schooling.

AVERAGE EDUCATION

On inspection what is again immediately evident is the considerably greater mobility in average education achieved over the two decades by the visible minorities (Blacks, Chinese, East Indians and Japanese), compared to all other ("white") groups. Most of the visible minority groups-by-city combinations experienced at least three years of education increase between 1951 and 1971 compared to about one to two years in the five cities as a whole. The British and French, along with the Italians, show meagre change, amounting on average to something over one year of schooling.

Toronto Italians were the only group to experience an actual decline in average schooling over the period — likely due to the large immigration of rural Italians during the 1950s. If one uses the city averages as a benchmark, only the British and Italians show a degree of educational mobility under that occurring in the city as a whole. Every other group-by-city combination is characterized by an above-average rate of upward adult educational mobility.

Two other trends evident in the earlier adult data are focused more sharply here. Educational change (and the levels of education upon which the change index is based) varies both *between* groups in the same city, and *within* the same group across cities. There are also slight differences in the change rate between cities as a whole. However, the absolute levels of education for a city (see Table 1), vary much more than these longitudinal mobility rates.

POST-SECONDARY EDUCATION

Table 5 also highlights the changes in proportions of groups with higher education in 1971, as compared to 1951. Here the lesser increase in the white ethnicities' post-secondary training is vividly contrasted with the gains achieved by the visible minority groups in every city. Among the latter (except for Blacks) the percentage with advanced education in 1971 increased by a factor of four to eighteen compared with twenty years earlier. The analogous increase among white ethnic groups was a factor of two to six. The longitudinal

TABLE 5: 1951 –1971 Change in Mean Years of Educational Attainment and Change in Percentage of Ethnicity with Post-Secondary Educational Attainment, by Ethno-racial-religious Group and City

	Black	*British*	*Chinese*	*East Indian*	*French*	*German*	*Italian*	*Japanese*	*Jewish*	*Scandinavian*	*Ukrainian*	*Entire city*
$\bar{X}$ Yrs. Educ.												
Halifax	162	118	321	233	125	126	112	211	129	130	128	120
Montreal	*	114	180	227	117	121	107	154	127	119	132	115
Toronto	*	120	218	184	119	126	94	152	163	127	130	114
Winnipeg	*	115	223	234	119	129	101	152	134	122	128	118
Vancouver	*	120	207	200	122	129	131	156	130	127	125	118
% with Post-2ry												
Halifax	290	277	1400	1640	467	400	273	1240	237	440	500	327
Montreal	*	258	467	1460	317	244	333	575	356	256	480	300
Toronto	*	207	640	569	267	229	200	400	391	259	300	215
Winnipeg	*	264	1400	1867	380	600	300	500	333	350	567	312
Vancouver	*	246	800	500	311	471	280	567	245	400	525	258

Notes: No 1951 data on the Greek or Portuguese groups.

The change index = 1971 educ/1951 educ × 100. An index above 100 indicates that the 1971 educational level was higher than the 1951 level; an index below 100 indicates that the 1971 level was below the 1951 level.

*No 1951 data; 1951 data on Halifax Blacks from Clairmont & Magill (1974).

mobility of Halifax Blacks in advanced education (well below that for the city as a whole) is in direct contrast to their relative greater advance in average schooling (considerably above the city level). This hints at the once prevalent structural and institutional discrimination to which Haligonian Blacks were subject. Their greater relative mobility in average schooling, moreover, can be attributed more to a decline in the proportion of Blacks possessing only elementary schooling than to an increase in the proportion with post-secondary education.

DISCUSSION

Some might argue that the post-secondary education change indices under-emphasize the educational accomplishment of groups that already had a high level of attainment in 1951 and which continued to improve in the following two decades. What this overlooks, however, is that groups such as the British, French and Germans occupied a lower position in 1971 with regard to advanced education than many of the other ethnic groups. On the other hand, in 1951, the visible minorities occupied positions near or at the bottom level of post-secondary attainment.

Elsewhere, moreover, I have shown that in no city during 1971 did the proportion of third and later generation members of the British group possessing post-secondary education rank the highest or even second-highest among the thirteen groups. Furthermore, in Halifax, Montreal and Toronto, the oldest generation British ranked no better than fifth. Third and later generations, of course, comprise the bulk of the British group in every city and it is just these generations that are reputed to have made most use of Canadian education to gain their reported socio-economic dominance (Herberg, 1982).

Thus, if there is any truth to the dictum that the level of education in a group portends its ability to successfully compete in the arenas of social and economic/political activity, these data suggest that important changes are underway. The new educational elite appear to be comprised of the visible minorities and the Jews. We should begin, therefore, to look for signs as to whether these groups are beginning to make greater inroads into social, political and economic life and leadership. Porter (1979, p. 279) and Reitz (1980, pp. 158–59), it should be noted, observed that in the mid-1970s this had not occurred in any significant manner. However, using national census data, it is evident that the Asians and Jews now surpass the British in the percentage of their number in the highly skilled professional-administrative jobs (Herberg, Forthcoming B). The 1981 census information, moreover will likely reveal further changes in, for instance, increased entry to the visible minorities into the professions and management as well as other economic advances. Hopefully, further research will focus on the extent to which groups following the educational change path of the visible minorities are penetrating spheres of influence and power previously occupied solely or primarily by the British group in Canada.

In the meantime, these data clearly support two hypotheses considered earlier: (1) the relativistic principle that each group is different in their use (and conceptualization) of formal education; and (2) that the socio-cultural environment of a city influences its residents in patterned ways. These propositions, while having most explanatory applicability to the post-secondary longitudinal mobility, also apply to the visible minorities and several other groups (including the Italians, Jews and probably the Scandinavians) in terms of mobility in average education.

Youth's Educational Attendance in 1971

It is very important to consider the extent of 1971 youth attendance at educational facilities, secondary and post-secondary, for two major reasons: First, the youth cohort is the only one for which we can be absolutely sure the educational experiences in question are relatively recent and were obtained in Canada. In contrast, even for Canadian-born adults, we can be sure that most of the education reported was not recently acquired, and, for adult immigrants, we must assume of course that much of their education was obtained before coming to Canada. In the second place, conceptually, the educational attendance of youth represents the continuation of adult educational patterns, providing next-generational insights into levels of education obtained. In thise sense, the 1971 data represents an important source regarding Canada's future, for the detailed 1981 census information on these matters will not be available to us for some years yet to come.

ATTENDANCE LEVELS

Table 6 presents 1971 data on the percentage rate of youth educational attendance by group, city and generation in Canada. On examination, we see that the adult patterns considered previously are accentuated even more distinctly. The visible minorities and the Jewish group possess levels of educational attendance that represent an even greater gap than existed in the adults data. Even more prominent is the conspicuously low educational attendance of first-generation Greek, Italian and Portuguese youth (except for Haligonian Portuguese and Vancouver Greeks and Italians). Furthermore, the variation *within* each group between cities (even to the extent of variation within the same generation) again confirms the validity of the relativistic principle that patterns of social behaviour vary between and within ethnic groups by locale.

EDUCATIONAL RANK

The listing of educational rank for each group in each city (see Table 7) strikingly illustrates the significance of youth patterns of educational attainment when compared to the data of adults' post-secondary rankings (see Table 5). There are two patterns of particular interest. First, youth attendance for the British, French, German and Scandinavian groups in many cases ranked lower than the achievement of their elders and do not demonstrate above average, let alone leading positions in these rankings. This, it could be argued, bodes poorly for these groups in the years ahead, especially when compared to the much higher rankings obtained by the visible minority and Jewish groups. Secondly, with only two city-by-group exceptions, Greek, Italian and Portuguese youth are at or near the bottom of the rankings — a similar position to that occupied by their seniors. These below-average rates of attendance serve to remind us of how strong intra-ethnic values and practices can be, under certain conditions, in determining children's futures — especially in terms of the relative weaknesses of the educational system to influence youths.

Even so, what might be termed the "ethnic determinism" of these three groups — so evident in 1971 — appeared to have begun adapting to a more Canadian or perhaps urban norm by the end of the decade. Caliste (1981), for example, reported that at the end of the 1970s education was perceived as the most important mobility channel for Ontario Italian and Greek youth. In another study, d'Ambrosio and d'Ambrosio (1980), found that nearly two-thirds of Toronto Italian youth–young adults were continuing to attend post-compulsory schooling, and that 68 per cent of this group were planning to attend post-secondary education. Of those no longer attending school, over one-fifth had already completed post-secondary training. In effect, then, well over half of the d'Ambrosio sample possessed or planned to complete post-secondary education (compared to 8 per cent of Toronto Italian adults who had higher education in 1971).

INTERGENERATIONAL MOBILITY

Patterns of intergenerational mobility (see Table 8) are rather different in many respects than those inferred from earlier comparisons of adult as opposed to youth statistics. Nevertheless, ratios for the British, French, German and Scandinavian groups are again com-

TABLE 6: Percentage of Educational Attendance in Cohort Age 15 –24 in the Five Cities, by Ethnicity and Generation in Canada, 1971

	Black	*British*	*Chinese*	*East Indian*	*French*	*German*	*Greek*	*Italian*	*Japanese*	*Jewish*	*Portuguese*	*Scandinavians*	*Ukrainian*	*Entire city*
Halifax	82	76	100	100	68	79	71	59	*	90	100	75	100	75
1A Gen.	*	100	100	100	*	*	75	46	*	*	100	0	*	81
1B Gen.	*	71	*	*	*	100	*	*	*	*	*	*	*	76
2nd Gen.	*	76	100	*	68	80	71	*	*	82	*	100	*	76
3rd, + Gen.	82	76	*	*	68	79	*	75		96	100	100	100	75
Montreal	80	64	79	78	58	63	61	58	100	79	43	72	78	60
1A Gen.	80	73	73	80	74	70	57	54	*	80	43	100	86	62
1B Gen.	*	67	90	*	60	57	52	52	*	69	25	*	58	59
2nd Gen.	80	63	93	*	63	70	86	74	*	81	*	70	85	72
3rd, + Gen.	*	63	93	75	57	57	75	58	100	79	43	67	68	58
Toronto	68	70	78	66	69	75	62	60	78	86	52	76	79	69
1A Gen.	70	70	74	67	86	70	58	54	100	89	53	100	83	63
1B Gen.	*	63	81	*	75	61	58	58	*	76	50	50	69	61
2nd Gen.	62	70	91	*	66	85	90	83	85	87	75	64	87	79
3rd, + Gen.	64	70	100	*	65	76	64	66	75	86	17	85	64	71

TABLE 6 continued

Winnipeg	67	70	84	100	64	75	40	61	71	85	31	67	71	70
1A Gen.	62	70	69	100	*	67	40	58	*	100	31	60	81	63
1B Gen.	*	66	*	*	*	58	*	35	*	78	*	*	70	60
2nd Gen.	*	66	91	*	68	84	33	82	67	82	*	64	72	74
3rd, + Gen.	*	71	78	*	64	73	*	62	71	86	*	68	71	70
Vancouver	87	71	83	67	67	75	84	71	76	79	65	65	71	73
1A Gen.	100	71	83	66	36	70	93	64	100	67	65	73	*	74
1B Gen.	*	60	73	25	83	71	*	62	40	64	*	41	*	62
2nd Gen.	*	69	86	82	64	80	67	85	75	80	*	66	75	73
3rd, + Gen.	83	73	78	71	70	73	100	69	80	81	*	66	69	73

Notes: 1A Gen. – Immigrated to Canada between 1956–1971.
1B Gen. – Immigrated to Canada between 1946–1955.
2nd Gen. – Born in Canada of immigrant parents.
3rd, + Gen. – Native-born of native-born parents.
*Group size insufficient to calculate statistic

TABLE 7: Educational Rank of the Ethno-Racial-Religious Group's Percentage of Youth Attendance at an Educational Facility, by City of Residence

	Black	*British*	*Chinese*	*East Indian*	*French*	*German*	*Greek*	*Italian*	*Japanese*	*Jewish*	*Portuguese*	*Scandinavian*	*Ukrainian*
Halifax	6	8	2.5	2.5	11	7	10	12	*	5	2.5	9	2.5
Montreal	2	8	3.5	5.5	11.5	9	10	11.5	1	3.5	13	7	5.5
Toronto	8	7	3.5	9	10	6	11	12	3.5	1	13	5	2
Winnipeg	8.5	7	3	1	10	4	12	11	5.5	2	13	8.5	5.5
Vancouver	1	8	3	10.5	10.5	6	2	8	5	4	12.5	12.5	8

Note: *Group size insufficient to calculate statistic.

paratively low, indicating less downward mobility in the youth generation. A similar situation occurs for Blacks in the four cities west of Halifax and the Jewish groups on the two coasts, each of which have experienced intergenerational stability or a decline in educational attendance.

The greatest upward mobility experienced by the youth–young adult generation occurred among the Chinese, Greek (except in Winnipeg), Italian (except in Halifax), Portuguese and Ukrainian groups east of Vancouver. Halifax Blacks are also included in this high mobility aggregate. Within these high intergenerational mobility groups, the range of increase in youth schooling at a conservative estimate, is about one-quarter to two and a half times that of adults with at least a Grade 9 education in 1971. By contrast, the mobility ratios within the other ethno-racial-religious groups, reflect, on average, just slightly greater youth schooling, when compared with adults.

Finally, while there seems to be a strong geographic variation intergenerationally both within and between groups, two ethnicities — the Chinese and Portuguese — are characterized by high mobility levels in every city. Three other groups — Greek, Italian and Ukrainian — also possess elevated mobility ratios in four of the five cities. Interestingly, these three groups are marked by downward mobility in the non-conforming location. Two groups — the British and Scandinavian — had ratios indicative of moderate downward mobility of youth in all five cities. Overall, however, the pattern was much less consistent among other low or downwardly mobile groups. Finally, we can point to perhaps another kind of ethnic outcome. Earlier similarities in educational patterns of adults were noted for the three white ethnicities (Greek, Italian and Portuguese) characterized by high post-1951 immigration levels. On the intergenerational mobility measure, these three ethnicities are among those showing the highest changes in youth upward mobility — the Portuguese in particular.

Conclusions

Five central conclusions emerge from the analysis presented in this paper. First, the position of each ethno-racial-religious group in the 1971 adult educational hierarchy in Canada differed considerably from those obtaining in 1951. In brief, the two charter groups and several of the other long-established ethnic groups have been displaced at the top of the "educational ladder" by the visible minorities, the Jews and, probably, the Ukrainians.

TABLE 8: Intergenerational Mobility Ratio of Percentage of Youth Age 15 –24 Attending Educational Facilities to the Percentage of Adults Possessing at least 9th Grade Education, by City and Ethno-Racial-Religious Group, 1971

	Black	*British*	*Chinese*	*East Indian*	*French*	*German*	*Greek*	*Italian*	*Japanese*	*Jewish*	*Portuguese*	*Scandinavian*	*Ukrainian*	*Entire city*
Halifax	134	97	155	105	98	96	137	88	*	101	132	90	116	97
Montreal	90	91	139	85	107	78	179	223	124	118	165	91	162	111
Toronto	82	91	126	69	102	95	177	231	101	109	260	90	152	106
Winnipeg	81	86	129	114	107	119	85	161	103	113	148	93	131	104
Vancouver	104	84	141	95	91	106	161	165	97	83	176	90	94	97

Note: A Mobility Ratio above 100 indicates that the youth–young adult attendance rate was higher than the percent of adults with at least 9th grade education. A ratio below 100 indicates the percent of adults with at least 9th grade was higher than the youth–young adult attendance rate.

*Too few cases to calculate statistic.

Secondly, in comparing the youth attendance standings with those pertaining to adult educational attainment, it appears that changes in the educational status of ethnic groups will have continued to shift during the 1970s. There is also evidence to suggest that some of the visible minorities and groups benefiting from recent immigration, whose adults possessed extremely low education in 1951 and 1961, were beginning to adapt an urban-Canadian norm by 1971. This is especially noticeable when one examines the increasing levels of youth attendance, compared to education possessed by adults.

Thirdly, very great differences can be observed in educational attainment between ethnic groups in the same city, not merely in the level of adult and/or youth education, or the amount of directional change in adults' educational status between 1951 and 1971, but also in terms of youth *versus* adult intergenerational shifts. Thus the relative value placed on formal education appears to vary greatly between ethnicities within the same social environment. Education also fulfills very different functions in some groups than others, especially with regard to the extent that past discrimination and the strength of discriminatory barriers were perceived as surmountable.

Fourthly, city contexts affected groups in different ways. Each ethnic group — and likely each one in each city — seems to be characterized by a unique set of internal social values and relations influencing the function of formal education within that group in that particular social-geographic context.

Fifthly, the relativistic principle enunciated here seems to be efficacious in summarizing the complex and intricate variations in educational outcomes covered in this article. Both function and accessibility, from the perspective of ethnic groups varies by city, group and period. There are, therefore, no fixed generalizations that can be applied unreservedly. It also suggests that the relationship of one generation in an ethnic group to extra-ethnic institutions, and the confidence that is accorded them, differs widely by group, city, period, etc.

Finally, to take up an issue raised in the introduction to this paper; if one accepts the notion that differences in educational attainment collectively comprise an ethnic hierarchy, then the hierarchical structure that existed in 1951 had within two decades been virtually reversed. By 1971, the leaders among the thirteen ethno-racial-religious groups covered here were the visible minorities, the Jews and, depending on the exact kind of index applied, perhaps the Ukrainians as well. The British group, on the other hand, and I suspect unknowingly, have dropped from their traditional position at the head of the hierarchy to a location somewhere in the middle ranks.

Further, it seems likely that ethnicity and race was a principal barrier for non-British groups to entry onto the upwardly mobile escalator of education before the mid-1960s or so. The "ethclass" notion is a conceptual capsulization of the ethno-racial discrimination, that Porter (1965), Isajiw (1975), Reitz (1980) and I agree existed in the past. Indeed, Reitz has gone so far as to revise the de facto cultural pluralism, combined with ethclass of the pre- and immediate postwar era, that Porter analysed as "exploitation" by the Anglo-Celtic group. Even if conscious exploitation existed, and I doubt it was planned, the discriminatory barriers by 1971 had fallen to the constant and concerted opposition by the Jewish and visible minorities. Those British (and French) who continue to view themselves to be masters of a Canadian ethno-racial hegemony are or will be the principal victims of their racist ideology. In fact, even the belief by charter group members that the future is theirs, by dint of their past and/or present status as charter member, will continue to prove a disservice to themselves and their ethnic peers. What was is no longer. Far from being the beneficiaries of an ethnic stratification system, and more particularly its customary reinforcing structures such as education, the evidence presented here suggests that they are suffering as victims.

Relative to the older generation, the causes of observed ethnic differences among the youth–young adult generation appears to vary. Those ethnic groups experiencing high youth educational mobility represent rather extreme variations in the influence exerted by immigration in the period following the Second World War. The Chinese, Greek, Italian and Portuguese communities received a relatively high proportion of immigrants, but this was not the case for the Haligonian Black and Ukrainian communities. Similarly, the East Indian community was characterized by very high immigration, but other groups experiencing the same general pattern of moderate to no shifts in mobility contained comparatively few recent immigrants. Thus, the degree to which post war immigrants formed part of an ethnic group does not seem to have been a generalized differentiating influence between marked upward mobility on the one hand, and stability or downward mobility on the other.

The origins of upward mobility between the youth and adult generations may well be the result of the changes in schooling that have taken place within each group since 1951, in concert with the unfolding of desegregated ethnic-specific adaptation processes in Canada among ethnic groups with heavy recent immigration — Greeks, Italians, Portuguese, and visible minorities. It definitely appears, moreover, that by 1971 the educational dominance of the British was over and that well-established ethnic groups such as the

French, German, and perhaps the Jewish and Scandinavian may also have reached their educational peak, and are being surpassed by the visible minorities.

Other than some of the visible minorities, it seems likely that the ethnic groups to next move up the educational attainment ladder will be those swelled by heavy immigration in the late 1950s through the early 1970s: the Greeks, Italians and Portuguese. One possible exception are the Ukrainians, who while characterized by lengthy residence, nevertheless exhibit educational mobility more akin to some of the visible minority groups or those benefiting from the influx of new immigrants. A possible explanation for this is that the Ukrainians have been a largely undereducated, rural people that have only lately begun adapting to residence in the urban centres of the country. In this connection, it seems clear that the greater youth mobility in education (compared to their elders) is part and parcel of the adaptation by rurally based cultures to the post-industrial values, structures and processes that were well-developed in Canadian cities by 1971.

On the other hand, members of those ethnic groups that much earlier had evolved a rather stable mode of adaptation to the Canadian circumstances (e.g., the British, French, German, Jewish and Scandinavian groups) may wrongly think they no longer need to depend so heavily upon formal education as the principal mechanism by which to achieve full social, economic and political participation in Canada. Finally, it is abundantly evident that the extent of education available to ethnic groups in post-industrial Canada is by no means limited by the amount of education another, or more "dominant" group possesses. The increases in the levels of educational attainment by the Jewish and visible minority groups are instances of the continuously evolving ethno-racial-religious mosaic in Canada.

Notes

1. The larger study of which this analysis forms a part was completed in 1980 prior to the collection and publication of the 1981 census data.
2. The criterion for the youth population of those residing in the parental/guardian's home was imposed so as to enable a directly relevant measure of parental socio-economic status as an influence on youth's attendance in schooling, an aspect not reported on here, but see Herberg (1982).
3. Gender inequalities are widespread and may have increased from 1951 to 1971. The complexities of these gender differences are analysed elsewhere (see Herberg "Gender, Ethnicity and Longitudinal Mobility: Women are still Undereducated," forthcoming A).

4. It is probably safe to say that Halifax, where the Black adult population has not changed its relative standing between 1951 and 1971, reflects a unique experience and setting.

References

Calliste, A. Paper presented at Canadian Ethnic Studies Association conference, October, 1981, Edmonton, Alberta.

d'Ambrosio, L.G. and d'Ambrosio, E.A.M. *Cultural Retention of Italian Canadian Youth*. Toronto: Canadian Business and Professional Association of Toronto, 1980.

Gordon, M.M. *Assimilation in American Life.* New York: Oxford University Press, 1964.

Herberg, E.N. "Gender, Ethnicity and Longitudinal Mobility: Women are still Undereducated," Forthcoming A.

______. *Ethnic Group Life in Canada: Adaptation and Transformation,* Forthcoming B.

______. "Ethnicity and Intergenerational Education Mobility: The Ascendance of the Minority Ethnicities," paper presented at the Canadian Society of Sociology and Anthropology Annual Meeting, University of Ottawa, June 1982.

______. "Education Through the Ethnic Looking-Glass: Ethnicity and Education in Five Canadian Cities. Ph.D. thesis, University of Toronto, 1980.

Hughes, E.C. "The Study of Ethnic Relations." *Dalhousie Review*, 27, no.4 (Winter 1968 –69), pp. 510 –20.

Isajiw, W.W. "The Process of Social Integration: The Canadian Context," in P.M. Migus, ed. *Sounds Canadian.* Toronto: Peter Martin, 1975, pp. 129 –38.

Kalbach, W.E. and W.W. McVey. *The Demographic Bases of Canadian Society.* Toronto: McGraw-Hill Ryerson, 1979.

Kubat, D. and D. Thornton. *A Statistical Profile of Canadian Society.* Toronto: McGraw-Hill Ryerson, 1974.

Porter, J. *The Vertical Mosaic: An Analysis of Social Class and Power in Canada.* Toronto: University of Toronto Press, 1965.

______. *The Measure of Canadian Society: Education, Equality, and Opportunity.* Toronto: Gage, 1979.

Reitz, J.B. *The Survival of Ethnic Groups.* Toronto: McGraw-Hill Ryerson, 1980.

Richmond, A.H. and W. Kalbach. *Factors in the Adjustment of Immigrants and Their Descendents.* Ottawa: Statistics Canada, 1980.

Heritage Languages and Canadian School Programs

JIM CUMMINS

During the past ten years a massive process of reorientation has begun in the school systems of major Canadian cities. Two developments have combined to bring out this reorientation process. First, the federal policy of multiculturalism, and second, the extremely rapid increase in the numbers of immigrant students in urban school systems. The aims of the multiculturalism policy as it affects education are to find effective ways of realizing the educational potential of culturally and linguistically diverse children and to develop social cohesion by promoting appreciation among all children of the varied contributions of different ethnic groups to the Canadian mosaic. The practical relevance of this policy has increased in recent years as the number of students who do not have English as a first language has grown to over 50 per cent in the Toronto school system and to around 40 per cent (at the elementary level) in the Vancouver system. This phenomenon is common to most of the western industrialized countries. Chaib and Widgren (1976), for example, estimate that by the year 2000 about one-third of the European population under thirty-five years of age will have an immigrant background.

The primary initial concerns of the reorientation process in Canadian schools have been to improve existing methods and materials in the teaching of English as a second language/dialect (ESL/D) and to develop curricula which promote cross-cultural understanding (Ashworth, 1975). Since command of the English language is a prerequisite to the adjustment of immigrant children to the school environment and to Canadian society as a whole, the strong emphasis on improving the effectiveness of ESL/D instruction is clearly

---

SOURCE: This article is a revised and expanded version of a paper entitled "The Language and Culture Issue in the Education of Minority Language Children" which appeared in *Interchange,* 10, no. 4 (1979–80), pp. 72–88. Reprinted by permission of the Ontario Institute for Studies in Education.

appropriate. However, there is a growing realization that ESL/D instruction cannot be treated as an isolated process but must be coordinated with an understanding of immigrant children's overall linguistic, psychological and educational development. Thus, in Canada as well as in the other western industrialized countries which have large numbers of immigrant children, educators have begun to broaden their focus in order to provide school programs which cater to the needs and strengths of the total child rather than just to deficiencies in the language of the host country.

Although virtually educators adhere to the principle of addressing the needs of the total child, consensus breaks down when attempts are made to translate this principle into educational practice. Depending upon the relative significance attributed to different factors in explaining the poor educational performance of many minority-group children (see, for example, Bhatnagar, 1976; Coleman *et al.*, 1966; Skutnabb-Kangas and Toukomaa, 1976; Verma and Mallick, note 1) the adaptations which educators decide are required in the educational treatment could range from relatively minor changes, such as greater sensitivity to the child's cultural background and learning style, to major changes, such as the use of the child's home language as the primary medium of communication throughout elementary school.

Obviously the political, social and administrative feasibility of different adaptations varies widely and these considerations must be balanced with an assessment of the specifically educational needs of immigrant children. However, because there is so little consensus as to what are the educational needs of immigrant children, and because very little research has been carried out on the topic, political, social and administrative factors have tended to play an overriding role in determining the extent of changes which have been instituted in schools systems not only in Canada but also in most of the other western industrialized countries.

Minority Languages in the School

The most contentious issue in the debates in virtually all the western industrialized countries has been whether, and to what extent, the home language (L1) of minority group children should be incorporated into the school curriculum (see, for example, Centre for Information on Language Teaching, 1976; Epstein, 1977; Masemann, 1978; Smolicz and Secombe, 1977). The complexity of the issue can be seen in the fact that although psycho-educational, social-policy and administrative/financial considerations must be weighed against one another, there is little consensus within any of these areas as to the probable effects of different options. For example, the primary rationale underlying bilingual education programs in the United States and Sweden is that the educational failure of many minority-group children is a consequence of the mismatch between the language and culture of the home and those of the school. The use of L1 as an initial medium of instruction is designed to ensure that academic progress is not retarded while the L2 is being learned. However, the validity of this rationale has been questioned on the grounds that the success of immersion programs for majority language children in Canada and elsewhere shows that language mismatch, in itself, is not a crucial factor (Bowen, 1977; Epstein, 1977).

The social policy debate has centred on the issue of whether a policy of cultural pluralism giving strong support for the maintenance of minority languages and cultures would lead to social fragmentation or, alternatively, encourage social cohesion (see, for example, *New York Times* editorial and debate in TESOL Newsletter, September 1977). Related to this issue is the question of whether or not societal institutions are prepared to relinquish assimilationist goals as opposed to making them more palatable.

The administrative and financial difficulties of providing instruction through the medium of L1 for children from a large variety of language backgrounds in the same school have often been advanced as an argument against any change in the linguistic status quo. However, there are many places throughout the world where administrative and financial considerations have not proved an insurmountable barrier to the recognition of children's L1 in the schools. For example, in Sweden it is obligatory for municipalities to organize mother-tongue instructions if the children or their parents want it. In 1977/78, 41 per cent of immigrant students were taught their mother tongue in the schools while 16 per cent received auxiliary instruction in other subjects through the medium of their mother tongue (Skutnabb-Kangas and Toukomaa, in press). In the United States, bilingual education for minority-language children is now widespread (see, e.g., Paulston, 1977) and a variety of bilingual programs for immigrant children also exist in Australia (Radio, 1977) and the EEC countries (e.g. Willke, 1975; Appel, note 2).

How have Canadian policy makers responded to the "language and culture" issue? The two major large-scale initiatives that have taken place in Canada during the past two years are the Heritage Language (HL) program in Ontario and the Programme d'Enseignement Langues d'Origines (PELO) in Quebec. The HL program involves teaching community languages either outside regular school hours or in the course of an extended school day (as in the Metropolitan Toronto Separate School System) for up to two and a half hours per week. In 1980–81 more than 76,000 children (figures supplied by Ontario Ministry of Education) participated in this program. The PELO project (Bosquet, note 3) involves teaching Italian, Portuguese, Greek and Spanish to children of these backgrounds for 30 minutes per day during regular school hours. In contrast to the HL program, the PELO is relatively small-scale, involving about 600 children in its third year of operation (1978/79).

The HL and PELO programs have incorporated minority languages into the school system as subjects of instruction. However, there also exist several programs in which minority languages are used as media of instruction. Among these are the Hebrew, English and French trilingual programs evaluated by Genesee, Tucker and Lambert (1978) and the Ukrainian-English and German-English bilingual education programs started in Edmonton in the early 1970s (Lamont, Penner, Blowers, Mosychuk and Jones, 1978) and now spreading in Manitoba. Unlike the majority of children in the HL and PELO programs, most of the children in these trilingual and bilingual programs are third-generation immigrants whose home language is English. For example, in the Edmonton Ukrainian-English program only about 10 per cent of children are fluent in Ukrainian on entry to the program. The aims of these programs are to give children an appreciation of the minority culture and to permit them to become functionally bilingual. Thus, the programs have similar aims to those of French immersion programs and can be categorized as "enrichment" programs in Fishman's (1976) terms.

Finally, there exist programs in which the minority language is used as an instructional medium in the initial stages of schooling as a "bridge" or transition to instruction through the L2. An example of this type of program in the Canadian context is the transition program operated by the Toronto Board of Education for Italian-speaking children in junior and senior kindergarten (Shapson and Purbhoo, 1977).

It is clear that each of these types of program embodies certain psycho-educational assumptions regarding the needs and potential strengths of minority-language children. How do these assumptions compare with those of alternative programs which have been rejected in the Canadian context on the basis of psycho-educational, administrative, social or political grounds? To what extent are different sets of psycho-educational assumptions supported by empirical evidence? In other words, what weight should be attached to different psycho-educational considerations in balancing them against possibly conflicting administrative, social or political considerations? If research were able to demonstrate convincingly that a particular form of educational adaptation (e.g., bilingual education) greatly increased the chances of educational success for certain types of minority-language children, then the moral imperative to institute that form of education would become harder to evade on other grounds.

Assumptions Regarding Educational Significance of Home Language and Culture

Two types of psycho-educational rationales have been advanced to justify the inclusion of minority children's L1 in the school curriculum. These rationales can be termed "L1 as transition" and "L1 as enrichment," respectively (see Fishman, 1976). These rationales each embody two components related to the development of cultural identity and conceptual-linguistic development of minority-language children. The "transition" rationale, which underlies U.S. and Swedish bilingual education policy, is that the use of L1 as an initial medium of instruction is necessary to bridge the cultural and linguistic gap between home and school. The "enrichment" rationale points to the beneficial personal, emotional and possibly cognitive effects of becoming highly competent in two languages and of being able to participate fully in two cultures. This type of rationale underlies immersion programs for majority-language children as well as maintenance programs for minority children (e.g., francophone minorities outside of Quebec). These programs clearly also have societal goals, but these goals are not of concern here. In general, transition program rationales reflect educators' perceptions of the needs of minority-language children, whereas enrichment rationales reflect the perceived potential of minority-language children.

Program Options

Table 1 presents the main types of educational programs for minority language children which are either in existence or have been proposed in terms of their assumptions (explicit or implicit) regarding the significance of L1 instruction for transitional or enrichment purposes. The purpose of making these assumptions explicit is to provide a basis for comparing different program options in terms of empirical research evidence and also to evaluate the extent to which different programs are likely to meet their psycho-educational goals.

The first alternative refers to the regular L2 program where no concessions are made either to the minority child's language or cultural background. This approach, which until recently was almost

TABLE 1: Assumptions Regarding Significance of Home Language and Culture in Programs for Minority Language Children

Programs	*Transition*		*Enrichment*	
	Cultural Identity	*Language*	*Cultural Identity*	*Language*
1. *"Regular" (submersion)* (L2 only, no cultural adaptations)	–	–	–	–
2. *Culturally Sensitive Regular* (L2 only, + cultural adaptations)	+	–	+	–
3. *Culturally Sensitive Regular + L1 Instruction* (L1 taught as subject, e.g. HLP)	+	(–)	+	+
4. *Culturally Sensitive L2 Immersion +L1 Maintenance* (L1 used as medium for about 30 per cent of time after L2 established)	+	–	+	+
5. *Transitional Bilingual* (L1 phased out as L2 established)	+	+	–	–
6. *Language Shelter* (L1 used as a major medium throughout schooling)	+	+	+	+
7. *Functional Bilingual* (L1-medium usage sufficient to develop fluent and literate L1 skills)			+	+

\+ = factor viewed as significant
– = factor viewed as not significant
( ) = with qualifications

universal, has been termed "submersion" both to highlight its "sink or swim" philosophy and to distinguish it from the approach used in immersion programs for majority-language children (Cohen and Swain, 1976). The approach is totally assimilationist, and children's home language and culture are viewed either as impediments to educational success or as having no functional significance.

The second type of program is perhaps the most common approach to minority-language education in western industrialized countries. Efforts are made to broaden the cultural base of the school system and to generate respect for cultural diversity. Educational difficulties which minority children encounter are viewed mainly as a function of their deficiency in the language of the host country combined with the cultural mismatch between home and school.

Provision of third-language instruction at the elementary level, as in the HL and PELO programs, has both cultural and linguistic goals. Culturally, it is intended to transmit a message to children that their language and heritage are worthwhile and valid and need not be rejected in favour of the dominant language and culture. The cultural gap between the home and school is narrowed and children are encouraged to develop a healthy identification with both cultures. From a linguistic perspective, third-language instruction is intended to encourage the child to maintain L1 skills and to become literate in that language. However, in general, the HL and PELO programs do not embody transitional linguistic goals since subject-matter instruction is through the medium of L2.[1]

The "Multilingual Project" (Radio, 1977, 1978) in Australia can also be classified under program option 3, although up to now it has been implemented only at the secondary level.[2] The project has developed parallel multimedia modules in both English and community languages on a variety of topics (e.g. Australian aborigines, computers, etc.) and children have the option of following the material in either language. Evaluation of the project has been very positive and the approach appears to have wide potential applicability.

The fourth alternative, suggested by Cohen and Swain (1976) and by Epstein (1977), involves introducing the L1 as a medium of instruction for part of the school day after basic proficiency has been attained in L2 through an "immersion" approach. This approach derives from the successful French immersion programs in Canada (Lambert and Tucker, 1972; Swain, 1974) and would involve, among other things, initial segregation of minority- and majority-group children, and use of teachers who understand children's L1. Thus, in the early stages of L2 acquisition, children would be enabled to use L1 for communication amongst themselves and with the teacher, although the teacher would speak only L2 to the children. In comparison with a regular "submersion" program this "immersion" approach is likely to lessen the cultural mismatch between home school; however, the academic aspects of linguistic mismatch are not considered significant. In other words, it is not considered necessary to teach subject matter in L1 while L2 is being acquired. As far as "enrichment" goals are concerned, the use of L1 is a medium of instruction in this program is likely to be more successful in promoting functional bilingualism than the teaching of L1 as a subject in, for example, the HL and PELO programs (see Swain, 1974).

Transitional bilingual programs (alternative 5) attach considerable significance to the initial cultural and linguistic mismatch between home and school and use the child's L1 in the initial stages to allow curriculum content to be assimilated while L2 is being learned. Maintenance of L1 is not a program goal since L1 is no longer used as an instructional medium when the child's L2 skills are judged to be adequate to assimilate curriculum content through that language.

Programs in which the minority language is used as the major medium of instruction and the majority language is taught as a second language (alternative 6) have been termed "language shelter" programs in Scandinavian countries (Toukomaa and Skutnabb-Kangas, 1977). Although, in terms of L1 and L2 usage in the early grades, language shelter programs may be indistinguishable from transitional programs, the goals and assumptions of the programs are very different. Proponents of language shelter programs (Hébert *et al.*, 1975; Toukomaa and Skutnabb-Kangas, 1977) argue that effective promotion of conceptual development in both L1 and L2 and reinforcement of children's identity can best be achieved by using L1 as the major medium of instruction throughout elementary and secondary school. Thus, for language shelter programs, transitional and enrichment assumptions are not clearly distinguishable.

The seventh program option is termed "functional bilingual" because the aim of such programs is to help children develop fluency and literacy in both L1 and L2 and to enable them to participate effectively in two cultural groups. The orientation of the program is entirely towards the enrichment potential of bilingualism and biculturalism, and transitional goals are not a major concern. Canadian examples of this type of program are the Ukrainian-English and German-English bilingual programs in Western Canada. The major difference between language shelter and functional bilingual programs is that, as the name implies, language shelter programs are designed for children whose L1 is in danger of replacement by L2 and who may also tend to perform poorly in an L2-only school context. By contrast, children in functional bilingual programs are not "at risk" in terms of academic achievement. For example, the majority of children in the Edmonton functional bilingual programs do not have fluent Ukrainian or German skills or entry to the program and for them the program is essentially an immersion program. Similarly, whether a French-language program for minority francophone children is more accurately characterized as a "language shelter" or "functional bilingual" program will depend on the specific context. Thus, although the seven program options are conceptually distinct, in practice they overlap to a certain extent.

Empirical and Theoretical Considerations

A first principle in examining the appropriateness of different program options is that immigrant and minority-language children do not constitute a homogenous group, either in terms of input to school systems or in terms of output. There are large differences both within the between groups of minority-language children on entry to school in terms of background factors, L1 and L2 abilities, motivation to learn L2 and maintain L1, as well as in other cognitive and attitudinal variables. Thus different forms of educational treatment will exert a differential impact on children with different input characteristics. In other words, there is an *interaction* between educational treatment and child input variables. It is only by making this assumption that it is possible to account for the fact that under any form of educational treatment some immigrant children appear to succeed relatively well whereas others fail.

If we ignore the fact that the seven program options outlined in Table 1 differ in the extent to which they attempt to exploit the enrichment potential of the child's home language and culture, and compare them only in terms of the major goal which they share, that is, the development of high levels of L2 skills, then it follows from the interaction assumption that the seven program options will be differentially effective in realizing this goal for students with different input characteristics. In other words, for some children who may, for example, be highly motivated to learn L2 and to identify with members of the dominant culture, a culturally sensitive L2 immersion program may be more effective, in terms of L2 learning, than a language shelter program that provides less intensive exposure to L2. However, for a minority child who is experiencing conflict and ambivalence vis-à-vis home and school cultures, a language shelter program may provide a better basis for L2 learning. In comparison with an L2 immersion program it would also, of course, allow the child to develop L1 literacy skills.

What evidence is there to support the transitional and enrichment rationales and what impact are the different program options likely to have on minority children's educational development?

CULTURAL IDENTITY AND EDUCATIONAL TREATMENT

There is a little controversy regarding the disruptive effects that cultural conflicts can have on minority children's academic adjustment (see, for example, Ashworth, 1975; Bhatnagar, 1976; Ramcharan, 1975) and most school systems in western industrialized countries have made efforts (sometimes only token) to narrow the cultural gap between home and school. Lambert (1967) has distinguished four possible ways in which minority-language children can work out their identity in relation to participation in two cultures:

1. harmonious identification with both L1 and L2 cultures;
2. identification with L2 culture, rejection of L1 culture (evidenced in, for example, unwillingness to speak L1);
3. identification with L1 culture, rejection of L2 culture;
4. failure to identify strongly with either culture.

These patterns of identification are intimately tied up with the learning of L1 and L2. For example, a child who identifies closely with both cultures is more likely to achieve high levels of proficiency in both languages than a child who identifies with neither.

In terms of enrichment goals only the first pattern of cultural identification is likely to promote comfortable participation in both cultures and high levels of L1 and L2 skills. Children who conform to the second pattern may perform well in school and gain high levels of L2 skills but at a cost to their L1 proficiency and possibly to familial harmony. Thus if cultural enrichment is perceived as a desirable and feasible goal for minority children, it is necessary to investigate the extent to which different program options lead to the first pattern of identification. If L1 cultural maintenance is not viewed as an important goal or is perceived as incompatible with L2 cultural identification, then the second pattern of identification would be considered acceptable or desirable. Informal observation suggests that this pattern is a common one among immigrant children in Canada and elsewhere. The extent to which initiatives such as the HL and PELO programs will promote a shift from pattern 2 to pattern 1 is an important issue in evaluating these programs.

The third and fourth patterns identified by Lambert seem to be associated with academic failure among minority children. An examination of the academic performance of different minority language groups in several countries shows a strong tendency for those groups who perform poorly in school to have ambivalent or negative feelings towards the L2 culture and often also towards their own culture. This pattern has been clearly documented for Finnish immigrants in Sweden by Skutnabb-Kangas and Toukomaa (1976).

For example, they quote Heyman's (1973) conclusion:

> Many Finns in Sweden feel an aversion, and sometimes even hostility, towards the Swedish language and refuse to learn it under protest. There is repeated evidence of this, as there is, on the other hand, of Finnish people — children and adults — who are ashamed of their Finnish language and do not allow it to live and develop. (Quoted in Skutnabb-Kangas and Toukomaa, 1976, p. 29.)

Given this ambivalence, it is not altogether surprising that Finnish children born in Sweden perform extremely poorly in school; nor is it surprising that Finnish immigrant children who arrive in Sweden at age ten or later who have not experienced this ambivalence and negative stereotyping in their preschool and early schooling years perform better in Swedish language skills within a relatively short time in comparison with those born in Sweden (Skutnabb-Kangas and Toukomaa, 1976).

It seems probably that the same ambivalence towards L1 and L2 cultures is a factor underlying the poor school achievement of many North American native groups. For example, Rosier and Farella (1976) report that, prior to the implementation of a bilingual program, Navajo Indian children in Rock Point and other Navajo schools were two years behind U.S. norms in English reading by the end of grade 6, despite intensive teaching of ESL.

The same factor might explain the poor academic performance of Franco-Ontarian students (Wright, 1971; King and Angi, note 4). The Toronto Board of Education (TBE) findings (Wright, 1971) are outlined in Table 2. Two questions immediately arise in relation to these data. First, why do the third-language groups at all SES (socio-economic status) levels show a greater proportion of students in high academic streams than the group whose mother tongue is English? Second, why does the French group show such a high proportion of students in low academic streams at both elementary and secondary levels? This tendency is again apparent across SES levels, but French-speaking students born outside Canada show no academic deficit (Wright, 1971).

The relatively high educational achievement of bilingual children born in Canada has been documented in other TBE reports (e.g., Ramsey and Wright, 1969, 1970) and by Bhatnagar (note 5) and it seems likely that high parental aspirations play a major role in explaining these findings. For these groups, any cultural conflicts that may have been experienced have clearly not proved debilitating as far as educational achievement is concerned. However, for the French group this is not thc casc, and it seems likely that their relatively low achievement is related to the ambivalence felt towards their own

TABLE 2: Class Placement of Low SES French, English, and Third-Language Mother Tongue Children in the Toronto School System Who Were Born in Canada

Mother Tongue	*Elementary* *% in Special Class (low academic)*	*Secondary* *% in Special Vocational Program*	*% in 5 Year (high academic) Program*
French	7.65	18.65	27.46
Third Language (range across groups)	0.08–2.96	0.54–8.84	58.04–78.84
English	4.99	10.33	40.65

Note: Adapted from tables 3 and 7 in Wright, (1971).

language and culture vis-à-vis the dominant English language and culture. This ambivalence on the part of parents is likely to affect both their patterns of interaction with and their aspirations for their children. These in turn may exert a negative effect on children's linguistic and academic development.

The notion of "bicultural ambivalence" is consistent with the structural analysis of minority student academic failure provided by John Ogbu (1978). Although Ogbu's analysis is not directly concerned with *linguistic* minorities or bilingual education, the patterns of minority school performance he identifies show clearly the futility of looking only at linguistic or school program variables for explanations of the effects of bilingual programs.

Ogbu first distinguishes between three types of minority groups, namely, autonomous, caste and immigrant minorities. Autonomous groups possess a distinct racial, ethnic, religious, linguistic or cultural identity and are generally not subordinated economically or politically to the dominant group. Jews and Mormons are current examples of autonomous groups in the United States.

Caste minorities, on the other hand, are usually regarded by the dominant group as inherently inferior in most respects. Their post-educational opportunities are restricted to the least desirable social and occupational roles and their failure to ascend the socioeconomic ladder is attributed to inherent characteristics of the group (e.g., "innate intelligence," "cultural deprivation," "bilingualism," etc.). Ogbu identifies Black, Indian and Hispanic groups in the United States as caste minorities and attributes their school failure to inferior education combined with the perception by the group of post-school economic barriers ("job ceiling") which limit the rewards to be gained from formal education. The perception of powerlessness or lack of mastery over their own fate may influence the patterns of parent-child interaction and the consequent cognitive, linguistic and motivational styles parents transmit to their children. Ogbu points out that

> caste minority children naturally acquire the linguistic, cognitive, motivational, and other skills or personal attributes adaptive to their adult roles. These skills may promote their failure in the dominant group's type of school success, but in that very way schooling improves their adaptability to the menial social and occupational roles they will play as adults (1978, p. 41).

Ogbu's analysis of the reproduction of inequality among caste minorities in the United States is strongly supported by the identification of similar patterns among caste groups in Britain (West Indians), New Zealand (Maoris), India (the scheduled castes), Japan (Buraku outcastes), and Israel (Oriental Jews).

The third type of minority group, immigrant minorities, differ from most caste minorities in that they have moved into a host society more or less voluntarily and tend to have instrumental attitudes towards the host society and its institutions. They tend to be less affected by the ideology of dominant group superiority than are caste minorities and often their lot appears very good compared to that of their reference group in the homeland. Ogbu gives Chinese and Japanese as examples of immigrant groups in the United States. He also points out that the status of minority groups may change. For example, immigrant minorities may develop into autonomous or caste minorities. The fact that recent Finnish immigrants to Sweden and Mexican immigrant workers in the United States manifest the characteristics of caste minorities is clearly a function of historically determined patterns of relationships between the two cultures. For example, Finnish immigrants to Australia are regarded as a high-status group and perform well academically (Troike, 1978) thereby fitting the description of "immigrant" rather than "caste" groups, in contrast to their counterparts in Sweden.

Ogbu's distinctions between different types of minority groups and his structural analysis of the causes of school failure among caste minorities are clearly compatible with the "bicultural ambivalence" notion and help explain the poor school performance of Franco-Ontarian students relative to other minority-language students in Ontario. They also permit the Canadian findings to be related to findings in other educational contexts.

Several recent research projects suggest that language shelter programs have been remarkably successful in promoting educational success for minority students who tend to fail in L2-only programs. Before reviewing these research findings, it is necessary to consider the role of linguistic factors as intervening variables in bilingual children's academic and cognitive development.

LINGUISTIC FACTORS AND EDUCATIONAL TREATMENT

Functional Bilingualism as Enrichment

There is no question that becoming fluent and literate in a language or languages other than one's mother tongue significantly increases an individual's potential for personal development. Much of the popularity of French immersion programs in Canada can be attributed to this factor, and throughout the world individuals spend vast amounts of time and money learning second languages. This activity is strongly promoted by educational and other institutions in order to increase the linguistic resources of the society. Given the obvious individual and societal benefits of bilingualism one might ask why the already developed linguistic resources represented by community languages are not cultivated to a greater extent. The major reasons in most cases are clearly socio-political; however, these socio-political reasons have often been cloaked in the garb of psychological rationalizations concerning the negative effects of bilingualism and bilingual education. Assimilationist educational policies have been justified on the grounds that bilingualism leads to academic retardation and language handicaps.

Certainly there has been empirical evidence to suggest that bilingualism was associated with lower levels of verbal intelligence (see Darcy, 1953, for a review of studies). However, there was, until relatively recently, little inquiry as to why these negative effects were always found among immigrant and minority language children in the process of being assimilated by a dominant majority, whereas the bilingualism of majority language groups (or "elitist" bilingualism — Fishman, 1976) had never been an educational problem. This phenomenon is exemplified in Canada in the success of French immersion programs. In Lambert's (1975) terms, educationally successful forms of bilingualism tend to be "additive" in that the individual adds an L2 at no cost to L1 proficiency. The bilingualism of minority language groups is termed "subtractive" in that the child's L1 skills are replaced or "subtracted" in the process of acquiring L2.

The findings of a considerable number of recent studies (reviewed in Cummins, 1978b, 1978–79) suggest that additive forms of bilingualism can positively influence academic and cognitive functioning. Specifically, children in French immersion programs have been found to pull ahead of comparison groups in some aspects of English skills (e.g. see Bark and Swain, 1978; Tremaine, 1975). There is also evidence that bilingual children are better able to analyse linguistic meaning and are more sensitive to aspects of interpersonal communication than unilingual children (Ben-Zeev, 1977a, 1977b; Cummins, 1978a; Cummins and Mulcahy, 1978; Feldman and Shen, 1971; Genesee, Tucker, and Lambert, 1975; Ianco-Worrall, 1972). A positive association has also been found between bilingualism and cognitive flexibility (Balkan, 1970) and some studies have reported that bilingual children are more advanced in general intellectual development than are unilingual children (Bain, 1975; Liedke and Nelson, 1978; Peal and Lambert, 1962).

While any cognitive advantages associated with additive bilingualism are likely to be fairly subtle and to not represent large-scale enhancement of cognitive growth, the evidence supporting such effects does add an extra dimension to the obvious personal advantages of functional bilingual skills. The educational policy implications of this analysis are embodied in the issue of how to change the educational environment of minority-language children so that additive rather than subtractive forms of bilingualism are developed. Program options 7, 6, 4, and 3 in Table 1 are the only ones that aspire to this type of "enrichment" objective. However, is it realistic to talk of "enrichment" objectives given the fact that many groups of minority-language children exhibit a high rate of school failure? The issues underlying this question are related to the transitional assumptions of the program options in Table 1.

L1 Instruction as Transition

Underlying the transitional assumptions of the six program options in Table 1 is the major issue of whether the educational failure of many minority-language children can be wholly accounted for by cultural mismatch between home and school, or whether linguistic factors also play a significant role for some children. It is possible to distinguish three basic positions on this issue. The position underlying options 1–4 is that minority children's conceptual and academic development can be adequately mediated by L2; consequently, it is not essential to use L1 as an instructional medium from the initial grades, although some instruction through L1 may be desirable for cultural identity reasons or to maintain basic skills in L1 (options 3 and 4). The position underlying transitional programs, on the other hand, is that academic and conceptual development can be adequately mediated by L2 only after a certain level of L2 skills has been attained. The theoretical and practical problem with this position is of course to specify what minimum level of L2 skills is required for a child to benefit from L2 instruction, and on this basis to establish entry and exit criteria for transitional programs. The language shelter approach takes the position that minority children's L1 should be the major medium of instruction throughout schooling, but especially in the early grades, since it represents the most effective means of promoting both secure cultural identity and overall conceptual development, thereby providing a basis for the assimilation of both L2 and academic content. For advocates of language shelter programs, functional bilingualism is the only realistic educational goal for minority language children; the alternative for many children, it is argued, is "semilingualism," that is, low levels of language proficiency (e.g., literacy skills) in both languages (Skutnabb-Kangas, 1978; Toukomaa and Skutnabb-Kangas, 1977).

At this stage it is not possible to draw any final conclusions on the validity of the theoretical assumptions underlying most of these program options. Whether options 3 and 4 would be successful in reducing the disproportionate numbers of children from some minority language groups who fail in school under options 1 and 2 is not known because examples of the third option are relatively recent and most have not yet been evaluated, while option 4 has not been put into effect in any minority-language situation. In general, transitional programs in the United States appear to have met with only limited success (see, e.g., Paulston, 1977). However, it is not possible to say what extent this apparent limited success is a function of invalid theoretical assumptions, poorly implemented programs, or poorly designed evaluations (e.g., the American Institutes for Research [note 6] study — see Leyba, note 7; Swain, note 8).

Language Shelter Programs

Several recent research projects suggest that the "language shelter" approach is particularly effective for children who are experiencing ambivalence vis-a-vis home and majority cultures. As noted previously, intensive teaching of the majority language has not produced encouraging results in minority language groups such as the Finns in Sweden, native Indian children in North America, or minority francophone children in some parts of Canada. This is illustrated in a quotation from a Swedish school psychologist: "After a certain amount of L2 teaching, it doesn't matter how much more such teaching you give some of the immigrant kids. They do not progress. It is as if they reach a cognitive limit" (quoted by Ekstrans, note 9, p. 63).

There is a striking contrast between this arrested state of cognitive and linguistic development under L2-only instruction and the progress made by some groups of minority children when L1 is used as a major medium of instruction in the early grades. Consider some examples.

The preliminary results of a large-scale longitudinal evaluation in Sodertalje in Sweden show that, by the end of grade 6, Finnish immigrant children who have been instructed initially mainly through Finnish, with Swedish becoming the major language of instruction (about 75 per cent of the time) from grade 3, perform almost as well in both Finnish and Swedish as Swedish-speaking children in Finland; this represents a considerable improvement in both languages compared to their performance in Swedish only programs (Hanson, note 10). The findings from other studies of bilingual programs for Finnish children are consistent with these results (Lasonen and Toukomaa, 1978: Toukomaa and Skutnabb-Kangas, 1977).

Bilingual programs for children of migrant workers have also been implemented in Holland with similar results. Appel (note 2), for example, compared the Dutch language proficiency of two groups of Turkish and Moroccan migrant workers' children (total N =57), one of which was receiving instruction mainly through L1 while the other received instruction either mainly or totally through Dutch. It was found that after eight months in school, children who were instructed mainly through L1 were just as proficient in Dutch as those instructed through Dutch.

The findings of the longitudinal evaluation of the bilingual program for Navajo students at Rock Point in the United States are also consistent with the assumptions of language shelter programs (Rosier and Farella, 1976). Since 1971 the school at Rock Point has operated a bilingual curriculum in which all initial literacy skills are taught in Navajo, and English reading is introduced only after Navajo reading skills are well established (in grade 2). The evaluators of the bilingual program at Rock Point compared how students in the program were performing relative both to students at Rock Point school before the program was instituted and also to other Bureau of Indian Affairs (BIA) schools in the Navajo area which did not have bilingual instruction.

It was found that by grades 5 and 6 the Navajo students whose L1 skills had been promoted by the school were performing at the National U.S. norm in English reading. Before the bilingual program was instituted students at Rock Point were *about one and a half years below the norm* in English reading despite intensive ESL instruction in the school. Similarly, the BIA schools which did not have bilingual instruction were more than two years below the national norm by the end of elementary school.

The grade 2 comparisons between Rock Point and the BIA schools are interesting. The Rock Point students who had been reading in English for only 5 months or less did just as well in English reading as BIA students who had at least two years of English reading experience. More important, however, is the fact that between grades 2 and 6 the Rock Point Students' rate of growth in English reading skills was about double that of students in the BIA schools. The authors attribute this increased rate of growth to bilingual instruction:

> It represents the cumulative effects of initial literacy in Navajo and the promotion of cognitive development through instruction in the native language. . . . The teaching of Science and of Navajo language may have given students practice in critical thinking beyond the level accessible to them in a monolingual English curriculum. (Rosier and Farella, 1976, p. 387)

Findings from studies of minority francophone students in Canada instructed through French show a similar trend. Carey and Cummins (note 11), for example, reported that grade 5 children from French-speaking home backgrounds in the Edmonton Catholic School System bilingual program (80 per cent French, 20 per cent

English, from K–12) performed at a level in English skills equivalent to that of anglophone children of the same IQ in either the bilingual or regular English programs. An evaluation carried out by Popp (1976) showed that grade 12 minority francophone students in Welland, Ontario, who had been instructed mainly through French in the primary grades and for about 50 per cent of the time in the secondary grades, performed as well as anglophone students (taught entirely through English) on measures of English reading comprehension, but less well on measures of English vocabulary.

A large-scale study carried out by Hébert *et al.* (1976) among grades 3, 6, and 9 francophone students in Manitoba also shows that there is no simple relationship between instruction through the medium of a language and achievement in that language. At all grade levels there was a significant positive relationship between percentage of instruction in French (PFI) and French achievement but *no relationship* between PIF and English achievement. In other words, francophone students receiving 80 per cent instruction in French and 20 per cent instruction in English did just as well in English as students receiving 80 per cent instruction in English and 20 per cent in French.

The success of these programs suggests that the development of deeper levels of linguistic proficiency in both L1 and L2 is closely bound up with children's overall intellectual development and that conceptual skills developed in one language can easily be transferred to another (see Cummins, 1979). Thus, the psycho-educational assumptions of language shelter programs appear to have some validity. However, on the basis of studies to date it is not possible to disentangle the effects of the linguistic factor from those of the "cultural identity" factor. In other words, the success of these programs could derive either from helping minority children resolve their ambivalence in relation to home and school cultures, or alternatively from the fact that "development of the child's first language up to a capacity for abstraction provides the best conditions for acquiring a good knowledge of the second language and consequently, in the long run, for a successful schooling" (Wilke, 1975, p. 367). Clearly, these alternative explanations are not mutually exclusive. Also, in the case of language shelter programs, transitional and enrichment rationales cannot be neatly separated; in other words, well-developed L2 skills could be due either to the initial use of L1 as an instructional medium (transition) or to positive conceptual–linguistic consequences which, recent studies suggest, can result from attaining high levels of bilingual skills.

Conclusions

It is clear that there exists a variety of psycho-educational rationales for providing mother-tongue instruction for minority children. These rationales often co-exist with socio-political rationales such as facilitating the free flow of labour between countries and the return of the migrant worker to the home country at some point (Michalski, 1977). For the minority group itself, cultural maintenance is usually the strongest motivating force. However, although the existence of a particular program is influenced by a large number of factors, it is possible on the basis of the experience to date to draw tentative conclusions regarding some of the psycho-educational factors at work in determining the educational development of minority children:

1. There exists considerable variation between minority language groups in the extent to which children are capable of succeeding in an L2-only school milieu. This variation is independent of SES and appears to be related to socio-cultural factors such as the degree of insecurity in relation to the home language and culture, and ambivalence towards the majority language and culture. These socio-cultural factors, in turn, result from socio-political and historical factors which have given rise to "caste-like" status for some minority groups.

2. The "language shelter" approach appears to be effective in reducing school failure among minority children who tend not to succeed in an L2-only setting.

3. The success of language shelter programs as well as of immersion programs for majority children suggests that in bilingual learning situations achievement in the majority language is minimally related to amount of instruction received through the medium of that language. This appears to be because the majority language is reinforced in the wider community and instruction in the minority language is effective in promoting children's overall conceptual skills. However, instructional time in the minority language *is* significantly related to achievement in that language.

4. The high level of academic achievement of minority children in some L2-only school settings (Bhatnagar, note 5; Ramsey and Wright, 1969, 1970) shows that bilingual or language shelter programs are not "necessary" for all minority children. However, there is considerable evidence that the attainment of functional bilingual skills can positively influence children's cognitive functioning. These findings add an extra dimension to the obvious personal advantages of bilingualism and suggest that school systems should explore ways of exploiting this potential strength of minority-language children. Highly successful functional bilingual programs of this type exist in Western Canada.

Thus recent research findings run counter to many of the intuitive assumptions of educators concerned with minority-language children. Specifically, the findings suggest that intensive teaching of the majority language is not necessarily the most appropriate form of educational treatment for minority children who are performing poorly in school. Educational policy makers should therefore adopt a flexible, open-minded approach which takes account of the psycho-educational needs and potential strengths of minority children as well as of the cultural aspirations of their parents.

Notes

Preparation of the original paper was made possible through financial support from the Multiculturalism Directorate of the Secretary of State, Ottawa. I would like to thank Jean Hanscombe, David Stern and Merrill Swain for their valuable comments on an earlier draft of this paper.

1. In some school systems (e.g., North York) the HL curriculum covers certain aspects of the regular curriculum and in this sense might be regarded as "transitional" since the same content is taught in L1 and in L2.
2. The Multilingual Project clearly differs from the HL and PELO programs in that the language is not taught as a subject but used as a parallel medium to teach content. However, it has been grouped in this category because the time allocation and consequent overall impact are likely to be similar.

Reference Notes

1. Verma, G.J., and Mallick, K. "Social, personal and academic adjustment of ethnic minority pupils in British schools." Paper presented at the International Congress of Applied Psychology, 1978.
2. Appel, R. "The acquisition of Dutch by Turkish and Moroccan children in two different school models." Research report, Institute for Developmental Psychology, Utrecht, 1979.
3. Bosquet, M. "Le P.E.L.O. au Québec: Les objectifs vises, les composantes de la phase expérimentale et l'évaluation." Paper presented at C.S.S.E. Conference, Saskatoon, 1979.
4. King, A.J.C., and Angi, C.E. *Language and Secondary School Success*. Report prepared for the Royal Commission on Bilingualism and Biculturalism, 1968.
5. Bhatnagar, J. "Linguistic behaviour and adjustment of immigrant children in French and English schools in Montreal." Paper presented at XIXth International Congress of Applied Psychology, Munich, 1978.
6. American Institutes for Research. *Evaluation of the Impact of ESEA Title VII Spanish/English Bilingual Education Programs*. Report submitted to U.S. Office of Education, 1977.

7. Leyba, C.F. *Longitudinal Study Title VII Bilingual Program, Santa Fe Public Schools, Sante Fe, New Mexico.* National Dissemination and Assessment Center, California State University, Los Angeles, 1978.
8. Swain, M. "Bilingual education: Research and its implications." Paper presented at the 13th annual TESOL convention, March, 1979.
9. Ekstrand, L.H. "Bilingual and bicultural adaptation." Doctoral dissertation, University of Stockholm, 1978.
10. Hanson, G. "The position of the second generation of Finnish immigrants in Sweden: The importance of education in the home language to the welfare of second generation immigrants." Paper presented at symposium in Split, Yugoslavia, October 1979.
11. Carey, S.T. & Cummins, J. *English and French Achievement of Grade 5 Children from English, French and Mixed French-English Home Backgrounds Attending the Edmonton Separate School System English-French Immersion Program.* Report submitted to the Edmonton Separate School System, April, 1979.

References

Ashworth, M. *Immigrant Children and Canadian Schools.* Toronto: McClelland & Stewart, 1975.

Bain, B.C. "Toward an integration of Piaget and Vygotsky: Bilingual considerations." *Linguistics*, 160 (1975), pp. 5–20.

Balkan, L. *Les effets du bilinguisme francais-anglais sur les aptitudes intellectuelles.* Bruxelles: Aimav, 1970.

Barik, H.C., and Swain, M. "Evaluation of a French immersion program: The Ottawa study through grade 5." *Canadian Journal of Behavioural Science,* 10 (1978), pp. 192–201.

Ben-Zeev, S. "The influence of bilingualism on cognitive development and cognitive strategy." *Child Development,* 48 (1977), 1009–1018. (a)

______. "The effect of Spanish-English bilingualism in children from less privileged neighborhoods on cognitive development and cognitive strategy." *Working Papers on Bilingualism,* 14 (1977), pp. 83–122. (b)

Bhatnagar, J. "Education of immigrant children." *Canadian Ethnic Studies,* 8 (1976), pp. 52–70.

Bowen, J.D. "Linguistic perspectives on bilingual education," in B. Spolsky and R. Cooper, eds. *Frontiers of Bilingual Education.* Rowley, Mass.: Newbury House, 1977.

Carringer, D.C. "Creative thinking abilities of Mexican youth: The relationship of bilingualism." *Journal of Cross-Cultural Pshchology*, 5 (1974), pp. 492–504.

Centre for Information on Language Teaching and Research. *Bilingualism and British Education: The Dimesnions of Diversity*. CILT Reports and Papers 14, 1976.

Chaib, M., and Widgren, J. *Invandrarbarnen och skolan.* Stockholm: Wahlstrom and Widstrand, 1976.

Cohen, A.D., and Swain, M. "Bilingual education: The immersion model in the North American context," in J.E. Alatis and K. Twaddell, eds. *English as a Second Language in Bilingual Education*. Washington, D.C.: TESOL, 1976.

Coleman, J.S., Campbell, E.Q., Hobson, C.J., *et al. Equality of Educational Opportunity.* Washington, D.C.: U.S. Government Printing Office, 1966.

Cummins, J. "Bilingualism and the development of metalinguistic awareness." *Journal of Cross-Cultural Psychology*, 9 (1978), 131–49. (a)

———. "The cognitive development of children in immersion programs." *The Canadian Modern Language Review,* 34 (1978), pp. 855–83. (b)

———. "Bilingualism and educational development in anglophone and minority francophone groups in Canada." *Interchange,* 9, no. 4 (1978–79), pp. 40–51.

———. "Linguistic interdependence and the educational development of bilingual children." *Review of Educational Research*, 49, (1979), pp. 222–51.

——— and Mulcahy, R. "Orientation to language in Ukrainian-English bilingual children. *Child Development,* 49, (1978), pp. 239–42.

Darcy, N.T. "A review of the literature on the effects of bilingualism upon the measurement of intelligence." *Journal of Genetic Psychology,* 82 (1953), pp. 21–57.

Epstein, N. *Language, Ethnicity and the Schools.* Washington, D.C.: Institute for Educational Leadership, 1977.

Feldman, C., and Shen, M. "Some language-related cognitive advantages of bilingual five-year olds." *Journal of Genetic Psychology,* 118, (1971), 235–44.

Fishman, J. "Bilingual education: What and why," in J.E. Alatis and K. Twaddell, eds. *English as a Second Language in Bilingual Education*. Washington, D.C.: TESOL, 1976.

Genesee, F., Tucker, G.R., and Lambert, W.E. "Communication skills of bilingual children." *Child Development,* 46, (1975), 1013–18.

Hébert, R., *et al. Rendement académique et lange d'enseignement chez les élèves franco-manitobians.* Saint-Boniface, Manitoba: Centre de recherches du College Universitaire de Saint-Boniface, 1976.

Heyman, A. *Invandrarbarn: Slutrapport.* Stockholm: Stockhoms Invandrarnamd, 1973.

Ianco-Worrall, A. "Bilingualism and cognitive development." *Child Development,* 43 (1972), pp. 1390–1400.

Lambert, W.E. "A social psychology of bilingualism." *Journal of Social Issues,* 23 (1967), pp. 91–109.

———. "Culture and language as factors in learning and education," in A. Wolfgang, ed. *Education of Immigrant Students.* Toronto: Ontario Institute for Studies in Education, 1975.

——— and Tucker, G.R. *Bilingual Education of Children: The St. Lambert Experiment.* Rowley: Newbury House, 1972.

Lamont, D., Penner, W., Blowers, T., Mosychuk, H., and Jones, J. "Evaluation of the second year of a bilingual (English-Ukrainian) program." *Canadian Modern Language Review,* 34 (1978), 175–85.

Lasonen, K., and Toukomaa, P. *Linguistic Development and School Achievement among Finnish Immigrant Children in Mother-Tongue Medium Classes in Sweden.* Research Reports No. 70, Department of Education, University of Jyvaskyla, 1978.

Liedke, W.W.A., and Nelson, L.D. "Concept formation and bilingualism." *Alberta Journal of Educational Research*, 14 (1968), pp. 225–32.

Masemann, V.L. "Multicultural programs in Toronto schools." *Interchange*, 90, no. 1 (1978/79), pp. 29–44.

Michalski, C. "Teacher education for a multicultural society: Some global trends and the Ontario Ministry of Education position," in V. D'Oyley, ed. *The Impact of Multi-Ethnicity on Canadian Education*. Toronto: The Urban Alliance on Race Relations, 1977.

Ogbu, J. *Minority Education and Caste.* New York: Academic Press, 1978.

Paulston, C.B. "Research viewpoint," in *Bilingual Education: Current Perspectives; Vol. 2. Linguistics.* Arlington, Va.: Centre for Applied Linguistics, 1977.

Peal, E., and Lambert, W.E. "The relation of bilingualism to intelligence." *Psychological Monographs,* 46 (1962), p. 546.

Popp, L.A. "The English competence of French-speaking students in a bilingual setting." *The Canadian Modern Language Review*, 32 (1976), pp. 365–77.

Ramsey, C., and Wright, E.N. "Students of non-Canadian origin: The relation of language and rural-urban background to academic achievement and ability." Research report No. 76, Toronto Board of Education, 1969.

———. "Language backgrounds and achievement in Toronto schools." Research report No. 85, Toronto Board of Education, 1970.

Rado, M. "The Multilingual project: A model of bilingual education." *RELC Journal,* 8 (1977), pp. 42–50.

———. "What bilingual education can tell us." *Ethnic Studies,* 2 (1978), pp. 48–58.

Ramcharan, S. "Special problems of immigrant children in the Toronto school system," in A. Wolfgang, ed. *Education of Immigrant Students: Issues and Answers.* Toronto: Ontario Institute for Studies in Education, 1975.

Rosier, P., and Farella, M. "Bilingual education at Rock Point — Some early results." *TESOL Quarterly, 10 (1976), pp. 379*–88.

Shapson, S., and Purbhoo, M. "A transition program for Italian children." *The Canadian Modern Language Review,* 33 (1977), pp. 486–96.

Skutnabb-Kangas, T. "Semilingualism and the education of migrant children as a means of reproducing the caste of assembly line workers," in N. Dittmar, H. Haberland, T. Skutnabb-Kangas, and U. Teleman, eds. *Papers from the First Scandinavian-German Symposium on the Language of Immigrant Workers and Their Children.* ROLIG-papir 12, Roskilde Universitetscenter, 1978.

——— and Toukomaa, P. *Teaching Migrant Children's Mother Tongue and Learning the Language of the Host Country in the Context of the Socio-cultural Situation of the Migrant Family.* Helsinki: The Finnish National Commission for UNESCO, 1976.

Smolicz, J.J., and Secombe, M.J. "A study of attitudes to the introduction of ethnic languages and cultures in Australian schools." *The Australian Journal of Education,* 21 (1977), pp. 1–24.

Swain, M. French immersion programs across Canada: Research findings." *The Canadian Modern Language Review,* 31 (1974), pp. 117–29.

Toukomaa, P., and Skutnabb-Kangas, T. *The Intensive Teaching of the Mother Tongue to Migrant Children of Pre-school Age and Children in the Lower Level of Comprehensive School.* Helsinki: The Finnish National Commission for UNESCO, 1977.

Tremaine, R.V. *Syntax and Piagetian Operational Thought.* Washington, D.C.: Georgetown University Press, 1975.

Willke, I. "Schooling of immigrant children in West Germany, Sweden, England." *International Review of Education*, 21 (1975), pp. 357–82.

Wright, E.N. "Programme replacement related to selected countries of birth and selected languages." Research Report No. 99. Toronto: Toronto Board of Education, 1971.

APPENDIX

The Official Languages Act (1969)

Multiculturalism Within a Bilingual Framework Policy (1971)

Bill 101: Charter of the French Language (1977)

Canadian Charter of Rights and Freedoms (1982)

The Official Languages Act (1969)

An Act respecting the status of the official languages of Canada

[*Assented to 9th July, 1969*]

Her Majesty, by and with the advice and consent of the Senate and House of Commons of Canada, enacts as follows:

SHORT TITLE

1. This Act may be cited as the *Official Languages Act.*

DECLARATION OF STATUS OF LANGUAGES

2. The English and French languages are the official languages of Canada for all purposes of the Parliament and Government of Canada, and possess and enjoy equality of status and equal rights and privileges as to their use in all the institutions of the Parliament and Government of Canada.

STATUTORY AND OTHER INSTRUMENTS

3. Subject to this Act, all instruments in writing directed to or intended for the notice of the public, purporting to be made or issued by or under the authority of the Parliament or Government of Canada or any judicial, quasi-judicial or administrative body or Crown corporation established by or pursuant to an Act of the Parliament of Canada, shall be promulgated in both official languages.

4. All rules, orders, regulations, by-laws and proclamations that are required by or under the authority of any Act of the Parliament of Canada to be published in the official gazette of Canada shall be made or issued in both official languages and shall be published accordingly in both official languages, except that where the authority by which any such rule, order, regulation, by-law or proclamation is to be made or issued is of the opinion that its making or issue is urgent and that to make or issue it in both official languages would occasion a delay prejudicial to the public interest, the rule, order, regulation, by-law or proclamation shall be made or issued in the first instance in its version in one of the official languages and thereafter, within the time limited for the transmission of copies thereof or its publication as required by law, in its version in the other, each such version to be effective from the time the first is effective.

5. (1) All final decisions, orders and judgments, including any reasons given therefor, issued by any judicial or quasi-judicial body established by or pursuant to an Act of the Parliament of Canada shall be issued in both official languages where the decision, order or judgment determines a question of law of general public interest or importance or where the proceedings leading to its issue were conducted in whole or in part in both official languages.

(2) Where any final decision, order or judgment issued by a body described in subsection (1) is not required by that subsection to be issued in both official languages, or where a body described in that subsection by which any final decision, order or judgment including any reasons given therefor is to be issued is of the opinion that to issue it in both official languages would occasion a delay prejudicial to the public interest or resulting in injustice or hardship to any party to the proceedings leading to its issue, the decision, order or judgment including any reasons given therefor shall be issued in the first instance in its version in one of the official lanuages and thereafter, within such time as is reasonable in the circumstances, in its version in the other, each such version to be effective from the time the first is effective.

(3) Nothing in subsection (1) or (2) shall be construed as prohibiting the oral rendition or delivery, in one only of the official languages, of any decision, order or judgment or any reasons given therefor.

(4) All rules, orders and regulations governing the practice or procedure in any proceedings before a body described in subsection (1) shall be made in both official languages but where the body by which any such instrument is to be made is satisfied that its making in both official languages would occasion a delay resulting in injustice or hardship to any person or class of persons, the instrument shall be made in the first instance in its version in one of the official languages and thereafter as soon as possible in its version in the other, each such version to be effective from the time the first is effective.

6. Without limiting or restricting the operation of any law of Canada relating to the conviction of a person for an offence consisting of a contravention of a rule, order, regulation, by-law or proclamation that at the time of the alleged contravention was not published in the official gazette of Canada in both official languages, no instrument described in section 4 or 5 is invalid by reason only that it was not made or issued in compliance with those sections, unless in the case of any instrument described in section 4 it is established by the person asserting its invalidity that the non-compliance was due to bad faith on the part of the authority by which the instrument was made or issued.

7. Where, by or under the authority of the Parliament or Government of Canada or any judicial, quasi-judicial or administrative body or Crown corporation established by or pursuant to an Act of the Parliament of Canada, any notice, advertisement or other matter is to be printed in a publication for the information primarily of members of the public resident in the National Capital Region or a federal bilingual district established under this Act, the matter shall, wherever possible in publications in general circulation within that Region or district, be printed in one of the official languages in at least one such publication appearing wholly or mainly in that language and in the other official language in at least one such publication appearing wholly or mainly in that other language, and shall be given as nearly as reasonably may be equal prominence in each such publication.

CONSTRUCTION OF VERSIONS OF ENACTMENTS

8. (1) In construing an enactment, both its versions in the official languages are equally authentic.

(2) In applying subsection (1) to the construction of an enactment,

(*a*) where it is alleged or appears that the two versions of the enactment differ in their meaning, regard shall be had to both its versions so that, subject to paragraph (*c*), the like effect is given to the enactment in every part of Canada in which the enactment is intended to apply, unless a contrary intent is explicitly or implicitly evident;

(*b*) subject to paragraph (*c*), where in the enactment there is a reference to a concept, matter or thing the reference shall, in its expression in each version of the enactment, be construed as a reference to the concept, matter or thing to which in its expression in both versions of the enactment the reference is apt;

(*c*) where a concept, matter or thing in its expression in one version of the enactment is incompatible with the legal system or institutions of a part of Canada in which the enactment is intended to apply but in its expression in the other version of the enactment is compatible therewith, a reference in the enactment to the concept, matter or thing shall, as the enactment applies to that part of Canada, be construed as a reference to the concept, matter or thing in its expression in that version of the enactment that is compatible therewith; and

(*d*) if the two versions of the enactment differ in a manner not coming within paragraph (*c*), preference shall be given to the version thereof that, according to the true spirit, intent and meaning of the enactment, best ensures the attainment of its objects.

DUTIES OF DEPARTMENTS, ETC. IN RELATION TO OFFICIAL LANGUAGES

9. (1) Every department and agency of the Government of Canada and every judicial, quasi-judicial or administrative body or Crown corporation established by or pursuant to an Act of the Parliament of Canada has the duty to ensure that within the National Capital Region, at the place of its head or central office in Canada if outside the National Capital Region, and at each of its principal offices in a federal bilingual district established under this act, members of the public can obtain available services from and can communicate with it in both official languages.

(2) Every department and agency of the Government of Canada and every judicial, quasi-judicial or administrative body or Crown corporation established by or pursuant to an Act of the Parliament of Canada has, in addition to but without derogating from the duty imposed upon it by subsection (1), the duty to ensure, to the extent that it is feasible for it to do so, that members of the public in locations other than those referred to in that subsection, where there is a significant demand therefor by such persons, can obtain available services from and can communicate with it in both official languages.

10. (1) Every department and agency of the Government of Canada and every Crown corporation established by or pursuant to an Act of the Parliament of Canada has the duty to ensure that, at any office, location or facility in Canada or elsewhere at which any services to the travelling public are provided or made available by it, or by any other person pursuant to a contract for the provision of such services entered into by it or on its behalf after the coming into force of this Act, such services can be provided or made available in both official languages.

(2) Every department and agency described in subsection (1), and every Crown corporation described therein that is not expressly exempted by order of the Governor in Council from the application of this subsection in respect of any services provided or made available by it, has the duty to ensure that any services to which

subsection (1) does not apply that are provided or made available by it at any place elsewhere than in Canada can be so provided or made available in both official languages.

(3) Subsection (1) does not apply to require that services to the travelling public be provided or made available at any office, location or facility in both official languages if, at that office, location or facility, there is no significant demand for such services in both official languages by members of the travelling public or the demand therefor is so irregular as not to warrant the application of subsection (1) to that office, location or facility.

11. (1) Every judicial or quasi-judicial body established by or pursuant to an Act of the Parliament of Canada has, in any proceedings brought or taken before it, and every court in Canada has, in exercising in any proceedings in a criminal matter any criminal jurisdiction conferred upon it by or pursuant to an Act of the Parliament of Canada, the duty to ensure that any person giving evidence before it may be heard in the official language of his choice, and that in being so heard he will not be placed at a disadvantage by not being or being unable to be heard in the other official language.

(2) Every court of record established by or pursuant to an Act of the Parliament of Canada has, in any proceedings conducted before it within the National Capital Region or a federal bilingual district established under this Act, the duty to ensure that, at the request of any party to the proceedings, facilities are made available for the simultaneous translation of the proceedings, including the evidence given and taken, from one official language into the other except where the court, after receiving and considering any such request, is satisfied that the party making it will not, if such facilities cannot conveniently be made available, be placed at a disadvantage by reason of their not being available or the court, after making every reasonable effort to obtain such facilities, is unable then to obtain them.

(3) In exercising in any proceedings in a criminal matter any criminal jurisdiction conferred upon it by or pursuant to an Act of the Parliament of Canada, any court in Canada may in its discretion, at the request of the accused or any of them if there is more than one accused, and if it appears to the court that the proceedings can effectively be conducted and the evidence can effectively be given and taken wholly or mainly in one of the official languages as specified in the request, order that, subject to subsection (1), the proceedings be conducted and the evidence be given and taken in that language.

(4) Subsections (1) and (3) do not apply to any court in which, under and by virtue of section 133 of *The British North America Act, 1867*, either of the official languages may be used by any person, and

subsection (3) does not apply to the courts of any province until such time as a discretion in those courts or in the judges thereof is provided for by law as to the language in which, for general purposes in that province, proceedings may be conducted in civil causes or matters.

(5) The Governor in Council, in the case of any judicial or quasi-judicial body established by or pursuant to an Act of the Parliament of Canada, and the Lieutenant Governor in Council of any province, in the case of any other court in that province, may make such rules governing the procedure in proceedings before such body or court, including rules respecting the giving of notice, as the Governor in Council or the Lieutenant-Governor in Council, as the case may be, deems necessary to enable such body or court to exercise or carry out any power or duty conferred or imposed upon it by this section.

FEDERAL BILINGUAL DISTRICTS

12. In accordance with and subject to the provisions of this Act and the terms of any agreement that may be entered into by the Governor in Council with the government of a province as described in section 15, the Governor in Council may from time to time by proclamation establish one or more federal bilingual districts (hereinafter in this Act called "bilingual districts") in a province, and alter the limits of any bilingual districts so established.

13. (1) A bilingual district established under this Act shall be an area delineated by reference to the boundaries of any or all of the following, namely, a census district established pursuant to the *Statistics Act,* a local government or school district, or a federal or provincial electoral district or region.

(2) An area described in subsection (1) may be established as a bilingual district or be included in whole or in part within a bilingual district if

(*a*) both of the official languages are spoken as a mother tongue by persons residing in the area; and

(*b*) the number of persons who are in the linguistic minority in the area in respect of an official language spoken as a mother tongue is at least ten per cent of the total number of persons residing in the area.

(3) Notwithstanding subsection (2), where the number of persons in the linguistic minority in an area described in subsection (1) is less than the percentage required under subsection (2), the area may be established as a bilingual district if before the coming into force of this Act the services of departments and agencies of the Government of Canada were customarily made available to residents of the area in both official languages.

(4) No alteration of the limits of any bilingual district established under this Act shall be made unless such district would, if the proposed alteration of its limits were made, continue to comply with the requirements of this section respecting the establishment of bilingual districts under this Act.

(5) No proclamation establishing or altering the limits of any bilingual district shall be issued under this Act before such time as the Governor in Council has received from a Bilingual Districts Advisory Board appointed as described in section 14 a report setting out its findings and conclusions including its recommendations if any relating thereto and at least ninety days have elapsed from the day a copy of the report was laid before Parliament pursuant to section 17.

(6) A proclamation establishing or altering the limits of any bilingual district shall take effect in relation to any such district on such day, not later than twelve months after the issue of the proclamation, as may be fixed therein in relation to that district.

14. (1) As soon as possible following the completion of each decennial census, or, in the case of the decennial census taken in the year 1961, forthwith after the coming into force of this Act, the Dominion Statistician shall prepare and send to the Clerk of the Privy Council a return certified by him showing the population of each of the provinces and census districts in Canada, categorized according to the official languages spoken as a mother tongue by persons resident therein as ascertained by that census, and as soon as possible thereafter the Governor in Council shall, pursuant to Part I of the *Inquiries Act,* appoint not less than five and not more than ten persons, selected as nearly as may be as being representative of residents of the several provinces or principal regions of Canada, as commissioners to constitute a Bilingual Districts Advisory Board for the purpose of conducting an inquiry as described in section 15.

(2) One of the persons appointed as described in subsection (1) shall be designated in the instrument of appointment to act as chairman of the Board.

(3) Forthwith upon the appointment of a Bilingual Districts Advisory Board, the Clerk of the Privy Council shall send a copy of the return referred to in subsection (1) to the chairman of the Board.

15. (1) Upon receipt by the chairman of a Bilingual Districts Advisory Board of the copy of the return referred to in subsection (3) of section 14, the Board shall, with all due despatch, conduct an inquiry into and concerning the areas of Canada in which one of the official languages is spoken as a mother tongue by persons who are in the linguistic minority in those areas in respect of an official language, and after holding such public hearings, if any, as it considers necessary and after consultation with the government of each of the provinces in which any such areas are located, prepare and submit to the Governor in Council a report setting out its findings and conclusions including its recommendations if any concerning the establishment of bilingual districts or the alteration of the limits of any existing bilingual districts in accordance with the provisions of this Act.

(2) In addition to its duties and powers under the *Inquiries Act* in respect of an inquiry as described in this section, a Bilingual Districts Advisory Board may be charged by the Governor in Council with the negotiation, on behalf of the Governor in Council, of a draft agreement with the government of a province for the purpose of ensuring that, to the greatest practical extent, the limits of any area that may be established as a bilingual district under this Act will be conterminous with any area similarly established or to be established in that province by such government.

(3) In carrying out its duties under this section, a Bilingual Districts Advisory Board shall have regard to the convenience of the public in a proposed bilingual district in respect of all the federal, provincial, municipal and educational services provided therein and where necessary recommend to the Governor in Council any administrative changes in federal services in the area that it considers necessary to adapt the area to a provincial or municipal bilingual area, for the greater public convenience of the area or to further the purposes of this Act.

16. The Dominion Statistician and the Director of the Surveys and Mapping Branch of the Department of Energy, Mines and Resources shall make available their services and the facilities of their respective offices, and render all such other assistance to a Bilingual Districts Advisory Board as may be necessary, in order to enable that Board to discharge its duties under this Act.

17. Within fifteen days after the receipt by the Governor in Council of the report of a Bilingual Districts Advisory Board submitted by the chairman thereof pursuant to section 15, or, if Parliament is not then sitting, on any of the first fifteen days next thereafter that Parliament is sitting, the Governor in Council shall cause a copy of the report to be laid before Parliament.

18. As soon as possible after the issue of any proclamation establishing or altering the limits of a bilingual district under this Act, the Director of the Surveys and Mapping Branch of the Department of Energy, Mines and Resources shall, in accordance with the descriptions and definitions set out in the proclamation, prepare and print

(*a*) individual maps of each bilingual district showing the boundaries of each such district;

(*b*) individual maps of each province showing the boundaries of each bilingual district therein; and
(*c*) individual maps of each local government or school district, portions of which are in more than one bilingual district.

COMMISSIONER OF OFFICIAL LANGUAGES

19. (1) There shall be a Commissioner of Official Languages for Canada, hereinafter in this Act called the Commissioner.

(2) The Commissioner shall be appointed by Commission under the Great Seal after approval of the appointment by resolution of the Senate and House of Commons.

(3) Subject to this section, the Commissioner holds office during good behaviour for a term of seven years, but may be removed by the Governor in Council at any time on address of the Senate and House of Commons.

(4) The Commissioner, upon the expiration of his first or any subsequent term of office, is eligible to be re-appointed for a further term not exceeding seven years.

(5) The term of office of the Commissioner ceases upon his attaining sixty-five years of age, but he shall continue in office thereafter until his successor is appointed notwithstanding the expiration of such term.

(6) In the event of the death or resignation of the Commissioner while Parliament is not sitting or if he is unable or neglects to perform the duties of his office, the Governor in Council, after consultation by the Prime Minister with the Speaker of the Senate and the Speaker of the House of Commons, may appoint a temporary Commissioner, to hold office for a term not exceeding six months, who shall, while holding such office, have all of the powers and duties of the Commissioner under this Act and be paid such salary or other remuneration and expenses as may be fixed by the Governor in Council.

20. (1) The Commissioner shall rank as and have all the powers of a deputy head of a department, shall devote himself exclusively to the duties of his office and shall not hold any other office under Her Majesty or engage in any other employment.

(2) The Commissioner shall be paid a salary equal to the salary of a puisne judge of the Exchequer Court of Canada, including any additional salary authorized by section 20 of the *Judges Act,* and is entitled to be paid reasonable travelling and living expenses while absent from his ordinary place of residence in the course of his duties.

21. Such officers and employees as are necessary for the proper conduct of the work of the office of the Commissioner shall be appointed in the manner authorized by law.

22. The Commissioner may engage on a temporary basis the services of persons having technical or specialized knowledge of any matter relating to the work of the Commissioner, to advise and assist the Commissioner in the performance of the duties of his office and, with the approval of the Treasury Board, may fix and pay the renumeration and expenses of such persons.

23. The Commissioner and the officers and employees of the Commissioner appointed as provided in section 21 shall be deemed to be persons employed in the Public Service for the purposes of the *Public Service Superannuation Act*.

24. The Commissioner shall carry out such functions and duties as are assigned to him by this Act or any other Act of the Parliament of Canada, and may carry out or engage in such other related assignments or activities as may be authorized by the Governor in Council.

25. It is the duty of the Commissioner to take all actions and measures within his authority with a view to ensuring recognition of the status of each of the official languages and compliance with the spirit and intent of this Act in the administration of the affairs of the institutions of the Parliament and Government of Canada and, for that purpose, to conduct and carry out investigations either on his own initiative or pursuant to any complaint made to him and to report and make recommendations with respect thereto as provided in this Act.

26. (1) Subject to this Act, the Commissioner shall investigate any complaint made to him to the effect that, in any particular instance or case,

(*a*) the status of an official language was not or is not being recognized, or

(*b*) the spirit and intent of this Act was not or is not being complied with

in the administration of the affairs of any of the institutions of the Parliament or Government of Canada.

(2) A complaint may be made to the Commissioner by any person or group of persons, whether or not they speak or represent a group speaking the official language the status or use of which is at issue.

(3) If in the course of investigating any complaint it appears to the Commissioner that, having regard to all the circumstances of the case, any further investigation is unnecessary, he may in his discretion refuse to investigate the matter further.

(4) The Commissioner may, in his discretion, refuse to investigate or cease to investigate any complaint if in his opinion

(*a*) the subject matter of the complaint is trivial,

(*b*) the complaint is frivolous or vexatious or is not made in good faith, or

(*c*) the subject matter of the complaint does not involve a contravention or failure to comply with the spirit and intent of this Act, or does not for any other reason come within his authority under this Act.

(5) Where the Commissioner decides to refuse to investigate or cease to investigate any complaint, he shall inform the complainant of his decision and shall give his reasons therefor.

27. Before carrying out any investigation under this Act, the Commissioner shall inform the deputy head or other administrative head of any department or other institution concerned of his intention to carry out the investigation.

28. (1) Every investigation by the Commissioner under this Act shall be conducted in private.

(2) It is not necessary for the Commissioner to hold any hearing and no person is entitled as of right to be heard by the Commissioner, but if at any time during the course of an investigation it appears to the Commissioner that there may be sufficient grounds for his making a report or recommendation that may adversely affect any individual or any department or other institution, he shall, before completing the investigation, take every reasonable measure to give to that individual, department or institution a full and ample opportunity to answer any adverse allegation or criticism, and to be assisted or represented by counsel for that purpose.

29. (1) Subject to this Act, the Commissioner may regulate the procedure to be followed by him in carrying out any investigation under this Act.

(2) The Commissioner may direct that information relating to any investigation under this Act be received or obtained, in whole or in part, by any officer of the Commissioner appointed as provided in section 21 and such officer shall, subject to such restrictions or limitations as the Commissioner may specify, have all the powers and duties of the Commissioner under this Act in relation to the receiving or obtaining of such information.

(3) The Commissioner shall require every person employed in his office who is directed by him to receive or obtain information relating to any investigation under this Act to comply with any security requirements applicable to, and to take any oath of secrecy required to be taken by, persons employed in any department or other institution concerned in the matter of the investigation.

30. The Commissioner has, in relation to the carrying out of any investigation under this Act, power

(*a*) to summon and enforce the attendance of witnesses and compel them to give oral or written evidence on oath, and to produce such documents and things as the Commissioner deems requisite to the full investigation and consideration of any matter within his authority under this Act, in the same manner and to the same extent as a superior court of record;
(*b*) to administer oaths;
(*c*) to receive and accept such evidence and other information whether on oath or by affidavit or otherwise as in his discretion he sees fit, whether or not such evidence or information is or would be admissible in a court of law; and
(*d*) subject to such limitations as the Governor in Council in the interests of defence or security many prescribe, to enter any premises occupied by any department or other institution of the Parliament or Government of Canada and carry out therein such inquiries within his authority under this Act as he sees fit.

31. (1) This section applies where, after carrying out any investigation under this Act, the Commissioner is of the opinion that an act or omission that was the subject of the investigation is or was or appears to be or have been
(*a*) contrary to the provisions of this Act;
(*b*) contrary to the spirit and intent of this Act but in accordance with the provisions of any other Act of the Parliament of Canada or any regulations thereunder, or in accordance with a practice that leads or is likely to lead to any involuntary contravention of this Act; or
(*c*) based wholly or partly on mistake or inadvertence.

(2) Where the Commissioner is of opinion
(*a*) that the act or omission that was the subject of the investigation should be referred to any department or other institution concerned for consideration and action if necessary,
(*b*) that any Act or regulations thereunder described in paragraph (*b*) of subsection (1) should be reconsidered or any practice described in that paragraph should be altered or discontinued, or
(*c*) that any other action should be taken,
the Commissioner shall report his opinion and his reasons therefor to the Clerk of the Privy Council and the deputy head or other administrative head of any department or other institution concerned and may in his report make such recommendations with respect thereto as he thinks fit, and, in any such case, may request the department or other institution concerned to notify him within a specified time of the action, if any, that it proposes to take to give effect to his recommendations.

32. In the case of an investigation carried out by the Commissioner pursuant to any complaint made to him, the Commissioner shall inform the complainant, and any individual, department or institution by whom or on whose behalf any answer relating to the complaint has been made pursuant to subsection (2) of section 28, in such manner and at such time as he thinks proper of the results of the investigation and, where any recommendations have been made by the Commissioner under section 31 but no action that seems to him to be adequate and appropriate is taken thereon within a reasonable time after the making of the recommendations, he may inform the complainant of his recommendations and make such comments thereon as he thinks proper and, in any such case, shall provide a copy of such recommendations and comments to any individual whom he is required by this section to inform of the results of the investigation.

33. (1) If within a reasonable time after the making of a report containing any recommendations under section 31, no action is taken thereon that seems to the Commissioner to be adequate and appropriate, the Commissioner, in his discretion and after considering any reply made by or on behalf of any department or other institution concerned, may transmit a copy of the report and recommendations to the Governor in Council and may thereafter make such report thereon to Parliament as he deems appropriate.

(2) The Commissioner may disclose in any report made by him under this section such matters as in his opinion ought to be disclosed in order to establish the grounds for his conclusions and recommendations, but in so doing shall take every reasonable precaution to avoid disclosing any matter the disclosure of which would or might be prejudicial to the defence or security of Canada or any state allied or associated with Canada.

(3) The Commissioner shall attach to every report made by him under this section a copy of any reply made by or on behalf of any department or other institution concerned.

34. (1) In addition to any report that may be made by him under section 33, the Commissioner shall each year prepare and submit to Parliament a statement relating to the conduct of his office and the discharge of his duties under this Act during the preceding year including his recommendations, if any, for any proposed changes in this Act that he deems necessary or desirable in order that effect may be given to this Act according to its spirit and intent.

(2) Every report or statement to Parliament made by the Commissioner under section 33 or this section shall be made by being transmitted to the Speaker of the Senate and to the Speaker of the House of Commons for tabling respectively in those Houses.

(3) The Commissioner may, instead of making a separate report to Parliament under section 33 on the matter of any investigation

carried out by him under this Act, include such report in his annual statement to Parliament made under this section unless, in his opinion, the nature of the report is such that it ought to be brought to the attention of Parliament without delay.

GENERAL

35. The Governor in Council may make such regulations as he deems necessary to effect compliance with this Act in the conduct of the affairs of the Government of Canada and departments and agencies of the Government of Canada.

INTERPRETATION

36. (1) In this Act,

(*a*) "court of record" means any body that, under the Act by or pursuant to which it is established, is or is declared to be a court of record;

(*b*) "Crown corporation" means a Crown corporation as defined in Part VIII of the *Financial Administration Act;*

(*c*) "enactment" means any Act of the Parliament of Canada including this Act and any rule, order, regulation, by-law or proclamation described in section 4; and

(*d*) "National Capital Region" means the National Capital Region described in the Schedule to the *National Capital Act.*

(2) For the purposes of this Act, the "mother tongue" spoken by persons in any area of Canada means, in relation to any determination thereof required to be made under this Act, the language first learned in childhood by such persons and still understood by them, as ascertained by the decennial census taken immediately preceding the determination.

(3) For the purposes of this Act, a reference to the institutions or any of the institutions of the Parliament or Government of Canada shall be deemed to include the Canadian Forces and the Royal Canadian Mounted Police.

(4) For greater certainty it is hereby declared that section 107 of the *Criminal Code* does not apply to or in respect of any contravention or alleged contravention of any provision of this Act.

37. In every Act of the Parliament of Canada, a reference to the "official languages" or the "official languages of Canada" shall be construed as a reference to the languages declared by section 2 of this Act to be the official languages of Canada for all purposes of the Parliament and Government of Canada.

38. Nothing in this Act shall be construed as derogating from or diminishing in any way any legal or customary right or privilege acquired or enjoyed either before or after the coming into force of this Act with respect to any language that is not an official language.

CONSEQUENTIAL AMENDMENTS

39. (1) Subsection (1) of section 3 of the *Regulations Act* is repealed and the following substituted therefor:

"**3.** (1) Every regulation-making authority shall, within seven days after making a regulation or, in the case of a regulation made in the first instance in one only of its official language versions, within seven days after its making in that version, transmit copies of the regulation in both official languages to the Clerk of the Privy Council."

(2) Subsection (1) of section 6 of the said Act is repealed and the following substituted therefor:

"**6.** (1) Every regulation shall be published in the *Canada Gazette* within twenty-three days after copies thereof in both official languages are transmitted to the Clerk of the Privy Council pursuant to subsection (1) of section 3."

(3) All that portion of subsection (3) of section 6 of the said Act preceding paragraph (*a*) thereof is repealed and the following substituted therefor:

"(3) No regulation is invalid by reason only that it was not published in the *Canada Gazette,* but no person shall be convicted for an offence consisting of a contravention of any regulation that at the time of the alleged contravention was not published in the *Canada Gazette* in both official languages unless"

ORDERLY ADAPTATION TO ACT

40. (1) Where upon the submission of any Minister it is established to the satisfaction of the Governor in Council that the immediate application of any provision of this Act to any department or other institution of the Parliament or Government of Canada (hereinafter in this section called an "authority") or in respect of any service provided or made available by it

(*a*) would unduly prejudice the interests of the public served by the authority, or

(*b*) would be seriously detrimental to the good government of the authority, employer and employee relations or the effective management of its affairs,

the Governor in Council may by order defer or suspend the application of any such provision to the authority or in respect of any such service for such period, not exceeding sixty months from the coming into force of this Act, as the Governor in Council deems necessary or expedient.

(2) Any order made under this section may contain such directions and be subject to such terms and conditions as the Governor in Council deems appropriate to ensure the earliest possible application of any deferred or suspended provision provided for in the order, and in addition may prescribe different periods, not exceeding in any case the maximum period provided for under subsection (1), for different operations carried on or services performed or made available by the authority, to or in respect of which the application of any such provision is deferred or suspended.

(3) A copy of any order made under this section, together with a report thereon by the Governor in Council setting forth concisely the reasons for its making, shall be laid before Parliament within fifteen days after the making of the order or, if Parliament is not then sitting, on any of the first fifteen days next thereafter that Parliament is sitting.

(4) In relation to the appointment and advancement in employment of personnel the duties of whose positions include duties relating to the provision of services by authorities to members of the public, it is the duty

(*a*) of the Public Service Commission, in cases where it has the authority to make appointments, and

(*b*) of the authority concerned, in all other cases,

to ensure that, in the exercise and performance of the powers, duties and functions conferred or imposed upon it by law, due account is taken of the purposes and provisions of this Act, subject always to the maintenance of the principle of selection of personnel according to merit as required by the *Public Service Employment Act.*

COMMENCEMENT

41. This Act shall come into force on the sixtieth day after the day this Act is assented to.

Statement by the Prime Minister in the House of Commons, October 8, 1971

I am happy this morning to be able to reveal to the House that the government has accepted all those recommendations of the Royal Commission on Bilingualism and Biculturalism as contained in Volume IV of its reports directed to federal departments and agencies. Honourable members will recall that the subject of this volume is "the contribution by other ethnic groups to the cultural enrichment of Canada and the measures that should be taken to safeguard that contribution."

Volume IV examined the whole question of cultural and ethnic pluralism in this country and the status of our various cultures and languages, an area of study given all too little attention in the past by scholars.

It was the view of the Royal Commission, shared by the government and, I am sure, by all Canadians, that there cannot be one cultural policy for Canadians of British and French origin, another for the original peoples and yet a third for all others. For although there are two official languages, there is no official culture, nor does any ethnic group take precedence over any other. No citizen or group of citizens is other than Canadian, and all should be treated fairly.

The Royal Commission was guided by the belief that adherence to one's ethnic group is influenced not so much by one's origin or mother tongue as by one's sense of belonging to the group, and by what the Commission calls the group's "collective will to exist." The government shares this belief.

The individual's freedom would be hampered if he were locked for life within a particular cultural compartment by the accident of birth or language. It is vital, therefore, that every Canadian, whatever his ethnic origin, be given a chance to learn at least one of the two languages in which his country conducts its official business and its politics.

SOURCE: Office of the Prime Minister (Press Release), October 8, 1971.

A policy of multiculturalism within a bilingual framework commends itself to the government as the most suitable means of assuring the cultural freedom of Canadians. Such a policy should help to break down discriminatory attitudes and cultural jealousies. National unity, if it is to mean anything in the deeply personal sense, must be founded on confidence in one's own individual identity; out of this can grow respect for that of others and a willingness to share ideas, attitudes and assumptions. A vigorous policy of multiculturalism will help create this initial confidence. It can form the base of a society which is based on fair play for all.

The government will support and encourage the various cultures and ethnic groups that give structure and vitality to our society. They will be encouraged to share their cultural expression and values with other Canadians and so contribute to a richer life for us all.

In the past, substantial public support has been given largely to the arts and cultural institutions of English-speaking Canada. More recently, and largely with the help of the Royal Commission's earlier recommendations in Volumes I to III, there has been a conscious effort on the government's part to correct any bias against the French language and culture. In the last few months the government has taken steps to provide funds to support cultural-educational centres for native people. The policy I am announcing today accepts the contention of the other cultural communities that they, too, are essential elements in Canada and deserve government assistance in order to contribute to regional and national life in ways that derive from their heritages yet are distinctively Canadian.

In implementing a policy of multiculturalism within a bilingual framework, the government will provide support in four ways.

First, resources permitting, the government will seek to assist all Canadian cultural groups that have demonstrated a desire and effort to continue to develop, a capacity to grow and contribute to Canada, and a clear need for assistance, the small and weak groups no less than the strong and highly organized.

Second, the government will assist members of all cultural groups to overcome cultural barriers to full participation in Canadian society.

Third, the government will promote *creative* encounters and interchange among all Canadian cultural groups in the interest of national unity.

Fourth, the government will continue to assist immigrants to acquire at least one of Canada's official languages in order to become full participants in Canadian society.

Mr. Speaker, I stated at the outset that the government has accepted in principle all recommendations addressed to federal departments and agencies. We are also ready and willing to work cooperatively with the provincial governments towards implementing those recommendations that concern matters under provincial or shared responsibility.

Some of the programs endorsed or recommended by the Commission have been administered for some time by various federal agencies. I might mention the Citizenship Branch, the CRTC and its predecessor the BBG, the National Film Board and the National Museum of Man. These programs will be revised, broadened and reactivated and they will receive the additional funds that may be required.

Some of the recommendations that concern matters under provincial jurisdiction call for coordinated federal and provincial action. As a first step, I have written to the first ministers of the provinces informing them of the response of the federal government and seeking their co-operation. Officials will be asked to carry this consultation further.

I wish to table details of the government's response to each of the several recommendations.

It should be noted that some of the programs require pilot projects or further short-term research before more extensive action can be taken. As soon as these preliminary studies are available, further programs will be announced and initiated. Additional financial and personnel resources will be provided.

Responsibility for implementing these recommendations has been assigned to the Citizenship Branch of the Department of the Secretary of State, the agency now responsible for matters affecting the social integration of immigrants and the cultural activities of all ethnic groups. An Inter-Agency Committee of all those agencies involved will be established to coordinate the federal effort.

In conclusion, I wish to emphasize the view of the government that a policy of multiculturalism within a bilingual framework is basically the conscious support of individual freedom of choice. We are free to be ourselves. But this cannot be left to chance. It must be fostered and pursued actively. If freedom of choice is in danger for some ethnic groups, it is in danger for all. It is the policy of this government to eliminate any such danger and to "safeguard" this freedom.

Bill 101
Charter of the French Language (1977)

[ASSENTED TO 26 AUGUST 1977]

PREAMBLE

WHEREAS the French language, the distinctive language of a people that is in the majority French-speaking, is the instrument by which that people has articulated its identity;

Whereas the Assemblée Nationale du Québec recognizes that Québecers wish to see the quality and influence of the French language assured, and is resolved therefore to make of French the language of Government and the Law, as well as the normal and everyday language of work, instruction, communication, commerce and business;

Whereas the Assemblée Nationale du Québec intends in this pursuit to deal fairly and openly with the ethnic minorities, whose valuable contribution to the development of Québec it readily acknowledges;

Whereas the Assemblée Nationale du Québec recognizes the right of the Amerinds and the Inuit of Québec, the first inhabitants of this land, to preserve and develop their original language and culture;

Whereas these observations and intentions are in keeping with a new perception of the worth of national cultures in all parts of the earth, and of the obligation of every people to contribute in its special way to the international community;

Therefore, Her Majesty, with the advice and consent of the Assemblée Nationale du Québec, enacts as follows:

CHAPTER I

THE OFFICIAL LANGUAGE OF QUÉBEC

1. French is the official language of Québec.

CHAPTER II

FUNDAMENTAL LANGUAGE RIGHTS

2. Every person has a right to have the civil administration, the health services and social services, the public utility firms, the professional corporations, the associations of employees and all business firms doing business in Qubec communicate with him in French.

3. In deliberative assembly, every person has a right to speak in French.

4. Workers have a right to carry on their activities in French.

5. Consumers of goods and services have a right to be informed and served in French.

6. Every person eligible for instruction in Québec has a right to receive that instruction in French.

CHAPTER III

THE LANGUAGE OF THE LEGISLATURE AND THE COURTS

7. French is the language of the legislature and the courts in Québec.

8. Legislative bills shall be drafted in the official language. They shall also be tabled in the National Assembly, passed and assented to in that language.

9. Only the French text of the statutes and regulations is official.

10. An English version of every legislative bill, statute and regulation shall be printed and published by the civil administration.

11. Artificial persons addressing themselves to the courts and to bodies discharging judicial or quasi-judicial functions shall do so in the official language, and shall use the official language in pleading before them unless all the parties to the action agree to their pleading in English.

12. Procedural documents issued by bodies discharging judicial or quasi-judicial functions or drawn up and sent by the advocates practising before them shall be drawn up in the official language. Such documents may, however, be drawn up in another language if the natural person for whose intention they are issued expressly consents thereto.

13. The judgments rendered in Québec by the courts and by bodies discharging judicial or quasi-judicial functions must be drawn up in French or be accompanied with a duly authenticated French version. Only the French version of the judgment is official.

CHAPTER IV

THE LANGUAGE OF THE CIVIL ADMINISTRATION

14. The Government, the government departments, the other agencies of the civil administration and the services thereof shall be designated by their French names alone.

15. The civil administration shall draw up and publish its texts and documents in the official language.

This section does not apply to relations with persons outside Québec, to publicity and communiqués carried by news media that publish in a language other than French or to correspondence between the civil administration and natural persons when the latter address it in a language other than French.

16. The civil administration shall use only the official language in its written communications with other governments and with artificial persons established in Québec.

17. The Government, the government departments and the other agencies of the civil administration shall use only the official language in their written communications with each other.

18. French is the language of written internal communications in the Government, the government departments, and the other agencies of the civil administration.

19. The notices of meeting, agendas and minutes of all deliberative assemblies in the civil administration shall be drawn up in the official language.

20. In order to be appointed, transferred or promoted to an office in the civil administration, a knowledge of the official language appropriate to the office applied for is required.

For the application of the preceding paragraph, each agency of the civil administration shall establish criteria and procedures of verification and submit them to the Office de la langue française for approval, failing which the Office may establish them itself. If the Office considers the criteria and procedures unsatisfactory, it may either request the agency concerned to modify them or establish them itself.

21. Contracts entered into by the civil administration, including the related sub-contracts, shall be drawn up in the official language. Such contracts and the related documents may be drawn up in another language when the civil administration enters into a contract with a party outside Québec.

22. The civil administration shall use only French in signs and posters, except where reasons of public health or safety require the use of another language as well.

23. The health services and the social services must ensure that their services are available in the official language.

They must draw up their notices, communications and printed matter intended for the public in the official language.

24. The municipal and school bodies, the health services and social services and the other services recognized under paragraph *f* of section 113 may erect signs and posters in both French and another language, the French text predominating.

25. The municipal and school bodies, the health services and the social services recognized under paragraph *f* of section 113 must comply with sections 15 to 23 before the end of 1983 and, upon the coming into force of this act, must take the required measures to attain that objective.

26. The school bodies, the health services and the social services recognized under paragraph *f* of section 113 may use both the official language and another language in their names and in their internal communications.

27. In the health services and the social services, the documents filed in the clinical records shall be drafted in French or in English, as the person drafting them sees fit. However, each health service or social service may require such documents to be drafted in French alone. Resumés of clinical records must be furnished in French on demand to any person authorized to obtain them.

28. In the school bodies, the official language and the language of instruction may be used as the language of internal communication in departments entrusted with organizing or giving instruction in a language other than French.

29. Only the official language shall be used on traffic signs. The French inscription may be complemented or replaced by symbols or pictographs.

CHAPTER V

THE LANGUAGE OF THE SEMIPUBLIC AGENCIES

30. The public utility firms, the professional corporations and the members of the professional corporations must arrange to make their services available in the official language.

They must draw up their notices, communications and printed matter intended for the public, including public transportation tickets, in the official language.

31. The public utility firms and the professional corporations shall use the official language in their written communications with the civil administration and with artificial persons.

32. The professional corporations shall use the official language in their written communications with their general membership.

They may, however, in communicating with an individual member, reply in his language.

33. Sections 30 and 31 do not apply to communiqués or publicity intended for news media that publish in a language other than French.

34. The professional corporations shall be designated by their French names alone.

35. The professional corporations shall not issue permits in Québec except to persons whose knowledge of the official language is appropriate to the practice of their profession.

Proof of that knowledge must be given in accordance with the regulations of the Office de la langue française, which may provide for the holding of examinations and the issuance of certificates.

36. Within the last two years before obtaining a qualifying diploma for a permit to practise, every person enrolled in an educational institution that issues such diploma may give proof that his knowledge of the official language meets the requirements of section 35.

37. The professional corporations may issue temporary permits valid for not more than one year to persons from outside Québec who are declared qualified to practise their profession but whose knowledge of the official language does not meet the requirements of section 35.

38. The permits envisaged in section 37 may be renewed, only twice, with the authorization of the Office de la langue française and if the public interest warrants it. For each renewal, the persons concerned must sit for examinations held according to the regulations of the Office de la langue française.

39. Persons having obtained, in Québec, a diploma referred to in section 36 may, until the end of 1980, avail themselves of sections 37 and 38.

40. Where it is in the public interest, a professional corporation, with the prior authorization of the Office de la langue française, may issue a restricted permit to a person already authorized under the laws of another province or another country to practise his profession. This restricted permit authorizes its holder to practise his profession for the exclusive account of a single employer, in a position that does not involve his dealing with the public.

CHAPTER VI

THE LANGUAGE OF LABOUR RELATIONS

41. Every employer shall draw up his written communications to his staff in the official language. He shall draw up and publish his offers of employment or promotion in French.

42. Where an offer of employment regards employment in the civil administration, a semipublic agency or a firm required under section 136, 146 or 151 to have a francization certificate, establish a francization committee or apply a francization programme, as the case may be, the employer publishing this offer of employment in a daily newspaper published in a language other than French must publish it simultaneously in a daily newspaper published in French, with at least equivalent display.

43. Collective agreements and the schedules to them must be drafted in the official language, including those which must be filed pursuant to section 60 of the Labour Code (Revised Statutes, 1964, chapter 141).

44. Where a grievance or dispute regarding the negotiation, renewal or review of a collective labour agreement is the subject of arbitration, the arbitration award shall be drawn up in the official language or be accompanied with a duly authenticated French version. Only the French version of the award is official.

The same rule applies to decisions rendered under the Labour Code by investigators, investigation-commissioners and the Labour Court.

45. An employer is prohibited from dismissing, laying off, demoting or transferring a member of his staff for the sole reason that he is exclusively French-speaking or that he has insufficient knowledge of a particular language other than French.

46. An employer is prohibited from making the obtaining of an employment or office dependent upon the knowledge of a language other than the official language, unless the nature of the duties requires the knowledge of that other language.

The burden of proof that the knowledge of the other language is necessary is on the employer, at the demand of the person or the association of employees concerned or, as the case may be, the Office de la langue française. The Office de la langue française has the power to decide any dispute.

47. Any contravention of section 45 or 46, in addition to being an offence against this act, gives a worker not governed by a collective agreement the same entitlement to vindicate his rights through an investigation-commissioner appointed under the Labour Code as if he were dismissed for union activities. Sections 14 to 19 of the Labour Code then apply, *mutatis mutandis*.

If the worker is governed by a collective agreement, he has the same entitlement to submit his grievance for arbitration as his association, if the latter fails to act. Section 16 of the Labour Code applies, *mutatis mutandis*, for the arbitration of this grievance.

48. Except as they regard the vested rights of employees and their associations, juridical acts, decisions and other documents not in conformity to this chapter are null. The use of a language other than that prescribed in this chapter shall not be considered a defect of form within the meaning of section 134 of the Labour Code.

49. Every association of employees shall use the official language in written communications with its members. It may use the language of an individual member in its correspondence with him.

50. Sections 41 to 49 of this act are deemed an integral part of every collective agreement. Any stipulation in the agreement contrary to any provision of this act is void.

CHAPTER VII

THE LANGUAGE OF COMMERCE AND BUSINESS

51. Every inscription on a product, on its container or on its wrapping, or on a leaflet, brochure or card supplied with it, including the directions for use and the warranty certificates, must be drafted in French. This rule applies also to menus and wine lists.

The French inscription may be accompanied with a translation or translations, but no inscription in another language may be given greater prominence than that in French.

52. The Office de la langue française may, by regulation, indicate exceptions to the application of section 51.

53. Catalogues, brochures, folders and similar publications must be drawn up in French.

54. Except as provided by regulation of the Office de la langue française, it is forbidden to offer toys or games to the public which require the use of a non-French vocabulary for their operation, unless a French version of the toy or game is available on no less favourable terms on the Québec market.

55. Contracts pre-determined by one party, contracts containing printed standard clauses, and the related documents, must be drawn up in French. They may be drawn up in another language as well at the express wish of the parties.

56. If the documents referred to in section 51 are required by any act, order in council or government regulation, they may be excepted from the rule enunciated in that section, provided that the languages in which they are drafted are the subject of a federal-provincial, interprovincial or international agreement.

57. Application forms for employment, order forms, invoices, receipts and quittances shall be drawn up in French.

58. Except as may be provided under this act or the regulations of the Office de la langue française, signs and posters and commercial advertising shall be solely in the official language.

59. Section 58 does not apply to advertising carried in news media that publish in a language other than French, or to messages of a religious, political, ideological or humanitarian nature, if not for a profit motive.

60. Firms employing not over four persons including the employer may erect signs and posters in both French and another language in their establishments. However, the inscriptions in French must be given at least as prominent display as those in the other language.

61. Signs and posters respecting the cultural activities of a particular ethnic group in any way may be in both French and the language of that ethnic group.

62. In commercial establishments specializing in foreign national specialities or the specialities of a particular ethnic group, signs and posters may be both in French and in the relevant foreign national language or the language of that ethnic group.

63. Firms names must be in French.

64. To obtain juridical personality, it is necessary to have a firm name in French.

65. Every firm name that is not in French must be changed before 31 December 1980, unless the act under which the firm is incorporated does not allow it.

66. Sections 63, 64 and 65 also apply to firm names registered under the Companies and Partnerships Declaration Act (Revised Statutes, 1964, chapter 272).

67. Family names, place names, expressions formed by the artificial combination of letters, syllables or figures, and expressions taken from other languages may appear in firm names to specify them, in accordance with the other acts and with the regulations of the Office de la langue française.

68. A firm name may be accompanied with a version in another language for use outside Québec. That version may be used together with the French version of the firm name in the inscriptions referred to in section 51, if the products in question are offered both in and outside Québec.

69. Subject to section 68, only the French version of a firm name may be used in Québec.

70. Health services and social services the firm names of which, adopted before the coming into force of this act, are in a language other than French may continue to use such names provided they add a French version.

71. A non-profit organization devoted exclusively to the cultural development or to the defense of the peculiar interests of a particular ethnic group may adopt a firm name in the language of the group, provided that it adds a French version.

CHAPTER VIII

THE LANGUAGE OF INSTRUCTION

72. Instruction in the kindergarden classes and in the elementary and secondary schools shall be in French, except where this chapter allows otherwise.

This rule obtains in school bodies within the meaning of the Schedule and also applies to subsidized instruction provided by institutions declared to be of public interest or recognized for purposes of grants in virtue of the Private Education Act (1968, chapter 67).

73. In derogation of section 72, the following children, at the request of their father and mother, may receive their instruction in English:

(*a*) a child whose father or mother received his or her elementary instruction in English, in Québec;

(*b*) a child whose father or mother, domiciled in Québec on the date of the coming into force of this act, received his or her elementary instruction in English outside Québec;

(*c*) a child who, in his last year of school in Québec before the coming into force of this act, was lawfully receiving his instruction in English, in a public kindergarten class or in an elementary or secondary school;

(*d*) the younger brothers and sisters of a child described in paragraph *c*.

74. where a child is in the custody of only one of his parents, or a tutor, the request provided for in section 73 must be made by that parent or by the tutor.

75. The Minister of Education may empower such persons as he may designate to verify and decide on children's eligibility for instruction in English.

76. The persons designated by the Minister of Education under section 75 may verify the eligibility of children to receive their elementary instruction in English even if they are already receiving or are about to receive their instruction in French.

Children whose eligibility has been confirmed in accordance with the preceding paragraph are deemed to receive their instruction in English for the purposes of section 73.

77. A certificate of eligibility obtained fraudulently or on the basis of a false representation is void.

78. The Minister of Education may revoke a certificate of eligibility issued in error.

79. A school body not already giving instruction in English in its schools is not required to introduce it, and shall not introduce it without express and prior authorization of the Minister of Education.

However, every school body shall, where necessary, avail itself of section 496 of the Education Act to arrange for the instruction in English of any child declared eligible therefor.

The Minister of Education shall grant the authorization referred to in the first paragraph if, in his opinion, it is warranted by the number of pupils in the jurisdiction of the school body who are eligible for instruction in English under section 73.

80. The Government may, by regulation, prescribe the procedure to be followed where parents invoke section 73, and the elements of proof they must furnish in support of their request.

81. Children having serious learning disabilities must be exempted from the application of this chapter.

The Government, by regulation, may define the classes of children envisaged in the preceding paragraph and determine the procedure to be followed in view of obtaining such an exemption.

82. An appeal lies from the decisions of the school bodies, the institutions mentioned in the second paragraph of section 72, and the persons designated by the Minister of Education, dealing with the application of section 73, and from the decisions of the Minister of Education taken under section 78.

83. An appeals committee is established to hear appeals provided for in section 82. This committee consists of three members appointed by the Government. Appeals are brought in accordance with the procedure established by regulation. The decisions of this committee are final.

84. No secondary school leaving certificate may be issued to a student who does not have the speaking and writing knowledge of French required by the curricula of the Department of Education.

85. The Government, by regulation, may determine the conditions on which certain persons or categories of persons staying in Québec temporarily, or their children, may be exempted from the application of this chapter.

86. The Government may make regulations extending the scope of section 73 to include such persons as may be contemplated in any reciprocity agreement that may be concluded between the Government of Québec and another province.

Notwithstanding section 94, such regulations may come into force from their date of publication in the *Gazette officielle du Québec*.

87. Nothing in this act prevents the use of an Amerindic language in providing instruction to the Amerinds.

88. Notwithstanding sections 72 to 86, in the schools under the jurisdiction of the Cree School Board or the Kativik School Board, according to the Education Act, the languages of instruction shall be

Cree and Inutituut, respectively, and the other languages of instruction in use in the Cree and Inuit communities in Québec on the date of the signing of the Agreement indicated in section 1 of the Act approving the Agreement concerning James Bay and Northern Québec (1976, chapter 46), namely, 11 November 1975.

The Cree School Board and the Kativik School Board shall pursue as an objective the use of French as a language of instruction so that pupils graduating frm their schools will in future be capable of continuing their studies in a French school, college or university elsewhere in Québec, if they so desire.

After consultation with the school committees, in the case of the Crees, and with the parents' committees, in the case of the Inuit, the commissioners shall determine the rate of introduction of French and English as languages of instruction.

With the assistance of the Minister of Education, the Cree School Board and the Kativik School Board shall take the necessary measures to have sections 72 to 86 apply to children whose parents are not Crees or Inuit qualifying for benefit under the Agreement.

This section, with the necessary changes, applies to the Naskapi of Schefferville.

CHAPTER IX

MISCELLANEOUS

89. Where this act does not require the use of the official language exclusively, the official language and another language may be used together.

90. Subject to section 10, anything that, by prescription of an act of Québec or an act of the British Parliament having application to Québec in a field of provincial jurisdiction, or of a regulation or an order, must be published in French and English, may be published in French alone.

Similarly, anything that, by prescription of an act, a regulation or an order, must be published in a French newspaper and in an English newspaper, may be published in a French newspaper alone.

91. Where this act authorizes the drafting of texts or documents both in French and in one or more other languages, the French version must be displayed at least as prominently as every other language.

92. Nothing prevents the use of a language in derogation of this act by international organizations designated by the Government or where international usage requires it.

93. In addition to its other regulation-making powers under this act, the Government may make regulations to facilitate the administration of the act, including regulations specifying the scope of the terms and expressions used in the act.

94. The regulations of the Office de la langue française or of the Government made under this act come into force from their publication in the *Gazette officielle du Québec* together with a notice of the date of their approval or adoption by the Government, whichever applies.

The Government, before adopting or approving a regulation under this act, must publish the draft regulation in the *Gazette officielle du Québec* at least sixty days previously, except regulations tabled in the National Assembly before the coming into force of this act.

If a regulation of the Office de la langue française or of the Government is amended, the amended text comes into force on its publication in full in the *Gazette officielle du Québec*.

Regulations ascribed by this act to the Office de la langue française, approved and tabled before the coming into force of this act, are deemed regulations of the Office de la langue française.

95. The following persons and bodies have the right to use Cree and Inutituut and are exempt from the application of this act, except sections 87, 88 and 96:

(*a*) persons qualified for benefit under the Agreement indicated in section 1 of the Act approving the Agreement concerning James Bay and Northern Québec (1976, chapter 46), in the territories envisaged by the said Agreement;

(*b*) bodies to be created under the said Agreement, within the territories envisaged by the Agreement;

(*c*) bodies of which the members are in the majority persons referred to in subparagraph *a*, within the territories envisaged by the Agreement.

This section, with the necessary changes, applies to the Naskapi of Schefferville.

96. The bodies envisaged in section 95 must introduce the use of French into their administration, both to communicate in French with the rest of Québec and with those persons under their administration who are not contemplated in subparagraph *a* of that section, and to provide their services in French to those persons.

During a transitional period of such duration as the Government may fix after consultation with the persons concerned, sections 16 and 17 of this act do not apply to communications of the civil administration with the bodies envisaged in section 95.

This section, with the necessary changes, applies to the Naskapi of Schefferville.

97. The Indian reserves are not subject to this act.

98. The various agencies of the civil administration, and the health services and social services, the public utility firms and the professional corporations referred to in this act are listed in the Schedule.

Canadian Charter of Rights and Freedoms (1982)

Whereas Canada is founded upon principles that recognize the supremacy of God and the rule of law:

GUARANTEE OF RIGHTS AND FREEDOMS

1. The *Canadian Charter of Rights and Freedoms* guarantees the rights and freedoms set out in it subject only to such reasonable limits prescribed by law as can be demonstrably justified in a free and democratic society.

FUNDAMENTAL FREEDOMS

2. Everyone has the following fundamental freedoms:
(*a*) freedom of conscience and religion;
(*b*) freedom of thought, belief, opinion and expression, including freedom of the press and other media of communication;
(*c*) freedom of peaceful assembly; and
(*d*) freedom of association.

DEMOCRATIC RIGHTS

3. Every citizen of Canada has the right to vote in an election of members of the House of Commons or of a legislative assembly and to be qualified for membership therein.

4. (1) No House of Commons and no legislative assembly shall continue for longer than five years from the date fixed for the return of the writs at a general election of its members.

(2) In time of real or apprehended war, invasion or insurrection, a House of Commons may be continued by Parliament and a legislative assembly may be continued by the legislature beyond five years if such continuation is not opposed by the votes of more than one-third of the members of the House of Commons or the legislative assembly, as the case may be.

5. There shall be a sitting of Parliament and of each legislature at least once every twelve months.

MOBILITY RIGHTS

6. (1) Every citizen of Canada has the right to enter, remain in and leave Canada.

(2) Every citizen of Canada and every person who has the status of a permanent resident of Canada has the right

(*a*) to move to and take up residence in any province; and

(*b*) to pursue the gaining of a livelihood in any province.

(3) The rights specified in subsection (2) are subject to

(*a*) any laws or practices of general application in force in a province other than those that discriminate among persons primarily on the basis of province of present or previous residence; and

(*b*) any laws providing for reasonable residency requirements as a qualification for the receipt of publicly provided social services.

(4) Subsections (2) and (3) do not preclude any law, program or activity that has as its object the amelioration in a province of conditions of individuals in that province who are socially or economically disadvantaged if the rate of employment in that province is below the rate of employment in Canada.

LEGAL RIGHTS

7. Everyone has the right to life, liberty and security of the person and the right not to be deprived thereof except in accordance with the principles of fundamental justice.

8. Everyone has the right to be secure against unreasonable search or seizure.

9. Everyone has the right not to be arbitrarily detained or imprisoned.

10. Everyone has the right on arrest or detention

(*a*) to be informed promptly of the reasons therefor;

(*b*) to retain and instruct counsel without delay and to be informed of that right; and

(*c*) to have the validity of the detention determined by way of *habeas corpus* and to be released if the detention is not lawful.

11. any person charged with an offence has the right

(*a*) to be informed without unreasonable delay of the specific offence;

(*b*) to be tried within a reasonable time;
(*c*) not to be compelled to be a witness in proceedings against that person in respect of the offence;
(*d*) to be presumed innocent until proven guilty according to law in a fair and public hearing by an independent and impartial tribunal;
(*e*) not to be denied reasonable bail without just cause;
(*f*) except in the case of an offence under military law tried before a military tribunal, to the benefit of trial by jury where the maximum punishment for the offence is imprisonment for five years or a more severe punishment;
(*g*) not to be found guilty on account of any act or omission unless, at the time of the act or omission, it constituted an offence under Canadian or international law or was criminal according to the general principles of law recognized by the community of nations;
(*h*) if finally acquitted of the offence, not to be tried for it again and, if finally found guilty and punished for the offence, not to be tried or punished for it again; and
(*i*) if found guilty of the offence and if the punishment for the offence has been varied between the time of commission and the time of sentencing, to the benefit of the lesser punishment.

12. Everyone has the right not to be subjected to any cruel and unusual treatment or punishment.

13. A witness who testifies in any proceedings has the right not to have any incriminating evidence so given used to incriminate that witness in any other proceedings, except in a prosecution for perjury or for the giving of contradictory evidence.

14. A party or witness in any proceedings who does not understand or speak the language in which the proceedings are conducted or who is deaf has the right to the assistance of an interpreter.

EQUALITY RIGHTS

15. (1) Every individual is equal before and under the law and has the right to the equal protection and equal benefit of the law without discrimination and, in particular, without discrimination based on race, national or ethnic origin, colour, religion, sex, age or mental or physical disability.

(2) Subsection (1) does not preclude any law, program or activity that has as its object the amelioration of conditions of disadvantaged individuals or groups including those that are disadvantaged because of race, national or ethnic origin, colour, religion, sex, age or mental or physical disability.

OFFICIAL LANGUAGES OF CANADA

16. (1) English and French are the official languages of Canada and have equality of status and equal rights and privileges as to their use in all institutions of the Parliament and government of Canada.

(2) English and French are the official languages of New Brunswick and have equality of status and equal rights and privileges as to their use in all institutions of the legislature and government of New Brunswick.

(3) Nothing in this Charter limits the authority of Parliament or a legislature to advance the equality of status or use of English and French.

17. (1) Everyone has the right to use English or French in any debates and other proceedings of Parliament.

(2) Everyone has the right to use English or French in any debates and other proceedings of the legislature of New Brunswick.

18. (1) The statutes, records and journals of Parliament shall be printed and published in English and French and both language versions are equally authoritative.

(2) The statutes, records and journals of the legislature of New Brunswick shall be printed and published in English and French and both language versions are equally authoritative.

19. (1) Either English or French may be used by any person in, or in any pleading in or process issuing from, any court established by Parliament.

(2) Either English or French may be used by any person in, or in any pleading in or process issuing from, any court of New Brunswick.

20. (1) Any member of the public in Canada has the right to communicate with, and to receive available services from, any head or central office of an institution of the Parliament or government of Canada in English or French, and has the same right with respect to any other office of any such institution where

(*a*) there is a significant demand for communications with and services from that office in such language; or

(*b*) due to the nature of the office, it is reasonable that communications with and services from that office be available in both English and French

(2) Any member of the public in New Brunswick has the right to communicate with, and to receive available services from, any office of an institution of the legislature or government of New Brunswick in English or French.

21. Nothing in sections 16 to 20 abrogates or derogates from any right, privilege or obligation with respect to the English and French languages, or either of them, that exists or is continued by virtue of any other provision of the Constitution of Canada.

22. Nothing in sections 16 to 20 abrogates or derogates from any legal or customary right or privilege acquired or enjoyed either before or after the coming into force of this Charter with respect to any language that is not English or French.

MINORITY LANGUAGE EDUCATIONAL RIGHTS

23. (1) Citizens of Canada

(*a*) whose first language learned and still understood is that of the English or French linguistic minority population of the province in which they reside, or

(*b*) who have received their primary school instruction in Canada in English or French and reside in a province where the language in which they received that instruction is the language of the English or French linguistic minority population of the province,

have the right to have their children receive primary and secondary school instruction in that language in that province.

(2) Citizens of Canada of whom any child has received or is receiving primary or secondary school instruction in English or French in Canada, have the right to have all their children receive primary and secondary school instruction in the same language.

(3) The right of citizens of Canada under subsections (1) and (2) to have their children receive primary and secondary school instruction in the language of the English or French linguistic minority population of a province

(*a*) applies wherever in the province the number of children of citizens who have such a right is sufficient to warrant the provision to them out of public funds of minority language instruction; and

(*b*) includes, where the number of those children so warrants, the right to have them receive that instruction in minority language educational facilities provided out of public funds.

ENFORCEMENT

24. (1) Anyone whose rights or freedoms, as guaranteed by this Charter, have been infringed or denied may apply to a court of competent jurisdiction to obtain such remedy as the court considers appropriate and just in the circumstances.

(2) Where, in proceedings under subsection (1), a court concludes that evidence was obtained in a manner that infringed or denied any rights or freedoms guaranteed by this Charter, the evidence shall be excluded if it is established that, having regard to all the circumstances, the admission of it in the proceedings would bring the administration of justice into disrepute.

GENERAL

25. The guarantee in this Charter of certain rights and freedoms shall not be construed so as to abrogate or derogate from any aboriginal, treaty or other rights or freedoms that pertain to the aboriginal peoples of Canada including

(*a*) any rights or freedoms that have been recognized by the Royal Proclamation of October 7, 1763; and

(*b*) any rights or freedoms that may be acquired by the aboriginal peoples of Canada by way of land claims settlement.

26. The guarantee in this Charter of certain rights and freedoms shall not be construed as denying the existence of any other rights or freedoms that exist in Canada.

27. This Charter shall be interpreted in a manner consistent with the preservation and enhancement of the multicultural heritage of Candians.

28. Notwithstanding anything in this Charter, the rights and freedoms referred to in it are guaranteed equally to male and female persons.

29. Nothing in this Charter abrogates or derogates from any rights or privileges guaranteed by or under the Constitution of Canada in respect of denominational, separate or dissentient schools.

30. A reference in this Charter to a province or to the legislative assembly or legislature of a province shall be deemed to include a reference to the Yukon Territory and the Northwest Territories, or to the appropriate legislative authority thereof, as the case may be.

31. Nothing in this Charter extends the legislative powers of any body or authority.

APPLICATION OF CHARTER

32. (1) This Charter applies

(*a*) to the Parliament and government of Canada in respect of all matters within the authority of Parliament including all matters relating to the Yukon Territory and Northwest Territories; and (*b*) to the legislature and government of each province in respect of all matters within the authority of the legislature of each province.

(2) Notwithstanding subsection (1), section 15 shall not have effect until three years after this section comes into force.

33. (1) Parliament or the legislature of a province may expressly declare in an Act of Parliament or of the legislature, as the case may be, that the Act or a provision thereof shall operate notwithstanding a provision included in section 2 or sections 7 to 15 of this Charter.

(2) An Act or a provision of an Act in respect of which a declaration made under this section is in effect shall have such operation as it would have but for the provision of this Charter referred to in the declaration.

(3) A declaration made under subsection (1) shall cease to have effect five years after it comes into force or on such earlier date as may be specified in the declaration.

(4) Parliament or a legislature of a province may re-enact a declaration made under subsection (1).

(5) Subsection (3) applies in respect of a re-enactment made under subsection (4).

RIGHTS OF THE ABORIGINAL PEOPLES OF CANADA

35. (1) The existing aboriginal and treaty rights of the aboriginal peoples of Canada are hereby recognized and affirmed.

(2) In this Act, "aboriginal peoples of Canada" includes the Indian, Inuit and Métis peoples of Canada.

EQUALIZATION AND REGIONAL DISPARITIES

36. (1) Without altering the legislative authority of Parliament or of the provincial legislatures, or the rights of any of them with respect to the exercise of their legislative authority, Parliament and the legislatures, together with the government of Canada and the provincial governments, are committed to

(*a*) promoting equal opportunities for the well-being of Canadians;

(*b*) furthering economic development to reduce disparity in opportunities; and

(*c*) providing essential public services of reasonable quality to all Canadians.

(2) Parliament and the government of Canada are committed to the principle of making equalization payments to ensure that provincial governments have sufficient revenues to provide reasonably comparable levels of public services at reasonably comparable levels of taxation.

CONSTITUTIONAL CONFERENCE

37. (1) A constitutional conference composed of the Prime Minister of Canada and the first ministers of the provinces shall be convened by the Prime Minister of Canada within one year after this Part comes into force.

(2) The conference convened under subsection (1) shall have included in its agenda an item respecting constitutional matters that directly affect the aboriginal peoples of Canada, including the identification and definition of the rights of those peoples to be included in the Constitution of Canada, and the Prime Minister of Canada shall invite representatives of those peoples to participate in the discussions on that item.

(3) The Prime Minister of Canada shall invite elected representatives of the governments of the Yukon Territory and the Northwest Territories to participate in the discussions on any item on the agenda of the conference convened under subsection (1) that, in the opinion of the Prime Minister, directly affects the Yukon Territory and the Northwest Territories.

PROCEDURE FOR AMENDING CONSTITUTION OF CANADA

38. (1) An amendment to the Constitution of Canada may be made by proclamation issued by the Governor General under the Great Seal of Canada where so authorized by

(*a*) resolutions of the Senate and House of Commons; and

(*b*) resolutions of the legislative assemblies of at least two-thirds of the provinces that have, in the aggregate, according to the then latest general census, at least fifty per cent of the population of all the provinces.

(2) An amendment made under subsection (1) that derogates from the legislative powers, the proprietary rights or any other rights or privileges of the legislature or government of a province shall require a resolution supported by a majority of the members of each of the Senate, the House of Commons and the legislative assemblies required under subsection (1).

(3) An amendment referred to in subsection (2) shall not have effect

in a province the legislative assembly of which has expressed its dissent thereto by resolution supported by a majority of its members prior to the issue of the proclamation to which the amendment relates unless that legislative assembly, subsequently, by resolution supported by a majority of its members, revokes its dissent and authorizes the amendment.

(4) A resolution of dissent made for the purposes of subsection (3) may be revoked at any time before or after the issue of the proclamation to which it relates.

39. (1) A proclamation shall not be issued under subsection 38(1) before the expiration of one year from the adoption of the resolution initiating the amendment procedure thereunder, unless the legislative assembly of each province has previously adopted a resolution of assent or dissent.

(2) A proclamation shall not be issued under subsection 38(1) after the expiration of three years from the adoption of the resolution initiating the amendment procedure thereunder.

40. Where an amendment is made under subsection 38(1) that transfers provincial legislative powers relating to education or other cultural matters from provincial legislatures to Parliament, Canada shall provide reasonable compensation to any province to which the amendment does not apply.

41. An amendment to the Constitution of Canada in relation to the following matters may be made by proclamation issued by the Governor General under the Great Seal of Canada only where authorized by resolutions of the Senate and House of Commons and of the legislative assembly of each province:

(*a*) the office of the Queen, the Governor General and the Lieutenant Governor of a province;

(*b*) the right of a province to a number of members in the House of Commons not less than the number of Senators by which the province is entitled to be represented at the time this Part comes into force;

(*c*) subject to section 43, the use of the English or the French language;

(*d*) the composition of the Supreme Court of Canada; and

(*e*) an amendment to this Part.

42. (1) An amendment to the Constitution of Canada in relation to the following matters may be made only in accordance with subsection 38(1):

(*a*) the principle of proportionate representation of the provinces in the House of Commons prescribed by the Constitution of Canada;

(*b*) the powers of the Senate and the method of selecting Senators;

(*c*) the number of members by which a province is entitled to be represented in the Senate and the residence qualifications of Senators;

(*d*) subject to paragraph 41(*d*), the Supreme Court of Canada;

(*e*) the extension of existing provinces into the territories; and

(*f*) notwithstanding any other law or practice, the establishment of new provinces.

(2) Subsections 38(2) to (4) do not apply in respect of amendments in relation to matters referred to in subsection (1).

43. An amendment to the Constitution of Canada in relation to any provision that applies to one or more, but not all, provinces, including

(*a*) any alteration to boundaries between provinces, and

(*b*) any amendment to any provision that relates to the use of the English or the French language within a province,

may be made by proclamation issued by the Governor General under the Great Seal of Canada only where so authorized by resolutions of the Senate and House of Commons and of the legislative assembly of each province to which the amendment applies.

44. Subject to sections 41 and 42, Parliament may exclusively make laws amending the Constitution of Canada in relation to the executive government of Canada or the Senate and House of Commons.

45. Subject to section 41, the legislature of each province may exclusively make laws amending the constitution of the province.

46. (1) The procedures for amendment under sections 38, 41, 42 and 43 may be initiated either by the Senate or the House of Commons or by the legislative assembly of a province.

(2) A resolution of assent made for the purposes of this Part may be revoked at any time before the issue of a proclamation authorized by it.

47. (1) An amendment to the Constitution of Canada made by proclamation under section 38, 41, 42 or 43 may be made without a resolution of the Senate authorizing the issue of the proclamation if, within one hundred and eighty days after the adoption by the House of Commons of a resolution authorizing its issue, the Senate has not adopted such a resolution and if, at any time after the expiration of that period, the House of Commons again adopts the resolution.

(2) any period when Parliament is prorogued or dissolved shall not be counted in computing the one hundred and eighty day period referred to in subsection (1).

48. The Queen's Privy Council for Canada shall advise the Governor General to issue a proclamation under this Part forthwith on the adoption of the resolutions required for an amendment made by proclamation under this Part.

49. A constitutional conference composed of the Prime Minister of Canada and the first ministers of the provinces shall be convened by the Prime Minister of Canada within fifteen years after this Part comes into force to review the provisions of this Part.

AMENDMENT TO THE CONSTITUTION ACT, 1867

50. The *Constitution Act, 1867* (formerly named the *British North America Act, 1867*) is amended by adding thereto, immediately after section 92 thereof, the following heading and section:

"Non-Renewable Natural Resources, Forestry Resources and Electrical Energy

92A. (1) In each province, the legislature may exclusively make laws in relation to

(*a*) exploration for non-renewable natural resources in the province;
(*b*) development, conservation and management of non-renewable natural resources and forestry resources in the province, including laws in relation to the rate of primary production therefrom; and
(*c*) development, conservation and management of sites and facilities in the province for the generation and production of electrical energy.

(2) In each province, the legislature may make laws in relation to the export from the province to another part of Canada of the primary production from non-renewable natural resources and forestry resources in the province and the production from facilities in the province for the generation of electrical energy, but such laws may not authorize or provide for discrimination in prices or in supplies exported to another part of Canada.

(3) Nothing in subsection (2) derogates from the authority of Parliament to enact laws in relation to the matters referred to in that subsection and, where such a law of Parliament and a law of a province conflict, the law of Parliament prevails to the extent of the conflict.

(4) In each province, the legislature may make laws in relation to the raising of money by any mode or system of taxation in respect of

(*a*) non-renewable natural resources and forestry resources in the province and the primary production therefrom, and

(*b*) sites and facilities in the province for the generation of electrical energy and the production therefrom,

whether or not such production is exported in whole or in part from the province, but such laws may not authorize or provide for taxation that differentiates between production exported to another part of Canada and production not exported from the province.

(5) The expression "primary production" has the meaning assigned by the Sixth Schedule.

(6) Nothing in subsections (1) to (5) derogates from any powers or rights that a legislature or government of a province had immediately before the coming into force of this section."

51. The said Act is further amended by adding thereto the following Schedule:

"THE SIXTH SCHEDULE

Primary Production from Non-Renewable Natural Resources and Forestry Resources

1. For the purposes of section 92A of this Act,

(*a*) production from a non-renewable natural resource is primary production therefrom if

(i) it is in the form in which it exists upon its recovery or severance from its natural state, or

(ii) it is a product resulting from processing or refining the resource, and is not a manufactured product or a product resulting from refining crude oil, refining upgraded heavy crude oil, refining gases or liquids derived from coal or refining a synthetic equivalent of crude oil; and

(*b*) production from a forestry resource is primary production therefrom if it consists of sawlogs, poles, lumber, wood chips, sawdust or any other primary wood product, or wood pulp, and is not a product manufactured from wood."

GENERAL

52. (1) The Constitution of Canada is the supreme law of Canada, and any law that is inconsistent with the provisions of the Constitution is, to the extent of the inconsistency, of no force or effect.

(2) The Constitution of Canada includes
(*a*) the *Canada Act,* including this Act;
(*b*) the Acts and orders referred to in Schedule I; and
(*c*) any amendment to any Act or order referred to in paragraph (*a*) or (*b*).

(3) Amendments to the Constitution of Canada shall be made only in accordance with the authority contained in the Constitution of Canada.

53. (1) The enactments referred to in Column I of Schedule I are hereby repealed or amended to the extent indicated in Column II thereof and, unless repealed, shall continue as law in Canada under the names set out in Column III thereof.

(2) Every enactment, except the *Canada Act,* that refers to an enactment referred to in Schedule I by the name in Column I thereof is hereby amended by substituting for that name the corresponding name in Column III thereof, and any British North America Act not referred to in Schedule I may be cited as the *Constitution Act* followed by the year and number, if any, of its enactment.

54. Part IV is repealed on the day that is one year after this Part comes into force and this section may be repealed and this Act renumbered, consequential upon the repeal of Part IV and this section, by proclamation issued by the Governor General under the Great Seal of Canada.

55. A French version of the portions of the Constitution of Canada referred to in Schedule I shall be prepared by the Minister of Justice of Canada as expeditiously as possible and, when any portion thereof sufficient to warrant action being taken has been so prepared, it shall be put forward for enactment by proclamation issued by the Governor General under the Great Seal of Canada pursuant to the procedure then applicable to an amendment of the same provisions of the Constitution of Canada.

56. Where any portion of the Constitution of Canada has been or is enacted in English and French or where a French version of any portion of the Constitution is enacted pursuant to section 55, the English and French versions of that portion of the Constitution are equally authoritative.

57. The English and French versions of this Act are equally authoritative.

58. Subject to section 59, this Act shall come into force on a day to be fixed by proclamation issued by the Queen or the Governor General under the Great Seal of Canada.

59. (1) Paragraph 23(1)(*a*) shall come into force in respect of Quebec on a day to be fixed by proclamation issued by the Queen or the Governor General under the Great Seal of Canada.

(2) A proclamation under subsection (1) shall be issued only where authorized by the legislative assembly or government of Quebec.

(3) This section may be repealed on the day paragraph 23(1)(*a*) comes into force in respect of Quebec and this Act amended and renumbered, consequential upon the repeal of this section, by proclamation issued by the Queen or the Governor General under the Great Seal of Canada.

60. This Act may be cited as the *Constitution Act, 1981*, and the Constitution Acts 1867 to 1975 (No. 2) and this Act may be cited together as the *Constitution Acts, 1867 to 1981*.

The Contributors

EDITORS

John Mallea is a Professor in the Sociology in Education Department at the Ontario Institute for Studies in Education. He has also taught at Queen's University and has been a Visiting Professor at Laval University and Monash University in Melbourne, Australia. He has written extensively on ethnicity and education as well as publishing in the area of comparative and international education.

Jonathan Young received his Ph.D. from the Ontario Institute for Studies in Education. From 1980-83 he lectured in Educational Administration and Research Methods at the College of the Bahamas. Current interests involve the application of ethnographic methods to research in minority group education.

CONTRIBUTORS

Ted Aoki is Professor and Head, Department of Secondary Education, University of Alberta.

Tom Blowers is Director, Program Review, Research and Liaison Branch, Edmonton Public School Board.

Barbara Burnaby is a Research Associate at the Ontario Institute for Studies in Education.

Bryan Connors is a Lecturer in the Department of Elementary Education, University of Alberta.

Jim Cummins is an Associate Professor at the Ontario Institute for Studies in Education.

Jorgen Dahlie is Professor and Head, Department of Social and Educational Studies, University of British Columbia.

Ed Herberg teaches sociology at the University of Toronto (Erindale).

Jim Jones is Supervisor, Second Languages, Edmonton Public School Board.

Olga Kuplowska is Manager, Office of Project Research, T.V. Ontario.

Wallace Lambert is a Professor in the Psychology Department at McGill University specializing in social and experimental psychology.

Dale Lamont is now a criminal justice educator for the John Howard Society, Calgary, but still retains an interest in bilingual education.

Vandra Masemann is a private consultant in ethnic relations and intercultural education with Inter-Cultural Associates, Toronto.

Harry Mosychuk is Assistant Superintendent, Monitoring Systems, Edmonton Public School Board.

Ken O'Bryan is Head of Development and Production, Addiction Research Foundation, Toronto.

The late **Robert Painchaud** was an Associate Professor of History at the University of Winnipeg.

Howard Palmer is an Associate Professor of History at the University of Calgary.

Wes Penner is Supervisor, Employee Relations, Edmonton Public School Board.

The late **John Porter** was one of Canada's most distinguished sociologists.

David Pratt is a Professor of Education at Queen's University.

Jeffrey Reitz is a Professor and Chairman of the Sociology Department, University of Toronto.

Guy Rocher is a Professor of Sociology, Centre de recherche en droit public, Université de Montréal.

Paul Robinson is President, Paul Robinson Education Services, Dartmouth, N.S.

H. H. Stern is Emeritus Professor, the Ontario Institute for Studies in Education.

Thomas Symons, founding President of Trent University, is currently Vanier Professor at that institution.

Walter Werner is Associate Professor in the Centre for the Study of Curriculum and Instruction, University of British Columbia.

June Wyatt is an Associate Professor and Director of Professional Development Programs, Faculty of Education, Simon Fraser University.

THE CARLETON LIBRARY SERIES

1. LORD DURHAM'S REPORT, edited and with an Introduction by Gerald M. Craig
2. THE CONFEDERATION DEBATES IN THE PROVINCE OF CANADA, 1865, edited and with an Introduction by P.B. Waite
3. LAURIER: A STUDY IN CANADIAN POLITICS, by J.W. Dafoe, with an Introduction by Murray S. Donnelly
4. CHAMPLAIN: THE LIFE OF FORTITUDE, by Morris Bishop, with a new Introduction by the author
5. THE ROWELL-SIROIS REPORT, *Book I,* edited and with an Introduction by Donald V. Smiley
6. THE UNREFORMED SENATE OF CANADA, by Robert A. MacKay, revised and with an Introduction by the author
7. THE JESUIT RELATIONS AND ALLIED DOCUMENTS: A SELECTION, edited and with an Introduction by S.R. Mealing
8. LORD DURHAM'S MISSION TO CANADA, by Chester New, edited and with an Introduction by H.W. McCready
9. THE RECIPROCITY TREATY OF 1854, by Donald C. Masters, with a new Introduction by the author
10. POLITICAL UNREST IN UPPER CANADA, 1815-1836, by Aileen Dunham, with an Introduction by A.L. Burt
11. A HISTORY OF TRANSPORTATION IN CANADA, *Volume I*, by G.P. deT. Glazebrook, with a new Introduction by the author
12. A HISTORY OF TRANSPORTATION IN CANADA, *Volume II*, by G.P. deT. Glazebrook
13. THE ECONOMIC BACKGROUND OF DOMINION-PROVINCIAL RELATIONS, by W.A. Mackintosh, with an Introduction by J.H. Dales
14. THE FRENCH-CANADIAN OUTLOOK, by Mason Wade, with a new Introduction by the author
15. THE WESTERN INTERIOR OF CANADA: A RECORD OF GEOGRAPHICAL DISCOVERY, 1612-1917, edited and with an Introduction by John Warkentin
16. THE COURTS AND THE CANADIAN CONSTITUTION, edited and with an Introduction by W.R. Lederman
17. MONEY AND BANKING IN CANADA, edited and with an Introduction by E.P. Neufeld
18. FRENCH-CANADIAN SOCIETY, *Volume I*, edited and with an Introduction by Marcel Rioux and Yves Martin
19. THE CANADIAN COMMERCIAL REVOLUTION, 1845-1851, by Gilbert N. Tucker, edited and with an Introduction by Hugh G.J. Aitken
20. JOSEPH HOWE: VOICE OF NOVA SCOTIA, edited and with an Introduction by J. Murray Beck
21. LIFE AND LETTERS OF SIR WILFRID LAURIER, *Volume I*, by Oscar Douglas Skelton, edited and with an Introduction by David M.L. Farr
22. LIFE AND LETTERS OF SIR WILFRID LAURIER, *Volume II*, by Oscar Douglas Skelton, edited by David M.L. Farr
23. LEADING CONSTITUTIONAL DECISIONS, edited and with an Introduction by Peter H. Russell
24. FRONTENAC, THE COURTIER GOVERNOR, by W.J. Eccles
25. INDIANS OF THE NORTH PACIFIC COAST, edited and with an Introduction by Tom McFeat

26. LIFE AND TIMES OF SIR ALEXANDER TILLOCH GALT, by Oscar Douglas Skelton, edited and with an Introduction by Guy MacLean
27. A HISTORY OF CANADIAN EXTERNAL RELATIONS, *Volume I*, by G.P. deT. Glazebrook, revised by the author
28. A HISTORY OF CANADIAN EXTERNAL RELATIONS, *Volume II*, by G.P. deT. Glazebrook, revised and with a Bibliographical Essay by the author
29. THE RACE QUESTION IN CANADA, by André Siegfried, edited and with an Introduction by Frank H. Underhill
30. NORTH ATLANTIC TRIANGLE, by John Bartlett Brebner, with an Introduction by Donald G. Creighton
31. APPROACHES TO CANADIAN ECONOMIC HISTORY, edited and with an Introduction by W.T. Easterbrook and M.H. Watkins
32. CANADIAN SOCIAL STRUCTURE: A STATISTICAL PROFILE, edited and with an Introduction and Commentary by John Porter
33. CHURCH AND STATE IN CANADA, 1627-1867: BASIC DOCUMENTS, edited and with an Introduction by John S. Moir
34. WESTERN ONTARIO AND THE AMERICAN FRONTIER, by Fred Landon, with a new Introduction by the author
35. HISTORICAL ESSAYS ON THE ATLANTIC PROVINCES, edited and with an Introduction by G.A. Rawlyk
36. A HISTORY OF JOURNALISM IN CANADA, by W.H. Kesterton, with an Introduction by Wilfrid Eggleston
37. THE OLD PROVINCE OF QUEBEC, *Volume I*, by A.L. Burt, with an Introduction by Hilda Neatby
38. THE OLD PROVINCE OF QUEBEC, *Volume II*, by A.L. Burt
39. GROWTH AND THE CANADIAN ECONOMY, edited and with an Introduction by T.N. Brewis
40. DOCUMENTS ON THE CONFEDERATION OF BRITISH NORTH AMERICA, edited and with an Introduction by G.P. Browne
41. ESKIMO OF THE CANADIAN ARCTIC, edited and with an Introduction by Victor F. Valentine and Frank G. Vallee
42. THE COLONIAL REFORMERS AND CANADA, 1830-1849, edited and with an Introduction by Peter Burroughs
43. A NARRATIVE, by Sir Francis Bond Head, edited and with an Introduction by S.F. Wise
44. JOHN STRACHAN: DOCUMENTS AND OPINIONS, edited and with an Introduction by J.L.H. Henderson
45. THE NEUTRAL YANKEES OF NOVA SCOTIA, by J.B. Brebner, with an Introduction by S.S. MacNutt
46. ROBERT LAIRD BORDEN: HIS MEMOIRS, *Volume I*, edited and with an Introduction by Heath Macquarrie
47. ROBERT LAIRD BORDEN: HIS MEMOIRS, *Volume II*, edited by Heath Macquarrie
48. THE CANADIAN MUNICIPAL SYSTEM: ESSAYS ON THE IMPROVEMENT OF LOCAL GOVERNMENT, by D.C. Rowat
49. THE BETTER PART OF VALOUR: ESSAYS ON CANADIAN DIPLOMACY, by John W. Holmes
50. LAMENT FOR A NATION: THE DEFEAT OF CANADIAN NATIONALISM, by George Grant, with a new Introduction by the author
51. CANADIAN FOREIGN POLICY, 1945-1954, by R.A. MacKay, edited and with an Introduction by the author

52. MONCK: LETTERS AND JOURNALS, edited and with an Introduction by W.L. Morton
53. HISTORICAL ESSAYS ON THE PRAIRIE PROVINCES, edited and with an Introduction by Donald Swainson
54. THE CANADIAN ECONOMY IN THE GREAT DEPRESSION, by A.E. Safarian
55. CANADA'S CHANGING NORTH, edited and with an Introduction by William C. Wonders
56. THE DEVELOPMENT OF CANADA'S STAPLES, 1867-1939, edited and with an Introductory comment by Kevin H. Burley
57. URBAN DEVELOPMENT IN SOUTH-CENTRAL ONTARIO, by Jacob Spelt
58. CULTURE AND NATIONALITY: ESSAYS BY A.G. BAILEY, by Alfred Goldsworthy Bailey
59. COMMUNITY IN CRISIS: FRENCH-CANADIAN NATIONALISM IN PERSPECTIVE, by Richard Jones, with a new Introduction by the author
60. PERSPECTIVES ON THE NORTH AMERICAN INDIANS, edited and with an Introduction by Mark Nagler
61. LANGUAGES IN CONFLICT, by Richard J. Joy, with a Preface by Frank G. Vallee
62. THE LAST FORTY YEARS: THE UNION OF 1841 TO CONFEDERATION, by J.C. Dent, abridged and with an Introduction by Donald Swainson
63. LAURIER AND A LIBERAL QUEBEC: A STUDY IN POLITICAL MANAGEMENT, by H. Blair Neatby, edited and with an Introduction by Richard T. Clippingdale
64. THE TREMBLAY REPORT, edited and with an Introduction by David Kwavnick
65. CULTURAL ECOLOGY: READINGS ON THE CANADIAN INDIANS AND ESKIMOS, edited and with an Introduction by Bruce Cox
66. RECOLLECTIONS OF THE ON TO OTTAWA TREK, by Ronald Liversedge, with Documents Relating to the Vancouver Strike and the On to Ottawa Trek, edited and with an Introduction by Victor Hoar
67. THE OMBUDSMAN PLAN: ESSAYS ON THE WORLDWIDE SPREAD OF AN IDEA, by Donald C. Rowat
68. NATURAL RESOURCES: THE ECONOMICS OF CONSERVATION, by Anthony Scott
69. "DOMINION LANDS" POLICY, by Chester Martin, edited and with an Introduction by Lewis H. Thomas
70. RENEGADE IN POWER: THE DIEFENBAKER YEARS, by Peter C. Newman, with an Introduction by Denis Smith
71. CUTHBERT GRANT OF GRANTOWN, by Margaret A. MacLeod and W.L. Morton
72. THE NATIVE PEOPLES OF ATLANTIC CANADA: A READER IN REGIONAL ETHNIC RELATIONS, by H.F. McGee
73. FREEDOM AND ORDER/COLLECTED ESSAYS, by Eugene Forsey, with an Introduction by Donald Creighton
74. THE CRISIS OF QUEBEC, 1914-1918, by Elizabeth Armstrong, with an Introduction by Joseph Levitt
75. STATISTICAL ACCOUNT OF UPPER CANADA, by Robert Gourlay, abridged, and with an Introduction by S.R. Mealing

76. THE ADVENTURES AND SUFFERINGS OF JOHN JEWITT CAPTIVE AMONG THE NOOTKA, edited and with an Introduction by Derek G. Smith
77. CAPITAL FORMATION IN CANADA, 1896-1930, by Kenneth Buckley, with an Introduction by M. Urquhart
78. BEYOND THE ATLANTIC ROAR: A STUDY OF THE NOVA SCOTIA SCOTS, by D. Campbell and R.A. MacLean
79. CONSOCIATIONAL DEMOCRACY, by K.D. McRae
80. PHILIPPE DE RIGAUD DE VAUDREUIL, GOVERNOR OF NEW FRANCE 1703-1725, by Yves Zoltvany
81. CANADIAN-AMERICAN SUMMIT DIPLOMACY, 1923-1973, by Roger Frank Swanson
82. HISTORICAL ESSAYS ON UPPER CANADA, by J.K. Johnson
83. THE CANADIAN BILL OF RIGHTS, by Walter Surma Tarnopolsky
84. SOCIALIZATION AND VALUES IN CONTEMPORARY CANADA, *Volume I, Political Socialization*, edited by Elia Zureik and Robert M. Pike
85. SOCIALIZATION AND VALUES IN CONTEMPORARY CANADA, *Volume II: Socialization, Social Stratification and Ethnicity*, edited by Robert M. Pike and Elia Zureik
86. CANADA'S BALANCE OF INTERNATIONAL INDEBTEDNESS, 1910-1913, by Jacob Viner
87. CANADIAN INDIANS AND THE LAW: SELECTED DOCUMENTS, 1663-1972, edited by Derek G. Smith
88. LIVING AND LEARNING IN THE FREE SCHOOL, by Mark Novak
89. THE CANADIAN CORPORATE ELITE: AN ANALYSIS OF ECONOMIC POWER, by Wallace Clement
90. MAN'S IMPACT ON THE WESTERN CANADIAN LANDSCAPE, by J.G. Nelson
91. PERSPECTIVES ON LANDSCAPE AND SETTLEMENT IN NINETEENTH CENTURY ONTARIO, edited by J. David Wood
92. MINORITY MEN IN A MAJORITY SETTING, by Christopher Beattie
93. CANADIAN-AMERICAN INDUSTRY, by Herbert Marshall, Frank Southard, Jr., and Kenneth W. Taylor
94. CAPITAL PUNISHMENT IN CANADA, by David Chandler
95. POLITICAL CORRUPTION IN CANADA: CASES, CAUSES, CURES, edited by Kenneth Gibbons and Donald C. Rowat
96. HISTORICAL ESSAYS ON BRITISH COLUMBIA, edited by J. Friesen and H.K. Ralston
97. THE FROG LAKE "MASSACRE": PERSONAL PERSPECTIVES ON ETHNIC CONFLICT, edited and with an Introduction by Stuart Hughes
98. CANADA: A MIDDLE-AGED POWER, by John W. Holmes
99. EIGHTEENTH CENTURY NEWFOUNDLAND: A GEOGRAPHIC PERSPECTIVE, by C. Grant Head
100. THE LAW AND THE PRESS IN CANADA, by Wilfrid H. Kesterton
101. THE AGRICULTURAL ECONOMY OF MANITOBA HUTTERITE COLONIES, by John Ryan
102. THE FRONTIER AND CANADIAN LETTERS, by Wilfrid Eggleston, with an Introduction by Douglas Spettigue
103. CANADIAN FOREIGN POLICY, 1955-1965, by A.E. Blanchette
104. A CRITICAL SPIRIT: THE THOUGHT OF WILLIAM DAWSON LESUEUR, edited and with an Introduction by A.B. McKillop

105. CHOOSING CANADA'S CAPITAL: JEALOUSY AND FRICTION IN THE 19TH CENTURY, by David B. Knight
106. THE CANADIAN QUANDARY: ECONOMIC PROBLEMS AND POLICIES, by Harry G. Johnson
107. KEYNESIAN ECONOMICS, by Mabel F. Timlin, with a biographical note by A.E. Safarian and a Foreword by L. Tarshis
108. THE DOUKHOBORS, by George Woodcock and Ivan Avakumovic
109. THE CANADIAN CITY: ESSAYS IN URBAN HISTORY, edited by Gilbert A. Stelter and Alan F.J. Artibise
110. DOES MONEY MATTER? by John Porter, Marion R. Porter and Bernard Blishen
111. WILLIAM LYON MACKENZIE: A REINTERPRETATION by William Dawson LeSueur, edited and with introduction by A.B. McKillop
112. THE DISTEMPER OF OUR TIMES, by Peter C. Newman
113. THE CANADIAN ECONOMY AND DISARMAMENT, by Gideon Rosenbluth
114. THE FARMERS IN POLITICS, by William Irvine with Introduction by R. Whitaker
115. THE BOUNDARIES OF THE CANADIAN CONFEDERATION, by Norman Nicholson
116. EACH FOR ALL, by Ian Macpherson
117. CANADIAN CONFEDERATION: A DECISION-MAKING ANALYSIS, by W.L. White, R.H. Wagenberg, R.C. Nelson and W.C. Soderlund
118. CANADIAN FOREIGN POLICY 1966-1976, edited by Arthur E. Blanchette
119. THE USABLE URBAN PAST, edited by Alan J. Artibise and Gilbert A. Stelter
120. ECONOMIC AND SOCIAL HISTORY OF QUEBEC, 1760-1850, by Fernand Ouellet
122. LAST OF THE FREE ENTERPRISERS: THE OILMEN OF CALGARY, by J.D. House
123. CONTEXTS OF CANADA'S PAST. Essays of W.L. Morton, edited by A.B. McKillop.
124. THE REDISTRIBUTION OF INCOME IN CANADA, by W. Irwin Gillespie
125. SHAPING THE URBAN LANDSCAPE: ASPECTS OF THE CANADIAN CITY-BUILDING PROCESS, edited by Gilbert A. Stelter and Alan F.J. Artibise
126. RECREATIONAL LAND USE: PERSPECTIVES ON ITS EVOLUTION IN CANADA, edited by G. Wall and J. Marsh
127. FEAR'S FOLLY (LES DEMI-CIVILISES) by Jean-Charles Harvey. Translated by John Glassco, edited by John O'Connor
128. THE ENTERPRISES OF ROBERT HAMILTON: Wealth and Influence in Early Upper Canada, 1776-1812, by Bruce G. Wilson
129. THE SOCIOLOGY OF WORK: Papers in Honour of Oswald Hall, edited by Audrey Wipper
130. CULTURAL DIVERSITY AND SCHOOLING IN CANADA: edited by John R. Mallea and Jonathan C. Young
131. ABORIGINAL PEOPLE AND THE LAW, edited by Bradford W. Morse

CARLETON CONTEMPORARIES

AN INDEPENDENT FOREIGN POLICY FOR CANADA? Edited by Stephen Clarkson
THE DECOLONIZATION OF QUEBEC: AN ANALYSIS OF LEFT-WING NATIONALISM by Henry Milner and Sheilagh Hodgins Milner
THE MACKENZIE PIPELINE: ARCTIC GAS AND CANADIAN ENERGY POLICY Edited by Peter H. Pearse
CONTINENTAL COMMUNITY? INDEPENDENCE AND INTEGRATION IN NORTH AMERICA Edited by W.A. Axline, J.E. Hyndman, P.V. Lyon and M.A. Molot
THE RAILWAY GAME: A STUDY IN SOCIO-TECHNOLOGICAL OBSOLESCENCE by J. Lukasiewicz
FOREMOST NATION: CANADIAN FOREIGN POLICY AND A CHANGING WORLD Edited by N. Hillmer and G. Stevenson

GENERAL LIST

1. DICCIONARIO DE REFERENCIAS DEL "poema de mio cid", compiled and arranged by José Jurado
2. THE POET AND THE CRITIC: A Literary Correspondence Between D. C. Scott and E. K. Brown, edited by Robert L. McDougall